Social Dancing in America

SOCIAL DANCING
in America

A History and Reference

VOLUME TWO

Lindy Hop to Hip Hop,
1901–2000

Ralph G. Giordano

Greenwood Press
Westport, Connecticut • London

Library of Congress Cataloging-in-Publication Data

Giordano, Ralph G.
   Social dancing in America : a history and reference / Ralph G. Giordano
     p. cm.
   Includes bibliographical references and index.
   ISBN: 0–313–33756–X (set : alk. paper)—ISBN 0–313–33403–X (vol. 1 : alk. paper)—
   ISBN 0–313–33352–1 (vol. 2 : alk. paper) 1. Ballroom dancing—United States—
   History. I. Title.
GV1623.G56 2007
792.3′3—dc22   2006026183

British Library Cataloguing in Publication Data is available.

Library of Congress Catalog Card Number: 2006026183
ISBN: 0–313–33756–X (set)   ISBN13: 978–0–313–33756–7 (set)
       0–313–33403–X (vol. 1)   978–0–313–33403–0 (vol. 1)
       0–313–33352–1 (vol. 2)   978–0–313–33352–1 (vol. 2)

First published in 2007

Greenwood Press, 88 Post Road West, Westport, CT 06881
An imprint of Greenwood Publishing Group, Inc.
www.greenwood.com

Printed in the United States of America

The paper used in this book complies with the
Permanent Paper Standard issued by the National
Information Standards Organization (Z39.48-1984).

10 9 8 7 6 5 4 3 2 1

Copyright Acknowledgments

Excerpts in Chapter 3 from *The Autobiography of Malcolm X*, by Malcolm X and Alex
Haley, copyright © 1964 by Alex Haley and Malcolm X. Copyright © 1965 by Alex Haley
and Betty Shabazz. Used by permission of Random House, Inc.

To
Thelma Lynn Olsen,
Debby Adams,
Rock-it, Gumball, Brandy,
and
All of those who live to dance

Those who dance are considered insane by those who can't hear the music.
—George Carlin, *Napalm & Silly Putty* (2001)

Contents

Acknowledgments

The quote "Those who dance are considered insane by those who can't hear the music" is often attributed to an anonymous source, but in 2001, comedian George Carlin chose it as the introductory quote to his book *Napalm & Silly Putty*. I must admit that I truly admired Mr. Carlin as he continually provided an ironic, truthful look at American culture and society. He looks at our own behavior and word patterns and, in turn, reveals some truths about ourselves. In many ways this selected dance quote by Mr. Carlin might also serve as the theme of dancing throughout America during the twentieth century. Having spent so much time myself not only researching the dances covered within this book, but also spending literally thousands of hours on the dance floor, I can honestly say that I know many others in my life certainly do not understand my insatiable desire to just go out and dance. Those same people have also questioned my own sanity, but in reality I know that it is they who certainly "can't hear the music."

As it turned out, the experience of participation in social dancing has provided me with a better understanding of the written historical works and film archives. Dance historian Lloyd Shaw probably said it best when he wrote:

> It isn't enough to read such books, you get only part of their impact. But if you put on a phonograph record, and dance, you get a moving, kinetic, living idea of what it's all about (34).

Shaw wrote that statement in 1948, but it certainly applies to social dancing throughout all facets of American history. In that same manner, there are so many aspects about social dancing that simply cannot be expressed in mere words or even photographs. Attached to it all is human emotion. How can one person describe the fun, the relaxation, the sociability, the friendships, and the exhilaration?

In 2004, a friend suggested that I read the local announcements of anniversary couples celebrating their 50th and 60th wedding anniversaries. I was amazed when she said, "Look how many of them first met at a dance." With that said, if writing a book is 1 percent inspiration and 99 percent perspiration, I have agreed to give my wife, Thelma Lynn Olsen, 1 percent of my royalties. In all seriousness, without my partner-in-life-in-dancing, my wife, this book certainly would not have been written, for it was through dancing that we first met.

Little did I know that as Thelma Lynn was growing up she always had a secret desire to "dance big" at a family wedding to Bobby Darin's hit song "Mack the Knife." Well, a short time after we met she fulfilled that dream with me as her dance partner. Since the mid-1990s we have danced together, and hardly a week has gone by without us dancing for a few hours. Granted, we continually dance in our hearts each day, and if given a choice we certainly would rather always be dancing. It was certainly a thrill for us to dance at the 100 Club at Oxford Circus in London—the very same basement venue where American servicemen danced the Lindy Hop during World War II. But we have also danced in over 20 states throughout America in literally hundreds of different dance venues, including Country, Shag, Swing, Ballroom, Social, Disco, Historical, and, of course, at family weddings and celebrations. At no time do we compete, for that would take all the fun out of the spontaneity of just getting up and dancing. However, I will admit that one time at a vacation resort in Jamaica we were awarded a "first prize" of a bottle of rum—which we still have not opened.

There are so many things about dancing that simply cannot be expressed in mere words or even photographs. Throughout the years, I have danced with many and have made many friends. So many of those individuals we would see on a regular basis. We would greet each other with a hug and a kiss on the cheek. "Hi Gail, hi Jason. Hey is Arnie here yet? I think I saw Eileen come in—where is she? Hey I haven't seen Rose in a while. I wonder where she is?" Occasionally someone outside the dance world might ask, "What do they do?" or "Where do they live?" Well the obvious answer to the first question is, "They dance!" On the other hand, regardless of what happens in the outside world, many of our dance friends are just that. We do not judge on political persuasion, economic status, or even sexual preference. The bottom line is "Do they dance?" Also, it matters little what their last name is or what their function is within American society, for the common attraction to the dancing is music and a dance floor. For almost all, the dancing and music serves as an escape from the outside world and in turn allows us to cope with the toils and tribulations of life itself.

Interestingly enough, as I traveled, whether alone or with Thelma, I would always seek out a local Country or Swing dance club. Within the dance world, I could always enter a similar type of dance place and not feel alone, I was always comfortable—I could not say the same for another type of establishment. How do you describe the exhilaration of dancing East Coast Swing within the Washington Redskins football stadium among 50,000 fans at an all-day country music festival? Or sitting in a bathroom in a Country & Western dance venue in New Jersey, and not seeing the individuals but overhearing a conversation? The first individual said to his friend, "Hey who was that guy you were talking to?" The friend answered, "Oh, he said he was a welder from Virginia." The first one replied, "For a southern boy he should be ashamed of himself, cause he can't dance a lick." Or being in Boot Hill in Rapid City, South Dakota, and seeing that the chair reserved for a "shoeshine" was not necessarily there for the pretense of keeping up appearances, but rather because some of the those who came to drink a beer and dance the Two-Step came right off working the ranch? The owners had the shoe-shine stand to ensure that no dirt or horse manure was transported to the dance floor. Or even forgetting which Texas dance club had the sign "Real men don't line dance—they Two-step"? Or first doing the Electric Slide at a Club Med in the Caribbean? The literally thousands of hours spent at two (now defunct) social dance clubs *Denim & Diamonds* in Manhattan and *The Pony Express* in Staten Island, New York? We moved on and spent over six years (and counting) once-a-week at the Whiskey Café in Lyndhurst, New Jersey. I would not trade those hours for anything.

During high school, I remember sneaking many Saturday afternoons all by myself to watch *America Bandstand* and *Soul Train*. I certainly admired all of those who could dance. During the late 1970s, during the height of the Disco craze, I did venture to some local discos, one time with friends, but mostly alone. My family did not know where I had learned to Hustle when I danced it at family weddings.

I also thank my family of Giordanos, Dattilos, Leavers, Kargos, Clarkes, Quat-trochis, Garcias, Merolas, and all the rest. It was mainly from my family that I first experienced the joy of social dancing. All of our family weddings certainly provided an amazing joyful experience of American social dancing. Little did I know while sitting with my grandfather, Antonio Dattilo, as he faithfully watched *The Lawrence Welk Show* on television so many years ago, that I would be writing about that very same show. When we were at a family wedding he was certainly one to do an Italian Waltz (which resembled a quick Polish Polka). I remember him, whether with my Grandma Anna Dattilo or one of his daughters, with his head down and deter-mined as he whirled around the dance floor. I fondly remember my Aunt "Chub-bie" and Uncle "Lucky" (known outside the family as Frederic and Maria Kargo) who were a professional dance team, invigorating the crowd at all family functions through their dancing.

All week long they could all toil through the tribulations of life—both good and bad—deal with family arguments, yet they never took those problems to the dance floor. And I must, of course, mention my own parents, Phyllis and Thomas Gior-dano—oh how they loved to dance. That experience was passed on to not only myself, but also to my brother Thomas Giordano, Jr., who is a Battalion Chief in the Fire Department of the City of New York. Both he and his wife, Helene, never miss an opportunity to enjoy a whirl on the dance floor. Many of us were extremely relieved after all those awful months following September 2001 when Tommy and Helene finally got back on the dance floor. In fact, they also attended many social dance functions sponsored by the Fire Department. On many an occasion, Tommy has told me that the organizers always remembered to include a "Lindy set for the Chief and his wife."

This second book would not have happened without a contract in place from Greenwood Publishing, and for that I am sincerely grateful. And, I cannot say enough about my "senior editor" Debby Adams at Greenwood. Her patience, dil-igence, and wonderful knowledge made this work a true partnership—especially her attention to historical detail in helping to organize the chapter introductions.

Acknowledgments

The author and his wife, Thelma Lynn, on the dance floor in Brooklyn, New York.   Leonard Yakir Photography.

Researching a book does not happen without the assistance of some very talented and dedicated people. First and foremost, my most heartfelt thanks and gratitude go to Angie DeMartinis who services the interlibrary loan section at the College of Staten Island Library. Her promptness and professionalism made the acquisition of some very difficult documents and publications an easy process. A grateful acknowledgment must go to the Music Division of the Library of Congress for their invaluable compilation titled *An American Ballroom Companion Dance Instruction Manuals Ca. 1490–1920*. The Web site contains a tremendous catalog of rare books and videos that otherwise would have been virtually unattainable.

Contributing sources for photographs include the Associated Press, the Catalina Island Museum Collection, the Library of Congress, Bettmann/Corbis, The Detroit News, Detroit Photographic Co., Getty Images, Phyllis Giordano, The Granger Collection, The Kobal Collection, Dolores Leaver, Thelma Lynn Olsen, Photofest, Michael Larsen-Elizabeth Pomada Literary Agents (Karen Lustgarten and Bernie Lustgarten), Lynne E. Riordan, Urban Archives Temple University, Leonard Yakir Photography, Kimberly Vollstedt of RBC Management, and Royal Crown Revue.

Individual thanks go to Carol Butler of Brown Brothers, Don Bowden at the Associated Press, Jeannine Pedersen, Curator of Collections at the Catalina Island Museum, Charlotte Massey and Patricia Zacharias at *The Detroit News*, and especially the crew at Photofest including Howard Mandelbaum, Ed Maguire, and Ron Mandelbaum. Photofest is a wonderful gem that holds over one million photographs located on East 31st in Manhattan. Yes, I agree with their philosophy that it is still better to search and flip through original 8 x 10 photographs rather than conduct a digital search.

Special thanks to those individuals who took time to provide personal interviews: Hilary Alexander, Dominick Dattilo, Phyllis Giordano, Betsy Greene, Maria Kargo, Mary Keil (go see her movie *Swing*, 2005), "Uncle Joe" Lanza, Dolores Leaver, Galt MacDermot, Vince MacDermot, Ann Merlino, Thelma Lynn Olsen,

Georganne Sassano, Carolyn Sgromo, Dave Snyder, Bob Soldivera, John Wakie, and Patricia Wakie.

And the joy of social dancing was certainly enhanced by friends Stella Bennardello, Greg Kmit, Sammie D., Donna, Lois Bilcher, Judy Dahl, Mrs. Rosemary's Dance Studio, Jason Kolucki and his "Evolution of Swing," Kristine Powell and her New Jersey Swing events, "Lenny Lounge," and the dance friends at the Whiskey Café in Lyndhurst, New Jersey. Also sincere thanks to all the bands that we ever danced to especially *Dem Brooklyn Bums* and *The Nashville Attitude* (Marc Sica, Sal Azzarelli, Sean Burns, and Dave Strickland) and their manager and photographer Lynne E. Riordan. Also, my thanks to Kathy Breit of BeaconPMG.

But mostly, I do wish to thank anyone who has had the gumption to open a "business" that included the fun of social dancing. And thanks to all of those who danced before me, those who dance with me, and especially those who will continue to dance after me. I sincerely hope you find somewhere within this book the common element that social dancing can provide within all our lives. I also hope that you enjoy this book, for dancing has certainly been a vital part in shaping the American way of life throughout our history.

Introduction

Social dancing was not new to the development of twentieth century America. Social dance traditions can be traced to ancient Greece and Rome, as well as to Biblical locales. In America, the emerging republic of the Founding Fathers held steadfast in the tradition of social dancing. While in Paris, in 1785, Thomas Jefferson wrote to Abigail Adams of a life "where we have singing, dancing, laughter and merriment." Historian Stephen Ambrose in *Undaunted Courage*, chronicling the adventures of Lewis and Clark, stated that social dancing was one of the important talents of Virginia gentlemen.

Throughout the nineteenth century American communities, cities, and the western territories regularly sponsored social activities that included dancing. The social elite attended dance functions at elaborate pavilions and resorts, where it was considered proper etiquette for a socialite to have a *dance card*. The dance card listed a set list of songs that would be played during the evening and a space where the names of gentlemen dance partners would be written in advance of the event. The predetermined dances were smooth flowing, dignified, sedate dances that emphasized a strict erect "carriage" between the partners and included Quadrilles, Lanciers, and some Waltzes. In order not to extend too much excitement, the typical dance format usually included a 10 to 15 minute rest after each dance. However, with the development of Ragtime music in the late 1890s, the music and the dances were faster and more energetic, and the rest periods were reduced (and eventually eliminated), which appealed mostly to the younger people.

By the twentieth century European immigrants brought traditional folk dances from their native countries and cultures, such as the Italian *Tarantella*, Jewish *Hora*, and Greek *Syrtos* and *Pidiktos*. Americans danced, young and old, male and female, mostly at communal events such as weddings. During the twentieth century, social dancing in itself offered a parallel of the social, economic, and cultural traditions of each particular time period. For example, segregation and the "Jim Crow" mentality was cemented in place all over the United States, so for most of the century dancing and dancing halls were strictly segregated. Segregation forced a mass migration from the South to northern cities, and with it came a transformation of the Delta Blues music into an American original—Jazz. Jazz gave birth to the Charleston Dance, as well as evolved into Swing music.

Economic uncertainty also played an important role in social dancing. Many individuals realized that dancing was a simple pleasure that for a few hours could alleviate the unwelcome stress of daily living. And some of the century's most prolific dance crazes occurred either during the two World Wars or during the Great Depression.

In the latter part of the century, with the technological advancement of television, shows such as *American Bandstand* (first aired in the early 1950s) followed by *Soul Train, Dance Fever,* and those watched by the MTV generation greatly influenced dance styles and the current "new" trend in dancing. The effects of advertising and media, including Hollywood and television, shaped what many believed to be popular, acceptable, and, in some cases, rebellious, or simply what was a "fad."

Many social dance books of the period simply provided descriptions and step-by-step instructions on "how to dance" as opposed to *why* people dance. Most, if not all, new dance trends started in the underground or as a public fad. Some dances simply faded out, and others became staples such as the Swing and the Fox trot. This book traces a consistent theme that contemporary dances and the associated music and fashion were more often than not initially perceived as "scandalous" and usually attacked by purists and religious groups as immoral. However, with time, each preceding dance moved from scandalous to public acceptance and respectability.

This book is not a book to teach people "How to Dance." There are literally thousands of publications and hundreds of dance studios available in the United States to do just that. This book is an attempt to provide a clear understanding of what was involved in the basic patterns and rhythms of the dance, the origins, and the popularity, but most importantly to place each in a historical and social context. This book is about the dances themselves and their importance in a social context. Therefore, each chapter contains a brief introduction of the social, political, and cultural climate. Although the book encompasses the twentieth century and covers many specific dances that had either broad appeal or negative repercussions, the book is about how individual Americans, mainly couples, interacted in a social dance setting. Some questions discussed throughout the book are as follows:

- What was the history of the most popular dances and where did they begin?
- What attracted men and women to social dancing in these periods?
- How did the historical, political, and cultural events influence dance styles?
- What was their ethnic and economic background?
- How was their dancing and choice of dance style viewed by contemporary society?
- How did social dancing influence fashion styles?
- What specific dances crossed over from "scandalous" to public acceptance?
- Which dances survived the test of time and why?
- What dances and dance venues were hindered by municipal regulations?
- What dances and dance venues were hindered by moral or religious objections?

Some points that should be noted are that some dance instruction manuals and historical texts list the names of the dances in lowercase. A significant number of dance manuals capitalize the names of specific dances. Since this book is about the dances and dancing in itself, I decided to capitalize the names of the dances throughout the text, such as Lindy Hop, Foxtrot, and Tango, for example, since they are nouns and are the names of dances but can also be a verb since dancing represents an action.

The spellings of most of the dances also vary, especially with Lindy Hop (sometimes Lindy hop, Lindy-hop, or just Lindy), Rhumba (sometimes Rumba), or Fox Trot (sometimes Foxtrot, Fox trot, or foxtrot). Most of the contemporary writings reference the dances as nouns, and therefore throughout the book the names of the specific dances are capitalized. I have chosen Rhumba with the "h" rather than the more common variant "Rumba" since the dance is Latin in origin and the pronunciation should roll the "R's." Rock 'n' Roll is another one that is often spelled many different ways such as "Rock and Roll," Rock & Roll, and Rock n' Roll. I have chosen "Rock 'n' Roll" for the reasons that are discussed at length in Chapter 4. With that said, I encourage you to read this book and hope that this history of social dancing in the twentieth century transcends your current understanding of why Americans choose to dance.

1

Animal Dances, The Castles, and Ragtime: 1901–1919

Here in America we are just beginning to wake up to the possibilities of dancing.
—Vernon Castle, 1914

The Political, Social, and Cultural Climate

At the turn of the twentieth century, America consisted of 45 official states, the District of Columbia, Indian Territory, and the territories of Oklahoma, New Mexico, Arizona, Hawaii, and Alaska. Its population was 76 million people. More than 45 million lived in rural areas and 30 million in cities.

America was in the midst of the Industrial Revolution as it began shifting from a rural-based economy to an industrialized urban economy. With the shift to urbanism, the need for new workers drastically increased, which led to massive immigration. During the period of 1890 to 1914, immigrants, almost exclusively from southern and western Europe, entered the nation at a rate of over 1 million per year. Most settled into overcrowded cities.

Of the total American working force of 29 million, more than 10.7 million were in agriculture (traditional farming) and 6.3 million in manufacturing (factory work producing products and goods such as steel for automobiles and buildings). The service industry of domestics, clerks, and secretaries accounted for 3.2 million. Working conditions, especially in the factories, were harsh (*This Fabulous Century*, 1969, 7–9).

Many worked a 10 to 14 hour day six days a week. To support the family, all the children had to contribute to the family income. Newspapers and investigative journalists (in a practice known as "muckraking") published stories of overcrowding in the cities and hazardous job conditions. Progressive Reformers, including clergy, politicians, and concerned individuals, attempted to provide legislation to correct what they saw as the immoral ills created by industrialization, immigration, and urbanization. Progressive Reform led to child labor laws and increased worker safety. Improved building codes were enacted by the investigative photo journalism of Jacob Riis in his expose *How The Other Half Lives* (1890, reissued 1901), and tragedies such as the 1903 Chicago Iroquois Theater and New York Triangle Shirt Waist Factory fires that killed 600 and 146 (mostly young women) individuals within minutes.

In August 1914, World War I began as Germany invaded France. At first, the German army moved quickly and threatened Paris. The advancing army was slowed at the Battle of the Marne. The war soon bogged down and remained a stalemate. No one could foresee that the trench warfare and horrible slaughter would continue for years. Millions of French, British, German, and Belgian soldiers were killed in battles at Ypres and the Somme.

In April 1917, the United States declared war on Germany and joined the world war started on the European continent three years earlier. From 1917 to 1918, the war changed American society. The draft process moved quickly, and the government enlisted the aid of many outside agencies and volunteers to support the mobilization. Immigration from Europe was halted, and all attention was turned towards the war effort. Immigrants, however, had been a major source of labor, and with the restrictions (and the draft) labor shortages occurred. During World War I, many women not previously working outside the home filled the workplace. The push to work in the labor shortage market sometimes meant working 14–16 hour days. These women replaced the men who left for the war in Europe to make the world, as President Woodrow Wilson declared, "safe for democracy."

Women suffragettes, led by the likes of Carrie Chapman Catt and others, also asked Wilson for democracy at home—for the right to vote. In 1915, over 26,000 women suffragettes marched in New York City. Many suffragettes were aided by the Women's Christian Temperance Movement and collectively campaigned not only for the right to vote, but also against vice and alcohol. In 1919, Congress approved, and in 1920 the states ratified the Nineteenth Amendment to the Constitution providing women nationwide with the right to vote.

By 1918, the European war had become part of every American's daily life. However, during that same year, Americans were struck on the home front by an unexpected terror with the onset of the Great Flu Epidemic. The first wave was in the spring, and within a three-month period many nationwide were sick; however, it was not necessarily fatal. In contrast, the outbreak of the flu epidemic in the fall of 1918 was devastating beyond compare. In total, the flu killed more than ten times the number of Americans than died on the battlefields of Europe. In fact, even in Europe the flu killed more American soldiers (over 57,000) than were killed in battle (over 54,000). On the home front the flu totally immobilized the entire country. No area was immune as the flu epidemic spread far and wide from rural towns to the big cities, and even to remote Eskimo villages. In total, within a three-month period more than one-half million people died an excruciating death and over 20 million were seriously ill. The global effect was equally astonishing as the estimates of those killed by influenza were placed at over 100 million. In total, more people died within a few short months than from any other single illness in the entire history of the world (Kolata 2001, 5, 22–23).

The flu was so deadly that almost all sorts of activities, both personal and work-related, ceased. The epidemic prevented people from enjoying a simple walk or attending a public event. In an attempt to slow the spread of the disease, schools, churches, theaters, and other places of amusement, including dance halls, were closed.

The combination of the Great War and the Great Flu epidemic affected every American—leaving many disenchanted and doubtful if life would even continue. *The Journal of the American Medical Association* noted in its final edition of 1918:

The [year] has gone: a year momentous as the termination of the most cruel war in the annals of the human race; . . . [and] unfortunately a year in which developed a most fatal infectious disease causing the death of hundreds of thousands of human beings (December 28, 1918, 2154, 2174–2175).

In addition to the war and the flu epidemic, African Americans had the additional burden of segregation. The 1896 Supreme Court Decision of *Plessy v. Ferguson* essentially declared segregation the acceptable law of America. Eleven of the former Confederate southern states enacted laws to separate all places of public accommodation. "Whites Only" and "Colored Only" signs were commonplace in cities and towns throughout the South. Oklahoma, a state for barely three years, joined the segregation crusade in 1910 (Trotter 2001, 289–290). Sadly, although not necessarily enforced by law, the segregation practice extended throughout the United States. Other areas, such as the Southwest and California, segregated Asians, Mexicans, and Native American Indians. These practices carried over into all phases of life, including places of public accommodations and entertainment facilities, especially dance halls.

To escape the long working days, low wages for the average working person, whether on the farm or in the city, and the problem of segregation, families would gather around a sing-along piano, singing songs popularized by barbershop quartets and marching bands such as John Philip Sousa. Vaudeville, nickelodeons, and Broadway's Ziegfeld Follies were popular. The neighborhood saloon was a place where many working class people and immigrants spent most of their leisure time. The development of cheap amusements such as penny arcades, amusement parks, and movie theaters also garnered great appeal.

Americans, especially the returning war veterans, were ready to put the awful past behind. The path was ripe for Americans to have fun and live recklessly—as the ensuing period of Prohibition and the Roaring 20s would prove. For many that involved having a drink, listening to music, and maybe dancing. Vernon Castle might have provided some foresight. In 1914, Vernon wrote,

People have altered the idea that only youth and dancing are synonymous; . . . it offers something as grateful to the old and middle-aged as to the young. . . . Here in America we are just beginning to wake up to the possibilities of dancing. We are flinging off our lethargy, our feeling of having time for nothing outside of business, and are beginning to take our place among nations who enjoy life (*Modern Dancing*, 38).

The Dances

For dancing is the loftiest, the most moving, the most beautiful of the arts, because it is no mere translation or abstraction from life: it is life itself.
—Maurice Mouvet, 1915

DANCE MASTERS AND DANCE INSTRUCTION BOOKS

During the first ten years of the twentieth century, it was not unusual for music to be played in the old nineteenth century tradition by a military band. Typical dances were mostly sedate Waltzes and Two-Steps, with a few Polkas, Quadrilles, Cotillions, and Lanciers. These dances and the format of the dance followed strict social etiquette guidelines from published sources by accomplished Dance Masters. In 1900, *Dancing and Its Relations to Education and Social Life* by Allen Dodworth, reissued from an earlier 1885 publication, was typical of the popular instructional dance booklets of the time. Simple illustrations demonstrated both the proper and the improper ways for a gentleman to hold a lady while dancing. In addition, instructions were given on how to properly conduct a dance. Dodworth, who died in 1896, had been America's most prominent dance instructor for over 50 years. The 1900 edition was only slightly revised and contained a new introduction by his nephew and successor T. George Dodworth.

During this time, Dance Masters, such as T. George Dodworth, Oscar Duryea, and Albert W. Newman, carried on the tradition set by Allen Dodworth, of teaching the set figures of Cotillions and Waltzes from the 1890s. Also, the Dance Masters taught only those dances considered acceptable to society. A full-page illustrated article on dance in *The Brooklyn Eagle* highlighted the "Latest Approved Position for Waltzing" by the Dancing Masters Association, as well as "Three Common Positions Which Have Been Officially Condemned" (July 7, 1901, 12). Many of the older dance masters also ridiculed many of the newer dances, especially if they were easy to learn and did not require intricate and expensive dance lessons.

Although "Dance Master" as a profession dated back to the European Renaissance, the first dance studio did not develop until the twentieth century. Ned Wayburn, a New York dancer, choreographer, and vaudeville entertainer was probably the first to open a series of dance studios. Marshall and Jean Stearns write that in the early 1900s Wayburn "had a monopoly on just about everything associated with the dance [and] operated the largest dancing school" (1994, 223). Around 1910, *Ned Wayburn Studios* were in operation in New York, Chicago, Atlantic City, and Florida. Wayburn also taught many famous celebrities and entertainers including Fred Astaire, Ann Pennington, Gilda Gray, Al Jolson, the Marx Brothers, and Marilyn Miller. Other professional dancers and teachers included Mr. and Mrs. John Murray, Louise Glaum, Wilma Winn and Everett Evans, and Dorothy and Carlos Sebastian (Dannett and Rachel 1954, 82).

For those who could not afford private lessons with a Dance Master, books and instruction manuals were plentiful. Caroline Walker's *The Modern Dances: How to*

Dance Them (1914), for example, provided "complete instructions for learning" the Tango, the One-Step, the Castle Walk, the Walking Boston (a waltz variation), the Hesitation Waltz, the Dream Waltz, and the Argentine Tango. Vernon and Irene Castle published *Modern Dancing* (1914) with not only dance instruction, but also advice on what to wear, what music to play, and how to properly arrange a dance. John Murray Anderson provided *Social Dancing of To-Day* (1914) with text, 29 diagrams and 52 illustrations. A few of the other dance instruction books included the following:

- Frank Leslie Clendenen, *Clendenen's Treatise on Elementary and Classical Dancing* (1903);
- J.S. Hopkins, *The Tango and other up-to-date Dances* (1914);
- Albert W. Newman, *Dances of To-day* (1914);
- Bales O'Donnell, *The Tango and the New Dances for Ballroom and Home* (1914);
- Eileen Swepstone, *The Tango: As Standardized and Taught by the Representative Dancing Masters of the North American Continent* (1914);
- George Hepburn Wilson, *A Study in Modern Dance Positions* (1916);
- Vivian Persis Dewey, *Tips to Dancers, Good Manners for Ballroom and Dance Hall* (1918); and
- Frank Leslie Clendenen, *The Art of Dancing; its Theory and Practice* (1919).

These dance instruction books allowed people to learn to dance within their home and accompanied by music.

During the 1890s and early 1900s, the popular form of home music was usually purchased as sheet music and played on a home piano. At the time automated player pianos became increasingly available. The player pianos were mechanical devices that could be wound like a clock. Upon insertion of a metal cylinder with dimples and projections into the player piano, the cylinders would raise and lower and strike the piano keys. Home music for sing-alongs or dancing could be attained without someone who actually knew how to play the instrument. The Victrola would eventually replace the player pianos.

During the late 1890s, a major technological breakthrough was the formulation of the Home Music Box and Thomas Edison's "Talking Box." Edison combined the reproduction of both the voice and music playable on one phonographic record. A short time thereafter, the Victor Talking Machine Company advanced Edison's phonograph concept into a record playing machine with a built-in horn speaker and finished wood cabinet. As a result, the Victrola enabled the American public to hear both the music and the singers within the comforts of a family living room. The "Victrola" was so widespread and popular that Americans adopted the term to describe record players of all kinds for the next half-century. The middle class especially began buying the Victrolas and recordings of popular artists. In turn, the Victrola also allowed Americans to host a dance party within the employment of musicians.

A September 24, 1904, *Saturday Evening Post* advertisement for the Victor Talking Machine, for example, promised it was "loud enough for dancing." By 1912 the double-sided disc, with one song per side, was an industry standard. Historian Donna R. Braden stated, "Discs were not only more portable and easier to operate

than [the previous wax] cylinders, but also had the technical capability to record more complex dance music'' (1988, 116). By 1914, the Columbia Record Company mass-produced the ''Double Disc'' that was playable on any manufacturer's record player. The advertisements of the day encouraged Americans to ''Dance!'' During World War I, however, relaxation with the new Victrola usually offered listening to only a choice of rousing patriotic songs such as ''Over There,'' ''You're a Grand Old Flag,'' or ''Let's All Be Americans Now'' (Braden 1988, 116; Panati 1991, 17; McCarthy 1971, 9).

This "Phonograph Ad" advertised the Columbia Double-Disc Records that encouraged Americans to "Dance!" The ad appeared in *Life* magazine in February 1914. The Granger Collection ID: 0007067.

THE TWO-STEP AND THE CAKEWALK

The Two-Step was one of the most popular dances in America dating from 1890 to 1910. (The Texas Two-Step and Country Two-Step were different variations and are discussed in Chapter 7.) As *The Complete Book of Ballroom Dancing* described, the "dance consisted of a series of chassés either forward or sideward to 2/4 or 4/4 music...a quick march with a skip in each step.'' A chassé is three changes of weight alternating each foot with a close of the free foot next to the foot supporting the weight. The Two-Step was popular at sedate elite balls and cotillions as well as in rural areas during barn dances and community socials and was done to the music of John Philip Sousa marches. At the time the Two-Step was popular and the Cakewalk dance was in decline (Stephenson and Iaccarino 1992, 19, 71).

The Cakewalk (sometimes Cake Walk) traced its origins to African American plantation slaves during the nineteenth century. The style was said to have developed from the slaves mimicking their masters dancing at a fancy ball. The Cakewalk was most popular during the 1890s, reaching its peak around 1896 or 1897 coinciding with Ragtime music. The dance involved a man and a woman side-by-side. The man held his hand out, and the lady placed her hand in his (sometimes they would interlock arms). They sauntered and strutted with their heads high, stepping in time to Sousa-type marches as well as incorporating elements of the Two-Step and Polka. It was common at an elite ball to have African Americans strut performance-like for the entertainment of the white elite, oftentimes in competition for a prize of a cake. The performances often resembled comedic antics involving wobbly knees, tipping high hats, and using canes as a prop. A 1903 American Mutoscope and Biograph Company film short *Cake Walk* illustrating a contemporary sampling from the period is viewable on *America Dances! 1897– 1948: A Collector's Edition of Social Dance in Film* (see bibliography) (McCarthy 1971, 9).

The Cakewalk, however, was not always accepted by mainstream society. The clergy was particularly harsh in denouncing it. An article in *The Brooklyn Eagle* newspaper on July 20, 1902, for example, reported on a Cakewalk contest at Coney Island in Brooklyn, New York. The article described the Cakewalk as "old-fashioned" and "one time popular." As if to imply the authenticity of the dance, they reported, "Every entry was a real Negro." In reality the statement revealed the segregation that existed nationwide ("A Plantation Cake Walk Makes Much Merriment," 4).

Implications of racial segregation and indifference to African American culture was so permeated in American society that statements such as reported in *The Brooklyn Eagle* were routine. In 1914, in *Social Dancing of To-Day*, for example, prominent dance instructor John Murray Anderson claimed that under proper tutelage all social dances could meet "the requirements for acceptance in Anglo-Saxon ballrooms" (31). Segregation and racial prejudice would unfortunately remain in music and dancing. However, it could not be denied that the development of the most popular American vernacular dances for the twentieth century would be introduced from either African American or Latin American traditions of dance and music.

THE TEXAS TOMMY, BALLIN' THE JACK, AND THE SLOW DRAG

In 1911, a theater production of *Darktown Follies*, which premiered in Washington, D.C., introduced the dances the Texas Tommy, Ballin' the Jack, and the Slow Drag. The dances, however, first originated around 1901 to 1905 and were performed on the rowdy stages of the Barbary Coast in San Francisco, California, and therefore were sometimes termed "tough dances." In 1913, the production moved to New York's Harlem's Lafayette Theater and popularized the dances for mainstream America. The New York production was such a hit that it is considered to have begun "the nightly migration [by wealthy whites] to Harlem in search of entertainment." The show moved downtown to Broadway in 1915 (Stearns and Stearns 1994, 125–127).

In 1912, Caroline and Charles Caffin in *Dancing and Dancers of Today* wrote, "The Texas Tommy dancers are perhaps more acrobatic than eccentric...the whirl which spins his partner towards the footlights with such momentum that without aid she must assuredly fly across them, must be nicely adjusted so that in neither force nor direction shall she escape the restraining grasp of his hand outstretched just at the right moment to arrest her...Poise and gentleness of handling must regulate the seemingly fierce toss of his partner, first in the air, then toward the ground" (269–271).

The Texas Tommy is the first known American social dance to incorporate the "breakaway" (dancing in an open position away from the partner). Therefore, it is considered the first swing dance and was the forerunner of the Lindy Hop (see Chapters 2 and 3). Dancer Ethel Williams described the Texas Tommy saying, "It *was* like the Lindy, but there were two basic steps—a kick and hop three times on each foot, and then add whatever you want, turning, pulling, [and] sliding." Dancer Willie Covan remembered, "The Texas Tommy had a different first step than the Lindy, or Jitterbug that's all" (quoted in Stearns and Stearns 1994, 128–129). A good version of the Texas Tommy was performed by dancers Fred Astaire and Ginger Rogers in the movie *The Story of Vernon and Irene Castle* (1939).

Another popular dance from the *Darktown Follies* was Ballin' the Jack. Historian Willis Laurence stated that the term "Ballin' the Jack" was a nineteenth century railroad expression that meant "traveling fast and having a good time." Songwriter Perry Bradford said he first heard the name in 1909 in Texas; however, African Americans had been dancing it for years before. It arrived in New York after 1910 and was described step by step in a song of the same name written by Bradford in 1913. The dance involved pulling both knees close together, swaying knees side to side, and then stepping in time around the dance floor. A part of the dance was considered risqué where the dancer twists around in a circle protruding the pelvis. This common African American hip movement from plantation days would influence the Twist during the 1960s and the Time Warp during the late twentieth century (Stearns and Stearns 1994, 98–99).

The ultimate dance to slower tunes that remained in vogue for the entire twentieth century was the Slow Drag. In 1901, dancer Coot Grant recalled that when she was 8 years old she saw couples dancing the Slow Drag in her father's Honky-tonk in Birmingham, Alabama. She watched through a peephole, "I remember the Slow Drag, of course, that was very popular—hanging on each other and barely moving" (quoted in Hazzard-Gordon 1990, 88). Charlie Love, a musician, recalls playing dances around 1903 in Louisiana and also remembered the Slow Drag. He said "They did the Slow Drag all over Louisiana, couples would hang onto each other and just grind back and forth in one spot all night" (quoted in Stearns and Stearns 1994, 21).

In 1911, famed ragtime composer Scott Joplin wrote the dance steps for the Slow Drag on the sheet music for a song he composed titled "Treemonisha." He advised to start the Slow Drag on the first beat of each measure of music. The foot movement was described, "When moving forward, drag the left foot; when moving backward, drag the right foot. When moving sideways to right, drag left foot; when moving sideways left, drag right foot." He advised if variations included prancing, the steps should be one step for each beat. Marching and sliding should correspond to the first and the third beats. Hops and skips on the second beat. The slower music could include the Schottische step doubled (McCarthy 1971, 8).

Mainstream America would not see the Slow Drag until 1929 in a Broadway play titled *Harlem*. The press was quite brutal in response to the dance. *The Brooklyn Eagle* chastised the "steaming couples, undulating with a great unholy violence never seen before" (February 21, 1929). *The New York World* lamented the "writhing lustily through their barbaric dances" (February 22, 1929). *The New York Daily News* was equally unsympathetic, warning that the police would stop the "orgiastic exhibition" (February 21, 1929). The *New York Sun* correctly assessed the Slow Drag, admiring "the slow sensual deeply felt rhythms which the Negro has brought to the white man and which the white man, however he may try, is always a little too self-conscious to accept" (February 21, 1929). The Slow Drag would eventually be known simply as a "slow dance" and remain in vogue for the remainder of the twentieth century, although it continually was chastised when performed by the youth.

RAGTIME AND THE DANCE BANDS

Many of the new youth dances of the early twentieth century were created in tandem with a new form of piano music called *Ragtime*. The music was firmly rooted in the African American tradition that began to replace the barbershop quartets and Sousa military bands. The music had a faster dance beat that younger adults enjoyed, but to which older adults objected. The distinguishing feature between the Sousa marches and Ragtime was the addition of syncopation. Syncopation added a beat in between the basic 1-2-3-4 so that the music would be played 1&2, 3&4 or described differently as "ba-da-bump" played within two beats of music. Agnes DeMille described syncopation and its relation to dancing. In *America Dances* she writes,

> A new kind of "rhythm" took over in the nation's songs and dances; the accent was placed, not on the downbeat as in European, *one*-two, but on the upbeat, or offbeat, one-*two*. This was African but it became American. Rhythmic beats began to be missed, and the accent slipped to unexpected counts....Now the Americans were clapping and stamping their dances on the offbeat (1980, 13).

Ragtime (sometimes simply referred to as "rag") was a music that reached across ethnic, social, and economic barriers. Many consider "Mississippi Rag" composed by William H. Krell in 1897 as the first "rag" song. Later that same year Tom Turpin released "Harlem Rag." The most noted of the Ragtime composers included Turpin, W. C. Handy, James Scott, Louis Chauvin, Joseph Lamb, and Scott Joplin (McCarthy 1971, 9). At first Ragtime was not well received by genteel society.

A first-page story that appeared on May 14, 1901, in *The Brooklyn Eagle* newspaper appeared under the headline "Oppose 'Ragtime' Tunes, Federation of Music Will Make Every Effort to Suppress Them." At its annual convention in Denver, Colorado, the American Federation of Musicians adopted a resolution calling Ragtime "unmusical rot" and would "make every effort to suppress and to discourage the playing and the publishing of such musical trash" (1). Regardless, Ragtime swept the nation, especially among the youth, and was the dominant dance music from the late 1890s until World War I. Along with Ragtime music came the onset of a dance craze that caused the development of bands and orchestras specifically for dancing.

Conflict exists in regards to labeling the Ragtime musicians as the first "dance bands," but in reality both the music and the dances accompanied each other. Therefore, it might just be a matter of acceptance of a definition of what a dance band actually was. Albert McCarthy in *The Dance Band Era* credits The Black and

Tan Orchestra in 1913, playing in San Francisco and Los Angeles, California, as most likely the first true dance band. The band included ten musicians, a large number for that time, and instruments of cornet, trombone, piano, two banjos, violin, string bass, and drums. The stringed instruments replaced the Sousa tuba, an innovation that was copied almost immediately (1971, 10–12). The Big Bands Database, on the other hand, speculates that in 1911 or 1912 "the very first leader to form a dance band" was Wilbur C. Sweatman, who formed an orchestra with a then unknown 21-year-old Duke Ellington on piano (Big Bands Database, http://nfo.net/usa/dance.html). In response to the claim of the Sweatman Orchestra, McCarthy states, "it seems more likely that what [Sweatman] played was a form of diluted ragtime....he was basically a vaudeville entertainer, whose forte was the playing of three clarinets at once" (1971, 10). But what is even more probable, is that there was no "one" orchestra or dance band, but rather a number of dance bands, in different regions, coming into being quite naturally in response to the public's desire to dance.

With the onset of the dance craze crossing ethnic, wealth, and generational lines, all sorts of venues opened for dancing. Since public dancing was in such high demand and the technology was not available for prerecorded music to be amplified to hundreds or even thousands of people at dances, the only option was live dance bands. As a result, for the first time, musicians could now earn a living playing dance music. In the early 1910s, many noted dance band members began their careers. Many of the musicians would achieve prominence continuing through the 1920s and some well past that time, including Charles Elgar, Charley Straight, Earl Dabney, Paul Specht, Fred Waring, Meyer Davis, Ted Lewis, Eddie Elkins, Art Hickman, Isham Jones, and Irving Berlin (McCarthy 1971, 10–11).

It was Ragtime music that accompanied the specific dances, and the syncopated rhythms worked hand-in-hand with the development of new dance steps. Sometimes the song came after the dance, sometimes the song came before the dance, and sometimes they developed concurrently. After 1910, as a result of the insatiable desire for dancing and the music for dancing, the music publishers became more insistent that a song must be danceable in order to achieve success (Spaeth 1948, 369). From that point on popular sheet music appeared "with parts for a dance band instrumentation." Some song titles reflected the types of dances, including "The Aeroplane Waltz" by Mamie R. Apple, "Maurice's Irresistible Tango" by L. Logatti, "The Maurice Syncopated Waltz" by D.D. Onivas, "My Tango Girl" by Arthur, Goetz, and Hirsch, and hundreds of others. Irving Berlin was one of many musicians who began composing Ragtime songs that catered to the dancing craze. They included "Show Us How to Do the Fox Trot" (1914), "The Syncopated Walk, Watch Your Step," and the "Chicken Walk." Berlin's most famous song of the dance period, "Alexander's Ragtime Band," although not solely a ragtime tune, was developed towards the end of ragtime and is considered by many as a transitional song toward the development of Jazz (McCarthy 1971, 9).

Ragtime and the new dances were lucrative to business owners of the many ballrooms in the cities as they encouraged the new dance craze. Professional dancer Irene Castle remembered, "When 'ragtime' swept the country [the] one-step came right along with it, killing off the waltz and the two-step." (Irene Castle, *Castles in the Air* 1980, 85). From the ragtime era to the end of the century, music and dance were intertwined.

ANIMAL DANCES, THE TURKEY TROT, GRIZZLY BEAR, AND BUNNY HUG

The dances that accompanied the ragtime music of the time had names such as the Turkey Trot, Chicken Scratch, Monkey Glide, Grizzly Bear, the Bunny Hug, and many other less significant; hence they were more commonly known as "Animal Dances." These simple easy-to-do fun dances quickly replaced the Cakewalk and the Two-Step mainly among the working class. These dances simply required walking around the floor in the embrace of your partner and did not involve the strenuous exercise or coordinated foot patterns of the nineteenth century dances. The Animal Dances received their name mainly because of the manner in which the dancing couple embraced each other, flailed their arms, or caricatured their dance steps, jaunts, or even hops like barnyard animals. Although the Animal Dances were a part of the working class for the previous few years, the society groups and mainstream America did not pick up on them until after 1911 (Chapman 1997, 99). The most popular of the Animal Dances were the Turkey Trot, Grizzly Bear, and Bunny Hug.

The Turkey Trot was an American vernacular dance, and unlike previous dances introduced to America, it did not have European traditions. It was most likely invented in San Francisco along the infamous Barbary Coast around 1900. The popularity was because it was simple, easy to learn, and fun—something that anyone could do—and it captivated the masses and created a nationwide (although mainly in the urban cities) mania of fast and fun dances.

As with the Turkey Trot, the Grizzly Bear and the Bunny Hug, along with the Texas Tommy, trace their origins

The "Turkey Trot" became a generic name used by the press for any of the Animal Dances. The illustration, published in the *Saturday Evening Post* in 1912, mocks the Animal dances. Library of Congress, Prints and Photographs Division CD 1—Johnson (H), no. 92 (DLC/PP-1970: R322.92).

To dance the Turkey Trot, the man and woman started in a face-to-face closed position. He would grasp his right arm around the lady's waist, and both would joyfully strut around the dance floor in single steps. At an opportune point in the music or during a musical break they would stop and proceed to alternate placing their heels out from their body (known as "heel touches") while at the same time flailing their elbows and arms emulating a turkey, hence the name. From 1911 to 1913, the dance "ruled the roost." At that time the Turkey Trot also became a generic name used by the press to describe any of the Animal Dances (Chapman, 14). Two other animal dances that achieved some staying power were the Grizzly Bear and the Bunny Hug.

to San Francisco's Barbary Coast. The Grizzly Bear was first introduced to Broadway in the Ziegfeld Follies of 1910 and quickly spread to other cities. The appeal laid in the fact that the dancers literally bear hugged each other, allowing them to get as close as possible with only the thickness of their clothing separating them. StreetSwing.com describes the dance as "basically a One Step, swaying shoulders back and forth on each step." A simple version involved taking a sway step to the side, holding each other in a bear hug "in correct imitation of a dancing bear," and proceeding to alternately step and sway to either side (StreetSwing.com, "Grizzly Bear," n.d.). Irving Berlin wrote a "rag" song titled "Grizzly Bear" intended for the Grizzly Bear dance. The illustrated cover of the sheet music portrayed a dancing couple in a "grizzly bear" hug.

The Bunny Hug was a similar dance as the man and woman held each other tightly and hopped, shimmied, and shook like a bunny rabbit, although it was usually danced to slower tunes. Another version was the "Bunny Hop," which included a kick and a series of hops like a bunny.

The Animal Dances ushered in a dance craze with many fad dances that quickly came and went, including the Chinese Ta-Toa, the Pickford Polka (named for film celebrity Mary Pickford), Pavlova Gavotte, Lulu Fado, and numerous versions of the Waltz and the Tango. Other dances of the period that quickly faded included the Eight Step (similar to a Tango), the Polka Skip (a Castle Walk done in polka time), the Media Luna, the Lame Duck, Buzzard Lope, the Fanny Bump, Fish Tail, Eagle Rock, Itch, Camel Walk, Chicken Scratch, Monkey Glide, Kangaroo Dip, Possum Trot, Bull Frog Hop, Buzz, Shimmy, Squat, Grind, Moche, Funky Butt, and hundreds of other dances of similar names that sought to capitalize on the dance mania. Musician Perry Bradford recalled, "Touring the South, I saw a million steps in a million [honky] tonks. The dancers had all kinds of names and [sometimes] no names for the dances" (Stearns and Stearns 1994, 103). At first, the Animal Dances were extremely popular among the young and the African Americans. They also became popular among all ages and spread to white society. With the popularity among mainstream America also came objections.

Most objected to the fact that the Animal Dances did not require training from a dance instructor since it appeared that all a gentleman had to do was grab a willing lady, pull her close, and twirl madly around the floor. Much of the attack might simply have been that these dances had origins among working class people and African Americans in bordellos, honky tonks, and saloons.

Objections to the Animal Dances varied from simple ridicule to severe penalties. StreetSwing.com notes, "On July 22, 1913, written on a dance card from the Exposition Park dancing pavilion in Conneaut Lake, [Pennsylvania] it was written that the Grizzly Bear Dance and Turkey Trot would not be tolerated" (StreetSwing. com "Grizzly Bear," n.d.). Editor Edward Bok fired 15 young women from *Ladies' Home Journal* magazine after he caught them dancing the Turkey Trot (Stephenson and Iaccarino 1992, 26). Irene Castle recalled a story of a New Jersey girl who "was arrested for Turkey Trotting down the street in a residential neighborhood." Upon demonstrating the dance in court the jury acquitted her (Irene Castle, *Castles in the Air* 1980, 85). Sylvia Dannett and Frank Rachel write in *Down Memory Lane* that a "Paterson, New Jersey, court imposed a fifty-day prison sentence on a young woman for dancing the turkey trot" (1954, 75). Close dancing in connection with the Turkey Trot was also unfavorable.

A publication edited by Beryl and Associates, *Immorality of Modern Dances* (1904), claimed an endorsement on its cover as "highly recommended by clergymen of the Roman Catholic and Protestant Churches as Well As By Jewish Rabbi." The language within the entire text preached with all fire and brimstone to "condemn dances which demand close bodily contact between man and woman" (28). Billy Sunday, the most prominent evangelist of the early twentieth century, preached against the evils of society including drinking, profanity, gambling, smoking, and promiscuity. Between 1906 and 1918, he preached to a combined total of over 80 million people. He was particularly harsh on dancing. Sunday was quoted on numerous occasions as saying, "I say, young girl, don't go to that dance; it has proved to be the moral graveyard that has caused more ruination than anything that was ever spewed out of the mouth of hell" (quoted in Erenberg 1981, 258–259).

The Congress of American Dancing Teachers meeting in 1915 posed "one momentous question...how far apart dancers should dance?" The question was still asked even though the previous year they approved "a distance of from three to six inches" ("Cabarets Confound the Dance Masters," September 12, 1915, 10). In response, many dance instructors changed the names of the dances and also toned down the "vulgar" parts of the dances. The Castles, for example, taught the One-Step, derived from the Turkey Trot by eliminating movement and wiggles at the shoulder and waist. As early as 1914, *The New York Times* claimed "that the turkey trot, as it was danced here about two years ago, when it started as a craze...has been trimmed, expurgated and spruced up until now it is quite a different thing. Gone are the wriggly wabbles, with the shoulders bobbing up and down" ("All New York Now Madly Whirling in the Tango"). After 1910, most of the Animal Dances were replaced by the One-Step, the Maxixe, the Hesitation Waltz, the Castle Walk, and two of the most distinctive social dances of the period, the Tango and the Foxtrot.

HARRY FOX AND THE FOX TROT

Dance historians Sylvia Dannett and Frank Rachel write in *Down Memory Lane* that the Fox Trot "was the dance that sought and proved to be so typically American in its rhythm that it pushed all the other dances into the background" (1954, 79). During the 1910s the Fox Trot, sometimes known as the "horsetrot" or "fishwalk," originated. (The spelling of the term varies widely, including "Foxtrot," "foxtrot," and "Fox-trot.") Some minor disagreement exists concerning the origin of the dance. The most consistent and plausible is that it originated from a working class vaudevillian performer named Harry Fox.

As part of his vaudeville act, Fox trotted on the stage and created steps to Ragtime music. Vaudeville at the time was mainly an entertainment venue for working class and immigrants. He sometimes alternated a slow walk with three trotting steps and the dance was called Fox's Trot. However, the continuous trotting was not necessarily a step that the dancing public could maintain on the social dance floor. In 1913, dance master Oscar Duryea was asked to develop Harry Fox's steps

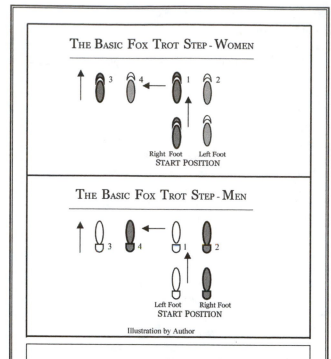

THE BASIC FOX TROT STEP - WOMEN

Right Foot   Left Foot
START POSITION

THE BASIC FOX TROT STEP - MEN

Left Foot   Right Foot
START POSITION

Illustration by Author

The Fox Trot was danced either in progressive line of dance around the floor or as a "spot dance." A spot dance simply meant that the dance couple danced within a particular spot or stayed within the same area of the dance floor. This was usually done when the dance floor was crowded. The Fox Trot is danced from a closed position in a 4/4 rhythm with a series a gliding steps sliding the feet on the floor. The man started on the left foot and the woman with her right foot. (This would remain a 20th century standard for all American social couple dances in a lead and follow face-to-face situation). The steps were walking in rhythm in a slow-slow-quick-quick pattern (Some versions reverse the pattern as quick-quick-slow-slow. Ballroom version and DanceSport competitors start "off the beat" on the rhythm or the "&1" and some also teach &1 with a reverse pattern of quick-quick-slow-slow). Due to the combination of slow and quick steps many stylized patterns lent themselves to easy adaptation within the dance. The Fox Trot also incorporated elements of the old Two-step and many pivot turns and glides of many other dances.

and refine them for social dancing (Dannett and Rachel 1954, 79). In 1914, the Congress of American Dancing Teachers adopted Duryea's standardized Fox Trot "in an effort to have it taught the same everywhere" ("Cabarets Confound the Dance Masters," 1915, 10).

The Fox Trot is an easy dance to learn and versatile enough to fit almost any style of twentieth century American popular music. This versatility and adaptability is the reason that many dance historians cite the Fox Trot as the dance that changed dancing as it was known throughout twentieth century America. It was the first dance to alternate between slow (two beats of music) and quick (one beat of music) steps. Amateur dance historian James Nicholson writes, "This flexibility also extended to musicians. The Fox Trot is basically from the Two-step, however, it's done with a broken instead of an even beat (Basically Slow-Slow-Quick-Quick). This syncopation rhythm gave musicians greater freedom in arrangements." In turn, the dancers had a greater range of freedom to incorporate whatever pattern they chose to dance. As probably the most enduring dance of the twentieth century, the Fox Trot pattern would be adapted to the Lindy Hop, Jitterbug, and Country Two-Step.

MAURICE MOUVET, THE TANGO, CABARETS, THE APACHE, AND THE MAXIXE

Maurice Mouvet was the dancer and dance instructor who successfully bridged the gap between the working class and fashionable society. Mouvet was born in Brooklyn, New York, into a working class family of Bavarian immigrants. He avoided the traditional immigrant role of factory work or small business ownership and worked at the art of social dancing. He was an accomplished social dancer by the time he was 14 years old. In 1907, he was sent by his father to Paris in order to expand his dancing knowledge.

At the time Paris was looked upon as the leader in social dance. Prior to his Parisian experience Mouvet, in his autobiographical dance instruction book *Maurice's Art of Dancing* (1915), wrote, "I could do the Polka and the Cake-walk and the Two-step, but I did not know how to Waltz" (12). He learned the Waltz by going to Parisian ballrooms. He continued his learning and honing his teaching style by traveling to Vienna, Austria, where he picked up on the Viennese Waltzes. Mouvet said, "In my eagerness to perfect the Viennese Waltz, I went whenever possible to places where I might have an opportunity of dancing with the women who had known the waltz since they were little children and who absorbed it, in some way so that it had become an expressive part of themselves" (15–16). Mouvet's pattern of development would serve all social dancers well in the twentieth century. Only so much could be learned in a dance studio or from an individual dance instructor. The essence and soul of dancing could be effectively learned only with many hours of patience and enjoyment of actually doing the dances.

Mouvet is credited with introducing the Apaché, the Brazilian Maxixe, and the Argentine Tango. These dances originated among the working classes of South American cities and Parisian saloons; however, Mouvet assisted in the transition of these dances from lowbrow to highbrow acceptance.

Some sources date the Tango to the early 1800s as the Spanish brought the dance to South America. Cyril Rice linked the Tango dance to African slaves in the Caribbean. Rice discovered an 1836 entry in Esteban Pichardo's Cuban Dictionary defining Tango as a "gathering of newly arrived Negroes to dance to the sound of their drums." It became popular in Argentina and Brazil around 1850. By 1880, the Tango was danced with a *con corte*, "a pause in the continuity of the movement [and a] sway of the hips and shoulders" (*The Dancing Times*, "The Tango Bombshell," 1937, quoted in Chapman 1977, 29–30). It was brought to Paris around 1900 where it became very popular about 1908–1909. In 1910, it was Maurice Mouvet who introduced the Tango to America by way of Paris ("The Tango," Library ThinkQuest.org, n.d.).

While in Paris, Mouvet learned the Tango from "a group of young South American boys...dancing their national dance." He refined the dance with eight steps "with only six steps and four figures (instead of the original eight)...the Promenade, Cortez, Media Luna, El Paso, L'éventail, Les Ciseaux, El Pados, and the Single Three" that became the standard American Tango for the twentieth century. The Tango is danced in 2/4 time with eight measures and 16 counts to each figure. The Tango rhythm is a slow-slow-quick-quick-close. The hold is a basic closed position with "the man's hand extending with the palm turned upward and the women's right [hand] resting lightly in it. The arms are always curved. The man's right arm is around his partner's waist, supporting her slightly." The Tango is the exception to the rule that all dances begin with the left foot for the man; the lead began with either foot (Mouvet 1915, 85–87).

Mouvet's description of one of the basic figures included the Promenade and the Half Cortez. The Promenade was both the man and woman walking forward. The Half Cortez involved a step forward with the right foot of the man pointing the left foot and slightly turning the body. The woman mirrored this pattern, only backwards. They would hold a count of two and reverse direction while the man "slightly bending the left knee and raising the right toe [and the woman] slightly bending the knees and raising the left heel" (1915, 87). Many have described dancing the Tango as telling a story, and the patterns are danced within the 16 or 32 beat phrasing of Tango music.

In reality the Tango was not danced all that often when first introduced to New York simply because it was difficult to learn and do. The dance couple of Vernon and Irene Castle popularized the Tango on the Broadway stage and in New York cabarets. Vernon Castle claimed "its too sensuous character was gradually toned down, and from a rather obscene exhibition…it bloomed forth a polished and extremely fascinating dance." Irene Castle cautioned a hostess in arranging a dance set that the Tango "is not generally known or danced, and therefore no more than one or two of these should be introduced in the afternoon's progress" (*Modern Dancing* 1914, 83, 158).

The Tango was featured in a few silent films of the period including *Tango Tangles* (1914) and *The Tango Queen* (1916). The Tango maintained steadfast popularity throughout the twentieth century—mainly shifting to ballroom aficionados. Other movies that included Tango scenes were *The Four Horsemen of the Apocalypse* (1921), *The Sheik* (1921), *Strictly Ballroom* (1992), *Evita* (1996), *The Tango Lesson* (1997), and *Tango* (1998). In *Assassination Tango* (2002), according to Internet Movie Database, "the tango scenes [are filmed] with the utmost respect [that] the dance commands…Fans of the Tango should not miss" (http://imdb.com/title/tt0283897/#comment). In the Hollywood movie *Scent of a Woman* (1992), the Tango is described by actor Al Pacino as "the easiest dance. If you make a mistake and get tangled up, you just Tango on."

The sensuality and closeness of the new dance infuriated moral reformers, and many cities banned the dance outright. In *Steppin' Out: New York Nightlife and the Transformation of American Culture 1890–1930*, music historian Lewis Erenberg writes, "To the dismay of moralists, men and women in the tango even brought legs and pelvic regions into intimate contact in the much feared dip portion of the dance, which placed women in a horizontal position reeking of sexual exploration" (Erenberg 1981, 155). Objections to the Tango were widespread and numerous. Between the years 1913 and 1915, *The New York Times*, for example, continually blared headlines denouncing the Tango. A few examples include the following:

- Chicago Mayor Carter H. Harrison "Bans Tango Restaurants" (November 30, 1913, 1);
- "Catholic Church Fighting the Tango, Cardinal Farley Has Inaugurated a Crusade Against the Modern Dances," (January 2, 1914, 9);
- "Mothers in Society Oppose the Tango" (January 11, 1914, 6); and
- "Tango Pirates Infest Broadway, Afternoon Dances Develop a New Kind of Parasite Whose Victims Are the Unguarded Daughters of the Rich" (May 30, 1915, SM16).

In 1914, *The New York Times* also reported that the Congress of American Dancing Teachers confronted a "big problem [on] what to do about the tango" ("All New York Now Madly Whirling in the Tango").

In defense of the Tango, Mouvet wrote, "A good many people have criticized the Tango because they have seen it improperly danced….For dancing is the loftiest, the most moving, the most beautiful of the arts, because it is no mere translation or abstraction from life: it is life itself" (1915, 71, 86). The attack on the sensuous nature of the dance would be a continuing cycle of criticism and objections to each of the new dance styles that emerged throughout the twentieth century. In 1958, Irene Castle said, "As I look back on the tango battle, it doesn't seem possible that so many people could have been so worked up over something so very foolish" (*Castles in the Air*, 1980, 86).

Another dance that Mouvet learned in Paris was *La valse Chaloupée*, more commonly known as the "Apaché." The Apaché was a theatrical dance that had roots among the rough and seedy underworld of Parisian clubs. Mouvet first saw it at a club named Caveau des Innocents and termed it a "dance of realism [and] primitive passion." He practiced this dance for six months before presenting it at an upscale Parisian club called the Café de Paris. In October 1910, he returned to New York and introduced the Apaché with partner Madeleine d'Arville at Louis Martin's upscale cabaret in Manhattan. At first he thought the dance would attract the attention of police; however, "fashionable" New Yorkers flocked to Martin's (Mouvet 1915, 28–30).

Mouvet described the Apaché as "a man leaning over one of the rough tables laid down his poker hand and, crossing the room, grabbed one of the girls. She did not seem willing to dance, but with simple persuasion he raised one of his hands and gave her a smart smack across her mouth. It was a novel way to begin a dance." Mouvet added, "she submitted to be taken into the middle of the floor, and the peculiarly vicious and savage dance commenced." The partners warmed to each other and embraced. At the conclusion, "with sudden violence he unloosed her hold and pushed her none to gently onto the floor near his table. Then he returned, picked up his poker hand, and continued the game as if there had been no interruption." Mouvet claims that his performance of the Apaché dance at Louis Martin's in October 1910 "was the opening of cabaret in New York." The general dancing public attempted to copy the dance, but the fad was short-lived. In 1911, Mouvet met and married Florence Walton. For the next ten years they danced as a very popular cabaret performance couple (Mouvet 1915, 28, 35).

The cabaret was the forerunner of the nightclub that featured a combination of food, entertainment, and dancing for its patrons. The cabarets attracted an upscale patronage seeking to satisfy their desire to dance. Music historian Lewis Erenberg writes, "In the cabaret there were few mechanisms to facilitate the mixing of people who did not know each other. The dance card was not in force, and the idea that one should never dance with the same person twice in succession was forever broken" (1981, 122–123, 155).

Numerous cabarets opened in quick succession. At first many thought the combination somewhat unconventional, but the dance craze of 1911–1915 made dancing and the restaurant business a common attraction. Some restaurants held out; however, by 1913, in New York City, for example, "if a restaurateur wanted to stay in business" he was also in the dance business (Chapman 1977, 40). Most of the establishments that transformed their eateries to accommodate bands and dancing catered to the wealthier clientele. Some simply opened dance floors and either hired lesser-known entertainers or none at all. The venues would provide an opportunity for professional dancers such as Maurice Mouvet and Florence

Maurice Mouvet and partner Florence Walton demonstrate the Maxixe dance.   Library of Congress.

Walton to set the pattern of "acceptable" dances for the upscale crowd and for amateur dancers to watch and learn. Mouvet was sought out as a dance teacher, and soon all were learning to dance the Apaché, the Tango, and the Maxixe.

The Maxixe (pronounced "mashish"), although short-lived, is linked closely to two later twentieth century dances popular in America—the Samba (see Chapter 3) and the Lambada (see Chapter 6). The Maxixe started as a couple dance in Brazil around 1870. It was not considered a dance of the elite but rather a dance of "the street." The dance position involved close full body contact at all points from foreheads pressed together to interlaced legs (a distinctive feature of the Lambada). Historian John Charles Chasteen claims "Maxixe was not a specific rhythm, it was a way of moving one's body and also a way of syncopating and accenting the performance of the music....one could maxixe to various kinds of music, including polkas, lundus, Argentine tangos, and ultimately, sambas." The Maxixe was similar to the Argentine Tango and had similar South American roots, hence the reason that the Maxixe was sometimes referred to as the Brazilian Tango, especially when it first reached Paris around 1912 and shortly thereafter in New York. Some claim it was derived from the Cuban dance Habanera, which is almost identical to the Argentine Tango (McDonagh 1979, 28; Chasteen, "The Prehistory of Samba: Carnival Dancing in Rio de Janeiro, 1840–1917," 1996, 39–40).

Both the Castles and Maurice Mouvet popularized the dance in America, providing a stylized version in 2/4 time. Strict attention was kept between the carriage of the head and the position of the arms. The Maxixe was a complicated dance and therefore short-lived. Maurice Mouvet described it as follows:

[It is] a double quick march or two step with a skip in each step, done as rapidly as possible, while moving forward, backward and turning....The kick is very hard to do. The girl must lift herself from the floor to a certain extent....While it is the kick that makes the Maxixe it is a variation from the motif of this dance...yet the Maxixe has numerous figures (1915, 98–100).

The Maxixe was also performed by dancers Fred Astaire and Ginger Rogers in the movie *The Story of Vernon and Irene Castle* (1939). Maurice Mouvet's place in social dance history, however, would be overshadowed by the most influential dance couple of the twentieth century, Vernon and Irene Castle.

VERNON AND IRENE CASTLE, THE ONE-STEP, THE CASTLE WALK, AND THE HESITATION WALTZ

More than any other individuals of the twentieth century, dancers Vernon and Irene Castle were most responsible for influencing dancing and making it acceptable for all classes of American society. Vernon and Irene developed a graceful, smooth dance style that eliminated the "vulgar" aspects of the Animal Dances. They also made it respectable to dance in public, at dance halls, and at restaurants. This also marked the transitional dance period where many still looked to Paris as the leader of the newest social dance trends. But from this point, because of the influence of the Castles, the role would reverse, as America, mainly New York, became the center of introducing new styles of social dance.

Irene Foote was born in New Rochelle, New York, in 1893. She met Vernon (born 1887 in England as Vernon Castle Blythe) in New York City during rehearsals for a Broadway show. They married in 1910 and sailed to Paris for their honeymoon. It was while honeymooning that they first began dancing together and received Parisian acclaim as a dance couple. Upon return to America (the dance craze was already on) they came with the advance billing of having taken Paris by storm (Erenberg 1981, 159).

The Castles were an instant success and quickly gained popularity. They were featured in numerous newspaper and magazine articles that featured photographs and illustrative dance steps so every one could dance the "Castle Way." In response to previous objections of dance, the Castles stated the aim of their dance style and book was "to uplift dancing, purify it, and place it before the public in its proper light" (1914, 18). They said, "Drop the Turkey Trot, the Grizzly Bear, and the Bunny Hug etc. These dances are ugly, ungraceful and out of fashion." Castle etiquette "for correct dancing" advised "do not wriggle the shoulders. Do not shake the hips. Do not twist the body. Do not flounce the elbows. Do not pump the arms. Do not hop—glide instead" (1914, 177).

Vernon and Irene Castle were successful in toning down what they (and reformers) saw as vulgar aspects of the Turkey Trot. In doing so, they refined some of the moves and changed the name to the *One-Step*. In associating the dance with the same Ragtime music the Castles called the One-Step "the dance for rag-time music." They added that the One-Step was one of "the most popular of all dances . . . it can be learned in a very little time by anyone" (1914, 43).

In 1912, they introduced a toned down version of the Two-Step termed the *Castle Walk*, which was basically a graceful walk. The Castle Walk was made up in connection with a song of the same name written specifically for the Castles by the James Reese Europe band. Vernon explained that one should walk in same manner as described in the One-Step, but "Now, raise yourself up slightly on your toes at each step, with legs a trifle stiff, and breeze along happily and easily, and you know

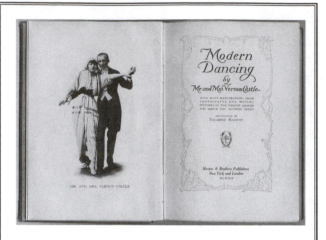

Vernon and Irene Castle's instructional dance book *Modern Dancing*, c. 1914. Author's Archives.

Vernon Castle, writing in *Modern Dancing*, described the One-Step as a basic closed position. But he warned,

> Don't stand too close together or too far apart... the gentleman starts forward with his left foot, and the lady steps backward with her right, walking in time to the music. Bear in mind this one important point: When I say *walk*, that is all it is. Do not shuffle, do not bob up and down or trot. Simply *walk* as softly and smoothly as possible, taking a step to every count of music (1914, 44).

And that was all there was to the One-Step. The main ingredient of grace and refinement was the key to the dance being executed properly—which is what the Castles so astutely demonstrated. Of the One-Step, Maurice Mouvet added, "It is marching without coming down smartly upon your heels; it is walking briskly, cheerfully, spiritedly on a smooth floor" (1915, 77).

all there is to know about the Castle Walk" (1914, 47). The Castles perfected this as their own and displayed it often in cabarets and society functions. They specialized in accentuating the dance as they turned a corner "leaning over slightly—just enough to make a graceful turn" (1914, 47). They would start with large graceful circles around the dance floor and continue to make smaller and smaller circles. As Vernon wrote, "It sounds silly and is silly. That is the explanation of its popularity" (1914, 47).

The Castles also refined and updated a version of the "old-fashioned Waltz." The Waltz dates to the early nineteenth century, and many versions transpired including the Viennese and the Boston. The Castles taught their version of the Hesitation Waltz, since Vernon admits, "Every one seems to do it differently." Vernon readily admits that neither he nor Irene invented the Hesitation Waltz, but knew "at least four persons" who claimed to have originated it. The dancers took a traditional closed position in the same manner as the traditional Waltz. Unlike the traditional Waltz, the man began on the right and the lady on the left mirroring the man's steps. Vernon describes, "Then the man steps back with the right foot, taking two steps on two counts, alternating the right and left foot; then he moves forward two steps—right foot, left foot—again allowing each step to fill in one count of the music....the steps should not be directly forward and backward...you should turn and travel just a little. For the next two counts the gentleman allows his [and his partner's] weight to rest on his left foot [and his partner on the right foot]." This adds the distinct hesitation or pause to the Waltz" (Castle and Castle 1914, 71–72). The Hesitation Waltz did not last long and would be replaced in the social dance scene with the standardized traditional steps of the Waltz during the 1920s.

By 1913, the Castles were in great demand as performers and as dance instructors to the wealthy of society. Their success led to the opening of Castle House, a

Manhattan dance studio located directly across the street from the fashionable upscale Ritz Carlton Hotel. They followed with a cabaret, the "Sans Souci." In 1914, they opened another dance studio named "Castles in the Air," and the following year a dance studio and ballroom "Castles-by-the-Sea" located at Coney Island in Brooklyn, New York. They also made a film titled *Social and Theatrical Dancing*, which might have been the first instructional dance movie (later called "an instructional dance video"). Also in 1914, they published their popular instructional book simply titled *Modern Dancing* (Erenberg 1981, 159–169).

Objections were even raised against the refined and graceful dancing couple, Vernon and Irene Castle. Irene Castle remembered, "By the fall of 1913 America had gone absolutely dance mad. The whole nation seemed to be divided into two equal forces, those who were for it and those who were against it. The battle of the newspapers began. Half of them condemned the new dances as not only unsightly, but downright immoral" (Castle, *Castles in the Air*, 1980, 85). In 1914, the influential *Ladies' Home Journal* "inaugurated a series of articles intended to show how dancing could be done with finesse—that is, in the fashion of Vernon and Irene Castle. Ironically, many of "the matronly readers raised such a moralistic hue and cry" the editor dropped the series after two articles. William Inglis of *Harper's Weekly* wrote, "I had seen drunken sailors cavorting in various parts in the world, but never anything like this in the presence of fathers, mothers and daughters" (Tompkins, *American Decades: 1910–1919*, 1996, 276, 278–279). The Reverend Joseph Silverman wrote an article in *The New York Times* titled "Denounces Modern Dances," saying, "The popularity of these obscene and so-called 'modern' dances lies not in any aesthetic qualities they possess, but purely and solely in the unlimited liberty that they give for indelicate proximity of the sexes" (5).

In response to the attack on dancing and in defense of her clients, the Castles, Elisabeth Marbury (a well-known influential producer and literary agent of the time) wrote, "These would-be reformers never see that they are tacitly admitting that it is ignorance of the dances, not knowledge of them that does the harm....If we bar dancing from the world, we bar one of the supreme human expressions of happiness and exultation (Castle and Castle 1914, 21, 26). Vernon Castle agreed with Marbury and also rebutted the critics. He wrote:

> Objections to dancing have been made on the ground that it is wrong, immoral, and vulgar. . . . It is possible to make anything immoral and vulgar; [it] all depends on how it is done....The modern dances properly done are *not* vulgar; on the contrary they embody grace and refinement (1914, 32–33).

Caroline Walker, writing in *The Modern Dances, How to Dance Them* (1914), echoed Vernon's statement with her own. She writes, "The new dances are not improper dances. On the contrary, they are just as proper and graceful as the time-honored waltz and two-step, and far more interesting." Walker also advised prospective students "If the poses shown in this book are carefully observed, and the instructions . . . are followed, these dances will be performed in a manner which cannot possibly provoke unfavorable criticism" (7–8).

Despite the objections, Americans of all walks of life rallied around the Castle style of dancing and contributed to the growing popularity of dancing during this period. Marshall and Jean Stearns write that the Castles were also a "major influence" on dancers Adele and Fred Astaire (see Chapter 3). Fred Astaire said of the Castles, "They were a tremendous influence on our careers." Fred and his sister Adele saw three Broadway musicals featuring Vernon and Irene between 1913 and 1914. They saw *The Sunshine Girl* at least nine times (Stearns and Stearns 1994, 225).

FASHION, THE GIBSON GIRL, AND IRENE CASTLE

Because of the widespread publicity of the Castles, Irene was one of the first celebrities to influence fashion in her clothes and hairstyle on a nationwide scale. The fashion styles for both men and women during the early 1900s followed Victorian era formality. In public, men wore long pant trousers, a waistcoat, a three-button jacket, a high collared shirt with a necktie, and a hat. Most times the hat was a derby, and the wealthy wore hats made of silk. In the summer months the hat was usually straw. Indoors the hat and jacket came off—but not the waistcoat.

Women, in all cases, were expected to act with proper etiquette and decorum. Their fashion style included a large hat, usually decorated with lavish feathers, ribbons, and bows. Their hair was long, but done up in a style to reveal the neck. The dress was expected to be long and cover the ankles, the hem usually dragging the ground. A prerequisite was a corset, a series of petticoats, a chemise (underclothes), and a shirtwaist. The 1900s brought a change in activities among women that necessitated changes in fashion. New fashions were required that would allow women to ride bicycles, play tennis, play golf, drive an automobile, and dance.

Prior to World War I, the *Gibson Girl* was the most popular fashion image. The image of the ideal American female was first drawn by illustrator Charles Dana Gibson for *Life* magazine in 1890. Because the image of the Gibson Girl was so influential, women between the ages of 15 and 30 copied her hairstyles and dressed as she did. Men were also captivated by her image. Therefore, even they copied the hairstyles and fashion attire of the men in the *Gibson Girl* ads. *The New York World* proclaimed, "before Gibson synthesized his ideal woman, the American girl was vague, and nondescript. As soon as the world saw Gibson's ideal it bowed down in adoration, saying 'Lo, at last the typical American girl'" (*This Fabulous Century, 1900–1910*, 1969, 183).

Gibson's image was fictional, but with dancers Vernon and Irene Castle the American public had real people to emulate. Irene Castle, more than any other individual of the period, was responsible for bringing about many fashion changes. Irene's dresses were elegant yet ever so slightly above the floor and loose enough to allow her movement to dance. Her short bob haircut and beaded head band (a practical application to keep her hair from getting in her eyes) was widely copied and predated the flapper fashion and hairstyles (Tompkins, *American Decades: 1910–1919*, 1996, 179). Young women influenced by the popular images of both Irene Castle and the *Gibson Girl* cut their hair and searched for similar dresses to wear. Men, likewise, were enamored of the popular image of the ideal "American Girl" and copied the fashion of Vernon with thoughts of attracting similar females.

The dance mania also changed fashions in shoes, hairstyles, hats, and other garments. The petticoats, corsets, and other restrictive undergarments were discarded in favor of clothes that allowed activity such as dancing. In a very short time the matronly Victorian era fashion styles were discarded, and the new ones began to resemble the flapper style of the 1920s. In 1914, Irene Castle started a national trend in both short hair and tight fitting hats. Supposedly, during a brief hospital stay, Irene was forced to cut her hair. In order to appear in public she purchased a "Dutch cap" which set off a nationwide trend.

Irene Castle, writing in *Modern Dancing*, also devoted a long chapter titled "Proper Dancing-Costumes for Women" to suggest eliminating "a gown that is stiff" and instead replacing it with a "plaited skirt of soft silk or chiffon [as] the most graceful to dance in." She further commented on other clothing and fashion items. For example, shoes "comfortable [and] fastened on securely"; "Big hats are

Vernon and Irene Castle set fashion trends that both American men and women emulated. In 1914, Irene started a national trend in both short hair and tight fitting hats. In this photo she wears short hair and a "Dutch cap," which set off a nationwide trend.   Library of Congress, Prints and Photographs Division LC- USZ62-120307.

unpleasant to dance in"; petticoats, stockings, blouses, and waistlines that "should always be high enough to eliminate the harsh line of the hips." Irene also endorsed a special corset made especially for dancing known as the "Castle Corset." Irene and Vernon also suggested proper dance music. Vernon Castle stated, "People can say what they like about rag-time. The Waltz is beautiful, the Tango is graceful, [and] the Brazilian Maxixe is unique...but when a good orchestra plays a 'rag' one has simply *got* to move." The Ragtime orchestra of choice for Vernon and Irene was James Reese Europe (1914, 43, 139–142, 147).

THE CASTLES AND JAMES REESE EUROPE

Regardless of who actually was the first dance band, the first of the prominent dance bands of the twentieth century was James Reese Europe and his "eighteen-piece all-black band." Europe, born in Alabama in 1881, traveled to New York in 1904 and worked as a piano player for a few years. He was well-established by 1910 and formed two clubs for African American musicians and entertainers, the Clef Club and later the Tempo Club. He was part musician and part agent as he booked hundreds of musicians at dances and social functions from New York to Chicago. By the time his band was hired in to accompany Vernon and Irene Castle for a 1914 Philadelphia engagement, he was an established ragtime performer. However, his association with them brought wider acclaim, and from that point on he was the dance band for the Castles (McCarthy 1971, 9).

As the Castles' dancing rose in prominence, so did Europe's band. Irene and Vernon felt that Europe's music complemented their dancing, and in a short time Europe began composing music specifically for Castle dances. One example was "Castle Walk" for the original dance of the same name. The Victor Record Company recorded Europe and his dance music with the label bearing the note "Recorded under the personal supervision of Mr. and Mrs. Vernon Castle" (McCarthy 1971, 10). It was apparent that Europe also had influence on some of the dances that the Castles learned. Irene said, "It was Jim Europe...who suggested the foxtrot to us" ("Swing Music and Popular Dance," *Dance Herald*, February 1938, quoted in Stearns and Stearns 1994, 98).

Unfortunately World War I would not only interrupt the appeal of dancing, it would also separate the Castles both from each other and from James Reese Europe. Prior to America's entry into the war, Vernon, a British citizen, volunteered as a flyer with the British Royal Flying Corp. In 1917, he returned to the United States as a flight instructor. During a routine flight, he crashed and died. Upon America's entry into the war, Europe enlisted as a member of the 369th Infantry (New York's famed "Harlem Hellfighters"). While in the Army, he formed an orchestra and was shipped overseas to play music for the American troops. Europe's band returned to acclaim at the end of the war and marched in the victory parade down Broadway in New York City. In 1919, Europe was stabbed during a dispute with a band member and later died (McCarthy 1971, 10).

Irene continued dancing and appeared in a few movies. She had a brief stint as a featured dancer at the 1939 New York World's Fair. In 1958, she wrote her autobiography *Castles in the Air*, mostly reminiscing about her dancing days with Vernon. In retrospect, she attributed her success with Vernon to "the sense of humor that permeated our dancing [and] the great sense of bubbling joy we shared when we danced." She died peacefully in 1969 (Castle 1980, 87).

The Places to Dance

Couples stand very close together, the girl with her hands around the man's neck, the man with both arms around the girl or on her hips; their cheeks are pressed close together, their bodies touch each other…they throw aside all restraint and give themselves to unbridled license and indecency.

—Louise De Koven Bowen, 1917

RURAL DANCE, AND NEIGHBORHOOD DANCE HALLS

Throughout America during the early twentieth century, social dancing was divided among social class. The elite continued the tradition of society balls. Rural inhabitants danced in one-room schoolhouses and barns, and immigrants danced in neighborhood social clubs and saloons. Although the dance mania after 1910 did not totally eliminate the class division, it did provide all Americans with a common interest in dancing.

Prior to the dance craze of 1911–1915, most dances were strictly social affairs for special occasions, such as a cotillion, an elite ball, or a barn dance. Charity balls during weekday evenings were strictly for the wealthy social classes. The Social Season was a standard affair among the wealthy elite from late fall until mid-May. The wealthy danced in the grand ballrooms of vacation resorts, and many had large grand ballrooms within their mansions. Fashionable vacation resorts for the wealthy existed in Atlantic City, New Jersey, Martha's Vineyard, Massachusetts, Saratoga, New York, Newport, Rhode Island, and Mackinac Island, Michigan, among many others. Dance cards were still in vogue. (The dance cards were pre-printed and sometimes distributed weeks before the actual dance.) The dance card listed the exact program of the music and types of dances scheduled to be played during the evening. Next to each dance was a space where the young lady could write in the name of a gentleman, thereby reserving a particular dance in advance. Social decorum of all classes dictated that the lady would reserve both the first and last dances for the gentleman who brought her, since a woman would never attend an event unescorted. It was also implied that it was not proper to dance two successive dances in a row with the same partner. This decorum also applied to dances in rural areas.

In most rural areas it was the one-room schoolhouse that served as a community center, of which more than 212,000 were in operation. During the week, it served as a school for the children. Sometimes in the evenings it would serve as a meeting hall, and on Sundays many were used for church services. Saturdays were usually reserved for dances. Rural areas also celebrated dances on special occasions, and almost everyone in the community attended them. Historian Andrew Gulliford noted that, "those too small to dance played outside until it got dark and then played hide-and-seek games underneath the school desks while their parents [danced] the schottische, the butterfly, the polka, and the waltz" (1992, 202).

The dance halls for the working class people and rural inhabitants were by no means similar to the grand ballrooms of the wealthy. The working class congregated within their own neighborhoods in smaller social halls and community centers, of which many were just a space to dance. Historian Kathy Peiss noted that working class families did not take part in the same recreational activities. She said, "Each family member sought recreation in different places outside the home, the father going to the saloons, adolescent daughters and sons attending dance halls, children flocking to the streets with only the mother staying at home" (Peiss 1986, 179). Many immigrants took part in communal social gatherings, sometimes impromptu, outside in the street or tenement yard.

A tenement was typically a four to six story masonry building about 20 feet wide by 60 to 80 feet long. Each floor had three or four small apartments that each housed an entire immigrant family. Sometimes there were four to ten family members crowded into a single room. The tenements were poorly ventilated, and sanitation was a problem. The backs of tenements were interconnected with yards that were surrounded by the buildings and were out of view from the street. The dancing in these yards was not publicized in the newspapers, but dancing did, in fact, go on.

A typical scene in a tenement yard was described by one individual in New York's Lower East Side as, "After they had practiced [dancing] they would play dance music, and all the girls and boys in the flats [apartments] would go in the yards and dance. How the people did enjoy that music! Everyone would be at their windows listening. Sometimes they would play old song tunes, so soft and so beautiful. Then the people would clap their hands; it was inspiring in a neighborhood like that" (Peiss 1986, 15). For indoor dancing, the tenement dwellers had access to mainly two types of dance establishments, the neighborhood social club or the neighborhood saloon.

Dances in a working class neighborhood were usually held in a social club. These social clubs typically had a saloon in front and a small area in the back for dancing. In New York City, for example, there were over 500 neighborhood dance halls. Unlike in the rural areas, the dances did not attract members of the entire family. They were usually attended by unmarried young women between the ages of 12 and 25 and young men who were just a little older. These dance halls were one of the few places that could provide social interaction without the chaperone of adult family members. For almost all couples, dancing together for a period of time usually ended with marriage. In the summer months, the working class has access to dancing at amusement parks such as Coney Island in New York (Peiss 1986, 88).

DANCING AT TURN-OF-THE-CENTURY AMUSEMENT PARKS

During the first decades of the twentieth century, Coney Island was an area of unparalleled amusement and attraction with its three amusement parks that included Steeplechase, Dreamland, and Luna Park. The beach and boardwalk offered inexpensive entertainment and attracted throngs of working class people. The area was a mecca for those seeking any sort of entertainment, and Coney Island was the first public area where different ethnic and social classes intermingled. A short distance away were three racetracks and fashionable hotels in Gravesend and Sheepshead Bay. The wealthy would venture to the amusement parks, and for the first time the social classes intermingled. An article in *The*

The dance halls for the working class people and rural inhabitants were by no means similar to the grand ballrooms of the wealthy. The working class congregated within their own neighborhoods in smaller social halls, community centers, and saloons.   Brown Brothers x 78.

Brooklyn Eagle newspaper on July 20, 1902, told of a new dancing pavilion opened by George Tilyou's Steeplechase Park at Coney Island. Almost 1000 people showed up to dance "in spite of the wind and rain, which drenched everybody... [they] filled the new dancing pavilion by 9:30 p.m." Dreamland (a neighbor to Tilyou's Steeplechase) also opened a ballroom. Similar dancing pavilions existed across America. In Utah, on the Great Salt Lakes, for example, were many dancing pavilions. Saltair, built in 1893 by the Mormons, was patterned after a Moorish temple and was probably the largest dance arena in America at that time. Garfield Beach, a popular resort near Black Rock, Utah, also had a large dancing pavilion built over the Great Salt Lakes. Both pavilions were also attractions for swimming and family amusements. Dancing was also a popular attraction at amusement parks nationwide.

By 1914, over 2,500 amusement parks were in operation. Two of the most famous were White City and Cedar Point. White City was a popular amusement park located in the south side of Chicago close to the elevated train of Chicago's

Salt Air Dancing pavilion, on the Great Salt Lake, Utah, c. 1901.   Detroit Photographic Company.

famous Loop. In 1905, two ballrooms were built at White City that could accommodate up to 1000 dancers and were often filled to capacity (Newman, "Jazz Age Chicago," 2000).

Cedar Point Amusement Park in Sandusky, Ohio, on Lake Erie also offered dancing for their guests at the Grand Pavilion and Cedar Point Coliseum. The Grand Pavilion offered elegant dining on the first floor and a dance hall on the second. However, dancing was so popular that another dance hall was located nearby in a building named the Coliseum. The Coliseum at Cedar Point was one of the largest buildings in the Midwest, with two floors for a combined total of over 90,000 square feet. The exterior measured 300 feet long and 150 feet wide and was topped by a series of distinct domes adding an additional 40 feet in height. The first floor had a dining hall, and the second floor a dance hall (Cedar Point Amusement Park: "A History of Cedar Point," n.d.).

The amusement parks were open only three or four months of the year, but the dance halls were open all year. However, almost all the dance halls throughout the

United States were segregated. In reality, segregation was worsening and extended to all places of public accommodation. It was especially severe in dance halls where African Americans certainly could not intermingle or dance as an integrated couple, and in most cases were denied entry if whites were dancing. By 1915, most cities instituted "whites-only" policies. African Americans, therefore sought to dance in Jook joints, Honky-tonks, and after-hours clubs (Nasaw 1993, 111).

JOOK JOINTS, HONKY-TONKS, AND AFTER-HOURS PLACES

"Jooking" was a slang term among African Americans for any social form of singing, playing, or dancing. Sociologist Katrina Hazzard-Gordon in *Jookin' The Rise of Social Dance Formations in African American Culture* writes that the term is most likely from the West African Bambara word *dzugu* or *jugu*, which means wicked or bad. It developed among African American slaves on American plantations and referred to singing and dancing. The word was also found among whites in northern Florida and Georgia who used it to describe "to go partying" (1990, 79–81).

In 1934, sociologist Zora Neal Hurston said, "Singing and playing in the true Negro style is called jooking" (quoted in *Jookin'* 1990, 63). Some differentiated that a jook joint was located in a rural area, a honky-tonk was located closer to a town, and an after-hours club was usually located in a city or on the outskirts. In any case they were some of the few places that either African Americans or low-income whites could attend freely. Patrons enjoyed dancing at these places regardless of their race, class, or gender. These places had no restrictions on the type of dance; therefore, the dances themselves were usually fast, simple, and fun. It was within these environments that dances such as the Slow Drag, Texas Tommy, the Black Bottom, Charleston, and hundreds of other dances would become popular across mainstream America.

The roots of the jook joints began shortly after the American Civil War. Although they could be found in mostly rural areas, some were in small towns, or even cities. Ambiance and décor was not the attraction; in fact, most were quite shoddy. A "jook joint" was defined by Zora Neal Hurston "as the word for a Negro pleasure house. It may mean a bawdy house. It may mean the house set apart on public works where men and women dance, drink, and gamble. Often it is a combination of all of these." Hazzard-Gordon adds the jook "was the only dance arena of its time that successfully accommodated the emerging regional culture among black freedman" (Hazzard-Gordon 1990, 79–82).

Another place for rural and low-income patrons to dance was the honky-tonk. The honky-tonk developed almost at the same time as jook joints but were closer to the urban areas and sometimes within cities. Honky-tonks offered the same elements of drinking, dancing, and music as the jooks, but they differed mainly in playing "more sophisticated music." The honky-tonk would also become associated with a style of music, which could be ragtime, blues, hillbilly, or the beginnings of jazz (Hazzard-Gordon 1990, 84–86).

The after-hours clubs developed after municipalities instituted licensing of public establishments such as amusement parks, saloons, and dance halls, about the early 1900s. The name was derived from the fact that they would stay open past the legally predetermined hour of closing set by municipal regulations. As with the jooks and honky-tonks, they were first and foremost businesses. Food and liquor were served, and music and dancing served as an attraction for customers. The locations of these places ranged from converted basements, storefronts, or small buildings on the outskirts of towns or in rural areas. The music could be as informal as a record-playing Victrola, a single musician, or even a small band. In one form or another, jook joints, honky-tonks, and after-hours establishments remained throughout the entire twentieth century (Hazzard-Gordon 1990, 88–90).

CONCERT-SALOONS, DANCE PALACES, AND MUNICIPAL DANCE HALLS

At the beginning of twentieth century America, social dancing was so popular that many establishments opened with the main purpose of offering dance bands and public dancing. During the years 1911 to 1915 in particular, Americans were engaged in a nationwide dance craze. The impetus of the dance craze was mainly in response to the lively music of Ragtime and early Jazz combined with the very easy Animal Dances including the Turkey Trot. However, according to historian Russel B. Nye, "The origins of the American public dance hall lay primarily in the nineteenth-century saloon" (1973, 14). Commonly known as the "concert-saloon," they appeared mainly in cities in the 1840s and 1850s, "reaching its height of popularity in the decades 1890–1910." In 1900, the Barbary Coast of San Francisco was reported to have over 300 such establishments in a six-block area. Chicago had over 285 (Nye 1973, 14). (Almost all the dance halls along the Barbary Coast were destroyed in the great San Francisco earthquake of 1905. The city was quick to rebuild, especially the profitable dance halls.) In New York City there were more than 500 neighborhood dance halls, in Chicago over 400, and in Cleveland 130 (Peiss 1986, 88). Most of these dance halls were open for only one reason—to sell alcohol. Some were disreputable, and a few offered prostitution. Nye concluded, "The association of dancing, music, liquor, and sex was well established in the public mind long before the close of the century (Nye 1973, 14).

With the dance mania, the emphasis shifted to larger venues that would provide only places for dancing. After 1910, many large dance halls in cities all across the United States began to replace the smaller neighborhood saloon dance halls. But what made them uniquely different was that they were elaborately decorated and furnished, fashioned after wealthy ballrooms and resorts. They were also opened to the public, and the attraction was dancing, not alcohol. They lived up to their name as "Dance Palaces" (see Chapter 2).

In 1911, the Grand Central Palace in New York City that could accommodate over 3,000 dancers was most likely the first of the grand ballrooms open to the public. The paid admission was not based on a single entry fee but was based on the number of dances. Tickets were purchased at 10 cents per dance or three for 25 cents. Some other dance halls would combine the per dance ticket price with an entry fee of between $1 and $1.50. Kathryn Murray recalled that the Grand

Central Palace was also "the first of the dance halls to provide hostesses to male patrons as dance partners at ten cents a dance." She also recalled that in 1912 her husband Arthur Murray (see Chapter 2) won a waltz contest at the same dance hall and began his career as a dance instructor (Murray 1960, 40).

Other cities such as Cleveland, Chicago, and San Francisco also opened similar ballrooms. In the city of Chicago alone it was estimated that at least 86,000 people attended a dance hall each evening, a number that exceeded the number of people attending a movie or any other form of entertainment. Other cities reported large numbers attending dance halls. For example, Kansas City reported an average weekly total attendance of over 16,500 people and Milwaukee estimated 9,300 on any given Saturday night (Nye 1973, 15).

Large ballrooms such as Roseland in New York City (which was open past 1:00 A.M. every day of the week) could accommodate 3,000 people on the dance floor. These halls were open and available for working and middle class people. Large dance halls of similar capacities opened in cities all across America including Chicago, Cleveland, Des Moines, Kansas City, Milwaukee, Newark, Philadelphia, and St. Louis. In Kansas City, municipal authorities counted over 49 dance halls (Nasaw 1993, 111).

Many municipalities followed suit and sponsored dance halls in public parks and public buildings. In 1912, in Cleveland, Ohio, for example, the Municipal Parks Department converted two park shelter houses into dance halls. The purpose as stated by a Cleveland dance hall inspector "was to offer an opportunity for dancing under the best possible conditions...our young people can spend a pleasant evening at dancing amid a wholesome surrounding." One at Edgewater Park on Lake Erie and adjacent to a manufacturing and tenement district had a dance floor 83 feet by 34 feet. Tickets were sold at the rate of three cents per couple for each dance. Opening night recorded 11,630 dance tickets sold. Another was opened at Woodland Hills Park and had a dance floor of 76 feet by 33 feet. Other municipalities followed Cleveland's successful example ("Cleveland's Municipal Dancing Pavilions," 1914, 34–35).

In 1913, Cincinnati sponsored a local music hall for public dances with a floor 85 feet by 280 feet. Children danced on Saturday afternoons from 2:00 to 5:00 P.M. and adults every Saturday night from 8:00 to 11:30 P.M. Twenty-two dances averaged 643 persons per dance. In 1914, the city of Chicago funded Dreamland Hall, located in Chicago's west side. Forty-three public dances were held with a total attendance of over 17,000 people. The municipalities of Denver, Milwaukee, San Francisco, and Seattle also sponsored successful dances (Rex 1915, 415–419).

Dance studios opened at as rapid a rate as places to dance did. But many of the dances were simple and quick to learn and did not always require expensive lessons. In 1913, a *New York Times* article "Dance Craze Stays But Amateurs Rule" quoted one manager as saying:

> Those who have not yet learned to dance seem to like the dancing of the skilled amateurs better than that of the professionals. Indeed, there are many men and women in New York now who dance for their own amusement whose dancing equals that of any of the best professionals (20).

With the public's desire to dance, many places offered dancing every night of the week, which extended into the late hours.

Unlike the earlier periods during the nineteenth century of dances only on a special evenings and long breaks between the actual dancing, the insatiable American desire was for continuous dancing. In an age before amplification and prerecorded music, the only opportunity for continuous music was provided by a live orchestra or band. Therefore, the larger venues usually hired two bands to provide continuous music, thereby eliminating the long breaks between music that was so prevalent in the years before the twentieth century. Some even offered afternoon dances termed "afternoon tea dances" or "tango teas," or *dansants*. In a very short time it seemed that everyone was dancing—at least in the cities. *Vanity Fair* reported "all you need do is walk up Broadway in the afternoon, evening or night, or browse around the hotels...There is dancing at all of them, and with it, exhibition dancers and teachers ("The Dance Craze—If Dying—Is a Remarkable Invalid," 1915, 34).

In 1914 a *New York Times* reporter sought information on the dance craze for a full-page article in the Sunday magazine section. During the course of one Saturday he visited 13 different dance halls from 1:00 P.M. in the afternoon until well past 3:30 A.M. the next morning—over 14 1/2 hours of continuous dancing. During the afternoon he found that women greatly outnumbered the men. He traveled from a "tea dance" to a "roof of a big hotel." He also traveled to a "tango tea" described as "a very private very select sort of affair" (*New York Times Sunday Magazine Section*, "Contemporary Dancing has Evolved the Concave Man," January 1914) (Chapman 1977, 93).

MUNICIPAL DANCE HALL REGULATIONS AND CHARITY GIRLS

An early advocate of the benefits of dance as physical education within the public schools was Luther Halsey Gulick. Gulick was also a founding member of the YMCA in Springfield, Massachusetts. In the early 1900s, he moved to New York City and continued in promoting recreation and physical education, especially in the public schools. In 1910, Gulick published *The Healthful Art of Dancing*, promoting social dance among the youth, adults, and elderly. He wrote,

> In America we have so completely forgotten the deeper possibilities of dance that the word in general use has come to have but one meaning, namely a man and a woman holding each other and performing an exceedingly simple whirling movement of music set in four-four or three-four time (quoted in Wagner 1997, 252).

Gulick was mainly an advocate of folk dancing and supported the cultural influence of dance by immigrants. He said that Americans did not "[understand], cared for, or even thought about the precious social heritage [immigrants] might give us—a heritage of art, of story, of music, of the dance....Dancing is not only the most universal of the arts, but the mother of all art." Other dance advocates of the time included:

- Dr. Thomas D. Wood, *The Ninth Yearbook of the National Society for the Study of Education* (1910);
- Emil Rath, *Aesthetic Dancing* (1914); and
- Louis H. Chalif's *The Chalif Text Book of Dancing* (1914).

As a result, many public schools in urban areas instituted mandatory physical education programs that included folk or social dancing. However, it was also apparent that many others simply misunderstood the word "dance" and still sought to regulate public social dancing (Wagner 1997, 252–253).

Most municipalities, including New York, Chicago, and Buffalo, enacted legislation regulating dance halls. A common concern, in an age before cities and states enacted uniform building codes, was the dangers of overcrowding and limited protection or exits in case of a fire. From 1909 to 1912, Belle Linder Israels (sometimes seen as Mrs. Charles H. Israels) of the Committee on Amusement and Vacation Resources for Working Girls continually pushed for regulation in New York City. In 1914, the City of Buffalo, New York, for example, issued "Ordinances Governing the Conduct of Public Dances and Dance Halls." The Buffalo ordinance provided for licensing and regulations including "the protection of the public health, for the safety of buildings and for the protection of the public from fire" (3). The ordinance also provided for the revoking of a license and closing a dance hall if "any indecent or immoral act is committed, or...vulgar character takes place" (5). The ordinance also prohibited any alcohol in "any dance hall, or in any room directly opening into such dance hall" (8). In response to the temperance movement, the Castles argued that "[p]eople who dance drink less" (33).

Similar legislation was enacted to prevent the sale of alcohol "under the same roof" as dancing. These were sometimes known as "Cabaret Laws." Establishments sought many creative ways to counter the restriction. Some simply held dances outside or up on the roof. An article in *Variety* reported that in Chicago, for instance, the following:

> A number of cabarets have gotten over this by taking the roof off. In other words they are running gardens, or outdoor cabarets, and the corporation council has held that this is in compliance with the letter of the law....Others have divided their places by glass partitions, thin enough to permit the noise of the music to be heard in the "booze" department of the resort. Others have used lattice partitions ("Beating Chi's Cabaret Law," 1918, 3).

In a fashion similar to those of Chicago, fashionable hotels such as the Waldorf-Astoria in New York City opened the roof terraces, and for the social elite a "roof season" was available. One *New York Times* article, "Admit New Dances to Roofs of Hotels," reported the opening of roof terraces offered a surprise welcome relief, especially during hot summer months. The article reported that the cool rooftop breezes provided the dancers "a chance to dance in the summer, where they would stand a chance of being swept by the breeze without having to go down to Coney Island" (1914, Sec. 2, 12).

However, many municipalities and moral reformers sought to close down these dance establishments. In 1917, for example, Louise DeKoven Bowen, under the direction of The Juvenile Protective Association (JPA) of Chicago, authored a report titled "The Public Dance Halls of Chicago." DeKoven Bowen stated the reason for the report was to respond to "so many complaints, regarding dance halls, from mothers whose children were attending these halls, or from neighbors who knew about conditions existing there" (3). DeKoven Bowen's report was a follow-up to a series of magazine articles written by herself and other advocates, such as Jane Addams of Chicago's Hull House, from 1911 to 1912. The articles by Addams and DeKoven Bowen were combined and published in 1912 in a book *From Dance Hall to White Slavery: The World's Greatest Tragedy* (Wagner 1997, 295).

In 1889 in Chicago, Jane Addams instituted the Settlement House idea at Hull House as a "community of women reformers." Addams and her fellow workers were part of a growing number of urban moral reformers. According to historian Linda J. Tomko, they "were deeply concerned with the perils the urban environment posed to immigrant children and working youths" (1999, 139). A similar idea was instituted by Lillian Wald at the Henry Street Settlement House in New York City. As a solution to the perceived urban "ills of society," Hull House and others provided neighborhood recreation, gymnasiums, and self-help courses in the English language, writing, sewing, crafts, and dancing.

At Hull House, Mary Wood Hinman taught the social dance classes that included an array of folk, ballroom, and historical dances. One Hull House attendee, Russian immigrant and textile worker Hilda Satt Polachek, remembered,

> We danced once a week in this carefree class, all winter...In June, the class closed for the summer with a gay cotillion...No matter where the members of the dancing class came from, dingy hovels, overcrowded tenements, for that one night we were all living in a fairyland.

Addams encouraged those such as Polachek who "worked too hard and needed some fun" (quoted in Tomko 1999, 137–139).

However, Addams in no way agreed with dancing at the municipal dance halls. In the preface to *From Dance Hall to White Slavery*, for example, she proclaimed, "The dance hall evil is a canker that the community must eradicate to save its future generations" (1). The publication under the "authorship" of John Dillon and H.W. Lytle further promised:

> Stories of actual events, places and persons that have had a part in bringing about the investigations conducted by various commissions and organizations of the dance hall evil in Chicago.

Dillon and Lytle cited "statistics" provided by the investigations of DeKoven Bowen and the Chicago Municipal Vice Commission that supposedly over 5,000 young girls each year were seduced in the municipal dance halls and abducted into "White Slavery" as prostitutes or, as society at the time called them, "fallen women" (8). Their summation, concurred with by Addams, DeKoven Bowen, and Dean Sumner, chairman of the Vice Commission, was that the dance was "the big key to vice in Chicago." He added, "Prolonged study has led them to the conclusion that the vice problem may not be solved without careful consideration of the dance hall evil" (13). DeKoven Bowen added,

> The combination of the community dance hall and the disorderly saloon is one of the mighty factors in the ruin of our young girls. We cannot afford to ignore this evil and maintain a shred of self-respect. (Dillon, 1).

DeKoven Bowen continued her crusade against the "dance hall evil" for many years after the publication of *From Dance Hall to White Slavery*.

In 1917, Louise DeKoven Bowen's JPA report of "The Public Dance Halls of Chicago" was a culmination of six years of study as well as attending all the known dance halls in Chicago from 1910 to 1916. In 1910, the JPA visited 328 halls and in 1916, 213, with the average number visited each year exceeding 200. The public dances were divided into two classes as "those given by the management or proprietors of the halls, and those given by clubs and societies" (6). The JPA observed in the saloon type dance halls the dances were usually four to five minutes in length with a long break in between, anywhere from 5 to 45 minutes. They claimed the idea was to encourage the sale of alcohol (6–12).

The JPA made some recommendations for the dance halls, such as to provide drinking water in lieu of alcohol, police in attendance, chaperones, and a curfew. In 1914, Chicago attempted to prohibit the sale of alcohol in 440 licensed dance halls. By 1916, DeKoven Bowen reported that the sale of liquor in dance halls was also prohibited in many cities including Kansas City, Cleveland, Pittsburgh, Cincinnati, Columbus, Detroit, Buffalo, Los Angeles, Minneapolis, Duluth, and Portland (8–12). However, the consistent fear of the reformers in regards to the dance hall was that young girls would lose their virginity as a result of dancing.

The JPA investigators often observed that the popularity of the dance halls attracted large crowds; therefore the dance space was crowded, and "the dancers are obliged to stand almost still and go through the motions of dancing only." DeKoven Bowen's description of what goes on during the close dancing rivals the most titillating romance novels of the day. She describes that it is common that "Couples stand very close together, the girl with her hands around the man's neck, the man with both arms around the girl or on her hips; their cheeks are pressed close together, their bodies touch each other; the liquor which has been consumed is like setting a match to a flame; they throw aside all restraint and give themselves to unbridled license and indecency" (5). The fears of sexual promiscuity seemed most prevalent when young white girls, in their search for fun and relaxation, innocently stepped onto the dance floor. (For black women, there was no widespread concern in regard to their sexual morality.)

Consequently, by the early twentieth century many of the anti-dance crusaders cited the growing societal fear of sexual promiscuity. In turn, many of the anti-dance publications were written not only by church leaders but also by moral reformists. Some of the publications included:

- The Reverend James W. Bonham, *The Temple of Pleasure* (1900);
- Pastor James Monroe Hubbert, *Dancers and Dancing; a calm and rational view of the dancing question* (1901);

- C.A. Davis, *Dances and Dancing School* (1902);
- The Reverend Mgr. Don Luigi Satori, *Modern Dances* (1910);
- Colonel Dick Maple, *Palaces Of Sin, Or The Devil In Society* (1902, reprinted 1910);
- Beryl and Associates, ed. *Immorality of Modern Dances* (1904);
- The Reverend Henry Brown, *"The Dance," The Impending Peril* (1904);
- W.H. Bates, *The Worldly Christian's Trinity: Cards, Theater, Dance* (1905);
- William E. Beederwolf, *The Christian Amusements: Is Dancing Sinful?* (1909);
- The Vice Commission of Chicago, *The Social Evil In Chicago* (1911);
- The Reverend Henry W. Bromley, *A Sermon On Popular Amusements* (1914);
- Thomas Dixon, *The Root Of Evil* (1914); and
- Mordecai Franklin Ham, *The Modern Dance; a historical and analytical treatment of the subject; religious, social, hygienic, industrial aspects as viewed by the pulpit, the press, medical authorities, municipal authorities, social workers, etc.* (1916).

In 1904, the *Immorality of Modern Dances*, as one example, also continued the same anti-dance themes of the late nineteenth century that included the bad effects upon health and the inconsistency within the Biblical Scriptures. The editors Beryl and Associates were especially harsh about the face-to-face round dances. In support of their claim of the "immorality" of social dancing, the editors Beryl and Associates inserted over 100 pages of supporting proclamations from clergy of all denominations of Protestants as well as Catholics and Jews.

In 1916, Thomas A. Faulkner not only reissued his notorious late nineteenth century anti-dance publication of *From the Ball-Room to Hell* (1892), he also saw fit to write another anti-dance treatise. Faulkner's simple reasoning for the reissue and for another new publication *The Lure of the Dance* (1916) was a direct result of the ongoing dance craze. He explained his reasoning as follows:

> Since writing my first book on the subject of dancing—"From the Ball Room to Hell"—I have realized to a greater extent the vast importance of this question, and as the dance craze has developed with such incredible rapidity during the last few years into one of the most irresistible and dangerous attractions in the form of amusements, I have decided to again bring the subject before the public. I shall endeavor to portray the evils resulting from this so-called "innocent" diversion in such a manner that the Christians, and especially the parents, of today will awaken to the deep sense of responsibility that I feel is resting upon them (7).

Faulkner not only cited the supposed association of sexual promiscuity with social dancing, he also invoked the fear that young women within dance halls were routinely kidnapped and ultimately forced into prostitution. His unfounded surprising claim was that it was the dance master who organized the "white slavery." Faulkner's wild accusation was as follows:

> One of the most astounding features in connection with this satanic traffic in human flesh is the revenue received by many dancing masters through an organized ring of thieves (92).

Unfortunately, the prevailing belief among many progressive moral reformers agreed with Faulkner's assumptions.

As a result, many dance halls, ballrooms, and cabarets enacted rules and restrictions, especially regarding females. One such restriction was placed upon spinning a dance partner, which was known as "Spieling." The reason it was discouraged was because it created physical excitement and therefore was perceived to encourage sexual activity. Some places refused entry to unescorted or individual women. It was also improper for a man to ask a woman sitting at a different table to dance. The idea continually stressed was for a heterosexual couple to enter, dance, and leave together as a couple. A large measure of success for Vernon and Irene Castle was based on the fact that they were a *married* couple.

The practice was simple, since society, at that time, viewed a woman alone as a prostitute, and the cabarets, in order to stay in business, avoided risking a vice raid or the wrath of public attention by the newspapers. A respected *Guide-Book for Travelers* to New York City written by Fremont Rider in 1916 warned "that single women were generally made to feel unwelcome in the cabaret" (Erenberg 1981, 136). Regardless of how dancing was done, to the reformers of the early twentieth century, however, the idea of close contact fast dancing of any kind was considered vulgar and obscene.

The reformers and clergy also expressed concern over so-called "charity girls." A charity girl was a term applied to a young working-class woman who was on a date (usually dancing). She was described as one who exchanged "flirtatious glances" or even "sexual favors" in return for her male partner paying for the cost of the date. The simple fact that the idea of a man paying for the entire cost of the date started because women were not in an economical position to do so. Because of either low wages or financial contributions to the family, or both, they were not able to afford such leisure pleasures as going to a nightclub or a ballroom dance. For many young working women, therefore, the only opportunity for social participation was as a "charity girl." The mere mention of the sexual immorality, however, was cause for immediate censure and sometimes closure of a place of establishment.

In reality, the fact that the reformers and investigators totally missed was that society was changing and no longer succumbing to the traditional roles of the nineteenth century. Most of their objections were based on what "might" happen in regards to sexual relations when, in fact, people danced for the enjoyment of dancing itself. Dancing offered a new freedom in public that broke from the traditional set ways of the previous generations. In previous years, when the dances occurred either within a rural community or at a society function, they were among those who knew each other in some fashion or had a common bond. The new fashion of public dancing was among individuals who did not necessarily know each other, allowing for class and ethnic mixing. Females, in particular, were discarding their matronly roles and exploring a new sense of individuality. The pattern would continue through the twentieth century, and dancing would continue to break new ground and fend off similar criticism.

2

The Charleston, Flappers, and Jazz: 1920–1932

The afternoon was already planned; they were going dancing—for those were the great days.

—F. Scott Fitzgerald, 1922

The Political, Social, and Cultural Climate

This time was considered an era of prosperity and was known as the *Roaring 20s* or the *Jazz Age*. Business was booming in urban areas and fortunes were made from investments in the Wall Street Stock Market. On the other hand, farms in rural areas were beginning to suffer hardship and were failing at a continuing rate preceding the Great Depression.

In 1920, the U.S. Census reported 106 million people living in the United States. The population was almost evenly split between rural areas and urban areas. Half of the total population was concentrated in the Northeast with some small suburban areas developing near cities such as Pittsburgh, Chicago, and New York. Over 90 million were listed as "white." About 40 percent of that number were either recent immigrants or children of immigrants. African Americans numbered 9.8 million with about 80 percent living in the South. Native American Indians and Asians numbered less than 500,000. Of the total working force of 48.9 million people, over 12 million were in agriculture and 12 million in manufacturing (Kyvig 2002, 7–9).

For working class Americans the average 6-day 60-hour workweek in 1919 decreased to a 5-day 48-hour workweek by 1929. The reduction in hours came mainly as a result of bitter labor disputes and violent strikes. As a result, additional time for leisure activities was available not only at the end of the workday but also on Saturdays and Sundays. The introduction of the idea of the weekend meant the opportunity for dancing on Saturday night and church worship on Sunday morning.

The situation for African Americans intensified in the South as a revitalized Ku Klux Klan terrorized them through beatings, lynchings, and the burning of churches and homes. Many African Americans sought relief from the southern terror by migrating North into cities including St. Louis, Chicago, Detroit, Philadelphia, and New York. Nationwide anti-immigrant sentiment continued as immigration from Southern and Eastern Europe was severely limited by the Congressional Johnson Quota Act of 1924. During the decade a total of only 4.1 million immigrants were allowed entry. Unlike the preceding years, most were white Europeans from Northern Europe, the British Isles, and Scandinavia. Moral reformers, who for years were attempting to control the private lives of individuals, made significant gains, especially with the limitation of immigration, the nationwide push for Americanization, and the enactment of Prohibition (Giordano 2003, 50–51).

On January 16, 1920, Prohibition officially took effect. The Constitutional Amendment made it illegal for "the manufacture, sale, or transportation of intoxicating liquors" throughout the country. Enforcement of the law, however, was very difficult, and many individuals simply scoffed at the law and continued to drink. The illegal manufacture and smuggling of alcohol gave way to the formation of gangland warfare and bootlegging. "Bootlegging" was the term applied to the operation of a business that sold illegal alcohol acquired either by illegally manufacturing it or by smuggling it from Canada. A replacement for the saloons, called "speakeasies," broadened on a large urban scale and became a fashionable nightspot not only for drinking but also for music, entertainment, and dancing.

American fads that swept the nation included mah-jongg, crossword puzzles, miniature golf, yo-yos, roller-skating, parlor games, and anything requiring endurance, including flagpole sitting and dance marathons. It was also an age of great American literature that included works by F. Scott Fitzgerald, William Faulkner, Thomas Wolfe, and Sinclair Lewis. African American culture in literature, art, music, and dance gave rise to the Harlem Renaissance and slowly was incorporated into American popular culture. Magazines were extremely popular among all classes, including *The Saturday Evening Post, Collier's,* and *National Geographic.*

The American public craved sensational headline stories of scandal, bootleggers, gangsters, and sports. In 1919, the first of the newspaper "tabloids," *The New York Daily News,* sought to satisfy the public's desire. The tabloids captured the public's imagination, and, as circulation reached phenomenal numbers, many other cities nationwide copied the format. The tabloids carried sensational stories of the murder trials of Sacco and Vanzetti (extending over seven years, 1920–1927) and Leopold and Loeb (1924). The Scopes Monkey Trial (1925) captivated the public's attention. The Scopes trial featured luminaries Clarence Darrow and William Jennings Bryant debating the theory of creation of the human race as derived from the Bible versus evolution as derived from the theory that the human race evolved from primates. Sports headlines included the Chicago "Black Sox" scandal of fixing the 1919 World Series, the gargantuan efforts of baseball player Babe Ruth, golfer Bobby Jones, and football player Red Grange. Magician Harry Houdini captivated crowds with death-defying acts, as did Admiral Richard E. Byrd's exploration of the Antarctic.

Americans were tired of the destruction and death of the Great War, the Great Flu Epidemic, labor strife, and nativists, as well as moral restrictions. Many of the urban youth and young adults embraced a world of flaunting the laws of Prohibition, idolizing gangsters, sporting hip flasks, or patronizing a speakeasy. The music of Jazz caught the attention of America's youth as well as dancing the Charleston. In 1927, the highly publicized aerial feat of Charles Lindbergh's solo airplane flight across the Atlantic in 1927 lent its name to the popular dance the Lindy Hop.

By the end of the 1920s more Americans lived in urban areas, as the city became the center of cultural influence among the American people. The automobile, the radio, and the mass media became a major part of the everyday lives of Americans. As a result, a homogenized version of American trends, fashion, and games expanded into all areas of the country. A major reduction in work hours allowed more time at the end of the day as well as entire weekends to be devoted to recreation and dancing. The dancing business was profitable, and dancing was gaining acknowledgment as a healthy and fruitful use of time. On October 29, 1929, however, the stock market collapsed.

The Stock Market Crash of 1929 was an economic catastrophe that drastically altered the lifestyles of all Americans. Millions became unemployed and over 40 million of the nation's 122 million people were living in poverty. Many of those who had jobs suffered a decrease in work hours and wages. Marriage rates declined as well as the birthrate. Even the movie theaters were not immune as attendance declined by almost half from 1929 to 1932. The depression hit dance halls in the same way. The inexpensive radio served as an alternative for dance music, and by 1932 many dance halls were desperate for customers.

The Dances

I'm shaking my shimmy, that's what I'm doing.

—Gilda Gray, 1922

RURAL DANCING AND CITY IMMIGRANTS

Dancing continued to be popular among all ages and reached new heights of popularity during the 1920s. Many adults took ballroom classes and also sent their children to tap and ballet classes (Steiner 1933, 114). The time also marked the beginnings of new interpretational forms of tap, jazz, and modern dance. In 1926, Martha Graham gave her first New York performance featuring 18 barefoot dancers in an original interpretation. Graham based her creativity on the legendary pioneer Isadora Duncan, who had been creating and interpreting modern dance since the turn of the twentieth century. Ironically, in 1927, Duncan was killed in a freak accident when her fashionably flamboyant scarf that she was wearing got caught in the wheel of an open topped automobile in which she was riding.

The commercial dance halls were everywhere from the urban commercial districts of cities such as New York, Chicago, and the San Francisco Barbary Coast to the New Orleans French Quarter. New dance halls were opened, enlarged, renovated, and constructed. Social dancing was available at community centers, social clubs, fraternal lodges, public parks, private country clubs, resort hotels, and private homes with a phonograph or radio. Most towns simply relied on a community building that served multiple purposes that included fairs, exhibits, lectures, Chautauquas, and social dancing (Steiner 1933, 163).

Dancing in rural areas continued and was considered an inseparable part of the social fabric of the regions. Families still attended barn dances, as well as dances in community buildings and ranch houses. Families were known to travel all day on a Saturday to attend a dance. In some ranch houses the furniture would be moved outside to make room for dancing. Sometimes after the children were finished playing, they would lie down and sleep on the couches or in the wagon outside under the stars (Rollin 1999, 59).

Some communities began playing Jazz and Texas Swing (see Chapter 3). But most still continued to dance in the traditions of the nineteenth century such as Square Dances, the Schottische, Waltz, Polka, and Virginia Reel. In 1926, in Cokesbury, South Carolina, Blanche Torrent wrote, "Farm women...realized the value of recreation in their community life [and] a continued popular activity was dancing the Virginia Reel." The Virginia Reel was a popular folk dance since the early nineteenth century that incorporated 6 or more couples in contra lines weaving in and about the other couples (*The Playground*, March 1926, Vol. 19, No. 12: 668–669).

In 1928, the National Urban League sponsored Charles Johnson to provide a sociological survey of areas with a heavy black population in the South and Midwest. Among African Americans, life in both the rural towns and cities still remained segregated, but the lifestyles and leisure pursuits remained similar to that of whites. Venturing out among white communities for the purpose of recreation, entertainment, or dancing, however, was not an option (74–76). Regardless of racial segregation, all the clergy (white or black) had objections to young people dancing the Charleston, Shimmy, or Black Bottom. In one Kentucky community, Johnson discovered "[a] popular program for young adults involved social dancing under supervision" was eliminated "by the public protestations of the Negro ministry" (74–76).

Similar to African Americans, immigrants still sought recreation and dancing among those of their own nationality. They attempted to maintain their heritage that was brought with them from their native country. Paul Sturman, a Czechoslovakian immigrant, described the leisure time enjoyed aboard ship as he traveled to America in 1920. He described,

> Time between meals was spent on deck if the weather was good. In the evening there was usually dancing and music. Some immigrants would always come out with a harmonica or some musical instrument and the dance would follow (Museum Text Ellis Island).

Typically, the same trend of entertainment would continue if a community had a significant population to continue with the old-world traditions including folk dancing and traditional standards. One such example was the *Norwegian Centennial Celebration* in Minnesota in 1925, which drew over 100,000 people, most of Norwegian ancestry (Museum Text Ellis Island). However, the area where the immigrant settled determined what type of dancing he or she would do.

Dancing in cities on the west coast included more Waltzes than the east coast cities. A 1923 survey of one Seattle dance hall reported an equal number of Waltzes as Fox Trots. On the east coast the Fox Trot and One-Step were favored, and Waltzes were held to a minimum. In many east coast halls the playing of a Waltz usually meant the last dance of the evening (Mason, "Satan in the Dance Hall," 1924, 179). One recent transplant from rural Colorado to the city life of Chicago said, "It's getting so a fellow can't get acquainted unless he can dance. Out in Colorado, where I come from, they all dance different from what they do here. They dance the old square dances and things like that" (Cressey 1932, 132). However, in order to dance in the city he needed to take lessons.

DANCE TEACHERS AND ARTHUR MURRAY

Dance instructors resisted teaching new dances and carried on the tradition of teaching standard and acceptable ballroom dances. They sought to encourage the standards such as the Fox Trot, Waltz, Tango, Polkas, Square Dancing, or ethnic folk dancing. Dancing for adults was also clearly defined in dancing manuals and mail order instruction booklets of ballroom standards written by dance instructors such as Charles J. Frank and Lawrence Hostetler. The dance instruction manuals and books followed a trend that the favored ballroom social dances of adults were based on the preceding decade and did not accept the new contemporary dances until the fad had usually passed. Sometimes the dance was simply a fad and just disappeared. Others, such as the Charleston, proved too popular to be ignored during their own time.

During the period numerous magazines were published catering to the growing public interest in both social dancing and dance as art. Many of the titles were very similar and offered step-by-step instructions. They included *The Dance*, *The Dance Magazine*, *The Dancing Master*, *Dance Lovers Magazine*, *Dance*, *Dancer*, and *The American Dancer*. In 1942, *Dance* and *The American Dancer* merged under the single title *Dance Magazine* and continued to publish throughout the entire twentieth century ("The First 75 Years," Barzel, 2002).

Dance instruction proved to be very much in demand, and for some it would also prove profitable. At this time Arthur Murray proved to be the name in dance instruction that would become synonymous with all standard American social dancing for the next 75 years.

Arthur Murray was born in Manhattan, New York, as Murray Teichman to Austrian immigrant parents. He first had thoughts of becoming an architect and worked as a draftsman for a few New York firms while attending Cooper Union and then Columbia University. He first learned social dancing as a way to meet girls and hopefully become more popular. In 1912, he won a Waltz contest at the Grand Central Palace, a large dance hall in New York City, which gave him the idea that he could make money by becoming a dance instructor. At that time, however, social dance instruction was not fully established as a general profession. He invested in a dance course taught by Vernon Castle (see Chapter 1) and learned to dance the "Castle Way" (Kathryn Murray 1960, 33–43).

In 1919, Murray began teaching ballroom standards in a studio in Atlanta, Georgia. He also began a mail-order business for home dance instruction but had limited success. He reasoned that potential dance students would not expect the latest dance trend to come from Georgia, so he moved to New York and opened a small dance studio at 68th Street and Madison Avenue. He also maintained a loft about a block away from his studio to operate the mail-order business. One single advertisement in *The New York Times* brought in 37,000 responses. The same full-page ad was placed in other national newspapers and monthly magazines. The advertisement, titled "How I Became Popular Overnight," humbly admitted,

> Girls used to avoid me when I asked for a dance. Even the poorest dancers preferred to sit against the wall rather than dance with me. But I didn't wake up until a partner left me standing alone in the middle of the floor. That night I went home feeling pretty lonesome and mighty blue. As a social success I was a first-class failure.

A coupon was printed below the ad for a free sample mail-order dance lesson declaring the respondent would "become sought after as a dance partner." He employed a staff of 30 to handle the demand for his home dance lessons that eventually taught some 5 million people (Kathryn Murray 1960, 56–60).

Many others copied Murray's mail-order dance instruction business. In 1922, Charles J. Frank, with studios in Brooklyn, New York, and Philadelphia, Pennsylvania, offered "The Latest Method Home Instruction Dancing Courses" by mail. His short instruction booklets (about 25 pages) were in ballroom standards including the Waltz and the Fox Trot. The astounding success of mail-order dance instruction

Newspaper advertisement, titled "How I Became Popular Overnight!" for *Arthur Murray* mail-order dance lessons, shows Arthur Murray dancing with partner Ann Forest. Note the mail-in coupon at the lower right. Library of Congress, Prints and Photographs Division LC-USZ62-70141.

had the International Association of Masters of Dancing (of which Murray was a past president) in a dither. They said, "Arthur Murray, who has established a dancing association to give instructions by mail, has no connection with our organization." The Dance Masters declared war on "so-called dancing instructors who claimed to be able to teach the art of dancing through the mails" (Stephenson and Iaccarino 1992, 38).

Murray continued to prove himself as an astute businessman and an innovator in social dance instruction. In 1924, he captured the imagination of the fledging radio industry by devising a radio show to promote his dance studios. At the time, radio shows were broadcast in front of a live studio audience. Murray would ask for an audience volunteer as a partner. While he danced he described the steps over the airwaves. His radio show was carried by WOR-Newark and covered the New York Metropolitan area. It was later networked to reach a large portion of the country. It was during one of these shows that he met his wife Kathryn, who was an audience volunteer. He was also writing regular newspaper articles on dancing, which were picked up by N.E.A., at the time the largest news syndicate in America (Kathryn Murray 1960, 62).

Dance instruction proved extremely lucrative, and Murray opened a larger dance studio on 43rd Street in Manhattan. His students included some of the wealthiest New Yorkers and foreign dignitaries. Murray insisted that all his instructors teach the same way. He established a method of testing the student's ability to dance without the aid of a teacher. His method was that if a student could do the dance in time with music—alone—he or she could then do the dance with any partner. He taught and standardized five basic dances: the Fox Trot, Waltz, Viennese Waltz, Tango, and the Quickstep. These five are all danced as a couple in a closed position (Kathryn Murray 1960, 1–4).

The daily display ads of *The New York Times* on any given day offered the prospective dance student many options to choose from. A sampling from March 8, 1925, listed Arthur Murray offering the "Largest staff of America's finest teachers of ballroom dancing. You can learn in six strictly private lessons." Mr. and Mrs. Oscar Duryea on 67th Street and Central Park West held a "class for high school boys and girls in ballroom dancing with Real Tango Tuition." C & D Studio at 103rd Street and Broadway advertised "a dancing school at highest repute for the family." Albert H. Harris at 637 Madison Avenue stated "real instruction ballroom dancing: no freakishness." Alviane Dance Studio at 43 West 72nd Street provided lessons on "correct carriage and poise." Fay Evelyn's Ballroom Dancing studio at 7th Avenue and 57th Street across the street from Carnegie Hall promised, "Advanced pupils learn the newest innovations" (*New York Times*, March 8, 1925, Section X, 16).

The standardized steps as taught by Arthur Murray in America and Victor Silvester in England would set the basic rules for ballroom dances. In 1924, the Imperial Society of Teachers of Dancing formed a Ballroom Branch, and it was at this time that ballroom and social dancing diverged from one another. Social dances such as the Charleston and the Lindy Hop were based on spontaneity, improvisation, and the ability to dance with a multitude of partners. Ballroom dancing is marked by a pursuit of perfection on set routines danced with the same partner. Eventually, competition levels were set in ballroom dancing, which forever set the distinction between it and social dancing. Ian Driver wrote, "Ballroom dancing survived the twentieth century not by competing with the new styles and trends in social dancing...but because it strictly defined and codified itself, and then sought excellence within a number of specialized styles" (Driver 2000, 143). For the remaining part of the twentieth century ballroom dancing slowly accepted the American dance innovations, but only after they had proven that they were popular enough to stay. However, the ballroom dance styles were heavily modified from the American vernacular dance styles that either originated in the United States or were imported, such as the later adaptations of the Rhumba, Samba, Swing, and Cha-Cha.

THE FOX TROT AND QUICKSTEP

Over the years, the Fox Trot had undergone several changes. By 1924, there were two main versions, the slow Fox Trot and the quick Fox Trot. In 1925, Arthur Murray's ballroom social dancing standardized them as the Fox Trot and the Quickstep. The slow Fox Trot was the standard, as it would remain throughout the twentieth century.

Standard patterns of the Fox Trot, phrased in 4, 8, and 16 counts, included the Promenade, Sideward Glide, Hesitation, Change-Step, Two-Step, and turns. The Promenade is a break in the walking pattern, stepping to one side, closing with the other foot, and continuing in rhythm. The Sideward Glide is similar to the Promenade incorporating quarter turns. The Hesitation adds a pause of one beat within the rhythm by making a definite stop during the forward or backward walk, usually on count 4. On the Change-Step the man takes a backward rocking step with the left foot (count 1), bringing the right together with the left (count 2), step forward left (count 3), and continue the forward walk with the right foot (count 4). On all the patterns, the woman mirrors the man's footwork beginning count 1 with her right foot (Hostetler 1936, 92–99).

The quick Fox Trot was known as the Quickstep, which was the same basic step although when done to quicker music some added a skip or syncopation. (Another popular dance of the time, the Peabody, might have also been the Quickstep with regional variations.)

THE MOVIES, RUDOLPH VALENTINO, AND THE TANGO

During the 1920s, the movie industry began promotional advertisements for feature films in numerous newspapers and mass-market magazines. As a result, the movie industry flourished, and it was no longer Broadway, but the films and the movie stars that became responsible for the way the average American dressed, talked, and danced in their daily lives. The popularity of dancing led to it being featured in several films.

In 1923, based on the popularity of the Apaché Dance (see Chapter 1), Hollywood released a silent era movie *The Apache Dancer*. The American Film Institute (AFI) plot summary reads like the dance itself. "After saving the life of an American girl in a Paris cafe, an apache dancer inherits a fortune and goes to America to persuade the girl to marry him. His suit is temporarily threatened by some evil-doers who would like to discredit him, but he emerges the winner after a terrific fight" (AFI.com, *The Apache Dancer*).

Not all Hollywood movies portrayed dancing in a positive light. One example was *On Your Toes* (1927). In the movie, the son of the heavyweight boxing champ is considered "sissified" by his boxer father because he is a dance teacher. He marries and moves to New York City to open a dance school, but his wife wants him to get a "man's job," first as a taxi-driver and then as a boxer (AFI.com, *On Your Toes*).

In 1921, Rudolph Valentino started a new interest in the Tango with a scene from his popular movie *The Four Horsemen of the Apocalypse*. Later that same year, *The Sheik* established Rudolph Valentino as a major Hollywood star. Up until his untimely death, at age 31, in 1926, from complications of a perforated ulcer, he was the most popular film star of the time. Valentino was the sex symbol of his age. His on-screen style, mannerism, and fashion provided romantic sexual fantasies that women craved and men sought to emulate. When Valentino danced the

In 1921, Rudolph Valentino started a new interest in the Tango with a scene from his popular movie *The Four Horseman of the Apocalypse*. From that point on, many movies throughout the century would be responsible for the popularity of a particular dance or dance fad.   Courtesy of Photofest.

Tango, everyone wanted to learn to dance the Tango. Although the camera featured more close-ups of Valentino's face rather than the actual steps of the Tango, it was his on-screen magnetism that stirred the interest in the dance itself (DeMille 1980, 81). From that point on, many movies throughout the century would be responsible for the popularity of a particular dance or dance fad.

Valentino dancing the Tango was responsible for an increase among the youth doing the dance, but it still remained favored among the adult ballroom set. The Tango was most popular in the cities and was very rarely seen in small rural town dance halls. Reports also revealed that the tango was danced much more frequently and more skillfully than before 1920 (Mason, "Satan in the Dance Hall," 1924, 179). Adults continued dancing to the soothing prewar standards, mainly the Fox Trot, the Tango, and the Waltz. The introduction of the Rhumba also appealed to adults.

THE BASIC RHUMBA BOX STEP

Left Foot   Right Foot
START POSITION

Illustration by Author

Lawrence Hostetler added the instructions on how to dance the Rhumba in a revised 3rd edition of his popular *The Art of Social Dancing: A Text Book for Teachers and Students*. He writes, "The rhumba, as the dance is generally known in [America], is steadily increasing in popularity and it makes a welcome addition to our repertoire of social dances." The Rhumba basic is done in the form of a square box, similar to the Foxtrot. There is a sideward movement and an accentuated hip sway. Hostetler describes the basic Rhumba step, counting 1&2, 3&4 staring with the leader:

> "Step to the left side with the left (count 1). Close with the right (count 'and'). Step forward on the left (count 2); pause (count 'and'). These three steps are taken quickly and with very small steps. The definite pause which follows is made with the feet separated. Reverse the figure by stepping to the right side with the right (count 3); bring the left foot to the right (count 'and'). Step forward (or back) with the right (count 4); pause (count 'and')."

The follower, or female, starts with a step to the right side with the right foot and mirrors the same pattern as the man (141-147).

THE RHUMBA

In 1930, at the annual convention, the Dancing Masters of America (formerly the International Association of Masters of Dancing) noted "a Spanish tendency in the air. Radio people are said to be going tango." They also stated that the Waltz was always fashionable but also predicted a rise in Latin dancing. The first of the Latin influenced dances was the Rhumba ("700 Dance Masters Ponder New Steps," *New York Times*, 1930, 14).

The Rhumba (sometimes spelled rumba) was originated in and was the national dance of Cuba. The native Cuban terms for the dance are the "son" and "danzón." In April 1930, at the Palace Theater in New York City Don Azpiazú's Havana Casino Orchestra introduced authentic Cuban music to the American public. During the performance, Azpiazú performed "The Peanut Vendor," and a dance team performed the Rhumba. The song was a nationwide hit, as was the Rhumba. The stage dance versions of the Rhumba included special Latin costumes that added to the flavor of the dance. Some orchestras also adopted a dress-up costume to perform Rhumba music. The orchestras also incorporated common Latin musical instruments including maracas, painted gourds, bongo drums, and claves (short wooden sticks that are stuck together to create a counter-rhythm) (Roberts 1999, 76–77).

The Rhumba was not as smooth as the Tango but employed a box step with a swaying motion of the hips. The swaying hip motion is achieved by keeping the feet close together. The upper torso and shoulders are held erect, and all movement is from the waist down. Variations to the basic step included a "running Step," a "circle Turn," and a "Balance Step." Hostetler listed some common mistakes as "taking the steps too long…Failure to make a definite pause between each figure [and] not allowing the hips to sway with each change of weight" (Hostetler 1934, 141–147).

Many, however, thought the Rhumba was just another fad. According to Kathryn Murray, Arthur Murray, for one, "didn't hurry to teach Latin American dances." When Murray first heard about the Rhumba craze, he and his wife, Kathryn, sailed to Cuba to study the native dancers. He did not like the extent of hip movements of the original Cuban dancers. He said they were "a little too genuine." He diagramed a toned down version of steps and hip movements for his instructors to teach back in Manhattan (Kathryn Murray 1960, 7). After World War II, Ballroom and DanceSport versions of the Rhumba danced the break step on beat 2, rather than on beat 1 as in the Social Rhumba. The Rhumba was a ballroom favorite among adults for the remainder of the century.

RADIO AND SWEET BANDS

In 1920, Pittsburgh radio station, KDKA, transmitted the first commercial broadcast. The radio quickly spread in national appeal for entertainment that eventually influenced almost the entire population. By the mid-1920s, telephone lines made it possible for simultaneous live broadcasting (known as *networking*) to reach most of the nation. Radio reached into the rural heartland as well as the city as networking proved to be an easy way to communicate information to a widespread audience. The radio was an inexpensive choice of entertainment, and the listener had an almost unlimited choice of programs including news, sporting events, musical concerts, comedy, drama programs, religious sermons, and dance bands. By 1930, over 600 stations regularly broadcast commercial programs to over 12 million households, over 40 percent of all American homes. By 1932, during the worst of the Depression, radio ownership increased by another 4 million sets (Steiner 1933, 119).

Radio and dance music were a natural combination. Radio provided the dance bands, and the record companies, with the largest possible listening audience, which contributed to record sales. These bands broadcast over the radio from ballrooms in fashionable hotels and ballrooms in cities such as New York and Chicago. The radio shows were also in cooperation with commercial sponsorship. Because of the commercial sponsorship of the radio programs, some of the dance bands were able to command high salaries from $5,000 to $10,000 per week.

At the time, many of the popular radio dance bands were white and played sedate music standards. Their repertoire included sentimental ballads, slow Fox Trots, and waltzes catering to the adult dancing crowd. They were known as "sweet bands." Popular music vocalists who accompanied sweet bands included Bing Crosby, Russ Columbo, Rudy Vallee, and Al Jolson. The sweet bands included the Wayne King Orchestra, Fred Waring's Pennsylvanians, Guy Lombardo and his Royal Canadians, and the Ted Lewis Orchestra.

Wayne King composed "The Waltz You Saved For Me" and many other waltzes that earned him the title "The Waltz King." Fred Waring's Pennsylvanians is credited with the first dance recording to feature a vocal chorus on "Collegiate" as well as the first Rhumba, "Oh, Donna Clara." The band was featured in the Hollywood movie *Syncopation* (1929). By 1933, Waring was reported to be the highest paid bandleader in radio and theater performances. The band continued playing sentimental dance music for over 50 years.

In 1923, Guy Lombardo and his Royal Canadians began playing in Cleveland and broadcast over a local radio station. In 1927, in Chicago the band was broadcast over WBBM networking to most of the country. The band was advertised as playing the "sweetest music this side of heaven." Shortly thereafter, the band accepted an engagement at New York's Roosevelt Hotel that lasted over 30 years.

Ted Lewis fronted a large dance band of 14 that included four brass, two saxophones, two clarinets, two violins, and a rhythm section of piano, banjo, brass bass, and drums. The band played mostly sentimental ballads and Waltzes. Lewis's recording of the Waltz ballad "Goodnight" recorded in 1927 best exemplifies the relaxed sound of the band and was one of the best-selling dance records of all time. While on stage he added a flair of showmanship dressed in tuxedo tails, top hat, and cane, usually adding his trademark statement to the mellow dance crowd "Is ev-'rybody happy? Yes sir!" The band was also featured in two Hollywood movies *Is Everybody Happy?* (1929) and *Here Comes the Band* (1935) (McCarthy 1971, 21–40).

JAZZ, HOT JAZZ, AND THE "KING OF JAZZ"

The sweet bands remained popular, but it was the music of Jazz that would become synonymous with the era and contribute to the new dances of the era. The name Jazz supposedly originated from a Chicago term, "to jass it up," which meant to either speed it up or add flair. (In the early years Jazz was sometimes spelled "Jass.") Some Chicagoans used the term to denote sexual activity. In San Francisco, "jazz" meant any vigorous behavior.

At the turn of the twentieth century, Jazz music had definitely been born and flourished in New Orleans. Jazz is rooted in African American folk traditions and French Creole and Old World European musical styles that intertwined in the New Orleans area of the United States. According to *Encarta Encyclopedia*, the Old World European "contributed specific styles and forms—hymns, marches, waltzes, quadrilles, and other dance music, light theatrical music, Italian operatic music—and also theoretical elements, in particular, harmony, both as a vocabulary of chords and as a concept related to musical form." ("Jazz," *Encarta Encyclopedia*, n.d.). The banjo sounds of jazz were derived from African American slave culture, the guitar from Spanish, and the piano style of the Midwest and Ragtime (see Chapter 1). The combination of Creole, Spanish, and African American rhythms with the musical influences of the New World immigrants including French and Italian as well as elements of Ragtime and Blues created a distinctly new American sound. The sound that emerged was known as "New Orleans Jazz" or "Dixieland Jazz."

As African Americans migrated north into cities including St. Louis, Kansas City, Detroit, and Chicago, they brought the New Orleans Jazz sound with them. They picked up additional musical elements along the Mississippi River Valley known as the Delta Blues. As Jazz settled in Chicago (sometimes known as the "Chicago Style") it flourished in the heavily segregated south side of Chicago, an area known as the "Black Belt." The Chicago style of Jazz was fast-paced music that encouraged improvisation and spontaneity among both the musicians and the dancers. Jazz, more so than Ragtime, emphasized the upbeat and syncopations necessary for dancing. The style is such that the melody of the music is played against a steady backbeat and the syncopation is not accentuated. The originators who first popularized Jazz were a quintet from New Orleans.

In 1915, the Original Dixieland Jazz Band (they were first known as the Original Dixieland *Jass* Band) introduced New Orleans style Jazz to Chicago and New York. The five-member band was composed of Italian Americans from New Orleans. The band members did not use written sheet music. Instead, they added improvisation, incorporated more syncopation, and played variations on popular ragtime songs and some original compositions. Instruments included the cornet, trombone, clarinet, piano, and drums. Their combination of Dixieland, Sousa marches, and Ragtime syncopation captivated the American dancing public, and they became a popular sensation (McCarthy 1971, 9–10).

Other early Jazz bands were composed of four to six members, and some included banjos as well as brass and wind instruments. Ragtime dance bands, such as James Reese Europe (see Chapter 1) depended heavily on their string sections for the dance beat. Of the new Jazz, music historian Albert McCarthy said, "The use of wind instruments for dance music in intimate night clubs and larger ballrooms alike was virtually unknown before the coming of the Dixieland Band" (1971, 14).

The music when speeded up was known as "Hot Jazz." Hot Jazz could be found on the south side of Chicago, in New York's Harlem, on the San Francisco Barbary Coast, and in the New Orleans French Quarter. Popular Hot Jazz musicians included "King" Oliver, "Jelly Roll" Morton and Bix Beiderbecke, and Louis Armstrong. Some of the popular black bands included McKinney's Cotton Pickers, King Oliver's Creole Jazz Band, Luis Russell, Bennie Moten, Fletcher Henderson, Louis Armstrong, and Duke Ellington. These bands were mostly regulated to the dance halls patronized by African Americans and some whites.

African American dance bands and "Hot Jazz" bands did not have the same lucrative commercial radio contracts as the popular commercial white bands. As a result, most Americans did not really dance to or listen to much Hot Jazz. Musician and bandleader Benny Goodman (see Chapter 3) recalled, "The big white bands, like Whiteman, Isham Jones and the rest didn't play what musicians considered real [hot] jazz. They used 'symphonic' arrangements, with fiddles, and all sorts of effects" (1939, 62).

Some of the most popular white Jazz bands included Benny Meroff, George Olsen, Ben Bernie, Art Hickman's Orchestra, Sam Lanin, Abe Lyman, Isham Jones, Ben Pollack (a band that included both Benny Goodman and Glenn Miller), Jean Goldkette, the Ipana Troubadours, the Coon-Sanders Nighthawks, Thelma Terry's Playboys, and the Vincent Lopez Orchestra. The Vincent Lopez Orchestra was extremely popular and was still in existence through the 1960s. The Lopez Orchestra combined symphonic Jazz, sentimental ballads, and a few "hot" performances. Thelma Terry's Playboys (one of the very few dance bands in any era that was led by a female) were nine members who "offered dance music that ran the gamut from cleanly sweet to piping hot" (McCarthy 1971, 21–35). However, the musician that made Jazz respectable was Paul Whiteman.

Paul Whiteman was born in 1890 in Denver, Colorado. He was the son of a director of musical education for the Denver city school system. He learned music at an early age, and by the age of 17 he was playing with the Denver Symphony Orchestra. In 1911, he moved to San Francisco and discovered Jazz. In his autobiography titled *Jazz*, he recalled, "We first met—jazz and I—at a dance hall dive on the Barbary Coast....And it hit me hard....But rhythmic catching...and spirit lifting" (quoted in McCarthy 1971, 19–20). In 1920, he moved to New York in search of commercial success. He played at the upscale Palais on Broadway, and he recalled seeing the wealthy elite of New York in his audience including the Vanderbilts, Biddles, and Goulds, dancing to his Jazz music. Most of his music, however, was not the Hot Jazz and was geared to commercial success. In 1922 the band was featured on the Broadway stage in *George White's Scandals of 1922*. By 1924, Whiteman's orchestra was an astounding commercial success commanding a weekly salary of $25,000 and also a significant amount of radio airplay. His astounding commercial success was the reason he was dubbed the "King of Jazz."

In 1924, Whiteman's orchestra experimented with "symphonic jazz." He featured his young piano player, George Gershwin, who premiered *Rhapsody in Blue*. Much of his commercial success after 1924 was mainly as a show band rather than a dance band. His popularity and fees placed him well beyond the average dance hall. After 1927, he was financially able to hire some of the best musicians in the business. He employed some soon to be legendary Jazz and later Swing performers including Bix Beiderbecke, Tommy and Jimmy Dorsey, as well as Hoagy Carmichael, Johnny Mercer, Bunny Berigan, Eddie Lang, and vocalist Bing Crosby. In 1930, he and his band were featured in a Hollywood movie appropriately titled *The King of Jazz* (McCarthy 1971, 18–21).

Jazz was most certainly the most popular music of the time. For the young listeners, the music captured a joy and sense of adventure that was an exciting and radical departure from the other music of that time. The music promoted close and fast-paced dancing. At first the people danced faster Fox Trots, but eventually new dances developed. However, not everyone was captivated by the music or the dancing. In May 1920, for example, the *Atlantic Monthly* magazine belittled the music and dancing of Jazz. The editors claimed that they "trot like foxes, limp like lame ducks, one-step like cripples, and all to the barbaric yawp of strange instruments which transform the whole scene into a moving picture of a fancy ball in bedlam" (Baughman 1996, 269).

The Association of Masters of Dancing, for example, was not in favor of the new Jazz music or the dances that accompanied them. In reporting on the Association of Masters of Dancing annual convention in 1923, a *New York Times* headline proclaimed that the dance instructors agreed on the impending demise of Jazz. The headline for the story read: "[Association of Masters of Dancing] Says Jazz will Sing its Swan Song Soon." The president of the Music Industries Chamber of Commerce said "music publishers were eager to produce music that [merits] the efforts of the dancing masters...to encourage better music and dancing...for the public has had too much jazz and according to the opinion of many in touch with conditions, will welcome this reform." The dance masters adopted as a rule, "Don't permit vulgar cheap jazz music to be played. Such music almost forces dancers to use jerky half-steps, and invites immoral variations." At their 1923 convention they vowed to continue their "fight against jazz and unseemly dancing" ("Dance Masters Fight Jazz," *New York Times*, 1923).

In August 1921, the widely read (about 6 million subscribers) and highly influential *Ladies' Home Journal* published an article by music professor Anne Shaw Faulkner titled "Does Jazz Put the Sin in Syncopation." Faulkner decried:

> Jazz disorganizes all regular laws and order...it is harmful and dangerous, and its influence is wholly bad....Jazz originally was the accompaniment of the voodoo dancer, stimulating the half-crazed barbarian to the vilest deeds. The weird chant, accompanied by the syncopated rhythm of the voodoo invokers, has also been employed by other barbaric people to stimulate brutality and sensuality. That it has a demoralizing effect upon the human brain has been demonstrated by many scientists...the effect of jazz on the normal brain produces an atrophied condition on the brain cells of conception, until very frequently those under the demoralizing influence of the persistent use of syncopation, combined with inharmonic partial tones, are actually incapable of distinguishing between good and evil, right and wrong. Such music has become an influence for evil (16, 34).

The *Ladies' Home Journal* was relentless in the attack on Jazz. In December 1921, it followed up with two articles written by editor John R. McMahon titled "Unspeakable Jazz Must Go!" and "Back to Pre-War Morals." In January 1922, it published an editorial "The Jazz Path of Degradation," which stated, "Jazz dancing is degrading. It lowers all moral standards." Despite objections, Jazz music flourished and energetic fast-paced dances emerged, including the Black Bottom, the Varsity Drag, the Shimmy, and the Charleston.

THE CHARLESTON

No one dance throughout American history has been so closely identified with a historical time period as the Charleston. It was the dominant dance craze of the time and was danced to the fast-paced music of Jazz. The Charleston was a short-lived dance fad, lasting about three years. During that time it was extremely

No one dance throughout American history has been so closely identified with a historical time period as the Charleston. The Charleston marked a significant departure from other types of American social dance. Note the "flapper" style fashion and "bob" haircut on the woman.   Courtesy of Photofest.

The Charleston was a fast-paced energetic bouncy dance with torso movement and many synchronized movements of the arms and legs. A 1925 instructional newsreel from Castle Films shows a good basic Charleston step as well as variations. The Charleston was danced in 4/4 time in a closed position face-to-face. The man's left hand is held up high and the right is placed around the lady's waist. The man steps forward left (count 1) and kicks forward right (count 2) with a slight twisting movement on the balls of both feet. He then steps backward right (count 3) and kicks left (count 4). The woman mirrors the basic steps starting back on the right. Some basic steps kept the feet low to the ground and alternated heels together and toes together with bent knees in opposite direction. This basic step was similar to the Mashed Potato that was popular in the early 1960s (see Chapter 5).

popular and newsworthy. Very little written dance instruction from the time was available on "how to" dance the Charleston. The Charleston was a simple fun dance that really did not require much formal instruction. After the basic step was learned, much was based on improvisation and reaction to the Jazz music. The Charleston most likely originated among African Americans around 1913 at the Jungles Casino in Charleston, South Carolina. In 1922, a version of the Charleston dance was part of an African American musical *Liza*. It was later rechoreographed by two black dancers Cecil Mack and James Johnson for an all-black Harlem show *Running Wild*. In 1923, Ned Wayburn (see Chapter 1) learned the basic step from a young African American and choreographed some variations for the *Ziegfeld Follies* (Dannett and Rachel 1954, 106).

The music that accompanied the dance included "Charleston" by Paul Whiteman and his Orchestra, "I'm Gonna Charleston Back to Charleston" by the Coon-Sanders Nighthawks, "Charleston Charley" by Birt Firman and his Carlton Hotel Dance Orchestra, "I'd Rather Charleston," by Fred and Adele Astaire with George Gershwin on piano, "Sweet Georgia Brown" by Ben Bernie and his Hotel Roosevelt Orchestra, "Yes Sir, That's My Baby!" by Ace Brigode and his Fourteen Virginians, and "Five Foot Two, Eyes of Blue" by Art Landry and his Orchestra. The music and the dance were all the rage and quickly became popular mainly among the energetic youth.

One Charleston variation was to break apart side to side. As they break, the woman kicks high and the man admires and claps hands in time. Some couples broke side to side and did high kicks in unison while swinging the arms side to side in rhythm with the steps. A popular step was to bend over the torso and place the hands on bended knees, wing-out the knees and then pull the knees together and crossing the hands repeating the pattern a few times giving the appearance that the legs were also crossing.

Some other variations included jumping feet apart, as in a jumping jack, and exaggerated twisting behind the legs. The Collegiate variation was an exaggerated version with high kicks and lots of torso bouncing energy. The "Scarecrow" mimicked cartoonish figures with the arms and knock-knees. The "Around the World" was kicking the leg in the air, keeping it up, and going in a circular motion. Some chose to do a "Precision," which was done in tandem with a partner or a series of other dancers incorporating timed freezes (known as "breaks") and doing the same patterns in unison.

The Charleston marked a significant departure from other types of American social dance. Dance historians Marshall and Jean Stearns in *Jazz Dance: The Story of American Vernacular Dance* write, "In the history of American popular dance, the Charleston marks two new departures: For the first time a step was taken over generally by men [and] the distinction between popular dances to watch, and popular dances to dance, was wiped out" (1994, 112). The dance itself also received a lot of media attention. Much was written in newspapers and magazines about the gyrations and antics of the dance itself. Many films and newsreels exist of people actually doing the Charleston.

The Charleston dance craze swept the country, and it seemed that just about everybody was doing it just about anywhere. Young schoolchildren did it in the schoolyard, and performers did it on Broadway and in Hollywood movies. People went Charleston crazy; they danced individually, as couples, and in chorus lines. They danced within their homes, inside ballrooms, on college campuses, outside, on roofs, on the boardwalks, on the beach, even with sailors on the decks of battleships. Charleston dance contests drew major media attention all across the country.

A 1925 newsreel "Charleston Dance Contests," narrated by Tom Hale, showed couples dancing in an airplane. And one daring barnstorming soul even danced the Charleston on the upper wing of a biplane. All sorts of variations and antics were added to the dance and endurance became important. At New York City's Roseland Ballroom one dancer continuously danced the Charleston for 17½ hours (*America Dances! 1897–1948: A Collector's Edition of Social Dance in Film*).

Some unfortunately were so quick to capitalize on the Charleston craze that tragedy occurred. On July 4, 1925, in Boston, a roof collapsed on the Pickwick Dance Club during a Charleston dance and 44 people were killed. Panati states, "The tragedy was blamed on the 'unnatural stress' that the dance's flailing put on the building." Fear that other dance halls—which had, of course, survived vigorous polkas, pounding square dances, and galloping fox trots—might succumb to the Charleston's swaying allowed a number of establishments to imaginatively ban the dance. One proprietor placed a sign outside his restaurant that stated, "This Building Cannot Withstand the Charleston" (Panati 1991, 134).

Contemporary films that featured the Charleston included *King on Main Street* (1925), *Social Celebrity* (1926), *The Crowd* (1927), and *Our Dancing Daughters* (1928). The popular mass media *Life Magazine* featured a John Held, Jr., illustration of the dance on its cover of February 18, 1926 issue titled "Teaching Old

Dogs New Tricks." The cover illustration shows an elderly gentleman in formal evening attire dancing the Charleston with a young flapper. The cover obviously insinuates that the dance was so popular that it spread among all ages (Baughman 1996, 35).

However, many dance instructors did not accept the tight holds or the energetic antics of the Charleston. Charles J. Coll and Gabrielle Rosiere in *Dancing Made Easy* cautioned "The woman who is incorrectly held cannot with grace or facility follow the leading of her partner and this deficiency in the instruction of the art of dancing is more pronounced since there is no striking new dance to attract the eye.... The right hand of the man should never pass higher than the waist of the lady and should only rest there lightly.... The lady places her left hand lightly on the back of the man so that he may have perfect freedom in his leading, at the same time giving the lady the correct position" (1922, 249–250). Professor Romayne De Forrest in *How To Dance and What To Dance* wrote, "No man can lead efficiently if bending too far back, as this throws the body out of line, and no woman can move gracefully and follow the changes of figures who has not unrestricted freedom of movement" (43). In 1930, Hostetler, writing in *The Art of Social Dancing*, decried "social dancing, an integral part of a nation's recreative life, enjoyed by millions of participants, has been allowed to drift aimlessly, and it is sometimes tossed about so recklessly by fickle, popular taste that one now and then wonders if it has not retroverted to its savage ancestry" (xiii–xiv). However, the dance proved so popular that the established dance teachers could not ignore it for long. The dance teachers modified the Charleston and added subtler variations. Kathryn Murray said of her husband, "Arthur didn't teach the Charleston until it had been accepted by the best people" (1960, 1).

In order to perform the fast-paced Charleston, women had to change clothing styles, so restrictive corsets and long dresses were discarded and hemlines rose, raising morality questions. Therefore, the older generations and ministers who were not in favor of the new dance or the music also denounced the Charleston. The New Orleans Morality League denounced the "fierce jazz dance invaders" and pressed for an "anti-vulgar dance ordinance" (Stearns and Stearns 1994, 114). An Oregon Evangelist preached, "dancing is the first step and easiest step toward hell. The modern dance cheapens womanhood. The first time a girl allows a man to swing her around the dance floor her instinct tells her she has lost something she should have treasured" (*Fabulous Century 1920–1930*, 1969, 41).

THE SHIMMY, THE BLACK BOTTOM, AND THE VARSITY DRAG

The origin of the Shimmy is unclear, although some similar versions were known among southern African Americans before 1900. Some even said that the belly dance performed by Little Egypt at the 1893 Chicago World's Fair was actually the Shimmy. In 1909, songwriter and stage performer Perry Bradford composed a song titled "Bullfrog Hop" that actually described the Shimmy, which consisted of shaking the shoulders and making the gesture of scratching an itch in rhythm. Bradford said, "I closed my act with that dance" (Stearns and Stearns 1994, 104).

According to popular culture historian Charles Panati, the Shimmy consists of shaking the shoulders and, "In its turning in of knees and toes the dance resembled the Charleston, while in its vigorous wiggling of the backside it displayed elements of the black bottom" (1991, 135). The Shimmy became a national dance craze in 1922, when Gilda Gray introduced it in the Ziegfeld Follies. Mae West also adapted the Shimmy and performed it onstage. Both dancers claim to have first performed the Shimmy around 1919 or 1920. Mae West admits to seeing a version of the Shimmy in Chicago and incorporated it in her act around 1919. She claimed, "I had suddenly started a great new dance fad in respectable circles" (Stearns and Stearns 1994, 105).

Although it appears with almost all of the American vernacular dances, it is quite hard to determine the exact origins of this particular dance. In Gilda Gray's obituary, *The New York Times* wrote that the Shimmy was Gray's "spontaneous invention in John Letzka's Saloon in Cudahy, Wisconsin around 1916" (December 23, 1959, quoted in Stearns and Stearns 1994, 105). Some claimed that when Gilda Gray sang she could not keep her body

The Shimmy became a national dance craze in 1922, when Gilda Gray introduced it in the Ziegfeld Follies. In this photo Gray demonstrates the dance that she simply described as, "I'm shaking my shimmy, that's what I'm doing." Courtesy of Photofest.

still. When asked what she called the dance she did while she sang, she replied "I'm shaking my shimmy, that's what I'm doing" (Dannett and Rachel 1954, 94). During this period, the Shimmy remained mostly a performance dance. However, it would resurface during the 1960s as part of freestyle (see Chapter 5).

The Black Bottom was a solo dance that was notorious for its slapping of the buttocks during the dance. It replaced the Charleston in sweeping the nation as a popular dance fad. Although it did not achieve the lasting connection with the 1920s as the Charleston did, it was very popular during its own time. Marshall and Jean Stearns wrote that the dance was "a well-known dance among semi urban Negro folk in the South long before 1919." In 1919, songwriter Perry Bradford's dance song titled "The Original Black Bottom Dance" contained dance descriptions of the Black Bottom. A later song titled "Black Bottom" written by Henderson, De Sylva, and Brown had different lyrics. The song performed by Johnny Hamp and his Kentucky Serenaders was a popular radio hit. The Black Bottom was first introduced to the public around 1924 and received notoriety by Ann Pennington in *George White's Scandals of 1926* (Stearns and Stearns 1994, 110).

A 1926 instructional silent era film titled "Let's Do Black Bottom" showed a performer demonstrating the Black Bottom. The film is quite stereotypical of its time as to how the film and media portrayed African Americans. A brief history stated, "funny how they got the Black Bottom idea—someone strayed from the Great White Way [Broadway] to the great open spaces and saw" the film cut to a scene of two young African Americans about 10 years of age dressed in overalls dancing in the mud. The film flashes, "The colored kids got it from a cow stuck in the mud."

In an age of silent films the steps of the Black Bottom were first described on screen and with intermittent visuals of a performer demonstrating the step with on screen instructions.

1. First Stamp your feet
2. Now do a "double Stamp"
3. Next combine the Swing and Dance Like this
4. Now do it again strutting forward at the same time
5. This is the most important part of the dance. It is known as the "box"—
6. First it is one to the right
7. Then, it is one to the left
8. Now one to the front—
9. And one directly back completes the "box"
10. Simple, isn't it?

The complete dance is shown "once more, so you won't forget—this time" in slow motion. In addition to the steps, the arms are extended to the side parallel with the ground and brought down at times slowly slapping and holding the backside. The female dancer rolls her eyes seductively and her head sways side to side. Slight arm motions are also used to either side as if fanning a flame. The prediction is "All the world will soon be imitating that cow stuck in the mud."

The film shows Americans of all ages and walks of life doing the dance. Two young African American girls are shown dancing the Black Bottom as well as two construction workers high above the ground on a steel beam. Described as "It's the new 'Noon hour wiggle,'" a police officer and a street sweeper also do the Black Bottom. Finally, "And finally the stage version as it was performed by famed Broadway dancer Ann Pennington" (Castle Films, "Let's Do Black Bottom," *America Dances! 1897–1948*).

The Varsity Drag was a short-lived fad dance mainly among the college age crowd. It was derived from the Zelma O'Neil version of the dance from the 1927 Broadway stage play *Good News*. It lived on longer in the song of the same name "The Varsity Drag," written by Henderson, De Sylva, and Brown, than the actual dance itself. The song performed by George Olsen with Fran Fret on vocals contains reference to college campus life and provided some direction on how to do the dance:

First Lesson right now, you'll love it an' how you'll love it
Here is the drag, See how it goes
Down on your heels, And up on your toes
That's the way to do the Varsity Drag.

The one line of instruction is all the song offered on how to perform the Varsity Drag (Stearns and Stearns 1994, 113). Very little written instruction is available on the dance. Most people improvised moves from the Charleston or relied on the Hollywood movie version of *Good News* (1927). A ballroom version was listed in *Dance Magazine* and illustrated by Albert H. Ludwig and Jean Morris that was based on the same one line instruction from the song (Dannett and Rachel 1954, 122).

A version of the dance appeared in the extremely popular 1950s television series *I Love Lucy*. In one episode characters Fred and Ethel Mertz (actors William Frawley and Vivian Vance) performed the Varsity Drag. Both appeared in "period collegiate costume," and they themselves were veterans of performing the original dance ("Lucy Has Her Eyes Examined," Episode #77; first aired December 14, 1953). Other fad dances that were introduced during this time period were Bambouca, Racoon Dance, the Toddle, the Sugar Foot, Kinkerjeu, Lindy Whirl, Yankee Prance, the Tragico Tango, the Collegiate Shag, the Murray Shag, the St. Louis Shag, and the Peabody (a fast Fox Trot). Also the Tangolio, a combination Fox Trot and Tango, as well as the Raggedy Ann (named after the doll), a combination shuffle step with a grizzly bear hold appeared briefly.

FASHION, FLAPPERS, AND THE GREAT GATSBY

In the 1920s college campuses became synonymous with freedom of the new youth, and pledging fraternities and sororities became a rage. Inspired by the Valentino movie, college men called themselves "sheiks" and females "shebas." Young men sought to fashion their image from the likes of Valentino. Beards and moustaches were no longer fashionable. Many also sported the amateur sportsman look patterned after the likes of famed amateur golfer Bobby Jones. They wore V-neck sweaters, open collared shirts, loose fitting slacks, or even knickers.

The Charleston and Varsity Drag were quite popular on college campuses. Also popular on campus was the "cut-in" dance. The idea was that more men than women would be invited to a dance. The men were expected to "cut-in" during the course of a dance as many times as possible with a different female during an evening.

The culture also produced a distinctive slang. For example, "hooch" was alcohol. Anything or any person considered good-looking was the "cat's meow," "cat's whiskers," or "cat's pajamas." A "lounge lizard" was a gigolo. An important person was the "big cheese," and a boring person was a "flat tire." In defiance of prohibition, young men sported hip flasks to hold their "hooch," and young women dressed in the image of the flapper.

Flappers were also in defiance of Prohibition. And they also broke some long-standing traditions of acceptable female behavior by drinking and smoking in public. In addition, they were also freely speaking of sexual relations. In doing so, they offended all that the adult generation stood for. Lucy Rollin, in *Twentieth-Century Teen Culture by the Decades*, described flapper fashion:

> Her clothes revealed her new freedom and sexuality. Necklines were lowered and soft-ened even on daytime dresses and blouses, sleeves disappeared for evening, waistlines dropped to an easy slimness around the hips, skirts shortened even for evening to reveal the ankles and calves, and stockings were rolled down to reveal bare knees. Favored fabrics for the popular short loose dresses were floating and sheer, occasionally with heavy beading on evening dresses, which were sometimes completely backless and softly draped (1999, 49–50).

Hair was cut short and bobbed, sometimes worn with a tight fitting bell-shaped hat. Long beads draped around the neck suitable for twirling during dancing. The women also began wearing makeup, rouge, and lipstick. In previous decades the idea of a "painted women" was associated with a prostitute. The symbol of the youthful slender, flat-chested flapper represented rebellion against previous notions of conformity and morals. The fun and carefree attitude was a dominant feature of the time, but it was not indicative of all young females. The flapper life-style was adopted mainly by young urban middle-class and wealthy women.

One young woman, Ellen Welles Page, defended the flapper in an article "A Flapper's Appeal to Parents" that appeared in *Outlook Magazine* on December 6, 1922.

> If one judges by appearances, I suppose I am a flapper. I am within the age limit. I wear bobbed hair, the badge of flapperhood....I powder my nose. I wear fringed skirts and bright-colored sweaters, and scarfs,...and low-heeled "finale hopper" shoes. I adore to dance. I spend a large amount of time in automobiles. I attend hops, and proms, and ball-games, and crew races, and other affairs at men's colleges....Think back to the time when you were struggling through the teens. Remember how spontaneous and deep were the joys...Give us confidence—not distrust—We are the Younger Generation. The war tore away our spiritual foundations and challenged our faith....The times have made us older and more experienced than you were at your age. It must be so with each succeeding generation...Make us realize that you respect us as fellow human beings...Believe in us, that we may learn to believe in ourselves...Is it too much to ask? (Page, "A Flapper's Appeal to Parents").

The flapper image was also perpetuated in Hollywood movies. Louise Brooks, one of the most popular Hollywood actresses of the time, personified the flapper image to the American youth in the film *A Social Celebrity* (1926). Clara Bow was another classic image of the flapper during the silent film era—earning the title the "It Girl." Another was actress Joan Crawford. Crawford earned fame offscreen as she was an accomplished dancer and won many Charleston contests, which first garnered her attention from Hollywood film makers. Crawford starred in many films of the era; one classic was *Our Dancing Daughters* (1928), which featured most of the contemporary dances of the day, including the Black Bottom, the Shimmy, and the Charleston. Of flappers and the youthful dancing generation in general, a full-page advertisement in the *Saturday Evening Post* stated:

You may regard the new generation as amusing or pathetic; as a bit tragic, or rather splendid. You may consider their manners crude, their ideals vague, their clothes absurd...But it is useless to deny that these youngsters have a definite bearing on the thought, literature and customs of our day. And particularly do they exert a powerful influence on buying habits and the movement of merchandise (quoted in Panati 1991, 117).

The defining contemporary written accounts of the period and the flapper generation can be found in the works of F. Scott Fitzgerald.

The term "flapper" first appeared in a Fitzgerald collection of short stories, *Flappers and Philosophers*, published in 1920. In the short story "The Perfect Life" in *The Basil and Josephine Stories*, he writes, "The afternoon was already planned; they were going dancing—for those were the great days" (158). His stories were contemporary and commented on the social climate, in many instances, on dancing. Fitzgerald's definitive novel of the period was *The Great Gatsby* (1925). Through a fictional narrator, Nick Carraway, he describes the life of Jay Gatsby, a wealthy society individual on his West Egg estate in Long Island, New York.

The contemporary novel tells tales of bootlegging, expensive automobiles, Jazz music, lavish parties, flappers, and dancing. Carraway describes his first impression at a Gatsby party, "There was dancing now on the canvas in the garden, old men pushing young girls backward in eternal circles, superior couples holding each other tortuously, fashionably and keeping in the corners—and a great number of single girls dancing individualistically...By midnight the hilarity increased" (Fitzgerald 1925, 51). At another party Carraway says, "The music has died down as the ceremony began and now a long cheer floated in at the window, followed by intermittent cries of 'Yea-ea-ea!' and finally by a burst of jazz as the dancing began" (Fitzgerald 1925, 135).

DANCE MARATHONS AND *THEY SHOOT HORSES DON'T THEY?*

In 1923, the first dance marathon was held in the Audubon Ballroom in New York City (see Chapter 5). The eventual winner, Alma Cummings, danced with a series of partners for 27 hours. *The New York World* reported, "Of all the crazy competitions ever invented the dancing marathon wins by a considerable margin of lunacy." In April of the same year in Cleveland, Ohio, the 27-hour record was extended by one couple to over 90 hours. The spectacles were very popular and attracted thousands of spectators. Dance marathon mania took hold as cities all across the country adopted the idea (Dannett and Rachel, 104).

In the dance marathons, dancers competed for prizes, mostly money. The rules stipulated that one couple had to maintain continuous motion. If a person tired and any portion of his or her body, other than the feet, touched the dance floor, he or she was disqualified. The couples usually danced in hourly increments of about 45 to 50 minutes with 10 minutes rest. Most of the time they shuffled and swayed slowly to the music, sometimes dozing, with the simple objective to keep moving. Usually once during the hour the couple was required to dance a specific dance such as the Fox Trot or Quickstep in order to stay in the competition.

The physical and mental toll taken upon dance marathon contestants was accurately captured in the 1969 Hollywood movie *They Shoot Horses Don't They?* In this scene a judge is ready to disqualify the contestants if any portion of their body, other than their feet, touched the dance floor.   ABC Pictures / Courtesy of Photofest.

In order to encourage the spectators, sponsors devised all sorts of devilish and brutal antics such as speeding up the music, adding relay races, and concocting elimination games. Prior to the antics, the MC was known to shout, "Yowsah, Yowsah, Yowsah." As the days passed and contestants tired, arguments would happen; some couples would slap and literally fight with each other. Dance marathons were a popular attraction and drew thousands of spectators. At one time or another every major city held a dance marathon and every major city attempted to ban the dance marathons.

Dance marathons continued during the early years of the 1930s. Many newsreels of the time featured stories highlighting the hundreds of hours of dancing and extreme exhaustion that the contestants encountered. For many depression era entrants, the reward was not so much the possibility of a cash prize, but, rather, the marathons offered a place to stay and free food. Contestants lucky enough to last a couple of weeks were usually sponsored by a local business that supplied them with much needed shoes as well as clothing emblazoned with the sponsor's name. The physical and mental toll taken upon dance marathon contestants was accurately captured in a 1935 novel by Horace McCoy and later Hollywood movie *They Shoot Horses Don't They?* (1969).

One of the most highly publicized dance marathons started on June 10, 1928, at Madison Square Garden in New York City. After 131 hours, 56 couples were still on the dance floor (most began to exhibit hate towards each other). After seven days the city's Board of Health decided to monitor the physical health of the remaining 13 couples. The commissioner of the Board of Health ordered the marathon stopped in its 428th hour with nine couples still moving about in front of 7,000 spectators (Panati 1991, 124–125).

Before that particular marathon was stopped, another marathon was going on at the Manhattan Casino (later renamed the Rockland Palace) also in New York City. Unlike the marathon event at Madison Square Garden, the Manhattan Casino event was *not* segregated. At one point, during the mandatory one hour of continuous movement, the dance music was speeded up. One dance contestant, George

"Shorty" Snowden, decided to improvise and do a version of the Breakaway. Two reporters for *The New York World* newspaper were on hand to report on the event. Fox Movietone News was also filming the event and focused in on Snowden's feet. An interviewer asked him what he was doing with his feet. Shorty replied, "the Lindy." Other reports quoted Shorty as saying, "I'm doing the hop just like Lindy" (Stearns and Stearns 1994, 315–316). With that simple improvisation and statement the Lindy Hop was born.

THE LINDY HOP

In 1927, the interest in aviation reached an incredible frenzy with the first solo transatlantic flight by Charles Lindbergh. The impact of Lindbergh upon aviation and popular public opinion cannot be understated. Very few Americans of any time received the attention and accolades afforded to "Lucky Lindy." All across the nation newspapers, magazines, and radio stations honored and hailed him as a hero, as did New York City, which held a ticket-tape parade attended by hundreds of thousands. Therefore, during the one moment of media attention afforded Shorty Snowden at the dance marathon, the reference to "Lindy's Hop" was understood all across America. Later, after the newsreel and newspaper reporters had left, Snowden said, "I was really doing the regular steps, just like we did them at the Savoy" (quoted in Stearns and Stearns 1994, 316). Snowden performed an early version of the Lindy Hop in a ten-minute Hollywood movie short *After Seben* (1929).

The Savoy Ballroom, in New York City's Harlem, opened the previous year on March 12, 1926. It covered an entire city block and could accommodate over 5,000 dancers. The ballroom was open seven nights of the week (until 3 A.M. on weekends) and held matinees on the weekends. The Savoy catered to a predominantly African American audience. They maintained a two-band policy so that the music never stopped. When one band took a break, the other played. It was at the Harlem Savoy that the Lindy Hop dance originated.

In the Jazz rhythm the partners rock back on the "& 8" count and forward on count 1; the pattern continues as noted above. Margaret Batiuchok describes the Jazz rhythm as follows: "The man rocks back [and] forward on counts /8 of the eight, or on counts 5/6 of the six. The woman steps on the right foot when he's on the left" (Batiuchok, *The Lindy: Origin and Development of the Lindy Hop 1927–1941*, 1988).

The hold in the Lindy Hop is different from the basic ballroom closed position. There are two basic holds: the closed position and the open

The Lindy Hop evolved as a purely original dance, but incorporated steps and movements from its predecessors, including the Charleston, Texas Tommy, and the Breakaway. The Lindy Hop was an eight-count dance counted out as 1-2, 3 & 4, 5-6, 7 & 8. In the basic step the man steps back on the left foot (count 1) and forward on the right foot (count 2), a slight rocking motion back and forward. He brings the left foot forward and to the side (count 3) steps side right (count &) and back on the left (count 4) completing a triple step left-right-left (three steps to two beats of music). He then steps side right (count 5) step side left (count 6) and repeats a triple step right-left-right (counts 7 & 8). The Lindy Hop was done in one spot on the dance floor as the partners developed a clockwise rotation during the eight-count rhythm. The Savoy style incorporated the Lindy Hop as an eight-count Jazz rhythm.

position. In the Lindy closed position, the leader takes the followers right hand in his left hand and holds her hand waist high as if he is going to kiss it. The man's right hand is behind the woman at waist level. The lead and follow are at waist level rather than shoulder height. In the closed position the partners mirror each other's footwork. The open position (or "Breakaway") drops the right hand from the lady's waist, and contact is by the single hand connection; man's left to lady's right. The open position allows each dancer to vary his or her own individual steps, or "play" within the rhythm. In other words, the partners can each improvise different step patterns within the eight count rhythm. Because of the improvisation and personal styling, the Lindy Hop would remain regional, and different styles developed as it became a national dance craze during the 1930s.

The Places to Dance

For the people to whom dancing has no appeal I have the deepest sympathy. They miss one of the greatest joys of life...A perfect partner, a perfect band, a perfect tune, and a perfect floor: what an appeal to one's sense of joy and happiness.

—A.M. Cree, 1920

CABARETS, SPEAKEASIES, AND ROADHOUSES

By the 1920s there were many places to dance. Public dancing was available at amusement parks, municipal sponsored park pavilions, and community centers. Dancing could also be found at private clubs, fraternal lodges, charity balls, and other traditional nineteenth century type social gatherings. Other places included dancing academies, dine-and-dance restaurants, hotels, cabarets, nightclubs, jook joints, honky-tonks, roadhouses, excursion boats, and, of course, home parlors.

Cabarets continued in popularity, especially with the advent of Jazz music. The prosperous crowd was mostly an older adult crowd, but younger people of college age were frequenting them more often than in the past. The big city cabarets of New York and Chicago flourished, and advertisements offered nightly entertainment and dancing. The *New Yorker* magazine advertised the dance team of Marjorie Moss and Georges Fontana performing "El Tango Tragico" at the *Club Mirador* at 200 West 51st Street (November 21, 1925, 28). The *New Yorker* magazine of January 2, 1926 advertised dozens of cabarets. For example, the *Rue Vignon* at 20 East 9th Street advertised "Dine and Dance." *Barney's* at 85 West 3rd Street also advertised "Dinner and Dancing." *The Kazrek* at 745 7th Avenue and 49th Street offered "Dining 6–10 P.M.; [and] Supper dancing at 11 P.M. All-star cabaret programme. Famous dancers and singers" (January 2, 1926, 47).

Speakeasies and nightclubs also featured the new Jazz bands. In 1923, one such club, the famed *Cotton Club*, opened in New York's Harlem. The *Cotton Club* served food and alcohol at high prices and presented cabaret style entertainment for a wealthy white audience. Although the Cotton Club was in Harlem, an African American neighborhood, the clientele was strictly white and the entertainers were always black. Very few establishments of any sort allowed intermingling of the races. The few that did were known as "Black and Tan" clubs. In Cleveland, for example, the only black-and-tan club, the *Cedar Gardens*, restricted African American patrons from Thursday to Saturday. The larger cities such as New York and Chicago did have cabarets and dance establishments that were solely for African Americans.

The small town equivalent of the speakeasy was the "roadhouse." Roadhouses were usually on the outskirts of a town or just outside the city limits. They were easily accessible by automobile and far from law enforcement. The roadhouses offered similar entertainment and dancing as the cabarets but not so elaborate. The patrons were more likely to be working class or African American (Steiner 1933, 114). The full extent of activities at the roadhouses and speakeasies during Prohibition can never be known. Although no accurate records were kept, since their operation was illegal, historian Eliot Asinof noted that in Detroit alone it was estimated that "the illegal importation of alcohol was a new business that escalated to $215 million a year, second only to the manufacturing of automobiles" (1990, 263).

COMMERCIAL DANCE HALLS AND DANCE PALACES

The overwhelming popularity of the large commercial dance halls, dance palaces, taxi-dance halls, and thousands of other dance establishments that flourished during the 1920s and lasted through the 1930s is indicative of the social and cultural times. At the time, dancing was one of the very few legal activities for nighttime public recreation or entertainment. The dance halls combined the attraction of the popular musical artist heard on the radio with dancing. The main location for public dancing was the commercial dance hall.

Overall, the number of smaller commercial dance halls actually declined, but because of the opening of large dance halls, each capable of accommodating 2,000 to 5,000 dancers at any one time, the overall numbers in attendance increased dramatically. Statistics borne out by the numerous agencies that visited and investigated the dance halls revealed that 14 percent of men between the age of 17 and 40 and 10 percent of females of the same age attended a dance hall at least once a week. In San Francisco the number was 25 percent. The statistics do not take into account those who danced at college fraternity parties, private functions, or in wealthy ballrooms (Mason, "Satan in the Dance-Hall," 1924, 176).

LeRoy E. Bowman and Maria Ward Lambin spearheaded a study by an Advisory Dance Hall Committee (representing 11 cooperating agencies including the Women's City Club) under the auspices of the New York City Recreation Committee. Their study reported 786 licensed dance halls in New York City, an increase of 40 percent since the 1920 report of 476 licensed dance halls. The dance halls were spread throughout the five boroughs almost in proportion to the population. In 1924, the attendance at the 238 Manhattan dance halls totaled 122,272 people per week, which amounted to a yearly total of over 6.1 million. The male to female ratio was about 60 percent male to 40 percent female. Attendance figures were not available for the other four boroughs of Staten Island, the Bronx, Queens, or Brooklyn. In all, they visited 105 dance halls, which included 13 closed halls, 21 restaurants, 9 dance palaces, and 12 social club dances. These numbers also do not include the 18 to 20 large hotels, settlement houses, and public schools that were exempt from licensing. Bowman and Lambin estimated that dances at community centers and settlement houses attracted another 189,000 to 200,000 per year. In that same year, Chicago dance hall admissions also numbered over 6 million ("Evidences of Social Relations As Seen in Types of New York City Dance Halls," 286–289).

A 1925 report by Collis Stocking, *A Study of Dance Halls in Pittsburgh*, tallied statistics of 155 licensed dance halls with a combined weekly attendance of over 37,000—a yearly attendance of 1.9 million. Cities all across America reported economic success with dance hall admissions. Large elaborately furnished dance halls opened, such as Denver's *Trocadero*, New York's *Roseland*, Cleveland's *Crystal Slipper*, Detroit's *Graystone*, Chicago's *Trianon*, Boston's *Raymor*, Indianapolis's *Indiana Roof*, and the Los Angeles's *Palomar*. They were known as Dance Palaces. Every major city had one or more elaborately styled large dance halls, and many small towns had a smaller version (Steiner 1933, 113).

The Dance Palaces employed the most popular orchestras of the time, sometimes two to provide continuous music. Couples were accepted, but no restrictions were placed upon groups of females or individual entry, and each was charged an admission fee. Most still employed a ticket-a-dance per couple plan. The price ranged from 5 cents to 15 cents per dance. The dance floors were roped off; some elaborate ones had a fixed railing and areas designated as admission to the floor. A ticket taker would take the ticket and allow the couple onto the dance floor. Some smaller dance halls had ticket takers who walked the floors in a fashion similar to a train conductor.

Many of the Dance Palaces offered a dance hostess with a price ranging from 35 to 45 cents for three dances. Although the hostesses usually received a "tip" as an extra, they were not considered immoral since the establishment type was considered respectable. A few also provided gentlemen hosts to dance with unescorted ladies; however, no prepurchased ticket was required. Almost anyone over the age of 16 who paid an admission fee was allowed entry, that is, except African Americans and many other ethnics and immigrants.

The *Savoy* in New York City's Harlem was believed to be the first and one of the very few integrated dance halls in America (see Chapter 3). In 1927, another *Savoy Ballroom* was opened in Chicago, Illinois, by dance promoter I. Jay Faggen that could accommodate over 4,000 dancers. Faggen was noted for partnering successful ballrooms including the *Savoy* in Harlem, the *Blue Bird Ballroom* and *Roseland*, both in Manhattan, and the *Rosemont Ballroom* in Brooklyn. The Faggen policy was to open the ballroom seven nights of the week with matinees on the weekend (Newman, "Jazz Age Chicago," 2000).

East Harlem in New York City was developing a strong Puerto Rican immigrant culture. In early 1930, the local Puerto Rican civic association rented the Golden Casino on 110th Street and Fifth Avenue and sponsored what is considered the first Latin dance in America. Other theaters and ballrooms in the area soon featured authentic Latin music and staged dances (Roberts 1999, 88).

Other dance halls throughout the country, however, were mostly segregated. Those that did allow blacks to enter were careful to keep black couples separate from white couples in "unofficial" segregated areas. Many blacks simply chose to dance in small speakeasies, social clubs, and private house parties that catered to blacks. Nevertheless, the large dance halls were popular and profitable (Trotter 2001, 424).

CHICAGO DANCE HALLS AND SANTA CATALINA ISLAND

Andrew Karzas was an entrepreneur who saw the potential of the dance hall as a profitable business. He invested huge sums of money into two of the most elegant ballrooms in America, both in Chicago. In 1922, Karzas opened the *Trianon Ballroom* located at 62nd Street and Cottage Grove Avenue. The location was adjacent to an elevated rail line and within a densely populated middle class neighborhood. The Trianon was a large ballroom that could accommodate 3,000 or more dancers. It was elaborately furnished in an opulent Turkish style typical of many of the posh and elegant hotels and ballrooms of the time.

Karzas did not want a bad association with his ballrooms; therefore, he maintained a dance policy that did not allow any immoral behavior, including drinking alcohol or dancing in a manner he deemed as vulgar. The Trianon was the first ballroom in Chicago to strictly enforce a dress code. Jackets and ties were required for men and appropriate evening attire for females. He had "floor walkers" dressed in tuxedos to enforce the rules. He also resisted having any fast or hot Jazz played and maintained a strict "white only" policy, which included the musicians in the dance bands. The adult evening crowd danced mainly to Waltzes, Two-Steps, and Fox Trots (Newman, "Jazz Age Chicago," 2000).

The success of the Trianon encouraged Karzas to open another dance palace in the northern uptown section of Chicago. The *Aragon Ballroom* was also located close to an elevated rail line and maintained the same dance policies as the Trianon. The elegant ballroom was over 80,000 square feet and was the largest place of amusement in Chicago. The Aragon offered slower paced music and formality in an elegant setting for an older adult clientele. Men were required to wear jackets and ties and women evening wear. The Aragon advertised, "Every facility to insure the complete comfort of dance lovers…Commodious checkrooms for both men and women, a handsomely appointed grande mirror salon for the convenience of milady, a clean wholesome refectory where appetizing refreshments are served by charming senoritas" ("Beauty of Old Spain Is Found At the Aragon," *Chicago Evening American*, July 15, 1926, 1).

Opening night at the Aragon on July 15, 1926, was covered as a page one story in the *Chicago Evening American*. Chicago Mayor William Hale Thompson presided over the opening ceremony as the ballroom filled to capacity. The Aragon and its grandeur rivaled any of the most lavish interior spaces in America. The interior was described as, "Tall, stately towers and minarets of silver gleaming above the blue skies; great granite walls covered with ancient arabesques of green, blue and gold; vaulted ceilings and archways, Moorish carvings and scrollwork; all the splendors of ancient Spain" ("Thousands Throng Great Aragon Ballroom," *Chicago Evening American*, July 16, 1926, 1).

The music from the ballroom was broadcast on Chicago radio station WGN every evening from 10 P.M. to 11 P.M. except Sunday. The weekly attendance totaled

An invitation to "Admit Two (Lady and Gentleman) as the guests of the management without charge whatsoever to the ARAGON or the TRIANON," ballrooms in Chicago, c. 1932. Author's Archives.

18,000 people. The Aragon continued to hold regularly scheduled dances until its closure in 1964. The hall continued to hold concerts and special sporting events through the end of the twentieth century (Newman, "Jazz Age Chicago," 2000).

The more youthful Chicagoans danced in places such as the *Arcadia Ballroom* located on Montrose Avenue west of Broadway. The Arcadia was faster paced and regularly employed African American bands playing Hot Jazz. Others included the *Rainbow Room* and *Green Mill Gardens*. The *Rainbow Room* could hold 2,000 for dining and 1,500 to dance. *Green Mill Gardens* also combined dining and dancing and had a large outdoor garden for dancing during the summer months (Newman, "Jazz Age Chicago," 2000).

Luxury resorts for vacations and dancing were still popular among the wealthy. Unlike previous years it became acceptable (and popular) for an unchaperoned female to attend a resort. In 1927, the influential magazine, the *Woman's Home Companion*, stated that it was "now quite the usual thing for a party of girls to go un-chaperoned to a summer resort" (Aron 1999, 228). One such resort was on Santa Catalina Island.

Santa Catalina Island, part of the Channel Islands, is 21 miles long and 12 miles wide and is located 22 miles off the coast of southern California. Most people arrived by one of the two steamships, the *S.S. Avalon* or the *S.S. Catalina*, that provided round-trip service from Wilmington, California. Many others arrived by private yacht. The island resorts such as the St. Catherine Hotel catered to a wealthy clientele and were popular for either a day at the beach, an extended stay, or a night of ballroom dancing. The favored location was the Catalina Casino Ballroom. It was not a gambling casino but an entertainment venue with a movie theater on the first level and a grandiose ballroom on the top level. The Catalina Casino opened in 1929, and during the 1930s the ballroom drew crowds of over 5,000 to dance and listen to popular bands of the day (Wade, "Santa Catalina Island, Southern California's swing-era paradise," n.d.).

TAXI-DANCE HALLS

On the other end of the economic scale, a popular place to dance was the Taxi-dance hall. Similar to the Dance Palaces, the Taxi-dance halls were usually located in the general downtown area of a city, usually close to major subway or elevated rail lines, such as Chicago's Loop District. The Dance Palaces and the Taxi-dance halls tried to maintain a standard that would not offend people. The Dance Palaces were mostly successful in that end. The Taxi-dance halls were not.

In 1932, Sociologist Paul G. Cressey, a caseworker for the Chicago Juvenile Protective Association, published a definitive contemporary study, *The Taxi-Dance Hall: A Sociological Study in Commercialized Recreation and City Life*. The study was the result of an in-depth personal observation of the codes of conduct and operation of Taxi-dance halls in Chicago during the 1920s. According to Cressey, the Taxi-dance hall was selected "because it was at the time a very new and questionable type of establishment with which even social workers were not familiar" (xxxiii). He defined a Taxi-dance hall as "a commercial public dance institution attracting only male patrons, which seeks to provide them an opportunity for social dancing by employing women partners, who are paid on a commission basis though the ticket-a-dance plan, and who are expected to dance with any patron who may select them for as few or as many dances as he is willing to purchase" (27).

The origins of paying for a dance can be traced to the 1849 gold rush in San Francisco, California. The practice continued until 1925 when it was outlawed in that city. The first of the ten-cents-a-dance policies was in New York City at the Grand Central Palace in 1911 (see Chapter 1). At first they did not have a name, and they were called "Closed Dance Halls" because they did not allow women patrons. Some called them "dime-a-dance halls," "stag dances," or "monkey hops." The name Taxi-dance hall was derived from the fact that hostesses could be rented for a service in proportion to time spent, similar to a taxicab.

Typically these halls held about 200 to 600 people. An admission fee of 50 cents to $1.50 was charged. The entry fee sometimes allowed about three dances. Once inside, male patrons purchased individual tickets usually at a cost of 10 cents per dance. Discounts were offered such as three dances for 25 cents. Upon being selected for a dance, the dance hostess would take the ticket and usually stuff it in her stocking. At the end of the evening she would cash-in her tickets with the management. A respectable dance hall would evenly split the profits with the hostess. The hostesses were nicknamed "nickel hoppers" since their take was half of the 10 cents a dance (Cressey 1931, 3–17). Dances were short in duration, about 40 to 60 seconds. Sufficient time was not always allowed to clear the dance floor to start the process again. It was not unusual for a hostess to dance 70 or 80 times in one evening (Mason, "Satan in the Dance-Hall," 1924, 178).

In 1923, Chicago had only two Taxi-dance halls operating the *Athenian Dancing Academy* on North Clark Street and the *American Dancing School* at Robey Street and North Avenue. They were profitable, and others quickly opened, including the *Ashland Dancing School* on Ashland Avenue and Madison Street, the *Madison Dancing School* six blocks west on Madison Avenue, and a second *American Dancing School* on Madison and Robey Streets. By 1927, cities all across America had licensed Taxi-dance halls. In 1930, a 12-minute short movie titled *Roseland* featured taxi dancers in the famed New York City dance hall. In July 1931, in New York City almost 100 Taxi-dance halls were operating in Manhattan and Brooklyn with a combined weekly attendance of 35,000 to 50,000 men, and over 8,000 female dance hostesses were legally employed (Cressey 1932, 214–222).

The Taxi-dance hall equivalent for working class females, however, simply did not exist. Another type of closed hall appeared in wealthy "refined" circles. At some fashionable hotels and most luxury resorts the management employed gentlemen hosts for dancing with unescorted females. The gentlemen hosts were not paid per dance nor did the women pay them, although it was reported that some upscale New York hotels did offer women a companion for dancing, shopping, and attending the theater, if so desired. It was customary for the gentlemen host to receive a tip of about $15 to $20 (Mason, "Satan in the Dance-Hall," 1924, 179).

From an outsider's point of view, the Taxi-dance hall was in complete contradiction to any traditional American entertainment venue. The idea that a woman was at the service of a complete male stranger could only be viewed by society as immoral behavior. One visitor recalled, "The girls themselves, were young, highly painted creatures, who talked little" (Cressey 1932, 31). Prior to this time only females of questionable moral behavior, such as prostitutes, wore makeup. During the 1920s, however, makeup in general was becoming a fashion statement for young females across America.

Cressey observed that any evidence of prostitution or immorality was hard to find. Although the pay for dancing was certainly much better than for a factory or clerical job, the pay was nowhere near what a prostitute could earn. One young dance hostess said, "After I had gotten started at the dance hall I enjoyed the life too much to want to give it up. It was easy work, gave me more money that I could earn in any other way, and I had a chance to meet all kinds of people." Cressey concluded that the Taxi-dance hall "may thus be viewed as a natural outgrowth of certain urban conditions rather than as a moral violation" (262). One reason is that the patrons had limited, if any, choices for recreation and entertainment other than the Taxi-dance hall (Cressey 1932, 32, 262–265).

In Chicago, for example, the population increased from 1.7 million people in 1900 to 3.4 million in 1930, many of them recent immigrants. Many immigrant males had left their native countries alone looking to make money to send for their wife and children. Others were young and single and sought to make enough money to start a family in America. Therefore, the males greatly outnumbered the females. Dancing was a simple recreational pleasure that immigrants found comfortingly similar to their own traditions in this new country. The elegant Dance Palaces did not allow them entry; therefore, the Taxi-dance hall satisfied not only the disparity in the male to female ratio but also alleviated the problem of loneliness in the city.

The Taxi-dance hall also provided dance partners for those individuals who were shunned by society and could not attend other dance halls, which included working class whites, Filipinos, Chinese, Mexicans, Polish, Italians, Greeks, Jews, and college and high school boys, as well as patrons with physical handicaps, "the dwarfed, maimed, and pock-marked." One group was totally excluded—African Americans. Unfortunately, segregation was routinely practiced throughout the United States, and African American men simply were not allowed to dance with white women (Cressey 1932, 10). In 1933, Stanley Walker, city editor of the *New York Herald Tribune*, simply said, "Its main purpose is to give the unattractive man a chance to have a good time," and they all found social acceptance (208–209). Therefore, the Taxi-dance hall was not a deliberate attempt to exclude female patrons but rather a business by which dance partners were available for men who could not otherwise obtain them.

In actuality, the public dance halls made the working class individual part of a social group and therefore socially significant, at least during the time spent dancing. In 1924, Gregory Mason observed, "At work he and she are just numbers on the payroll, cogs in the human machinery of a vast office or vaster factory. But in the dance-halls such youths and maidens become somebodies. To the same music they dance the same steps as their luckier [wealthy] cousins in Newport [Rhode Island]" (180). Despite the innocent need, objections to the Taxi-dance halls, commercial dance halls, and dancing in general were numerous, and municipal regulations were enacted.

MUNICIPAL DANCE HALL REGULATIONS

In 1929, the U.S. Department of Labor published the results of a national study to investigate the public "dance-hall problem in cities" throughout the United States (1). The study, supervised and authored by Ella Gardner, was titled *Public Dance Halls: Their Regulation and Place in the Recreation of Adolescents Bureau Publication No. 189*. Over 400 cities (with population in excess of 15,000) responded to a series of questions and also sent copies of existing state legislation regulating dance halls. One question posed was whether children, especially females, should be allowed into the public dance halls, and if so, what "safeguards" should be implemented (1).

In 1925 and 1926, Bureau agents visited 15 cities to make personal observations. They visited dance halls in Butte, Montana; Chicago, Illinois; Dayton, Ohio; Detroit, Michigan; Duluth, Minnesota; Houston, Texas; Los Angeles, California; New Bedford, Massachusetts; Ottumwa, Iowa; Paterson, New Jersey; Portland, Oregon; Rochester, New York; San Francisco, California; Seattle, Washington; Wichita, Kansas; and New York City, New York. The dance halls visited included outdoor pavilions, rented halls, amusement parks, cafés, cabarets, dance academies, dancing schools, armories, dance palaces, and taxi-dance halls.

All the cities visited and 28 states had regulations on dance halls. The most common included restrictions on Sunday dancing, municipal supervision by local police, and hours of closing, usually 1 A.M. or 2 A.M. Some ordinances allowed an extension of the closing hour on special holidays and New Year's Eve. The regulations also stipulated lighting and exit requirements, moral conduct, and type of dances. Violation of the ordinances carried monetary fines and in some cases imposed a prison sentence. Most restricted entry to unmarried unescorted people under the age of 16 to 18 (2–3).

Some individual restrictions, such as in El Paso, Texas, prohibited the "attendance of women known to be immoral." Port Arthur, Texas, as did many other cities, permitted only dances approved by the National Association of Dancing

Masters. They also named specific dances not permitted, including the Bunny Hug, Turkey Trot, Texas Tommy, and Grizzly Bear. Lynn, Massachusetts, did not allow "unrefined dancing." Lincoln, Nebraska, made it unlawful "for any person to participate in a dance of a coarse or vulgar character or offensive to public morals and decency" [and restricted] "undue familiarity between partners." They also defined the standard dance position as "the lady shall place her left hand on the gentleman's right shoulder or arm and her right hand on the gentleman's left hand, the gentleman's right hand on the lady's back, and at all times the patrons shall keep their bodies at least 6 inches apart." Sheboygan, Wisconsin, allowed the owner of the dance hall the "power to use necessary and reasonable force to suppress indecent and boisterous dancing" (12–13). Cleveland, Ohio, specified, "Dancers are not permitted to take either exceptionally long or short steps." Cheeks were not allowed to be too close and definitely prohibited from "touching." Cleveland also prohibited "Vulgar, noisy, jazz music" (Mason, "Satan in the Dance Hall," 1924, 181). One proposal was to wear a "bumper" belt around the waist of the female, complete with protruding sticks, to prevent close body contact.

Woman wearing a "bumper" belt to prevent close body contact of her male dance partner, c. 1923.   Photo by Topical Press Agency / Courtesy Getty Images 2665076.

During the years 1924–1925, Francis H. Hiller studied dance halls throughout Wisconsin in the counties of Brown, Columbia, Dane, Douglas, Fond du Lac, Iron, Jefferson, Kenosha, La Crosse, Milwaukee, Racine, Waukesha, and Winnebago. The unique approach of the state of Wisconsin to dance hall legislation enabled the county boards to enact ordinances and licensing procedures at the county rather than the state level. The regulations were similar to those of other American cities. For example, Kenosha County permitted only dances approved by the National Association of Dancing Masters and required the rules to be clearly posted in each public dance hall. In Oshkosh, Wisconsin, dancing men and women partners were not allowed to look into each other's eyes.

The nature of supervision and enforcement of the public dance hall regulations varied widely. Some of the inspectors employed by the counties included farmers who did not dance and did not know what should or should not be permitted. In certain instances two inspectors commenting on the same dancing couple disagreed, one claiming the dancing couple was "improper" and the other inspector saying "he saw nothing wrong with it." In Kenosha County instances were reported of rules of the Association of Dancing Masters broken by 5 out of 6 couples, who were issued warnings. In Iron County, however, the deputy sheriff reported arresting dance couples for the same offense (Hiller, "The Working of County Dance Hall Ordinances in Wisconsin," 1927, 7–10).

The Music Division of the Library of Congress provides an excellent catalogue of the municipal regulations, popular dance instruction booklets, and anti-dance literature published during the 1920s titled *An American Ballroom Companion: Dance Instruction Manuals Ca. 1490–1920*. One example of anti-dance literature was the Reverend Thomas Faulkner's *From The Ballroom to Hell*. It was first published in 1894 and was resurrected three times including in 1916 and 1922. The Reverend Dr. R.A. Adams, in *The Social Dance* (1921), bluntly dedicated himself to "the great work of saving the young men and young women from the inevitable effects of the Social Dance" (2). The Reverend John Roach Straton of New York City published two anti-dance books, *The Dance of Death, Should Christians Indulge?* (1920) and *Fighting the Devil in Modern Babylon* (1929).

From 1918 until 1929 the Reverend Straton was the pinnacle of religious opposition to entertainment and dancing and received a lot of media attention. The Reverend Straton's Calvary Baptist church was in the heart of midtown Manhattan on West 57th Street located on the same block as two dancing schools. Stanley Walker, city editor of the *New York Herald Tribune*, said Straton "was opposed to virtually everything in the way of amusement that was going on in New York." The list of objections included cardplaying, drinking, Jazz music, the theater, low-cut dresses, divorce, novels, overeating, stuffy rooms, Clarence Darrow, evolution, the Museum of Natural history, boxing, the private lives of actors, modernism, and even poodle dogs. He particularly abhorred dancing. Unlike other clergy who preached from the pulpit, Straton was known to disguise himself and actually visited restaurants, speakeasies, and dance halls to gather "first hand" information for his Sunday sermons. He was also successful in preaching over the airwaves of the fledging radio industry (177–184).

Straton met with many of those in New York who simply laughed off his accusations, but he did endear himself to the millions of people outside of New York who had the same opinion. Therefore, as Stanley Walker wrote, Straton was viewed as "a symbol of righteousness to the rest of dry, Puritan America" (181). It might be with some irony that Straton died of a stroke on the morning of October 29, 1929, the day of the Stock Market Crash that began the Great Depression (Stanley Walker, 177, 181).

Gregory Mason reviewing the New York City dance halls for *The American Mercury* wrote, "Nearly always, however, the attempts to censor dancing are conceived in hysteria and carried out to absurdity…the most immoral thing about the public dance-hall is probably the dead, pallid boredom that it begets, the absolute crushing out of any such slight spontaneity as these young male and female products of our industrial civilization may have yet possessed when they entered its doors.

The very steps of the fox-trot [sic] and one-step are appallingly monotonous" (Mason 1932, 179–182).

Other prominent clergy in opposition to dancing included Catholic Patrick Cardinal Hayes, Rabbi Stephen S. Wise, Methodist Reverend Dr. Christian Fichthorne Reisner, Baptist Reverend Dr. Harry Emerson Fosdick, and Episcopalian Bishop William T. Manning. The concerns about Saturday night dancing had mixed reactions from the clergy. Bishop William T. Manning, for example, who favored rejoicing and relaxation, said, "It is not a mortal sin to dance after 12 o'clock Saturday night, but it is not advisable to do so. We cannot well begin our Sunday in the right way, by being at the early celebration of the Holy Communion, if we dance after midnight Saturday night" ("Manning Rules Out A Puritan Sunday," *New York Times*, February 26, 1926, 16). In Dearborn, Michigan, parents and the First Evangelical Church of Dearborn presented a petition signed by over 200 parents "demanding that the teaching of the dances be stopped in the schools." Ironically, the dances in objection were "old-fashioned dances" sponsored by Henry Ford, himself an outspoken critic of Jazz and modern dancing ("Ford Townsmen Object to His Dances," *New York Times*, 1926, 22).

Objections to dancing from the pulpit continued. However, the reasoning and logic applied by the religious zealots to the prohibition of dancing sometimes defied all reason and logic. They usually supported their sermons with purely fictional "statistics" or sensationalized "stories." Some of the reactions bordered on the ridiculous. The indomitable Reverend Dr. R.A. Adams actually tried to blame dancing as the cause of marriage infidelity, promiscuity, loss of physical strength, early death, and even abortion. He wrote:

In fact, the dance is the mother of abortion—and it is a prolific mother too. Heated in the dance, burning with passion, with modesty dethroned as the result of sexual embraces, intoxicated by wine and passion, oftentimes, the girl not only yields to the wrong, but, losing all control actually makes openings. Then, when the departures have been made and she realizes that what has been done cannot be repaired, she gives herself up to the enjoyment of sexual pleasures out of wedlock. Then, when she finds herself on the road to maternity, she attempts to hide her shame and save her parents from disgrace, by means of abortion; and there have been thousands of cases in which the girl ended her own life, as well as that of the unborn child (21–22).

The Reverend J.W. Porter assessed, "The wave of licentiousness, now sweeping over the country...is due in large measure to the ballroom...and will, if unchecked, be the ruin of our own country." He also decried that "liquor and the dance-hall are responsible for fifty percent of the murders of America." In 1928, California Evangelist Harry O. Anderson said that due to dancing "there are 5,000 girls lost every twelve months in the city of Chicago...[in Los Angeles] 5,000 girls slip out of sight never to be seen again." He somehow provides a mathematical deduction that over 7 million girls "in a century" are "lost in a life of shame and sorrow" (Wagner 1997, 272–273). The Reverend Dr. R.A. Adams also bellowed:

Danceland Dance Hall in New York City during the Depression advertised "50 Dances 50¢," c. 1932.   © Bettmann/Corbis.

Tell if you think Jesus Christ would go to a dance [and] dance the tango, the turkey trot and the buzzard lope. Do you believe He would go to a dance and hug up and waltz all night? Be honest and tell if you would for a moment believe that Jesus could be induced to do a thing like that? Even as worldly as you are, you answer NO! Then, be assured that you cannot follow Jesus and do these things (1921, 27).

Curiously this quote would be recycled by clergy in opposition to dancing throughout the twentieth century (see Chapters 4 and 6).

At the time, publisher H.L. Mencken, writing in *The American Mercury*, cynically stated religious people lived "in mortal fear that somewhere, somehow, someone might be enjoying himself" (Baughman 1996, 383). A.M. Cree, writing in his *Handbook of Ball-Room Dancing*, added "For the people to whom dancing has no appeal I have the deepest sympathy. They miss one of the greatest joys of life...A perfect partner, a perfect band, a perfect tune and a perfect floor: what an appeal to one's sense of joy and happiness" (1920, 21–22). Those who danced would continue to enjoy the pleasures of dancing throughout the twentieth century. Critics would also continue to attack dancing, even during the onset of the Depression during the 1930s.

From 1929 until 1932, social dancing was also in a depression and almost non-existent. Cabarets, nightclubs, vacation resorts, ballrooms, and dance halls all reported a severe drop in business. In late 1930, a *Variety* magazine headline read "Dance Halls All Starving" (November 12, 1930, 1). By 1932, many dance halls were desperate for customers. In order to stay in business, many of the ballrooms drastically reduced the admission fee. Taxi-dance halls such as Danceland in New York City advertised "50 Dances 50¢," and stayed open from 8 P.M. to 3 A.M. As the Depression wore on, many Americans needed to find activities to temporarily alleviate the economic worry, and dancing served as a means to alleviate their concerns. However, during World War II, dancing achieved newfound importance and gained recognition as a patriotic cause.

3

The Lindy Hop, Jitterbug, and Swing: 1932–1947

Jitterbugs are the extreme swing addicts who get so excited by its music that they cannot stand or be still.

—*LIFE* Magazine, 1938

The Political, Social, and Cultural Climate

The stock market crash of 1929 triggered a worldwide depression. In America, the effects were mind boggling as unemployment nationwide was over 25 percent and production of goods came almost to a halt. Wages were either nonexistent or drastically reduced; therefore, families could not pay the rent or the mortgage. As a result, millions were homeless as many Americans lost their homes and farms. Some simply packed up their families and moved away in search of work to support and feed family members. The bread lines and food relief were common sights in most cities. The population growth came almost to a standstill.

During the 1930s, while America was still in the depths of the Depression, many Americans were unemployed and had little or no money. People spent more time at home and listened to the radio. With what little extra money they had, Americans escaped to the movies, with fantasy themes such as musicals and elaborate dance performances. During the period, movie attendance averaged over 90 million per week. Some of the famous films included *The Wizard of Oz*, *Gone With the Wind*, *Casablanca*, and *Citizen Kane*. Some of the Hollywood movie stars included Shirley Temple, Clark Gable, Humphrey Bogart, Carole Lombard, Katherine Hepburn, and the comedy teams of the Marx Brothers and Abbott and Costello. (By comparison, after World War II, with the advent of television, attendance dropped to 25 million per week and in the year 2000 was about the same.) During the

Depression and especially during World War II, dancing also served as a relief from worry and as a way to pass time.

The Depression marked the first time that the federal government showed a serious interest in public recreation and leisure time programs. President Franklin D. Roosevelt and the New Deal established many federally funded programs that created jobs to help the economy and society. In 1934, Roosevelt created the Federal Emergency Relief Administration, the Works Progress Administration (WPA), and the Civilian Conservation Corps (CCC). The WPA constructed and improved numerous roads, hiking trails, lakes, and campsites in the National Parks and forests through the organization of the CCC. The WPA also built and renovated recreation facilities and dance pavilions. A Recreation Section of the WPA employed over 50,000 people nationwide to administer and conduct community activities. Dancing of all sorts was taught, including ballroom, tap, folk, and square dancing (Wrenn and Harley 1941, 224–227).

By 1940, the U.S. Census reported the population of the United States was 132 million. More than 74 million lived in rural areas and 57 million in cities. More than half of the total population was concentrated in the Northeast. The work force was 56 million with the main occupations split between manufacturing and agriculture (Lingeman 1970, 13).

At the beginning of 1940, Americans were slowly emerging from the devastating effects of the Depression. In Europe, however, war was raging throughout the continent as Hitler conquered most of the continent. At first, most Americans were too preoccupied with the economic recovery at home to worry about involvement in another European war. However, the surprise attack by the Japanese government upon the American military base at Pearl Harbor in Hawaii on December 7, 1941, suddenly thrust the United States into the world war with both Japan and Germany.

The suddenness of America's entry into the war and the widespread paranoia created a perceived "real threat" of invasion on either coast of the United States mainland. In the event of an attack, an air raid siren would warn Americans, thereby requiring them to go into a total "blackout." During a blackout, all the streetlights were shut off and any homes or businesses either had to shut off the lights or have "blackout curtains" on the windows to prevent light from showing on the exterior. By June 1942, government mandated blackouts were in effect along both coasts. Because Americans particularly feared an invasion upon the Pacific coast, anyone of Japanese ancestry was immediately suspected as a spy or potential saboteur. Therefore, in early 1942, President Franklin D. Roosevelt signed Executive Order #9066 that instituted the forced relocation of all Japanese Americans from the West Coast of the United States. Literally within days of the order, the entire Japanese American population (over 120,000 people) were removed from their homes and businesses and relocated to inland states including Montana and Nevada. Most were kept in the "Interment" camps until late 1944. Upon returning to the coast, when the war was over, almost all found their homes and businesses no longer available (Nash 1985, 149).

World War II instantly became the main focus of American society. The government shifted its focus from the depression era work agencies towards the war. In the process they also convinced Americans to contribute and sacrifice to the war effort. The shift in industrial production also proved to be the economic stimulus that brought the country out of the Depression. Millions of workers who were previously unemployed were suddenly in high demand. Many of those found work in the new war material production factories. The war also required a need for an unfathomable number of soldiers, so the United States instituted a Selective Service draft system. Between 1940 and 1946, over 34 million males registered and over 16 million served in active duty.

By 1942, unemployment was virtually nonexistent. Unlike the Depression when jobs were few, American industry was operating at production levels unlike any in history, and labor shortages prevented meeting the demands of wartime production. Production was at an all time high, but the goods were solely for the military and the war effort. Shortages of basic necessities on the home front required the introduction of a rationing system. Rationed items included gasoline, rubber, coffee, tea, sugar, butter, meat, and almost every other food and consumer product. Americans were issued ration coupon books that assigned "point values" to rationed products. Therefore purchasing a product required not only money but also the addition of coupon points.

As Americans sacrificed to support the common cause, rationing and coupon points became part of everyday life. Americans were also asked to conserve and lend a hand by providing needed items to recycle by instituting "scrap drives" and growing their own vegetables in backyard "Victory" gardens. During the remaining war years, the tasks at hand did not change.

Since the economic prosperity could not be used for the purchase of material goods, many used the additional income for entertainment. Record numbers went bowling or went to the movies. The entertainment industry also supported the war effort. The Hollywood movies of the time produced numerous musicals and film fare carefully designed to continually remind the American public of the need to support the war effort. To some, with the war at hand, fun and frivolity were viewed with a sense of urgency. Splurges on nightclubs and dancing became commonplace, since many felt that they might not live to see tomorrow.

The Dances

But for the most part the public was still doing the same sort of gliding dances that had been popular for a long time, except maybe in Harlem where the "Lindy Hop" and such were popular.

—Benny Goodman, 1939

THE DEPRESSION AND DANCE MARATHONS

As the Depression wore on, dancing served as a means to alleviate the economic uncertainties. Those desperate for any means to earn money entered dance marathons. However, in 1933, in order to alleviate the health hazard associated with the marathons, the governor of New York State signed a law making any continuous dancing beyond eight hours a criminal offense. Many other cities followed, and dance marathons soon faded out (Panati 1991, 125).

After 1932, social dancing slowly regained its popularity at resorts, hotels, and commercial dance halls. Ballroom standards, especially the Fox Trot, were the main choice among older adults. Dance instructor Lillian Ray acknowledged, "Most women adore dancing with a response to rhythm and gaiety that is as natural as liking sunshine. The music, the lights, the flattery, the chance to wear frivolous clothes that have no relation to daytime duties, are too irresistible to be foregone easily." Women especially adored dancing if it was with their own husband. With very little money and much more time available than ever before, dancing was an inexpensive form of entertainment that could alleviate the worry of the depression. Ray said to the husbands of America, "It is no longer smart...to give up dancing for the lazy comfort of slippers and newspaper...dancing is part of [your] necessary social equipment" (1936, 19).

During the late 1930s, as the depression subsided, dance studios once again prospered. A survey of the Sunday *New York Times* advertisements during 1937 and 1938 revealed entire pages devoted to dance instruction. Almost all offered instruction in the Rhumba, Waltz, Tango, and the Fox Trot. They included well-established teachers including Arthur Murray, Ned Wayburn, Louis H. Chalif, Betty Lee, and Miss Dale. In 1940, in Chicago, for example, over 180 dancing schools for adults were listed in the telephone directory (Chicago, Vol. II, 139). A major factor was that people wanted to dance like those in the Hollywood movies. The new dance couple that many sought to emulate was Fred Astaire and Ginger Rogers.

FRED ASTAIRE AND GINGER ROGERS

Up until 1932, Fred Astaire had danced as part of a team with his sister Adele for over 25 years. After Adele's retirement, Fred headed to Hollywood where his association with dance partner Ginger Rogers began. Throughout the 1930s, Astaire and Rogers gracefully danced their way through nine Hollywood movies, *Flying Down to Rio* (1933), *The Gay Divorcee* (1934), *Roberta* (1935), *Top Hat* (1935), *Follow the Fleet* (1936), *Swing Time* (1936), *Shall We Dance* (1937), *Carefree* (1938), and *The Story of Vernon and Irene Castle* (1939). They exuded an elegance and grace on the Hollywood screen that was unmatched. Astaire was very concerned that their onscreen dancing appeared natural and real to the movie audiences. In order to ensure that the dance scenes did not appear faked by camera trickery, he had a clause in his contract that when dancing, he and his partner must be filmed head to toe.

The elegant leading of Astaire and graceful following of Rogers was a sight that the public fantasized to imitate. Dance instructor Lillian Ray advised, "Never should the so-called gentler sex be quite so gentle and acquiescent as when dancing. No matter what her views on suffrage and feminism may be, it is a woman's duty to let the man lead on the ballroom floor. He is the guiding spirit; hers, the following. He is the pacemaker; she, the responsive shadow" (1936, 41).

Ginger Rogers and Fred Astaire dancing in a scene from the movie *Carefree*, 1938.   Courtesy of Photofest.

Ginger Rogers's dancing prowess certainly matched that of Astaire. She has often been quoted, "I did everything Fred did only backwards and in high heels." The notoriety of the dance couple was so widespread that it was very common throughout the remainder of the twentieth century for a very good amateur dance couple dancing at a wedding, social event, or vacation resort to be called out to as "Hey Fred and Ginger."

One scene between Fred and Ginger in the movie *Flying Down to Rio* featured a new dance called the Carioca that many people wanted to learn. Dance instructor Lawrence Hostetler attempted to analyze the dance but commented that the Carioca "has no definite form which could give it the distinction of being called a new ballroom dance." Hostetler suggested, "When dancing to the 'Carioca' one can use either a rhumba movement or variations of the fox-trot" (1934, 156). The Carioca, however, was only a stylized ballroom version of the Samba, and rather than develop a new dance step, instructors taught students the simple Brazilian dance.

THE SAMBA, THE CONGA, AND VELOZ AND YOLANDA

The Samba traces its origins to Brazil as a carnival street dance in Rio de Janeiro. It is also closely linked to the Afro-Brazilian Folk dance the Batuque. The Batuque is a circle dance that forms around one dancer and calls out a dancer from the circle

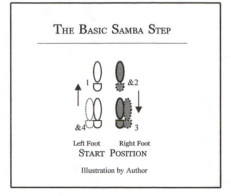

THE BASIC SAMBA STEP

1 &2

&4 3

Left Foot   Right Foot
START POSITION

Illustration by Author

The Samba described "as a suave voluptuous dance with subtle movements" is danced in a syncopated 2/4 rhythm as 1&2, 3&4. The basic is a bouncy step forward with the left (count 1) and a bounce forward with the right (&2). The weight remains on the left foot with the right foot touching next to the left with the heel slightly raised and both knees slightly bent. The right foot steps backward (count 3) and a bounce step back with the left as it touches next to the right foot with the left heel slightly raised. The Samba contains a step called the Maxixe, consisting of a step and point. Other figures include Walks, Turns, Rocks, Rolls, and Corta Jaca (Dannett and Rachel, 147).

The Samba's prominence was boosted by performances by Latin American dancer and actress Carmen Miranda in her Hollywood films that included *Down Argentine Way* (1940), *Weekend in Havana* (1941), *The Gang's All Here* (1943), and *Copacabana* (1947). Miranda was typified in each of these movies wearing distinctive hats of exotic flowers and fruits as well as exaggerated Latin American costumes from the Bahia region of Brazil (Driver 2000, 76–77).

to exchange places. Some reports said that the dancer in the center pointed to the next dancer and shouted "Samba" as they exchanged spots. During the nineteenth century the word "samba" was used by poor Brazilians as a general reference to polyrhythmic dance accompanied by percussion instruments. Historian John Charles Chasteen states, "It was more an event (as in 'an all-night samba') or a style of body movement than a particular step." Some other sources link the Samba to the secular part of an African religious ritual dance, the *candomble*, from the northeast region of Bahia (Chasteen, 1996, 30–31).

The Samba that eventually reached America was inspired by the 1917 Brazilian song hit "Pelo Telefone." (Some music historians debate that the composition might have actually been for the Maxixe dance.) The Samba, as with other Brazilian street dances including the Batuque and Maxixe, involved "people of mixed race" and "racial mixing." Chasteen points out "since social dancing—a shared activity, by definition—resonates pleasurably in the personal experience of so many...the most powerful meaning of samba as a national symbol is its implied bridging of a racial divide, as white and black Brazilians come together in mutual appreciation of Afro-Brazilian culture" (1996, 47).

Throughout the 1920s and 1930s, many native Brazilian groups known as *escolas de samba* (samba schools) were formed. The main goal of each school was to place first during Rio de Janeiro's carnivals. Therefore, numerous steps were added, including the closed ballroom hold (see Chapter 1). As a result, the Samba dance achieved international notoriety as a cultural symbol of Brazil. The Samba was "officially" introduced in America at the 1939 New York World's Fair and quickly became popular (Driver 2000, 75).

In late 1938, another Latin import, the Conga, was fashionable. It initially started as a couple dance but soon developed into a group dance as a "Conga chain" or "Conga line." In the Conga line, one individual stood in front as others formed a single line behind. Each person would place his or her hands on the hips of the person directly in front. The basic rhythm was a simple one-two-three-kick. The couple or group would perform the basic pattern in unison. They began: step left foot (count 1), cross right over left (count 2), step left (count 3), and kick right. Followed by step right foot (count 1), cross left over right (count 2), step right (count 3), and kick left. The Conga line of men and women would serpentine along the dance floor picking up people as it went along.

In 1941, an excellent contemporary example of the Conga was in the movie *Hellzapoppin'*, a zany comedy starring Olsen and Johnson. The movie featured quite a few contemporary dance styles, including the Fox Trot, the Cut-in dance, smooth style Lindy Hop, and aerial Lindy Hop. The Conga, however, closed the show. It was featured as both a partner dance and a Conga line led by actress Martha Raye. The Conga was especially enjoyed during World War II, but the fun and frivolous dance soon ended with the end of the war. It was revived in the mid-1950s as the Bunny Hop (see Chapter 4) and became a staple at weddings, catered affairs, and vacation resorts for the remainder of the twentieth century (see Chapter 6).

The hip movement in the Latin Dances was an unnatural movement for Americans, but the music and the movement was catchy, fun, and enjoyable. Latin American dances including the Rhumba, Samba, and Tango quickly became the rage. Latin music was in demand and many orchestras incorporated Rhumbas, Congas, Tangos, and Sambas in their repertoire. The door was open for Americans to enjoy authentic Latin music.

In 1937, singer and maraca player Frank "Machito" Grillo immigrated to New York. In 1940, he teamed with clarinetist Mario Bauza to form the Afro-Cubans orchestra. The band of three saxophones, two trumpets, bass, bongó, and timbales combined American Jazz with authentic Cuban rhythms. They developed a new sound that set the pattern for Latin music for many years to come. The band later added more wind instruments, employing non-Latin musicians to authenticate American Jazz. According to Latin music historian John Storm Roberts, in 1940, the forming of the Afro-Cubans was "the single most important event of the decade for Latin music's development" in the United States (Roberts 1999, 101–102).

Dance teams such as Frank Veloz and Yolanda Casazza-Veloz (a popular performance couple of the time known professionally as Veloz and Yolanda) focused on Latin American styles. In 1939, their publication *Tango and Rumba: The Dances of Today and Tomorrow* described the dances in depth. The book contained numerous photographs of the dance couple in each step pattern. On October 30, 1939, they were also a *LIFE* magazine cover story as the "Greatest Dancing Couple." Other prominent Hollywood and nightclub performance dance couples included Ramon and Rosita, and Renee and Tony DeMarco (Dannett and Rachel 1954, 126–127). The Latin dances were all the rage and were the most requested dances to learn at the dancing schools including Arthur Murray's.

ARTHUR MURRAY TEACHES "DANCING IN A HURRY"

At the onset of the Depression, Arthur Murray cut back his studios from a once thriving 12 floors in midtown Manhattan to just two floors. He remarketed his business and continued to place ads in popular magazines and newspapers for printed mail-order instruction manuals. His business, as did dancing in general, continued to pick up. Murray's 1937 illustrated booklet *Let's Dance* provided 20 easy dance lessons to learn at home. The manual included numerous illustrations and his trademark "Murray Footprints." Students were encouraged to make their own footprints by tracing a pair of their own shoes on cardboard. The left foot diagram is kept clear and the right foot darkened in. There was a "start pair" (both left foot and right foot together) plus an additional six footprints numbered 1, 3, and 5 for the left foot and 2, 4, and 6 for the right foot. Murray claimed, "If you have never danced at all up to now, you will find them indispensable." He suggested that the student lay out the footprints in the same manner as the illustrated diagrams throughout the booklet; therefore, the student could practice the foot pattern by simply placing their own feet over the cardboard cutouts. Murray cautioned, "When you are thoroughly familiar with the step you are learning—then, *and only then*, pick up the footprints and practice the step without them" (35).

Tips for dancers included "Important Things to Know About Dancing," such as how to do walking steps, balance, hold your partner, correctly position the feet, and gain confidence, and secrets of leading and following were also shared. He called the Fox Trot "America's most popular dance," and provided instruction for the standard ballroom version as well as the One-Step, Waltz, Tango, and Rhumba. At the time, Murray did not think the Lindy Hop fashionable enough to teach; therefore, he recommended the One-Step for "any fast or 'Swing' type of [music]" (1937, 5–7).

The booklet also offered instruction for some dance steps popular among the college age crowd, including the Shag. The basic step of the Shag (also known as the "Flea Hop") was described as, "Hop, Hop, 1-2-3 short steps, with a 'hop' and kick on 3rd step. The short steps are taken to side, first left, then right.... This basic step may be varied by turning forward or backward, or turning to right or left. The degree of 'hop' and 'kick,' of course, depends entirely on how much pep and go the dancers put into it" (1937, 27).

By 1937, the Arthur Murray name was established for dance instruction; however, he had yet to achieve nationwide prominence. In 1941, Johnny Mercer wrote a song for the Hollywood movie *The Fleet's In* titled "Arthur Murray Taught Me Dancing in a Hurry." At first Arthur did not like the lyrics, but he was convinced by his friend, comedian Groucho Marx, who said, "Look, Arthur, who listens to lyrics—in fact, who listens? All anyone will remember is your name." Marx was right. Kathryn Murray proclaimed, "that song brought more international publicity than all the write-ups and promotions we had ever had." Their gross business in 1941 was $2 million, but by 1946 it had increased to over $12 million. She attributed the phenomenal increase to the business and prestige provided by the song and also as a result of two fad dances, the Lambeth Walk and the Big Apple (1960, 104–105).

THE LAMBETH WALK AND THE BIG APPLE

The Lambeth Walk was an extremely popular fad dance in America at the end of the 1930s. It was said to have originated in England and was introduced to America in 1938 by Arthur Murray. It was mainly a walking dance as a couple linked arms and strutted with a jaunt in their step. A popular Broadway musical, and subsequent Hollywood movie *For Me an My Gal*, featured the song "Lambeth Walk." The published sheet music of the song included dance step instructions written by Arthur Murray. The simple dance started with the man's left foot and the woman's right foot as follows:

1. Partners march side-by-side, gentlemen on the left. Strut forward 8 steps; swing the arms, walking jauntily in cockney fashion.

2. Link right arms, walk around in a circle to right 4 steps. Quickly reverse, linking left arms and walk 4 steps in circle to left.

3. Strut side by side again 8 steps (same as figure 1). Partners separate; face each other, taking short step back ward. Close heels on 4th count.

4. Slap knees in time to music.

5. Ending with pointing thumb over shoulder, in hitchhike fashion; and yell loudly, "Hoy!" Repeat [the] beginning. It is necessary that the steps fit the music. The dancers should start on the very first beat of the chorus (StreetSwing.com, "Lambeth Walk," n.d.).

The simplicity and fun of the Lambeth Walk appealed to dancers of all ages and society. Another fad dance would prove to be even more of a sensation.

Around 1938, Murray read a small article in *The New York Times* about a popular dance in South Carolina called the Big Apple. He sent a dance instructor to investigate and see the dance firsthand. The instructor was not impressed but reported it did have possibilities. Murray pondered over the report and choreographed his version of the Big Apple as a circle dance that incorporated many familiar dance steps of the day. The dancers began by marching in a circle. A caller (similar to Square dancing) shouted out a particular step and the group followed. The typical steps included Suzy-Q, Trucking, Applejack, Spank the Baby, Charleston, Boogie Woogie, and the Shorty George. Some callers improvised even including Square Dance steps. If the caller called out "shine," one couple would enter into the center of the circle and perform some of their best dance steps. The dance typically ended as all the participants joined hands, headed towards the center of the circle, and shouted "Praise Allah!"

Many newsreel footages highlighted the Big Apple with the Shag, Trucking, Suzy-Q, Charleston, and Shine steps. The movie *Keep Punching* (1939) featured an energetic version of the Big Apple dance ("Big Apple Basics," *America Dances! 1897–1948*). Other fad dances sprung from the Big Apple. The Little Apple was a couple's dance version of the Big Apple. Others included Peelin' the Peach, the World's Fair Walk, and the Boomps-a-Daisy. During World War II, fad dances inspired by the war included the Black-Out Stroll, the Draft-Away, the Thumbs Up, and Praise the Lord and Pass the Ammunition. These were mainly pantomime dances and were usually associated with just one particular song (Dannett and Rachel 1954, 154–157).

The popularity of the Big Apple among the fashionable set prompted the hotel manager of Staler Hotels to ask Murray to provide dance instructors in their hotels.

This was the beginning of the idea by Murray to initiate a dance studio franchise. In order to obtain a franchise, an individual had to have been an instructor in the Arthur Murray studios for at least one year. Upon achieving a franchise, the owners were required to pay Arthur Murray 10 percent (later reduced to 8 percent) of the gross annual billings. In exchange, the studios were sent management manuals and specific film instructions on how to teach the same style and steps of each dance according to "Arthur's method." The instructional films were produced and directed by Murray, and featured him demonstrating the dance techniques. Instructors were also required to travel to New York once a year for a brush-up course. Within a few years, Arthur Murray franchise studios were in 47 cities nationwide. By 1946, there were over 200 studios in major cities throughout the United States, a long way from his radio dance instruction days (Kathryn Murray 1960, 104–105).

RADIO, THE BIG BANDS, AND THE "KING OF SWING"

By 1940, over 90 percent of American homes owned at least one radio (Steiner 1972, 95). Radio was an inexpensive form of entertainment that allowed Americans an opportunity to momentarily forget the realities of the Depression and escape into a fantasy world of laughter and entertainment. The format of dramas, adventure, and music shows was basically the same through the 1930s and 1940s, although during World War II news occupied more airtime. But dance music consumed more radio airtime than any other type of program.

Hillbilly music (also known as Country and Western) was mainly popular in the southeastern portion of the country. The radio transmission of the Grand Ole Opry, from Nashville, Tennessee, reached about one-third of America. Many of the artists included dance bands such as Milton Brown and his Brownies, and Bob Wills and the Texas Playboys, among many others playing Hillbilly music or Texas Swing. Many of the bands toured the Southwest, including Oklahoma and Texas, playing in honky-tonks, roadhouses, county fairs, and dance halls. Music historian Ernie Smith said they played "a lively mixture of traditional country square dancing, ballroom, the Fox Trot, and in later years, the addition of the Lindy Hop...it was immensely popular with regional dancers" (Miller and Jensen 1996, xx). In the early 1940s Clyde "Spade" Cooley and his band played similar dance music including Rhumbas and Jitterbug. Cooley coined the phrase of his diverse musical style "Western Swing" ("Western Swing Bands: A History," n.d.).

Many of the sweet dance bands of the 1920s continued into the 1930s and 1940s, including the Vincent Lopez Orchestra, Guy Lombardo and his Royal Canadians, and Paul Whiteman. Whiteman's band was still literally the biggest of them all, consisting of 30 musicians playing a combined 88 different instruments. Whiteman's band played popular tunes, waltzes, hot specialty numbers, with vocalist and ensemble singing. In relation to other popular bands of the day, Whiteman "either preceded, taught, hired or survived them all" (Norris, "Long Lives The King," 1938, 49).

The Casa Loma Orchestra was a firmly established cooperative group managed by Glen Gray and was one of the best known dance bands from the late 1920s through the 1940s. It was popular among the college age listeners for playing a mix of sweet ballads and up-tempo tunes to keep the crowd dancing. The band played regularly at the prestigious Glen Island Casino in a wealthy part of Westchester County, New York. The band was also featured on the nationwide *Camel Caravan Hour*, which at the time was the most important radio showcase that a dance band could secure (Collier 1989, 122–123). However, it was an offshoot of jazz that defined the entire era—it was known simply as "Swing."

Bandleader Duke Ellington was credited with naming the musical style in the title to a 1932 popular song "It Don't Mean a Thing if It Ain't Got that Swing." Swing differed from jazz in that it was accentuated by resounding drum beats and the addition of more brass instruments of horns, trombones, and saxophones. By 1934, the typical dance band included three trumpets, two trombones, four saxophones, piano, guitar, drums, and bass, resulting in the subsequent name of the "Big Band" sound. Other bands added the clarinet and other reed instruments. Also at this time the banjo was replaced by the guitar, a stand-up string bass replaced the tuba, and the fiddle (or violin) was seen only in the sweet bands or Western swing bands (Goodman 1939, 138). The change in instruments allowed the music to "swing" and gave the music a "jump" that appealed to the dancers. But trying to describe swing is like trying to define "left" or "right." Bandleader Benny Goodman explained,

> Those who have asked for a one-word or one-sentence definition of swing overlook the fact that it was originally a term used among musicians to identify something they all recognized. How, for example, would you describe *red* for a child, who did not know what it was? You would point to something that was red, and say: "That is red." . . . Similarly with swing—it can be identified in an actual performance or on a record, and then recognized when it recurs in another performance, but it cannot be defined as a component of such and such elements. In a word, swing is a property of music played in a certain way, rather than a definite kind of music itself (1939, 174).

It was Benny Goodman who is credited as the musician who set the pattern for the great dance bands of the period and for bringing swing into national prominence. Goodman was conscious that his band did not only swing but also attached great importance to danceable tempos (1939, 163).

Goodman's first break came shortly after he formed his own band. In late September 1934, the *Let's Dance* radio program sought to restructure its programming on Saturday night. The idea was to have three bands of different dance styles alternating each half-hour. During the audition, the bands played in a studio while the music was played in an audition room where the "informal" jury danced (Collier 1989, 129). Kel Murray was chosen as the "sweet" band, Xavier Cugat as the Latin Orchestra, and Benny Goodman for the "hot" band. The three-hour dance program was broadcast live and networked by 53 stations from coast to coast from 11 P.M. until 2 A.M. EST. On the west coast the *Let's Dance* was heard from 8 P.M. to 11 P.M., garnering a large share of the teenage listening audience (Goodman 1939, 146–153).

In early 1935, Benny Goodman and his Orchestra set out to tour the country playing swing music. Throughout the tour they were mildly received, in many cases even criticized and fired. They were very often accused of playing too loudly. The hotels that the band were booked in provided expensive dinner shows, and the people tended to be a bit older than the youthful swing audience. At an engagement at New York's Roosevelt Hotel, the stomping grounds of the Guy Lombardo Orchestra, Goodman received a request, "Just by way of *contrast*—something sweet and low." According to Goodman, this type of comment came almost everywhere they played. Usually a waiter would immediately motion "not to play so loud." Goodman recalled, "These folks didn't appreciate this or anything else connected with the kind of music I wanted to play" (Goodman 1939, 183).

The band worked its way west stopping for one-nighters and extended engagements—a week at the Stanley Theater in Pittsburgh, one-nighters in Columbus, Ohio; Toledo, Ohio; Lakeside, Michigan; and two days in Milwaukee, Wisconsin. The band had booked a four-week engagement in Denver at Elitch's Gardens; however, the owner wanted them fired after the first night.

What the band did not know was that Eltich's was a Taxi-dance hall. Goodman's band played long arrangements; some of their songs lasted three, four, five, or even six minutes. "One O'Clock Jump," for example, ran over seven minutes. The management was expecting short dances, under a minute, and was losing money. The manager also criticized the music, saying, "What's the matter—can't you boys play any waltzes?" Goodman wanted to disband and go back to New York. However, they had a few more bookings in Salt Lake City and a few one-nighters in San Francisco, California before heading to Los Angeles (Goodman 1939, 191–193).

In Los Angeles, at the Palomar Ballroom, they were met with a crowd of over 2,500 enthusiastic dancing teenagers and a nationwide radio audience. To Goodman's surprise, the teenagers "had been listening to the 'Let's Dance' program all the previous winter." In addition, most of them were very familiar with Goodman's hottest numbers that played in the late 1:30 to 2:00 A.M. time slot on the East coast but in California were on a little after 10 P.M. The four-week booking was doubled to eight weeks, setting attendance records for the Palomar Ballroom (Goodman 1939, 199).

After Los Angeles, the band members played their way east, traveling through Amarillo and Dallas, Texas. They moved north to Goodman's hometown of Chicago for a four-week booking at the Congress Hotel, one of the top name places for dance bands in the city. The Congress Hotel was the first to advertised them as a "swing band." They were met with a responsive crowd, and their booking was extended to a couple of months. At that time writers in Chicago and national magazines including *Time*, *Collier's*, *Vanity Fair*, and *Harper's* began using the term "King of Swing" (204–210).

After almost one year on the road, the band members returned to New York. Their success garnered them the regular spot on the *Camel Caravan Hour*, replacing the popular Casa Loma Orchestra. They also played at the Pennsylvania Hotel and at the Paramount Movie Theater. At the Paramount, the band performed five shows a day. The response from the youthful audience was overwhelming as the teens literally danced in the aisles. As a result of Benny Goodman's efforts, swing music, the big bands, and dancing were in demand (1939, 216).

By 1939, NBC radio broadcast 49 dance bands and CBS 21 as part of its weekly programming. Major sponsorship increased the salaries of the bands, and remote broadcasts from the big hotels in New York, Chicago, and Los Angeles were spread nationwide. By the 1940s, well over 100 top name bands were playing regular engagements and lucrative one-night stands, including Jimmie Lunceford, Chick Webb, Jimmy Dorsey, Tommy Dorsey, Count Basie, Ozzie Nelson, Charlie Barnet, Artie Shaw, Woody Herman, Shep Fields, Stan Kenton, Kay Kyser, Harry James, Gene Krupa, and Glenn Miller (Erenberg 1998, 164–165).

Swing music offered both a fresh new appeal to those who wanted to dance and even for those who just wanted to listen. A columnist for *The New York Times* observed, "swing differs from other great contemporary trends in having nothing repressive about it. It gives free exposure to the player's individualism. The best things he does are not in the written score at all. It encourages a style of dance... which has more exuberance than pattern" ("Hot Music At Carnegie," 1938, 22). In his 1939 autobiography, Goodman recalled:

> Then too, it's always been a fact that styles in dancing follow the styles in music...that puts a certain dance across. But for the most part the public was still doing the same sort of gliding dances that had been popular for a long time, except maybe in Harlem where the "Lindy Hop" and such were popular. It wasn't until quite some time after this that the...other dances which really went with the kind of music we played came in (143).

The Lindy Hop was the dance that really went "wild" and matched the music of swing.

THE LINDY HOP, THE ZOOT SUIT, AND THE JITTERBUG

Unlike the bouncy predecessors such as the Charleston and Animal dances, the Lindy Hop was a smooth flowing rotating spot dance that stayed low to the ground. The distinctive feature of the dance was the breakaway that allowed the dancer to improvise steps that "swung" with the music. In the spring of 1936, the Lindy Hop took on a different variant that achieved its main distinction—the aerial. An "aerial" is a dance step where one or both of the dancers' feet leave the floor.

Aerials had been performed in other dances before 1935. The Nicholas Brothers used leaps and flips in their tap dance routines in the early 1930s. Also, lifting a dance partner was not new. Irene and Vernon Castle incorporated lifts in their performances around 1914. In ballroom dancing the lift is graceful and smooth, and usually only the female partner is lifted and held in a position before being gently placed down on the dance floor in rhythm. In a Lindy Hop aerial the move is quicker and acrobatic with either the male or female partner being lifted. Sometimes both would jump in unison. The aerial in the Lindy Hop developed during a dance contest at the Savoy Ballroom in Harlem, New York.

Shorty Snowden and his partner Big Bea had created a signature show step for the competitions where he would go back-to-back with Big Bea, lift her, and carry her off. Sometimes she would even carry him off. During one dance contest, a young dance couple, Frankie Manning and Frieda Washington, went one better,

An instructional booklet for "Swing Steps," c. 1943.   Author's Archives.

incorporating the same move as Snowden but adding a complete back flip. It was called "Over the Back." In a televised interview, Manning cheerfully remembered "we didn't know what to do because they didn't have any dance schools or anybody who knew how to teach this step." He described the move, "she's back to back with me and I flip her over my back and she lands on her feet in front of me. So we call it over-the-back because that's the trajectory she takes. She comes over my back and lands in the front" (City Arts, "The Uncut Interview with Frankie Manning," n.d.).

With the over the back flip aerial, the crowd went wild. Thereafter in competitions, showcases, and Hollywood movies, the aerial was a distinguishing feature of the Lindy Hop. After 1937, there were two distinctive styles: a smooth Lindy Hop in which the feet did not leave the floor and a jump version incorporating aerials, coordinated kicks, hops, dips, flips, lifts, turns, and just about any improvised move within the rhythm of the music. Some variations included the Suzy-Q (sometimes "Suzi-Q" or "Susie Q"), Truckin', and line dances.

Truckin' was a dance that was uniquely stylized by the individual. Some did it as a step within the Lindy Hop. Truckin' was described as "the shoulders are often hunched up, one above the other, the hips sway in Congo fashion, and the feet execute a variety of shuffles while the index finger of one hand wiggles shoulder-high at the sky. The movement tends to be more or less straight ahead (Stearns and Stearns 1994, 41).

Swing line dances that incorporated early jazz and some tap steps included the Jitterbug Stroll, the Shim Sham, and the Trunky Doo. The Shim Sham was a standard showbiz tap routine that the Savoy Lindy hoppers adapted as a ballroom line dance. The dance had specific steps that included the Cross Over, the Tacky Annie, the Half-Break, Boogie Backs, Boogie Forwards, and Shorty George steps, after which each dancer grabbed the nearest person to dance until the song was finished (Stearns and Stearns 1994, 195–196).

Competition among the Lindy Hoppers became standard on most Saturday nights or sometimes late in the evening. Civil rights leader Malcolm X described a typical competition among Lindy Hoppers, "All the other dancers would form a big 'U' with the band at the open end. The girls who intended to compete would slip over to the sidelines and change from high heels into low white sneakers. In competition they could never survive in heels" (72–73). Many of the younger dancers quickly embraced the aerials, but most dance halls did not permit aerials except during a competition or a jam circle. The reason was simple: somebody could get hurt, especially another dance couple that might move into the space where the airborne dancer was about to land. For that reason, many dance halls did not allow the Lindy Hop or the Jitterbug.

Jitterbug became a term that was widely used to describe both dancing to fast swing music and the dancers themselves. In 1934, bandleader Cab Calloway described some Lindy Hop dancers "like the frenzy of jittering bugs." In 1938, he compiled and published *Cab Calloway's Hepster Dictionary: The Language of Jive*. Within the "dictionary" he used the term "Jitterbug" and also provided slang phrases for the swing generation such as "daddy-o," "hepcat," and "Zoot suit." The youth adopted the language of jive and applied it to their dancing. A "hepcat" was a devotee of swing music. An "ickie" was someone who was critical of swing. A "jitterbug" was one who danced to the music. "Cutting the Rug" applied to dancing (Cab Calloway Web site, n.d.).

At that time it was readily apparent that swing music, jitterbug dancing, the language of jive, and the Zoot suit were definitely a part of the youth culture. In his autobiography, Malcolm X described that his first Zoot suit "was just wild: sky-blue pants thirty inches in the knee and angle-narrowed down to twelve inches at the bottom, and a long coat that pinched my waist and flared out below my knees" (59). The Zoot suit was very popular among teenage youth of African American, Mexican American, Italian American, and other ethnic groups. For females, the fashion was short tight skirts and sweaters (usually black in color), high heels, and styled hairdos.

Some artists and cartoons of the time even ridiculed the Zoot suit. One example in 1942 was the Kay Kyser song "A Zoot Suit (For My Sunday Gal)" for Columbia Records. The tune is about the problems associated with wearing the garish, exaggerated "hep" fashion. Newspapers at the time were not very kind to those who wore Zoot suits. People in Zoot suits were continually harassed, made fun of, and cursed at. Dominick Dattilo, an Italian American of immigrant parents, living in Brooklyn, New York, said, "I remember being in Times Square [Manhattan] one day dressed in my version of a Zoot suit and having some servicemen harass me and they chased me. I couldn't tell anyone of the incident because I was playing hooky from school" (Giordano interview, 2001). In June 1943, in Los Angeles it was taken to the extreme as racial tensions among servicemen and Mexican American teenagers wearing Zoot suits erupted in violence. The Mexican American youth nicknamed Pachucos were harassed and physically beaten by U.S. sailors and soldiers in an event that became know as the Zoot Suit Riots.

In 1938, *LIFE* magazine proclaimed, "Jitterbugs are the extreme swing addicts who get so excited by its music that they cannot stand or be still…They must

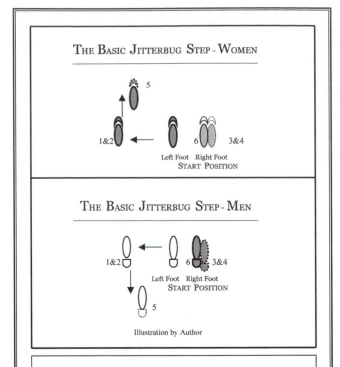

THE BASIC JITTERBUG STEP - WOMEN

5

1&2   6   3&4

Left Foot   Right Foot
START POSITION

THE BASIC JITTERBUG STEP - MEN

1&2   6   3&4

Left Foot   Right Foot
START POSITION

5

Illustration by Author

The Jitterbug is a fast moving bouncy six-count rhythm to handle the faster tempo swing music. The two basic hand holds for the closed position and the open position are the same as in the Lindy Hop (see chapter 2). However, the Jitterbug rhythm is slow-slow-quick-quick or 1&2, 3&4, 5, 6. The leader starts by shifting the hips and weight to the left side and steps down on the left foot and holds (counts 1&2). He then shifts the weight to the right side and steps down on the right foot (counts 3&4). The leader steps back on the left ball of his foot (count 5) and rocks forward and steps down on the right foot (count 6).

prance around in wild exhibitionist dances or yell and scream" (August 9, 1938). In 1943, *LIFE* magazine added, "a jitterbug was anyone who bounced, wiggled and jumped in time to hot music without any particular knowledge of what he was doing" ("The Lindy Hop: A True National Folk Dance Has Been Born in U.S.A.," 95).

During the time period the Jitterbug was never fully understood among those who were not young. Meyer Berger wrote in the widely circulated *Collier's* magazine, "Psychologists thought the recent jitterbug jamboree was an expression of adolescent bewilderment brought on by war... The kids laughed off these theories—and theorists. They said, 'That's the way with *oolie droolies*. They ain't hep. They ain't solid. They ain't set and groovey like a five-cent movie. Which is the hep cats' way of saying the older generation doesn't understand or respond to hot [music]'" (Berger, "Jive Bombers Jamboree," 1943, 18).

The Jitterbug was actually an adaptation of the Lindy Hop that allowed the dancers to stay with the faster swing music. It also encouraged improvisation in the "breakaway" position and incorporated lifts, jumps, and aerials. Both dances were done to the swing bands and were similar looking, which is why the term came to be used interchangeably. Although the terms "Lindy Hop" and "Jitterbug" were used interchangeably, there is a distinction. The Lindy Hop is an eight count syncopated smooth basic step (see Chapter 2).

Most Americans saw the Lindy Hop only in newsreels of the Harvest Moon Ball competitions and in movies such as *A Day at the Races* (1937), *Buck Privates* (1941), *Hellzapoppin'* (1941), *Ride 'Em Cowboy* (1942), *Groovie Movie* (1944), a nine-minute movie short, and *Killer Diller* (1948). Each provides some of the best acrobatic performance and smooth style versions of the dance ever filmed. The acrobatic aerial dance movements were eye-catching stellar performances by the best professional Lindy Hop dancers in the country. They were extremely fast paced, were choreographed for maximum effect on the movie scene, and definitely were not for simple enjoyment on a social dance floor.

The comedy *A Day at the Races*, starring the Marx Brothers, did well at the box office. At the time, the Marx Brothers were one of the top Hollywood box office attractions. Scenes in the movie offer excellent contemporary singer Alan Jones singing in the "crooning" style made popular by Bing Crosby. In various dance scenes Groucho Marx performs a Tango, Fox Trot, Rhumba, and Charleston. The film also has an ensemble dance scene between Harpo Marx and some African American children and another scene of African American adults performing the Lindy Hop. Unfortunately, a large segment of America did not get to see either the Harpo scene or the Lindy Hop scene. Since these scenes involved "racial mixing," they were censored out of distribution copies throughout the South and other areas of the United States. (At that time, this was a common practice for all Hollywood movies.) Copies with deleted scenes continued to air well into the 1970s on television stations. It was not until the very late twentieth century that the movie was shown intact. By that time the age of the movie relegated it to specialty cable stations dedicated to movie buffs who consigned the segregation to obscure trivia status.

It is quite possible that many thought the entire dance incorporated wild antics when, in fact, it was pure showmanship for both the movie screen and dance competitions. Therefore, this resulted in some jerky strenuous arm tugging and partner pushing and pulling for the uninitiated who tried to copy the Hollywood movies. In addition, the youthful exuberance of the dance was difficult to categorize, and older adults either could not perform the acrobatics or considered the athleticism of the dance not stylish or graceful. In either case, it definitely shocked and confused the established dance instructors and ballroom dancers.

In 1934, dance instructor Thomas E. Parson wrote in the *American Dancer*, "Several [dance] teachers were of the opinion that the Lindy Hop was merely a passing fancy; it was a dance fit for only a certain element of dancers; it wasn't [suitable] for the ballroom. To sum it up, the Lindy Hop was taboo!" Parsons, who also broadcast a radio dance program on WOR in New York, "was besieged with request to teach the Lindy Hop over the air." He ignored the request for over a year mainly because he could not find any ballroom dance instructors to teach him the dance. He said, "they thought it too vulgar for the ballroom." Parson learned the Lindy Hop by watching others and eventually taught it on his radio broadcasts (Parson, "News from New York," 10).

Lindy Hop and Jitterbug dance festivals became common, especially in the big cities. In 1939, a Los Angeles Jitterbug contest attracted over 100,000. In 1940, a Universal Pictures Newsreel reported, "200,000 Jitterbugs Go Slap-Happy at Swing Jamboree" in Chicago, Illinois. In 1941 a promoter staged a Dance Carnival in New York's Madison Square Garden. A triple bill of Benny Goodman, Larry Clinton, and Charlie Barnett attracted a crowd of over 31,000 on the first weekend (Lingeman 1970, 16).

In 1943, the very popular *LIFE* magazine featured the Lindy Hop on its cover and proclaimed "after 16 years of evolution and accretion, the Lindy Hop has become America's national dance." The nine page photographic essay by photographer Gjon Mili provided many excellent stills of Stanley Catron and Kaye Popp performing "Floor Steps," and Leon James and Willa Mae Ricker performing

Willa Mae Ricker and Leon James demonstrate an "Air Step" from *LIFE* magazine, August 23, 1943. Ricker and James were one of the Lindy Hopping couples in the movie *A Day At the Races.*   Photo by Gjon Mili / Time-Life Pictures / Courtesy of Getty Images 50478645.

"Air Steps." Catron and Popp were professional dancers appearing in *Something for the Boys* on Broadway. James and Ricker were part of the Congaroo Dancers, a group of professional dancers from the Savoy Ballroom ("The Lindy Hop: A True National Folk Dance Has Been Born in U.S.A.," 95–96).

Catron and Popp demonstrated the Jig-Walk, Twist, Peckin', The Tip, Truckin', the Boogie, Shorty George, the Suzy-Q, and the Swing-Out. The Swing-Out photographs provided excellent reference for the caption description that read "1) The boy steps back with left foot but does not shift weight; 2) Brings Left forward, pivoting on right; 3) Sweeps right around behind left as girl steps away; 4) Completes swing-out" (96–97). Leon James and Willa Mae Ricker demonstrated Air Steps including the Over the Back, a reverse Jump, as well as the Round-the-Back. Coincidentally, the article on the very next page is titled "The House of Savoy," but it is actually about the prominent historical Italian dynasty and not the Harlem ballroom.

During World War II, the Jitterbug was spread far and wide, mainly by American troops all over the country and even overseas. Since very few dance instructors taught the Lindy Hop and no standard written instructions of the dance were available, many regional styles of the Lindy Hop arose. As the GIs brought the dance to England, the British adopted a version that they called Jive. Jazz bands and later swing bands in the 1930s were fairly common in England and were regularly broadcast over the British BBC radio network. By the time American soldiers arrived in England during 1942–1943, the country was ready to embrace the American big bands and Jitterbug.

Some other dances that were done to very fast tempo music that evolved from the Lindy Hop and Jitterbug were the Balboa, Boogie Woogie, Collegiate Shag, St. Louis Imperial Swing, St. Louis Shag, Carolina Shag, Houston Push, Dallas Whip, Washington D.C. Hand Dancing, and Flea Hop. In fact, many New York dancers never even saw the other regional versions and vice versa.

By 1943, the Lindy Hop could no longer be ignored, but the ballroom dance instructors were still confused by the Lindy Hop. It appeared difficult to fit into set structured steps, patterns, and rules. In fact, the Lindy Hop *did* break all the rules of ballroom dancing by incorporating all sorts of individual steps and literally hundreds of variations. It was not until late 1943 that the New York Chapter of Teachers of Dancing, Inc., began teaching the Lindy Hop and Jitterbug. It was simplified, and almost all the energetic jumps and swivel hip movements were removed. They changed from the swing hold to the basic closed position ballroom hold that eliminated much of the improvisation on the breakaway. Eventually dance instructions adapted a toned down version called Triple Swing or sometimes East Coast Swing (see Chapter 6).

DEAN COLLINS, JEWEL MCGOWAN, CUTTING-IN, AND "MUSICAL HITLERISM"

The Lindy Hop was a dance that provided youngsters of different ethnic, racial, and class boundaries to have a common dance forum to embrace with swing music. The importance of dancing, especially the Lindy Hop, was emphasized by African American Civil Rights leader Malcolm X. Recalling his days in Harlem during the 1940s, he admitted, "But I still harbored one secret humiliation: I couldn't dance. I can't remember when it was that I actually learned how—that is to say, I can't recall the specific night or nights. But dancing was the chief action at those 'pad parties,' so I've no doubt about how and why my initiation into lindy-hopping came about" (64).

In California and other areas of the United States, segregation also applied to Mexican Americans. They were relegated to "Mexican Only" nights in the same manner as African Americans. Not unlike other teenage ethnic youth of the time they were also heavily influenced by Swing and the Lindy Hop. In East Los Angeles, for example, rather than stay within the ethnic barrio, the Mexican American youth left the neighborhood to seek American swing culture. Historian Eduardo O. Pagán said, "As soon as they would get out of the house they would bee line straight to Central Avenue [in Los Angeles]. A lot of Jazz clubs were there and they would go there to listen to jazz artists and to dance the swing" (quoted in PBS Video *Zoot Suit Riots*).

John Lucchese, a noted dancer and dance instructor of the 1940s and 1950s, recalled his first introduction to dancing. "I was introduced to dancing the way most Italian kids were, at weddings. The fathers would go into the back and play pinochle while the mothers would dance with the kids." As for the dance venue, Lucchese stated that New York City had many places to dance the Lindy Hop other than Harlem's Savoy Ballroom. Some of his favorite places included Clinton Hall in Queens and Club Fordham in the Bronx (Crease, "John Lucchese," n.d.).

Dean Collins (born Saul Cohen) was attracted to dance during his teenage years. Collins said, "Young people in those days took their dancing very seriously. They spent a lot of time with their partners, learned the steps, invented new ones." At 14 he traveled from New Jersey to the Savoy Ballroom in Harlem to learn to dance the Lindy Hop. By the time he was 18 years old, he was featured on the cover of *The New Yorker* magazine as its "Dancer of the Year." In 1939, Collins moved to

Hollywood with hopes of turning his amateur social dancing into a professional career. At that time he changed his name from Cohen thinking that a "Jewish sounding" name would prevent him from a dancing career (Loomis, "The Dean of Style," 2001).

In California, Collins discovered that the regional swing dance styles included the Balboa and the Camel Hop. He frequented the local ballrooms and is credited with bringing the Savoy style of Lindy Hop to the west coast and also introducing the Shim Sham to them. According to biographer Peter Loggins, in 1939, Collins choreographed a few dance sequences in the movie *Let's Make Music* that began a long movie career. Between 1939 and 1960 Collins danced in or choreographed over 100 movies with a dance scene featuring the Lindy Hop, "making him one of the most filmed 'Lindy Hoppers' on the movie screen." Collins developed a distinctive smooth style of Lindy Hop that some termed "Hollywood style." He also created a stylized version of the Swing-Out known as the Whip. Loggins describes the Whip: "[it] is a regular swing-out done in a narrow slot and when the follow comes around the lead, he uses his hand to push her out, creating a bit of momentum for the follower. This technique makes the follower look like she is smoothly and effortlessly gliding and allows for a whip executed at fast tempos." Dean Collins executed the Whip to perfection with partner Jewel McGowan in many Hollywood movies (Loggins, "Dean Collins, n.d.).

Jewel McGowan was probably the best female Lindy Hop dancer appearing in Hollywood films. She was noted for a distinctive "swivel" on her breakaway, and her contemporaries called her the "greatest female swing dancer ever" (Loomis, "The Dean of Style," 2001). She danced with Dean Collins in many other movies including *Dance Hall* (1941), *Playmates* (1941), *Buck Privates* (1941), *Ride 'Em Cowboy* (1942), *Springtime In The Rockies* (1942), *The Talk Of The Town* (1942), *Always A Bridesmaid* (1943), *Kid Dynamite* (1943), and *Living It Up* (1945). McGowan also danced in *The Get-Away* (1941), *Pot o' Gold* (1941), *Ten Cents a Dance* (aka *Dancing Ladies*) (1945), and *Talk About a Lady* (aka *Duchess of Broadway*) (1946).

During this time, it seemed that just about any Hollywood movie had at least one dance scene. Many had a dance scene with a slow Fox Trot that also had an individual "Cutting In" on a dancing couple. The scene was especially prevalent during World War II when there simply were not enough women partners at military dances. Although the custom could be annoying to leave a partner that you were enjoying dancing with for either a partner you did not like or possibly no partner at all, it was continually reinforced that it also was the patriotic thing to do. Dance instructors Billie and Earl of Billie's Dancing School proclaimed, "Cutting in during dances has become a recognized practice. The man who wishes to cut in taps the girl's partner on the shoulder quietly. The dancer must relinquish his partner courteously and cheerfully. The girl has no choice in the matter" (Ray 1936, 238–239).

America, however, was in a panic over the moral implications of Swing and its dancing jitterbugs. Religious leaders expressed outrage. Cardinal O'Connell of Boston expressed his "revolting disgust." The archbishop of Dubuque said, "We permit, if not freely endorse by our criminal indifference, 'jam sessions,' 'jitterbugs,' and cannibalistic rhythmic orgies to occupy a place in our social scheme of

Universal Studios promotional photograph for the movie *Buck Privates* (1941). Dean Collins and Jewell McGowan are the couple in the center.   Courtesy of Photofest.

things wooing our youth along the primrose path to hell." A University of Chicago professor decried that "Swing is musical Hitlerism." New York Philharmonic conductor Arturo Rodzinski called swing "one of the greatest causes of delinquency among American youth today." However, newspaper editor William A. White decried that each generation must have "its own rowdy modern music" (quoted in Stowe 1994, 1, 23–26). *New York Times* columnist Larry Clinton reasoned, "Swing is the voice of youth striving to be heard in this fast-moving world of ours ...Swing is the tempo of our time" (February 26, 1939, E9).

Swing music and the Lindy Hop portrayed very well the tempo of the time and inspired some notable contemporary painters and sculptors. Painter Stuart Davis's *Swing Landscape* (1938) was a WPA funded mural for the Williamsburg Housing Project in Brooklyn. In 1939, famed sculptor Richmond Barthe created *Lindy Hop*. Barthe was known for his love of contemporary dance that inspired his creations. Painter Piet Mondrian was a leader in the De Stijl movement (a radical abstractionism) who enjoyed dancing, Jazz music, and Swing. Three of his most famous works included *Fox Trot* (1929), *Broadway Boogie Woogie* (1943), and *Victory Boogie Woogie* (1944).

Musicians also responded to the tempo of the time and were conscious of the music they created for dancing. Musician Dicky Wells said, "for the dancer, you know what will please him...when you get that beat he's right there saying: 'Play that again!'" Musician Eddie Barfield remembered, "When you went to a dance you could hear the feet on the dance floor. Everybody was beating in time, it was one of those things, you could hear the patting of the feet right along, with the music" (quoted in Spring, "Swing and the Lindy Hop," 1997, 191–192). Band-leader Duke Ellington recalled, "We're always very happy when they ask us to play proms, weddings, country clubs, ballparks. You see, this way we get to have most of the fun, because the dancers are not just sitting there watching; they're having a ball" (Albert Murray, "The Blues as Dance Music," 1990, 68).

The Places to Dance

I'd been lindying previously only in cramped little apartment living rooms, and now I had room to maneuver.

—Malcolm X, 1943

TAXI-DANCE HALLS AND THE 1933 CHICAGO WORLD'S FAIR

By 1932, many cities enacted legislation to close Taxi-dance halls. In Chicago, all Taxi-dance halls were closed by order of the mayor and police commissioner. The citywide ban was mainly because of lobbying efforts by the Chicago Juvenile Protective Association (JPA) under the direction of Jesse F. Binford. Some Taxi-dance halls still tried to operate under the guise of a "dancing school" license. But all dance license applications had to be reviewed by Binford and the JPA. Those dancing schools actually operating as Taxi-dance halls were soon closed. Binford did not necessarily object to dancing in general. He and the JPA supported the "large very attractive" supervised ballrooms. He even wrote, "Dancing will perhaps always be one of the most popular of recreations." What was objectionable were the small unsupervised ballrooms and those that he felt led to immoral behavior such as the Taxi-dance halls. These objections even became the center of attention at the 1933 Chicago World's Fair (Binford, "Taxi-Dance Halls," 1933, 502, 506).

In 1933, the City of Chicago announced the opening of the Century of Progress World's Fair. The fair eventually attracted over 39 million paid admissions and featured a giant screen movie theater, an entertainment midway featuring games, rides, and attractions including the risqué burlesque dancer Sally Rand. By the time the fair opened many other objections arose. The *Cleveland Plain Dealer* newspaper accused the Century of Progress as "the most colossal aggregation of vulgarity ever assembled under the benign American sky." The *Chicago Daily News* was amazed that "the proprietors of the shows who hire foul-mouthed barkers and who induce young girls to exhibit themselves naked in public for a price" were allowed to operate (quoted in Binford "Taxi-Dance Halls," 1933, 508–509). The naked young girl in question was Sally Rand and the exhibition the highly provocative Fan Dance.

It was at Chicago that burlesque performer Sally Rand introduced America to the Fan dance. As she danced, Rand continually moved some handheld fans around and over her body with the continuous suggestion that she would reveal her nudity at any time. Her clever use of the fans in time to the music, however, did not reveal any nudity whatsoever, though it did appear that she was totally nude with only the fans that covered her. Although at one point she was arrested for public indecency, the event was not banned. The Fan dance became a popular burlesque show and continued for many years thereafter. Many creative versions appeared including numerous Las Vegas stage shows (Giordano 2003, 94).

On May 27, 1933, the *Chicago Tribune* added, "More than two hundred girls have been recruited during the last few days as taxi-dancers in the World's Fair Streets of Paris [exhibition]." In planning the fair, a Committee on Protective Services was formed that included Jesse Binford and the Chicago JPA. The mission of the committee was to protect the community "from the degrading and demoralizing influences that break down individual and family community life" (508). The Committee directed its first protest against the two planned Taxi-dance halls that were advertised in Chicago newspapers on the same day as the *Chicago Tribune* announcement. The group was successful. A June 8, 1933, article in the *Chicago Herald Examiner* declared that Taxi-dancing was effectively "banned due to a complaint by the Chicago JPA and Reverend Philip Yarrow" (Binford 1933, 502).

As it turned out, the only success by the Committee on Protective Services was against the Taxi-dance hall. Executive JPA director Jesse Binford said, "to our surprise and bewilderment we found it absolutely impossible to close many objectionable concessions at the Century of Progress. Just why the exposition officials banned the taxi-dance halls, but found it impossible to eliminate these other concessions is difficult to understand" (1933, 509).

DANCING IN RURAL AREAS, WPA BALLROOMS, AND OPEN-AIR DANCING PAVILIONS

In rural areas, hit especially hard by the Depression, dancing was an inexpensive form of entertainment for the entire family and continued to serve as an important social activity. One Nebraska resident recalled, "People in the 1930s knew that the only things you needed were a few instruments, a dance floor—sometimes permanent, sometimes temporary—and a bunch of people who wanted to have a good time....Neighbors hosted barn dances, especially in the spring before the barn's haymow (or loft) was filled with the season's hay" ("Having Fun Dancing," n.d.).

In Shelby, in Polk County, Nebraska, local dances were advertised as "Old Time" that included Square dancing, Polkas, Schottisches, and Waltzes; "New Time" that included Round dancing (sometimes Jitterbug and Latin) to popular contemporary music; or "Mixed Dancing" that included a little bit of both. Shelby resident Jeanne Cook Walsh remembered that the American Legion held their dances on the second floor above a store. She recalled, "A big crowd dancing to a lively tune would cause the ceiling to move up and down in that building. One could actually see and feel the floor give to the beat of the music and dancers' feet" (Walsh, "Dancing Through the Depression," n.d.).

Eller's Dance Hall, located north of Shelby, in the Platte Valley was built specially as a dance hall. At Eller's dancers of all ages attended, including children and infants. At the far end of the dance hall was a place for the babies to sleep.

Other young children played, some sliding on the smooth dance floor, others running in and out of the dancing couples. Some other young children hopped around behind their parents learning to dance. If the hall was rented for a wedding, the entire town would have an open invitation to the dance (Walsh, "Dancing Through the Depression, n.d.).

Some towns benefited from dance halls built by the Works Progress Administration (WPA). The WPA built ballrooms and community recreation centers in cities and rural areas throughout the country. In 1933, a dance hall was built on the site of a former ballroom at Glen Echo Park in Maryland. The Spanish décor building could accommodate 1,800 dancers on its 7,500 square foot dance floor. It was open every night except Sunday with live music from 9 P.M. to midnight. Schuyler's Oak Ballroom in Nebraska was built in 1936 during the height of the Depression and featured Lawrence Welk's band on opening night ("The Spanish Ballroom at Glen Echo Park," n.d.).

During the 1930s, many open-air dance halls were built throughout Utah. Some were built as part of Mormon culture and others by neighboring communities. The outdoor pavilions had names such as "The Rendezvous," "The Purple Haze," and "The Starlight." One dance hall in Midvale, Utah, named the Rooftop Gardens was actually built upon a flat roof above a Mormon Church. One outdoor dance hall in Sanpete County, Utah, was built on a ridge between the Palisade Lake and a precipice with a sheer drop of hundreds of feet to a valley below. During World War II, war workers in Wendover danced on a concrete floor in the Jukebox Cave, an open-air pavilion near the Bonneville Salt Flats. All the dance halls were built for the same reason: "the sheer love of dance" (Craig Miller 2000, 53).

Dancing was a popular year-round recreational social activity in Muncie, Indiana. Sociologists Robert and Helen Lynd reported that dancing was "a prominent feature of the leisure and social life of Middletown people of all classes under thirty, with some following among the older group." During the summers of 1935 and 1936 amusement programs sponsored by the WPA provided free dancing programs and social dancing opportunities in the city's parks. Throughout the year Muncie residents danced in small informal dance halls with the music provided by a radio, phonograph, or jukebox. Many Muncie teenagers congregated in soda fountains (also known as soft-drink parlors) to dance (Lynd and Lynd 1937, 269).

SODA FOUNTAINS, JUKEBOXES, AND RENT PARTIES

The "Soda Fountain" was a service counter, usually located in a drugstore or a general convenience store, that served up food, ice cream, and soda. Some of the establishments enlarged the counter areas to include tables and chairs. The soda fountain was especially popular among the youth. Public establishments that catered to the middle and working class adults included diners and restaurants. Some of the soda fountains, diners, and restaurants also offered other recreational features such as pinball, ping-pong, billiards, or even miniature golf. These features encouraged patrons to linger long enough to purchase food and drink. Most of these places did not charge an admission fee; they also provided music by either a radio or a jukebox, and some allowed dancing.

The music played on jukeboxes was a dominant force and did much to promote the dance bands and dancing. Over 400,000 existed nationwide and played over 5 billion songs per year (Panati 1991, 198). Many commercial establishments, such as soda shops, diners, roadhouses, social clubs, jook joints, and honky-tonks, installed jukeboxes to solicit business. These places became popular, especially among teens who wanted to listen or dance to the music. The term "juke joint" became a slang term among whites for the presence of a jukebox in any commercial establishment. Among African Americans the term "juke joint" became interchangeable as slang with "jook joint" (see Chapter 1).

In 1940, a new development combined the film short with the jukebox, termed "Soundies." A Soundie was a 2–3 minute musical short that predated the MTV generation music videos (see Chapter 6). In addition to the movie theaters, a company founded by Jimmy Roosevelt (the president's son) produced Panoram Jukeboxes that allowed the jukeboxes to be equipped with a small movie screen. The Soundies, therefore, could be viewed in any saloon, social club, or soda fountain that had a jukebox. Some Soundies with notable dance performances included *Cottontail* (1940), *Hot Chocolate* (1941), *Outline of Jitterbug History* (1942), and *Harlem Rhumba* (1942). During World War II, shortages and rationing of raw material for the war curtailed almost all civilian manufacturing, including the production of Panoram Jukeboxes. Combined with the advent of television during the postwar period, they quickly became obsolete.

A distinctive street culture that developed among urban youth were "cellar clubs." The cellar clubs were usually loosely organized social clubs providing themselves with social and recreation programs including sports and dancing. Its members were youth between the ages of 16 and 25, numbering from 6 to 100 members Some of the clubs were well organized. The Harlem Swing Club, for example, held dances every Sunday evening from 10 P.M. until 2 A.M. The club held its dances in a hall on the first floor of a building located at 41 West 124th Street in New York City. The dances were geared to teenagers and featured the Lindy Hop and Big Apple. The social clubs were found among all ethnic groups, social classes, and age groups. Some social clubs had a fraternal or political association and most averaged about 100 to 1000 members. The common thread was that almost all sponsored social activities among their members that included dancing.

The role of the church in regard to recreation was drastically changing. Starting in the early 1920s, churches began taking an active role in social and recreational activities, sponsoring women's clubs, men's clubs, and youth groups. Many of the recreational activities included social dancing.

A unique entertainment form of the social club that first developed among urban blacks was the "rent party." Rent parties were not limited to African Americans; in rural areas they were called "house parties." Rent parties in urban areas dated from the 1920s when blacks first migrated to northern urban areas, but as the economic situation worsened they became common during the Depression. The idea was to provide entertainment and dancing in exchange for a small donation or "admission fee." The money collected would be used to pay the rent. Civil rights leader Malcolm X described a rent party that he attended in Harlem.

> I went to one of these—thirty or forty Negroes sweating, eating, drinking, dancing, and gambling in a jammed, beat-up apartment, the record player going full blast, the fried chicken or chitlins with potato salad and collared greens for a dollar a plate, and cans of beer or shots of liquor for fifty cents (85).

Rent parties became a regular source for urban social entertainment. Some other names for the rent parties included "blue Monday affairs," "house shouts," "chittlin' struts," and "too-bad parties" (Hazzard-Gordon 1990, 94–96).

Organizations such as the Phyllis Wheatley Association thought that the commercial dance hall was exerting an "evil influence upon the morals of the Negroes." Therefore they promoted and provided wholesome dances for African American teenagers and high school students in every major city. In Cleveland, the Universal Negro Improvement Association provided a dance hall for the local community of working class and poor African Americans. They continued through the 1930s and through World War II (Hazzard-Gordon 1990, 132–135).

THE GOLDEN AGE OF DANCE PAVILIONS AND THE "QUEEN OF SWING"

In 1914, with the onset of the first big dance craze in America two new ballrooms were built in Detroit, Michigan, the Arcadia Dance Hall on Woodward Avenue and the Bob-Lo Island Pavilion located on the Detroit River. The Arcadia closed in 1941, but the Bob-Lo lasted until 1955. The Bob-Lo Island Pavilion was one of the largest ballrooms in America accommodating 5,000 dancers. During the late 1930s and 1940s it was usually "at full capacity."

Other large Detroit dance pavilions included the Vanity, Walled Lake Casino, Edgewater Park, Jefferson Beach Pavilion, Grande Ballroom, and the Graystone. The Graystone attracted an older dance crowd and afforded the big bands including the Casa Loma Orchestra, Guy Lombardo, Ozzie Nelson, Jean Goldkette, and Benny Goodman. Monday was reserved as "colored night." Detroit resident Hank Zeck recalled,

> Times were tough, but everybody was broke. People loved to dance and have a good time. It didn't matter if you were working or not. The only thing fellow partners wanted to know was "could you jig [jitterbug]" One night at the Vanity ballroom Zeck was banned from the dance hall for one year for in his own words putting "too much 'jig' in my jitterbug" (Zacharias, "When Detroit Danced to the Big Bands," n.d.).

Detroit also had three large dance pavilions in Electric Park: the Pier Ballroom, the Ramona, and the Palais de Dance. Eastwood Gardens was a Detroit dance pavilion located at an amusement park at Gratiot and Eight Mile Road. Amusement parks did not have the money to invest in new rides or attractions; therefore, many advertised the beaches and refurbished their ballrooms. In 1939, in Cedar Point Amusement Park in Sandusky, Ohio, the management renovated the

Exterior of the Bob-Lo Island Pavilion in Detroit, Michigan, c. late 1930s. The Bob-Lo was one of the largest dance halls in America.   Courtesy of The Detroit News.

Coliseum dance hall. They hired the big bands popular of the day including Count Basie, Les Brown, Bob Crosby, Jimmy Dorsey, Duke Ellington, Woody Herman, Harry James, Ozzie Nelson, and Glenn Miller. Some performances from Cedar Point were broadcast nationwide on NBC radio (Cedar Point, "A Historical Perspective," n.d.).

Los Angeles, California, had the Palomar Ballroom (formerly the Rainbow Ballroom) at Vermont Avenue and Second Street, where Benny Goodman met success in 1935. A fire in October 1939 destroyed the Palomar Ballroom. Although no one was hurt, the Charlie Barnett Band lost all their instruments and most of their valuable dance charts. The Palomar was not rebuilt. The Los Angeles area had many other large dance pavilions, including the Mandarin Ballroom on the Redondo Beach Pier, the Venice Ballroom on Venice Beach, the Casino Gardens on Ocean Park Pier, the LaMonica Ballroom on Santa Monica Pier, the Casino Ballroom on Catalina Island (see Chapter 2), and the Rendezvous Ballroom on Balboa Island ("The Palomar Ballroom, Los Angeles," n.d.).

The Rendezvous Ballroom opened in 1928 with a 12,000 square foot dance floor with a capacity of 1,500 dancing couples. It, like so many ballrooms, suffered through a devastating fire in January 1935. It was quickly rebuilt as the swing and dance craze was spreading nationwide. The Rendezvous was known for developing a unique dance known as the Balboa. The Balboa was a versatile dance that could be done to very slow or fast music. It could be done on a crowded dance floor since it required little space. Located near a beach, the Rendezvous was a popular destination for teenagers and college students during the spring break. They could combine a day at the beach and dancing to top name swing bands until 1:00 A.M. On June 18, 1938, a local radio personality, Al Poska, organized a seven-day nonstop big band dance marathon that attracted nationwide media attention. The

Interior of the Bob-Lo Island Pavilion in Detroit, Michigan, c. late 1930s. Note the large dance floor and the live orchestra at the far left.   Courtesy of The Detroit News.

promotional event to celebrate the end of the school year was covered by *LOOK* magazine, a widely read mass-media magazine. Within the article the Rendezvous Ballroom was nicknamed the "Queen of Swing" ("The Rendezvous Ballroom: Queen of Swing," n.d.).

By 1940, dancing was a lucrative business and hundreds of ballrooms existed in cities and towns throughout the United States. Some notable examples were the Surf Ballroom in Clear Lake, Iowa; the Corn Palace in Mitchell, South Dakota; the Prom Ballroom in Minneapolis, Minnesota; the Pier Ballroom at Buckeye Lake, Ohio; Ocean Pier in Wildwood, New Jersey; Summit Beach, Akron, Ohio; and the Pla Mor in Lincoln, Nebraska. Many cities had a Ballroom named Roseland, including New York and Boston.

After learning to dance the Lindy Hop in small apartments at rent parties, Civil Rights leader Malcolm X recalled his teenage years at the Roseland State Ballroom, a large dance hall in Boston. At the time the Roseland State Ballroom was one of the largest and best-known ballrooms in the New England area. He said, "I'd been lindying previously only in cramped little apartment living rooms, and now I had room to maneuver. Once I really got myself warmed and loosened up...I was

Exterior of the Casino Ballroom on Catalina Island, California, c. 1937. The ballroom opened in 1929 and continued to sponsor dance events into the twenty-first century.   Courtesy of the Catalina Island Museum Collection.

whirling girls so fast their skirts were snapping.…Boosting them over my hips, my shoulders, into the air.…After that, I never missed a Roseland Lindy-hop as long as I stayed in Boston" (67).

The opening of the Palladium in Los Angeles coincided with when the dance band business and dancing were at an economically lucrative peak. The Palladium was designed and built solely for dancing to the big bands. It opened on October 29, 1940, featuring the Tommy Dorsey Orchestra. It was an immediate success and booked the top-name contemporary bands including Glenn Miller, Artie Shaw, Stan Kenton, and Harry James. Most nights the floor was filled with 4,000 to 5,000 dancers. Tables and chairs and balcony seating could accommodate thousands more. The social and economical climate for dancing appeared to be bright.

In 1996, looking back on the golden age of dance halls, dancers, and swing music, vocalist Joe Williams, who worked with many big bands, including Count Basie, fondly reminisced,

Dancers inside the Casino Ballroom on Catalina Island, California, c. 1940. During the 1930s and into the 1940s, the ballroom drew crowds of over 5,000 to dance and listen to popular bands of the day. Courtesy of the Catalina Island Museum Collection.

When we came along, we were lucky enough to come along when the bands played for dancing in the dance halls...All over the country wherever you went there were dance halls, and the people went to them to dance...and it felt so good that the dancers would dance from the first number to the very last note....All of that was together at one time, it was one great communication, and it never has been like that since....It was a party, it was the best (quoted in Miller and Jensen 1996, 215).

THE HARVEST MOON BALL

The Harvest Moon Ball was the best-known amateur dance competition in America. The first event was originally scheduled in 1927 in New York's Central Park. However, an estimated 75,000 people showed up causing disorganization and confusion, so the contest was postponed. The official start, sponsored by the *New York Daily News*, was in 1935 in Madison Square Garden. The preliminary competitions were held in ballrooms throughout the five boroughs of New York City. The headline of the *New York Daily News* on August 23, 1935, read "Dance Thrill Awaits 18,500 at Garden." Reporter Jack Turcott wrote,

All kinds of dancing—dreamy Waltzes, smooth Fox Trots and swashbuckling Tangos to twisting Rhumbas and snappy Lindy Hops will be done to perfection by the finest amateur dancers in the metropolitan area...No Matter how you like your dancing, you'll be thrilled by the performances of the eighty-two couples who've come through the eliminations to battle before 18,500 spectators for the terpsichorean crowns awaiting the winners (quoted in Miller and Jensen 1996, 74).

An "All Around Champion" was selected from the five division winners.

The competition was based on ballroom rules. In the ballroom standards partners' feet always had to remain on the dance floor, and the partners always had to remain in contact with each other. In the first contest the Lindy Hoppers were required to conform to the same rules, but at least they had appropriate music. The contest had two different bands, the Abe Lyman Orchestra for the ballroom standards and the Fletcher Henderson Orchestra for the Lindy Hop (Miller and Jensen 1996, 72, 155).

By 1940, the rules changed to allow the Lindy Hoppers to compete in a less inhibitive style. Since the dance judges were totally unfamiliar with the Lindy Hop, contestants thought the way to win was to catch the judge's eye. As a result, many steps were exaggerated and all sorts of acrobatics, aerials, and pantomimes were created in order to win the Lindy Hop contest. The contestants for the Waltz, Rhumba, Fox Trot, and Tango dressed in formal attire. Women wore high heels and long flowing dresses. Men wore dark suits, usually black tie and tuxedo tails. The Lindy Hoppers, in contrast, wore sneakers and clothing more appropriate for the acrobatic, athletic, and energetic nature of the dance.

With the Depression still in its depths, the Harvest Moon Ball offered an opportunity to escape. The contestants were amateur dancers from all walks of life. Contestant Norma Miller recalled that "Most of the contestants held low-income jobs, dancing was their way of escaping" (81). Anyone winning could not compete the following year, since they were deemed professional. But the winners were asked to perform their winning routine on the stage of the Lowe's State Theatre in Manhattan. The event, hosted by radio personality Ed Sullivan (who would later achieve fame as a television host), led many towards professional dancing careers and Hollywood movies.

The event was extremely popular at Madison Square Garden from its inception through the 1950s, usually selling out the arena. In following years, the Lindy Hop division name was changed to Jitterbug and Rock 'n' Roll. The 1937 and 1938 Harvest Moon Balls featured a Collegiate Shag Division. During World War II, the contest was expanded to include a Serviceman's division. Although the event continued in New York through the end of the century, it did not draw the same crowds. Other cities, such as Houston, Chicago, and Los Angeles, also hosted versions of the Harvest Moon Ball championships.

IRENE CASTLE AND THE 1939 NEW YORK WORLD'S FAIR

Dancing of different sorts was a major portion at the most publicized fair of the decade—the 1939 New York World's Fair. With the Depression ten years old, the New York World's Fair of 1939 promoted a hope for a "better tomorrow." The most notable item introduced was the television. In the first season, 25 million visitors went to the fair. Opening day in 1938 featured the Paul Whiteman Orchestra, dancer Irene Castle, the Brazilian Samba, and the Lindy Hop (Norris, "Long Lives The King," 1938, 49).

After a 16-year retirement, Irene Castle danced with new partner Alex Fischer before a cheering crowd of over 6,000 people. One performance of the Waltz evoked memories of her pre-World War I days dancing with her husband, Vernon. Calling Irene Castle "one of the great creative artists in the history of American dance," *LIFE* magazine reminisced that both her and Vernon's "grace and charm colored an era of American social history and...they left behind a memory which has kept its fragrance through the years" ("Life on the Newsfronts of the World," 1939, 18). However, the fair was not about the past but about the future. Two contemporary dances featured were the Samba and Lindy Hop.

The Brazilian Pavilion supplied both a native Samba orchestra and Brazilian dancers. The Samba dance was the featured attraction, and it was at the fair that most Americans were first introduced to it. The Lindy Hop was represented in its own pavilion modeled after the Savoy Ballroom.

THE SAVOY BALLROOM, "HOME OF HAPPY FEET"

Very few dance halls had the distinction of being so closely related to a dance style than the Savoy Ballroom in Harlem, New York. The Savoy was the place to not only dance but also to see the best Lindy Hop in New York City. As with most of the large ballrooms across the country, the Savoy maintained a policy of two live bands at all times. The "house band" during the early years was Chick Webb and his Orchestra and later Al Cooper's Savoy Sultans. During its 33 years in existence, over 250 top name bands played the Savoy, including Duke Ellington, Benny Goodman, and Cab Calloway. Many historical accounts seem to portray that *only* the Lindy Hop was danced at the Savoy and that the only music played was hard driving swing. In fact, *all* the bands mixed in the sentimental ballads, including the Fox Trot and Waltz. One noted Savoy regular known as "The Sheik" (because of his slicked down conked hair in Valentino fashion) was noted for his Fox Trot and Tango. Even some of most noted sweet bands of the period played there, including Rudy Vallee, Paul Whiteman, Bennie Moten, and Guy Lombardo. Lombardo had the distinction of setting the all-time attendance record for a single night appearance (Stearns and Stearns 1994, 316–317). However, it was the Lindy Hop that provided the Savoy with its legendary status.

The grandeur of the Savoy Ballroom matched that of any of the large Dance Palaces of the day. Lindy Hopper Leon James described his first time at the famed dance hall,

> Upon entering the Savoy Ballroom...you climbed two mirrored flights of marble steps until you found your self in a teeming crowd at the middle of a block-long dance floor. Directly opposite, a raised double bandstand gleamed with instruments, and one of two bands was up there in full swing. My first impression was that I had stepped into a different world. I had been to other ballrooms, but his was different—much bigger, more glamour, real *class* (Stearns and Stearns 1994, 321).

Malcolm X also vividly remembered his first visit. "The ballroom made the Roseland in Boston look small and shabby by comparison. And the Lindy-hopping

The interior of the Savoy Ballroom in New York City. It was nicknamed the "Home of Happy Feet" and was the birthplace of the Lindy Hop. Note the two bandstands at the right side of the dance floor.   Courtesy of Photofest.

there matched the size and elegance of the place.. . .Probably a third of the sideline booths were filled with white people, mostly just watching the Negroes dance; but some of them danced together...I had never seen such fever-heat dancing...those people just about tore the Savoy roof off" (83–84).

The Savoy was open seven nights a week. Special nights included Monday as "Ladies Night." Tuesday was reserved for the "400 Club," a select group of the best dancers among the Savoy regulars. Thursday was "Kitchen Mechanics" night, the traditional night off for domestics, kitchen workers, and maids. Saturday night was when the Savoy was most crowded. Sunday was usually the night celebrities would show up. One night actress Lana Tuner entered the Savoy and called it the "Home of Happy Feet." The nickname stuck.

The Savoy regulars took to "showing off" the Lindy Hop for the tourists with what appeared to be impromptu dance competitions. Savoy regular, Norma Miller revealed that, "When the tourists came to the ballroom, they saw what they thought was a spontaneous exhibition by a regular group of dancers, simply in a ballroom to enjoy social dancing. But that wasn't the case, what they were watching was rehearsed and choreographed dance" (63).

In 1942, famed African American author Langston Hughes thought that the performance by the Savoy regulars was a "deal with the devil." He critically wrote, "The Lindy-hoppers at the Savoy even began to practice acrobatic routines, and to do absurd things for the entertainment of the whites, that probably never would have entered their heads to attempt merely for their own effortless amusement. . . .

Then Harlem nights became show nights for the Nordics" (Hughes, 226 quoted in Spring 1997, 207).

However, the elegant Savoy Ballroom was the exception to the rule for African Americans. Nationwide dance halls and dancing in general remained strictly segregated. Some of the big ballrooms allowed African Americans entry one night a week, typically a Monday night. In many cases the admission price was higher than on the nights when whites were admitted.

Those Savoy regulars who occasionally traveled from Harlem were in for a rude awakening. Norma Miller was such a great Lindy Hop dancer that she became a member of Whitey's Lindy Hoppers. The professional dance team performed at the 1939 New York World's Fair, appeared in Hollywood movies, and traveled the world. In November 1942, after performing in Brazil, she and her fellow Lindy Hoppers arrived in Miami Beach, Florida. She sadly remembered,

> It was the first time I had personally experienced the prejudices we had heard about in the South. Black people were completely segregated; I couldn't believe it. Nothing I had experienced prepared me for this. I had known segregation existed, but it wasn't until I saw it first hand that it became real to me. We had traveled all around the world, had been embraced by countless people who loved us, so to face this in our own country was a real shock (182).

Throughout the South, African Americans continued to dance in jook joints, honky-tonks, or makeshift dance halls located either in "undesirable" parts or on the outskirts of towns. The Rhythm Nightclub in Natchez, Mississippi, was one example. The name "nightclub" is a misnomer. The dance hall was a crude 200 foot long one-story corrugated iron building with only one entry/exit. The windows were boarded to prevent anyone attempting to avoid paying the admission fee and a highly flammable material of "hanging moss" was on the walls and ceilings for decoration. The conditions for tragedy were ideal.

On the night of April 23, 1940, an overflow crowd had come to dance to Walter Barnes and his Orchestra. At some point during the evening a fire started at the front of the building, blocking the exit trapping many people inside. As a result of the fire over 200 people died, including all but two members of the Walter Barnes Orchestra. The following day *The Natchez Democrat*, the local newspaper, grimly reported, "As the front exit to the building was blocked the Negroes turned and thundered to the back only to be met with the corrogated [sic] iron side of the building. They piled upon each other and there they died, some due to the flames and others due to suffocation." The extreme evidence of segregation is evident by the statement that the dead were taken "to the Negro undertaking establishments which were within a block of the dance hall." ("Cries of Burning Negroes Heard for Blocks," NatchezSites.com, 1940).

Throughout the United States segregation of dance halls was common practice. In 1945, at the Los Angeles Cotton Club Norma Miller danced to the Count Basie Orchestra with a friend named Milton. She recalled, "People were staring at us in an odd way, and we wondered why. It didn't occur to us until later that it was over my being black and his being white. Los Angeles was not accustomed to integrated dancing in 1945. The Savoy was a long way away" (Miller and Jensen 1996, 194).

The exterior of the Rhythm Nightclub in Natchez, Mississippi, on the day after a tragic fire killed over 200 African American dancers in April 1940. © Bettmann/Corbis.

During World War II, the Savoy Ballroom was a well-known place to servicemen. It was also no secret that interracial dancing occurred. In early 1943, however, Deputy Police Commissioner Cornelius O'Leary served notice to the Savoy ownership that "effective 12:00 noon Wednesday, March 24, 1943" their dance hall license would be revoked because of immorality and vice charges. The action to close the Savoy was hastened by a complaint by U.S. Army and Navy military officials lodged to New York City Health Department officials. The military claimed that between June 1942 and March 1943 164 sailors and soldiers had contacted venereal disease from women encountered at the Savoy (Capeci, "Walter F. White and the Savoy Ballroom Controversy of 1943," 1981, 19–20).

The charges and actions by the police, military, and New York City municipal authorities shocked Harlem residents. The Savoy had maintained an impeccable reputation among the estimated 10 million patrons who had paid admission to the ballroom since opening in 1926. The Savoy secured a temporary restraining order to remain open. However, in April 1943, the Appellate Division of the New York State Supreme Court rejected the appeal. The following day, on April 21, 1943, the doors to the Savoy Ballroom were padlocked (Capeci 1981, 13, 16–18).

Many African American leaders called the Savoy closing blatant racial discrimination and claimed the real issue was "interracial mixing." In all likelihood, it appears that Commissioner O'Leary simply used the military complaint as a convenient excuse to close the ballroom to prevent the interracial dancing. At the time, NAACP Executive Secretary Walter F. White bluntly charged that prior to the closing, the Deputy Police Commissioner had also exerted his municipal authority to eliminate any Savoy advertisements in white-read newspapers and also discouraged white bands from playing there. Historian Dominick J. Capeci, Jr., discovered that in the months preceding the order to close, O'Leary had made repeated requests of the Savoy management to prohibit interracial dancing. The Black Press, including the *Baltimore Afro-American, The Chicago Defender*, and the *New York Amsterdam News* closely followed the proceedings. The *New York Amsterdam News* claimed "that the United States Army ordered the Savoy closing to reinforce its Jim Crow policies." The major white-owned newspapers mostly ignored the incident. Military support of the war effort took precedence, and very few, if any, newspapers would counter a military decision or request (Capeci 1981, 18–19).

At the time, the United States military held strict segregation policies. The segregation was so strict that the military mandated that all blood donations to the American Red Cross be carefully separated so as not to mix the blood between whites and African Americans. In addition, white nurses were prevented from caring for African American soldiers (Giordano 2003, 110).

However, racial unrest and blatant violence on the home front garnered a major share of the newspaper headlines. Nationwide racial tensions were high, and violence erupted in over 50 U.S. cities, including New York and Los Angeles. In Detroit, Michigan, problems arose at the Federal Housing Administration built Sojourner Truth Housing Project. The housing was intended to house African American war workers in a predominantly white neighborhood. In June 1943, a mob of angry whites attacked black residents. In two days of battling 34 people were killed and 675 injured. The racial unrest took the combined efforts of both the local police and the U.S. military to end. As a result, the Savoy closing did not attract national attention, and neither did its reopening. In October 1943, after continual persistence by the NAACP, a license renewal was quietly granted, and the Savoy reopened (Capeci 1981, 24).

DANCING DURING WORLD WAR II, THE USO, AND NIGHTCLUBS

During World War II, dancing achieved a prominent status in society as an integral part of supporting the war. Although groups, such as the clergy and some older adults objected, they could not effectively voice their objections for fear of being viewed as hampering the war effort. Dancing was a valuable recreational diversion for servicemen, servicewomen, war workers, and civilians. As early as 1941, during peacetime, it was noted that military training needed to be supplemented with recreation. The most widely recognized military entertainment unit of the war was the United Services Organization (USO). The most popular USO event was dancing.

For those in military service and for their loved ones at home, there was no guarantee that they would survive the war. Therefore, dancing provided a welcome relief to forget the misery of the war. Journalist Lucy Greenbaum of the *New York Times* observed a servicemen's dance at Sloane House Y.M.C.A. in New York. She wrote, "Many of the men regard dancing as a regular Saturday night peacetime pursuit. The reversion to a familiar habit, even for an evening, makes them feel more secure, takes them away from thoughts of war" (Greenbaum, "Fighters With a Boogie Beat," 1942, 11).

Dance critic John Martin of the *New York Times* visited the Stage Door Canteen in New York City. He wrote, "the war is nothing to dance about, and you can say that again; but what I mean it sure is something to dance on account of." The live bands catered to the diverse preferences of both American and foreign servicemen by playing a mix of sweet and hot including Waltzes, Rhumbas, Fox Trots, Jitterbug, and Conga. English and Australian soldiers on leave were known for their preference for the Waltz. Young American soldiers from the cities preferred the

Servicemen's USO Dance during World War II, c. 1942. Note the abundance of uniformed servicemen in the background waiting to dance with a USO hostess.   Author's Archives.

Jitterbug and older soldiers usually the Fox Trot. The Stage Door Canteen did not allow civilian personnel entry unless they were female dance hostesses.

A Hollywood movie appropriately titled *Stage Door Canteen* (1943) recreated the vibrant USO atmosphere of the actual club. The movie portrayed the young female USO hostesses as always being sympathetic to the soldiers in uniform. For example, in one scene a young hostess says, "Sure, soldier, I'll be your girl tonight. Would you like to hold my hand?" The movie musical also featured many famous Hollywood stars of the day playing themselves, including Katharine Hepburn, Tallulah Bankhead, Helen Hayes, George Jessel, and Harpo Marx. Of particular note were the renowned bands including Count Basie, Xavier Cugat, Benny Goodman, Kay Kyser, Guy Lombardo, and Freddy Martin ("Stage Door Canteen," IMDb. com, n.d.).

Dancing, for many young women, was perceived as a patriotic duty. The hostesses were instructed never to say "no" to a dance with a serviceman. They were also encouraged to ask them to dance. One request came from a young hostess to an older soldier, "Don't you dance, soldier?" The soldier replied, "Sure I dance. But not jitterbug. Out where I come from in the Middle West you don't see so much of it as you do [in New York]. We don't think it's dignified. That's high school stuff" (John Martin, "The GI Makes With the Hot Foot," 1944, 14).

Dancing was so popular that over 2,000 war production plants nationwide had facilities for dancing during lunch or breaks. In addition, many of the plants were located near roadhouses, juke joints, and dance halls that were frequented by the workers. Towns and cities near the war plants and army bases regularly sponsored dances, many supported by the USO, churches, community centers, and Y.M.C. A.'s, among others (Lingeman 1970, 292). At faraway places such as Honolulu, Hawaii, the Royal Hawaiian Hotel was commandeered by the military as a Rest and Relaxation resort for service personnel. With the sunny Hawaiian weather soldiers and sailors were treated to regular dances on the open lawn of the hotel situated on Waikiki Beach in view of the famous Diamond Head volcano. Dance floors became more crowded. In some areas of the West Coast the dance floors were so crowded with servicemen and war workers that those doing the Jitterbug simply did not have enough room. Variations ensued, and some began dancing in a slot, straightening the dance so as not to take up so much room.

Nightclubs were a wartime favorite and almost every city had more than one. Without the ability to purchase material goods because of shortages and rationing, people spent their money on entertainment and enjoyed the fun of music, dancing, and nightclubs. *Downbeat* magazine noted that, "Working people newly burdened with war production pressure at home, and with casualty reports from abroad, are seeking the [lighter fun] atmosphere of clubs for entertainment and relief." Nightclubs billed top name vocal entertainers and the big bands. Prices were high, business was good, and nightclubs were not adversely affected by the wartime-imposed 20 percent federal tax on entertainment. Nightclubs could not handle the demand and many were overcrowded (Erenberg 1998, 146).

In November 1942, an overcrowded nightclub in Boston, Massachusetts, had tragic consequences. At the famed *Coconut Grove*, over 800 patrons crowded into the nightclub. During the course of the evening a fire occurred, and in the ensuing panic over 480 people died, including several members of the Mickey Albert Band that was playing there that evening (Leo Walker 1990, 97). The fire caused concern, and many cities enacted restrictions and midnight curfews. Ironically, no restrictions were placed after the 1940 Rhythm Nightclub fire in Natchez, Mississippi. At Natchez all of the dead were African American; at the Coconut Grove all the dead patrons were white.

IN THE MOOD FOR GLENN MILLER AND FRANK SINATRA

Swing was the music that was most closely associated with World War II. The music itself was enlisted to aid in the war effort, and nowhere was that more evident than in the music of Glenn Miller. His song hits included "Little Brown Jug," "Chattanooga Choo Choo," "Moonlight Serenade," and "In The Mood." Miller first achieved prominence with his orchestra in 1939. By the following year, his nationally syndicated radio show was heard by millions of Americans, and his live appearances set attendance records. In Missouri, for example, at St. Louis his band drew over 5,400 and in Kansas City over 7,800. Miller said, "it's an inspiring sight to look down from the balcony on the heads of 7,000 people swaying on a dance floor" (Erenberg 1998, 169). Miller, however, felt that his services would be better put to use if he enlisted.

In September 1942, Captain Glenn Miller was placed in command of the 418th Army Air Forces Band (AAF). Miller convinced the military to let him play the popular music that most of the young enlisted men preferred, which was swing music. Within the AAF, he organized a 42-man marching military band. But he added a unique "swing" to the marching band, incorporating two drummers placed upon jeeps. He also organized a 19-piece dance big band and a small jazz combo, and aired a radio show (Erenberg 1998, 182).

Unfortunately, in December 1944, Miller was lost in an airplane accident over the English Channel. Nevertheless, Glenn Miller's army band was credited as being just as instrumental in the war effort as any other American industry of that time. *Billboard* magazine regularly tracked the most popular dance bands and ranked them in a top-ten order. The list represented hot, sweet, and in-between, but during the war years Miller's band was tops:

1938	1940	1942
1. Benny Goodman	1. Glenn Miller	1. Glenn Miller
2. Tommy Dorsey	2. Kay Kyser	2. Tommy Dorsey
3. Hal Kemp	3. Tommy Dorsey	3. Harry James
4. Guy Lombardo	4. Benny Goodman	4. Benny Goodman
5. Kay Kyser	5. Orrin Tucker	5. Jimmy Dorsey
6. Casa Loma	6. Jan Savitt	6. Vaughn Monroe
7. Horace Heidt	7. Guy Lombardo	7. Sammy Kaye
8. Sammy Kaye	8. Sammy Kaye	8. Kay Kyser
9. Jimmie Lunceford	9. Hal Kemp	9. Charlie Spivak
10. Wayne King	10. Jimmy Dorsey	10. Woody Herman

Ironically, it was the war that was most responsible for the end of swing music. The Selective Service declared musicians as "non-essential" to the home front war effort; therefore, many were drafted into military service, which caused most bands to break up. On the other hand, the Selective Service deemed the Hollywood film industry and its employees as "essential" to the war effort, and therefore they were exempt from the draft. Others in the entertainment field declared "non-essential" included all professional ballplayers, such as baseball and football players. Touring bands had to curtail their lucrative engagements due to the gasoline rationing and travel restrictions. The final stroke was a musician's strike from mid-1942 until late-1944 that prevented any new commercial recordings. (Many bands did record previously released tunes, however, only on government issued "V" discs intended for servicemen overseas.) As a result, individual singers, who were not part of the musicians' union, and, therefore, not on strike, replaced that of the bands.

As the war dragged on most music sought was "G.I. Nostalgia" a termed labeled by bandleader Kay Kyser. Kyser starred in a few wartime Hollywood musicals that featured swing music and dancing, including *Around the World* (1943) and *Swing Fever* (1944). Some of the other bandleaders like Harry James played longer sweeter ballads for a slow Fox Trot and allowed the dancers to hold on to their partner for just a little bit longer. It was clear that dancing was changing towards more sentimental ballads by vocalists such as Dick Haymes, Bob Eberly, and a young skinny Italian singer from Hoboken, New Jersey, Frank Sinatra (Lingeman 1970, 299).

Prior to Sinatra, the band was the star attraction and the vocalist was a featured attraction. In 1939, Sinatra started as a vocalist with the Tommy Dorsey Orchestra. In 1942, however, the blue-eyed singer set out on his own and created a never before seen sensation that was called "Sinatra-mania." Screaming young female fans called "bobbysoxers" (due to their fashion style of knee length dresses, white crunched up socks, and two-toned saddle shoes) were known to faint as Sinatra crooned and swooned. Although they crowded the bandstand, they did not dance. It would take the explosion of a new type of music to get the kids dancing again.

4

The Mambo, American Bandstand, and Rock 'n' Roll: 1947–1960

Rock 'n' Roll is really swing with a modern name....It's the rhythm that gets the kids. They are starved for music they can dance to after all those years of crooners.
—Alan Freed, 1957

The Political, Social, and Cultural Climate

In August 1945, World War II ended with the atomic bombs dropped on Hiroshima and Nagasaki. Although much of the world was literally in ruins, mainland America was relatively intact. The war production had provided the United States with its most significant economic growth of the entire twentieth century. American workers earned significant wages and had more money per person than ever before. Over 12 million American servicemen and women were reintroduced into civilian life. Soldiers back from the war wanted to get on with their lives, go to school, get back to work, and start families. In 1946, with the immediate end of the war, over 3 million women left the work force and were newly married or reunited with soldier husbands. Birth rates increased dramatically, and the baby boom began. Delivering a baby, however, came with the fear that the baby might contract polio.

Similar to the outbreak of the influenza epidemic in 1918, polio also came without warning, and for the most part the cause was unexplainable. At the time it was incurable and could also affect adults. Polio could paralyze or incapacitate its victim by accumulation of mucus in the lungs. During an epidemic, public places were closed and social contact was severely limited. Wheelchairs and braces needed to support the victim were heavy, clumsy, and difficult to come by. Therefore, many polio victims were confined to the home. In 1954, Jonas Salk discovered an effective vaccine administered by injection. The vaccine was announced to the

American public via television. In 1956, an oral vaccine was developed by Albert Sabin, and polio was slowly coming under control.

The end of the war introduced Americans to the G.I. Bill, which provided veterans with significant amounts of money for college education and job training. Because of the educational opportunity, the former servicemen were better prepared to enter into the workforce. The transition occurred over a ten-year period, thereby avoiding "flooding the job market." The G.I. Bill also offered the opportunity for veterans to apply for a Veterans' Administration (VA) 30-year mortgage to purchase their own homes. Many of those loans were applied to single-family homes in suburban developments (Giordano 2003, 141).

Magazines and television continually portrayed a new idealized "American Dream" of suburban middle-class living. The image stressed home ownership, marriage, family, and consumerism. Goods, many never before available, were plentiful and most Americans could afford to buy them. A glut of purchases "on credit" included washing machines, air conditioners vacuum cleaners, home appliances, and automobiles. New toys and games, including the Frisbee, Silly Putty, Mr. Potato Head, Lego Toy Bricks, and Hula Hoops, were huge fads.

In 1947, the Soviet Union exploded its own atomic bomb, and Americans were worried about the threat of a nuclear war. In that same year, the Truman Doctrine abandoned the United States policy of peacetime isolationism and committed itself to the point of no turning back in the new "Cold War" against the Soviet Union and Communism. A widespread and popular notion was that American Communists were conducting atomic espionage for the Soviet Union. The Congressional House Un-American Activities Committee (HUAC) launched multiple investigations into Communist infiltration of organized labor, the Federal government, and most audaciously—Hollywood. In 1947, the *Hollywood Ten* comprising 10 motion-picture producers, directors, and screenwriters appeared before the HUAC. They refused to answer questions regarding allegations of possible communist affiliations and were sent to prison for contempt of Congress. Upon their release they were blacklisted from working with the Hollywood studios.

By 1950, Senator Joseph McCarthy seized the newspaper headlines, falsely warning Americans that they were endangered by Communist infiltration in Hollywood and government. During later hearings by McCarthy and the HUAC in 1951, the "naming-of-names" became the watchwords. The widespread paranoia that engulfed the entire country became known as the "red-scare." The question "Have you now or ever been a member of the Communist Party?" was routinely asked upon job applications and even for fishing licenses. The fear of Communism resulted in a rise in patriotic, fraternal, and religious affiliations. In 1954, as an affirmation against the atheistic beliefs of the Soviets, Congress added the words "one nation under God" to the Pledge of Allegiance.

The nation was also divided by segregation, although the barriers of segregation were slowly coming down. In 1947, both Jackie Robinson in the National League and Larry Doby in the American League broke "the color barrier" in major league baseball. The 1954 Supreme Court decision of *Brown v. the Board of Education of Topeka, Kansas* effectively ended school segregation. And in 1955, Rosa Parks refused to give up her seat on a bus, igniting a year-long boycott in Montgomery,

Alabama, that received national media attention and was successful in weakening the legal barriers of segregation.

In 1957, the Soviets launched "Sputnik," the first satellite in space. As a result, Americans were not only afraid of a nuclear war, but also the Soviet "threat" from outer space. Americans by the thousands built backyard fallout shelters for protection in the event of a nuclear attack. Schoolchildren were taught to "stop, drop, and cover" when and if the bomb would fall. It was within this political and social climate that Rock 'n' Roll music and Elvis Presley exploded upon America. By the mid 1950s, teenagers were dancing to Rock 'n' Roll music inspired by the song " (We're Gonna) Rock Around the Clock" by Bill Haley and the Comets. Teenagers by the millions hurried home every day after school to watch teenagers dancing on the television show *American Bandstand* hosted by Dick Clark. Of the music, Clark said:

> Kids hadn't been dancing since the end of the swing era. Suddenly, this spirited tune with a bouncy, rhythmic beat had the kids clapping and dancing (Uslan and Solomon, 1981, 17).

The Dances

It makes you want to dance. With a waltz you have to be in a good mood to dance to it. But with Rock 'n' Roll no matter what your mood is, it gets you.
—Teenager Vivian, 1958

DANCE INSTRUCTION

In 1947, the incomparable Paul Whiteman (see Chapters 2 and 3) wrote in reflection of his experiences of seeing Americans dance for the preceding 50 years. He said, "As a leader of dance orchestras for many years, I've observed thousands upon thousands of dancers....I like to watch them—to feel that my music is helping them have a good time. And the ones who have always had the most fun at the places where I've played have been those who could dance well" (Murray 1947, 5). Whiteman, however, could not foresee the immediate future.

Between 1947 and 1954, dance music and dancing was in a state of transition. The big bands were out; mellow pop standards and Bebop jazz were in. Bebop was created purposely off the standard dance beat so people would sit and listen —not dance. The reason most people did not dance to Bebop was because the music itself did not have a method of applying a repeatable dance rhythm and in turn lacked a continuous metronome beat that the dancers could count out. This is not to say that people did not dance to Bebop—it was just that the music itself was a bit too complicated to apply to any of the standard dances. The development of Bebop was in effect a rebellion in music by African American artists. According to musical composer Galt MacDermot (see Chapter 5), "Black musicians were sick of the social system. So they created music that was not necessarily off the beat but, was too complicated for white people to understand. I don't know why they wanted to do that but they did" (Giordano interview 2004).

In January 1949, in an article titled "Bebop: Music or Madness?" in *Our World*, self-described as "A Picture Magazine for the Whole Family," proclaimed "dig the new dances the cats are cooking. That should squash the deadpans who say Bebop isn't danceable." The magazine provided illustrations for the Applejack and Bebop dances. The Applejack was an individual dance with variations titled the Corkscrew Crawl and Upright, a Half Nelson Pose, and the Swing Kick. The Bebop was a couple's dance that incorporated underarm turns, an exaggerated dip, and a slide. Each dance incorporated a "freeze" step or a slide step to compensate for the complicated Bebop rhythm. In 1985, Bebop historian Ira Gitler added, "It was said that black people didn't dance to bebop and, for the most part this was true, but black people figured out a way to make those fast tempos by cutting the time in half whether they were doing a new dance called 'The Apple Jack' [sic] or the older Lindy Hop" (McQuirter 2002, 83–85).

Dancing was still popular but mainly among adults who danced to the prewar standards and the sedate orchestras of Lawrence Welk, Guy Lombardo, and Fred Warring. Sedate popular vocalists, known as "crooners" and vocal harmony groups ruled the radio airwaves. They included Perry Como, Rosemary Clooney, Doris Day, Gail Storm, Eddie Fischer, the Fontaine Sisters, the Mills Brothers, Dean Martin, Anita O'Day, Jo Stafford, and Patti Page. Page, for example, had a monstrous hit with the quaint and sedate *The Tennessee Waltz*, selling 6 million copies (James Miller 1999, 47).

Up until that time, Arthur Murray had an exclusive on the nationwide dance studio franchise. In 1947, dancer Fred Astaire (see Chapter 3) lent his name to a national franchise chain of *Fred Astaire Dance Studios*. In an attempt to publicize that the studio was not like other dance studios, he choreographed a new dance called "The Astaire." It combined elements of the Jitterbug, Fox Trot, and other earlier dances. The dance did not catch on. However, the Astaire franchise studios provided ample competition to the Arthur Murray nationwide chain. But the Astaire studios taught the same ballroom standards with little variations.

Some other well-known social dance instructors included D'Avalos and Aleida, "Killer Joe" Piro (see Chapter 5), The Herbert Taylors, Beale Fletcher, and Marge and Gower Champion. The Taylors were credited with introducing the "champagne hour" to the elegant hotel ballrooms of Chicago, New York, and Florida. The idea of a "champagne hour" was to have an audience participation dance contest. The MC (or the Taylors) would place his hand above each participating dance couple's head asking for audience response. The couple with the loudest audience response was given a bottle of champagne (Dannett and Rachel, 165).

On the other hand, learning the popular dance steps could also be accomplished at home. The suburban transformation also brought with it the idea of numerous "Do-it-yourself projects" that could be done at home. Do-it-yourself dance instruction was available as a complete package with a dance instruction book, foot diagrams, and record albums from many mail-at-home sources.

However, the Arthur Murray name was so synonymous with dance instruction that American popular entertainer Bob Hope once joked, "I used to take dancing

Do-it-yourself dance instruction was available as a complete package with a dance instruction book, foot diagrams, and record albums from many mail-at-home sources.   Author's Archives.

lessons from Arthur Murray until I found out it was more fun dancing with a girl." Perennial TV host Bert Parks explained, "If the audience sees me stumble and I say 'I learned that in dancing school,' no one would laugh. But if I say, 'I learned that from Arthur Murray,' they love it!" (quoted in Kathryn Murray 1960, 94–95).

Immediately after World War II the G.I. Bill even lent itself towards dance instruction. Arthur Murray secured a large contract to teach veterans how to dance. The demand of ex G.I.'s wanting to learn how to dance required the purchase of an additional building on 44th Street in Manhattan and the hiring of an additional 250 teachers. Shortly after the program began Congressmen attacked it for a supposed "waste of money." The VA suspended the dance instruction program after one year and held up payment. Murray initiated litigation in court and waited for over ten years to get paid.

The end of the program caused the immediate release of almost all the additional dance instructors. Those instructors who remained complained to the Murrays regarding unfair labor practices. In 1947, the Arthur Murray instructors sought to unionize with the United Office and Professional Workers of America. Grievances included fines for being late, strict grooming requirements, and no pay for waiting or a client's cancellation. The instructors added a new twist to the picket line as they publicized their cause by dancing the Conga on the street outside the New York studio. After 13 weeks of picketing the attempt at unionization failed, but Murray did make concessions to the staff, including increased wages and the elimination of nitpicking fines (Kathryn Murray 1960, 112–113).

The most notable new dance couple of the period was Marge and Gower Champion. They stared and danced their way through many 1950s Hollywood musicals including *Showboat* (1951), *Lovely to Look At* (1952), *Give a Girl a Break* (1953), *Three for the Show* (1955), and *Jupiter's Darling* (1955). The Champions cited that their inspiration to dance came from seeing Fred Astaire and Ginger Rogers on the Hollywood screen (see Chapter 3). In fact, Marge Champion had an uncredited role as a dancer in the Astaire and Rogers movie *The Story of Vernon and Irene Castle* (1939). They noted that Astaire and Rogers probably "inspired more people to dance than anyone in history" (Thomas 1954, 19). However, it was television that first gained them national prominence.

In 1949, the Champions appeared as regulars on an early television variety show *The Admiral Broadway Revue*. The appearance provided them with the notoriety to continue their dancing career in Hollywood movies. In all likelihood, they were the first dance couple to achieve success directly from the medium of television. In 1957, they hosted the NBC-TV prime-time *The Marge and Gower Champion Show*. It was not a show about dance instruction, although the theme song was "Let's Dance, Let's Dance, Let's Dance." In fact, it was a situation comedy, where Gower played the role of a choreographer and Marge a dancer, and the show always featured at least one scene with them dancing (Dannett and Rachel 1954, 184).

In August 1954, they premiered their own dance, The Champion Strut, at the Dancing Masters of America convention in Los Angeles. In their own words, "America hasn't had a screwy dance since the Lambeth Walk (see Chapter 3). The dance was "simple enough so that the non-dancer could pick it up easily." However, the simple dance never did catch on. At the time, Rock 'n' Roll music and dancing (see later this chapter) was about to explode upon America and create a new wave of dance hysteria upon the American teenagers (Thomas 1954, 45).

In the years preceding 1954, dance instruction for teenagers and young adults offered the sedate ballroom version of the Fox Trot and Waltz. Dance instructors Marge and Gower Champion favored the Tango, but acknowledged, "Few people do the tango any more, and orchestras seldom play one" (Thomas 1954, 29). In *Let's Dance with Marge and Gower Champion* (1954), they wrote:

> We discovered that the children...had no recreation facilities in the town and had decided to do something about it. They acquired an old army barracks and pitched in to clean it up and decorate it as a clubhouse....The townspeople had donated a juke-box, but none of the kids seemed inclined to dance. That amazed us. We grew up in a dance-happy generation. So we arranged for a dance teacher and two assistants to visit the clubhouse regularly (7).

In 1956, Beale Fletcher's *How To Improve Your Social Dancing* provided some insight that times were changing. Fletcher wrote, "Social dancing is more popular now than ever before. People have time for it...more time is available to cultivate the artistic and social aspects of life....The ability to dance develops personality, and above all—it is *fun*" (2). In addition to instruction in the standard ballroom variants, his book did include the popular contemporary dances such as the Cha Cha Cha, Mambo, Merengue, Polka, Folk Dances, and Square Dancing.

SQUARE DANCING, THE POLKA, AND THE TARANTELLA

Square dancing is a term loosely applied to almost all forms of traditional American folk dancing. Its roots are traced to the European English Country-dances and French Contredanse. The English Country-dances the Round and Square Eight containing set figures and patterns made their way to France in the late seventeenth century. The French transformed the two English dances into the Contredanse (later called the Cotillion) to include sets of two and four couples in a square. A later adaptation of the Contredanse was the Quadrille. The Quadrille was a set figure dance performed by both the French and the English in varying combinations of couples in a square. Colonial America adapted the dances of their European ancestors, and the Quadrille was the forerunner of the American Square Dance. It continued through the first half of the twentieth century mainly in rural areas at barn dances and in small towns (Harris et al., 2000, 125–127).

During World War II, American soldiers were transported to training areas all over the country. Soldiers in basic training camps in areas including Nebraska,

Community Square Dancing in Dallas, Texas, c. 1949.   Author's Archives.

Oklahoma, and Texas were introduced to Square Dancing as a Saturday night recreational activity. In these locations they also heard Country and Western music and Western Swing (see Chapter 3). In 1941, the widely popular Hollywood comedy team of Abbott and Costello even featured a Square Dance scene in the movie *Ride 'Em Cowboy*.

After World War II, Y.M.C.A.s and physical education programs throughout the nation's schools promoted Square Dancing as a healthy recreational activity. As a result, Square Dancing at community events gradually increased. Square Dances and Barn Dances became regular occurrences, rather than in the past when they were reserved for a special occasion or Saturday night. In a short time, people young and old all over the country were enjoying Square Dancing. Square Dance festivals arose that attracted between 5,000 and 10,000 participants. In addition, the dances were no longer held only in small towns or rural areas. Square dancing was enjoyed in towns of every size, including large cities. In 1946, for example, over 3,000 New York City residents, both young and old, attended an outdoor Square Dance held on the mall of the Bethesda Fountain in Central Park (Dannett and Rachel 1954, 175).

By the late 1940s, publications such as *Foot 'n' Fiddle* and *Sets In Order* (later known as *Square Dancing Magazine*) chronicled the Square Dance movement in America. Hollywood capitalized on the popularity with *Hollywood Barn Dance* (1947), *Square Dance Jubilee* (1949), *The Arkansas Swing* (1949), and *Square Dance Katy* (1950). Later twentieth century movies included *Square Dance* (1987) and *Son in Law* (1988).

Regional versions of Square Dances and callers varied widely, resulting in a move to standardization. In 1952, the first annual national Square Dance convention was held. During the decade, the conventions attracted between 15,000 and 20,000 people. In 1956, dance instructor Beale Fletcher described a typical Square Dance. He wrote,

This cover from *Sets In Order, the Official Magazine of Square Dancing* provides a good sample of four basic formations for Square Dancing including Grids, Stars, Circles, and Lines, c. June 1964. Used by permission of Bill Boyd and *Sets In Order Magazine*.

The Square Dance starts with the couples all joining hands in a large circle facing the center. Each boy has a girl partner on his right side...The music, which is in fast tempo...starts to play and the caller yells, "Circle—Left!"

The entire circle moves to the left while holding hands. The call is usually followed by: "Half-way back to the right!" The circle starts back in the other direction....When the caller says, "Odd Couples on your go!"...This movement breaks the large circle, and in its place we now have a group of small circles or "squares" (Fletcher 1956, 119).

Four couples each form a side of a square facing the inside of the square. The couples respond to the caller's heed for a particular figure that the set performs. Typical calls include "Honor your partner," "Promenade your partner," or "Do-sa-do" (sometimes spelled Do-si-do).

Honor your partner is sometimes called "Bow to your Partner." And it is just that, as the partner's turn face-to-face and bow. The Promenade is a dance position taken by the partners, who move counterclockwise around the circle. In the Promenade position partners stand side-by-side, man on woman's left. They hold cross hands in front of them; man's right hand over the top of the lady's left arm to lady's right hand and partner's left hand to left hand. In Do-sa-do, the partners face each other and pass each other right shoulder to right shoulder and "move around each other back to back and return to original position facing partner" (Harris et al., 2000, 137).

By 1960, 30 basic movements (or "sets") were standardized and published by *Sets In Order*. Conventions continued through the end of the century and attendance continued to grow. By the 1970s, the conventions drew over 40,000 people. By 1994, estimates ranged as high as 6 million people regularly Square Danced (Harris et al., 2000, 129).

Another traditional American folk dance was the Polka. The Polka was originally a Czechoslovakian dance believed to originate in the nineteenth century around 1830. In Czech, *Pulka* translates to half step for "the rapid shift from one foot to the other." It was introduced to Paris around 1840 and became a popular dance in the Parisian dance academies and ballrooms. In the 1850s, the dance was introduced to the United States. After World War II, a greater number of Polish immigrants entered the United States, adopting the Polka as their dance. In the early 1950s, Polka dance songs achieved a fair amount of radio airplay. One example was "Papa Won't You Dance with Me?" As a prelude to her hit song, Gale Storm spoke the words, "There is one dance more exciting than the rest. I like the Polka best."

The old world dance traditions of immigrant Americans were different from the American social traditions. Inhibitions within Anglo-European American culture continued to set a pattern that only a heterosexual couple could dance together. On the other hand, for immigrants from southern Europe such as Italy, Greece, Yugoslavia, and Hungary it was not unusual for dance and wedding celebrations to include solo dancing, group dancing,

Polka is a couple's dance done in either a closed dance position or side-by-side in 2/4 time in the count of 1,2,3 and 4,5,6. Staring with the left foot with a slight hop (count 1) followed by quick short *chassé* steps right foot (count 2), and left foot (count 3) the pattern repeats with the right foot with a slight hop (count 4) followed by quick short *chassé* steps left foot (count 5), and right foot (count 6). During the first half of the twentieth century, the Polka could be found at some rural barn dances but was almost nonexistent on the social dance floors. The Polka was popular at community dances, social gatherings, and wedding celebrations ("Polka History of Dance," n.d.).

or even men with men or women with women. Historian Richard Gambino states, "To be more precise, men had no inhibitions about dancing solo or with one or more men. Men and women commonly danced together in large groups, but coed duets were often limited to married or courting couples" (1974, 141).

The Tarantella is one example that is typical of the European folk dances in both style and origin. The Tarantella is a "high-spirited dance" of the Mezzogiorno region (southern portion) of Italy that varied from town to town. The dignified dance posture kept "the shoulders and hips fixed," yet allowed for individual interpretation and improvisation. The name of the dance was derived from the town of Tarentum (Taranto) in southern Italy. Local legend claims that the dance originated "as a superstitious ritual to cure the poisonous bite of large spiders called *tarantula*." The dance style holds the arms high above the shoulders. The feet are lifted and crossed over the body and stepping to the ground as if stepping on a spider (Gambino 1974, 141).

THE HOKEY POKEY AND THE HULA

In 1947, Larry La Prise reportedly introduced the novelty dance the Hokey Pokey at the Sun Valley Ski Resort in Idaho. Conflicting sources of the origin of the words and music for the Hokey Pokey might predate La Prise. Shakers in Kentucky might have performed a song with similar lyrics. One Kentucky resident claimed authorship in 1944. During World War II, American servicemen in England reportedly did an English dance the *Okey Cokey*. In 1950, Roy Acuff, however, secured the publishing rights for his Acuff-Rose Opryland Music Company. Many musical artists, groups, and novelty acts recorded the song. The dance quickly became a favorite party dance across America.

The Hokey Pokey is a circle dance, similar to a square dance in that the dancers respond to a caller. The dancers form a circle, and it is easy for anyone to get involved. No previous dancing experience is necessary. Partnering is not necessary. The mix can be any combination of male, female, adults, teens, and children. During the course of the song and dance, the caller indicates movements such as placing your right foot in towards to the center of the circle and then placing it to the outside of the circle. The dancer is told to put the right foot back towards the center and shake the leg. They are then told to turn the body about and shake their arms above their heads. After 1950, doing the Hokey Pokey was one dance that many Americans performed at one time or another at a social dance function. Many other party novelty dances followed including the Limbo, Alley Cat, Chicken Dance, Hands Up, and the Hula.

The native Hula dance actually is an intricate dance that interprets Hawaiian stories through the use of hand, body, and facial expressions (see Chapter 6). Non-natives who saw the Hula did not understand the dance and created simplified versions. In 1959, with Hawaii achieving statehood, many Americans nationwide held "Welcome Hawaii" themed parties. The parties encouraged Hawaiian attire and Hula dancing. The American adaptation, however, was not nearly representative of any intricate dance pattern. Some even danced with a Hula Hoop. (The simple plastic hoop was inspired by the Hawaiian Hula dance and was one of the biggest toy fads of the twentieth century, selling over 100 million units.) In fact, American Hula dancing usually involved a few individuals simply placing a Hawaiian lei around the dancers' necks, and they solo danced in any manner they pleased.

THE "KING OF THE MAMBO," THE CHA-CHA-CHA?, AND THE MERENGUE

From 1920 to 1959, Cuba was the central Latin musical influence in the Caribbean and the United States. The major musical influence was the development of the Mambo. America's relationship with the largest of the Caribbean islands was quite good, and immigration from Cuba to American cities such as New York, Chicago, Miami, San Francisco, and Los Angeles was common. Cuba, especially the city of Havana, was a major tourist attraction for well-to-do Americans. The vacation resorts featured excellent native entertainment and dancing. It was not until after the 1959 revolution led by Fidel Castro that relations between the United States and Cuba became strained.

Many sources rely on dance historians Sylvia Dannett and Frank Rachel who claim that the origin of the word "mambo" is a name for a Haitian "voodoo Priestess." They are also widely quoted that the Mambo "was originally a Haitian dance introduced to the West in 1948" (1954, 170). The origin of the music and the dance that became an American favorite is traced to Cuba. In Cuba, the word "mambo" did not necessarily have a specific meaning. However, it might have been applied to the dance from the phrase *abrecuto y guiri mambo,* which translated to "open your eyes and listen." During the 1930s, Cuban bandleader Orestes López was known to shout out "*Mil veves mambo!*" (A thousand times mambo) to his orchestra (Driver 2000, 86).

In 1937, Cuban bandleader Antonio Arcaño led a "charanga" named Arcaño y sus Maravillas. A charanga is defined as "a Cuban dance orchestra consisting of flute backed by fiddle, piano, bass, and timbales [ranging] from large society units to small street-bands" (Roberts 1999, 259). In 1938, as a band member of Arcaño y sus Maravillas, pianist Orestes López composed the song "Mambo." In the recording, which was a traditional Cuban danzon (similar to Rhumba), he added an American Jazz-like ending that became known as a Mambo rhythm. López described the "origin of the mambo" as follows:

> I introduced the rhythm with the intent of enriching [the] music...because before they used to play the final part real short, and didn't give any instrument the chance to enjoy themselves. Now with the mambo, a different spirit began among the dancers: they waited for this part, content that it would be long and pulled out all these steps (quoted in Waxer, "Of Mambo Kings and Songs of Love," 1994, 150).

In the early 1940s, many other Cuban bandleaders combined Latin rhythms with American Jazz. The style developed into the mambo rhythm that led to the development of the dance. In New York, the Latin bands drew on the ethnic diversity of Puerto Ricans, Dominicans, Cubans, African Americans, and Anglos to form a distinct New York Latin sound. Latin music historian Lise Waxer said, "The New

York sound was indeed different. Flashier, faster, brassy, and more agitated than Cuban music" (1994, 162).

The origin of the Mambo as a dance is unclear. Some say that Cubans danced the basic Mambo steps many years before in native Cuba. Others claim it was derived from the native *son* and *danzon* dancers. Others claim it was danced in native Haiti. Contemporary accounts such as in *Downbeat* magazine described it as "rumba with jitterbug" (Roberts 1999, 131). The Mambo was also described as a "charge step version of the rumba basic step" (Dannett and Rachel, 170). However, the Mambo, as danced in America, was strictly a New York City creation. The music developed in New York before the dance, and Latin Americans developed the dance style to fit the music.

In 1946, the first of the large Latin dances was held at the Manhattan Center. The dance was organized by record producer Gabriel Oller, who hired five groups catering to Latin Americans including Machito's Afro-Cubans. The dance drew over 5,000 enthusiastic Latin dancers. Another East Harlem promoter, Federico Pagani, took the idea downtown to the Alma Dance Studios at 53rd Street and Broadway. He convinced the owners to sponsor special Latin dance nights. It was within these dance environments that the Mambo developed as an American dance style (Roberts 1999, 112).

Latin music historian John Storm Roberts dates 1947 as the beginning of the Mambo craze in the United States. At that time, both Tito Puente and Tito Rodriguez each formed a *conjunto*. (The literal translation is "combo.") The Cuban conjunto combined vocals, trumpets, piano, bass, congas, and bongó. The Puerto Rican conjunto consisted of a cuatro (a small ten string guitar), guitar, and guayo scraper (a notched gourd played with a stick), accordion, and sometimes trumpets and clarinet. The Chicano conjunto consisted of an accordion, guitar, bass, spoons, and bongó (Roberts 1999, 260–262).

Tito Puente was born in New York City of Puerto Rican parents. Puente lived up to his public relations hype as "King of the Mambo," recording over 120 albums during his lifetime, and presented a big band Mambo sound. Pablo "Tito" Rodriguez was a singer and percussionist. He was born in 1923 in Puerto Rico. He came to the United States and sang with popular Latin Orchestras including Xavier Cugat, Noro Morales, and José Curelo before forming his own band (Roberts 1999, 125–130).

The success of the Mambo was overwhelming as the studios went almost exclusively Latin. The Alma Dance Studios was renamed the Palladium Dance Hall. By 1952, the Palladium was an all-Latin format, and it became the center of Mambo in New York regularly featuring Tito Puente, Tito Rodriquez, and Machito. Throughout the 1950s until its closing in 1966, the Palladium was "the Mecca of mambo." It featured Latin music every night of the week. Each night had a decidedly ethnic flavor: Wednesday nights attracted a large mix of Jewish and Italian Americans; Friday was a complete mix; Saturday was almost exclusively Latino and Latina; and Sunday was heavily African American and Puerto Rican (Boggs, 147).

However, it was Pérez Prado who introduced most Americans to Mambo music. Prado adopted the charanga sound of Cuban bandleader Antonio Arcaño for use with a big band jazz sound and heavily publicized the word "Mambo" to describe his sound (Waxer 1994, 152). Prado recorded mainly in Mexico and released songs through RCA for the American market. In 1951, Prado toured the west coast of the United States playing a big band style of Mambo, attracting crowds from 2,500 to 3,500 dancers. Prado was known for many popular instrumental Mambo songs including "Mambo No. 5," "Mambo No. 8," "Mambo No. 10," "Que Rico El Mambo," "Moliendo Café," and "Caballo Negro." Many American based groups covered his songs (Roberts 1999, 126–127).

By 1954, the Mambo dance became a rage, mainly among adults in the big cities of New York, Chicago, Miami, Los Angeles, and San Francisco. "Mambo Baby," a song by Ruth Brown, placed No. 1 on the *Billboard* Rhythm and Blues chart. Non-Latin singers charted Mambo hits on the Pop charts including Perry Como's "Papa Loves Mambo" and Rosemary Clooney's "Mambo Italiano." Venezuelan born Edmund Rios and His Orchestra recorded two popular albums for Latin dancing. *Ros Mambos* in 1955 contained music strictly for Mambos including "More Mambo," "Mambo Jambo," and a remake of Perez Prado's "Mambo No. 5," and in 1956 *Ros Album of Sambas* including "Amour," "Yankee Doodle Samba," and "Madalena."

Other popular Latin dance bands included Merced Gallego, the Californian dubbed "King of the Mambo," Alfredito (Brooklyn born Jewish Al Levy), and Alfredo Mendez (Jewish born Alfred Mendelsohn). Latin music historian John Storm Roberts states, "Like the links between Latin and black musicians, the

Perez Prado and his Orchestra perform for Mambo dancers in a scene from the movie *Cha-Cha-Cha Boom* (1956).   Columbia Pictures / Courtesy of Photofest.

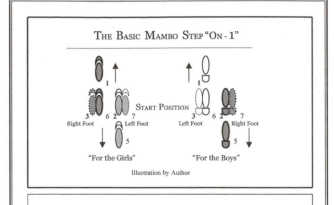

THE BASIC MAMBO STEP "ON - 1"

START POSITION

3 6 2 7   3 6 2 7
Right Foot Left Foot   Left Foot Right Foot

5   5

"For the Girls"   "For the Boys"

Illustration by Author

The Mambo basic is performed in 4/4 rhythm from a closed position and danced in one spot on the dance floor. To start the woman backwards, the man exerts a slight push forward with his left hand. To bring his partner forward, he pulls slightly with his right hand on her shoulder blade. The Champion's described the basic Mambo as follows:

For the Girls:

1. Move right foot backward - Count 1 -
2. Step in place with left foot - Count 2 -
3. Close with right foot   - Count 3 -
4. Hold in place.
1. Move left foot forward.   - Count 5 -
2. Step in place with right foot -Count 6 -
3. Close with left foot.   - Count 7 -
4. Hold in place.

For the Boys:

1. Move left foot forward.
2. Step in place with right foot.
3. Close with left foot.
4. Hold in place.
1. Move right foot backward.
2. Step in place with left foot.
3. Close with right foot.
4. Hold in place.

Jewish connection in New York Latin music is a strong one.. . .Latin music in New York always had a strong Jewish public...in fact, Latin music's hard-core non-Latin audience was almost entirely 'ethnic'—largely Jewish and Italian—and black" (1999, 130).

Of the Mambo, dance historians Jane A. Harris, Anne M. Pittman, and Marlys S. Waller, writing in *Social Dance* said, "The rhythm is difficult and has spurred controversy as to whether the rhythm is off-beat [count 2] or on-beat [count 1], that is, quick, quick slow or slow quick quick. Because of its highly syncopated beat, it has been a difficult rhythm to learn" (1998, 111).

In 1954, dance instructors Marge and Gower Champion wrote in *Let's Dance* that the Mambo should begin on the first beat (count 1). They added, "Some mambo fanciers believe the hold should come on the first beat. To each his own." Unlike in most other dance instruction booklets, the Champions included dance step instructions side by side for both the male and female, or in their case, which was aimed at the teenage audience, the "girls" and "boys."

To support the joy of dancing the Mambo, the Champions added, "Too many people filter off the floor when a Latin tune is played. They're making a mistake, because there are few ways to get more enjoyment from dancing than doing a rumba [sic], samba, or mambo well. Especially if you are more than slightly in love with your partner" (Thomas 1954, 29-37).

In 1955, Betty White's *How to Mambo* and, in 1956, Beale Fletcher's instructional book *How To Improve Your Social Dancing* both contradicted the Champions instructions, White and Beale preferring to "pause on the first beat of the music." Fletcher wrote, "There is a disagreement among dance authorities as to which beat in the music should take the open beat or pause in the dance" (90). White said the Mambo should begin on "2" with a prep step. She described the prep step as, "Leader steps to the left side (count 1), steps back on the right (count 2) and steps forward on the left foot and close right" (9–12). The contradiction and difficulty of the rhythm might be the reason why the Mambo faded in popularity among the American public. The difficulties of the Mambo rhythm led to the development of the easier Cha-Cha—or was it?

In 1953, the Cha-Cha (Latin origins spell it "chachachá") swept Cuba. Latin music historian Lise Waxer claims one reason for the "immense popularity" of the dance "was the intimate connection between the dance step and the rhythmic impulse of the music." Her research claims that the first "chachachá" was "*La engañadora*," written in 1953 by Enrique Jorrín and recorded in America. Jorrín said he wrote the music in response to the sound of the dancer's feet. He said, "I realized that the dancers, dragging their feet across the floor, made this sound: cha-cha-cha...Now, when you hear two hundred people making this noise at the same time, you catch onto it...cha-cha-*cha*, one-two, cha-cha-*cha*" (translation quoted in Waxer, "Of Mambo Kings and Songs of Love," 1994, 159–160). The following year the Cha-Cha was introduced in New York and Miami by Latin musicians, and it quickly became a craze in the United States.

The Cha-Cha is a simple version of the Mambo, adding a triple step or a chassé in place of the hold step in Mambo. (Some term the dance the "Triple Mambo.") In the basic 1950s Cha-Cha, the steps are taken "on beat" in time with the first beat of the music. The count is 1,2, 3&4, 5,6, 7&8 or, more commonly, as so many students of the dance remember, "1,2, cha-cha-cha, 3,4, cha-cha-cha." The leader starts step forward left foot (count 1), steps back in place with the right foot (count 2), chassés step triple rhythm (three steps to two beats of music, step left, step right, step left—counts 3&4), hence the cha-cha-cha. The leader steps backward right foot (count 5), steps back in place with the left foot (count 6), chassés step triple rhythm (step right, step left, step right—counts 7&8).

The upper body is held still and perpendicular to your partner. The steps are accentuated and led from the hip as the knees bend on the left step forward (count 1) and straightened as the right foot steps in place (count 2) and the left foot comes back in place (count 3). The bent knee and straighten technique is repeated on the backward steps. This hip movement is known as Cuban Motion. Variations include an "open break," "cross over steps," and a chassé turn sometimes known as the "chase and follow." This basic on-beat version of Cha-Cha would also be the standard of the line dance, couple, and choreographed Round dance in Country Dancing during the 1990s.

The Cha-Chas played by New York musicians blended the big band style with native Cuban charanga. Some of the early New York compositions were "El Campesino" by Machito and José Curbelo's "El Pescador." Tito Puente's "Happy Cha Cha Cha" and "Cha Cha Cha de Pollos" also maintained original charanga sounds. Perez Prado provided one of the first crossover Cha-Cha hit songs "Cerazo Rosa (Cherry Pink, and Apple Blossom White)." Sam Cooke's song "Everybody Loves to Cha Cha Cha" was also a popular hit (Roberts 1999, 132).

It was Arthur Murray who changed and standardized the Cha-Cha as a ballroom variant for his dance studios. At first he taught it as the on-beat basic count of "one-two-cha-cha-cha." He felt that it worked in practice with verbal instruction, but claimed that it was "impossible to diagram." According to his wife, Kathryn, "He changed the name of the dance to cha cha and the count to one-two-three cha-cha. The two 'cha-chas' are said very quickly, making one beat, or a total of four beats to the measure" (Kathryn Murray 1960, 9). The ballroom version introduced a prep step taking the dance off of the solid accentuated beat of the rhythm. The prep step is similar to the Mambo and is taken to the left side on the first beat of music (count 1) step back with the right (count 2) and forward left (count 3). The dance proceeds with the count of 4&1, 2,3; 4&1, 2,3 or quick-quick-slow, slow-slow; quick-quick-slow, slow-slow (Harris et al., 2000, 105).

The offbeat rhythm Cha-Cha starts with a back basic step from the standard ballroom closed position. On the backward step the man's lead is with his right hand pulling with slight pressure on the lady's back. On the forward basic step the man's lead is a slight push with the left hand. The prep step and the back basic step begin as: Step left foot to the side (count 1, slow), step backward with the right foot (count 2, slow), step forward left foot in place (count 3, slow), step right foot in place next to the left foot (count 4, quick "cha"), step left foot in place (count &, quick "cha"), step right foot in place (count 1, slow "cha"). Continue with a forward basic step. Step forward with the left foot (count 2, slow), step backward right foot in place (count 3, slow), step left foot in place next to the right foot (count 4, quick "cha"), step right foot in place (count &, quick "cha"), step left foot in place (count 1, slow "cha").

The inclusion of a prep step in the offbeat ballroom version, however, makes the dance restrictive so that the partners cannot "play" (a term for improvisation) as they can within the basic on-beat Cha-Cha rhythm. It also led to discrepancy as to whether the name of the dance was the Cha-Cha or Cha-Cha-Cha. Ballroom dances maintained the offbeat rhythm Cha-Cha for the remainder of the century.

Some other Latin dances that were popular at the time, though to a lesser extent, included the Zapateado, the Spanish Flamenco, Calypso, and Paso Doblé. The Calypso was a Dance of Trinidadian West Indian origin, made popular in conjunction with the Harry Belafonte song hit "Calypso." The origin of the words or dance is unclear. But it is certain that the dance was performed to native Calypso-type beats. In 1957, the short-term fad encouraged a Hollywood low budget film aimed at the teenage market titled *Bop Girl Goes Calypso* (Panati 1991, 275).

The Paso Doblé (Spanish translation means "two step") was more common among ballroom dance competition teams than on the social dance floor. One category of DanceSport competition (see Chapter 6) is the Latin group of the Cha-Cha, Samba, Rhumba, Paso Doblé, and Jive (English version of the Jitterbug). The competition division dances are all on the offbeat. Ballroom dance instructors continued to teach the competition version offbeat rhythm rather than the on-beat version that is so much easier for social dance occasions. This is probably the most plausible reason why ballroom dancing faltered and social dancers embraced the dances that did not require stuffy rules or restrictions to body and torso movements. One such dance was the Merengue.

The Merengue originated on the Caribbean Islands and is the national dance of the Dominican Republic. It developed sometime during the mid-nineteenth century among the native tribes. Legend abounds that a victorious general returned from battle with a leg wound and attempted to dance at a celebration in his honor. Rather than embarrass the general, others followed the limp step. Another story said that the dance developed from the sliding step motion of slaves working in the sugar cane fields who were chained together at the feet. Merengue music was played in New York during the 1940s; however, it was not until the early 1950s that the music and the dance developed in America. Luis Alberti's instrumental "Compadre Pedro Juan" was the classic Merengue song. It provided an upbeat joyful rhythm that dancers loved. The native dance is a little quicker rhythm than the American social dance version. The American adaptation is only slightly different from the native versions (Driver 2000, 89).

Unlike the other Latin dances that were danced either off-beat and on-beat, the Merengue is danced on-beat. It is a simple dance that can be learned very quickly and quite easily. The music is lively, playful, and upbeat in 4/4 time with a prominent beat. The steps are in constant rhythm counting 1, 2, 3, 4 without any syncopation or chasses, simply one step to match one beat of music. The basic Merengue rhythm begins in a closed dance position with the feet flat on the floor, with weight on the balls of the feet. The man takes a short step (a sliding or gliding motion) slightly to the left with the left foot (count 1), step with the right foot closing next to the left (count 2), step side to the left with the left foot (count 3), and step with the right foot closing next to the left (count 4). The woman mirrors the man's footwork. The dance is even easier when the couples simply perform the basic step or any variations to a count of 1,2,3,4,5,6,7,8 staying in time with the 8 beats of the bar of music. The variants and turns are performed within the 8 count beat allowing the dancers more time to complete the move but also allows for stylization and improvisation to fit the occasion or mood of the music. The simple on-beat rhythm is what made dancing to Rock 'n' Roll music (see later this chapter) so popular, especially among teenagers.

BOB HORN'S "BANDSTAND," AND THE BUNNY HOP

During the 1950s, television was most responsible for introducing teenagers to dancing. In 1951, Bob Horn, a local Philadelphia radio disc jockey, began broadcasting a daily dance party titled *Bandstand* on WIP radio. The show grew in appeal among teenagers. The following year, rival radio station WFIL enticed Horn to move his popular radio show to their network for a twice-a-day broadcast. WFIL also had a television station, and soon Horn was also the host of a televised version of *Bandstand*. Debuting on October 6, 1952, *Bandstand* broadcast from the WFIL-TV studios located on 46th and Market Streets in West Philadelphia, Monday to Friday, from 3:30 to 4:45 P.M. The WFIL-TV news release listed the simple format:

> The kids come in and dance while the cameras pick up human interest shots that never seem to tire the audience. The new dance steps, the new records, and daily flow of guest stars keep the show rolling along with a fresh outlook each day ("WFIL-TV Biography Bob Horn," 1954).

The dance show was an instant hit, attracting over 1,500 Philadelphia teenagers to the TV studio on the first day. The dancers were between the ages of 14 and 18, and most came from the local area high schools. At first the dancing was Jitterbug to fast records and Fox Trot to slower songs. During the course of the show, a promotional spot featuring one or two musical artists or groups would appear live to lip-sync a record. Lip-syncing was the act of an artist mouthing the words and

Teenagers dancing on *Bandstand* in Philadelphia. Host Bob Horn can be seen in the background, c. 1955.   Courtesy of Urban Archives Temple University.

pantomiming while the actual record was played on the air. Another method of record promotion was the Rate-A-Record segment (Jackson 1997, 18).

For the Rate-A-Record feature, Horn arbitrarily selected two teenagers from the studio audience to provide an off-the-cuff comment on a new song heard for the first time on the show. They could give the record a "score" on a scale of 35 (the low) to 98 (the high). The characteristic of the record most important to the teenage judges was whether it was danceable. The often repeated phrase "I'll give it a ninety-eight because it's got a great beat and it's easy to dance to" gave rise to the slogan most associated with the show. It was also during Horn's tenure as host that *Bandstand* realized its potential to influence new nationwide dance crazes via television (Jackson 1997, 18–19). A WFIL-TV news release recounted Horn's influence regarding dance styles:

His knowledge of popular music, both old and new, has resulted in terrific jumps in record sales when Horn has gone overboard for a new record. Ray Anthony's "The Bunny Hop" climbed well into the hit class in a few days when Horn started his kids doing the dance on "Bandstand" ("WFIL-TV Biography Bob Horn," 1954).

In 1953, the first influential television dance craze was the Bunny Hop danced to a song of the same name by bandleader Ray Anthony. Dance historians Sylvia Dannett and Frank Rachel claim the Bunny Hop originated in a San Francisco high school to a song titled "The Blacksmith Blues." Reportedly, bandleader Ray Anthony saw the dance and wrote a specific tune for the dance titled "The Bunny Hop" (1954, 187).

The Bunny Hop was very similar to the Conga (see Chapter 3). The dance started with as many teenagers as were willing to line up in a Conga line with both hands placed on the hips of the kid in front of them. The left foot/heel would be placed out to the left followed by the right foot/heel placed out to the right, then hopping with feet together forward in unison three times. The hop was repeated three times backward and the pattern was continually repeated (Shore and Clark 1985, 55). Adults also took a liking to the simple and fun Bunny Hop. As the years followed, the actual "hopping" disappeared as well as the Conga rhythm with intermittent kicks. Both dances meshed into a very simplified Conga line where the entire line just placed their hands on the hips of the person in front of them and followed along without any sense of unified rhythm or dance pattern.

Bandstand continued to garner high ratings in the Philadelphia region. However, in June 1956, Horn was arrested for drunk driving, and the publicity combined with rumors about other inappropriate behavior by the popular host caused the producers to drop him from the show. At the time, the television show was still seen only in the Philadelphia area, and many teenagers till relied upon the radio for music.

RADIO DISC JOCKEYS, RHYTHM AND BLUES, AND ALAN FREED

At the end of the war, the nation still relied on millions of radios for entertainment and news. At first, radio continued its format of national network broadcast of radio dramas, comedies, news, and music. By 1950, television (TV) was a dominant force and devastated the radio industry. TV transformed the radio format into a visual spectacular that radio could not match to stay financially viable. With the advent of television, radio did not so much disappear as it went through a transition. The network programs were replaced by regional disc jockeys (DJs) who created their own formats and a market dominated by music.

During the mid 1930s, Al Jarvis in Los Angeles and Martin Block in New York each originated a radio format playing only records for dancing. (Some say Jarvis was the first in 1935.) The "Make Believe Ballroom" replicated the sounds of the sweet bands that routinely played the elegant hotels (see Chapters 2 and 3). During the postwar period with radio losing its programming to television, radio stations searched for similar new creative formats. But rather than a calm and dignified

"Make Believe Ballroom," the new radio DJs were rancorous, jovial, bantering, and joking. The first was Dewey Phillips.

In 1948, Memphis, Tennessee, radio station WDAI was "the nation's first radio station to feature all-black music played by an all-black staff of disc jockeys." WDAI was one of most popular in Memphis. However, Memphis was a southern city as strictly segregated as they come. The WDAI broadcast of Rhythm and Blues artists was limited to daylight hours (Miller 1999, 37).

Dewey Phillips listened to WDAI and began playing the same songs on his evening radio show. On October 29, 1949, Dewey Phillips broadcast his first *Red Hot 'n' Blue* radio show on WHBQ in Memphis. His late-night 45-minute show aired from 10:15 to 11:00 P.M. five nights a week. Phillips had an upbeat flamboyant delivery, and his show garnered more and more white teenage listeners. He soon reached an audience of 100,000 listeners, about one-third the population of Memphis, and the show was extended from 9:00 P.M. to midnight. He quickly became a regional star of broadcasting, creating what was the first "celebrity disc jockey." *Red Hot 'n' Blue* continued for over ten years "changing forever, the way white people would hear black music" (Miller 1999, 34, 36–37).

At the same time, a new development in smaller inexpensive transistors produced radios that were smaller and portable. Unlike the television, which was bulky, expensive, and barely one to a home, the transistor radio was small and inexpensive. As a result, more radios were literally in the hands of many teenagers. Therefore, a teenager could retreat to an out-of-the-way place and listen to a radio program of choice. In order to listen to late-night DJs such as Dewey Phillips, some teenagers would take the small handheld transistor radio and listen while under the covers in their beds. More and more late-night white DJs began playing Rhythm and Blues records by African Americans.

The New York Times described Rhythm and Blues, "as a music of the Thirties and Forties that aimed primarily at the Negro market; that music emphasized the second and fourth beats of each measure [of music]" (Samuels, "Why They Rock 'n' Roll—And Should They?" 1930, 16). Some of the early Rhythm and Blues was sometimes known as "jump blues." Jump blues was an extension of the 1940s big bands (see Chapters 3) and songs such as Count Basie's "One O'Clock Jump." Music historian James Miller described it as "a simplified and superheated version of old-fashioned swing, often boogie-woogie based, usually played by a small combo of piano, bass, and drums, with saxophones and trumpet" (1999, 29). Early proponents included Louis (pronounced "Louie") Jordan and Wynonie Harris.

Jordan began his own band during World War II. He was one of the first artists to have his songs cross over into different segments of society. In 1944, Jordan's "G.I. Jive" became the first song charted by *Billboard* to place at the No. 1 slot in all three charts Pop, Race, and Folk. Other Jordan song hits included "Caldonia," "Choo Choo Boogie," and "Saturday Night Fish Fry." In 1948, *Billboard* changed the name of the three main record charts to Pop, Rhythm and Blues (R&B), and Country and Western. They maintained a separate chart for "Most-Played Juke Box Race Records" and "Best Selling Retail Race Records" (Miller 1999, 30).

In March 1948 the No. 1 record on the Billboard R&B charts was Wynonie Harris's "Good Rockin Tonight." Many have considered it as the first Rock 'n'

Roll song. In April 1949, he had another No. 1 with "All She Wants to Do Is Rock." Throughout 1948, many other R&B hit songs appeared with the word "Rock" in the title, including Jimmy Preston's "Rock the Joint," Roy Brown's "Rockin' at Midnight," and Bill Moore's "We're Gonna Rock, We're Gonna Roll," as well as "Rock and Roll." The problem was not just that African Americans sang them but that the slang for "rock" or "rocking and rolling" meant fornication. Record producer Henry Glover explained that at the time the music "was considered filth" (Miller 1999, 31). On the other hand, the songs were mainly bouncy, spirited, jump blues reminiscent of swing and definitely danceable.

In 1950, a Cleveland record store owner of *Record Rendezvous*, catering mainly to the African American music market, told his friend of the number of white teenagers in his shops buying Rhythm and Blues. He said, "The beat is so strong, that anyone can dance to it without a lesson." His friend was a local radio disc jockey named Alan Freed (Time-Life Books, *Rock & Roll Generation*, 1998, 18).

In 1951, Alan Freed began airing the late night *Moondog Show* on WJW-850 AM, a 50,000-watt Cleveland radio station. He geared his music to the teenage listening audience, playing mainly Rhythm and Blues records by artists including the Treniers, Moonglows, Cadillacs, Chuck Berry, Fats Domino, and Little Richard. He steadfastly refused to play white cover versions (see later this chapter) of any of the original R&B songs. He drew a faithful audience of teenage listeners, both black and white. At that time, he also began sponsoring live stage shows, bringing together many of the same acts he played on the radio. During a time of strict segregation, Freed's stage shows were the first time that music and dancing were presented to racially mixed audiences.

On March 21, 1952, Freed's first show held in the Cleveland Arena, billed as the *Moondog Coronation Ball*, drew a sold-out crowd of over 10,000 teenagers. Thousands of others were turned away, causing a near riot. Around this time Freed began using the on-air term "Rock and Roll" and sometimes "Rock 'n' Roll" to denote the music. In 1954, he moved to the WINS music radio station in New York City.

In New York, Freed called his radio show the *Rock and Roll Party*. One sound byte from an introduction to an early 1955 show began with, "Hello, everybody, yours truly, Alan Freed, the old king of rock and rollers, all ready for another big night of rockin' and rollin', let 'er go! Welcome to *Rock and Roll Party* number one!" (quoted in James Miller 1999, 84–85).

In 1955, Freed's first New York area stage shows on January 14 and 15 were billed as a "Rock 'n' Roll Ball." Music historian James Miller reports that this might be the first use of the phrase with apostrophes (1999, 86). The phrase, when used with the word "and" denoted both to "rock" and "roll." At the time the word was still a slang for fornication and having a good time. Actually, one could either "rock" or one could "roll," one could be done without the other. When the apostrophes linked the two words it became one singular word to denote the music. After Freed's move to New York, most contemporary newspaper and magazine stories spelled it with the apostrophes and began crediting Freed with coining the phrase "Rock 'n' Roll."

On September 2, 1955, Freed held a week-long "Rock 'n' Roll" stage show at the Brooklyn Paramount Theater, once again bringing together a racially mixed audience. The headliner was Chuck Berry. His numerous hit songs included "Maybelline," "Johnny B. Goode," "Sweet Little Sixteen," and "Roll Over Beethoven." Berry clearly remembered that show as a defining moment; he said:

> I doubt that many Caucasian persons would come into a situation that would cause them to know the feeling a black person experiences after being reared under old-time southern traditions and then finally being welcomed by an entirely unbiased and friendly audience, applauding without apparent regard for racial difference (quoted in James Miller 1999, 107).

Freed's stage shows quickly became legendary. The teenage faithful eagerly awaited each and every show.

In 1957, the New York show at the Manhattan Paramount Theater turned out the largest crowd in the 31-year history of the theater. The two-day event, on February 23 and 24, advertised seven screenings of the premier of the movie *Don't Knock the Rock*. The movie starred Freed, as himself, and also many musical performers. The movie contained some memorable contemporary Rock 'n' Roll dance scenes, including teenagers dancing the jitterbug on furniture and some dramatic aerials. The dancing on the furniture scene has an air of spontaneity and, in fact, it was. One of those teenager dancers was Joe Lanza. In an interview in 2004, Lanza remembered,

> It was all unrehearsed impromptu dancing. I had no idea of jumping on the furniture a moment before I did it. None of the Swing dancing was choreographed. It was all improvised. The day before I did my original [aerial] "Jumping Jack's" was admonished by the dance director not to do any aerials, but he was off the set that morning so I just went for it when the camera came on me, so two of my original aerials, my back flip [during the song] "Rippin' it Up" which was followed by original Jumping Jack, almost would never have been recorded (Lanza interview, 2004).

In between screenings of the movie *Don't Knock the Rock*, six live stage shows featured 12 groups of top Rock 'n' Roll performers backed by a 20-piece orchestra. In anticipation of the 8:15 A.M. opening, over 5,000 teenagers were already in line. (They had begun lining up as early as 4:00 A.M.) The theater quickly filled to its capacity of 3,650. During the day, a continuous stream of teenagers, a total of 15,220, waited to see the shows—the line lasted for 18 1/2 hours. Having a good time was the order of the day—watching the movie—listening to music—and dancing.

The New York Times reported, "Inside the theater, boys and girls danced in the aisles, the foyer, and the lobby, [they] stood in their seats and jumped up and down, screamed with delight as performers were announced, stamped their feet in time with the music and sang with the singers." At one point the vigorous feet stamping in the balcony worried the theater owners prompting them to call in both the Fire Department and the Buildings Department. As a precautionary measure over 1,000 youngsters were removed from the protruding balcony sections (Asbury, "Rock 'n' Roll Teen-Agers Tie Up the Times Square Area," 1957, 1, 12).

The following day over 16,000 showed up for the extravaganza. In anticipation, 279 New York City Police officers plus an additional 25 theater police were assigned to the theater—both inside and outside. Outside the police patrolled on foot and on horseback to keep the crowd at bay behind wooden barricades. The theater owners asked the New York City Police Department to patrol the aisles. During the course of the performances, *The New York Times* reported, the "men and women police patrolled the aisles, chasing would-be dancers back to their seats and ordering those who stood up in their seats to sit down...the police managed to thwart attempts to repeat Friday's dancing in the aisles. The youngsters kept trying, however." (Asbury "Times SQ. 'Rocks' For Second day," 1957, 37). For some reason beyond the realm of teenage thought, adults and the authorities just could not accept teenagers dancing and having a good time.

In response to the Rock 'n' Roll show staged by Freed, a *New York Times* headline proclaimed, "Experts Propose Study of 'Craze' Liken it to Medieval Lunacy, 'Contagious Dance Furies' and Bite of Tarantula." Psychiatrist Dr. Joost Meerlo likened the Rock 'n' Roll events to the "contagious epidemic of dance fury" that swept through Europe during the fourteenth century. He likened it to Tarantism "related to a toxic bite by the hairy spider called tarantula" that caused its victims' "breaking into dancing" (Bracker, "Experts Propose Study of Craze," 1957, 12).

In defense, Freed said, "Rock 'n' roll is really swing with a modern name....It's the rhythm that gets the kids. They are starved for music they can dance to after all those years of crooners" (Asbury 1957, 1).When questioned about the so-called lunacy of Rock 'n' Roll dancing, famed dance instructor Arthur Murray quietly replied, "the craze led to an influx of teen-age pupils that had raised total registration 10 percent" (Hammer, "Fad Also Rocks Cash Registers," 1957, 12).

In July 1957, Freed was offered a nationally broadcast television dance show titled *Alan Freed's Big Beat.* The weekly half-hour show was intended to bring the flavor of his theater stage shows to a nationwide audience. However, an innocent incident involving dancing led to furor and subsequent cancellation after the third show. One segment featured the affable and energetic Frankie Lymon. Lymon, an established Rock 'n' Roll singing star, had many hits with his group, the Teenagers, including "Why Do Fools Fall In Love," "I'm Not a Juvenile Delinquent," and "Goody Goody." The energetic Lymon was positioned on a raised platform in the middle of enthusiastic dancing teenagers. At one point, Lymon innocently reached down into the audience and brought up a young white girl to dance a Jitterbug. The producers were appalled, especially ABC's southern affiliates at the so-called "blatant" disregard for the rules of segregation. The show was cancelled immediately (Jackson 1997, 55–56). Freed's subsequent Rock 'n' Roll stage shows were met with resistance even before they began.

In 1958, Alan Freed's scheduled "Big Beat Rock 'n' Roll Show" at the Boston Arena in Massachusetts drew 6,000 fans. However, the show turned into a wild "melee" as local police would not let Freed's show play with the house lights off. *Variety,* the trade journal of the musical and entertainment business, reported

Police had refused to have the Arena lights turned down during the show which he emceed and which headlined Jerry Lee Lewis. Freed announced to audience: "I guess the police here in Boston don't want you to have a good time."

The crowd grew insistent that the house lights be turned down and a confrontation occurred between the teens and the Boston Police. A local Boston newspaper reported that in the ensuing confusion and melee 15 people were "stabbed, slugged, beaten, or robbed by a berserk gang of teenage boys and girls following the jam session."

A follow-up show in Hartford, Connecticut, brought similar results as disruptive behavior ensued. It is unclear, but many eyewitness reports indicated that it was local authorities who prompted "rioting" by the teenagers, causing cancellation of future shows. Boston Mayor John B. Hynes said:

> These so-called musical programs are a disgrace. They must be stopped and they will be stopped here effective at once....I am against rock and roll dances....This sort of performance attracts the troublemakers and the irresponsible....Future requests for dance licenses will be closely examined by the police, the licensing department, and the city censor.

As a result, many of Freed's scheduled Rock 'n' Roll shows were quickly cancelled, including a CYO benefit show on May 6, 1958, in Troy and a May 8 show at the Rensselaer Polytechnic Institute ("Boston Common to Hoot Mon Belt They Rock 'n' Riot Out of This Veldt," *Variety*, May 7, 1958, 1, 58).

Freed was also scheduled for a live stage show in Jersey City, New Jersey. The town council thought otherwise. Mayor B.J. Berry of Jersey City announced at a televised news conference:

> It's our feeling here in Jersey City that this rock and roll rhythm is filled with dynamite. And we don't want the dynamite to go off in the Roosevelt stadium of Jersey City.

Jersey City Commissioner of Public Safety Lawrence Whipple added,

> My department made a very thorough investigations of these so-called [Rock 'n' Roll] programs. We had telephone conversations and correspondence with various munici- palities. Included among these being Hartford, Connecticut; Orange, New Jersey; Asbury Park, and the city of Hoboken. And we find that these programs are not for the good of the community and that's why I ordered them banned (*Rock and Roll: The Early Days*, 1984, video).

However, a May 5, 1958, show did go on as scheduled in Lewiston, Maine, playing to a crowd of 2,500. The only incident concerned a 14-year-old boy, who was arrested for climbing onto the stage—and dancing ("Boston Common to Hoot Mon Belt They Rock 'n' Riot Out of This Veldt," *Variety*, May 7, 1958, 1, 58).

Prior to Alan Freed, the *Billboard* music charts clearly delineated between sedate Pop, rollicking Rhythm and Blues, and down-home Country and Western. The Rhythm and Blues chart was definitely reserved for the segregated African Ameri- can market. Freed's presentation of the so-called "Rock 'n' Roll" was merely a dif- ferent name for Rhythm and Blues. However, during an interview with *Rolling Stone* magazine, singer Ruth Brown was asked to identify the time when Rhythm and Blues became Rock 'n' Roll. She simply replied, "When the white kids started to dance to it." The record that started them dancing was "(We're Gonna) Rock

Around the Clock" (Troy Johnson, "How Dancing in Rock Became Uncool," 2003).

ROCK AROUND THE CLOCK, WHITE COVER VERSIONS, AND "THE KING OF ROCK 'N' ROLL"

As early as 1952, the musical group of Bill Haley and the Comets played a mix of Country and Western, Rhythm and Blues, and Country Swing. Some called it Rockabilly and others called it Rock 'n' Roll. In May 1954, the band achieved moderate success at No. 23 on the *Billboard* Pop chart with the song "(We're Gonna) Rock Around the Clock." The following year, in March 1955, the song was featured during the opening credits for the Hollywood movie *The Blackboard Jungle*. The film itself did not include scenes of teenagers dancing. In fact, the movie represented the serious problems of teens at an inner city high school in New York City. As the credits rolled, however, the song "(We're Gonna) Rock Around the Clock" blared loudly. The kids reacted and for two and a half minutes they literally danced in the movie theater aisles. "(We're Gonna) Rock Around the Clock" quickly went to No. 1 on the *Billboard* Pop charts selling over 6 million records by the end of the year (Miller 1999, 91–93).

The song kicked off a new wave of teenage inspired dancing. Dance historian Ian Driver points out that the singular song "reaffirmed the role of dancing as part of the social ritual of boy-meets-girl, which had been the case in ballrooms and dancehalls since the turn of the century" (2000, 184). Music legend Dick Clark (see later this chapter) remembered, "its initial impact was incredible. Kids hadn't been dancing since the end of the swing era. Suddenly, this spirited tune with a bouncy, rhythmic beat had the kids clapping and dancing" (Uslan and Solomon 1981, 17). Very soon thereafter, teenagers all over America were dancing to Rock 'n' Roll music to artists including Jerry Lee Lewis, Chuck Berry, Little Richard, and Buddy Holly.

Unlike Swing and Jazz that assigned drums and bass to play rhythm, Rock 'n' Roll used those instruments to play a heavy beat that "drove" the sound of the music. Similar to Rhythm and Blues, the accent was on the second and fourth beats of music. The prominent lead instrument was the solid body electric guitar. In 1950, Leo Fender introduced the solid-body *Telecaster* Electric Guitar (revised in 1954 as the *Stratocaster*). Prior to the solid-body instrument, guitars were deep bodied with a hole under the strings to allow the music to resonate. The solid body enabled the music to be picked up electronically and transferred to an amplifier, thereby allowing a heavier downbeat and louder sound. The solid-body guitar would become the trademark of Rock 'n' Roll bands.

Teenagers loved the music and went Rock 'n' Roll crazy, and they danced, and danced, and danced. They appropriated a new slang, incorporating some of the old but mostly new, to describe Rock 'n' Roll. In response to the question "what is it about Rock and Roll?" teenage answers included, "Rock 'n' Roll is crazy music man," "That music sends me," and "Rock 'n' Roll is cool daddy and you know it" (*Rock and Roll: The Early Days*, 1984, video). The music and dance craze led to many Hollywood movies capitalizing on the teenage fad. They included *Rock Around the Clock* (1956), *Rock, Rock, Rock* (1956), and *Don't Knock the Rock* (1957). A movie filmed in two weeks, *Rock Around the Clock* starred Bill Haley and the Comets and DJ Alan Freed, featured nine songs by Haley, and preached the innocence of the music.

The teenage fashion for girls included rolled up jeans, bobby socks, and saddle shoes. For a dress-up dance, girls wore below the knee dresses and bouffant styled hair held in place with lots of hair spray. Boys sported collared button-down shirts, slacks, and crew cuts. For a dress-up dance, boys wore either a sport jacket, shirt and tie, and matching slacks or a suit. Some young teenage males wore "ducktail" haircuts, jeans, and white t-shirts. Tight black jeans and a leather jacket was the sign of a true "teenage rebel" (Hammer, "Fad Also Rocks Cash Registers," 1957, 12). In order to groom a ducktail, the hair was grown a little longer. Styling and shaping the hair was achieved by the use of hair wax, Vaseline, or Brylcreem, leading to the term "greasers." Greasers were known to continually whip out a pocket comb and keep the hair in place. Both groups sported white socks (Time-Life Books, *Rock & Roll Generation*, 1998, 86–87).

Adults, however, were in a panic over the new music. Newspapers nationwide blared headlines such as "Rock-and-Roll Called Communicable Disease," "Teenage Music Craze Has Parents Worried 'We're losing control of our own children!'" The newspaper headlines asked, "Does Rock and Roll Cause Delinquency?" "Why They Rock 'n' Roll—And Should They?" and "Music or Madness? Rock and roll music has stirred up a whirlwind of adult protest" (*Rock and Roll: The Early Days*, 1984, video). FBI director J. Edgar Hoover called the music "a corrupting influence." *Time* magazine related the concerts to "Hitler mass meetings." A Baptist preacher called it a "new low in spiritual degeneracy" (quoted in Time-Life Books, *Rock & Roll Generation*, 1998, 44–45). The Reverend Jimmy Snow bellowed:

> I know how it feels when you sing it. I know what it does to you. And I know the evil feeling that you feel when you sing it. I know the lost position that you get into and the beat. Well, if you talk to the average teenager of today and you ask them what it is about Rock and roll music that they like. The first they'll say it's the beat, the beat, the beat (*Rock and Roll: The Early Days*, 1984, video).

The New York Times decried, "Rock 'n' roll exploits this same heavy beat [as Rhythm & Blues]—by making it heavier, lustier, and transforming it into what has become known as The Big Beat. It is a tense, monotonous beat that often gives rock 'n' roll music a jungle-like persistence." Former crooner and teen idol Frank Sinatra (see Chapter 3), obviously forgetting the admiration shown him by teenage bobby-soxers and the adult attacks of his own crooning during World War II, said "Rock 'n' roll smells phony and false. It is sung, played, and written for the most part by cretinous goons and by means of its almost imbecilic reiteration, and sly lewd, in plain fact, dirty lyrics" (Samuels, "Why They Rock 'n' Roll—And Should They?" 1958, 16).

In reality, much of the protest stemmed from the fact that many of the recording artists were African American. In a filmed television statement, the Executive Secretary of the Alabama White Citizens Council decried, "The obscenity and vulgarity of the Rock and Roll music is obviously a means by which the white man and his children can be driven to the level of the 'nigra.'" His cohort, the Chairman of the Alabama White Citizens Council, a local business owner of a used car lot, arrogantly displayed a sign that read, "We serve WHITE customers Only." He steadfastly added, "We set up a twenty man committee to do away with this vulgar and cannibalistic nigger rock and roll bop" (*Rock and Roll: The Early Days*, 1984, video).

In a *New York Times* interview, one young brown-haired teenager named Vivian simply rebutted, "The main thing about this music is that it's truly lively—it's not dead. It makes you want to dance. With a waltz you have to be in a good mood to dance to it. But with rock 'n' roll no matter what your mood is, it gets you" (Samuels, "Why They Rock 'n' Roll—And Should They?" 1958, 17–19). However, Rock 'n' Roll music was just too popular and profitable to be ignored. To reduce some of the negative aspects of the music, record producers hastily began recording "white cover" versions of popular Rhythm and Blues hits.

A white cover version was created when a white artist or group was chosen to record a song that was previously recorded by an African American artist. At first, white radio listeners were not even aware that another version existed. Basically white DJs played white recording artists. Prior to 1956, African Americans had limited radio airplay and were relegated to segregated sections of record stores (in many instances in a totally separate store in a segregated neighborhood). For example, during the 1950s in downtown Hollywood, California, the large record stores would not stock records by black artists (Macías 2004, 707). In order to capitalize on the demand for R&B records, one African American entrepreneur, John Dolphin, hired a disc jockey to broadcast from his 24-hour record store, Dolphin's of Hollywood. Located in South Central Los Angeles on Central Avenue, the idea of the store was to "bring Hollywood to Negroes." The rollicking fun attracted youths of all ethnic backgrounds to travel, some as far as 30 miles, to purchase R&B records and to hear live recording acts. In many instances, however, the Los Angles police would enter Dolphin's store and roust whites to leave the store, citing that "Central Avenue was too dangerous for white people." The *Los Angeles Sentinel* reported that on one night at least a dozen officers "formed a human chain at the front door [further] terrifying Caucasian customers...and rousing them from the neighborhood" (Macías 2004, 707–710).

Disc jockey Alan Freed was one of the few white radio disc jockeys who refused to play white cover versions. White cover versions were common from 1954 to 1956. In 1954, The Crew Cuts had two successful hits with cover versions of "Earth Angel" and "Sh' Boom." Not many people had even heard or known that "Earth Angel" by The Penguins and "Sh' Boom" by The Chords were Rhythm and Blues hits before the Crew Cuts recordings (*Rock and Roll: The Early Days*, 1984, video).

Sometimes the original R&B version was a bit too risqué. For example, Etta James's "Roll With Me Henry" had overtones of sexual fornication. The white cover version by Georgia Gibbs had the lyrics and the title changed to "Dance With Me Henry." Gibbs also had a hit with a cover of LaVern Baker's "Tweedle Dee." Sometimes, as in the case of singer Lloyd Price's song "Stagger Lee," a white cover version was not needed, but the lyrical content needed changing. In 1957, prior to his national appearance on *American Bandstand* (see later in this chapter), Price was asked to change the lyrics because of the violent content. The watered-down version became known as the "Bandstand version."

Pat Boone was one artist who capitalized on white cover versions. Boone presented a wholesome image of devoted husband and father. He was extremely popular during the 1950s, selling over 20 million records. He also had a television show and wrote a best-selling book *Twixt Twelve and Twenty: Pat talks to teenagers* (1958). The book provided teen advice on going steady, kissing ("kissing for fun is like playing with a beautiful candle in a room full of dynamite"), finances, and spirituality (Time-Life Books, *Rock & Roll Generation*, 1998, 46–47). Boone explained why white cover versions were necessary. He said:

> It was at that time an absolute wall an impenetrable wall between pop and R&B [Rhythm & Blues]. There were R&B stations, R&B artists [and] there was R&B music. But, it was not gonna get played in its original form on pop stations. It was just too ragged. "Oh in some cases it was a little suggestive or more in some cases even explicit" (*Rock 'n' Roll Explodes*, 1995, video).

But Boone's "Rock and Roll" did not expend much stage energy beyond some foot tapping and occasionally loosening his tie and finger snapping to an up-tempo cover of Little Richard's "Tutti Frutti." The absurdity of the cover versions was Boone's own attempt to cover Fats Domino's "Ain't That a Shame." Boone wanted to change the title to a grammatically correct "Isn't That a Shame." He was convinced otherwise and recorded the song as written by Domino. But in concert, Boone actually took to explaining the grammatical correctness of the song. In later years he took it as a joke and good-naturedly made fun of his own early ingressions (Miller, 102). Boone might not have been a true Rock 'n' Roll singer, but there was one person who certainly epitomized the music—his name was Elvis Presley.

More than any other artist, Elvis Presley defined the image of Rock 'n' Roll. Presley's music crossed the cultural barrier between black and white and transcended segregation. According to singer and 1950s Rhythm and Blues legend Ruth Brown,

> Where Elvis was concerned there was no color line, because everybody liked his music. And Elvis Presley was what they were looking for to get that music, not necessarily accepted because it was already accepted, but permissible for the white kids to listen to openly (*Rock 'n' Roll Explodes*, 1995, video).

In addition to the music, Elvis moved and danced in a way that no other white entertainer had done before. Musician and songwriter Hank Ballard (see Chapter 5) said of Elvis,

> See in white society the movement of the butt—shakin' the leg, all that was considered obscene for white folk. And here is this white boy and that grind—rollin' his butt and shakin' that notorious leg [laughs]...I hadn't even seen a black dude doin it—Elvis he had some movements I had never witnessed (*Rock 'n' Roll Explodes*, 1995, video).

In 1955, at separate performances in San Diego and Florida, authorities warned Presley that if he moved at all during his show "he would be arrested on obscenity charges" (Troy Johnson, "How Dancing in Rock Became Uncool," 2003).

Presley's national television debut came on January 28, 1956, appearing on Tommy and Jimmy Dorsey's *Stage Show.* At the time, musician and record producer Quincy Jones was a writer for the Dorsey brothers' show. He recalled that the studio musicians of the Swing era Dorsey brothers band could not play Presley's Rock 'n' Roll songs. Jones remembered, "The band was pissed off. They couldn't get into it or play with each other." Presley's manager, at the time Sam Phillips, sent for the band in Memphis, and Elvis performed brilliantly. However, Tommy Dorsey did not think much of Presley or Rock 'n' Roll. After Presley's performance, he said, "This Dude he'll be outer here tomorrow." One critic called the performance "the kind of animalism that should be confined to dives and bordellos." But the next day the station received over 8,000 fan letters (Time-Life Books, *Rock & Roll Generation,* 1998, 64).

On April 3, 1956, Elvis made another national television network appearance on Milton Berle's *The Milton Berle Show.* Berle told a nationwide viewing audience, "It's no secret that Elvis Presley is the fastest rising young singer in the entertainment industry today." On the Berle show, Elvis was allowed to perform as he wished. On his follow-up performance on June 5, 1956, he sang an upbeat Rock 'n' Roll version of a Rhythm and Blues No. 1 song titled "Hound Dog." Actually Elvis chose the song (a No. 1 R&B Hit for "Big Mama" Thornton) simply to have fun. Fronting a small combo of stand-up bass, rhythm guitar, and drums, his whole body was shown, performing and dancing as only Elvis could with gyrating pelvis and hip movements (*Rock and Roll: The Early Days,* 1984, video). "Hound Dog" became an immediate hit with his fans, but the media fallout was predictable.

Television critic Jack Gould of *The New York Times* declared, "[Presley] is a rock-and-roll variation of one of the most standard acts in show business: the virtuoso of the hootchy-kootchy…that heretofore has been primarily identified with the repertoire of the blonde bombshells of the burlesque runway" (May 23, 1993, B6). Congressman Emanuel Celler decried, "the bad taste that is exemplified by the Elvis Presley 'Hound Dog' music, with his animal gyrations which are certainly most distasteful to me, are violative of all that I know to be in good taste" (quoted in Miller, 132–133). Television sought to censor him.

On July 1, 1956, Presley made another national television appearance to sing "Hound Dog." This time on *The Steve Allen Show.* However, Allen said, "I will not allow him to do anything that will offend anyone" (Miller, 135). In doing so, they insisted that Presley appear wearing a tuxedo and sing to a dog. It was also explicitly added that any suggestion of pelvic movement was "against the rules" and was to be eliminated. Elvis felt snubbed and vowed to never succumb again to restraint. A few weeks later Elvis made the first of three appearances on the Ed Sullivan Show and became a sensation of the likes that had never been seen before (*Rock 'n' Roll Explodes,* 1995, video).

On September 9, 1956, an estimated 42 million people saw Presley's Sunday evening performance on *The Ed Sullivan Show* (over 82 percent of the television viewing audience). However, Sullivan thought Presley's gyrations were vulgar and refused to allow his wiggling hips to be broadcast to a national audience.

Therefore, on January 7, 1957, during Presley's third and final appearance on *The Ed Sullivan Show*, the producers instructed the cameras to close in on Elvis and only show him only from the waist up ("Parental Advisory: Music Censorship in America: Censorship Incidents 1950s," n.d.).

Despite the attempt to censor him, Elvis continued to sell records. In 1957, the biggest selling song of the year was Presley's "All Shook Up," selling an astonishing 2.45 million copies. Before the decade was over, Presley had sold over 28 million records (Samuels, "Why They Rock 'n' Roll—And Should They?" 1958, 16). Presley also made a series of successful movies, beginning with *Love Me Tender* (1956), *Loving You* (1957), *Jailhouse Rock* (1957), and *King Creole* (1958) (Stearns and Stearns 1994, 3).

The popularity of Elvis Presley and Rock 'n' Roll cannot be underestimated. Although reporters, critics, and the media relentlessly attacked Elvis and his "dirty body movements," Elvis represented a cultural phenomenon unlike any other. According to historian David Halberstam, beginning with Elvis Presley "the new music had entered the mainstream of American culture" (2001, 479). Dubbed the "King of Rock 'n' Roll" Elvis was just too profitable to be ignored. Elvis Presley was certainly the most recognizable name in Rock 'n' Roll. Therefore it was no coincidence that on August 5, 1957, host Dick Clark opened the national broadcast of the teenage dance show *American Bandstand* playing Elvis Presley's "Teddy Bear."

DICK CLARK AND "AMERICAN BANDSTAND"

On July 9, 1956, with little fanfare, Dick Clark replaced the embattled Bob Horn as host of the regional *Bandstand*. At the time of Bob Horn's troubles, WFIL also had Dick Clark under contract as a radio disc jockey. Clark's clean-cut wholesome image presented a likeable quality that seemed to magnify under the scrutiny of the television cameras. His youthful "boyish" looks (Clark was born in 1929) appeared little beyond the years of any teenager on the show. Under Clark's guidance, who served as coproducer, the show combined the ideas of television, music, and dancing together in a unique presentation and format.

Starting with Bob Horn and continuing with Dick Clark, *Bandstand* featured many African American musical groups and singers. Although the city of Philadelphia had a significant African American population, very few African Americans were ever allowed into the studio. When they were, it was expressly apparent that no interracial dancing would occur. The nature of television of the time period was an idealized version of a white nonethnic environment. The show itself would feature numerous ethnic and African American performers, but the dancers remained white. A significant number of the regulars and performers were Italian Americans of working class parents.

In 1957, Clark was especially busy. He continued to do *Bandstand* each weekday afternoon, and the show was successful enough to expand the broadcast from 2:30 to 5:00 P.M. He also made over 180 personal appearances at record hops and prepared to expand the regional show to a nationwide audience. In addition, ABC-TV made the decision to broadcast the show across the entire nation. In

Teenagers line up outside WFIL-TV studios in Philadelphia waiting to get on *American Bandstand*, c. 1959.   Courtesy of Urban Archives Temple University.

preparation for the nationwide broadcast, ABC-TV changed the name of the show to *American Bandstand* (Jackson 1997, 127).

The show continued from the Philadelphia WFIL-TV studios, and the national broadcast picked up the show at 3:00 and ended it at 4:30 P.M. Local Philadelphia TV still aired the full 2:30 to 5:00 P.M. slot ("Music Show Bows On A.B.C.-TV Aug. 5," 1957, 53). Within weeks, *American Bandstand* had an audience of over 20 million viewers. The large majority were teenagers who rushed home from school to watch the late afternoon show (Jackson 1997, 65).

However, television critic J. P. Shanley of *The New York Times* was not too praiseworthy of the first national broadcast. He wrote, "Viewers who are beyond voting age are not likely to derive much pleasure from 'American Bandstand,' the disc jockey show that began yesterday on Channel 7." He added that adults might find the 90-minute show "of music and dancing to be something of an ordeal." Shanley obviously did not think highly of the opening Elvis Presley song, "Teddy Bear," cynically stating that after the opening song, "Some of the subsequent records were less atrocious." Shanley did credit Clark as "well-groomed." He added, "There were no motorcycle jackets and hardly a sideburn in the crowd.... The girls wore pretty gowns and the boys were dressed conservatively." In response to the dancers, he quipped, "The quality of dancing was poor." ("TV: Teen-Agers Only," 1957, 42).

But that was the point. The appeal of the show was that any teenager sitting in his or her living room anywhere throughout the United States could identify and even emulate the average kid on *American Bandstand*. All the dancers *were* amateurs. In fact, no professional dancers were allowed on the show, and any regular who turned professional was not allowed back on the show. With the national broadcast of *American Bandstand* reaching so many viewers, the regulars became celebrities in their own right and received fan mail by the thousands. Television viewers had their favorite "couples" including Bob Clayton and Justine Carelli, as well Kenny Rossi and Arlene Sullivan (Jackson 1997, 70–71).

The regulars also introduced fashion trends that were usually copied. One fashion trend was the emergence of the "Philadelphia collar." Many viewers wrote in about the unique style of collar worn outside the sweater among the females on the show. Unbeknownst to the viewers, the collars were actually part of school uniforms. Although the local area Catholic high schools could not forbid the students from dancing on the show, they did forbid the wearing of school uniforms on television. Since the start of the show coincided with the end of the school day, many regulars could not go home first. Therefore, they either changed in the bathroom or simply put a sweater over their school uniforms (Jackson 1997, 70–72).

Under the national spotlight the show slowly shifted to a clean-cut mage of white teen idols including Frankie Avalon, Bobby Rydell, Fabian Forte (Philadelphia neighborhood kids), Bobby Darin, Annette Funicello, and Connie Francis (coincidentally all Italian Americans). *American Bandstand* historian John A. Jackson claims, "By using *Bandstand* to introduce young white singers less offensive than 'Elvis the Pelvis,' [Clark] did more than any other non-performer to change the face of rock 'n' roll" (1997, 41).

The immediate success of the show gave rise to an ABC-TV Monday night version of *American Bandstand*. In the fall of 1957, Clark hosted an hour-long evening show from 7:30 to 8:30 P.M. It appeared that the nighttime slot was a bit too ambitious in competition with the adult viewing audience, and it was switched. The first Saturday evening show aired February 15, 1958, from 7:30 to 8:30 P.M. but soon was streamlined to one-half hour. The Saturday night *Dick Clark's Beechnut Show* (sponsored by Beechnut chewing gum) was broadcast from the Little Theater in Manhattan. It was a fast-paced half-hour of recording stars aimed at the teenage market. However, the weekend evening show hardly ever featured teenage dancing on camera. On one show in November 1959, Clark sat in the audience and talked with the kids in the audience about his own book for teenagers titled *Your Happiest Years*. The Saturday night format ended in August 1960 when the Beechnut contract expired (Jackson 1997, 199).

Teenagers dancing on the nationally televised *American Bandstand*. Host Dick Clark can be seen in the background.   Courtesy of Photofest.

Once again the older adult critics were quite harsh. In February 1959, critic J.P. Shanley wrote that the performers on the Saturday night show were "egocentric incompetents, entirely lacking in talent but wallowing in wealth and adulation because of their hypnotic effect on their young worshippers" (Shanley, "Television," 1959, 587). In April of that same year, Bill Ladd of the *Louisville Courier-Journal* said the show "might be a documentary on incipient idiocy" ("Teen-Agers' Understanding Big Brother," 1959, 1). Despite it all, *American Bandstand* continued its popularity among the teenagers and was widely copied.

Other similar *Bandstand* type regional shows included *Detroit Bandstand*, *Connecticut Bandstand*, former bandleader Ted Steele's *Teen Bandstand* in New York, *Bandstand Matinee* hosted by Jim Lounsberry in Chicago, as well as *Milt Grant's Record Hop* in Washington, D.C., on WTTG-TV, The *Grady and Hurst Show* on WPFH-TV in Wilmington, Delaware, *The Art Laboe Show* on KTLA-TV in

149

Los Angeles, *The Buddy Deane Show* in Baltimore, and George Edick's *Party Time* on KTVI-TV in St. Louis, Missouri.

Despite all the other regional teenage dance shows, *American Bandstand* was the only show broadcast nationwide. Therefore, it remained the most influential. It inspired many songs including the notable "Queen of the Hop" by Bobby Darin. The song tells of a 16-year-old teenager who dances and watches *American Bandstand* every day. It also mentions contemporary dances including the Chicken, the Bop, and the Stroll.

THE STROLL, THE FISH, THE HAND JIVE, THE MADISON, AND THE BOP

The Stroll was a slow Line dance commonly enjoyed in African American communities within the major cities. The dance was inspired by the Chuck Willis Rhythm and Blues song "C.C. Rider." The Philadelphia *Bandstand* kids picked up on it, and once they performed it on television it spread among teenagers nationwide. In response to the newfound dance, Dick Clark suggested to a group called the Diamonds that a song should be written specifically for the dance. In a short time, they recorded a song appropriately titled "The Stroll." The song had a slower arrangement than "C.C. Rider," but it had a sensual catchy rhythm that made it the classic song to accompany the dance (Shore and Clark 1985, 58).

American Bandstand regulars continued to set the pattern for dancers that teenagers nationwide would copy. Joanne Montecarlo recalled one of her favorite dances to do on the television show was the Circle Dance. As an alternative version of a Square Dance, Montecarlo described,

> About six or eight regulars would form a circle and dance around the back of someone and take their hand and go to the next one, and so on. Say, a girl would start, and she would turn around and take the arm of a guy and dance around the back of the circle, outside of it, making hand contact with

Dick Clark described the Stroll as "a hip update of the old Virginia Reel." Two contra lines were formed, males on one side and females on the other. Each line performed a series of stylized steps. The stylized steps were simply a repeated 12-count segment. Boys started with their feet together touching the left foot diagonally forward (count 1) and bringing the left foot back touching next to the right foot (count 2). They proceeded down the line to the boys left with a 4-count vine step. The vine step placed the left foot diagonally forward putting all the weight on the left foot (count 3), stepping right crossing behind the left leg (count 4), stepping side left (count 5), and touching the right foot next to the left foot (count 6). Going back down the line to the boy's right; touch right foot diagonally forward (count 7), and bring the right foot back touching next to the left foot (count 8). Proceed down the line stepping with a 4-count vine step to the boy's right. Step diagonally forward putting all the weight on the right foot (count 9), step left crossing behind the right leg (count 10), step side right (count 11) and touch the left foot next to the right foot. The girls started with the right foot and mirrored the boy's footwork. The lines would continue moving side to side.

The couple at the far end of the line (boys right side and girls left side) stepped toward the center in the stroll rhythm of the six-count diagonal vine step. The boy and girl met face-to-face in the center of the contra lines and "sashayed in their coolest, most low-down fashion between the two lines." At the end of the line, they would separate and join the end of their respective gender line and continue in the "stroll" rhythm while couples at the far end of the line would enter the center to "stroll down the lane" (Shore and Clark 1985, 58).

everyone, and then she would end up in line and the next person would go. And it was all done in circular fashion (quoted in Shore and Clark 1985, 59).

The Circle Dance did not last long, though one dance that never went out of style was the slow dance.

Slow dancing continued as a regular dance among both teenagers and adults. Many teenagers had learned the simple Fox Trot from their parents (see Chapter 1) and applied it to the slower ballads. However, during this time teenagers began dancing a risqué version that was called the Fish. Actually, the Fish was just a new name given to an updated version of the Slow Drag (see Chapter 1). In the Fish, the dancers did not necessarily concentrate on any step pattern as much as the young male partner concentrated on trying to slowly grind his pelvis area on the thigh of his female partner. *American Bandstand* was quick to notify the dancers that the Fish would not be tolerated. In addition, at teenage dances nationwide, chaperones were quick to separate any teenagers attempting to dance the Fish.

In the summer of 1958, the Hand Jive was the rage. The hand dance was done to the Johnny Otis song "Willie and the Hand Jive." It was a 16-count hand dance that could be done as a couple or even sitting down. The simple dance started as both hands slap the thighs (counts 1, 2), clap hands (counts 3, 4), cross right hand palm down under left hand (counts 5&6), repeat with right hand over left hand (counts 7&8), make a fist with each hand, tap right fist on left fist (counts 9, 10), tap left fist on right fist (counts 11, 12), make hitchhike motion with right thumb over right shoulder (counts 13, 14), repeat with left thumb (counts 15, 16), and the sequence is continuously repeated. Some versions had slight variations. The movies *American Graffiti* (1974) and *Grease* (1978) each featured a sock hop dance scene (see later in this chapter) featuring the Hand Jive.

Another Line dance that the *American Bandstand* regulars performed on television was the Madison. The teenage television viewing audience "picked up" on the dance fad at the end of 1958, and it lasted until 1960. The dance first appeared among working class African Americans in midwestern cities. It is unsure whether the dance originated in an African American section of Baltimore, in a Detroit dance hall, or in a Cleveland bar. It is known that it was danced to the Ray Bryant song "The Madison Time." In the song itself, Bryant acts in the same manner as an American Square Dance caller. The recorded song called out steps performed in a sequence of short counts. *Time* magazine described the dance as follows:

A simple two-step, the dance lends itself to any music with a steady 4/4 beat—and allows innumerable variations: after the basic Madison step is completed, the caller can ask for the Big M...for a snatch of Charleston, for some cha cha cha, or for the step known as the "Jackie Gleason"...When a pattern is finished he may call: "Erase it," *i.e.* repeat the pattern in reverse. The variations often have a sports flavor, as in "the Wilt Chamberlain Hook," [Hall of Fame basketball player] in which the dancer suddenly goes stiff-legged and completes his shuffle with a Chamberlain-style hook shot. Baltimore devotees like "the Unitas," [the football quarterback of the Baltimore Colts] in which the dancer shuffles around with arm cocked as if to forward pass ("The Newest Shuffle," 1960, 44).

It did not require a lot of space and was danced at sock hops, in bars, in soda fountains, or at just about any place that had music or a jukebox. When the song was performed live, the band could call out any number of different dance steps.

A picture perfect example of the complete dance was prominently featured in the movie *Hairspray* (1988). The movie incidentally parodied *Bandstand* type teenage dance shows of the 1950s, specifically *The Buddy Deane Show* from Baltimore, Maryland. Deane's show was the top rated regional television dance program in the United States. However, it maintained a strict "whites only" program. Their answer to the race situation was to have a "Negro day" once a month (Jackson 1997, 141–142). Ironically, most, if not all, the new teenage dance fads originated among African Americans, but the dances did not become nationwide fads until they were "premiered" by white dancers on the television dance shows such as *American Bandstand*.

Many musical groups began the pattern of trying to write a song to fit a new dance fad. It was also apparent that by the time a song was written, recorded, and then released the particular dance fad might well be over. One example was the Rock 'n' Roll song "At the Hop" by Danny and the Juniors. In response to the Bop dance, they wrote a song titled "Let's All Do The Bop." Dick Clark, who by this time had developed a keen sense of the teenage trend, suggested a title change. The group changed the title and recorded "At the Hop." Clark was correct, the Bop dance quickly faded. However, the spirited upbeat "At the Hop," a song about dancing and dance fads, was an enduring hit. It was a favorite at weddings and social gatherings well into the beginning of the twenty-first century. Many, who either long ago forgot about the Bop, or never learned it, simply danced a fast Rock 'n' Roll version of the Jitterbug.

The Bop was a dance where the partners hardly ever held each other in a closed dance position. It originated in southern California in response to Gene Vincent's song hit "Be-Bop-a-Lula." It was later done to another Vincent hit "Dance to the Bop" and the Danny and the Juniors classic "At the Hop." Dick Clark first saw it when some teenagers visiting from California were dancing it in a corner of the studio. He asked them to teach the dance to some of the *Bandstand* regulars. During the ensuing weeks, it was danced almost daily, and teenagers nationwide quickly copied the dance. Clark described the pogo-style movement, "In the Bop, the partners faced each other and jumped up and down in place, grinding their heels back and forth each time they landed. It was a physically demanding dance so holding hands was virtually impossible for more than a few moments into it" (Shore and Clark 1985, 55–58).

Many other fad dances followed, but not with quite the same lasting impression. They included the Walk, the Shake, the Slop, and a combined Cha-Cha and Calypso called the "Cha-lypso." Also a new host of Animal dances (see Chapter 1) with names such as the Chicken, the Monkey, the Birdland, and the Pony. Two Animal dances considered too risqué for *Bandstand* were the Alligator and the Dog. Other than the Cha-lypso the fad dances did not involve touching your partner, thus setting the stage for the following decade when the Twist would break from all the past traditions of American social dancing (Shore and Clark 1985, 58–59).

The Places to Dance

To put a little fun in your life—try dancing!

—Kathryn Murray, 1950

I'd rather dance than eat.

—Pauline Sadowski, 1957

COMMERCIAL DANCE HALLS, ROSELAND, AND "THE FEMININE MYSTIQUE"

In the postwar years, bandleaders and musicians who had been away at war sought to pick up where they left off. Older bands were reformed, and even some new bands formed. Initially, the locations and engagements were plentiful. In 1947, Tex Beneke (with the remnants of the Glenn Miller Orchestra) opened at the Hollywood Palladium and drew an astounding 6,750 dancers. However, the Beneke engagement might have been the last significant time that a band and dancers would congregate in a commercial dance hall for the pure enjoyment of dancing to the music of a live orchestra. Dance band historian Leo Walker wrote, "The ten year period comprising the 1950s was one of steady decline of the dance band business from its once top position as a form of live entertainment to a situation where only a few of its former great names could prosper" (1990, 113, 211).

Initially, adults continued to frequent the nightclubs to enjoy an evening of dinner, entertainment, and dancing. Unfortunately, the wartime imposed 20 percent entertainment tax was still in effect, and the cost of an evening in a nightclub was expensive. (In 1946, the ballroom owners formed the National Ballroom Operators of America. One agenda item was to repeal the wartime entertainment tax, which was not rescinded until 1951.) By mid-1947, attendance figures at nightclubs and commercial dance halls began to decline. Many establishments that had previously been opened six nights a week cut back to four or five nights and then to only weekends. Eventually many closee up completely. In 1947, the Trianon and Aragon Ballrooms in Chicago (see Chapter 2) claimed, "more dancers each week than all other Chicago ballrooms combined." However, during the 1950s, both ballrooms maintained a strict "whites only" policy. At a time of growing nationwide sympathy towards desegregation, Civil Rights groups routinely picketed the ballrooms. Rather than compromise its policy, in 1954 the Trianon was closed to dancing (Leo Walker 1990, 107–108).

The famed Savoy Ballroom in New York City remained open until 1958 when the social and political climate rendered its closing. It was torn down to make way for a retail store and apartment housing. In 2002, a dedication plaque was placed at the site, which read in part, "During a time of racial segregation and strife, the Savoy was one of the most culturally and racially integrated of institutions, and its fame was international....It was a catalyst for innovation where dancers and musicians blended influences to forge new, widespread and long-lasting traditions in music and dance."

Dancers at the famed Savoy Ballroom in New York City in 1953. The ballroom that gave birth to the Lindy Hop was torn down in 1958 and replaced with a retail store and apartment housing.   Photo by Hans Von Nolde. AP/Wide World Photos.

By 1954, the Taxi-dance halls were almost nonexistent. A study by sociologist Clyde Vedder found that only six of the 50 largest cities still had Taxi-dance halls. For example, New York, which in 1930 had 27 Taxi-dance halls, had but only 10 in 1954. At the same time, in Los Angeles only two of nine remained since 1930. One dance hall that eliminated the Taxi-dance hall concept in 1951 but still thrived on couples social dancing was Roseland (Frank, "They'd Rather Dance Than Eat," 1957, 24).

Throughout the postwar period, Roseland Dance City (more commonly known as the Roseland Ballroom) in New York City was one of the few dance halls that continued to offer dancing every evening as well as weekday matinee sessions. The large dance floor at 60 feet by 185 feet could accommodate 1,250 couples. Since its opening in 1919, it was also under the same continuous ownership of Louis J. Brecker, and more than 20 million customers had passed through its doors. During that time, Roseland served as an elegant Dance Palace that also employed 150 Taxi-dance hostesses. By 1951, only four hostesses remained, and the concept of Taxi-dancing at Roseland was soon eliminated.

By the mid-1950s, Roseland continued to attract customers and maintained a "refined atmosphere" among its dancing clientele. The mainstay dances included the Waltz, Fox Trot, Rhumba, Mambo, Samba, Cha-Cha, and an occasional Paso

Roseland Ballroom on Broadway and 51st Street in New York City. Since opening in 1919 more than 20 million customers had passed through its doors. This photo was taken in 1945. In 1952, it moved around the corner and continued regular dancing through the end of the twentieth century.   Courtesy of Photofest.

Doblé. In 1957, Brecker counted over 500 "Roseland regulars" (most over the age of 40 years old) who danced at least twice a week. He boasted, "You won't find a better-behaved crowd anywhere." Roseland dancer Harry Silbert, a 54-year-old furrier said, "I love dancing. It's my life. I met my wife here. I bring my son and daughter to enjoy dancing. It's the only hobby I have. I don't drink, smoke, or play cards. Dancing is the only social outlet I need." Pauline Sadowski, a department store salesperson, added, "I'd rather dance than eat. I skip lunches and go without other luxuries. All my money goes on clothes for dancing. It's my life."

As part of its "refined atmosphere," Roseland also resisted the influx of Rock 'n' Roll dancing (see earlier in this chapter). A house rule was strictly maintained that "excludes youngsters more effectively: rock 'n' roll, the jitterbug and similar antics are prohibited." A restrained version of the Lindy Hop was allowed; however, an observer noted, "but the gentleman's feet never leave the floor and the lady never winds up in the chandelier." In October 1957, reporter Stanley Frank of the *Saturday Evening Post* spent an entire week observing the Roseland dancers. He concluded that, "Roseland is a valuable repository of wacky Americana, but it serves a more useful purpose today by teaching us to endure the aberrations of the

Roseland "regulars" Lucky and Maria Kargo practice in the upstairs dance studio, c. 1954.   Courtesy of Dolores Leaver.

younger generation" (Frank, "They'd Rather Dance Than Eat," 1957, 24–25, 114–120, especially 116).

Roseland, however, was one of the very few ballrooms across America that was able to survive. Ballrooms all across America experienced a severe decline in attendance. Former bandleader Paul Whiteman claimed that the transition from the band as the focal point to that of the vocalist attributed to the decline. In June 1958, in an article in the *Los Angeles Mirror News*, he said,

> I told them boys, you're digging your own graves' when they started featuring their singers and got the crowds ganged around the stand to listen instead of dance. They began to quit playing dance numbers....This may sound strange when you remember that I was the first leader to feature singers, however, I insisted that all of them sing in dance tempo so that they would not distract or interrupt the dancing (quoted in Leo Walker 1990, 301–303).

Many other bandleaders added complaints that the decline was attributed to the newer jazz style Bebop bands that did not play in "dance tempo." However, by that time most Americans were captivated by television and were firmly entrenched within their single-family homes in the newly developing suburbia.

At the time, many of the downtown areas were being deserted by the "white flight" as the Anglo Americans fled to the suburbs. Most of the federal funding was directed towards the construction of the Federal Interstate Highway system and for VA mortgages for suburban housing. Therefore, the inner cities were neglected by federal funding and quickly became run-down. With the transition to the suburbs, many were not in close proximity to dancing establishments or near public transportation. In addition, the car culture was taking over, and many of the old downtown dance palaces simply did not have adequate parking facilities. With the development of suburban malls, shopping centers, and entertainment spots such as drive-in movie theaters, the suburbanites rarely had any need to enter the downtown areas. The consumer culture of buying material goods never before available, such as home appliances, televisions, and, of course, single-family homes in suburbia, was replacing the active entertainment culture in the cities and towns.

However, the consumer culture and life in suburbia brought with it a new dilemma. The post–World War II period carefully reconstructed the roles that each gender was required to maintain in American society. The feminine "role" changed from the self-sufficient World War II "Rosie the Riveter" to that of a

"Happy Homemaker." During the 1950s and early 1960s, magazines and television continually portrayed and advertised the glory and happiness of middle-class motherhood and marriage.

The new American woman was one who devoted herself to raising a family, being a homemaker, and supporting her husband. Historian David Halberstam recalled that, "Gender, not talent, was the most important qualification....The boys in the family were to learn the skills critical to supporting a family, while daughters were to be educated [on how] to get married" (2001, 589). The specific roles of men and women were clearly delineated. Gender specific roles for men included construction workers, doctors, lawyers, soldiers, and police officers, to name a few. The feminine definition of a woman was as weak and sentimental. Gender specific roles included secretary, nurse, and ballet dancers. The masculine definition of a man was portrayed as strong and rugged.

Betty Friedan's noted book *The Feminine Mystique* (1963) documented the social "problem with no name" among young suburban housewives. Friedan's work made other women aware that they shared similar problems. (Friedan's expose would launch the National Organization for Women.) The common complaint was that they were not content to be at home in suburbia doing the housekeeping and child rearing, as well as buying and using consumer products. In general, Friedan observed that the suburban housewife lacked fulfillment. Some wanted to go out and work and have their own careers. In reality, women wanted an opportunity to express their talents and shape the world more profoundly than just doing the laundry or going to the supermarket.

The gender roles were so specific and separate that they also came between a husband and wife dancing together. However, the dancing may have proven that the togetherness and the equal partnership needed to dance together could reduce the need or obligation of the gender stereotyping. Interestingly enough, the dance book titled *Let's Dance with Marge and Gower Champion*, written in 1954, suggested that, "Many a happy marriage can be made happier if the husband and wife will relive the romance of their earlier years on the dance floor" (Thomas 1954, 7).

OLD WORLD TRADITION MEETS AMERICAN TRADITION AT WEDDING CELEBRATIONS

The traditions of old world dancing and American social dancing first came together in family celebrations such as weddings. Some claim that the wedding celebrations that became larger and more elaborate was a way of showing the other ethnic group that they were better off than they were. (Many people can also retell tales that these celebrations of culture mixing could also ignite into fisticuffs.) Prior to World War II, large gatherings of 100 to 400 people at a wedding celebration were usually confined to the wealthy. After the war, the economy was such that working and middle class families holding wedding celebrations of similar size was not uncommon. At a wedding celebration only one orchestra was hired and played continuous music. Staten Island bandleader Bob Soldivera recalled, "Our standard engagement was four hours....At most we might take a fifteen minute break so the caterers could serve dinner" (Soldivera interview, 2004).

Top: Phyllis and Thomas Giordano dance the traditional first dance at their wedding celebration in 1952. Middle: Both of them dancing at their son's wedding 30 years later in 1982. Bottom: Phyllis dancing with her son at a family wedding in 2000.   Courtesy of Phyllis Giordano.

Wedding celebrations could turn into a lively mixture of American social dances mixed with the old world traditional folk dances. Midwest and rural traditions combined British Isles *Scottish Waltz*, Irish *Step* or *Jig*, the German *Kanonwalzer* and *Krüz König*, and the Norwegian *Seksmannsril*. European folk dances included the Polish *Mazurka* or *Polka*, Lithuanian *Kalvelis* or *Klumpakojis*, the Israeli *Hora* and *Hava Nagila*, the Greek *Syrtós*, and the Greek-American *Misirlou*. The lively musical mixture would test the talents of the wedding band playing contemporary dance tunes for Fox Trots, Merengue, Rhumba, Lindy Hop, Waltz, and the traditional Folk dances. Soldivera remarked, "As an orchestra we had to be able to handle a request for anything and everything from an ethnic song to a Peabody or a Waltz. Some would be specific and say, 'Can you do the *Pennsylvania Polka?*' and we would have had to be prepared." As a result, Soldivera's orchestra maintained an extensive repertoire that included thousands of songs. However, with such a diverse range to draw upon, he added, "If you didn't play [Glenn Miller's] 'In the Mood' you were out of business [laughs]."

One first-generation Italian American remembered, "It was the live bands that made it exciting." She added, "How do you express the emotion with dancing that goes hand-in-hand with the music? Music, especially for Italians, it was so much a part of our culture and family life" (Giordano interview, 2004). Americans, many for the first time, saw an accurate portrayal of an Italian-American wedding feast (without the prejudicial stereotypical inclusion of the fictional organized crime connection) in the widely acclaimed Hollywood movie *The Godfather* (1972). The wedding scene is complete with a combination of American style Fox Trot and Lindy Hop as well as traditional Italian Folk songs and the Italian *Tarantella*.

With wedding celebrations across all ethnic and economic classes, the tradition of the newly married couple's "first dance" gained prominence. The traditional first dance between the married couple would sometimes be an excellent display of dancing as almost all young adults and their relatives knew how to dance. Many married couples continued to dance at family gatherings and weddings. Staten Island resident, Phyllis Giordano and her husband, Thomas, danced together at family weddings for over 35 years. She recalled,

It seems that after my own wedding in 1952, I danced with my husband at every wedding we went to until he passed away [in 1989]. We must have went to over one hundred family weddings alone [laughs] we have a very big family. We even danced in nightclubs like the Copacabana in New York, and the Log Cabin in New Jersey (Giordano interview, 2004).

TELEVISION DANCE PARTIES, "THE ARTHUR MURRAY PARTY," AND LAWRENCE WELK

It was television, more than any other technological development of the twentieth century, that drastically changed American social and leisure habits. In 1947, only 9,000 or so television sets existed nationwide. By 1950, the number quickly jumped to 3.9 million households (9 percent of the total population) and by 1960 over 45.8 million households had at least one television set. Almost immediately studies revealed that the average American was watching TV over 5 hours a day. As a result, other forms of "going out" entertainment, such as going to restaurants, to the movies, and dancing, experienced a sharp decline (Panati 1991, 240).

Television shaped a powerful image of popular culture. The television shows of the 1950s reflected the social conformity of the period and were careful to exclude stories and portrayal of minorities. TV portrayed homogenous white nonethnic suburban families where the mother was a housewife and the father worked at some unnamed job and always came home for dinner. The best-known shows of the period included *The Adventures of Ozzie and Harriet* (1952 to 1957), *Father Knows Best* (1954 to 1960), and *Leave it to Beaver* (1957 to 1963).

At one point or another each of the shows featured an episode with a theme centered on dancing. One episode of *Leave it to Beaver* portrayed the main character, Theodore "the Beaver" Cleaver, attending dancing school in preparation for a dance. He was taught the Fox Trot and the Waltz. In one *Ozzie and Harriet* episode the entire Nelson family, Ozzie, Harriet, and sons David and Ricky, prepared for a dance at the local country club. The episode featured the Fox Trot and even the Cut-in dance (see Chapter 3).

The highest rated show of the period, *I Love Lucy* (1951 to 1957), featured the indomitable comedy of Lucille Ball and her husband, Cuban bandleader Desi Arnaz. *I Love Lucy* averaged more than 70 million viewers each week and was the top-rated TV show of the period (Panati 1991, 302). Arnaz played the character Ricky Ricardo, a bandleader and owner of the fictitious "Tropicana" nightclub. In one 1953 episode, Lucy danced a Jitterbug at the Tropicana and characters Fred and Ethel Mertz performed the Varsity Drag (see Chapter 2) ("Lucy Has Her Eyes Examined," Episode No. 77; first aired December 14, 1953).

Television became a catalyst in promoting dancing to the public. In 1949, in Philadelphia, Paul Whiteman, the former "King of Jazz" (see Chapter 2), at the age of 62, hosted a teenage dance show called *TV-Teen Club*. It was broadcast locally over WFIL-TV and in the early 1950s nationally by the fledging ABC-TV network. Whiteman's was considered the first television show to feature teenagers dancing. They danced to a live band doing mostly Jitterbug and Fox Trot. In

1950, *Grady and Hurst's 950 Club* was the first television show to introduce the simple format of teenagers dancing only to records.

In the case of *American Bandstand* (see earlier in this chapter) over 20 million teenagers learned the latest dance craze in front of television sets in their own living rooms. As a result of the mass audience, a new dance could sweep the nation literally overnight. However, because of the nature of segregation and the image of Rock 'n' Roll in general, *American Bandstand* had to be careful not to upset the homogenous image of television. The origin of the new dances could not be credited to African Americans or ethnic neighborhoods. Therefore, many viewers assumed either the *American Bandstand* regulars or a particular musical artist originated the "newest dance sensation." At the same time, television dance shows also catered to adults.

In July 1950, Arthur Murray purchased five 15-minute television spots on CBS-TV and persuaded his wife, Kathryn, to host. The idea was to use television to promote his dance studios and stay one step ahead of the competitive *Fred Astaire Dance Studios*. In fact, the show amounted to being the first "infomercial." Before the third show aired, Arthur bought a half-hour summer series on ABC-TV and titled it the *Arthur Murray Dance Party*. By the summer of 1952, TV ratings climbed, and they signed with their first sponsor, General Foods. The format combined comedy sketches, musical guests, dance instruction, and a celebrity dance contest.

Celebrity dance contests included baseball legend Mickey Mantle, Broadway star Helen Hayes, and boxers Rocky Graziano and Jake LaMotta. The celebrity winner was judged by audience applause. On one show, October 6, 1960, the celebrity dance contest included actor Fernando Lamas with instructor Marilyn Gret performing a Tango, Arlene Dahl (Fernando's wife) danced a Waltz with instructor Frank Kaufman, and actor Farley Granger and actress Janice Rhule danced a Charleston. *American Bandstand* host Dick Clark was scheduled to dance the Jitterbug with actress Shelly Winters but had to cancel. At one time Clark's family were neighbors with Kathryn and Arthur Murray in Mt. Vernon, New York. At times Kathryn even baby-sat for the young Clark (Jackson 1997, 3).

On the same show, Arthur Murray demonstrated the basic Samba step in under a minute. He told his television audience, "The Samba is the easiest of all the Latin dances. You start with the left foot as usual. And all you have to do is this. [The TV camera focused on his feet] Step forward on the left [feet together] and step backward on the right [feet together]. Now in addition to stepping forward and back, you just bounce up and down like this as you step." He then stepped up to a female hostess and proceeded to show the television viewing audience how easy it was. The Arthur Murray Dancers followed with a theatrical version of the Samba.

During its run, from 1950 to 1961, *The Arthur Murray Dance Party* alternated on four different television networks, ABC, Dumont, CBS, and NBC. The show attracted millions of adult television viewers, many of whom also signed up for lessons at Arthur Murray Studios throughout the country. Each show would close with the signature line by Kathryn, "Until then to put a little fun in your life try dancing," as Arthur approached and waltzed her away (Kathryn Murray 1960, 10).

For the most part, the other contemporary television shows featured established music and dances from the big band era such as the Fox Trot, Samba, Lindy Hop, Rhumba, and Tango. In 1951, the first national television show featuring a dance band was *The Freddy Martin Show*. It was an all-band show without any dancing and lasted only two seasons (Jackson 1997, 12–13).

In the fall of 1952, Los Angeles had seven area television stations doing band shows at least once a week. One example was the *Weekly Dance Party*, a one and one-half hour live broadcast from the Hollywood Palladium. The television broadcast simply placed television cameras in the ballroom aimed at the band and the dancers. In 1955, the popular east coast Meadowbrook broadcast an hour long *The Cavalcade of Bands* (Leo Walker 1990, 183). Some bandleaders of the 1930s and 1940s, including Kay Kyser, Sammy Kaye, and Guy Lombardo, had limited TV success. Bandleader Lawrence Welk, however, flourished under the television cameras.

Lawrence Welk started in 1925, and, although his band had continued success, it was not until television that he became one of America's biggest musical attractions. Unlike other television shows, *The Lawrence Welk Show* did not attempt to capture the new youth market. Welk stuck with his proven formula and audience

Lawrence Welk started in 1925, and, although his band had continued success, it was not until television that he became one of America's biggest musical attractions. In this photo dating from the mid-1950s, Welk appeared at the Hollywood Palladium in Los Angeles for his weekly television show.   Courtesy of Photofest.

from years past. During his entire career his tempo and format changed very little, playing Fox Trots, Polkas, Rhumbas, and Waltzes.

In 1953, Welk first aired on local Los Angeles television broadcasting from the Santa Monica, California, Aragon Ballroom. Two other television dance band shows also broadcast from the same ballroom were Harry Owen's Hawaiians and Ina Ray Hutton's all-girl band. Hutton's show lasted four years and was one of the top rated west coast shows. In the summer of 1955, Welk's show was broadcast nationwide on ABC-TV. The first title was *The Dodge Dancing Party*, later changing to *The Lawrence Welk Show*. Eventually the show was moved out of the Aragon Ballroom and into a television studio for better production value (Leo Walker 1990, 181).

Ironically, the national debut of *American Bandstand* (see earlier in this chapter) on August 5, 1957, caused a one week cancellation of the Welk television show. Set to air on Monday evening at 9:30 P.M., the Welk show was cancelled because of a dispute by ABC technicians. Technicians in New York, Chicago, Los Angeles, and San Francisco stopped work in protest of the premiere of *American Bandstand*. According to *The New York Times*, "The union charged that the employment of local station technicians [in Philadelphia] had deprived their own members of work." The dispute was quickly resolved, and Welk was on the following week ("Welk Show Kept Off TV By a Network Dispute," 1957, 42).

Welk's show lasted on national television until 1971. It continued in syndication with new shows until 1982. The show continued in reruns well into the twenty-first century, over 50 years on television. In retrospect, Lawrence Welk said, "Our own success speaks for itself. I believe it came because we never forgot it was the dancers who paid our salaries and we always tried to give them what they came to hear" (quoted in Leo Walker 1990, 302).

COTILLIONS, DINNER/DANCES, AND DANCE SOCIALS

A 1959 Gallup Poll reported over that 32 million participated in some form of recreational dancing. Many people danced within the home, at family gatherings, and at weddings. Some continued the tradition of dancing at formal cotillions. The cotillion was a formal dance where young debutantes of the social elite were typically "introduced" into society. One example was the Cotillion Ball held annually in the Waldorf-Astoria Hotel in New York City. At a cotillion it was proper that the debutante held a dance card (see Chapter 1) and the first and last dances were reserved for the escort who she came with. The event was centered on dancing to a live orchestra and dinner was usually served.

Social functions that included dinner and dancing were not limited to debutante balls. Many organizations held social events that included dinner and dancing. The event might be either to raise money for a charitable cause or to acknowledge employee contributions to a company. In all but very rare cases, they included dinner and dancing. In 1953, the first Pink and Red Versailles Ball was held at New York's elegant Waldorf-Astoria Hotel. The annual event was attended by prominent members of the social, political, and diplomatic elite of New York City and Washington, D.C. The event was initiated to raise money to restore an historic

Royal Chateau near the city of Paris, France. An orchestra provided live music, and the main entertainment was dancing. On September 8, 1953, the United Nations (UN), an organization formed after World War II to preserve world peace, held its first United Nations Staff Day. Over 3,000 employees, guests, and family members danced to the live music of a 17-piece orchestra in the main lobby of the General Assembly Building. At the time it was the largest social event in the young history of the UN (Dannett and Rachel 1954, 188).

In 1957, E. Franklin Frazier noted in *Black Bourgeoisie* that African American fraternal organizations, churches, and community groups maintained a social life patterned after the white population of America. They held debutante balls as well as the annual "Pink Cotillion" in Philadelphia, Pennsylvania. The events were held in fashionable, although segregated hotels, included dinner and dancing to a live orchestra. Frazier noted that the ability to enjoy a social life similar to the white population "became identified with the condition of freedom" (1957, 202–203).

The bands that catered to the upscale hotels and resorts continued to do well, including those of Sammy Kaye, Wayne King, Jan Garber, Charlie Spivak, Ralph Flanagan (a new band), Lawrence Welk, and Guy Lombardo (see Chapters 2 and 3). Lombardo said, "For us the slump never occurred. We've always had more work offered us than we could handle and we still got good money for it" (quoted in Leo Walker 1990, 302). Lombardo continued to play the Roosevelt Hotel that dated to the 1920s. On November 18, 1955, he had the distinction of presiding over a birthday dance for Mrs. Mary Andrews in celebration of her 100th birthday. She credited her longevity to keeping active dancing.

Orchestra leader Bob Soldivera fondly remembered his ongoing association with similar type events. Soldivera, who was born in Staten Island, New York, began playing as an orchestra leader in 1954. His love of music, initially encouraged by his father, led to a career as a full-time professional big band dance orchestra leader until the year 2000. At one time or another he played every hotel in Manhattan, including the "Windows of the World" at the top of the World Trade Center. Most of the time his band consisted of 8–10 pieces, sometimes as many as 24. As a club date musician, he played at commercial dance halls, private parties, dinner dances, and corporate functions. Some of his fondest memories were of events held in his hometown on Staten Island.

Soldivera noted that he had a long-standing engagement with many companies that held an annual dinner/dance for their employees. But it was not the food that they came for. He said, "You could serve sandwiches, they didn't care. They knew how to dance and they enjoyed themselves responding to my music and all type of tempos." In order to set the dancing mood, the orchestra would usually start the first set with a slow ballad such as "Stardust," "As Time Goes By," "Moon River," or a popular song of the day. He noted, "You never went wrong playing songs like these."

A song that never went wrong was Glenn Miller's "In the Mood." In fact, when Soldivera's orchestra played Miller's song the dance floor was usually packed, and they usually turned it into a four-song medley. He said, "we knew we hit a chord with 'In the Mood.'. . .We would continue the medley and then go into say 'Chattanooga Choo Choo' or 'One O'Clock Jump' and they still wouldn't get off the [dance] floor."

At other times, a song just might not appeal to a particular crowd and nobody was dancing. Therefore, Soldivera said, "I would decide we better bail out and go on to something else." But for the most part, if the music was right, people did not need any prodding to hit the dance floor. In fact, at that time it was not unusual at all events that included music to see couples dancing. But it was not just the annual events that had people dancing. Many halls sponsored regular dances, most with a live band on Friday and Saturday evenings.

For local Staten Island residents, Friday and Saturday nights offered many choices for social dancing, including the Mays Hotel in South Beach, the Svea Hall in West Brighton, and Harmony Park in Grasmere, that also had an adjacent picnic area that would have bands so people could dance outside. In the summer it was pizza, a beer, and a dance band. All the venues had live bands, but the main attraction was social dancing. For many young adults it was also a way to meet someone of the opposite gender either as a dance partner or a date. But a young woman did not go alone; the young women went as groups to the social dance places. In addition to the social dance halls, some teenages danced at amusement parks.

PALISADES AMUSEMENT PARK, PROMS, AND SOCK HOPS

In 1919, over 2,500 urban amusement parks existed throughout America. Almost all contained some form of indoor or outdoor pavilion for public social dancing. By 1960 only about 245 of the old amusement parks remained. One urban example was Palisades Amusement Park (first opened in 1908), located in Fort Lee, New Jersey (Giordano 2003, 156). During the 1950s and early 1960s, the park achieved its legendary prominence mainly due to teenagers, live Rock 'n' Roll music, and dancing. The events were broadcast on a local television affiliate in New York City. The show was hosted by New York radio disc jockey Murray Kaufman, known to his legion of fans as "Murray the K." As a result, Palisades Park attracted as many as 150,000 teenagers in a single day. Between 1947 and 1971, the average yearly attendance was over 6 million people. (In 1969, they set an all-time high with over 10 million admissions.) However, the neighboring community criticized the park for attracting mainly teenagers and not providing a wholesome family atmosphere. In 1971, community pressure hastened its closure (Gargiulo 1995, 101, 142).

In 1955, Disneyland redefined the amusement park as a theme park. The park was located in suburban Anaheim, California, far from the inner urban areas and accessible only by automobile or excursion bus. It provided a clean family atmosphere free of social, political, or economical conflicts of the time. Disneyland was an immediate success, attracting over 1 million customers in its first six months. Unlike the earlier urban amusement parks, however, Disneyland did not include an area for public dancing.

Teenagers and young adults continued to congregate at soda fountains, roller-skating rinks, bowling alleys, diners, and drive-in burger joints. Many of these establishments provided music by means of a jukebox. A new jukebox addition was a "wallbox." The wallbox was a compact tableside selection device that allowed individuals to select songs controlled by the jukebox. In many of these locations, teenagers would dance to music played on the jukebox.

Dances designed specifically for teenagers were Proms and "Sock hops." The Prom was a formal dance affair to signify the end the high school. Many of the proms were held in the high school gymnasium. The "unofficial" uniform for the boy was a white dinner jacket, shirt, tie, and dark tuxedo pants. For the girl, it was a strapless elegant dress, with a corsage affixed to wrist or pinned to her dress. Adult chaperones, composed of teachers and parents, were ever-present. Close dancing was not allowed, and Rock 'n' Roll music was usually forbidden. During the course of the school year, dances held in the gymnasium were known as Sock hops or Record hops (Time-Life Books, *Rock & Roll Generation*, 1998, 92–93).

A Sock hop received the name from teenagers who went to school or church sponsored dances usually held in a gymnasium. In order not to dam-

Teenagers dancing, dressed in prom attire, under the watchful eye of adult chaperones in the balcony, c. 1956.   Author's Archives.

age the gym floor, the teens were encouraged to remove their shoes and dance in their stocking feet. A band composed of fellow high schoolers or a local band usually provided the music. The Hollywood movie *American Graffiti* (1973) featured a "Sock hop." The Record hop was a teenage dance that hired a local celebrity radio DJ to spin the latest hit records. In 1957, *American Bandstand* Dick Clark made well over 180 personal appearances at Record hops (Jackson 1997, 127).

In 1959, Dick Clark organized a touring version of the *American Bandstand* television show called the *Caravan of Stars*. Clark usually arranged for about 14 to 16 of the current favorite Rock 'n' Roll acts to perform live stage shows for teenagers across the nation. They traveled by bus and performed in old theaters, roller-skating rinks, gymnasiums, community centers, open fields, and just about anywhere. The nature of a segregated society, however, was always apparent. Clark recalled,

> In the southeast we had to play before divided audiences—sometimes blacks upstairs and whites downstairs, sometimes split right down the middle with whites on one side and blacks on the other.... We couldn't sleep in the same hotels or eat in the same restaurants as the black artists.... We finally stopped traveling in the southeast because it got to be such a terrible hassle (Uslan and Solomon 1981, 61).

The municipalities continually tried to enforce segregation. But the reality was that through the live Rock 'n' Roll shows and television, for the first time both black and white teenagers were sharing the same experiences in music and dancing.

A scene from the Hollywood movie *American Graffiti* (1973) featured a "Sock hop." In order not to damage the gym floor, the teens were encouraged to remove their shoes and dance in stocking feet.   Universal Pictures / Courtesy of Photofest.

TEENAGERS, JUVENILE DELINQUENTS, AND "WEST SIDE STORY"

With the establishment of Rhythm and Blues and Rock 'n' Roll as a viable music market, many small independent distributors such as Chess, Imperial, Atlantic, Sun, and Essex, among dozens of others, were able to produce and distribute records to a new market distribution audience—the teenager. By 1956, estimates placed the number of teenagers at over 13 million. Teenagers, more so than during any other preceding period, also had a defined demographic as a powerful purchasing force.

By the end of the 1950s, over 400 new record labels were producing LP's and 45's. The introduction of the Long Playing 33 1/3 RPM (LP) record album, 45 RPM (45) record, and portable record players allowed the youth the privacy of listening to the preferred music of their choice. A slumber party or open house party was almost sure to have a portable record player and a "stack" of 45's for dancing. In 1950, Americans as a whole purchased almost 190 million records. By 1960 the number of records sold exceeded 600 million, and portable record players were selling at a rate of 10 million per year. The teenage market was responsible for almost 70 percent of all record sales (Kammen 1999, 180).

However, most of mainstream America likened any teenager that listened to Rock 'n' roll music as a juvenile delinquent. The Hollywood movie industry portrayed the teenage juvenile delinquent in movies including *The Blackboard Jungle* (see earlier in this chapter), *The Wild One* (1954), *Rebel Without A Cause* (1955), *Crime In The Streets* (1956), and *High School Confidential* (1958). The movie poster for *High School Confidential* claimed "behind these 'nice' school walls A TEACHERS' NIGHTMARE A TEEN-AGE JUNGLE!" The ad for *Crime In The Streets* asked, "How can you tell them to be good when their girl friends like them better when they're bad." Parents and municipal and religious leaders linked juvenile delinquency, teenage gangs, and Rock 'n' Roll as the cause for all the blame (Time-Life Books, *Rock & Roll Generation*, 1998, 122–123).

In 1957, teenage gang life was portrayed in a Broadway musical *West Side Story*. (The Hollywood movie version in 1961 garnered ten Academy Awards.) *West Side Story* described for Americans the problems of a cross-cultural relationship of a teenage Anglo boy and teenage Latina girl torn between rival New York City street gangs. The young teens of different ethnic backgrounds meet at a local dance and fall in love. The show, choreographed by Jerome Robbins, elevated stage dance to a new level, incorporating elements of ballet and contemporary Mambo and Bebop. The acting was also within the dancing to express emotion and tell the story. The fight scenes, expressed in dance, actually advanced the plot of the story and added to racial tension among the teenage gangs (Driver 2000, 174). *West Side Story* actually portrayed a reality of American life that continued to exist, simply that the races or ethnic groups should not mix. Adults looked to blame teenagers, but, in reality, many adults were scared of change, scared of nonconformity, scared of heightened sexuality, scared of rebellion, and mostly scared of the weakening of segregation.

In August 1944, the City Council of Los Angeles established the Bureau of Music to recognize the "social power of music," offering music in the schools, in communities, and as summer concert series in many of the city's parks. In 1952, the Los Angeles Metropolitan Recreation and Youth Services Council promoted wholesome recreation among the youth including "dancing." The program was successful as long as interracial dancing was not a factor and R&B or Rock 'n' Roll music was not included.

In 1956, as a result of teenagers dancing to Rock 'n' Roll music, the Los Angeles County Board of Supervisors resurrected a Progressive Era law that prohibited public dancing in parks and public open spaces. One political official claimed that it "would lead to a lot of dancing in the darkness [and] might contribute to increased juvenile delinquency." They added that all public dances required prior approval by the Board of Education. In effect, dances had to be held on school grounds, thereby allowing maximum control and chaperonage, and thereby prohibiting Rock 'n' Roll music or interracial dancing. A similar law in the city of Atlanta banned teenagers from dancing in public "without the written consent of their parents" (Macías, "Bringing Music to the People," 2004, 696–709).

Sponsors of Rock 'n' Roll music and dance shows, including radio DJs Johnny Otis and Art Laboe, began shows in the Long Beach Shrine auditorium about 19 miles south of Los Angeles. At a time of increased youth ownership of automobiles and the development of the U.S. Interstate highway system, teenagers were able to travel the 19 miles with little trouble. Otis and Laboe also staged shows at the American Legion Stadium in the city El Monte about 12 miles east of Los Angeles. The shows in Long Beach routinely attracted over 3,000 to 4,000 teenagers, and the Friday and Saturday evening dances in El Monte Legion Stadium regularly drew over 2,000 teenagers of mixed ethnic groups including Mexican, Anglo, and African Americans. At El Monte, Mexican Americans influenced the creation of dance steps called the Pachuco Hop and the Corido Rock. For a brief time the El Monte City Council, citing "rock and roll creates an unwholesome, unhealthy situation," revoked the dance permit. The promoters argued that the ordinance was simply "racism, under the guise of all-American morality." The City Council was eventually pressured to rescind the ban (Macías, "Bringing Music to the People," 2004, 710–711).

Many religious leaders, including the Reverend Norman Vincent Peale, the Reverend Billy Graham, and Catholic Bishop Fulton Sheen, continued to condemn the simple leisure pursuit of teenagers dancing, especially to Rock 'n' Roll music. In fact, Sheen, Peale, and Graham were national celebrities. Each had syndicated newspaper columns, best-selling books, and television programs. In 1952, Bishop Sheen's TV show, *Life is Worth Living*, was seen in prime time on Tuesday evenings from 8 to 8:30 P.M. The show was an unscripted combination of Biblical stories and moral statements that reached over 25 million Americans. In 1952, sales of the Bible, the best-selling book of the period, sold over 26.5 million copies within one year. Reverend Peale's *The Power of Positive Thinking* (1953) sold 2 million copies. Graham's column was carried in over 125 newspapers, his weekly television show was viewed by an estimated 50 million people, and he was receiving over 10,000 letters per week. Among the "vices" of contemporary society Graham preached against was dancing (Whitfield 1996, 77–84, 117).

In January 1955, a notable Christian magazine, *These Times*, responded to the question of dancing as recreation. The rhetoric echoes the Reverend A.M. Cree and Thomas Faulkner from the 1920s (see Chapter 2). The editor stated,

> Can you imagine the Lord Jesus dancing the modern social dances?...rhythm and music in the dancing of men and women together serve only one purpose—the gratification of the sensual passions....The Bible plainly teaches that impurity is a matter of thoughts. Can the thoughts be pure in the atmosphere of the dance hall? At once someone will say, "Confine the dancing entirely to the home." [However] there is a very short step from home to hell. The young person who has been taught to dance at home is sent out into the world without moral armor....Will the Holy Spirit dwell in his heart while his body sways to the rhumba or other "hot" music? To ask is to answer the question (Kaplan 1960, 150–151).

Despite the warnings of the clergy, some churches at the time were relaxing their views on dancing. Many Catholic churches regularly sponsored dances for both adults and teenagers. In Mexican-American districts of Los Angeles the CYO under the auspices of the Catholic Church sponsored weekly block parties called "jamaicas." Neighborhood residents drew upon their ethnic diversity, dancing traditional Mexican Folk dances known as *rancheras*, as well as Polkas and the Jitterbug. In 1950, Augustana College, strictly run by the Lutheran church simply decided to leave the issue of dancing up to the individual. The college administration of Augustana Lutheran issued the statement that "the problem of dancing is but one of the symptoms of the inroads of secularism upon the Church. There are greater, more fundamental problems" (Wagner 1997, 336–337). During the tumultuous 1960s, society, indeed, had more fundamental problems to worry about than dancing.

5

The Twist, Doing Your Own Thing,
and A Go-Go: 1960–1969

In our dancing, as in our ideology and diplomacy, we show who we are, and what America is in the twentieth century.

—Marshall Fishwick, 1962

The Political, Social, and Cultural Climate

In 1960, the American population was 179.3 million people. At that time, the immigration pattern was changing, as the flow of immigration opened with new immigrants coming from the Caribbean, Asia, and the Middle East, most settling in the major American cities. During the same period, over 40 million Americans moved from the cities and rural areas to the new suburban developments. By 1964, the American population was almost evenly divided in thirds among the suburbs, cities, and rural areas. The ability to move to the suburbs was predicated on securing a federally sponsored 30-year mortgage. The loans were used mainly for single-family homes in suburban developments. On the other hand, housing for the inner cities and urban areas received little federal funding, which eventually led to the massive "urban decay" of the inner cities (Foner 1998, 267).

In October 1962, the Cuban Missile Crisis created a standoff between the United States and the Soviet Union. The United States announced that the Soviets had placed nuclear missiles in Cuba, posing a threat to national security. The United States responded with a naval blockade of the island and directed its own nuclear warheads at Cuba. A standoff ensued with each nation threatening a nuclear attack. After a tense 12 days, the Soviet Union removed the missiles with an assurance that the United States would not invade Cuba. The singular incident represented the closest time during the twentieth century that nuclear war might become a reality.

The crisis, however, hastened American fears of an imminent nuclear attack. Civil Defense posters were in schools and public places claiming, "You can protect yourself from...Radioactive Fallout, get the facts! From Your Civil Defense Director." In the event of a nuclear attack, schoolchildren were taught to stop, duck, and cover and actively participated in Civil Defense drills. Almost all schools had fallout shelters and many homeowners constructed one in their basement or in the backyard. Historian Kenneth Rose estimated that by 1964, at least 60,000 back-yard home fallout shelters existed. However, since many homeowners kept their fallout shelters a secret, the real number might have been as high as 200,000 (2001, 191, 202).

The growing interest in missiles, satellites, space exploration, and the possibility of placing an American on the moon captured the imagination of Americans. In 1962, an estimated 135 million people watched Astronaut John Glenn's televised launch and subsequent earth orbit. By 1969, America had, in fact, placed two men on the surface of the moon and safely returned them to earth (Hilliard and Keith 2001, 174).

At the time, segregation was still a common practice. In early 1963, Alabama's new pro-segregationist Governor George Wallace of Alabama steadfastly proclaimed, "Segregation now! Segregation tomorrow! Segregation forever!" In contrast, President John F. Kennedy favored an end to segregation, which he described as "a moral crisis." On June 12, 1963, Kennedy spoke to a national television audience stating that he would seek Congressional legislation to provide equal accommodations for all Americans in public establishments. Sadly, on that same night, civil rights leader Medgar Evers was assassinated in Jackson, Mississippi. Later that same year, on November 22 President Kennedy was assassinated in Dallas, Texas. During the following days, the entire nation was in mourning (Williams 1987, 195).

Within days, the former vice president, Lyndon B. Johnson, stated, "no memorial or eulogy could more eloquently honor President Kennedy's memory than the earliest possible passage of the civil rights bill" (Williams 1987, 226). On July 2, 1964 the federal Civil Rights Act was officially signed into law. The law made it illegal for racial discrimination in places of public accommodation. However, the federal law did not eliminate the practice of segregation as many southern states, and even northern states, refused to acknowledge the federal legislation. In 1965, President Johnson further strengthened the Civil Rights Act by securing Congressional approval of the Voting Rights Act for all citizens in federal, state, and local elections. Johnson also outlined his plans for the Great Society program. The program declared a "war on poverty" and an extension of social programs. One program expanded Social Security, adding Medicare and Medicaid (Williams 1987, 254).

A tool for inner city neighborhoods to aid in the war on poverty was the federally funded Community Action Programs (CAP). The CAP established that recreation activities were "essential to individual and community well-being, to be planned for and made available to everyone irrespective of their ability to pay" (Kraus

1971, 39). For the most part, however, the necessary funding for inner city recreation was not fully available. Tensions continued during the following years as both Civil Rights leader Martin Luther King, Jr., and presidential hopeful Robert Kennedy were assassinated.

Selective Service had been an active part of young American men's lives since World War II. A significant number of soldiers continued to be drafted and deployed to Europe and other parts of the globe to deter any Soviet action during the continuing Cold War. In 1965, the United States increased its troop strength in Vietnam and intense fighting ensued. By 1968, the United States committed over 543,000 troops in an all-out war in Vietnam. Later that same year, the North Vietnamese launched the Tet Offensive and turned the course of the war against the Americans. In response, the United States extended its bombing raids beyond Vietnam into Laos and Cambodia. The mounting death toll of American soldiers (in all, over 58,000 died in Vietnam) and the unprecedented bombings ignited massive antiwar protests and an upheaval within American society.

By 1969, antiwar protests and unrest on college campuses extended nationwide. In protest incidents, students occupied administration buildings on over 50 college campuses including Harvard, Cornell, Columbia, and Berkeley. On May 4, 1970, during a protest at Kent State University in Ohio, the National Guard fired into a crowd and killed four student protestors. Less than two weeks later, at Jackson State University in Mississippi, the National Guard also killed two protestors. In response, more than 100,000 Americans from all walks of life marched on the nation's capitol in Washington. Across the country, thousands more joined in solidarity at over 500 college campuses (Foner, 304).

This turbulent period of change in American society was also reflected in its dancing. A generational gap both in society and the dance floor separated the dancing public. Older adults continued to dance ballroom and traditional couple's dances. The younger set twisted off into expressionistic and individual solo dancing. At first, a whole slew of nonpartner dances came and went. In a short time, the dances did not even have names, nor for that matter did they have any set patterns. After 1969, as a result of the success of Woodstock (see later in this chapter), rock music moved to the point of large stage shows where the audience went to watch the performers dance and the crowd simply swayed along. As the years increased, the gap between traditional partner social dancing and freestyle expression widened. Filling in the gap was an emerging young adult generation that did not dance. In 1962, sociologist and cultural historian Marshall Fishwick proclaimed, "In our dancing, as in our ideology and diplomacy, we show who we are, and what America is in the twentieth century" (Needham 2002, 123).

The Dances

"Let's Twist Again (Like We Did Last Summer)"
—Chubby Checker song title, 1961

THE DAY THE MUSIC DIED AND "PAYOLA"

In the fall of 1958, teenage Rock 'n' Roll icon Elvis Presley was drafted into the U.S. Army. Not too long thereafter, in the early hours of February 3, 1959, three notable Rock 'n' Roll artists, Buddy Holly, Ritchie Valens, and J.P. Richardson, were killed in a plane crash in Clear Lake, Iowa. The event made headline news and became known as "the day the music died." After both Presley's induction and the plane crash, the rebellious side of Rock 'n' Roll music gave way to the popularity of the "teen idols" who included Annette Funicello, Frankie Avalon, Fabian, Paul Anka, and Bobby Rydell.

Also in 1959, the U.S. House Oversight Committee began to investigate deejays who took gifts and cash payments from record companies in return for playing records on their shows. It was termed "Payola." Though a number of deejays and program directors were caught in the scandal, the committee decided to focus on Alan Freed (see Chapter 4). In November 1959, WABC radio in New York asked him to sign a statement confirming that he had never accepted payola. Freed refused to sign "on principle" and was fired. On February 8, 1960, a New York Grand Jury began looking into commercial information in the recording industry, and on May 19, 1960, eight men were charged with receiving illegal gratuities ("Alan Freed Is Out in 'Payola' Study," 1959, 1).

In March 1960, Congressional hearings were held to investigate the payola scandal. Federal Trade Commission chairman Earl W. Kintner reported "that record companies had made payments to 255 disc jockeys and other broadcasting personnel in more than 56 cities in twenty-six states." Two prominent names mentioned were *American Bandstand* host Dick Clark and radio disc jockey Alan Freed. Clark was mentioned as having financial interest in 17 music companies and might have provided preferential treatment to commercial advertisers. By the time of the investigations, however, Clark had divested himself of outside interests and escaped retribution.

As it turned out, Alan Freed was the only deejay subpoenaed by the Oversight Committee. Despite being given immunity, Freed refused to testify and was put on trial. In December 1962, he eventually pleaded guilty to numerous counts of commercial bribery. Although the charges were really criminally serious, he was only required to pay a $300 fine and received a six-month suspended sentence. However, his career was finished. In March 1964, while living in California, Freed was charged by the IRS for failure to pay back taxes during his radio career in New York. In January 1965, before any action could be taken, Freed contacted uremia and died at the age of 43 (Morthland 1980, 103).

Critics, however, charged that the investigations were really a convenient excuse by the U.S. Government to stem the tide of Rock 'n' Roll music and the dancing that they felt was corrupting the American youth. Rock 'n' Roll music historian David Hinckley wrote, "it had taken a couple of years, but by the summer of 1960, grownups saw some encouraging indications that they had finally tamed this rock 'n' roll menace" (Hinckley, "Not the Soda Fountain Type," 2004).

DANCE STUDIO FLEECING, LIFETIME DANCE CONTRACTS, AND "DANCE WITH ME, HERMAN"

In 1958, the New York State Legislature sought "To authorize strict control over ballroom dancing studios for adults." Assemblyman Malcolm Wilson questioned the apparent standard practice of "high-pressure sales techniques." The reason was cited that district attorneys statewide had filed reports "by patrons of some of the studios who claim to have been [swindled] of their life savings." One instance noted a woman who paid over $9,000 for a series of lifetime lessons. Another case involved an elderly woman who cashed in her life insurance savings for a long-term contract ("State Curb Asked On Dance Studios," 1958, 8).

In 1959, New York State Attorney General Louis J. Lefkowitz began a yearlong investigation into the business practices of dance studios. Lefkowitz's case was based on the premise that many dance students statewide had been "induced to sign life-time contracts far in excess of their [own] ability to pay." During the investigation, it was discovered that many dance studios employed dubious methods "of inducing dance students to sign contracts." And in doing so, dance students had unknowingly signed "open-ended" lifetime contracts. In particular, he cited that three major dance studios, the Arthur Murray Dance Studios, Fred Astaire, Inc., and the Dale Dance Studios had "failed to perform or to have violated agreements for lessons."

The results of the investigation prompted new state legislation and revised business practices for the dance studios. Lefkowitz announced that the three major dance studios (Arthur Murray Dance Studios, Fred Astaire, Inc., and the Dale Dance Studios) had "signed agreements to abide by a code of ethics." The code required "all contracts be in writing and in the case of life-membership agreements, approval of an officer of the dance corporation must be obtained." Cancellation provisions were required and be clearly indicated on the contract, as well as the actual amount of money required to be paid ("Ethics Code Signed By 3 Dance Studios After Sate Inquiry," 1959, 47).

In late 1962, California's Attorney General Stanley Mosk began a statewide effort to curtail improprieties in the dance studio business. He cited a 1961 law that limited dance studio contracts not to exceed "$500 or more than a seven-year term are illegal." Mosk charged that many of the dance studios, especially the established studios under the franchise of the Fred Astaire and Arthur Murray chains, with "racketeering." The charges stemmed from the 10 to 15 percent franchise fees of yearly profits, high-pressure sales techniques, and unscrupulous promotional sales techniques. Subpoenas were immediately served in Pasadena, Glendale, Sacramento, and Oakland. Mosk indicated that the studios had probably collected "many millions of dollars from gullible persons," not just in California but throughout the whole country. Using words such as "racket" and "fleecing," the state charged that the unknowing dance students were unaware of the sales promotions that were "set forth in minute detail in manuals up to 100 pages." In exchange for a promise of "ballroom proficiency" many students had signed away for "lifetime" contracts. Mosk did note that there were many "legitimate dance studios," but it was "necessary to take action against those studios which have been consistently violating our law against long-term service contracts" ("Dancing Studios Face Coast Study," 1923, 35).

In 1960, Arthur Murray and Kathryn Murray were confronted by allegations that some of their customers had been pressured into signing "lifetime contracts" requiring an up-front payment in excess of $12,000 or more. The Murrays were also criticized for their continued practice to run down a list of names in the local telephone book, informing the individual that he or she had won free dance lessons. The Federal Trade Commission eventually ordered the Arthur Murray studio to stop its high-pressure sales techniques. In 1964, Arthur and Kathryn Murray divested their interest in over 500 studio franchises and retired to Hawaii. Arthur died in 1991 at the age of 95. In 1999, Kathryn died at the age of 92 (Allen, "Kathryn Murray Dies at 92; Coaxed Many to 'Try Dancing,'" 1999, 39).

By the mid-1960s, regulation and control over dance studios provided for consumer protection. As a result of the Federal Trade Commission investigation, most cities issued reports on the dance studios, forcing local studios to revamp their advertising campaigns and restructure business practices. Many dance schools in Washington and California were forced to close down. New York City's Better Business Bureau, for example, offered a free fact sheet report providing basic solvency information and comparable rates for dance studios to anyone requesting it by mail. One bit of advice was "to read all documents carefully" and not be misled into thinking that the name of a celebrity such as Fred Astaire was actually associated with a particular studio (Bosworth, "At Honka Monka and Roseland, Dancing Their Troubles Away," 1971, 62). In 1964, the New York State Legislature passed a law requiring, "Limitation on contracts by dancing studious, gymnasiums and other social training facilities by requiring that they may not exceed $500 and must be for a definite period" ("Summary of Principal Bills," March 30, 1964, 24).

The situation involving dance studio manipulation was so widely known among Americans that it became the subject of a prime-time network television show. One 1965 episode, titled "Dance with me, Herman," of the highly rated prime-time television show *The Munsters,* parodied not only the current freestyle dance crazes, but also the insinuation of high pressure sales by dance studios. In the episode Herman (actor Fred Gywnne) does not want to embarrass himself at a parents' night dinner dance at his niece Marilyn's school. He reads a newspaper advertisement for dancing lessons and decides to secretly enroll. At the dance studio, the dancing school instructress convinces him that he is a "Natural born dancer." A thoroughly flattered Herman agrees to sign up for lessons that "extend over a ten-year period." In the end, however, the dance school owners think that the all-to-willing Herman is actually an undercover police investigator and eventually release him from his contract.

CHUBBY CHECKER AND "THE TWIST"

In the early 1960s, one new *American Bandstand* couple, Jimmy Petrose and Joan "Buck" Keine introduced the dance "the Strand" on national television. The Strand, described as a "slower bluesy version of the Lindy Hop," was performed as a graceful slow couple's dance. Petrose and Buck had learned the dance from their Philadelphia African American high school classmates. However, their access to the national television audience credited them with the new dance that inspired teenagers across the nation to copy their style. The Strand, however, would be the last of the traditional partner dances for quite awhile. The nation soon went crazy over a new dance sensation called "The Twist" (Mann documentary, *Twist*, 1992).

Some trace the origin of the word "twist" to a 1912 Perry Bradford song titled "Messin' Around," which contained lyrical directions to twist around. Dancer Al Minns described the Mess Around twist motion, "by placing hands on hips while [the] pelvic region is moved side to side and in and out." In 1926, an early Duke Ellington Jazz recording was titled "Harlem Twist," and in 1927 Jelly Roll Morton recorded a jazz era song titled "Turtle Twist." The following year, The New Orleans Owls recorded "New Twister." Although these song titles contain the word of the popular 1960s dance, they did not necessarily have a dance associated with them that resembled the latter day Twist (Dawson, 4).

In August 1961, *Ebony* magazine called The Twist "an evolution from the old Lindy Hop." During the breakaway in the Lindy Hop, many of the female dancers swiveled their feet in a twisting motion similar to the 1960s Twist. One example was dancer Jewell McGowan (see Chapter 4) who could be seen in many movies of the 1940s performing such a move. Regardless of whether The Twist might or might not have been new, it certainly created a new dance sensation unlike anything mainstream American social dance had ever seen before ("Popular Dances from Cakewalk to Watusi," 1961, 33, 38).

The song that inspired the dance "The Twist" was originally written in 1958 by Rhythm and Blues singer Hank Ballard. The song was first recorded and released by his group Hank Ballard and the Midnighters as the flip side to a slow tempo ballad named "Teardrops on Your Letter." After the release, record hop DJs (see Chapter 4) took to turning the 45 rpm record over and began playing the up tempo danceable song "The Twist." As a result, in April 1959, the Ballard version achieved mild success topping at No. 16 on the *Billboard* R&B charts.

During live shows, the Midnighters, who were well known for providing energetic dancing and antics during all their songs, did perform some twisting movements with both balls of the feet on the ground. However, it did not contain the complete motions that would characterize The Twist sensation. Cal Green, one of the original Midnighters, said, "all that other stuff came later." According to Hank Ballard, The Twist as a dance started during a performance at the Royal Theater in Baltimore. The kids in the audience emulated the stage antics and danced it on the Buddy Deane television show (see Chapter 4). At first Deane was shocked by the dance, but then called his friend Dick Clark and told him he should see the new dance (Dawson 1995, 13, 35).

In May 1960, Hank Ballard and the Midnighters appeared on *American Bandstand*, not to sing "The Twist," but to promote their newest single "Finger

Poppin' Time." The national TV exposure helped push the song onto the prestigious *Billboard* Pop charts, thereby providing Ballard with his first Top Ten single. Their chart success caused King Records to attempt a re-release of Ballard's original version of "The Twist." The re-release hovered around the bottom of the Top 100 on *Billboard's* Pop charts. However, Dick Clark chose not to promote Ballard's version of the "Twist." Clark, decided instead to ask a producer friend named Bernie Lowe at Cameo Records to record a "cover version" (see Chapter 4) with a likeable 19-year-old teenager named Ernest Evans.

Evans had attended South Philadelphia High School, the same school that many of the *Bandstand* dance regulars attended. After graduation from high school, he tried working odd jobs while trying to break into a show business career. He caught the attention of Clark and appeared from time to time on *American Bandstand* doing impressions of famous recording artists of the day. Supposedly Clark's wife, Barbara, heard Evans's impression of singer Fats Domino and playfully said that Evans was a younger version and nicknamed him "Chubby Checker" (Dawson 1995, 28–30).

In the summer of 1960, Checker's version of "The Twist" was so faithful to the original, right down to the vocal stylization and musical arrangement, that when Hank Ballard first heard it on the radio he thought it was his own version with the Midnighters. In 1992, Hank Ballard recalled,

Chubby Checker performs The Twist, c. 1962. Courtesy of Photofest.

I was in Miami during the time...taking a swim. And I heard this record *The Twist* blasting across white radio ...I said wow [punching his fist] I'm finally getting some white airplay. I'm going to be a superstar. But it was Chubby Checker [laughs] I thought it was me. Chubby had done such a beautiful clone of my record...and I'm grateful that he did...Look I thought it was me...to almost the end of the record...But if Chubby hadn't recorded *The Twist* it wouldn't have been as big as it is today [pause] that's for sure (Mann documentary, *The Twist*, 1992).

The first time that Chubby Checker demonstrated The Twist as a dance was in front of a live teenage audience of over 3,000 at The Ice House in Haddonfield, New Jersey. The first televised performance was filmed at Palisade

Amusement Park (see Chapter 4) for a regional television show, *Clay Cole's Record Wagon.* On each occasion the teens went wild and danced along with Checker ("The 'King of Twist' Tells How It All Started," 1962, 13). It was not until a week later that The Twist would be introduced to teenagers nationwide. On August 6, 1960, host Dick Clark chose to introduce Chubby Checker and the new dance on his nationally televised Saturday evening version of *American Bandstand.* Checker not only lip-synched the song, he also demonstrated how to do The Twist.

Variations were plentiful, such as waving one hand in the air or turning or twisting all the way down as low to the floor as possible and twisting back up. In a special magazine issue titled *The Twist,* television host Clay Cole with partner Vicky Spencer demonstrated "13 simple steps." The simple basic step was described as "plant one foot forward, most of your weight on it. Holding hands hip-high, now TWIST your shoulders in one direction, hips in the other. Don't rush. And GET THAT BEAT!" ("How to Twist," 1962, 22–25).

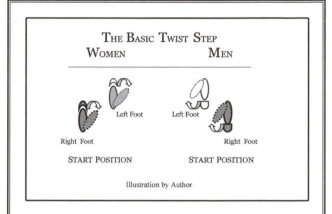

THE BASIC TWIST STEP

WOMEN   MEN

Left Foot   Left Foot

Right Foot   Right Foot

START POSITION   START POSITION

Illustration by Author

As a dance, the Twist was actually quite simple. First and foremost, no partner was needed; therefore it did not matter that partners had to mirror each other's footwork or dance in coordinated rhythm with each other. The individual dancer lifted slightly on the balls of both feet and swiveled both the hips and feet in unison. The arms were kept slightly away from the body at waist level. Checker's description was equally as simple. He suggested, "Just pretend you're wiping your bottom with a towel as you get out of the shower and putting out [something] with both feet." Unlike the gyrations of Elvis Presley a few years earlier (see chapter 4), Checker, himself, mastered a simple subtle hip swivel that did not appear obscene or vulgar. Twist historian Jim Dawson said, it "was simplicity itself, so elemental in its execution that anybody, no matter how awkward or uncoordinated, could finesse his or her way through it. The Twist was probably the world's easiest dance" (Dawson, 34).

By mid-September of 1960, Checker's version of "The Twist" rocketed to No. 1 on the *Billboard* Pop charts. Checker's album, *Twist with Chubby Checker,* released in the fall of 1960 remained on *Billboard's* Top 40 Album charts for 42 weeks (Dawson 1995, 43, 79). As popular as The Twist was, it could not have achieved the quick rise to mass appeal without the nationwide television audience. Chubby Checker admitted, "I may have started the nation twisting, but I couldn't have done it without Dick Clark and *American Bandstand*" (Shore and Clark 1985, 121). Clark added, "Most of the country first saw it done on *American Bandstand.* All anyone had to do was tune in between 3:30 and 5:00 [P.M.] to see it live from Philadelphia. The Twist was the rage and we had the patent on it" (quoted in Dawson 1995, 27).

Chubby Checker would have over 20 Top 40 song hits, many associated with short-lived dance fads, such as the Hucklebuck, the Pony, the Fly, and the Limbo. The Limbo quickly became a popular American party dance, thanks in part to a hit record by Chubby Checker titled "Limbo Rock."

THE LIMBO AND "LET'S TWIST AGAIN"

The Limbo was derived from a funeral ceremonial dance from Trinidad in the South Caribbean. This Trinidadian ritual was danced in hopes that the soul of the deceased would pass directly into heaven without being regulated to "Limbo" (a place of indecision between Heaven and Hell). Broadway dancer and choreographer Geoffrey Holder described it as "mourners bend backwards in supplication and take turns passing under a bamboo pole" and pass in front of the deceased.

In the late 1940s, dancer Boscoe Holder (Geoffrey's brother) claimed to have used the funeral ritual as a creative dramatic stage dance performance in Trinidad. The Trinidad dancers were garbed in traditional attire that was described as "half-naked." The dance was well received by American tourists and was performed in the nightclubs and resorts throughout the Caribbean. Upon returning home, Americans described the bent-over-backwards scantily clad natives to their friends and relatives. However, upon seeing the Limbo performed in America, Geoffrey Holder was embarrassed that, "Ladies removed their hats and mink stoles, pulled their dresses above their knees and snaked under curtain rods to show the folks back home at parties the marvelous native dance they had picked up in the Caribbean."

Despite Holder's remarks, doing the Limbo quickly became a new dance fad among all ages from the very young to just about anyone who could slightly bend backwards. The Limbo was also packaged by the Wham-O Manufacturing Company as a complete "do-it-yourself party kit." (Wham-O was the same toy company that produced the Hula Hoop and the Frisbee, both huge fads in the late 1950s and 1960s.) The package came with a set of support posts, a limbo pole, an accompanying record, and "detailed instructions." And believe it or not, Holder was actually quite critical of the harmless Wham-O game box claiming, "Nothing is missing but the corpse and coffin" (Holder, "The Twist? It's Not a Dance," 1961, SM78).

However, unlike other dance fads, the Limbo never fully faded away. In fact, it became an almost regular occurrence at all sorts of parties including weddings, birthdays, backyard barbecues, and block parties. In actual use, many did not even bother with the support posts; in fact, just about anything, including a broomstick handheld by an individual on either side, served as a "Limbo kit." It was certainly a fun party dance, but prior to getting people up to do the Limbo, it was usually preceded by a dance that everyone would get up and do quite willingly and without prodding—The Twist.

In 1961 and 1962, The Twist, which many thought was just another passing dance fad, reached unfathomable proportions and swept Americans both young and old. It was prompted once again by Chubby Checker, who recorded a follow-up song to "The Twist" titled "Let's Twist Again (Like We Did Last Summer)." The song quickly went to No. 1, and The Twist dance was once again all the rage. Checker had another Top Ten hit with the song "Slow Twistin'," which he recorded as a duet with Dee Dee Sharp. A repackaged Checker album by Parkway Records titled *Your Twist Party* was on *Billboard's* Top 40 Album charts for over 30 weeks. Parkway also released two other Checker albums titled *Let's Twist Again* and *For Twisters Only.*

By the end of 1961, the 20-year-old Chubby Checker was a nationwide sensation among both young and old. He was in huge demand for personal appearances and for providing instruction on how to dance The Twist. In November 1961, five-minute instructional clips by Checker himself were broadcast on local television affiliates nationwide. In New York City, for example, Channel 9 aired the five-minute segments Monday through Friday at 10:55 A.M.

Critic Milton Esterow of *The New York Times* tried to figure out the sociological significance of Chubby Checker and the new dance sensation. After witnessing a live performance, Esterow seemed puzzled. He wrote:

> He sings neither better nor worse than many of today's teen-age idols. He has a sense of rhythm and does the twist to different tempos—slow, medium fast, fast, faster and what can only be described as utter chaos.
>
> As the pace quickens, he weaves a spell over young and old. Hundreds of people snap their fingers, clap their hands, stamp their feet, sway from side to side sitting down and shout "Yeah, yeah." Through the tumult, Chubby twists (Esterow, "Chubby Checker Twists Upward," 1962, 34).

The Twist would continue to spiral upward.

In January 1962, Chubby Checker's "The Twist" was re-released and once again reached No. 1 on the *Billboard* Pop charts. (Checker's distinction of having a recording hit No. 1 on two separate occasions was the only non-Christmas record of the entire twentieth century to do so.) In February 1962, two weeks after reaching No. 1, it was displaced by the "Peppermint Twist—Part 1" recorded by Joey Dee and the Starliters (Dawson 1995, 65). Dee's version of The Twist dance added a few leaps and arm gyrations, but was essentially the same as Checker's version. But the sensation of The Twist became bigger than the previous year—as did The Peppermint Lounge.

THE PEPPERMINT LOUNGE AND THE JET SET

Joey Dee (Joseph DiNicola) was born in Passaic, New Jersey, of Italian immigrant parents. At the time, his band Joey Dee and the Starliters was noted as one of the top regional bands in northern New Jersey. But it was not until they played in New York City at a small club named the Peppermint Lounge that they would achieve lasting fame. In the fall of 1961, Dee (22 years old at the time) remembered that on one particular rainy night "we had some people come in and very fashionably dressed, I knew they were people of means." Two couples and one gentleman sat at "a table off in the corner." At one point during the show, they played "The Twist" and the kids got up and danced. Apparently on a dare, one of the couples got up and danced The Twist among the "roughnecks" and "rowdies." Dee thought nothing of it until the following day.

Apparently two of the people at the table were socialite Hope Hamilton and society newspaper columnist Cholly Knickerbocker. Knickerbocker's column the "Smart Set" was carried by the *New York Journal American* and was widely read among the social elite. On Friday, September 22, 1961, Knickerbocker wrote, "The Twist is the new teen dance craze. But you don't have to be teenage to dance it." As a result, that very same evening, Dee recalled, "about ten people [came] in from the theater." The next evening "about 20 and then 40 and it just escalated until the place was inundated with [society] people" (Mann documentary, *Twist*, 1992).

Almost overnight the Peppermint Lounge became *the* place to Twist. Located on West 45th Street in Manhattan, in the heart of the Broadway theater district, it took The Twist and introduced it to the Jet Set. The Jet Set (also known as "Café Society") consisted of celebrities and affluent individuals. They traveled to the small club adorned in minks, diamonds, gowns, black tie tuxedos, and designer clothes. At the Peppermint, they mingled with sailors, soldiers, and "leather jacketed drifters." However, *New York Times* columnist Arthur Gelb was not impressed. He called it,

> a grotesque display every night from 10:30 to 3 o'clock....The elite of the social set and celebrities of show business have discovered the Twist, performed to rock 'n' roll, and are wallowing in it like converts to a new brand of voodoo. Café society has not gone slumming with such energy since its forays into Harlem in the Twenties (Gelb 1961, 39).

On the other hand, celebrity newspaper columnist Earl Blackwell said, "The rhythm is contagious. It makes you want to get up and dance. What's most important is that it's an easy dance to do. Everyone can do it" (Gelb 1961, 37). A televised New York City *Telenews* report of the day said,

> Here and now the slumming is at a little bar called the Peppermint Lounge. It's nestled in a rather unimposing little Manhattan neighborhood...For the regulars at the Peppermint, the Twist is not new, but then society discovered it. Almost overnight the Rolls Royce set began to mingle with the motorcycle set. Now they rub elbows with the mobs that line up every night outside the Peppermint Lounge. The mink stole has become as common as the bulky sweater and the black leather jackets....Sometimes even high social standing can't even get you in. As many as 1,000 customers are turned away every night" (Mann documentary, *Twist*, 1992).

The reality of it all was that the Peppermint Lounge had a very small dance floor and the entire place could accommodate only 200 patrons at any one time. Twist historian Jim Dawson surmised,

> What fed the ongoing notoriety of the Peppermint Lounge story was the press's fascination and puzzlement with the idea of the international jet set hanging out at a working-class rock and roll bar. There didn't seem a precedent for it in America, at least not since the twenties, when Prohibition made people do a lot of crazy things in a lot of strange places (1995, 52–53).

Janet Huffsmith was a waitress at the Peppermint Lounge when all the interest began. One night she simply "got up on this little wrought iron railing and stared dancing." She remembered that the people "just went nuts they went crazy." Word of mouth spread and others coming into the lounge wanted to see the person who danced on the railing. Her boss encouraged her to duplicate the feat each night. At

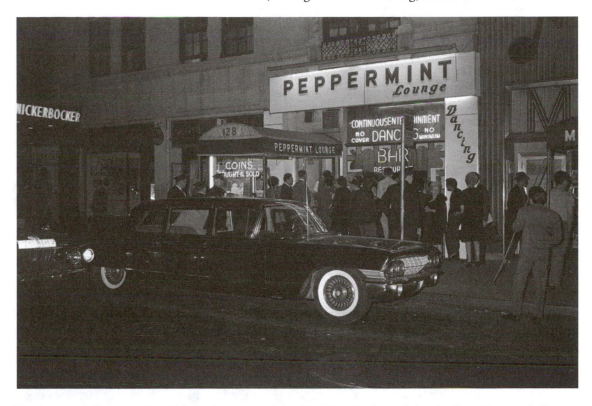

The Peppermint Lounge in New York City became *the* place to Twist. In this photo taken in October 1961, note the limousines and the well-dressed patrons waiting to enter.   © Bettmann/Corbis.

first she would just freestyle whatever Twist motions that she felt like doing. Soon thereafter, as the Peppermint Lounge grew in notoriety, a choreographer was brought in as were additional dancers, and they became "The Peppermint Twisters." The attire for the four women in similar beehive bouffant hairdos was short dresses with lots of fringe on their "fannies" to accentuate the twist. The media attention was so scrutinous that some newspaper columnist supposedly "clocked" the fringes "to go 80 miles an hour" (Mann documentary, *Twist*, 1992).

The lure of The Twist spread to high-end celebrity fund-raisers throughout New York City. In November 1961, for example, it was danced at such elite occasions as a champagne dinner at the elegant Four Seasons restaurant to benefit Girls Town, a charity ball at the swank Plaza Hotel in Manhattan, a gala event at the Metropolitan Museum of Art, and a victory ball for New York City's Mayor Robert Wagner at the Astor Hotel (Gelb, "Habitues of Meyer Davis Land Dance the Twist," 1961, 37). In turn, the amount of publicity devoted to the Jet Set at the Peppermint Lounge made The Twist acceptable to adults nationwide.

The Twist did not require much floor space, so just about any club, large or small, could spin a few records and offer Twist dancing. Many places hung signs "Come On In and Do the Twist" and "Patrons Twist at your Own Risk." The energy required usually meant that even if the floor was crowded, the dancers would not stay out there very long without needing a rest. In some nightclubs, some people just stood up where they were sitting pushed the chair back a little and twisted in place. Small's Paradise in Harlem, New York (a club harkening back to the Lindy Hop days of the 1930s), started a Tuesday night Twist contest. One group, Mama Lu Parks and the Parkettes, won so many Twist contests they were eventually billed as the "World's Greatest Twisters."

As a result of the massive amount of publicity, The Twist spread to the elite west coast clubs including the Crescendo Club and the Peppermint West (a franchise of New York's Peppermint Lounge) both in Los Angeles, as well as to The Scene in Chicago. Soon just about every major city had an "in" place to go Twisting. But The Twist was not limited to just the cities or elite clubs. The Twist appeared at just about every school dance and catered affair. In the South, for example, one magazine reported "that guys and dolls who Twist below the Mason-Dixon Line put the emphasis on knee-action, rather than hip-twisting. A Southern twist is more of a squat than a swivel" (*The Twist Magazine*, 1962, 56).

TWIST AROUND THE CLOCK, HEY, LET'S TWIST!, AND EVERYBODY'S TWISTING

Twist movies were rushed into production. Two low budget films, each filmed in late 1961, *Twist Around the Clock*, starring Chubby Checker, and *Hey, Let's Twist!*, starring Joey Dee and the Starliters, were released within one week of each other in January 1962. The promotional advertising placard for *Hey Let's Twist!* proclaimed: "Right Out of New York's Famed Peppermint Lounge, the Temple of the Twist. . . .With The Stars And Music That Started It. . .Filmed Where It Happens Every Night—The Story, The Sensation That's Sweeping The Nation—Into The Hearts Of Young And Old!" *The New York Times* called *Twist Around the Clock* "obviously a rush job to cash in on the current dance craze." The dance scenes of The Twist were described as "lively, buoyant, and limber." During that same year, other low budget quick production movies quickly followed, including *Twist All Night*, *Doin' the Twist* and a London production titled *It's Trad, Dad* (Thompson, "Producers Rush Movies on Twist," 1962, 13).

In the fall of 1962, a sequel to *Twist Around the Clock*, also staring Chubby Checker, titled *Don't Knock the Twist*, was also rushed into production. In connection with the promotion of both *Don't Knock the Twist* and *Hey, Let's Twist!*, the Fred Astaire Dance Studios combined with movie theater managers to set up local promotions including dance contests and certificates for free dance lessons (Dawson 1995, 111–114).

Not to be outdone, the *Arthur Murray Dance Studios* picked up on the sensation and offered Twist lessons throughout their nationwide chain of dance studios. They also teamed with legendary Rhythm and Blues artist King Curtis to produce a single and an album titled *The Arthur Murray Twist*. Curtis also provided instrumental versions of "The Twist," "The Peppermint Twist," and "Let's Twist Again (Like We Did Last Summer)." In 1962, Curtis also had his own hit with "Soul Twist" that he recorded with his group His Noble Knights (Dawson 1995, 93).

In late 1962, *Twist All Night* starred musician and singer Louis Prima with Sam Butera and the Witnesses. A *Variety* review called it "a rambunctious celluloid

People dance The Twist outside of a Brooklyn movie theater before the premier of the movie *Twist Around the Clock*.   Library of Congress, Prints and Photographs Division LC-USZ62-126081.

rumble into which a slim, shopworn story has been loosely constructed around periodic outbursts of the new dance." Part of the promotion for *Twist All Night* was a five-minute color instructional film titled *How to Twist* (Dawson 1995, 115).

Instructional dance books were quickly rushed to publication such as *Doing the Twist*, which sold over 125,000 copies in ten days. *Let's Twist!*, a paperback by Pyramid Books written by George Carpozi, Jr., included instructions for the dance and advertised "16 pages of photographs of the Twist and other dance crazes." Dancer John Lucchese wrote *Joey Dee & the Story of the Twist* (1962).

The insatiable public desire to Twist prompted the release of all sorts of Twist record albums and magazines. Many singles that were quickly recorded and became hits included Sam Cooke's "Twistin' the Night Away," the Isley Brothers' "Twist and Shout" (covered in 1964 by The Beatles), Joey Dee and the Starliters' "Peppermint Twist—Part 1" and "Hey, Let's Twist," Danny and the Juniors' "Twistin' U.S.A.," and Gary U.S. Bonds' "Dear Lady Twist" (Dawson 1995, 7).

Bonds attempted to combine both The Twist craze and the late 1950s Calypso phase (see Chapter 4) with an album titled *Twist Up Calypso*. The Marvellettes, who had a hit song titled "Mr. Postman," tried to capitalize on The Twist fad by recording "Twistin' Postman." The Dovells did the same with "Bristol Twistin'

The insatiable public desire to Twist prompted the release of all sorts of Twist record albums and magazines.   Author's Archives.

Annie" (a follow-up to their dance hit "The Bristol Stomp"). Other song titles included "Kansas City Twist," "Tequila Twist," "Short Shorts Twist," "Guitar Boogie Twist," "Twistin' Bells," "Big Bo's Twist," "The Alvin Twist," "Limbo Twist," "Percolator (Twist)," "Twist on Little Girl," "Twistin' Matilda," "The Spanish Twist," and hundreds more.

It also seemed that just about every musical artist tried to cash in on The Twist by devoting entire albums to the dance. Albums included *Dance The Authentic Peppermint Twist with Joey Dee*, *Twist with B.B. King*, *Twist with Etta James*, *Twist with Jimmy McCracklin*, *Twist with Bobby Darin*, *Do the Twist with Ray Charles*, *Doin' the Twist with Louis Prima*, *The Crystals Twist Uptown*, *Chuck Berry Twist*, *Bo Diddley's a Twister*, *Twist with Bobby Freeman*, *Twistin' with the Cadillacs*, *Twistin' with Duane Eddy*, as well as *Meyer Davis plays the Twist*, JoAnn Campbell's *Twistin' and Listenin'*, and Ray Bryant and his Combo's (of Bunny Hop fame; see Chapter 4) *Dancing the Big Twist*. Orchestral Twist arrangements included "Twist-ing" by the Irving Fields Orchestra and "Twistin' in High Society" by Lester Lanin and his Orchestra. Famed Mambo composer Perez Prado (see Chapter 4) even got into the act with his released "Now Twist Goes Latin." It was an undisputable fact that The Twist had certainly transcended the generations and crossed into mainstream America when even the indomitable Frank Sinatra recorded "Everybody's Twisting."

The Twist became a major merchandizing fad. One *New York Times* headline proclaimed "Twist Looms Biggest Merchandising Bonanza Since Davy Crockett

Fad." (During the mid-1950s, *Davy Crockett* was a popular children's television show that triggered a major merchandising extravaganza of items associated with the TV show.) The Twist, in itself, became packaged to sell things and the word Twist began to appear everywhere on everything including rings, bikinis, hats, books, hairdos, hair tonic, underwear, dolls, dresses, and shoes. A milk commercial sponsored by The American Dairy Association promoted milk to provide the "vitality" needed to dance The Twist.

By the end of 1962, America was in the midst of a Twist dancing frenzy. The Twist could be seen in many episodes of both daytime and evening prime-time network television shows. Two of the most highly rated TV shows of the period parodied the dance. *The Dick van Dyke Show* called it "The Twizzle" (February 28, 1962), and *The Flintstones* called it "The Twitch" (October 12, 1962). One evidence of note was the physical change in Chubby Checker. Photographers noticed that, because of the constant attention and performances, he was losing weight and actually slimming down due to the exhaustive performance schedule. As a result, diets and weight loss programs promoted by Twisting were advertised nationwide ("Twist and Get Healthy," 1962, 35).

The Twist pushed social and ballroom dancing to the brink of extinction. John Lucchese, a prominent dance teacher in New York City, recalled,

> I thought [the Twist] would spark a renewed interest in dance and bring new people onto the dance floor, which it did. But I also thought the end result would be an interest in all kinds of dancing, including ballroom. That was a sad mistake. Interest in ballroom dancing began to wane, and it cut into my business (Crease, "John Lucchese," 2004).

Interest in ballroom dancing might have faded, but The Twist phenomenon became the first teenage dance craze to transcend the generations. Twist historian Jim Dawson said, "kids and their parents were Twisting in gymnasiums, ballrooms, dance halls, auditoriums, armories, church basements, even in bathrooms" (Dawson 1995, 72).

In the process, The Twist achieved the distinction of being the first dance craze that spread equally across mainstream America. Cultural historian, Charles Panati said, "from the standpoint of social dance it was important for two reasons: It was the first dance strictly for the individual and not the couple, and it was the first dance of the rock era to cross the generation gap from teen to trendy adult" (1991, 332). All in all, The Twist provided a sense of euphoria and youthful enjoyment, so adults wanted to learn how to do it and emulate the apparent fun. Waitress/dancer Janet Huffsmith added, "A lot of...publicity that it got called it vulgar, because of the gyrations. But it wasn't. It was fun—uninhibited. That's what made it what it was. They [adults] wanted to get out there...And just have one helluva good time" (Mann documentary, *Twist*, 1992).

"RISK IN THE TWIST" AND A "BRAVE NEW WHIRL"

The Twist had hardly reached its peak popularity when it was being criticized in newspapers and magazines nationwide. Comedian Bob Hope joked, "A guy froze to death doing the Twist; they couldn't bury him, they had to screw him into the ground." In December 1961, Broadway dancer and choreographer Geoffrey Holder said he would not dance The Twist, calling it "dishonest" and "embarrassing." He proclaimed that "Social dancing was never meant to supply vicarious kicks for spectators." He further stated, "It's synthetic sex turned into a sick spectator sport. . . . What you twist remains largely unmentionable. . . . The oldest hootchy kootchy in the books has become the latest thing. Who would believe it?" It appears that although he felt that when "young kids" did it—it was "cute." But Holder was appalled at "a contortion for children which got taken up by adults" ("The Twist? It's Not a Dance," 1961, SM78).

Also, in December 1961, a *New York Times* headline warned, "Risk in the Twist Cited by Surgeon." Buffalo, New York, orthopedic surgeon Dr. Bernie P. Davis said that knee injuries "were caused by the vigorous rotation of the knee required by the dance." The problem, however, was that he claimed the young did not even know if they were causing any damage to themselves. He explained, "in the Twist, teenagers seem to be hypnotized by the music and the rhythm and don't realize the strain on the knee." In Linden, New Jersey, Dr. Emanuel Mandell, president of the Society of New Jersey Chiropractors, concurred with Dr. Davis and recommended it would "be wise to practice moderation instead of excess because casualties are occurring" (1961, 134).

The editors at *Newsweek* magazine said The Twist turned America "into a national excursion into no-mind's land." The editors of *Ballroom Dance Magazine* called it "the biggest nothing dance of the twentieth century." *New York* Magazine devoted a cover story to the headline "Twist Dance Craze Hits Café Society, The Most Vulgar Dance Invented." They lay blame on the dance for the "deterioration of manners taste and the reaction to the Twist has been about as violent as the Dance itself" (Mann documentary, *The Twist*, 1992).

The stoic Roseland Ballroom (see Chapter 4) that prided itself on its "refined atmosphere" outright banned The Twist. One local newspaper declared, "Roseland Dance City Rules Out the Twist: The new dance, the Twist has been banned at Roseland." Louis Brecker, owner of the Roseland Ballroom, decried that the "[The Twist] is not, in our opinion, a ballroom dance. It is lacking in true grace, and since we have previously outlawed rock and roll as a feature at Roseland, we likewise will not permit the Twist to be danced" (Kotlowitz, "Roseland: The Eternal Prom," 1967, 133).

In early 1962, New York Catholic Bishop Burke expressly prohibited parochial school students from dancing The Twist. Bishop Burke considered the dance "to be lewd and un-Christian" ("Censorship Incidents 1960s," n.d.). In June 1962, *Senior Scholastic* magazine questioned, was it an "American Twist or Twisted Americans?" That same month, *TV, Radio Mirror* magazine asked, "Is the Twist Immoral?" (p. 72).

In 1962, Fred M. Hechinger, the Education Editor of *The New York Times* teamed with his wife, Grace Hechinger, to write the book *Teen-age Tyranny*. (The paperback release in 1963 was widely circulated.) The book was a self-described "shocking study of an American subculture—and of America's dangerous tendency toward becoming a teen-age society." The authors asked the question, "Are adults abdicating their rights and privileges for the convenience of their immature off-spring?" In particular, the Hechingers attacked The Twist. They said The Twist "has the elements of bump-and-grind exhibitionism on an amateur level [and] a flagrant example of a teenage fad dominating the adult world." The Hechingers also had something to say about the social elite who danced The Twist at the Peppermint Lounge. They called them "synthetic socialites and decadent aristocracy" (94–95).

Noted psychologist and author Dr. Albert Ellis, even paid a firsthand visit to the famed Peppermint Lounge. He said The Twist "Is a violent expression of today's youth in a world full of troubles." Dr. Ellis added, "there is sex implied in it, no doubt about that…But it is not a social sex urge. The sex image is confined to the individual; the partner might as well be lost" ("The Psychiatrist Who Analyzed The Twist," 1962, 21).

Former President Dwight D. Eisenhower was also not a fan of The Twist. In May 1962, *The New York Times* proclaimed, "Eisenhower Discerns a Decline in Morality." At the dedication of the Eisenhower Library in Abilene, Kansas, he spoke to an audience estimated at over 25,000 people. Eisenhower said, "that American concepts of beauty, morality, and decency were declining." He specifically singled out "the twist dance craze for special scorn" (Wehrwein 1962, 1). Eisenhower's former vice president, however, might have seen The Twist in a different way. During Richard Nixon's 1962 campaign for Governor of California, his campaign workers, known as "The Nixonettes," were smiling and dancing The Twist while passing out literature and balloons (Mann documentary, *Twist*, 1992).

In 1962, sociologist and cultural historian Marshall Fishwick's smartly titled article "The Twist: Brave New Whirl," in *The Saturday Review*, provided a logical rational analysis of the contemporary Twist sensation. He wrote,

> Sociologists have begun to document the change from the Protestant ethic to the social ethic; from individualism to togetherness…the remnants of the Puritan tradition dictated a rigid cultural conscience repressing those impulses…The favorite parental target in 1962 is the new dance rage, the Twist…Parents forbid it individually, and some towns communally. The dance draws such descriptive epithets as barbaric, erotic, inhuman, and satanic. Listening to a group of local ladies sound off recently, I realized that I had heard a remarkably similar description myself once—when I learned how to jitterbug! So did my father, he admitted privately—when he did the Charleston (Needham 2002, 123–125).

The Twist was, in fact, a sociological phenomenon. *American Bandstand* host Dick Clark stated:

> One of the biggest moments in rock and roll and its most socially significant period to date was when the twist hit. Adults could dance and publicly show that we weren't afraid to like this music. Rock and roll had now become socially acceptable to the sophisticated and the rich. That's why the twist was so terribly important. It didn't have so much to do with the dance itself as much as the fact that everybody was dancing it (Uslan and Solomon 1981, 77).

When Chubby Checker was asked about the sociological significance of The Twist dance sensation, he simply replied, "People do it and they forget things....I never had so much fun in all my life" (Esterow, "Chubby Checker Twists Upward," 1962, 34).

THE WATUSI, MASHED POTATO, FRUG, SWIM, MONKEY, JERK, AND THE FREDDY

When just about every source had been analyzed and all was said and done about The Twist, it was Chubby Checker who provided a definitive observation. He said, "Before the Twist came, everyone danced together. I'm the guy that started people dancing apart. You know, I taught the world how to dance as they knew it today" (Panati 1991, 331). The Twist certainly changed the way Americans of all ages danced and would dance for the remainder of the twentieth century. The Twist spawned a host of other nonpartner fad dances such as the Watusi, Mashed Potato, Frug, Swim, Monkey, Jerk, the Freddy, and a slew of others.

In the summer of 1961, singer Bobby Rydell's hit song "The Fish" was promoted as one of the "latest dance records." When he premiered the song on *American Bandstand*, he did not demonstrate the dance since he did not know what the dance was about. Bandstand regulars created a simplified solo dance with some pantomime fishlike movements. The dance, however, was no relation to and was a far cry from the slow dance version of the Fish from the late 1950s (see Chapter 4). The improvised pantomime movements, however, would be the new trend in fad dances.

The 1962 album, *Twist with Chubby Checker* by Cameo-Parkway Records, was released at the height of The Twist craze, but only three of the 12 songs on it were for The Twist. The other nine tracks were for specific fad dances, including the Stroll, the Strand, the Chicken, the Hucklebuck, the Madison, Chalypso, the Slop, and the Pony. The back cover of the album promised,

> The Beginning and The End for Your Swingin' Dancin' Party. EVERY NIGHT IS SATURDAY NIGHT! With this Chubby Checker album...perfect for parties... delirious for dancin'...and rockin' all the way! Whether you wanna twist—shimmy— stroll—chicken—madison—hucklebuck—slop or just have fun listenin'; put this album on from the beginning to the groovy end and go!!! 'cause EVERYTHING SWINGS (Album Cover Notes).

The trend in the new dance crazes was simplicity and freestyle. The movement was basically freestyle, which meant that the dance did not have basic set patterns and many of the motions were improvised. All the dances had a commonality of minimal (if any footwork) and pantomime arm movements. Another common element was that they were spot dances (did not travel along the dance floor), and were performed solo without touching one's dance partner. Dance historian Ian Driver noted, "The hands played an important part and the common hand movement... alternately brought the curved arm up from hip level to halfway across the chest and back again" (2000, 95).

The Hullabaloo Discothèque Dance Book described the dances as "almost anything goes in these dances, so long as you keep loose, and keep the beat" (1966, 7). As for the suggestion of learning either to follow or to lead your partner, the *Hullabaloo* answer was "Forget it. Except for, say, the Watusi, you hardly ever have to follow or lead your partner, so you can feel freer. Great not to worry about stepping on toes!" (1966, 11).

The Watusi (sometimes known as the Waddle or Wobble) was one of the very few of the 1960s "discothèque dances" that suggested following your partner. The *Hullabaloo Discothèque Dance Book* suggested, "Whoever starts first is the leader." In 1961, the group The Vibrations' hit song "The Watusi" introduced the dance of the same name. The tune was based on the Hank Ballard and the Midnighters' song "Let's Go, Let's Go, Let's Go." The following year, Ray Barretto had a hit with "El Watusi," and the Orlons' hit song "Wah-Watusi" peaked at No. 5 but remained on the charts for over 13 weeks (Flores, 84–85).

> To dance the Watusi, the feet were slightly apart, the hands were held waist high, and the body was slightly bent forward towards your partner. The basic count was "slow-quick, quick, tap/slow—quick, quick, tap." When the male and female partners faced each other, the foot pattern was: Man: Step left, step right, step left, tap right. Step right, step left, step right, tap left. Woman: Step right, step left, step right, tap left. Step left, step right, step left, tap right. Foot pattern variations included doing the basic step backward, forward, and adding turns. The variations involved different hand patterns including the Popeye, Sightseer, Rowing the Boat, Dracula, or a pantomime of a famous actor, actress, or singer. The Watusi could also be turned into a group dance with the leader calling out different patterns and variations "square-dance style" (*Hullabaloo*, 1966, 44–45).

In early 1961, some kids were spotted doing a new dance on *American Bandstand*. In order to capitalize on the public's desire for new dances, Cameo Records producers Kal Mann and Dave Appell quickly recorded a song with singer Dee Dee Sharp titled "Mashed Potato Time." Sharp said, "The Ironic part [laughing] was I couldn't do the dance." When she appeared on Bandstand, she faked a few steps and some of the better Bandstand regulars danced alongside. Sharp added, "I did just enough to jump back out of the way" (*Twist* documentary, 1992).

The Mashed Potato (sometimes known as "The Mashed Potatoes") was popular in late 1961 and early 1962. It was a variation of The Twist but was also quite similar to the basic Charleston of the 1920s (see Chapter 2). Unlike the Charleston, which stepped forward and back, the Mashed Potato stepped to the side. The count was 1&2, 3&4, and both male and female did the same foot pattern without partnering. The *Hullabaloo Discothèque Dance Book* described the basic steps as follows:

1. Step to the right with your right foot.
2. Place your left toe to the heel of your right foot, simultaneously turning your right heel inward.
3. Step left.
4. Right toe to left heel as you turn your left heel inward (30).

Ron Mann's 1992 documentary titled *Twist* on DVD, provides an excellent dance instructional titled "Let's Learn to Dance with Laney Cross." The segment includes instruction on how to do the Mashed Potato as well as how to dance The Twist, the Pony, Shake Your Tail Feather, the Monkey, and the Madison (see Chapter 4).

The Frug (sometimes known as Surf, Big Bea, and Thunderbird) was one of the most common of the freestyle dances. The feet were slightly apart "at whatever distance feels comfortable." The weight is on the left foot and the right knee is slightly bent. The hands are held waist high. The basic movement was described as "Just keeping in time with your right knee, bending and straightening as much as possible—as much as the rapid beat of the music will allow." The hands alternate one in front and one in back, each with two beats of the music. Some variations included simply keeping both feet on the floor and using a slight sway of the body from side to side and sometimes a hip swivel somewhat similar to The Twist and performing some arm movements (*Hullabaloo*, 1966, 12).

The Swim, popular in 1964, was just a variation of the Frug. The difference is that the arms make a motion of a person making a swimming stroke in the water. Cultural historian Charles Panati described the Swim "with feet largely stationary and arms pantomiming a breaststroke, backstroke, crawl, or dog paddle, or out stretched to simulate floating" (1991, 333). Another variation was the Bug (sometimes known as the Fly) where the dancers flap their hands as if they were shooing a bug away. The Hitchhiker variation held the thumbs up and motioned in hitchhiker fashion (*Hullabaloo*, 1966, 15–18).

The Monkey was a popular dance fad in 1963 and 1964. The dance mimicked the motions of a monkey climbing a tree and scratching its body. The basic body movement involved ending the torso forward and then backward as the arms continually made a motion as if a monkey were climbing a tree. In 1963, musician Major Lance had a hit song for the dance titled "The Monkey Time" (Panati 1991, 334).

In the mid-1960s, the Jerk "involved snapping your body forward with a jerking motion while the lower portion remained relatively stationary." The Jerk was the same body movement as the Monkey but the arm movement was different. The hands come together and cross in front at face level as if "leading a band." The arms and hands are then pushed outward in a sweeping motion away from the body (*Hullabaloo*, 1966, 24).

The Freddy (sometimes spelled "Freddie") was inspired by the British group Freddy and the Dreamers. The lead singer performed a pantomime dance of extending out the left arm and leg to the left side while leaning to the right side and placing them both down on the side. And raising the right arm and leg to the right side while leaning to the left side. The dance when done by a couple involved them being face-to-face; the man would start on the left foot and the woman on the right side.

So many other dance fads came and went, including the Bug, Fly, Hitchhike, Elephant Walk, the Pony, the Pony Tail, the Fish Tail, the Surfer's Stomp, the Peter Gunn, the Locomotion, the Slop, the Mouse, the Boston Monkey, the Bird, the Ginza, the Bombay, the Buzzard, the Shing-a-ling, the Hully Gully, and the Funky Chicken. They were all simple and easy to follow, and, if necessary, anything could be faked or simply made up at the time. By the mid-1960s, the dances ceased to have any specific names or defining gestures. The dances were simple, the steps seemed to disappear, and they simply became known as "doing your own thing."

THE PACHANGA, "BLAME IT ON THE BOSSA NOVA," LA BOSTELLA, AND THE BOOGALOO

While The Twist was sweeping the country and attracting major media attention, the Latin sounds and dances were also transforming. After 1960, the political accession of Fidel Castro in Cuba led to the breakdown of diplomatic relations with America. The ability of musicians to freely travel back and forth to Cuba was suddenly ended. As a result, so did the musical sounds of Cuban refugees in Miami and New York as they became more influenced by American Jazz and South American rhythms. The bands were consolidating the Charangas (see Chapter 4), and the Latin sound of the Rhumbas, Mambos, and Cha-Chas were coming together. These sounds would combine with American Jazz and fuse into a culture sometimes known as "Cubop." By the mid-1960s, one result was that the Charangas suddenly disappeared from the Latin music scene. This continuing musical development would lead to Salsa and eventually the mainstream adaptation of Disco and the Hustle dance (see Chapter 6). At the time, the dance associated with the new Latin rhythms was the Pachanga (Roberts 1999, 162–163).

In August 1961, *Ebony* magazine called the Pachanga the "Latest Latin dance craze." The Pachanga was a solo partner dance incorporating "elements of Charleston and Lindy Hop" ("Popular Dances From The Cakewalk To The Watusi," 1961, 36). On the other hand, the *Hullabaloo Discothèque Dance Book* recommended a "one-two count" as each person did a "stomp/swivel." The stomp/swivel was simply stomping the left foot and turning the left toe out and repeating it with a stomp of the right foot and turning the right toe out. It was also recommend to add "a little style by emphasizing the hip motion" (1966, 34). The Pachanga, as most dances of the time, quickly faded from the social dance scene. In November 1962, as the nationwide Twist dance craze was also finally waning, *Newsweek* magazine predicted that the next "national craze to replace the twist" would be another Latin dance—the Bossa Nova.

Bossa Nova music (sometimes called "Jazz Samba" or "Jazz Bossa") was a distinctly South American cultural music form that had its roots firmly planted in America. The word origin is from the Portuguese; loosely translated, Bossa means "boss" and Nova means "new." As a Brazilian term, it has a loosely defined meaning as either "new touch" or "new feeling." Throughout the twentieth century, Brazilian musicians continually looked to modernize the culturally significant Samba beat (see Chapter 3). The experimentation led to combining the Brazilian Samba with American Jazz. The result was Bossa Nova music. Therefore, the resultant musical influence upon America was actually a result of America's own distinct culturally diverse musical development ("The Bossa Nova," 1962, 82).

In 1959, composer Tom Jobin and poet Vinicius de Moraes wrote what was most likely the first written Bossa Nova, the musical score for the movie *Black Orpheus*. In early 1961, American Jazz guitarist Charlie Byrd, while touring South America and Brazil on a cultural exchange program, discovered the Brazilian

Jazz-Samba sounds. Byrd is credited with introducing the Bossa Nova rhythms to fellow Jazz musicians in New York upon his return to America. In June 1962, Byrd, along with saxophonist Stan Getz, released the album *Jazz Samba*. One single named "Desafinado" quickly rose to No. 1 on the *Billboard* Pop charts (Roberts 1999, 170–171). In early 1962, as a result of a grant from the International Cultural Exchange, the Paul Winter Sextet spent six months traveling throughout Latin America studying the Bossa Nova sounds. Paul Winter, a 22-year-old from Altoona, Pennsylvania, explained, "Bossa Nova is a mood, not a new beat. [In Brazil] we lived, drank, and ate bossa nova for a month" ("The Bossa Nova," 1962, 82).

During the last week in November, the Bossa Nova received its first national attention as a result of a concert at the White House and the famed Carnegie Hall. The White House program was part of a series of "Musical Programs for Young People by Young People." By November 1962, over 50 Bossa Nova albums were available. Musical artists included Antonio Jobim, Sergio Mendes, Herbie Mann, and Dizzy Gillespie (Roberts 1999, 172). One of the better-known Bossa Nova songs was "The Girl from Ipanema," recorded by Stan Getz and João Gilberto, and sung by Astrud Gilberto. Brazilian singer and guitarist João Gilberto was "the acknowledged master of the [Bossa Nova] movement" in the United States. Other popular songs included an Elvis Presley recording "Bossa Nova Baby" as well as a Top 40 Pop hit by Eydie Gorme titled "Blame It On the Bossa Nova" (Driver 2000, 79).

Bossa Nova music became quite lucrative and popular among the mainstream American public. The dance, however, did not catch on as many thought it would. The reason was a combination of the new trend in nonpartner dancing and the music itself. Dance historian Ian Driver said, "The music was in syncopated 2/4 time, as opposed to the 4/4 time" (2000, 79). The music editor at *Newsweek* magazine explained that the Bossa Nova beat "is not simple, but tricky and syncopated." One American radio disc jockey, however, said the music was "like nothing but a broken Samba beat." Musician Vinicius de Moraes claimed that American Bossa Nova musicians were actually playing and listening to the wrong beat. Americans were used to the heavy Rock 'n' Roll beat based on simple 4/4 time accentuated on the 2nd and 4th beat; whereas "the proper Bossa Nova rhythm was accentuated on the weak beat of 1 and 3." Dancing on the "weak beat" would be the equivalent of dancing on the "two" rather than the "one" (see discussion on Mambo in Chapter 4). In November 1962, the music editor at *Newsweek* correctly surmised "this subtlety may very well keep [Bossa Nova] from becoming as big a craze as the twist" ("The Bossa Nova," 1962, 82).

At the time, mainstream American social dancing was also gravitating towards partner separation in their dancing and not the closed couple partnering required of the Bossa Nova. However, the most plausible reason might be that the Bossa Nova did not have a specific dance to accompany the music. At first many encouraged a slowed down version of the Samba.

Just about the only consistency of teaching a Bossa Nova dance was in the closed dance position (see Chapter 1) as a spot dance moving forward, backward, sideways, and incorporating turns. The dance instruction for the basic Bossa Nova varied. Dance instructor "Killer Joe" Piro (see later in this chapter) described it as a "Samba without the jump." Arthur Murray said it "had the lilt of the Samba with the more earthy feeling of the Rumba motion." Audio Fidelity Records produced an instructional Bossa Nova album claiming it was "a smooth sophisticated Samba." Instructor John Monte, of the Fred Astaire Dance Studios, recommended, "doing the Twist to bossa nova rhythm, which comes out like a mambo" ("The Bossa Nova," 1962, 82).

In 1966, *The Hullabaloo Discothèque Dance Book* offered directions for the Bossa Nova "in regular dance position," and politely asked the teenage reader, "Remember *that?*" The dance was described as "a shift of weight from one foot to the other, in a little back-and-forth and side-to-side pattern." They suggested "the vertical motion" of the Samba and "the Cuban hip motion of the Rumba." The basic step was similar to the Samba, but offered an eight count basic with four counts front to back and four counts side-to-side. The basic pattern step forward left foot (count 1), tap right foot next to left (count 2), step backward right foot (count 3), tap left toe next to right (count 4), step side with the left foot (count 5), tap right foot next to left (count 6). Step side with the right foot (count 7), tap left toe next to right (count 8) (50–52).

In 1969, John Youmans' *Social Dance*, an instructional book designed for physical activity and recreation programs in schools, said it was different from the Samba. He described the difference that Bossa Nova "is smooth, subtle, and sophisticated with its slow tempo, whereas Samba is fast, bouncy and plebian." Youmans counted the rhythm as 1&2, 3&4. His Bossa Nova basic was described as: step forward left foot (count 1), slight hop or jump forward with right foot (count &), slight hop or jump forward with left foot (count 2), Step backward right foot (count 3), slight hop or jump backward with left foot (count &), slight hop or jump backward with right foot (count 4) (69–70).

In 1979, Karen Lustgarten's *The Complete Guide to Touch Dancing* provided a retrospective on earlier American partner dances. The Bossa Nova was described as "the Samba's tempo was slowed down and a 'Bossa Nova beat' was introduced by new Brazilian composers. The steps remain the same [as the Samba], only the tempo and type of sound are different" (1979, 72).

In 1963, Joe Lanza, a noted Hollywood dancer and choreographer, claimed an original Bossa Nova dance. Beginning in 1949, Lanza owned and operated The Hollywood Dance Club and taught many people in the Hollywood, California, area how to dance. One of his specialties was teaching the "Dean Collins" smooth style of swing dancing (see Chapter 3). Lanza himself danced in over 75 Hollywood movies and television shows including the movie *Don't Knock the Rock* (see Chapter 4). In 1963, he taught the Bossa Nova in the Los Angeles public school system ("LindyByLanza.com," n.p.).

Lanza explained, "we were at a loss as to what dance form to use to express this animated, fun-feeling rhythm.... The modified Mambo and Samba have been tried but without success." He made it clear that his Bossa Nova version was a "substitute" dance since no one dance style was accepted and "has no resemblance to any other ballroom dance." Lanza's Bossa Nova began with a tripe step chassé to the left side (count 1-2-3) a triple step chassé to the right (count 4-5-6). Side step seven steps to the left (similar to the Merengue; see Chapter 4), on the last count the right foot is free, and the pattern is reversed beginning with the right foot. Variations were added including turns and dips (Lanza 1963, 1–2).

However, the Bossa Nova never did catch on among the American youth. The Bossa Nova, although lively and bouncy, was contained to a small group of adult social dancers. In July 1963, columnist Allen Hughes of *The New York Times* added, "The furor of the twist has died down and exhausted oldsters have come to realize that it was never right for them....Bossa Nova, a musical style indigenous to Brazil was imported to this country, made-in-America dances were devised for it and weary old twisters found a new fad to release them from the swiveling orbit" ("Though the Fad is Gone, Twisting Lives On," 1963, 72).

In 1965, the Bostella (sometimes "La Bostella" or "La Bostela") was another short-lived dance fad. The dance was supposedly created in Paris, France. As the story goes, magazine editor, Honoré Bostel, a nondancer, tripped and fell while in a Parisian discothèque. Upon seeing him fall, other dancers "apparently taken by the innovation, dropped to the floor" (Mee, "Discotheque Man," 1966, 106).

In February 1965, dance instructor "Killer Joe" Piro introduced the dance at the affluent Shepheard's discothèque in the Drake Hotel. The high point of the dance was to go down to the floor. Prior to the floor antics, columnist Philip Dougherty of *The New York Times* observed that the dance "appears to be pure Spanish folk dancing with much hand-clapping, finger-snapping, hip-holding, and some heel-stomping. There is no confusing footwork." Piro said the dance was like the kid's dance Ring-Around-a-Rosy which had the kids dancing and then all falling down. Piro's version had couples "braced back to back, sink slowly [to the floor] with varying degrees of grace" (Dougherty, "Now the Latest Craze Is 1-2-3, All Fall Down," 1965, 43).

The dance became a fad and was performed at many events and parties. The prelude involved all sorts of freestyle antics. The end was usually the same as everyone would all fall down to the floor or two dancers would go back-to-back and slide slowly down to the dance floor. *The Hullabaloo Discothèque Dance Book* suggested the music from the Mexican Hat Dance, a traditional folk dance from Mexico. As far as the dance, the suggestion was, "You can really do anything else you care to do, so long as it fits the beat and is very lively." But the "whole point of the Bostella" was the ending as "Everyone falls down!" (1966, 63–64).

In 1966, the famed Manhattan Palladium Ballroom (see Chapter 4) closed, signifying an end of an era of Latin Mambo and Cha-Cha dancing. In that same year, musician Jimmy Sabater remembered playing regularly one night a week at the "black dances" at the Palm Gardens Ballroom in Manhattan. During one of those dances, The Joe Cuba Sextet was playing a series of Mambos and Cha-Chas but "nobody was dancing." Sabater suggested that they play a new song of theirs titled "Bang Bang." Joe Cuba recalled, "Suddenly the audience began to dance side-to-side like a wave-type dance, and began to chant 'she-free, she-free,' sort of like an African tribal chant and dance." What the band witnessed was the beginning of the Boogaloo (Flores, 75–76).

Latin cultural historian Juan Flores described that the flavor of the song "Bang Bang" was "very much a party...thus getting the black audiences involved and onto the dance floor." "Bang Bang" was not necessarily the first Boogaloo song, but it definitely was the first to bring the music and dance to popular attention. Some claim that musicians as early as the 1950s were performing a similar sound, but the true Boogaloo sound and dance did not materialize until 1966. Some claim Herbie Hancock's "Watermelon Man" as the original Boogaloo, or even Ricardo "Richie" Ray's "Se Soltó—On the Loose" in 1966 and "Jala Jala y Boogaloo" in 1967.

The heyday of Boogaloo (sometimes "bugalú") lasted about three years from 1966 to 1969. The Boogaloo sound, however, was more than just a musical fad. In reality it reflected a melding of cultures among African Americans and Puerto Ricans in New York City. Flores added, Boogaloo music and dancing in general "was intended to constitute this meeting between Puerto Ricans and blacks, and by extension, between Latin music and the musical culture of the United States." The song and dance reflected the social coupling of African Americans and Latin Americans dancing at the same clubs and listening to the same music (77–78).

The fusion of the music, which was reflective of Afro-Cuban and American influences, coincided with the development of a first generation of Puerto Ricans born and raised in New York as Americans. Musician Willie Torres used the term "Nuyoricans" reminding others that he was not only of Puerto Rican heritage but was born and bred in New York, therefore spoke mainly English and was also heavily influenced by his own American culture. An important factor were musicians such as Willie Torres and Nick Jiménez who composed Latin dance music with English lyrics including a Cha-Cha version of "I've Got You Under My Skin" and "Mambo of the Times." Other popular Boogaloo song hits included "At the Party" by Hector Rivera, "I Like It Like That" by Peter Rodríguez, "Gran Combo's Boogaloo" by El Gran Combo, "Boogaloo Blues" by Johnny Colón, "Watusi Boogaloo" by Willie Rosario, "Boogaloo Down Broadway" by Fantastic Johnny C, and "Funky Broadway," "Mustang Sally," and "In the Midnight Hour" by Wilson Pickett (Flores, 77–80, 84–86).

Although African Americans and Latin Americans shared a common musical and dance connection, the two groups shifted their interests in different directions. African Americans gravitated towards Soul music and Latins towards Salsa. The Pachanga, the Bossa Nova, La Bostella, and the Boogaloo all came in with high expectations but never did connect with nationwide dance influences. The music and dancing appealed to a somewhat older generation and never did connect with the youth. Mainstream American youth still preferred Rock 'n' Roll, especially when "four lads" from Liverpool, England, came to America.

THE BEATLES, HIPPIES, WOODSTOCK, DOING YOUR OWN THING, AND *HAIR*

In September 1963, Dick Clark premiered a new song by a group from England titled "She Loves You." The Rate-A-Record (see Chapter 4) jury of three gave it low marks of 77–65–70. Comments included, "It doesn't seem to have anything" and "it's not all that easy to dance to." In addition, upon seeing a photograph of the four lads from Liverpool, "The kids all snickered." Those four lads, John Lennon, Paul McCartney, George Harrison, and Ringo Starr, also known as The Beatles, soon took America by storm (James Miller 1999, 213).

On Sunday evening February 9, 1964, their television appearance on the *The Ed Sullivan Show* was seen by over 70 million people. (Coincidentally, after the show, The Beatles traveled a few blocks and visited the Peppermint Lounge to Twist.) Sullivan's simple introduction of "Ladies and Gentlemen, The Beatles," was drowned out by an audience of screaming teenage and preteen fans. With a count of "a, 1-2-3-4" The Beatles launched into their first set that included "All My Loving," "Till There Was You," and "She Loves You." Their second set included "I Saw Her Standing There" and "I Wanna Hold Your Hand." Those songs sold millions of copies—mostly to "frenzied" teenage fans. In April of that year, five songs by The Beatles placed at No. 1 through No. 5 on *Billboard's* Music Pop Charts. All told, they had 14 singles in the Top 100. By end of 1964, they placed 30 singles on the year-end Top-100 *Billboard* charts, and Beatles' records alone accounted for over 60 percent of all the single 45 rpm's sold in America (Panati 1991, 341).

In 1965, The Beatles released an album titled *Rubber Soul.* Its significance was that they had created a concept album rather than a collection of singles aimed for Top 40 airplay. From that point on, the focus of Rock 'n' Roll music shifted to album-based music and away from Pop tunes aimed at the teenage dance market. Other albums followed, including *Sgt. Pepper's Lonely Hearts Club Band* and *Let It Be*. The Beatles continued to record until the end of the decade. They officially broke up in 1970, but continued to record individually.

The success of The Beatles opened the door for a host of British groups to gain airplay in America. They included Herman's Hermits, Freddy and the Dreamers, the Rolling Stones, the Dave Clark Five, and Peter and Gordon. In addition, they led the way for a revolution not only in music but also in American cultural freedom of expression symbolized by the hippie movement.

"Hippie" was a term that was first used in 1965 and applied towards a new "counterculture" lifestyle that rejected the conventional American lifestyle. They practiced a participatory communal lifestyle that included music, expressionistic dancing, and the "use of mild drugs for mind expansion and for collective consciousness." They also attempted to promote the value of peace, love, and understanding though large public gatherings. In July 1967, one such gathering was held in the Haight-Asbury district of San Francisco, and *Time* magazine termed this period the "Summer of Love." Haight-Ashbury and Greenwich Village in New York City were communities among themselves that served as a refuge for the hippie lifestyle. Two clubs, the Fillmore in San Francisco and the Fillmore East in New York City, operated by Bill Graham became the havens for the counterculture music and dancing. During the following years, the gatherings, known as "be-ins," would be repeated in most major cities with the main theme of music and expressionistic dance. The social expression of dance was reflected in the Broadway stage production of *Hair* (Ibrahim 1991, 219).

It was the counterculture that gave rise to the freestyle expression in dance. In many of the new dances the partners never touched. Dancers could go on the dance floor solo, or in a group, and "do their own thing" to the music. A large majority of the dancers simply swayed to the music with a freedom of expression and creative body movement. Some critics charged that the dancing was the result of being in a "drug stupor." *American Bandstand* host Dick Clark recalled, "As the hippie movement gained momentum nationwide, dances ceased to have faddish names. Many teens, stoned, simply moved to the music impressionistically, or exhibitionistically, as the drug they were on inspired them" (quoted in Shore and Clark 1985, 134).

LSD and marijuana were two recreational drugs that were a part of life for many of the counterculture. The use of marijuana (nicknamed "pot") became common and widely acceptable at music concerts and peaceful gatherings. LSD was a mind altering psychedelic drug (it did not become an illegal substance until 1966) that received national attention. LSD, nicknamed "acid," became associated with the harder driving psychedelic sound and music that became known as "Acid Rock." Recreational drug use was not limited to just hippies. It was also more commonplace throughout American society, especially in the white upper class and suburbia. In 1970, statistical research proclaimed that over 20 million people had used marijuana at least once. In addition, over 7 million Americans had experimented with LSD and other types of hallucinogenic drugs.

Opponents, however, viewed the nonconformist counterculture and drug use as a threat to traditional American values. Dance historian Don McDonagh noted that, "The generation gap set old (over 30), against young (under 30), in music, politics, and sexual freedom. 'Doin' your own thing' became the alternate lifestyle and on the dance floor it meant that no one touched" (1979, 93). For those under 30 years old, sometimes a dance floor was no longer necessary—as Woodstock proved.

In August 1969, over 450,000 gathered for "Three Days of Peace and Music" at the Woodstock Music Festival in Bethel, New York. The communal event was displayed by the sharing of food and drugs. The event overall was characterized by a sense of joy, the ability for unrestricted freedom of expression, and dancing. During the three-day festival, the music started at dawn and played well into the late evening. The event opened in glorious sunshine. As the music played, many of the attendees simply got up and danced. Observers tried to apply names to the freestyle dance expression and applied such as the "Woodstock Mudslide" and "Woodstock Sungrope." Some reached towards the sky as if attempting to touch the sun, providing the descriptive title of Woodstock Sungrope for the freestyle dance expression. Journalist Abe Peck of *Rolling Stone* magazine and editor of the book *Dancing Madness* described the dance actions as they "Raise their arms in the air and move their bodies in any way that feels good doing the…Woodstock Sungrope" (1976, 116).

Dance historian Don McDonagh wrote, "It was a dance of life at the time; it no longer required a dance floor, partners, or a certain pattern of steps. The dancers swayed, swooped, and twirled in a formless expression of ecstasy or sometimes despair" (1979, 103). The despair might have been misinterpreted as rain seemed to mar the event. As the music continued to play on, the attendees frolicked and danced in the mud. As a result, some simply termed that freestyle expression as the "Woodstock Mudslide."

The peaceful event was not without its harsh critics. Outcries came from many media sources, legislators, and religious organizations. In September 1969, for example, the Catholic Church in Seattle, Washington, purchased a two-page advertisement in the *Seattle Post Intelligencer*. The advertisement condemned "rock festivals and their drug-sex-rock-squalor culture." They even called for criminal prosecution of any "rock musicians" who induced individuals to act in the manner that they did at Woodstock ("Censorship Incidents 1960s," n.d.).

In 1970, a conservative political action group known as the Movement to Restore Democracy appealed to ban "rock music to end the spread of Socialism in America." State legislators across the country also sought to eliminate large rock music festivals. In 1972, Indiana enacted state legislations to "get tough" on large rock festivals and concerts that the State Attorney General Theodore Sendak called "drug supermarkets." (Ironically, the legislation was so poorly worded that it actually outlawed any large outdoor gathering including the Indianapolis 500.) In 1973, New York Senator James Buckley wrote a scathing federal report linking drug use and rock music. He put emphasis on the recording industry to eliminate "drug-endorsing rock musicians" with the threat of intervention by the federal government (Censorship Incidents 1970s," n.d.).

Despite the attacks, music and dancing could not be separated from American culture. Staten Island architect and part-time musician Vince MacDermot said, "Dance and the music is so important." Vince's father was Galt MacDermot, the composer of the Broadway musical *Hair*.

Nowhere was the trend more apparent that American social dancing was rapidly changing than in the Broadway musical *Hair*. The story of *Hair*, created by James Rado and Gerome Ragni, and produced by Michael Butler, sought to replicate the "reality" of the Hippies living in New York City's East Village at that same time. On October 17, 1967, *Hair* was the first production at the newly opened Public Theater in Manhattan. After a scheduled limited engagement, it was moved temporarily to a discothèque named *Cheetah*, located on Broadway between 45th and 46th Streets. The show "officially" opened on Broadway at the Biltmore Theater on April 29, 1968. It ran for an astounding 1,742 performances, finally closing on July 1, 1972. The show would also spawn two popular hit songs, "The Age of Aquarius" by the Fifth Dimension and "Hair" by the Cowsills. *Hair* was so successful that 14 national touring companies performed the musical at the same time it was running on Broadway. However, some cities including Boston, Massachusetts; Chattanooga, Tennessee; and St. Paul, Minnesota, sought court injunctions to prevent the stage play from opening. Other cities sought to restrict the show's content ("How Hair Came to Broadway," n.p.).

At the time, *Hair* was in total contrast to what the American public was used to seeing. The Broadway show reflected the changing times of the period, with themes including hippies, drugs, and sexual freedom. The play also contained scenes of nudity, the use of Rock 'n' Roll music, nonprofessional dancers, and defiance of the American flag. According to Galt MacDermot, the show's musical composer, most of the Broadway old guard and some of the American public "didn't like it." MacDermot added, "It had quite a lot of antipathy. It was antiwar in a country that was supposedly for the war. The attitudes toward sex, drugs, the government, and even the flag. That was pretty shocking to a lot of people at that time" (Giordano interview, 2004).

By 1960, MacDermot saw that the music in America was changing. For the most part, it was changing more to his liking "which was African." He added, "I had just come back from Africa (where I had lived for a few years) and was interested in the Rock 'n' Roll and Pop sounds....There was a tremendous amount [of] music coming out of Detroit and I became interested in the music of the time, which was 'funk.'" In developing the musical score for *Hair*, MacDermot selected Rock 'n' Roll and Funk musicians for the Broadway stage band. "It was important to select the right musicians," he explained. "If you don't have the right music, you don't have the right dancing."

The dancing and fashion used in the show was unlike anything Broadway had previously done. The show's producers and choreographer Julie Arenal desperately wanted an authentic look and feel of the contemporary time period. MacDermot remembered the audition process,

> We were trying to get a new look on Broadway....We looked everywhere for kids. First we wanted to make sure they looked right—specifically the hippie look. Then if they could dance and we hoped they could sing....If they couldn't sing we didn't hire them.

Also, up until that time, Broadway had basically ignored contemporary social dancing. In order to maintain a reality, the producers of *Hair* did not hire experienced Broadway dancers trained in the professional style. MacDermot explained,

> We were definitely involved in a social time study. As far as the sense of the story about contemporary kids of the 60s, that was the way kids danced in those days. These were kids who liked to dance socially but they had no training. It certainly gives you a sense of the time, of the people. It was real people doing real dancing.

MacDermot admitted that he was very conscious of dance beats while writing his music. He said,

> Dancing has to be an individual expression for it to be real. I'm very aware of rhythm as a physical thing and used it to express the *feel* of the music....We didn't have any labels for the specific dances....Dancing is whatever you make it. You hear the music you want to move....For instance, in the breakaway in swing dancing, you can see the relationship of the dancers to the music and everybody had their own style. Presley had his own way, and that's why it looked good....I think that dancing is probably the most important thing a person can do. Expressing themselves individually is what dancing is about.

In comparison to the Broadway stage version and the 1979 Hollywood movie version, MacDermot added,

> I preferred seeing the kids dance in the play. The movie version was ten years later. The choreography by Twyla Tharpe superimposed the dancing as part of the Hollywood movie. But, by that time, however, the social times had changed and it really didn't matter (MacDermot interview, 2004).

The social times were indeed changing. The freestyle dancing caught on in all walks of life. It became common at a social function for individuals to freestyle dance to all types of music and the trend continued throughout the remainder of the twentieth century and well into the twenty-first century. Although in the late 1970s the return of partner dancing would be heralded with the introduction of Disco music and the Hustle, it was Freestyle dancing that would be the mainstay of the Disco era.

The Places to Dance

When they dance, they smile all the time. It is a kind of inspired solution.
—Robert Kotlowitz, 1967

I believe the dance is in the Devil's territory.
—The Reverend William W. Orr, 1960

Sex is inseparable from the dance. That is what makes dancing wrong.
—The Reverend Don Humphrey, 1963

In any case, the young will create the dances they need if the old will only stay out of the way.

—Alan Hughes, 1964

RETIREMENT VILLAGES, CRUISE SHIPS, BALLROOMS OF YESTERYEAR, AND MALCOLM X

For the most part, the standard public venue for dancing completely changed. In the past there had been commercial dance halls, community centers, local school gymnasiums, and town halls. After 1960, the venues switched to smaller discothèques and eventually, with freestyle dancing, to just about anywhere including a park or a beach. Older adults had the opportunity to dance in retirement villages and gated communities.

On January 1, 1960, a retirement community specifically designed for people over the age of 55 years opened at Sun City, Arizona. Within the suburban development, a recreation center included a place for the inhabitants to hold regular Saturday evening dances. By the end of the 1970s, the population at Sun City was over 45,000 people. The Sun City development company built two others in Arizona, two in California, and one each in Nevada, South Carolina, Texas, Florida, and Illinois totaling over 80,000 homes. Similar communities opened all over the country. By the mid-1970s, over 700 retirement communities containing over 350,000 people were just in the state of California.

Leisure World Retirement Village, for example, opened on both coasts, including California, Maryland, and New Jersey. They advertised "A world of indoor recreation, [and] cultural and social activities…[all] within a gated community." A gated community was a self-contained community that hired a 24-hour security service to monitor the entry into the development. Almost all these gated communities offered recreational social dancing. Adults in these communities continued to dance the Fox Trot, Cha-Cha, and Waltzes (Giordano 2003, 175).

Social dancing for adults was also available on cruise ships. By 1960, the cruise ship industry began to include vacation packages for working and middle class adults and families. The lure of the cruise ships was plentiful food, nightly live entertainment, and social dancing. In addition, guests could learn any multitude of dances as the cruise ship companies hired dance instructors. At one point, the Arthur Murray studios had as many as 80 teams of dance instructors on cruise ships and at resort hotels.

When back on land, however, the opportunity for similar type social dancing in ballrooms was scarce. The ballrooms of yesteryear were rapidly closing and were either torn down or converted to other uses. On February 9, 1964 (the same night that The Beatles first appeared on Ed Sullivan), the famed Aragon Ballroom in Chicago (see Chapter 3) closed its doors for good. It was both fitting and sad that Wayne King played "The Waltz You Saved for Me" as the last song at the closing. King played the dance song using the same saxophone that he played at his Aragon debut 35 years previously. A UPI story said,

> Grandmas and grandpas who did their courting under the Aragon's make believe stars, swayed to the strains of the waltz king's theme song, "The Waltz You Saved for Me." The sky was synthetic, as usual, but some of the tears were real. The Aragon... closed its doors on the big band era shortly after midnight (quoted in Leo Walker 1990, 218).

In 1966 the Aragon was converted into a discothèque named "The Cheetah," which closed within six months of its opening. It was later converted to a roller-skating rink (Banks, "The World's Most Beautiful Ballrooms," 1973, 212–215).

Other ballrooms were converted to shopping centers, car dealerships, or simply torn down. The Trianon, also in Chicago, which closed in 1954, was torn down in 1967 for an urban renewal project. The famed Savoy Ballroom in Harlem closed in 1958. During the early 1960s, it was torn down to make way for a retail store and apartment housing. In 1966, the famed "Queen

The Audubon Ballroom on 166th Street and Broadway in Harlem, New York. This photograph was taken on February 21, 1965, shortly after Civil Rights leader and former Lindy Hop dancer Malcolm X was assassinated. The Audubon Ballroom was the same venue that held the first dance marathon in 1923. It was also where, in 1976, DJ Grandmaster Flash perfected the art that made the turntable an instrument by creating longer music breaks giving rise to Breakdancing.   AP/Wide World Photos.

of Swing" Rendezvous Ballroom (see Chapter 3) was destroyed by a fire. Rather than rebuild the ballroom that had opened in 1928, an apartment building was built on the site. The closings were hastened by the decline in social couple dancing during the 1960s. At the time, most of America's remaining 500 ballrooms and dance halls were relegated to weekend or seasonal schedules.

In order to make up for the decline in revenue, many of the ballrooms began renting their facilities for meetings, social gatherings, and even religious functions. The Audubon Ballroom, in Harlem, sought to supplement its revenue by sponsoring meetings for Community Action Programs. Famed Civil Rights leader and former Lindy Hop dancer Malcolm X (see Chapter 3) held one such meeting. On February 21, 1965, Malcolm X , by this time an internationally known Negro Nationalists leader, was scheduled at the Audubon Ballroom to discuss his plans for a community action program in Harlem. Tragically, just as he stood behind the podium and was about to deliver his message, he was viciously gunned down and killed.

MEMORIZERS, TERRORISTS, FANTASISTS, EXHIBITIONISTS, ONLOOKERS, AND NATURALS

By 1967, it appeared that Roseland, self-proclaimed as "The World's Most Famous Ballroom," might also have been "the world's only famous ballroom." In 1956, the Roseland Ballroom on West 51st Street and Broadway was slated for demolition and a hotel was built on the site. In order to remain open, it moved its operation one block north to West 52nd Street. The ballroom continued to attract its regular clientele, but, as they got older, there was not a significant number of the younger generation coming in behind them to replenish the base. At the time, however, despite the closing of ballrooms nationwide, Roseland continued to provide dancing seven days a week and also continued to maintain its afternoon dance (see Chapter 4).

In November 1967, Robert Kotlowitz, on assignment from *Harper's Magazine*, observed the unique sociological time capsule maintained by Roseland Ballroom. He claimed that Roseland tried to maintain an atmosphere that it was "always 1943, more or less." Kotlowitz provided a vivid description of the interior. He wrote,

> The heart of Roseland is a vast, lightly sanded, perfectly polished maple dance floor. It is set in front of a bandstand [big enough to hold two bands at once] decorated by endless drooping folds of golden drapery...Roses are everywhere. Real ones sit in tall vases on the bandstand. Plaster roses are carved four feet high on the walls....Full-length mirrors are spotted around the huge room, reflecting roses. In one dark corner of the ballroom is a television set on which tired or discouraged patrons watch sporting events. Comfortable armchairs face the dance floor...there gentlemen and ladies sit and watch other couples dance while ladies who are alone wait for invitations. Many people come to Roseland alone and most come regularly (Kotlowitz, "Roseland: The Eternal Prom," 133).

Kotlowitz grouped the Roseland dancers into one of six categories. "Memorizers" were those couples who have memorized every dance step in their head. He claimed, memorizers often did not "hear the melodies the band is playing" and their "bodies cannot sense the rhythm." Therefore, there is "at least one lapsed beat between the sound of the music and the performance of the dance." The second group, termed "Terrorists," were those friendly smiling dance couples "who sail around the ballroom floor" without regard to who they "ram" into. The "Fantasists" were not necessarily good dancers, but in their own minds they had "an idealized image of what they look like on the dance floor." On the other hand, "Exhibitionists" usually tried to show off some unusual dance move. Most exhibitionists were distinguished by their gaudy fashion attire such as "a woman in her sixties in a psychedelic mini-dress." With such an eccentric group of dancers there were the "Onlookers," those people who came not to dance but "to observe, watch, and sometimes nap." And, of course, there were a precious few "Naturals." The naturals were simply "Couples who are born to dance" (1967, 135–136).

To add to his observations, Kotlowitz interviewed many of the Thursday afternoon regulars. Most preferred to remain nameless. One elderly woman said, "This place is done with dignity.…Why, a lady can't get a drink at the bar if she's unescorted." An elderly gentleman added, "I've been coming here for forty-four years, twice a week.…People come here until they die" (1967, 134). A grandmother of 22 offspring said, "my husband goes fishing and drops me off here first. I hear music I have to dance." The self-imposed reputation might have hidden a whimsical anecdote as one unnamed regular said,

> One year, a big magazine…came up here and took pictures on a Thursday afternoon. At the first click, all the married men ran off the dance floor. Me, too. I've been coming here alone for eight years on Thursday afternoon and my wife still doesn't know (1967, 133).

Kotlowitz surmised that for better or worse Roseland seemed to inspire an allure of an "Eternal Prom." And when the patrons are dancing, "There they lose their real selves and find better—or at least other—ones for the moment. When they dance, they smile all the time. It is a kind of inspired solution" (1967, 136).

Within the tumultuous period of social change both in society and on the dance floor, some older traditions resurfaced, although on a much smaller scale. Some of the swankier hotels and the few remaining traditional dance ballrooms in the larger cities reinstituted the afternoon "tea dance" or *dansants* (see Chapter 1). Some hotels harkened a bit of nostalgia offering "Special Tea Dance Menus." One hotel advertised, "After work take a sentimental journey into the twenties, thirties, and forties with those great big band sounds in our Atrium Park Lobby" (Driver 2000, 116).

Society and charity functions also continued to maintain the social dance traditions. The military services academies at West Point and Annapolis had continued to include social dancing as part of the training regime since its inception in the early nineteenth century. The idea was to introduce the cadets to the proper etiquette of the ballroom in order to be proper gentlemen and also to act as ambassadors while stationed in foreign countries. However, with the rising social tensions and the situation concerning the Vietnam War, the academies would eventually drop their programs (Driver 2000, 112).

AMERICAN BANDSTAND GOES TO CALIFORNIA AND BEACH MOVIES

On Friday August 30, 1963, *American Bandstand* made its last five-days-a-week live broadcast and switched one week later, on September 7, 1963, to Saturday afternoons at 1:30 P.M. For the first time, the show was taped and ceased to be aired live. But, *American Bandstand* was still the premier showcase for teenagers, dancing, and new dance fads. Georganne Sassano and Carolyn Sgromo both watched the show during 1960 to 1964 to learn the new dances. Each day after school they anxiously rushed home to watch the show. Sgromo exclaimed,

> My after school activity was *Bandstand! Bandstand* was before homework. The books were out in case my parents came home, but I didn't do homework. After *Bandstand* was over I was supposed to cook supper. But since I had to then do my homework, sometimes supper was late and I got into trouble from my father [laughs]....And of course the topic in school the next day was always, did you watch *Bandstand* yesterday?

Sassano watched the show a bit longer from 1960 to 1968. She said,

> When I first started watching *Bandstand* I was only about ten years old....I watched for the clothes and to learn the new dance steps. I remember that I danced in front of the TV. Sometimes by myself. Sometimes with my sister and mother.

But even after the show was over, they would get out their records and continue dancing.

Both Sassano and Sgromo put their *Bandstand* dance practice to use. Each attended regular Friday night and Saturday night dances in the gymnasium at the local high schools. Sassano remembered,

> Almost all the girls danced, sometimes with each other. And most of the boys danced. But if one of the boys didn't ask a girl to dance the girls would just dance with each other. If not we would just sit in the bleachers and wait for a boy to ask us to dance. Only a few of the boys could do the fast dances, but almost all of them asked a girl for a slow dance. During a slow dance if we got too close the chaperones would separate us or just push us back a bit

Sgromo remembered a similar experience. She added,

> I remember meeting these two Brooklyn Tech [high school] students on the train. I really liked this one guy Marvin, because he was so good looking. But his friend Billy was the one that asked me to the dance. As it turned out, Billy was the one who could really dance. And when we went to the dance, Billy and I won a Lindy contest!

At the time, however, most of the teenagers stopped dancing after high school. Sgromo remembered it was not necessarily the coming of The Beatles or the British invasion but rather marriage that interrupted her dancing. She said, "After I graduated high school, I got married. And at the age of twenty I had kids and that was the end of my dancing days [laughs]."

News, also paid a seemingly endless amount of attention to the dance crazes in the gossip columns, entertainment pages, and sometimes even headlines. One individual who achieved a fair share of headlines was Frank "Killer Joe" Piro.

Frank Piro was born of Italian immigrant parents in East Harlem, New York. I[n] 1942, he achieved acclaim as "the first non-Negro" to win the Jitterbug in the Ser[-] viceman's Division of the Harvest Moon Ball Dance Contest (see Chapter 3). H[e] supposedly earned the nickname "Killer Joe" because of the fact that his tireles[s] energy wore out numerous dance partners. After World War II, he frequente[d] the Latin music dance halls and was making a name for himself as a dance instruc[-] tor. In the early 1950s, he taught the Mambo and Cha-Cha at the famed Palladiu[m] (see Chapter 4). Piro maintained a studio at 54 West 55th Street in Manhattan[.] Unlike other dance instructors, he did not advertise nor did he franchise his studi[o.] Throughout his career (he died in 1989 at the age of 68) he preferred to handl[e] only the number of students that he could personally instruct and preferred to sta[y] directly involved.

"Killer Joe" Piro with partner Olga Varvaro at Roseland Ballroom in New York City, c. 1966. © Bett-mann/Corbis.

In early 1964, *American Bandstand* and Clark left the Philadelphia WFIL-TV studios and moved the entire production to California. The first California show aired on Saturday afternoon, February 8, 1964. The next night the famed Aragon Ballroom in Chicago closed, and The Beatles made their first national American network appearance on *The Ed Sullivan Show*. This one solitary weekend represented a changing of the old guard in American social dancing (Jackson 1997, 229).

In Hollywood, California, the *American Bandstand* once-a-week amateur dancers were looking more professional and were hogging the camera. With the change in Rock 'n' Roll music leaning more to the British flavor of The Beatles, *American Bandstand* sought to maintain its dancing theme. By 1965, the show programmed more Motown and Soul music. At the same time, *Bandstand* introduced its first regular African American dance couple Famous Hooks and June Strode. (In the past, the show had infrequent appearances of African American couples but none were regulars.) In September 1967, *Bandstand* finally aired in color, the last television show on ABC-TV to do so (Jackson 1997, 243). According to *Bandstand* historian Michael Shore, "The look of the show was changed [and] the show simply became that much less of a fixture in the lives of its viewers" (Shore and Clark 1985, 92).

During the late 1950s, ABC-TV had a hit afternoon lineup that featured *American Bandstand* and followed the dance show with the *Mickey Mouse Club*. The *Mickey Mouse Club* combined with the opening of Disneyland in California and quickly became a perennial favorite among America's children. The show also had a group of regulars known as the "Mouseketeers." One of those regulars was a very young Annette Funicello who would later branch out into a singing and movie career. As a teenager Funicello had quite a few hit records and regularly appeared as a guest on *American Bandstand*. The notoriety led her into a Hollywood movie career typified by starring in a series of Southern Californian "Beach movies." Funicello's costar in many of those movies was another frequent *American Bandstand* guest, Frankie Avalon. Their movies included *Beach Party* (1963), *Bikini Beach* (1964), *Beach Blanket Bingo* (1965), and *How to Stuff a Wild Bikini* (1965). The movies all had a similar theme of teenagers at or near the beach and sometimes included surfing. The movies had simplistic scripts, and the attraction was the singing and dancing. The dancing was either featured on the beach or in a discothèque. The dancing was freestyle and included the Watusi, Mashed Potato, Frug, Swim, Monkey, Jerk, and the Freddy.

CLAY COLE, SHINDIG!, WHERE THE ACTION IS, AND EVERYTHING'S "A GO-GO"

During the early 1960s, regional television markets still sought to capitalize on teenage dance shows that copied the format of *American Bandstand*. In 1961, Jack Spector, a New York radio disc jockey hosted his own *Bandstand* type show. *The Jack Spector Show* was broadcast over WPRO-TV channel 12 in Providence, Rhode Island. In 1962, *The Dave Sennett Dance Party* was also broadcast from Rhode Island on WPRO-TV. The shows featured amateur teenage kids dancing to records of Rock 'n' Roll hits of the day as well as live guests lip-synching to their hits. However, in Baltimore, *The Buddy Deane Show* (see Chapter 4) was one teenage dance show that refused to integrate. They did offer to expand the "Negro Day" from once a month to "three or four days." Civil Rights groups applied constant pressure, but the producers refused to yield. Rather than allow blacks and whites to dance side-by-side, the station simply cancelled the show (Jackson 1997, 231).

One of the few regional teenage dance shows that had a continued run through most of the 1960s was hosted by Clay Cole. Beginning on September 10, 1959, Cole (himself a teenager at 19 years old) hosted a seven-days-a-week *Rate the Records* on local New York/New Jersey affiliate channel 13. His audience was drawn from the large metropolitan tri-state area of New York, New Jersey, and Connecticut. In 1960, almost immediately after The Twist craze broke, Cole had the distinction of having Chubby Checker on to demonstrate The Twist before the *American Bandstand* national broadcast. In October 1963, after channel 13 was sold, he negotiated to host *The Clay Cole Show* on channel 11. He downplayed the rebellious side of music saying, "The kids like so-called rock 'n' roll because adults don't." Cole continually stressed the wholesome side of the show saying, "We want the kids to look like [the] Sunday-school type, not the soda-fountain type. We want them to show up as ladies and gentlemen, not mugs." However, as the 1960s progressed with the heightening involvement of young people in the counterculture and growing their hair long, the "wholesome" teenager was hard to find. The show ended in December 1967 (Hinckley, "Not the Soda Fountain Type," 2004).

The format of a teenage dance show was still an idea that attracted television producers. In September 1964, ABC-TV aired *Shindig!*, the first of the newer trendy national prime-time network dance shows. The format was to showcase the current pop stars combining a mix of American and British musical artists including Frankie Avalon, Bobby Rydell, Marvin Gaye, Nancy Sinatra, Gary Lewis and the Playboys, Lesley Gore, Paul Revere and the Raiders, Jackie DeShannon, Peter and Gordon, and Dusty Springfield. Unlike the earlier type dance shows that featured amateur teenage dancers, *Shindig!* hired high-energy professional dancers who appeared on stage behind the guest musical act. The show was an instant hit and the following season was aired two nights a week for one-half hour. The style of the show was fast-paced as was the dancing. The quick energetic style of the dancers led to the term "Go-Go dancers."

The television networks sought to capitalize on the new fad. The formats were basically all the same, especially with each new show featuring its own professional "Go-Go" dancers. Other television shows included *Hullabaloo, The T.A.M.I. Show, Hollywood a Go-Go, Shivaree,* and *Let's Go-Go.* In June 1965, Dick Clark sought to recapture the five-day weekday afternoon teenage audience with *Where the Action Is.* The show was also broadcast on ABC-TV in the former afternoon time slot of *American Bandstand* (Jackson 1997, 237–238).

It seemed that just about anything and everything was supplemented with the ending of "A Go-Go." Many of the highly rated prime-time network television shows parodied the "Go-Go" theme and the trend of the new fad dances. In September 1965, the "talking horse" *Mister Ed* series featured an episode titled "Ed A-Go-Go." During the course of the episode, the cast danced the Watusi, the

Frug, and the Swim. Mister Ed skateboarded and wore a Beatles wig. The cast even introduced a new dance called "The Mule." In December 1965, the prime-time cartoon *The Flintstones* also parodied the Go-Go type dance shows, with an episode titled "Shinrock A-Go-Go." In the episode, Fred Flintstone accidentally drops a bowling ball on his foot. As he is hopping around in pain a producer thinks that Fred has created a brand new teenage dance. Fred is asked to perform the "Frantic" on the television show "Shinrock!" at the dance club "Bedrock A-Go-Go."

Many other highly rated prime-time television shows echoed the contemporary culture of "Go-Go dancers." The parodied television shows all had a similar theme that the teenagers were in a trance-like state controlled by the music such as the "Groovy Guru" on *Get Smart!* Others included dances such as the "Bat-tusi" and the "Bat Twist" on *Batman* and psychedelic dancers on *The Addams Family, Lost in Space, The Flying Nun,* and *Laugh-In.* The prime time "Go-Go" shows did not last very long. *Hullabaloo* went off the air in August 1966, *Shindig!* ended in January 1966, and *Where the Action Is* lasted until 1967.

Most of the shows did feature dancers of different racial ethnicity, but because of the nature of the freestyle nontouch dancing, they were tolerated. Sadly, although federal legislation was in place with the 1964 Civil Rights Act, many Americans still showed outward signs of racial prejudice. In 1968, during a singing duet on a network television entertainment show, host Petula Clark gently placed her hand on Harry Belafonte's arm. The "interracial touching" between a man and a woman sent corporate sponsors (mainly in the southern affiliates) "into an uproar." threatening "to pull their advertising support" ("Censorship Incidents 1960s," n.d.).

DISCOTHÈQUES, "KILLER JOE" PIRO, AND GO-GO DANCERS

Discothèques originated in Paris, France, before World War II. Unlike the other nightclubs and dance halls of the time that hired live bands, one Parisian club named "La Discotheque" took to playing songs from the large selection of records that they kept on the premises. The name "discothèque" was derived from the French term for library *bibliotheque*, which housed books; therefore, a club that housed a record disc music library was referred to by the French as a *discothèque.* After World War II, as a result of the influx of American soldiers, the Parisians danced the Jitterbug to the records of swing music. One of these clubs was the widely acclaimed and fashionable Whiskey A Go-Go. Eventually, the discothèque idea spread from France to England and then to America (Panati 1991, 385).

In America in the fall of 1961, the affluent Jet Set discovered the Peppermint Lounge and The Twist in New York City (see earlier in this chapter). As The Twist dance craze spread, many other clubs opened and began playing records instead of hiring live bands. The clubs did not require much space since a bandstand was not required, nor was much space needed for the freestyle type dances. The discothèque scene was fueled by the notoriety attended to the celebrities and high society who adorned the pages of influential magazines including *LIFE, LOOK,* the *Saturday Evening Post,* and *Harpers.* Newspapers, including *The Los Angeles Times,* the *Washington Post, The New York Times,* and the *New York Daily*

In early 1964, *American Bandstand* and Clark left the Philadelphia WFIL-TV studios and moved the entire production to California. The first California show aired on Saturday afternoon, February 8, 1964. The next night the famed Aragon Ballroom in Chicago closed, and The Beatles made their first national American network appearance on *The Ed Sullivan Show*. This one solitary weekend represented a changing of the old guard in American social dancing (Jackson 1997, 229).

In Hollywood, California, the *American Bandstand* once-a-week amateur dancers were looking more professional and were hogging the camera. With the change in Rock 'n' Roll music leaning more to the British flavor of The Beatles, *American Bandstand* sought to maintain its dancing theme. By 1965, the show programmed more Motown and Soul music. At the same time, *Bandstand* introduced its first regular African American dance couple Famous Hooks and June Strode. (In the past, the show had infrequent appearances of African American couples but none were regulars.) In September 1967, *Bandstand* finally aired in color, the last television show on ABC-TV to do so (Jackson 1997, 243). According to *Bandstand* historian Michael Shore, "The look of the show was changed [and] the show simply became that much less of a fixture in the lives of its viewers" (Shore and Clark 1985, 92).

During the late 1950s, ABC-TV had a hit afternoon lineup that featured *American Bandstand* and followed the dance show with the *Mickey Mouse Club*. The *Mickey Mouse Club* combined with the opening of Disneyland in California and quickly became a perennial favorite among America's children. The show also had a group of regulars known as the "Mouseketeers." One of those regulars was a very young Annette Funicello who would later branch out into a singing and movie career. As a teenager Funicello had quite a few hit records and regularly appeared as a guest on *American Bandstand*. The notoriety led her into a Hollywood movie career typified by starring in a series of Southern Californian "Beach movies." Funicello's costar in many of those movies was another frequent *American Bandstand* guest, Frankie Avalon. Their movies included *Beach Party* (1963), *Bikini Beach* (1964), *Beach Blanket Bingo* (1965), and *How to Stuff a Wild Bikini* (1965). The movies all had a similar theme of teenagers at or near the beach and sometimes included surfing. The movies had simplistic scripts, and the attraction was the singing and dancing. The dancing was either featured on the beach or in a discothèque. The dancing was freestyle and included the Watusi, Mashed Potato, Frug, Swim, Monkey, Jerk, and the Freddy.

CLAY COLE, SHINDIG!, WHERE THE ACTION IS, AND EVERYTHING'S "A GO-GO"

During the early 1960s, regional television markets still sought to capitalize on teenage dance shows that copied the format of *American Bandstand*. In 1961, Jack Spector, a New York radio disc jockey hosted his own *Bandstand* type show. *The Jack Spector Show* was broadcast over WPRO-TV channel 12 in Providence, Rhode Island. In 1962, *The Dave Sennett Dance Party* was also broadcast from Rhode Island on WPRO-TV. The shows featured amateur teenage kids dancing to records of Rock 'n' Roll hits of the day as well as live guests lip-synching to their hits. However, in Baltimore, *The Buddy Deane Show* (see Chapter 4) was one teenage dance show that refused to integrate. They did offer to expand the "Negro Day" from once a month to "three or four days." Civil Rights groups applied constant pressure, but the producers refused to yield. Rather than allow blacks and whites to dance side-by-side, the station simply cancelled the show (Jackson 1997, 231).

One of the few regional teenage dance shows that had a continued run through most of the 1960s was hosted by Clay Cole. Beginning on September 10, 1959, Cole (himself a teenager at 19 years old) hosted a seven-days-a-week *Rate the Records* on local New York/New Jersey affiliate channel 13. His audience was drawn from the large metropolitan tri-state area of New York, New Jersey, and Connecticut. In 1960, almost immediately after The Twist craze broke, Cole had the distinction of having Chubby Checker on to demonstrate The Twist before the *American Bandstand* national broadcast. In October 1963, after channel 13 was sold, he negotiated to host *The Clay Cole Show* on channel 11. He downplayed the rebellious side of music saying, "The kids like so-called rock 'n' roll because adults don't." Cole continually stressed the wholesome side of the show saying, "We want the kids to look like [the] Sunday-school type, not the soda-fountain type. We want them to show up as ladies and gentlemen, not mugs." However, as the 1960s progressed with the heightening involvement of young people in the counterculture and growing their hair long, the "wholesome" teenager was hard to find. The show ended in December 1967 (Hinckley, "Not the Soda Fountain Type," 2004).

The format of a teenage dance show was still an idea that attracted television producers. In September 1964, ABC-TV aired *Shindig!*, the first of the newer trendy national prime-time network dance shows. The format was to showcase the current pop stars combining a mix of American and British musical artists including Frankie Avalon, Bobby Rydell, Marvin Gaye, Nancy Sinatra, Gary Lewis and the Playboys, Lesley Gore, Paul Revere and the Raiders, Jackie DeShannon, Peter and Gordon, and Dusty Springfield. Unlike the earlier type dance shows that featured amateur teenage dancers, *Shindig!* hired high-energy professional dancers who appeared on stage behind the guest musical act. The show was an instant hit and the following season was aired two nights a week for one-half hour. The style of the show was fast-paced as was the dancing. The quick energetic style of the dancers led to the term "Go-Go dancers."

The television networks sought to capitalize on the new fad. The formats were basically all the same, especially with each new show featuring its own professional "Go-Go" dancers. Other television shows included *Hullabaloo*, *The T.A.M.I. Show*, *Hollywood a Go-Go*, *Shivaree*, and *Let's Go-Go*. In June 1965, Dick Clark sought to recapture the five-day weekday afternoon teenage audience with *Where the Action Is*. The show was also broadcast on ABC-TV in the former afternoon time slot of *American Bandstand* (Jackson 1997, 237–238).

It seemed that just about anything and everything was supplemented with the ending of "A Go-Go." Many of the highly rated prime-time network television shows parodied the "Go-Go" theme and the trend of the new fad dances. In September 1965, the "talking horse" *Mister Ed* series featured an episode titled "Ed A-Go-Go." During the course of the episode, the cast danced the Watusi, the

Frug, and the Swim. Mister Ed skateboarded and wore a Beatles wig. The cast even introduced a new dance called "The Mule." In December 1965, the prime-time cartoon *The Flintstones* also parodied the Go-Go type dance shows, with an episode titled "Shinrock A-Go-Go." In the episode, Fred Flintstone accidentally drops a bowling ball on his foot. As he is hopping around in pain a producer thinks that Fred has created a brand new teenage dance. Fred is asked to perform the "Frantic" on the television show "Shinrock!" at the dance club "Bedrock A-Go-Go."

Many other highly rated prime-time television shows echoed the contemporary culture of "Go-Go dancers." The parodied television shows all had a similar theme that the teenagers were in a trance-like state controlled by the music such as the "Groovy Guru" on *Get Smart!* Others included dances such as the "Bat-tusi" and the "Bat Twist" on *Batman* and psychedelic dancers on *The Addams Family*, *Lost in Space*, *The Flying Nun*, and *Laugh-In*. The prime time "Go-Go" shows did not last very long. *Hullabaloo* went off the air in August 1966, *Shindig!* ended in January 1966, and *Where the Action Is* lasted until 1967.

Most of the shows did feature dancers of different racial ethnicity, but because of the nature of the freestyle nontouch dancing, they were tolerated. Sadly, although federal legislation was in place with the 1964 Civil Rights Act, many Americans still showed outward signs of racial prejudice. In 1968, during a singing duet on a network television entertainment show, host Petula Clark gently placed her hand on Harry Belafonte's arm. The "interracial touching" between a man and a woman sent corporate sponsors (mainly in the southern affiliates) "into an uproar." threatening "to pull their advertising support" ("Censorship Incidents 1960s," n.d.).

DISCOTHÈQUES, "KILLER JOE" PIRO, AND GO-GO DANCERS

Discothèques originated in Paris, France, before World War II. Unlike the other nightclubs and dance halls of the time that hired live bands, one Parisian club named "La Discotheque" took to playing songs from the large selection of records that they kept on the premises. The name "discothèque" was derived from the French term for library *bibliotheque*, which housed books; therefore, a club that housed a record disc music library was referred to by the French as a *discothèque*. After World War II, as a result of the influx of American soldiers, the Parisians danced the Jitterbug to the records of swing music. One of these clubs was the widely acclaimed and fashionable Whiskey A Go-Go. Eventually, the discothèque idea spread from France to England and then to America (Panati 1991, 385).

In America in the fall of 1961, the affluent Jet Set discovered the Peppermint Lounge and The Twist in New York City (see earlier in this chapter). As The Twist dance craze spread, many other clubs opened and began playing records instead of hiring live bands. The clubs did not require much space since a bandstand was not required, nor was much space needed for the freestyle type dances. The discothèque scene was fueled by the notoriety attended to the celebrities and high society who adorned the pages of influential magazines including *LIFE*, *LOOK*, the *Saturday Evening Post*, and *Harpers*. Newspapers, including *The Los Angeles Times*, the *Washington Post*, *The New York Times*, and the *New York Daily*

News, also paid a seemingly endless amount of attention to the dance crazes in their gossip columns, entertainment pages, and sometimes even headlines. One individual who achieved a fair share of headlines was Frank "Killer Joe" Piro.

Frank Piro was born of Italian immigrant parents in East Harlem, New York. In 1942, he achieved acclaim as "the first non-Negro" to win the Jitterbug in the Serviceman's Division of the Harvest Moon Ball Dance Contest (see Chapter 3). He supposedly earned the nickname "Killer Joe" because of the fact that his tireless energy wore out numerous dance partners. After World War II, he frequented the Latin music dance halls and was making a name for himself as a dance instructor. In the early 1950s, he taught the Mambo and Cha-Cha at the famed Palladium (see Chapter 4). Piro maintained a studio at 54 West 55th Street in Manhattan. Unlike other dance instructors, he did not advertise nor did he franchise his studio. Throughout his career (he died in 1989 at the age of 68) he preferred to handle only the number of students that he could personally instruct and preferred to stay directly involved.

"Killer Joe" Piro with partner Olga Varvaro at Roseland Ballroom in New York City, c. 1966.   © Bettmann/Corbis.

Piro reached celebrity status after adults and high society embraced The Twist craze. He was described by *The New York Times* as "a dance instructor to high society and popularized many of the steps of the discothèque era." In fact, many of his clients were affluent celebrities and those among high society. In February 1965, he received banner headlines when he introduced the dance La Bostella (see earlier in this chapter) to the affluent "Jet Set" at Shepard's discothèque at the Drake Hotel. Famed author Gay Talese called him a "tireless dancer" (1964, 88). In 1965, *LIFE* magazine carried a full page ad of "Killer Joe" featuring a new dance called "the Mule." In January 1966, columnist Charles L. Mee of *The New York Times* called him "Discotheque Man." He called Piro "the pre-eminent performer, teacher and lay analyst of the Twist and all its descendants: the Shake, Jerk, Slop, Monkey, Dog, Frug, Swim, Watusi, Bug, Mule, and Hully-Gully" (1966, 92). Mee witnessed Piro's club hopping and mingling among the dance crowd, which most of the time meant spending seven nights a week at various dance clubs.

At the time, New York City flourished with discothèques including The Dom, Hippopotamus, Sybil Arthur, Ondine, Il Mio, L'Interdit, and Discothèque-au-Go-Go. In February 1965, *The New York Times* journalist Philip Dougherty wrote, "The common denominator of the discothèque is darkness, a small dance floor and the beat" (43). "Murray the K's World" was one of the few exceptions. It was a large discothèque in an abandoned airplane hanger at Roosevelt Field in Queens, New York. It also contained one of the first multimedia sound and light presentations that accompanied the music, an element that would be a distinctive feature of the Discos in the late 1970s (McDonagh 1979, 93). Sybil Arthur, which became known simply as Arthur's, received such media attention, due to the celebrity clientele, that it became the first of the discothèques to restrict entry by use of velvet ropes and a doorman. A franchise branch was opened in Los Angeles. The exclusivity, however, came under attack by the Human Rights Commission and Arthur's was closed in June 1969 (Lawrence 2003, 16–17).

During the late 1960s, the discothèques had the music played by DJs who began using two turntables and created a continuous stream of music by mixing the end (or sometimes middle) of a song into another of similar beats. The good DJs were able to create a smooth transition that kept the freestyle dancers on the floor for long periods of time. Some of the club DJs began offering "discothèque-to-take-out," which was the precursor to the late twentieth century development of the mobile DJ for weddings and catered affairs. The 1960s were a step up from the Record hops of the 1950s (see Chapter 4) that had simple record players and limited amplification. By 1965, turntables, speakers, and amplifiers were improving. The promise was "to turn home, club, or hotel into a discothèque." At the time three mobile DJs advertised in Manhattan: Slim Hyatt (the resident DJ for Shepard's discothèque at the Drake Hotel), dance instructor Killer Joe Piro, and a group called the "Porpoise" (Dougherty, "Now the Latest Craze Is 1-2-3, All Fall Down," 1965, 43).

In 1964, the Arthur Murray Dance Studios released an album titled *Arthur Murray presents Discotheque Dance Party*. The 12 song 33 1/3 LP contained five songs for the Fox Trot, two for Twisting, one each for Merengue, Cha-Cha, Mashed Potato, Hully-Gully, and Jamaica Ska. In reality the dances on the album were not the same dances that were danced in the new discothèques. The purpose of the album was to capitalize on the current trend. The album also sought to inform the potential record buyers and those curious about the growing nationwide discothèque scene, including one in the small town of Stockbridge, in the Berkshire Hills of western Massachusetts. The album notes promised,

> A happy choice of tempos...there are two separate bands to duplicate the changing moods of a Discotheque program. Victor Gerard's smooth style alternates with the swinging hi-jinx of The Hip City Five. The variety of styles and the sequence of the numbers are calculated to make your own living room into a real Discotheque. Just roll back the rug, turn down the lights, jam-pack the floor, and send your folks to a movie (Album notes).

In June 1964, *Glamour* magazine hosted a party for over 1,000 discothèque dancers at the Palladium. Journalist Robert Alden covered the event and provided a first-hand account. He noted,

> The dance floor was swaying. The bombastic drive of the rock 'n' roll music had the dancers pounding the floor in unison, and under the impact the sturdy dance floor bent, but fortunately did not give. On display was the twist and a large group of dances derived from the twist—the Frug, the wobble, the surf, the Hully-gully, the uncle willy, the Jamaican ska, the mashed potato, and the smashed banana (Alden, "1,000 Twisters and One Floor Swing at Venerable Palladium," 1964, 28).

By 1965 over 5,000 similar type discothèques were in operation throughout the United States (Stearns and Stearns 1994, 5).

A short-lived fashion fad from the discothèque era for men was the Nehru jacket —a lapel-less jacket buttoned to the neck with a square cutout at the neck, similar to a priest collar. A turtleneck sweater or shirt was usually worn underneath the jacket. Pants styles included bell-bottoms for both men and women. Skirts were extremely short as evidenced by the miniskirt. The short skirts were usually accompanied by high on the calf "Go-Go" boots. The Go-Go boots were popularized by the television shows such as *Shindig!*, *Hullabaloo*, and *Where the Action Is*, as well as by the Go-Go dancers in the discothèques.

Go-Go dancers were young women who were paid to dance on a stage or on a perch within the discothèque. In 1965, the Whiskey à Go Go nightclub in Hollywood, California, for example, provided a suspended cage-like platform high above the dance floor. Usually three scantily clad female dancers occupied the perch and performed while the public danced on a floor below. Many other discothèques had similar arrangements. In 1966, the Ginza Nite Club in New York City provided a suspended platform hung from the ceiling by chain link. The supporting chains spaced about 12 inches apart gave the appearance of a gilded cage. The Go-Go dancers eventually faded from the social dance scene, as did the discothèques. The main reason was that the social times were changing, and women dancing as objects on a platform or as "prisoners" in discothèque cages were fast becoming not socially acceptable.

"Go-Go dancers" on a suspended platform dance above the crowd at the Whiskey à Go Go nightclub in Hollywood, California. In this photo taken in January 1965, the dancers are sporting short skirts and bare midriffs. Note the fringes on the outfits that accentuated the fast-paced body action of the dancers was derived from The Twist dresses.   AP/Wide World Photos.

"WHAT MAKES DANCING WRONG?" AND "TWISTING LIVES ON"

By the 1960s, many religious organizations had relaxed their views on dancing. But, on the other hand, there were still a significant number of religious leaders and groups that would not give up the attack. Up until 1960, the main thrust of religious objection had to do with the face-to-face embrace of the closed position required of most social dances. A logical deduction would lead to the fact that with a dance such as The Twist, and subsequent freestyle dances, that the solo dancing would alleviate the objections. But that just did not happen.

At the time, most of the Catholic churches sponsored "Conforturnity" on Friday night in either their gym or recreation hall. The idea of Conforturnity was a place for the teenagers to congregate and socialize. The main recreational activity was music and dancing. But they were not allowed to do The Twist. As discussed earlier in this chapter in "Risk in the Twist and a Brave New Whirl," parochial school students in the archdioceses of New York City, for example, were forbidden by the Catholic Church to dance The Twist. Catholic Bishop Burke's rhetoric and disdain for The Twist was also echoed by many other moralists and media sources.

Even though The Twist separated the partners from the "deplorable" embrace of partner dancing, objections still mounted. The gyrations and movements of the hips and pelvic area of the body while Twisting appalled the moralists and religious factions. In 1962, at the time that Bishop Burke issued his edict, The Twist was in the midst of its greatest popularity among mainstream adults. But at that time, unlike the previous decades, they had both the kids and the adults alike enjoying the fun, frenzy, and frivolity of "objectionable" dancing.

In 1960, the Reverend William W. Orr in Chicago published *The Christian and Amusements*. Within his treatise he commented on just about all the mainstream fads, toys, games, music, and television shows that were enjoyed by mainstream Americans. He held particular disdain for dancing, and his argument was against the mainstream direction that social dancing had attained. He wrote,

> I know very well that dancing is overwhelmingly popular, and just about everybody dances....I am also aware that you will seldom find a voice raised against it, even in some Christian circles. But...I believe the dance is in the Devil's territory, and I believe it is away [sic] out of bounds for followers of Christ....In many cases it soils lives and could cause immorality of the worst sort....Those who are devotees of the dance claim many things, but I have not yet heard them claim that dancing is to the glory of God. Nor have I ever heard of a dance being opened with "All Hail the Power of Jesus' Name," or stopped in the middle for prayer, or even terminated by an earnest invitation for the ones present to receive the Lord Jesus Christ as personal Saviour [sic] (99–102).

The good Reverend was so adamant that he even dismissed any dancing within the privacy of the home stating it "has a way of growing into something else." Unlike the editor of the Christian magazine *These Times* (see Chapter 4) and the Reverend A.M. Cree and Thomas Faulkner from the 1920s (see Chapter 2), the Reverend Orr stopped just short of the often repeated statement, "there is a very short step from home to hell" but the same thought is implied. The Reverend Orr felt that the only answer was complete abstinence from dancing. He did offer some alternative suggestions to suppress the urge to engage in social dancing. Some alternatives to do at home included playing board games like Monopoly, Parcheesi, or even the card game Old Maid. He was serious when he suggested, "Perhaps you could pull taffy and get all stuck up!" (1960, 104).

With the popularity of Square Dancing, the Reverend Orr felt he should also comment. He felt that the use of the word "dancing" was somewhat misnamed. He actually likened Square Dancing to "a game rather than a dance." His reasoning was that the partners in Square Dancing did not assume the positions so objectionable in other forms of dance such as face-to-face and the close proximity of the partners. He did caution, however, that to avoid any objections the square dance should always be held in a well-lit area under quality supervision. Orr did note that if a person was not careful, the appeal of Square Dancing might just well lead others astray to venture towards social dancing. He cited numerous accounts of young people who began "their downfall with their participation in square dancing which has led them into the evils of ballroom [nee social] dancing" (1960, 105–106).

In 1963, the Reverend Don Humphrey of Great Bend, Kansas, in his publication *What Makes Dancing Wrong?* posited that the thesis of his book "will attempt to prove that dancing causes sin" (2). Humphrey invoked the common twentieth century attack on dancing harkening back to the days of the Reverend Billy Sunday, the Reverend Thomas Faulkner, and the Reverend A.M. Cree (see Chapters 1 and 2) decreeing that "sex is inseparable from the dance. That is what makes dancing wrong" (3). In defense of his argument, he devoted almost half his book to chapters titled "Emphasis in Dancing is Sexual," "Dancing is Sexually Arousing," and "Dancing is an Expression of a Sexual Outlet." He disputed the fact that although over 39 million Americans (both young and old) danced and many religious denominations sponsored dance socials—dancing was "morally wrong." He added that if an individual chose to dance, it "may result in the losing of their souls" (2).

Unlike the Reverend Orr, Humphrey conceded that "married couples are free to enjoy together anything of a sexual nature they both desire" including dancing. Once again he echoed the erotic sensual description of his Christian predecessors. He continued to provide writing in a descriptive manner that rivaled some of the best romance novels of the day—only he was serious. He emphasized,

> A normal man cannot hold a girl in his arms, their bodies pressed against each other dancing cheek to cheek, and not have his emotions stirred sometimes to desire her body …it is physical contact that sends the blood racing through their being and makes them feel desirous all over their bodies.…In dancing, physical positions are employed that should be reserved for the marriage state (1963, 16–19)

Humphrey's marital concession, however, came with the admonishment that added "only if it is in privacy and does not influence those who are not married" (1963, 12). In other words, a married couple could only dance in the privacy of their own home where no else could see them—including their own children.

In a later chapter, however, Humphrey's marital concession was examined with the question "why is it that after marriage people seldom dance as much as before?" (1963, 15). Curiously, Humphrey did not actually ask the opinions of anyone who danced, either married or unmarried. Rather, he said, "we shall never quote any human being to prove anything as right or wrong. Always it shall be the Bible that either substantiates or condemns" (1963, 2). Although Humphrey quoted Matthew, Mark, Luke, and Samuel, he missed the fact that teenagers at the time were more likely to quote John, Paul, George, and Ringo. In addition, an ad-hoc sampling of loving relationships of adults that have transgressed through the social, political, and economical turmoils of twentieth century America produced a simple fact: Those who dance together, with all their heart, soul, and, yes, even their feet—shared an equal 50/50 partnership not only on the dance floor but in the realities of life.

In actuality, the Reverend Humphrey's beliefs might not really have been as devoutly Christian in nature as they appeared. In reality, close examination of his attack on dancing might reveal that his true intentions were a devout fascist belief. His summation echoed the chilling words, "Dancing will never be right until we can regiment people's intelligence and be sure that they only think certain things" (1963, 27).

A 1964 article in *The New York Times*, titled "Though The Fad Is Gone, Twisting Lives On," might have not only summed up the end of The Twist fad, but might also have provided a good analogy, Alan Hughes wrote,

> Indeed, social dancing may be one of the greatest assets to healthy growing up that exists for the young nowadays. Not the kind of social dancing that begins in Miss Prim's weekly classes, where courtly manners, white gloves, and a host of other artificialities prevail, but the social dancing the young discover for themselves...In any case, the young will create the dances they need if the old will only stay out of the way (72).

Twisting did, in fact, live on. The separation of partners on the dance floor became the mainstay of social dancing throughout the remainder of twentieth century. The simple fun and frivolity of The Twist era, however, was nothing compared to the extravagance of the Disco era.

6

The Hustle, Saturday Night Fever, and Disco: 1970–1979

I like to think that once they start dancing they stop believing they have troubles. And isn't that what most people want to do these days?

—Marty Arret, 1971

The Political, Social, and Cultural Climate

In the 1970s, there was a considerable change in American society as evidenced by the anti-Vietnam sentiment, recreational drug use, and Affirmative Action. The average workweek was 35 to 40 hours, and the 9 A.M. to 5 P.M. Monday to Friday job was commonplace. During this time, retirement among individuals over the age of 55 increased, as did travel vacations, and leisure activities (Kraus 1971, 310).

Cultural pride was outwardly displayed by many ethnic groups, including Puerto Ricans, Mexicans, and Italian Americans. Equality movements surfaced through Gay Liberation, Women's Liberation, and the American Indian Movement. It was also a time of sexual freedom. Books that challenged the status quo of America's sexual mores became nationwide best sellers. They included *Everything You Always Wanted to Know About Sex but Were Afraid to Ask*, *The Sensuous Woman*, *Fear of Flying*, *I'm O.K., You're O.K.*, *Any Woman Can*, *The Joy of Sex: A Gourmet Guide to Love Making*, and *More Joy of Sex*.

The war in Vietnam escalated and student protests joined by other Americans from all walks of life reached massive proportions. As a result, the view towards Vietnam among government officials in Washington, D.C., was slowly changing. They realized that the war could not be won and it was also tearing apart the fabric of American society. As a result, President Nixon laid plans for a systematic withdrawal of American soldiers by 1973. In that same year, the United States eliminated the mandatory draft process through Selective Service and instituted a policy of an "all-volunteer" army. In 1974, as a result of the Watergate scandal Richard Nixon resigned as President of the United States. (His vice president, Spiro Agnew, had also previously resigned.) Gerald Ford, who had been selected as a replacement vice president, assumed the presidency.

The increased prosperity of the post–World War II period was less evident. By the mid-1970s, the United States was in a wide-sweeping recession. Gasoline shortages nationwide led to long lines at the gas stations. In many instances, gasoline purchases were rationed and in some cases were not even available. Many of the major cities, long since ignored by substantial federal funding, were also faced with impending bankruptcy. New York City, for example, petitioned the federal government for assistance and was turned down by President Gerald Ford. A famous headline carried by the *New York Daily News* read "Ford to City: Drop Dead."

In 1976, the nation prepared for the Bicentennial (the 200th anniversary of the ratification of the Declaration of Independence). Americans were instilled with a new patriotism as they embraced the coming of the Bicentennial. Television began the countdown to 1976 a full year in advance with daily 60-second educational tidbits of American history titled *Bicentennial Minutes.*

Television was still the overwhelming choice when spending leisure hours. One of the top rated weekly programs, *All in the Family,* represented a breakthrough by providing stories on contemporary social issues including integration, bigotry, the Vietnam War, women's liberation, and homosexuality. Television continued to provide viewers with sensitive social issues, including segregation and genocide. In 1977, *Roots* dealt with the plight of African American slavery in America. It was presented as a 12-hour miniseries over eight consecutive evenings and watched by over 130 million people. The following year, a four night miniseries *Holocaust,* seen by over 120 million, revived the issue of genocide and the survivors of Nazi persecution.

Some of the harsh topics, graphics, images, and language in these television programs created concern among conservative parental groups. Pressure was placed upon the Federal Communications Commission to designate the time period from 7:00 P.M. to 9:00 P.M. as "Family Viewing Time." In other words, any program deemed inappropriate for small children would not be allowed in that time slot. In 1974, the videocassette recorder (VCR) provided a new option in family home entertainment. The VCR was attached by a cable to a home television set thereby providing the viewer the ability to tape a televised program. The VCR could also be programmed to record while a person was out of the house so they could view a program at their leisure. By the 1980s, Hollywood movie studios began marketing current and classic movie titles available for home rental or purchase.

In the summer of 1975, *Jaws* became the highest grossing film to date. The movie, set at a summer beach community, told a tale of a shark that viciously attacked swimmers. The tension and terror created by the movie gave moviegoers a fear of going into the water. In 1976, the movie *All The President's Men,* based on the Watergate scandal and Nixon's subsequent resignation, was the year's most profitable film.

In 1977, there was a symbolic end to the internal strife created by the Vietnam War as President Carter officially announced an "unconditional pardon" to all Americans who had evaded the Selective Service draft. However, in January 1979, Carter's presidency was marred by turmoil in Iran that led to a second major gasoline shortage in America. Lines at gas stations were once again part of American's lives. Service at gasoline stations was regulated to matching up the odd and even number day of the week with the odd and even number on the license plates of cars. In a short time gasoline prices doubled. In November of that year, Iranians overtook the American embassy in Tehran and kidnapped 52 Americans. The hostages would remain captive until January 1981.

In 1977, new technology combined with spectacular special effects compelled audiences to see the science fiction movie *Stars Wars*. Also in 1977, *Saturday Night Fever* popularized the Hustle dance and the Disco craze. Each became surprise hits that filled the movie theaters. In 1978, a simple fun movie, the Hollywood release of *National Lampoon's Animal House*, spurned an interest in "toga parties." Happiness was spread throughout the country with the ever-popular "smiley face" button. In 1971, during a six-month period over 20 million buttons were sold. The button became associated with a trendy slogan as Americans wished each other to "Have A Nice Day" (Panati 1991, 377).

As a result of the success of Woodstock (see Chapter 5), Rock music was performed in large stage shows by the likes of Mick Jagger of the Rolling Stones and David Bowie, where the audience went to watch the performers dance and the crowd swayed along. On the other hand, by the mid-1970s, the new music genre Disco had teens and adults returning to partner "touch" dancing with the Hustle. In the late 1970s, Disco also had a multitude of meanings: It was a dance style, it was used to describe an entire new genre of music, it was the name of a nightspot for dancing, and it represented a freewheeling sexual lifestyle.

During the tumultuous time of recession and cities faced with impending bankruptcy, the continuing war in Vietnam, student unrest on college campuses, and the flourishing hippie counterculture, it might not have been a total surprise that many people sought the fun of Disco dancing. In 1971, dance instructor Marty Arret, who also led a dance contest at Corso's, a trendy Latin Club on East 86th Street in Manhattan, said, "I like to think that once they start dancing they stop believing they have troubles. And isn't that what most people want to do these days?" (Bosworth 1971, 62).

The Dances

Women love men that can dance, it's just a proven fact.

—Deney Terrio, 1977

The fact is, if you can walk, you can dance.

—K-tel, 1978

A DANCE RECESSION

After 1970, there was a great disparity in American social dancing. Most of the dancing styles were divided across the generations. Many displayed their dancing ability at a family celebration such as a wedding. Abe Peck, editor of *Rolling Stone* magazine observed, "At a wedding, the old folks Waltz and Tango and Fox Trot; the parents of the group Rumba and Charleston and Jitterbug; aunts and uncles call for Cha-Cha, Mambo, Merengue and Twist; and 'the kids' raise their arms in the air and move their bodies in any way that feels good" (Peck 1979, 116).

For the most part, during the early 1970s, there was no major dance craze nor were there many available dance venues, and public dancing in itself was at a low point. However, some small segments of the American public sought relief from bad headlines by learning ballroom dances and old traditional standards. In March 1971, John Salonz, owner of the Fred Astaire Dance Studios in New York and Pennsylvania, said that his experience was that, "In spite of the recession, in spite of a general feeling of gloom, people it seems are dancing." He said that "disco-theque dancing" was still the most common "because it's the easiest to fake." He also felt that the popularity of the Twist made people "aware of their bodies," but after such a long period of dancing apart he thought that adults were "tired of dancing alone." He observed a general trend in a return to what he termed "slow 'together' dancing." As a result, some adults were returning to the dance studios for lessons. During the first two months of 1971, at his Manhattan school alone, he had over 200 new applicants sign up for lessons, and his business had almost doubled since 1969. Most of those wanted to learn the Tango and Viennese Waltz. A few even requested to learn the Hula.

Other dance studios reported a similar upswing in students taking ballroom lessons. In all, about 10,000 people in New York City were enrolled in dance studios, about 40 percent male and 60 percent female. Salonz said the "Women stick to classes longer because it makes them feel so good. Men tend to learn a few steps and then stop. We also have a few customers who don't enjoy dancing at all. What they want to buy is some self-confidence."

Beyond the dancing schools, very few public dancing facilities were available. Roseland Ballroom in New York City, for example, was having a hard time attracting new dancers. Most of their steady clientele had simply grown old and either died or were incapable of making it onto to the dance floor. Mr. and Mrs. Don Colettis echoed the reality of the social climate. The Colettis said they took continuous dance lessons and enjoyed the Samba on Saturday nights at New York's Roosevelt Hotel. They said, "it makes us forget—for a minute—that we have a son over in Vietnam" (Bosworth 1971, 62).

SOUL TRAIN, THE BREAKDOWN, THE SCOOBY DOO, THE LOCKERS, AND *BANDSTAND* REUNIONS

In 1971, producer Don Cornelius provided a "hipper all-black" version of *American Bandstand* titled *Soul Train*. In 1970, the show actually started on WCIU, a small UHF station in Chicago, and was an instant hit among the city's African American population. The following year, the show was moved to California and syndicated to 33 cities on a weekly basis nationwide. The ratings were very good in cities such as Atlanta, Chicago, Cleveland, Detroit, New York, and Philadelphia. At the time, Cornelius claimed it was the most watched TV show by African Americans, in more than 2 million homes each week.

Basically, *Soul Train* followed the same format as *American Bandstand*. The dancers danced to prerecorded music and the musical guests lip-synched. In questions on comparisons to *American Bandstand*, Cornelius, the show's creator, producer, and host said, "A dance show is a dance show, is a dance show. We've always realized that we were doing *American Bandstand* or whoever did this before us." Cornelius's media-relation side might have been a bit humble, since in reality he was the show's creator, producer, writer, host, and personally selected the music and guests. As such, this placed him as one of the very first African Americans to hold that distinction in the American media culture of television. Also in 1971, Don Cornelius asked record producers Gamble and Huff (see later this chapter) for an

Soul Train was a televised dance program that combined both the music and culture of African Americans. In this photo, host Don Cornelius (at the far right) introduces dance contest winners. The Lockers, a high-energy dance team that were noted for their brightly colored dazzling costumes, are the first six on the left. Courtesy of Photofest.

upbeat theme song for the show. The Philadelphia producers responded with the song "T.S.O.P. (The Sound of Philadelphia)" by the group MFSB. (The song would also go to No. 1 on the R&B *Billboard* chart.) The addition of the "Philly Sound" earned *Soul Train* the distinction as the trendy new "hip" television dance show (Meisler 1995, D7).

In February 1973, Clayton Riley's eloquent review in *The New York Times* termed the show as "a grooving, swinging, moving thing of beauty." The music played was Soul and Rhythm and Blues "incorporating very fundamental dance beats into its structure." The essence of cultural pride is evident in Riley's description of the show. He proudly exclaimed,

> Each week a group of Black young people from the Los Angeles area get it on to live and recorded Black music, exhibiting in addition to the most fabulously creative dance steps extant in the land today, a personal and glorious sense of *self* that they realize in a very visceral place, a place beyond any intellectual measure.

Soul Train combined both the music and culture of African Americans for the first time. Riley added that *Soul Train* was an extension of a long-standing tradition. He described the cultural significance of *Soul Train* as:

> The constant reflection of a social milieu that includes children *and* adults whose understanding of one another is based on the common denominator of dance music and language. Black social dancing remains a way of living out a set of historical realities that have always been at once familiar to Black grammar school kids as is to their grandparents.

Riley did note a very significant connection to the tradition of *American Bandstand* when he added, "But the kids *are* the show" (Riley 1973, 121).

The kids, indeed, were the show, but the selection process was quite unique. Auditions were held only the first time the show went to California. After that, the only way to get on the show was to have a recommendation from one of the show's current dancers. Cornelius explained the reason. He said, "People who dance well, dress well, are well groomed and know how to behave seem to know others who dance, dress, and behave well" (Strauss 1995, TE3).

Two *Soul Train* dancers, Don Campbell and Damita Jo Freeman, were responsible for introducing three popular dances of the time—the Lock, the Breakdown, and the Scooby Doo. For the Breakdown, Freeman suggested an exaggerated step back on one leg and swinging the opposite arm and repeated the motion with the other leg and opposite arm. Actually, the alternate arm and leg was the natural motion that a person did in a regular walking step. The Breakdown did not involve any movement of the feet. She said, the "only movement is in your hips, knees and arms and, of course, your head." Freeman described the Scooby Doo as "a jump-kick dance which is frantic." The simple dance added the exaggerated movements of the cartoon character of the same name (Freeman 1976, 98–103).

Don Campbell developed the dance known as the Lock (sometimes called "Locking" or "Popping"). The dance was a robotic style of dance moving and stopping in a freeze, giving a mechanical or robotic appearance. The Lock was described in *Dancing Madness* as "kicking out a knee, thrusting back with the opposite hip, rolling his wrist and pointing and locking every four beats" (Peck 1976, 58).

Both Campbell and Freeman went on to a professional dance career with a dance group that they formed called the Lockers. The Lockers were a high-energy dance team that was noted for their brightly colored dazzling costumes. The Lockers were extremely influential in the stage dancing career of Michael Jackson, as well as influencing the Break Dancing styles of the Electric Boogaloo and Hip Hop (see Chapter 7).

In October 1993, Cornelius decided to step down as host of *Soul Train*. He thought that after 22 years the show needed a new look. Thereafter, each week a new guest host presided over the dancers and introduced the musical guest. However, Cornelius continued to produce the show, select all the music, as well as introduce the guest host. Although he might have never said so publicly, Cornelius must have had the same foresight that Dick Clark had when he boasted of an *American Bandstand* run of over 30 years. *Soul Train* matched the 30-year run and still aired first run shows as the twenty-first century began (Rule 1993, C18).

Throughout the 1970s, *American Bandstand* continued on network television as a fixture on Saturday afternoons. At the time, the show was no longer aired live, but rather it was taped every six weeks with three shows on a Saturday and three shows on a Sunday. The show still had its regulars, but the dancers appeared more professional and continually hogged the camera. In addition, the age limit was raised to 21 and then continued upward (Shore and Clark 1985, 154–155).

At the time, however, *American Bandstand* was developing a reputation as a nostalgic memory of dancing times gone by. On February 4, 1977, Clark hosted a special televised *American Bandstand's 25th Anniversary*. The Friday evening show, broadcast on the ABC television network on Friday evening from 9:00 to 11:00 P.M., was billed as "a special two-hour presentation commemorating the quarter-century mark of the popular teen dance program." The show featured over

The February 4, 1977, ABC-TV promotional photo press release for *American Bandstand's 25th Anniversary* featured Dick Clark in front of dancers costumed from the decades of the 1950s, the 1960s, and the 1970s. The nostalgia show was advertised as "a special two-hour presentation commemorating the quarter-century mark of the popular teen dance program." Courtesy of Urban Archives Temple University.

75 performers who took "a happy look back to the days when Bandstand was a Philadelphia fixture." The ABC-TV promotional photo press release featured a close-up of Clark "backed by three lovely ladies." Each of the "lovely ladies" was dressed in a costume reminiscent of a teenage dancer from the decades of the 1950s, the 1960s, and the 1970s (ABC Photo Release 1977). But at the very time that the general mood of American society towards dancing seemed ambivalent, a new world for mainstream American social dancing appeared—it was called Disco.

DISCO, "THE PHILLY SOUND," VAN MCCOY, AND THE HUSTLE

The word "Disco," to describe the music and the dance clubs, first came into use around 1974. No specific instance or person can be attributed to the first use of the word. Some claim that it was simply a shortened version of the word "discothèque." According to cultural critic Stephen Holden (at the time Holden wrote a regular Pop Culture column for the *New York Daily News* and was a featured columnist for *Rolling Stone* magazine), the term came from record companies who had heard of records becoming dance club hits. So they hired "disco consultants" to track the play to cross them over to radio airplay (1979, 29).

Disco was first known as "party music," and its main radio outlet was WBLS-FM in New York. At the time, WBLS-FM was New York's top black radio station and its top DJ was Frankie Crocker. Holden called Crocker "the Alan Freed of disco" (see Chapter 4). Crocker frequented the dance clubs and played many of the same songs over the radio airwaves. In the summer of 1973, he played an obscure hit, a French import titled "Soul Makossa" by Manu Dibango, that is often credited with being the first such crossover Disco hit. Crocker also played dance club hits songs in celebration of gay culture including "I Was Born This Way" by Carl Bean and "To Each His Own" and "Lovin' Is Really My Game" by transvestite singer Sylvester. Crocker also played music known as the "Philly Sound" (Holden 1979, 29).

In 1971, Kenny Gamble and Leon Huff began producing records in Philadelphia, Pennsylvania, under the company name of Philadelphia International Records. With the new record label, Gamble and Huff sought to bring their own musical background to capitalize on the "emerging black music market." At the time research demographics indicated that African Americans were buying more record albums than their white counterparts. The artists leading in sales were R&B and Soul music makers who included Curtis Mayfield, Isaac Hayes, the Temptations, and Diana Ross and the Supremes (Lawrence 2003, 117).

Gamble and Huff's music production continued in the same tradition of Rhythm and Blues, Motown, and Soul that emanated out of the cities, including Detroit and Chicago. In the process they created a new sound that became known as the "Philly Sound." Their productions included songs such as "Love Train" and "I Love Music" by The O'Jays, "When Will I See You Again," by the Three Degrees, "The Love I Lost" by Harold Melvin and the Blue Notes, "Don't Let the Green Grass Fool You" by Wilson Pickett, and "T.S.O.P. (The Sound of Philadelphia)" by MFSB. All the songs had a heavy bass beat and were danceable. The pattern was repeated in dance club hits including "Rock the Boat" by the Hues Corporation, "Rock Your Baby" by George McCrae, and "Love's Theme" by Barry White and the Love Unlimited Orchestra.

Barry White had his first hit in mid-1973 with "I'm Gonna Love You Just a Little More Baby," which topped at No. 3 from his debut album *I've Got So Much to Give.* His songs were described as "a series of sexy hit records...erotic, romantic fantasies." In early 1974, Barry White's "Never, Never Gonna Give You Up" was on the charts at the same time as the instrumental hit "Love's Theme" that he had arranged, composed, and conducted for a 41-piece orchestra. [The previous year he also wrote the hit song "Walkin' in the Rain (With the One I Love)" for Love Unlimited.] Other hits by White included "Can't Get Enough Of Your Love Babe" and "You're My First, My Last, My Everything." All of these songs from the "Philly Sound" crossed over into mainstream popularity and not only sold millions of records but also became American pop classics. In particular, White's "You're My First, My Last, My Everything" had couples returning to partner dancing (Uslan and Solomon 1981, 344).

In 1975, a song simply titled "The Hustle" by Van McCoy and the Soul City Symphony kicked off the national Disco dance craze. At first, people (mainly Hispanic, blacks, and gays) in areas such as New York and San Francisco were dancing the dance but it did not have a name. The song "The Hustle" gave the dance its name. The catchy instrumental music with a resounding danceable beat rising intermittingly to exciting crescendos and limited lyrics sensuously enticed dancers to do the Hustle. By the summer of 1975, the song quickly went to No. 1 on the *Billboard* charts and eventually sold over 10 million copies. The Hustle dance was soon all the rage. Harkening back to "(We're Gonna) Rock Around the Clock" (see Chapter 4), in just one song Van McCoy was able to transform an underground dance style and make it popular among mainstream Americans (Panati 1991, 385).

The Hustle was, in fact, a Latin dance, but more specifically it was purely an American invention created by Hispanics in New York City. Therefore, the Hustle had the distinction as the first Latin dance indigenous to America. Latin dances had maintained a century long tradition as part of American social dance beginning with the Tango in the early twentieth century and continuing with the Rhumba, Samba, Conga, Mambo, and the Cha-Cha. Unlike the Hustle, all of those dances were imported. Most cite the Hustle's origin to the Upper East Side of Manhattan in an area known as Spanish Harlem or sometimes called "El Barrio" (Driver 2000, 109).

In 1975, journalist Dena Kleiman of *The New York Times* cited the origin of the dance to about 1970 in "the black and Puerto Rican bars of Queens." She said that although the dance was performed to many different songs "it is most often done to Van McCoy's 'The Hustle,' which is the 1970s equivalent of the Chubby Checker classic, 'the Twist'" [see Chapter 5].

The Hustle incorporated turns, dips, and moves reminiscent of swing, merengue, and other Latin dances. Some even compared it to a smoothed out Lindy Hop. And, in fact, it developed as a hybrid of the Latin dances and the Lindy Hop. Dance historian Ian Driver said, "Structurally, the hustle is not unlike the Lindy hop: it has a basic step structure, which is then enlivened by more elaborate improvised moves that are unique to each dancing couple. But its sensuality and rhythm give it a decidedly Latin feel" (2000, 207). The Hustle also required a return to dancing in partnership and actual touching once again, and the style was called "touch dancing."

In July 1975, as "The Hustle" song was a nationwide radio hit, *The New York Times* announced, "The Hustle Restores Old Touch to Dancing." In fact, the article read like a "how to" instruction booklet complete with photographs and foot diagrams. The eight-count "Beginner's Hustle" started from a closed position. The basic was described as follows:

> Leader starts tap left toe to the left side and turn head and torso slightly to the left (count 1), bring foot back to start position (count 2), repeat toe tap and head turn to right side (count 3), return right foot to start position (count 4). Walk forward with left foot (count 5) walk forward with right foot (count 6), bring left foot next to right (count 7), hold for one count (count 8). The follower starts with the right foot and mirrors the leaders footwork.

Kleiman observed that the Hustle was danced not only in discothèques but also at graduation parties, weddings, sweet sixteen parties, and proms. But what was most important and surprising to her was that "dance partners are...touching each other once again." Kleiman added, "It calls for two people with a good sense of rhythm and high energy levels who are undaunted by intricate footwork and turns ("The Hustle Restores Old Touch Dancing," 1975, 16).

Because of the "intricate footwork and turns," the Hustle also brought a resurgence of students into the dance studios to learn touch dancing and Hustle techniques. In the previous years there had been nothing to teach since the dancers were "doing their own thing" and simply made it up as they went along. With the Hustle, individuals once again needed to learn how to dance with a partner.

SATURDAY NIGHT FEVER, 2001 A "DISCO" ODYSSEY, AND THE BEE GEES

By mid-1977, however, the Hustle did not necessarily appear to be anything other than just another passing dance fad. In the fall of 1977, as *Saturday Night Fever* wrapped the filming, soundtrack editor Bill Oakes remembered delivering the music to the editors in California. He said, "I was driving down Hollywood Boulevard and in front of me a truck had a bumper sticker saying 'Death to Disco' and in the back of my car I had what was the result of nine months work. And I'm thinking 'we're too late.' Why are we making a movie about a phenomenon that's dying?" In fact, rather than represent a movie at the end of an era, *Saturday Night Fever* signified the birth of a new nationwide American dance craze and a whole new social movement (*VH1 Behind the Music*, documentary, 2001).

In June 1976, a new Saturday night ritual among working class individuals was revealed in a *New York Magazine* cover story titled "Tribal Rites of the New Saturday Night." In the article, writer Nik Cohn described the goings-on within a real-life Disco dance club in Brooklyn named "2001 Odyssey." The story centered on Vincent, a working class Italian American, who in Cohn's words was "a flamboyantly dressed fellow" who by day worked a dead-end job in a hardware store. But on Saturday night, Vincent was "somebody." Cohn wrote,

> So the new generation takes few risks. It goes through high school, obedient; graduates, looks for a job, saves and plans. Endures. And once a week, on Saturday night, its one great moment of release, it explodes....When Saturday night came round and [Vincent] walked into 2001 Odyssey, all the other faces automatically fell back before him, cleared a space for him to float in, right at the very center of the dance floor (31).

In 1997, Cohn admitted that the central character of his story was not actually a real person. Cohn had briefly seen the character that he named "Vincent" in the doorway of the 2001 Odyssey Disco, but he never did get the chance to interview or see him again. Therefore, "Vincent" was a combination of the many dancers whom Cohn observed in the Disco (Errico, "Writer Admits Faking 'Saturday Night Fever' Story," 1997).

However, the paintings by illustrator James McMullan that accompanied the article were quite factual. According to a *New York Magazine* story in 2006 commemorating the 30th anniversary of Cohn's article, McMullan's illustrations "were drawn closely from photos he took during multiple trips to the Bay Ridge Disco called 2001 Odyssey" at the same time that Cohn researched the article. Therefore, although Cohn's article might have been a compilation of fiction, "The paintings are, in essence, fact." Nevertheless, both the "factual" illustrations and the "fictional" story became the basis for the hit movie *Saturday Night Fever* (Sternbergh, "Inside the Disco Inferno," 2006, 98–99).

As for the star of the movie, producer Robert Stigwood had only one person in mind to play the lead role and that was John Travolta. At the time, the 23-year-old Travolta was a teen idol known for his character Vinnie Barbarino from his television show *Welcome Back Kotter* (1975–1979). Since the character "Vinnie" was also from Brooklyn, Stigwood did not want Travolta to have the same cast name. Therefore, he asked screenplay writer Norman Wexler to change the name Vincent to "Tony Manero."

The movie *Saturday Night Fever* was filmed in the actual Bay Ridge, Brooklyn neighborhood in which the story took place. Bay Ridge resident, Thelma Lynn Olsen, who worked at White Castle at the time, vividly remembered the scene filmed within the hamburger restaurant. She said,

> When I first saw Travolta I was behind the counter and he came in on the 5th Avenue side door. I thought he was very, very handsome. But, I wasn't awestruck, I was more amazed by the whole interesting scene of making the movie...When it came out I did go see it. But, primarily to see the scenes that I recognized. Because [laughs] I really wasn't into the Disco scene (Olsen interview, 2004).

On the other hand, there were those who were into the Disco scene but were not so lucky to see the actual filming of the movie. Brooklyn resident Patricia Wakie recalled,

> I remember hanging out every Friday and Saturday night at the disco named "2001 Odyssey." We would go out about 10 P.M. and we would get dressed as if we were going

to a wedding. We never went out in jeans. One Friday night when we went to the disco it was closed. They told us that they were filming a movie. We were really mad. Now, because of that stupid movie, *Saturday Night Fever*, we had to go somewhere else (Wakie interview, 2004).

However, at the time that *Saturday Night Fever* was ready for nationwide release, director John Badham remembered that Paramount Pictures movie studios did not think it would do well. One Paramount executive said, "this [movie] is terrible. It's a vulgar little movie. There's all kinds of bad language in here, nudity and rape scenes and God knows what all." In fact, the movie reflected the harsh reality of life with nonchalance towards coarse language, drug use, discussion of abortion, casual sex, a rape scene in the back of a car, and a priest abdicating from the church. The film's portrayal of Tony Manero was more than that of being the best dancer. Manero is a complex deep character who is egotistical, homophobic, misogynistic, racist, narcissistic, and pessimistic about his future. And it was with some reluctance and pessimism that Paramount Pictures premiered the movie on December 7, 1977, in Hollywood. Despite the pessimism, it was an instant hit and topped the box office, eventually making $285 million dollars.

In December 1977, movie reviewer Frank Rich said the movie "succeeds in capturing the animal drive of disco music and the social rituals of the people who dance to its beat...where working-class kids slave all week so that they can dress up and boogie on Saturday nights" (1977, 69). Film critic Roger Ebert described the movie as

The poster for the movie *Saturday Night Fever* with actress Karen Lynn Gorney and actor John Travolta dancing, c. 1977. Paramount Pictures Corporation / Courtesy of Photofest.

A dark tale about a dead end kid who seeks glory on the dance floor...this movie kinda shook free from the general depression and drabness of the political and musical atmosphere of the seventies and remembered that was what music was really about, especially if you're young. It's having a good time, going out there and dancing. Its Saturday night (*VH1 Behind the Music*, documentary, 2001).

But it was Travolta's dancing that most people remembered about the movie.

In order to prepare for the dance scenes, Travolta worked with dance coach Deney Terrio. (Terrio would later go on to star in a nationally syndicated Disco dance show titled *Dance Fever*—see later in this chapter.) For seven months prior to the actual filming, Travolta danced three hours a day and ran two miles—and in the process also lost 20 pounds. Terrio said, "he was easy to teach." He added, "Women love men that can dance, it's just a proven fact. And I wanted the women to love John not because he was John Travolta or Barbarino but because he could move" (*VH1 Behind the Music*, documentary, 2001).

In fact, one of the most memorable dance scenes in the movie was Travolta's solo dance in the center of the dance floor—to much adoration from the females in the dance club and in movie audiences. At first, the scene was not even scheduled to be part of the movie. At Travolta's insistence the solo dance scene was added. He said, "I had to enforce that scene. They were basing this movie on his being the best dancer, and he didn't have a solo. I had to prove to the audience that he was the best" (Hanson 1978, 166). However, the first time Travolta saw the finished cut of the scene he "was in shock." He said, "my solo dance that I had worked for nine months had been cut to close-up. I cried when I saw it." Upon Travolta's insistence, the scene was reedited to show the whole body from head-to-toe and only one brief close-up. This quintessential dance scene was aided by the multicolored blinking square lights of the dance floor itself.

The lighted dance floor at 2001 Odyssey was actually an addition for the movie. Badham said it "was our most expensive item in the movie." It was made by a company in New York that specialized in lighted dance floors at a cost of $15,000. (In 2005, the floor was sold at an auction.) The movie crew also thought the background did not photograph well. Therefore, they applied standard rolls of aluminum foil to the walls. They also added strings of white Christmas tree lights "to give a glowing effect." It was the Disco 2001 Odyssey that was at the center of Manero's life and being the best dancer was proven through a dance contest ("Director's Commentary," *Saturday Night Fever* DVD).

During the dance contest, Tony and Stephanie (actress Karen Lynn Gorney) performed a dance that was totally opposite those of the other high-energy dance contestants. Badham said, "they go soft and romantic" as the camera followed them through the Bee Gees song "More Than a Woman." Some of the scene was shot in slow motion, but the director was constantly conscious of the dancing and filmed it in a way that stayed "on the beat." It is also the only dance scene where Travolta wore the three-piece white suit.

Following Tony and Stephanie were the last contestants, Puerto Rican "Couple No. 15," Hector and Maria. Movie director John Badham said, "These guys are so hot that they just…burned up the whole floor…[and] broke through any kind of camera angle we had." Therefore, they were filmed similar to Fred Astaire's head to toe method (see Chapter 3). Badham commented that if they were not such great dancers it would have been "deadly to photograph them in the wide shot."

Prior to Tony and Stephanie's dance, an African American couple performed in the dance contest at 2001 Odyssey to the taunts of "Go back to your club!" Badham remembered that at the time he asked some of the regulars at 2001 Odyssey, "What would you do if you saw dancers…that were this good that were African

American? They said, 'We'd walk away; we wouldn't watch them. You're asking us to stand here and watch them and we wouldn't do that.'"

The reality of the time, however, was that ethnic neighborhoods produced ethnic clubs and very rarely did the cultures integrate. Only in instances such as the dance contest did couples venture to another Disco. And in instances of dance contests, the winner was usually selected from one of the regulars. Such is the case in *Saturday Night Fever* as Tony and Stephanie were awarded the first prize. However, Tony knows that the Puerto Rican couple "out danced" them and, therefore he presented them the first prize check and trophy. His partner Stephanie disagreed. Manero countered, "Stephanie, that was rigged. It's like family. They can't give it to no 'spic' [ethnic slur] or no stranger. What are you crazy?" Badham explained,

Nowhere in the movie is this kind of racism and prejudice exposed as clearly as it is in this moment and...we can see something has happened to Tony Manero's character that he realizes...how it's totally wrong probably because he appreciates the quality of the dancing so much and he knows...that he didn't win this contest he didn't win first prize...Both of the other couples were better than him" ("Director's Commentary," *Saturday Night Fever*, DVD).

Travolta's film character, Tony Manero, was in stark contrast to the innocent lovable television character Vinnie Barbarino from the series *Welcome Back Kotter*. In fact, the movie posed a critical question as to whether parents should let their preteen daughters see the movie starring their "idolized heartthrob" (Mann, 1978, D1). *Newsweek* magazine film critic Susan Cheever Cowley added, "While an adult viewer can understand the message of the movie, a 12-year-old caught up in the music, the photography, the sensual rhythm of it may not" (1978, 97).

In order to capitalize on the built-in preteen market, Paramount Pictures released an edited toned down version of the movie, in all removing five minutes of the film. The edited PG (Parental Guidance Suggested) version made it more acceptable for the parents of teenagers and the preteen fans. The sex scenes were eliminated, the coarse language dubbed, and the references to drug use softened. It was this edited version that many remembered about the film.

In 1978, the Hustle dance and "Disco Fever" spread nationwide. However, the mainstream image that perpetuated from *Saturday Night Fever* was Travolta's index finger pointed high in the air and the white three-piece suit with the collared shirt opened over the lapels of the jacket. *Newsweek* magazine announced, "the cleaned-up slicked-back, white-suited look of John Travolta in the film 'Saturday Night Fever' has infected the youth of America. Thousands of shaggy-haired, blue-jeaned-clad youngsters are suddenly putting on suits and vests, combing their hair and learning to dance with partners." Department stores reported opening special sections just for Disco attire. One Brooklyn department store labeled its section "Night Fever." Clubs nationwide encouraged *Saturday Night Fever* look-alike contests. Young men strove to look like John Travolta's "Tony Manero" and young women as Karen Lynn Gorney's "Stephanie" (Cowley, 1978, 97).

The three-piece suit was not the only American classic, so was the movie soundtrack album. In 1978, the soundtrack double album to the movie *Saturday Night Fever* sold an unprecedented 25 million copies and remained at No. 1 on the

Billboard Album charts for an astonishing 24 consecutive weeks. At the time, it became the biggest selling album in music history. The numbers were so staggering because it sold more than the previous three all-time best selling albums combined.

The album had eight No. 1 singles, including "You Should be Dancing," "Jive Talkin'," "How Deep is Your Love," "More Than A Woman," "Stayin' Alive," and "Night Fever" by the Bee Gees, "If I Can't Have You" by Yvonne Elliman, and "A Fifth of Beethoven" by Walter Murphy. Other songs from the album that hit the top ten were "Disco Inferno" by The Trammps, "Boogie Shoes" by K.C. and the Sunshine Band, "Open Sesame" by Kool and the Gang, and another version of "More Than a Woman" by Tavares. The impetus aided Disco music in dominating the radio airwaves. In 1978, the Bee Gees were awarded a Grammy for "Best Album of the Year" for *Saturday Night Fever* (Tobler, "Liner Notes," 1995).

Both the soundtrack album and the movie inspired people to take to the dance floor. The dances included those from the movie, including freestyle Disco, the New York Hustle, the Latin Hustle, the Tango Hustle, and a line dance, the Bus Stop. To dance was to participate and to participate was to belong. But in order to dance one needed to learn how to dance.

A young couple in a dance studio imitates the Disco style and clothes inspired by the movie *Saturday Night Fever*, c. 1978. Photo by Frank A. Cezus / Courtesy of Getty Images 1906833.

HUSTLE DANCE INSTRUCTION, KAREN LUSTGARTEN, AND THE REEMERGENCE OF TOUCH DANCING

In fact, in 1976, editor Abe Peck of *Rolling Stone* magazine had the foresight to publish *Dancing Madness*, which included the Hustle as well as instruction by Karen Lustgarten. Also in 1976, Groove Sound Records released an instructional record album titled *Learn Disco Dancing*. Side one provided vocal voice-over by dance instructors Jeff and Jack Shelley. Side two provided music to practice by. Written dance instruction and illustrations were also included on the back cover for three partner dances—the American Hustle, Latin Hustle, Foxy Trot Hustle—and two line dances—the Walk and the Bus Stop. In addition to dance instruction, many publishers rushed instructional "how to" dance books into publication.

In 1978, K-tel combined a record album with an instructional book titled *Let's Disco!* K-tel advertised, "A complete instructional system for disco dancing." The simple advice provided for the novice Disco dancer said,

> The fact is, if you can walk, you can dance. Basically speaking, those great dancers you've admired on the dance floor or in the movies exhibited three qualities: a sense of rhythm; a love of music; and a willingness to learn, loosen up, and let go (9).

Some other dance instruction books included Kitty Hanson's *Disco Fever* (1978) and *Touch Dancing* (1978), Jack Villari and Kathleen Sims's *The Official Guide to Disco Dance Steps* (1979), Carter Lovisone's *The Disco Hustle* (1979), and Karen Lustgarten's *The Complete Guide to Disco Dancing* (1978) and *The Complete Guide to Touch Dancing* (1979).

In San Francisco, dance instructor Karen Lustgarten had been teaching Disco dancing, both partner and freestyle, since March 1973. At the time, the music and dancing were not mainstream and were considered "underground." At first she advertised it as "fad dancing" since she said at the time "few people knew what the word 'disco' meant." (She later termed it "fast dancing.") Lustgarten learned the dance by frequenting the gay nightclubs in San Francisco, Los Angeles, and New York. She kept a notebook and wrote down the various steps and styles. In her studio, she broke down the steps, variations, and styling, and gave them names

Some of the numerous instruction books and record albums to learn how to Disco dance including *The Complete Guide to Disco Dancing* by Karen Lustgarten at the far right.   Author's Archives.

to teach beginners. She compiled her notes and wrote a book on the Disco dance steps, but she was continually rejected by publishers.

However, in 1978, after the release of the movie *Saturday Night Fever*, her book was sought after by publishers clamoring for anything related to Disco dance instruction. Lustgarten's *The Complete Guide to Disco Dancing* was a runaway best seller and made the New York Times Best Seller List for 13 weeks, climbing to No. 10. In turn, her classes quickly grew to over 250 students. She added, "thanks in big part to that unmentionable movie" (Lustgarten 2002).

In *The Complete Guide to Touch Dancing* (1979), Karen Lustgarten predicted, "It won't take long before you discover that there's something irresistible about touching someone close to you when you dance" (14). Within her book, she reintroduced some of the old-time American social dances, with some "spiced up" new names. The old favorites with new names included the Tempestuous Tango, the Lemon Merengue, the Sensuous Samba (which she subtitled the Bossa Nova), and the Hot-Cha-Cha.

In describing the Hot-Cha-Cha, Lustgarten said it was "a spinoff of the Mambo." In comparing the Mambo derivative to the Cha-Cha for application on the Disco dance floor, Lustgarten harkened back to the discussions of dancing on the off-beat (count 2) or on-beat (count 1). (See discussion on Mambo in Chapter 4.) She suggested, "As long as you keep the basic 'one, two, cha-cha-cha' step....You may find this dance easier than the Mambo because you're dancing *on* the beat" (Lustgarten 1979, 90–94).

In 1980, Lustgarten's success and notoriety increased so much that she earned an invitation as the "Official Disco Dance Instructor" at the Winter Olympics in Lake Placid, New York. The ultimate honor, though, might have come in 1999 when the United States Postal Service issued a commemorative "Disco Music" stamp as part of the "Celebrate the Century" series. The image on the stamp is that of Lustgarten from the cover of her 1978 dance instruction book, *The Complete Guide to Disco Dancing*. Her partner is decked out in a three-piece white suit and black shirt reminiscent of the Tony Manero character from the movie *Saturday Night Fever* (Lustgarten 2002).

After the movie, dance instructors nationwide were soon besieged by students wanting to learn the Hustle. In August 1978, journalist John Rabb of *The Washington Post* spent six weeks researching dancing schools in the Washington, D.C., area. Some of the dance schools that he visited in this area included The Flather and Three, A Dance Studio, The Dance Factory in Arlington, Virginia, the Dushor Dance Club, and Dance World, both in Bethesda, Maryland. All the dance studios were open weekdays from either 10 or 11 A.M. in the morning to 10 or 11 P.M. at night. Most offered Saturday lessons, and all offered group and private lessons. But observation was different from actually taking dance lessons.

Rabb revealed that, "It was time to come out of the closet and learn how to hit the dance floor with style and expertise." To Rabb, that did not mean a reference to homosexuality, but rather "disco dance lessons." In an article which he titled, "How I Stopped Feeling Guilty, Started Jiving, and Got Down to Gyrating and Grooving On the Hardwood," he said that in regards to dancing he always "conjured up long-repressed childhood fears of a time when dancing was for sissies."

However, with the introduction of the on-screen "manliness" presented by John Travolta in *Saturday Night Fever* that no longer applied.

For his first venture into the world of dance instruction, Rabb chose the Vic Daumit Dance Studio located at Connecticut Avenue in Washington, D.C. The second floor studio was reached by a set of "poorly lit stairs," which he climbed with some reluctance. Upon reaching the top, he said,

> Right at that moment I was opening the studio door. The soothing strains of the Bee Gees' "How Deep Is Your Love" filled the mirrored studio where seven or eight couples and their instructors executed and re-executed the steps and turns of the New York and Latin Hustle. Ranged casually around the wooden floor were other students, waiting with encouraging nonchalance for their half-hour in the limelight. In the corner, an effervescent Latin woman patiently drilled a middle-aged black couple on the correct timing for a multiple turn. At the center a small elderly woman whirled effortlessly in the arms of a handsome young instructor while her graying husband watched carefully....Everyone appeared to be having a grand time. They were serious about their dancing and the competent, encouraging instructors seemed to have allayed all fears, real or imagined.

Rabb seemed somewhat surprised and taken aback by the whole atmosphere. His gaze was interrupted by a female instructor who asked "Are you ready to try it yourself?" He eloquently described his first dance lesson as follows:

> She grasped my sweaty hands with a professional firmness, led me to the corner of the floor by the full-length mirrors and lost no time in attempting to teach me the six-step rudiments of the New York hustle....And so it went, to the end of the first half-hour and on into the next week's lesson (1978, 1).

The pattern, as described by Rabb was repeated more and more throughout the country as many adults took dance lessons. In 1978, *Newsweek* magazine reported, "dozens of dance studios have doubled the enrollment of their hustle classes" (Cowley 1978, 97).

THE AMERICAN HUSTLE, LATIN HUSTLE, AND NEW YORK HUSTLE

The Hustle developed not only as a regional dance particular to Los Angeles, San Francisco, and New York City, but it also developed as individual neighborhood variations. There was the Beginner Hustle (sometimes known as the American Hustle), the Latin Hustle, and the Brooklyn Hustle, as well as the California Hustle, the L.A. Hustle, the Tango Hustle, the Foxy Trot Hustle, the Continental Hustle, the Swing Hustle, the Latin-Swing Hustle, and many more. Almost all of the Hustle variations were danced in a six-count basic in 4/4 time.

All the partner Hustle dance variations added spins, turns, dips, drops, and lifts. Many of the moves were the same as those used in traditional American social dances such as the Fox Trot, Tango, Lindy Hop, Mambo, and Cha-cha. The lifts were smooth and graceful, more similar to ballroom lifts and not as acrobatic as the

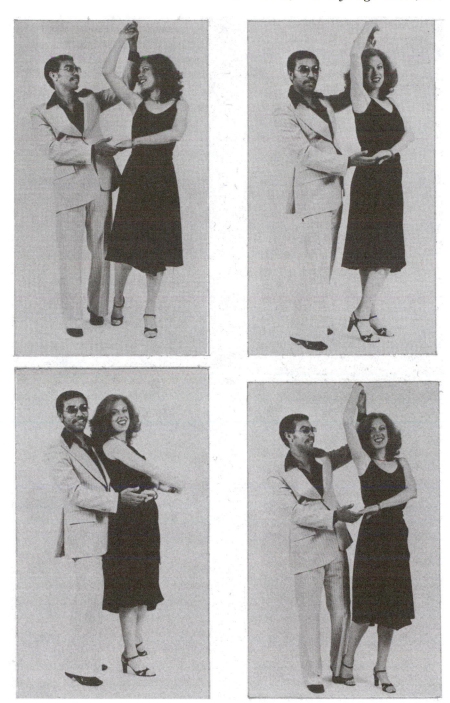

Dance instructor Karen Lustgarten and partner demonstrate one of the many moves for the Hustle dance. This one is the "Wrap-Unwrap Turn." (From *The Complete Guide to Disco Dancing* by Karen Lustgarten. Photographs by Bernie Lustgarten, pages 114–115.)   Courtesy Michael Larsen–Elizabeth Pomada Literary Agents.

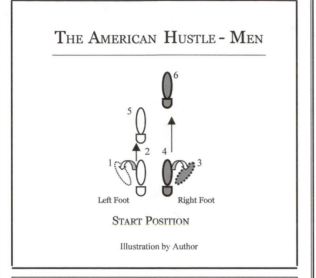

THE AMERICAN HUSTLE - MEN

Left Foot   Right Foot

START POSITION

Illustration by Author

The American Hustle was very similar to the Beginner Hustle (see earlier this chapter). The difference was in substituting a toe tap and torso turn with a side touch. In the American Hustle, the partners face each other in a closed dance position. The six-count basic is: The male leader begins with: Touch left foot to the side (count 1), bring left foot together (count 2), touch right foot to side (count 3), bring right foot together (count 4), walk in place left foot – right foot (counts 5, 6). All the variations take place on the counts of 4, 5, 6. The female follower mirrors her partner's steps beginning with: Touch right foot to the side (count 1). A "Progressive Step," added a little movement: The first three counts remain the same but a walk forward right – left – right (counts 4, 5, 6) is added for the leader and walk backward left – right – left (counts 4, 5, 6) is added for the follower.

Lindy Hop. The similarities included the basic "closed" dance position (see Chapter 1) and the reintroduction of the role of a leader and a follower. Dance instructor Karen Lustgarten offered an historical reference point, "If you can recall how Fred [Astaire] and Ginger [Rogers] danced together in the old-time movies you'll immediately be able to assume this position" (1978, 92). The most common of the partner Hustle dances were The American Hustle, Latin Hustle, and New York Hustle.

Dance instructors Jeff and Jack Shelley on their instructional dance album *Learn Disco Dancing* (1976) and Karen Lustgarten in her book *The Complete Guide to Disco Dancing* (1978) both described the Latin Hustle the same way, including separate headings of "Her Version" and "His Version." The six-count basic for the male leader: Tap left foot to left side, or tap left foot in place (count 1), do a Cha-Cha-Cha stepping left-right-left (counts 2 & 3), walk (either in place or traveling) step right, step left, step right (counts 4, 5, 6). And the six-count basic for the female follower: Tap right foot to right side, or tap right foot in place (count 1), do a Cha-Cha-Cha stepping right-left-right (counts 2 & 3), walk (either in place or traveling) step left, step right, step left (counts 4, 5, 6). Lustgarten commented "that the footwork to this variation is by far the most challenging and the most beautiful. At first this step may seem too complicated but don't be discouraged! It does take practice and commitment, so expect to lose the step every so often at first" (1978, 102).

The New York Hustle (which was sometimes also called the Latin Hustle) was the most common and also became the standard Hustle that was taught throughout the remainder of the twentieth century. It was also a six-count basic but added a syncopated count of "And 1, 2, 3; And 4, 5, 6." Although it was counted as a six-count basic, it was simply a repeated pattern of the first section. Therefore it was really a three count dance to four counts of music. The rhythm is counted &1, 2, 3. There is a pause (or a hold) on count 4, but it is not counted in the rhythm.

The leader steps back on the left ball of the left foot and does a quick rock step putting all the weight on the right foot (count &1), step left (count 2), step right (count 3), and pause (count 4). The follower steps back on the right ball of the right foot and does a quick rock step putting all the weight on the left foot (count &1), step right (count 2), step left (count 3), and pause (count 4). The syncopation of the &1 count allows a subtle push and pull that is similar to the Jitterbug. Therefore the "push and pull" allows the leader to prep his partner for a turn or a variation. As with the other partner Hustle dances, the turns and variations happen on the counts of 2 and 3. Other patterns and variations were added in combinations of six and eight counts.

There was an early version of a partner Hustle dance also called "The New York Hustle." It was a four-count basic step with a simple tap-step tap-step rhythm. The basic was tap left foot to left side (count 1) step left foot in place (count 2), tap right foot to right side (count 3) step right foot in place (count 4). The follower mirrored the pattern beginning with the right foot. There was also a Four Step Hustle that incorporated walking steps. K-tel's dance instruction book *Let's Disco!* described a four-beat pattern with the leader alternating walking steps left-right-left-right and the follower alternating right-left-right-left. Variations included dips, underarm turns, and eight-count patterns similar to the other Hustle dances (K-tel 1978, 44–55). Other Disco dances included line dances.

THE L.A. HUSTLE, THE NEW YORK BUS STOP, AND DISCO LINE DANCES

The L.A. Hustle (also known as the Bus Stop, the California Hustle, and the Los Angeles Hustle) was a line dance that was done to Disco music. Dance instructor Karen Lustgarten claimed,

> This is the line dance that launched a thousand others. It debuted in Summer '75 in a small disco in Los Angeles, and enjoyed instant popularity. It didn't become a national breakout until Spring '76 when it hit the East Coast under the name the 'Bus Stop.' Some of the steps were modified during the migration, and after a while enough spin-offs were created to make line dances a permanent part of everyone's disco dance repertoire (1978, 86).

Line dancing had earlier precedents in the 1950s—Madison and the Stroll as well as the Shim Sham in the 1930s. In line dancing the individual dancers did not touch. They lined up in rows with equal spacing between the dancers. All the dancers started on the same foot and moved in unison (hopefully) all in the same direction. But unlike, the earlier line dances that faced only one direction, the L.A. Hustle incorporated a turn at the end of each sequence. Lustgarten described the sequence pattern for the L.A. Hustle as "The dance breaks down into four parts: first backward and forward; then side to side; then short jumps topped off with a chicken flap; and finally standing in place, poking around with your right toe—winding up with a kick, which leads into the first step of the set again." Upon completing the sequence, the entire group would turn in unison and repeated the sequence again, facing a different location in the dance club (1978, 105).

The New York Bus Stop was a modified version of the L.A. Hustle with a 24 beat repeating sequence. Many other line dance variations existed that included many of the walking forward and back and side-to-side sequences of the L.A. Hustle. They included the Walk, the Rollercoaster, the Hollywood Line Hustle, the Lust Hustle, the Saturday Night Fever Line Dance, and the Hot Chocolate. The Hot Chocolate was a "16 beat repeating line dance with one quarter-turn that was almost exactly the same as the Electric Slide (see Chapter 6) (K-Tel 1978, 30).

DISCO FASHION, FREESTYLE, AND THE BUMP

But dancing well also included dressing well. In July 1975, journalist Dena Kleiman of *The New York Times* reported a noticeable change in fashion on the dance floors of the Discos. She wrote,

Unlike their older brothers and sisters who took pride in a pair of dungarees, free flowing, unkempt hair and "hang-loose" dances, today's young people value sleek clothes, fancy high-heeled shoes and a more stylized, structured form of dancing. It's no longer "anything goes" but what looks good (56).

Many men were influenced by Travolta's three-piece suit from *Saturday Night Fever*. Similar suits were available in a wide array of bright pastel colors. The three-piece suit included wide jacket lapels, a buttoned vest, and bell-bottom pants. An unbuttoned collared shirt was worn over the suit jacket collar. Regardless of wearing either a suit or no jacket and vest at all, the polyester shirts were worn open from the neckline down to the mid-chest. Some of the shirts did not even have buttons six to eight inches below the neckline. The outfit was completed by platform shoes with a front sole of an inch or more thick and a heel 2 to 3 inches high.

Women also wore platform shoes in gaudy colors and bulky shapes, but the heels and front soles were sometimes as high as six or seven inches. Some women wore designer jeans or "Hot Pants," which first became fashionable around 1970. Cultural historian Charles Panati described the Hot Pants as "scandalously short shorts...[that] revealed more leg and lower cheek than the shortest mini [skirt] ever had" (1991, 369).

In 1979, music critic Judith Glassman described some of the fashion that she had seen worn on the Disco dance floors. She observed,

Women in bare, slinky dresses with thigh-high slits or shiny clinging jeans and backless mules [halters] weave and whirl. Their partners, in sleek three-piece white suits, pull them in and twirl them out. Bare chested men in balloon topped trousers, pegged at the ankles (44).

The common element was that all the dancers dressed to be seen, and each imagined he or she was Disco dancing similar to those in the movies.

In reality, the Hustle and touch dancing were a small part of Disco dancing in general. Most of the dancing done in Discos was freestyle. For many adults who had grown up with the traditional closed dance position of the syncopated rhythms of the Cha-cha and Lindy Hop, the transition to learn the Hustle was not that difficult. On the other hand, other than the Twist, many of the mainstream older adults had simply ignored the stylistic expression of the nonpartner dances of the 1960s; therefore they had to learn the basics freestyle dance movements.

Dance instructor Karen Lustgarten commented, "The beauty of disco dancing is that once you learn the basics, the variety of combinations is limited only by your

Here's one of the easiest of the hip moves that is practically germane to disco dancing. Your feet don't move on the first 3 counts; all the action is in your hips, so let them loose and keep them liquid smooth.

H. THE SWAY

Dance instructor Karen Lustgarten demonstrates one of the basic Freestyle dance moves. This one is "The Sway." (From *The Complete Guide to Disco Dancing* by Karen Lustgarten. Photographs by Bernie Lustgarten, page 52.)   Courtesy Michael Larsen–Elizabeth Pomada Literary Agents.

Disco freestyle dancing appealed to both young and old. Here an older couple, Lilo and Dom Dattilo, dances at a family wedding, c. 1979.   Author's Archives.

The basic pattern for nonpartner freestyle Disco was a four-count step-tap step-tap (sometimes known as the Single Touch Step) or a step-step-step-tap usually counted out for a full eight beats to match the music.

A simple step-tap included step left foot (count 1) tap right foot next to left foot (count 2) step right foot (count 3) tap left foot next to right (count 4) step left foot (count 5) tap right foot next to left foot (count 6) step right foot (count 7), tap left foot next to right (count 8). Each pattern could also be started with the right foot.

The step-step-step-tap included a step side left with left foot (count 1) step or slide right foot next to left (count 2), step side left (count 3), tap right foot next to left (count 4), step side right with right foot (count 5), step or slide left foot next to right (count 6), step side right (count 7), tap left foot next to right (count 8).

imagination. Let yourself go!...you have complete freedom to perform any of the steps, styles, and variations that your little feet desire" (1978, 15). But freestyle Disco dancing did appeal to older adults and therefore required a transition for them to learn the basic steps. Therefore, with the freestyle Disco dancing there was a reorientation of rhythm that was required.

The patterns could be continually repeated throughout the entire dance adding in hip shaking and other body movements. Combinations of the step-tap and the step-step-step-tap could be intermingled as long as the body kept moving and danced with the beat. Lustgarten advised, "they all flow together like the music, without beginning or end" (1978, 38). Other variations included exaggerated slide steps, crossing, steps, walking steps, foot swivels, alternate knee lifts, body leans, sways, turns, hip swirls, and hip bumps.

One of the easiest of all the Disco dances, if not all of the twentieth century dances, was The Bump. The Bump did not have any steps and was done during Disco freestyle and sometimes incorporated in the Hustle partner dances. To do the Bump, the partners stood side-by-side and bumped their hips against each other. The Bump was usually done in multiples of two or four counts. (Although any combination worked as long as it was on the beat.) Abe Peck in *Dancing Madness* said, "The idea is to bump against your partner on the on beat and swing away for the off-beat. If you bump twice in and twice out, you're doing the Double Bump; bump on every beat and you've transformed it into the Electric Bump" (1976, 61). Some other fad dances included the Freak (see later in this chapter) and Kung Fu. The Kung Fu was based on martial arts moves and inspired by the 1974 song by Carl Douglas titled "Kung Fu Fighting." However, one of the most recognizable songs of the era was "Last Dance" by Donna Summer.

DONNA SUMMER, "THANK GOD IT'S FRIDAY," AND "LAST DANCE"

In 1975, Donna Summer (born La Donna Andrea Gaines) recorded "Love to Love You Baby" for the fledging Casablanca Records. The song, produced by Giorgio Moroder, became a monstrous worldwide hit and was later remixed to over 12 minutes in length for the Disco dance clubs. The song styling was originally termed "Euro-Disco," which combined a European record producer with an American singer. However, unlike the voice and guitar driven Rock music of the day, Moroder introduced a resounding bass drum as the main drive of the dance mix. He recalled, "Why not help the dancers to dance even better by making the drum into more of a stomping sound?" But in essence the main hook of the record was the over four minutes of sensuous "orgasmic groaning" that the freestyle dancers loved (Lawrence 2003, 173–174).

Other Disco song hits for Summer included "I Feel Love" (1977), "MacArthur Park" (1978), and "Heaven Knows" (1979). In early 1979, her album *Bad Girls* produced three No. 1 songs, "Bad Girls," "Dim All the Lights," and "Hot Stuff." By the end of 1979, she released a *Greatest Hits* album that produced another No. 1 single "On the Radio" (Uslan and Solomon 1981, 447–449). However, the best remembered of all Summer's classic hits was "Last Dance" from the movie *Thank God It's Friday.*

A simple, fun, and innocent movie of the Disco era was *Thank God It's Friday* (1978). The tale was set in a popular fictitious Los Angeles Disco named "The Zoo." The simple plot was described by IMDb.com as follows:

> It's Friday and everyone is going to the hot new disco. The Commodore's are scheduled to play if Floyd shows up with the instruments and Nicole dreams of becoming a disco star. Other characters are there to win the dance contest ("Thank God Its Friday," IMDb.com).

A large portion of the film took place within the Disco and featured many different dance experiences. The movie captured the flavor of a young suburban couple wanting to "experience" the Disco dance world that they were hearing and reading about. Two underage teenagers sneak into the club in an attempt to win the dance contest. One of them teams with a local dancer and does, in fact, win the dance contest. Added to the mix are a host of other colorful characters and an appearance by the musical group the Commodores. But the highlight of the film is that of an aspiring singer named Nicole (played by Donna Summer) who introduced and sang the song "Last Dance."

Summer's song became a major hit and became an instant classic. (In 1979, "Last Dance" also won an Academy Award Oscar for best song.) It was routinely played as the closing and "last song of the night" in Discos and at parties all across the country. Throughout the remaining years of the twentieth century, it became a very popular song at weddings and social affairs for DJs to play as the "last dance" of the evening (see Chapter 7). Another song that was also routinely played during the course of an evening and became an anthem of the Disco era was "I Will Survive" by Gloria Gaynor.

"I WILL SURVIVE," MECO, AND DISCO TAKES OVER

In 1975, Gloria Gaynor recorded the first Disco album that put an entire side of an extended mix of Disco songs together as one seamless medley. The album, released through Polydor Records, was a 20-minute mix of three Gaynor songs, "Honeybee," "Never Can Say Goodbye," and "Reach Out, I'll Be There," and became extremely popular in the Disco dance clubs. In late 1978, Polydor promoted Gaynor's new extended single "Substitute" as her next big hit. However, many of the club DJs and dancers preferred the "B" side titled "I Will Survive." The song became a huge hit and defined the era, particularly for African American women (Jones and Kantonen 2000, 6–9).

In 1977, the female trio First Choice, composed of Rochelle Fleming, Annette Guest, and Joyce Jones, released the self-titled album that yielded the hit "Let No Man Put Asunder." Another trio, Odyssey, composed of three sisters Carmen, Lillian, and Louise Lopez, had hits with "Native New Yorker" and "Easy Come Easy Go." In 1978, the mixed-ethnic female trio Musique released an extended four song LP titled *Keep On Jumpin'* with the infamous 8 minute and 20 second pulsating and sexually suggestive "In The Bush." Many radio stations nationwide banned the song. In 1979, Sister Sledge, another group of sisters, recorded the hits "Got To Love Somebody," "He's the Greatest Dancer," and "We Are Family" (1979). Solo Disco divas included Vickie Sue Robinson with "Turn the Beat Around" (1976), Alicia Bridges with "I Love the Nightlife" (1977), Thelma Houston with "Don't Leave Me This Way" (1977), Yvonne Elliman with "If I Can't Have You" (1977), Chaka Khan with "I'm Every Woman" (1978), Bonnie Pointer with "Heaven Must Have Sent You" (1979), Anita Ward with "Ring My Bell" (1979), France Joli with "Come to Me" (1979), and Amii Stewart with "Knock on Wood" (1979).

On the male side, The Trammps (voted the Top Disco Group by *Billboard* magazine in 1975, 1976, and 1977) had their biggest hit with "Disco Inferno" from the movie *Saturday Night Fever*. In early 1977, they played the Roseland Ballroom as part of a five-hour Disco dance celebration for over 3,000 people as did the group Tavares. The five-brother group Tavares had hits with "Heaven Must Be Missing An Angel" (1976), "More Than a Woman" (also included on the *Saturday Night Fever* soundtrack), and "Whodunit" (1977). Other musical groups included MFSB, Barrabas, The Ritchie Family, the Commodores, and the ethnically mixed KC and the Sunshine Band (Jones and Kantonen 2000, 134).

Many other record producers applied the Disco format and began producing extended remixes in the production studios. In 1977, the producer simply known as "Meco" took the theme from the summer blockbuster movie *Star Wars* and remixed it with a Disco beat. In October the song reached No. 1 on the *Billboard* charts. Meco also remixed the themes to many science fiction movie releases of

Some of the many popular Disco record albums.   Author's Archives.

the time, including *Close Encounters of the Third Kind* and *Superman*. He also applied the same format to song classics from *The Wizard of Oz* (1978). During that same year, the female trio Tuxedo Junction combined the Disco concept with Glenn Miller and some Swing era classics (see Chapter 3), including "Chattanooga Choo Choo," "Moonlight Serenade," and the title cut on *Tuxedo Junction* (1977). The producers actually used some of the original members of the Glenn Miller Orchestra, who interpreted the complicated original string charts. In 1979, their follow-up album contained Disco remixes of "Begin the Beguine," "Stardust," "That Old Black Magic," and the title cut of the Duke Ellington classic *Take The A Train* (Jones and Kantonen 2000, 93).

By 1979, radio discovered that Disco music could also be good for ratings. After New York radio station WKTU-FM changed to an all-Disco format, it went from an almost obscure station to the number one radio show in the number one market in America. Shortly thereafter, over 200 radio stations nationwide switched to an all-Disco format. During that same year, Motown Records got in on the Disco scene with a "Long Playing 12" Disco Single" with a ten-minute mix of a medley of 1960s song hits from Diana Ross and the Supremes. They followed with many other remixes of Motown artists (Glassman 1979, 46).

As a result of the phenomenal success of Disco music and dancing, in April 1979, a cover story of *Newsweek* magazine proclaimed "Disco Takes Over." During that same month *Rolling Stone* columnist Stephen Holden added, "Everyone here knows that 1979 will go down in history as the year Disco became the biggest thing in pop since Beatlemania and possibly since the birth of rock & roll" (29).

During 1978 and 1979, Disco songs dominated the sales charts as well as the prestigious *Billboard* Pop chart. By the end of each of the years of 1978 and 1979 Disco songs occupied seven and eight spots, respectively, on *Billboards* Top Ten Songs of the Year.

Top Ten Songs of the Year (* denotes Disco song).

1978	1979
1. * "Night Fever" / Bee Gees	1. "My Sharona" / The Knack
2. * "Shadow Dancing" / Andy Gibb	2. * "Le Freak" / Chic
3. * "Stayin' Alive" / Bee Gees	3. * "Bad Girls" / Donna Summer
4. "You Light Up My Life" / Debby Boone	4. * "Do Ya Think I'm Sexy" / Rod Stewart
5. "Kiss You All Over" / Exile	5. * "I Will Survive" / Gloria Gaynor
6. * "Three Times a Lady" / The Commodores	6. * "Y.M.C.A." / The Village People
7. * "How Deep Is Your Love" / Bee Gees	7. * "Hot Stuff" / Donna Summer
8. * "Love Is Thicker Than Water" / Andy Gibb	8. * "Ring My Bell" / Anita Ward
9. "Baby Come Back" / Player	9. "Sad Eyes" / Robert John
10. * "Boogie Oogie Oogie" / A Taste of Honey	10. * "Reunited" / Peaches and Herb

Although nowhere near as influential as the Beatles, the one single musical act that stood out as probably the most recognizable group of the Disco era was the Village People.

THE VILLAGE PEOPLE, "MACHO MAN," "Y.M.C.A.," AND "IN THE NAVY"

In June 1977, the self-titled debut album *Village People* contained four songs that praised the gay lifestyle titled "Fire Island," "Greenwich Village," "Hollywood," and "San Francisco." The album did not receive any mainstream radio airplay but was No. 1 on the Disco dance club charts. The first song from the album, "San Francisco," sold over 100,000 copies. The modest number of sales was enough to prompt another album and a tour. However, like many of the Disco hits of the day, it was a studio produced album. And, in fact, no actual group existed as the producer Jacques Morali employed male models for the album cover. Therefore, a real live group was needed.

In early 1977, Morali first conceived the idea of the group upon seeing Felipe Rose dancing in a Greenwich Village Disco while dressed in an American Indian outfit. He envisioned a six member vocal group that exaggerated the American male stereotypes of a Cowboy, Construction Worker, Indian, Policeman, Motorcycle Biker, and a Soldier. As it turned out, he employed Felipe Rose to sing as part of the studio production and kept him in the role of the "American Indian." Two of the other studio musicians were also retained. Victor Willis was given the role of the "Policeman," and Alexander Briley was chosen to portray the Soldier and was known as "The GI."

In order to fill the remaining three roles, Morali held over 200 auditions. He eventually selected the final three members: Glenn M. Hughes, who was working as a toll collector at the Brooklyn Battery Tunnel, was selected as "Leather Man," the leather suited motorcycle biker with a bushy mustache. Randy Jones, the "American Cowboy," was from an Agnes DeMille Dance production company. David Hodo, the "Construction Worker," replete with hard hat and cool sunglasses, was simply unemployed. Willis, who co-wrote many of the songs, was the only straight member of the group (Peck 1976, 13).

The Village People as a musical group were so campy and fun to watch that they appealed to both the gay crowd and the straight crowd as well as the young and old. As the group's success grew, their songs maintained a balance of trying to portray a "tongue in cheek" for the straight audience and at the same time playing up to the gay audience. In fact, many critics themselves were not always sure what was going on. On one hand, music historians Michael Uslan and Bruce Solomon expressed an opinion that, "The songs were not blatantly gay, but they could lend themselves easily to a gay interpretation" (1981, 422). *Rolling Stone* magazine music critic Lester Bangs said, "These singers are happy clichés who make other folks happy by demonstrating that it's more than enough to *be* merely a happy cliché." Lead singer Policeman Victor Willis explained, "The group has never performed gay. Nobody has ever come out in drag. The group performs a masculine show. It's a male-image show. Gay people like us, straight people like us. But we're not a gay group." Leather Man Glenn Hughes added, "We're six very positive male, energetic symbols. We are definitely gonna have a gay following" (Bangs 1979, 92).

In 1978, the Village People released their second album titled *Macho Man*. The first single "Macho Man" was released in February 1978. Very soon thereafter, it received heavy airplay on mainstream American radio and went to the top of the *Billboard* sales charts. The song continually chanted the words "body" while glorifying the male narcissistic approach of viewing his own body. But, the main appeal of the song lied in the easy to sing-along anthem-like chorus that repeated the title "Macho Man." Abe Peck, editor of *Rolling Stone*, said, "The lyrics were broad based enough for both gay and straight males to accept as either gospel or goof." Lead singer and cowriter Willis suggested that if anyone actually listened closely, he or she would find that, "There's nothing in 'Macho Man' lyrically that's gay." That may have been the reason that the Village People had their biggest success among the straight clubs and record buyers. In 1979, promoter Kenn Friedman of Casablanca Records told the *Village Voice*,

> "Macho Man" did not happen in gay clubs but in straight ones. The Village People is the first gay-to-straight "crossover" group, a group with an originally gay image and following that's made it in straight discos. The funny thing is that straights don't really believe the group is gay. They love 'em in Vegas and in tacky suburban dinner theaters in Midwestern shopping centers....The straights don't see the gay culture, they've only seen what they've made—the styles (Kopkind 1979, 14).

The same format was followed on the single, from their next album *Cruisin'*.

In late 1978, with a simple title reference of a well-known American institution, the Village People achieved lasting distinction in American social dance with the song "Y.M.C.A." Once again, *Rolling Stone* editor Abe Peck felt that "['Y.M.C.A.'] is the all-American success, the simple song that's open to tongue-in-cheek interpretation." Leather Man Glenn Hughes said, "'Y.M.C.A.' has the hook. They can hear the song once, and they're walking out of the room going [he sings] 'Y.M.C.A.'" (Peck 1976, 12–14).

And the hook to the song is what made "Y.M.C.A." the biggest and most well-known song hit for the Village People, eventually selling over 12 million copies. All told, the Village People sold an astonishing 65 million records (Uslan and Solomon 1981, 422). The Village People performed a rendition of the song in their movie *Can't Stop The Music* (1980). (Prior to the movie, lead singer and songwriter Victor Willis suddenly quit and was replaced by Ray Simpson.) During the performance of the song "Y.M.C.A.," the group frolicked and traversed through a Manhattan YMCA. The health club was stocked full of muscular semi-nude virile young men performing all sorts of athletic endeavors including wrestling, swimming, running, and gymnastics. (The irony of the scene is that only one woman is present. In order to have the Hollywood movie not appear "gay," the producers wrote in a character of a supermodel played by actress Valerie Perrine.) During the chorus of the song, an entire gymnasium full of men are led by the Village People as they held their arms high in the air mimicking each of the letters "Y," "M," "C," and "A."

The success of both the song and the dance was carried over onto social dance floors all across America. From weddings to bar-mitzvahs, baptisms, anniversaries, graduations, proms, block parties, senior centers, and just about anywhere a party was held—it was only a matter of time before the DJ would play the record and the entire dance floor would fill. Grandmothers would join their young offspring; men and women of all ages would all join in and sing-along and mimic the letters Y – M – C – A. In later years, some DJs would add in choreographed dance steps to perform during the entire song. Nevertheless, it became a new American classic standard social dance that stood equally alongside "The Twist," "(We're Gonna) Rock Around the Clock," and "In The Mood."

From 1978 through 1979, the Village People played to sold-out audiences all across America. They made an appearance in the Macy's Thanksgiving Day Parade as well as on *American Bandstand* and *Soul Train*. In March 1979, they even played the once stoic Roseland Ballroom in New York City. In mid-1979, they released their fourth album titled *Go West*. They had another hit with the title song as well as the song "In the Navy."

In order to promote the song "In the Navy," they were granted permission by the actual U.S. Navy to film aboard the frigate *U.S.S. Reasoner*. For the occasion, backup singer Alex Briley, "The GI," dropped his soldier outfit and dressed as a Shore Patrol Navy Sailor. Lead singer "Policeman" Victor Willis decided to dress as a Navy Admiral. In an age long before the "Don't Ask, Don't Tell" response about gays in the military (see Chapter 7), the U.S. Navy welcomed the Village People with open arms. During the filming, Navy spokesperson Lt. Commander Fred Gorell was present and officially welcomed the group aboard the ship. He said that he was "familiar with the group," had heard the song, and therefore approved the use of the navy frigate for filming. When asked, "How would you rate the record?" he harkened back to the early days of *American Bandstand* and said, "I'd say it has a good beat, and I'd give it a ninety-eight." When asked about the recruitment possibilities, Lt. Commander Gorell replied, "I would say that the Navy has an interest in communicating opportunities in the service, and the Village People seem to fit in very well with the young people" (Peck 1976, 14).

REGGAE, NOSTALGIA, THE TIME WARP, AND TOGA PARTIES

In 1976, Abe Peck, editor of *Dancing Madness* wrote, "Disco is not the only dancing madness loose in the land. The Puerto Rican and Brazilian rhythms of salsa music have turned the Big Apple into the Big Mango. The strains of Jamaican reggae are heard on every college campus." With the increase in leisure time and travel packages, overseas vacation travel by Americans became a regular occurrence. At the time, Club Med, with locations throughout the Caribbean Islands and Mexico, catered mainly to the meeting and gathering of "singles" on vacation. A significant part of their socializing methods included dancing such as the Twist, Limbo, Hands Up, Crazy Signs, various line dances, and aerobics. Other popular vacation destinations were Caribbean spots including Puerto Rico, the Dominican Republic, and Jamaica. Within these islands, Americans were entertained by local musicians and were usually encouraged to participate in cultural dances including the Merengue, Reggae, Rock Steady, and Jamaican Ska (Peck 1976, 7).

Reggae, Rock Steady, and Jamaican Ska were indigenous to the island of Jamaica. The Jamaican Ska (sometimes known just as "Ska") was a simple step-tap, step-tap. The body and arm movements were slower subtle versions of the basic Frug and Jerk, but with lots of relaxed Jamaican attitude. Jamaican musician Frederick "Toots" Hibbert said, "When we play in Jamaica, everybody is up dancin'—nobody just sit and watch." Reggae was a nontouching partner dance that could also be done solo. It stayed in one place and had very little movement on the dance floor. Hibbert explained that the basic Reggae dance was as follows:

> When you dance, you dance right on the beat. It's a feeling—if you can't feel the beat, you can't do the dance. You dance it however you want to dance—with your feet or with your hands. The key is: Follow the bass. The drum beat will lure you, but straddle it and the bass will carry you along (Peck 1976, 87).

Rock Steady is a slight variation to a slower Reggae beat. The dancer stays in one place and slowly rocks to each side of the body. Reggae and Rock Steady had many different moves, many applied from the daily life of Jamaicans, such as Ride-a-bike and broom sweeping (Hibbert 1976, 87–91).

At home, when not on vacation, America was in the midst of a nostalgia craze for 1950s Rock 'n' Roll music (see Chapter 4). In 1972, the Broadway musical *Grease* harkened back to the music of the 1950s. (The stage show ran until 1980, setting a record run of over 3,300 performances.) In the same year that *Grease* opened, New York radio station WCBS-FM adapted the first format to play music from the 1950s and early 1960s, which was termed "Oldies." The show quickly became one of the highest rated stations in America, and the Oldies format was quickly adapted nationwide.

In 1973, the nostalgia fad continued with the movie *American Graffiti*. The soundtrack had movie audiences clapping hands and leaving the theaters singing along to their favorite "Oldies" tunes. The movie opened with the blaring original 1950s rendition of Bill Haley and the Comets' "(We're Gonna) Rock Around the Clock." However, it did not have the same effect on the 1970s audiences, as there was no dancing in the aisles. The movie was a financial success, but most audiences missed the basic theme of the movie. According to the film's writer and director, George Lucas, it was, "about teenagers moving forward and making decisions about what they want to do in life. But it's also about the fact that you can't live in the past" (James Miller 1999, 315).

Nevertheless, the nostalgia fad continued in the 1974 television show *Happy Days*. Similarly, numerous Rock 'n' Roll revival stage shows were sponsored by the likes of Richard Nader and Dick Clark; however, they did not attract people to dance. In 1978, the nostalgia for the 1950s continued as a Hollywood movie version of *Grease* was released. The movie musical contained numerous dance scenes and also stared John Travolta. Although the movie was an outstanding success at the box office, it did not have anywhere near the same impact on social dancing as did *Saturday Night Fever*.

Another 1950s Hollywood movie that did not necessarily fare well at the box office was *American Hot Wax* (1978). The film was a semi-fictitious biography of one week in the life of radio disc jockey Alan Freed (see Chapter 4). Music critic Greil Marcus said, "the film may have jumbled the facts, but it was the most *emotionally* accurate rock and roll movie ever made. It caught what early rock felt like; it made you understand why and how it changed so many lives" (400).

One film that did inspire a new dance was *The Rocky Horror Picture Show* (1975). The pseudo-musical touched on themes of transsexualism and homosexuality and satirized the 1950s drive-in science fiction movies. When the movie was first released, it did not fare well. However, in 1978, one New York theater owner decided to show the film at midnight on Friday and Saturday evenings. In a short time, the midnight shows developed a cult following as audiences acted out the movie and verbally interacted with the on-screen characters. The audience members also took to bringing props to the theaters and dressing like their favorite characters. The cult phenomenon was picked up by over 50 movie theaters nationwide. As the first audience participation film, the ultimate experience was to dance the Time Warp.

The Time Warp was similar to a line dance but was more of a group participation dance. The song contained instructional lyrics for the dancer to do a short jump with both feet together to the left side. Both the right hand and right foot go out to the side and back to the body two times. With some campiness, both hands were put on the hips. The knees were pulled tight together and performed a thrusting motion with the pelvis. The head performs a circular motion looking skyward and the hands were thrown up in the air as they jumped and quarter turned around the room.

Historians Sally Banes and John Szwed point out that the Time Warp was "a camp parody" of the song "Ballin' the Jack" that was written and performed in the *Ziegfeld Follies of 1913*. "Ballin' the Jack" was a dance instructional song that

The cast from the movie *Rocky Horror Picture Show* (1975) dances the Time Warp that spawned a popular party dance. 20th Century Fox / Courtesy of Photofest.

instructed dancers to put the knees close and tight together and sway to the left side and the right side. In that position of the dance step—there was a direction to twist and put the arms up in the air (from "'Messin'-Around' to 'Funky Western Civilization," 2002, 175, 198).

In 1978, the Hollywood release of *National Lampoon's Animal House* spurned an interest in "toga parties." One scene in the movie featured a fraternity house party to which participants were encouraged to come dressed in bed sheets, reminiscent of an ancient Roman Toga. In September of that same year, *Newsweek* magazine reported over 100 college campuses sponsored toga parties. During the Toga Party in *Animal House*, the musical group Otis Day and the Knights performed a rendition of the Isley Brothers hit song titled "Shout!" The movie scene involved the Toga dressed college students following the instructions of the lead singer to get a little lower as they lowered themselves to the floor (which was a college fraternity dance known as the Gator) and then were instructed to get louder and jump up. The movie mimicking and Toga Party were copied at colleges, vacation resorts, and cruises, among others through the remainder of the century.

The Places to Dance

Disco has brought back the Hangout, a place to go for a few hours that doesn't cost too much.

—Cindy McEhrlich, 1976

Living the disco life is knowing that as long as you stay inside these glowing, flashing walls, absolutely nothing will change: neither the beat nor your relations with the people around you.

—Lester Bangs, 1979

TRADITIONAL BALLROOMS

At the end of the 1960s, some establishments, such as the St. George Hotel ballroom in Brooklyn, the Roseland Ballroom in Manhattan, and the Honka Monka in Queens, held onto the old traditional American social dances. In the early to mid-1970s, they continued providing opportunities to dance to the big band sounds of the 1930s and 1940s.

A contemporary movie that captured the essence of the period was *Queen of the Stardust Ballroom* (1975). The movie was filmed in Myron's Ballroom in Queens, New York, and was choreographed by Marge Champion (see Chapter 4). Other establishments held on to the same traditions at the same time that the general climate of American society was in a flux and dancing was still segregated (Bosworth, "At Honka Monka and Roseland, Dancing Their Troubles Away," 1971, 62).

BLOCK PARTIES AND HOUSE PARTIES

Soul music and Rhythm and Blues were still mainly confined to African American audiences and neighborhoods. Soul music went hand-in-hand with the burgeoning Black Pride movement in America. In 1968, the movement was given a rallying cry with the James Brown hit song "Say it Loud, I'm Black and I'm Proud." Brown was known as an innovative dance performer on stage and was sometimes controversial. In 1966, during a concert in Detroit, local police attempted to shut down his show. They claimed that Brown's dancing was "obscene" ("Parental Advisory: Music Censorship in America: Censorship Incidents 1960s," n.d.).

However, it was Brown's dancing that made him unique. He danced in quivering body movements and exciting footwork. His style was widely copied and influential among African Americans. His 1972 release and live stage dance performance of the song "Get on the Good Foot" was widely copied and spawned a dance known as the "Good Foot." The dance was characterized by Brown's trademark drops, spins, and knee bends. The Good Foot was considered the forerunner for the urban dance style that became known as Breakdancing (see Chapter 7) (Driver 2000, 197).

During the 1960s, Motown music, derived from Detroit, Michigan, typified the new urban sounds of African American artists. Motown groups including The

Temptations, the Four Tops, The Contours, and Smokey Robinson and the Miracles were known for their vocal harmonies and tightly choreographed dance steps. Their precision dance steps were borrowed from Jazz, Tap, and Lindy Hop routines. Outside the house, one Motown classic "Dancing in the Streets" by Martha Reeves and the Vandellas was a song version of an urban practice known as a block party.

Block parties involved entire families of ethnic neighbors partaking in an outdoor party where a city block was closed off to vehicular traffic. In many cases relatives and friends from other neighborhoods were invited. All enjoyed food, games, and music. Many times they included dancing. A phonograph supplied by one of the residents usually provided the music. Typically, many of the neighbors contributed their favorite record albums. In order to ensure a safe return, they would write their names in the upper corner of the record album sleeve. Later in the century, sound systems became quite elaborate and the block parties would hire a specialty DJ to provide the music.

For African Americans, in particular, dancing at neighborhood block parties was a significant part of the urban culture and also part of the emergence of "Black Pride." Famed author Maya Angelou fondly recalled her excitement at a neighborhood block party during her youth. She described that as the music began,

> I started dancing, rushing into movement, making up steps and changing direction. There was no story, no plan; I simply put every dance I had ever seen or known into my body and onto the stage. A little rhumba, tango, jitterbug, Suzy-Q, trucking, snake hips, conga, Charleston and cha-cha-cha. When the music was finished I had exhausted my repertoire and myself (Angelou 1976, 56).

Famed novelist Ralph Ellison also proudly stated, "Part of my pride in being what I am is that as a dancer, as a physical man...I bet you I can outdance, outriff most of those [other] intellectuals" (Ellison and McPherson 1970, 50).

Another development was the "House Party." Typically, a house party was given on a Friday or Saturday night and invitations were usually transmitted by word of mouth. The name was derived from the simple fact that the party is given at somebody's home. During the late 1940s and 1950s, they developed on a larger urban scale and became a common occurrence among American teenagers both white and black. They were also called, "Get-together's," "jam," "gig," and "set."

In the case of urban African Americans, the teenage house dance party was a comparatively new occurrence. Over a 14-month period from January 1972 to February 1973, sociologist Roy Milton Clark visited 27 teenage dance parties. The age of the participants ranged from 11 to 20 years old. Clark, himself in his early twenties, acclimated to the environment and dressed appropriately. He said he was "clean shaven. I had on tight fitting bell bottom pants, a 'body shirt' which was slightly open at the top in the front, a pair of brown suede boots, and I was wearing a large 'Shaft' hat which was tilted to one side." (*Shaft* was one of the newly emerging films starring African American actors in the lead roles. The hat was a flamboyant stylized cross between a fedora and a Zoot suit tando hat).

Clark observed a commonality that the dances were held in one of the teenager's homes and were supervised by one or more parents. In some cases the parent went to a neighbor's house, but routinely checked in about every half-hour. He also noted that only a small number of people attended a house party, and the setting was smaller and more intimate. Clark said, "The house party takes place in a relatively small area usually not larger than 15' by 15' [in a] living room or basement."

Preparation for the party involved either moving all the furniture out of the living room or basement or pushing it all to the perimeter to create a makeshift dance floor. Records were accumulated by borrowing from friends and neighbors. The lighting was dimmed and the main activity was usually dancing the "Slow Drag" (see Chapter 1). The Slow Drag sometimes developed into the "Grind." Clark described the Grind as a dance that involved "both people holding each other closely while rhythmically, slowly, rubbing their bodies against one another in what can be described as very sensual movement." Clark noticed that during the house party dancing, there was a noted distinction between African Americans and Anglo Americans. He said, "One complaint blacks have made about white parties is that whites frequently want to talk while dancing thereby interrupting the absorption and involvement in the physical movement" (Clark, "The Dance Party as a Socialization Mechanism," 1974, 145–149).

Sometimes the participants did not even need music to dance. If the music stopped, someone might shout, "We don't need no music" and individuals would square off in opposite gender lines. One male and one female entered the lane and "came on down" the middle of the line, similar to the 1950s Stroll (see Chapter 4). Shouts of encouragement were offered by the likes of "go ahead girl," "do your own thing," "right on," and "you go girl." It was known as the "Soul Train Line" (Hazzard-Gordon, "African-American Vernacular Dance," 1985, 442).

"THE PILL," THE GAY LIBERATION MOVEMENT, AND STONEWALL

During the 1960s, the freedom of expression on the dance floor coincided with the escalation of the Women's Equality Movement. The issue of the Women's Equality Movement (sometimes known as Women's Liberation) created heated discussion, mainly by male dominated conservative and religious organizations. Many in this opposition also strongly opposed the use of "Enovid," an oral birth control pill that was known simply as "The Pill." The birth control pill allowed a woman to freely engage in sexual intercourse for recreation and pleasure without the consequence of an unwanted pregnancy. In 1975, many radio stations across the country even refused to play the song "The Pill," by country music singer Loretta Lynn, because of its references to birth control. With the debate came concerns that arose over sexual freedom, especially among college age students and women of all ages. Many conservatives argued that sexual promiscuity would lead to communal living and homosexuality.

Many women attempted to find solace and sensual pleasure through Disco and freestyle dancing. At least on the dance floor the nonpartner dancing of "doing your own thing" allowed women the same equality as men. Unlike the past patriarchal role in society, in freestyle dancing women were able to break free from the traditional follower role. Women also found acceptance dancing among homosexual men.

At the time, any man interested in dancing, especially as a career, was cause for concern. In April 1965, a *Time* magazine article claimed, "Even today, if a boy hints that he might like to be a dancer, he becomes the playground freak, and Daddy goes rushing off to consult the family psychiatrist." Several years before, noted film actor and dancer extraordinaire, Gene Kelly starred in a television program titled "Dancing Is a Man's Game." In June 1966, in an article in the *National Observer* he described his reasons for the TV special. He said, "Dancing is a form of athletics and I'd like to see it attract strong young men who can experience the value and the sheer joy of it." But Kelly expressed his concern that the real reason for "the paucity of men entering the dance field, [was] for a reason no one wants to talk about—the feeling that the field is dominated by homosexuals" (Bell 1966).

Homosexuality was a word and a lifestyle preference that American society had tried to keep a secret. Some Hollywood movie screen actors, for example, hid their secret and carefully chose screen roles to amplify their masculinity. It was important to keep their lifestyle secret for they would certainly not only be banished from Hollywood, they might also possibly be jailed. During the 1950s, for example, attorney Roy Cohn, aide to Senator Joseph McCarthy, was extremely instrumental in working closely with the FBI during the Red Scare in American society (see Chapter 4). During the Red Scare, the mere hint of being a Communist was only one notch lower than being labeled a "homosexual." Ironically, Cohn himself was a closeted homosexual. During the late 1970s, Cohn turned up as a regular at Studio 54 and later acted as legal counsel for the owners in their battles with the IRS (see later in this chapter).

At the same time, New York City had a growing homosexual population. Cultural historian Charles Kaiser in *The Gay Metropolis* discovered that after World War II, "New York City became the literal gay metropolis for hundreds of thousands of immigrants from within and without the United States: the place they chose to learn how to live openly, honestly, and without shame" (ix).

But even in New York City, municipal laws prohibited any establishment from serving liquor "if there were more than three homosexuals present." In addition, any place that featured dancing had to have at least one female on the dance floor for three men. Although the liquor law was changed in 1965, and upheld by the State Appellate Division in 1967, police harassment was routine. The dance quota law lasted until 1971 (Driver 2000, 206).

The discovery of the discothèque scene during the 1960s and the advent of nonpartner dancing allowed homosexuals an equal opportunity to enjoy the pleasures of social dancing in public. The traditional methods of social dancing in a closed dance position with another man was certainly not allowed in any of the public dance halls of the past. Therefore, the nonpartner dancing allowed them the opportunity to enjoy social dancing without either being scrutinized or accused of being homosexual.

In an essay titled "Saturday Night Fever: An Ethnography of Disco Dancing," historian David Walsh's discussion and research disclosed the important part that the discothèque played "in the homosexual—particularly male homosexual world" (1993, 114). According to Walsh, the dance clubs served as "self-liberation as well as a venue for enjoyment, companionship, and meeting" (1993, 116). Across the board, the main attraction of freestyle dancing, to either gender or sexual preference, was that the learning of intricate steps or partnering was not necessary. Since the solo dance motions were actually "asexual," neither gender was required to assume a set partner dance or gender role. Regardless of dance style, however, homosexual dance clubs could flourish only in communities that accepted them. In the case of New York City, it took to literally physically fighting back to affirm the right to dance in public.

In 1969, the issue of homosexuality gained national attention as a result of a New York City bar known as Stonewall. Located in New York's Greenwich Village, Stonewall was a central meeting place for homosexuals, and the main activity was dancing. But living as a homosexual in New York City was not without harassment, physical beatings, and even arrest by police officers. However, in June 1969, during one routine "raid" on Stonewall, homosexuals were finally fed up and decided to fight back. During the confrontation, many of the patrons were brutally beaten and arrested. Unlike previous times, the incident received major media attention. "Stonewall" became a major turning point and rallied the cause for homosexuals nationwide. As a result, over 1,000 gay and lesbian groups throughout America made themselves public and organized under the name of the "Gay Liberation Movement." They also told accounts of similar harassment and brutal treatment by police officers in many of the major U.S. cities. The group led a nationwide push for equal protection under the law and to end discrimination in all areas of life. Despite the national attention, Americans still did not accept a public display of homosexuality (Lawrence 2003, 27).

THE BIRTH OF DISCO DANCE CLUBS

In February 1970, DJ David Mancuso held a Valentine's Day dance party in his large loft apartment at 674 Broadway in Manhattan. The space was about 1,850 square feet and could squeeze in a couple of hundred people. His parties were by invitation only, and he entertained a mix of straights, gays, and ethnics. The parties became a weekly event that lasted from midnight to 6 A.M., and his place simply became known as "The Loft." Since the dance parties were within his private home and did not sell alcohol, his was one of the very few Manhattan nightspots that could stay open all night (Lawrence 2003, 1, 250).

Shortly thereafter, in early 1970, The Sanctuary opened in a former Catholic church on West 43rd Street as the first Manhattan discothèque that publicly accepted homosexuals. The Sanctuary had a large dance floor and also attracted a significant number of the straight crowd. It quickly became a popular nightspot to dance and had lines outside waiting to get in. In 1971, the Hollywood thriller *Klute* filmed a portion of the movie within the Sanctuary. Other similar New York establishments that catered mainly to homosexual dancers were the Snakepit, Le Jardin, Salvation, and the Continental Baths in Manhattan and the Sandpiper and Ice Palace on Fire Island (Lawrence 2003, 18–19).

However, the New York State law was still in effect that "asserted that all-male dancing was illegal and that discothèques should contain at least one woman for every three men." On Fire Island, for example, New York City Police routinely patrolled the clubs and arrested any man dancing with another man. At the Ice Palace, for example, in order to maintain the lawful 3:1 ratio, the club had "a corral" to pass through to ensure an accurate count. Ice Palace owner Michael Fesco said, "The lesbians who lived on the island made up the numbers" (Lawrence 2003, 39–40).

The owners at clubs such as the Sanctuary were also careful to maintain the quota and admitted at least the required number of females. Many of those females were straight and were termed "Fag Hags." The term, although repulsive to some, and complete with a derogatory association towards homosexuals, became a badge of honor to some females. Texas transplant Hollywood DiRusso, a Manhattan publicist and a self-proclaimed "fag hag," proudly said,

> I make a decent salary, honey, but at least three-quarters of it goes for rent and the rest I spend on discotheques dancing my cute little tush off...I had already made up my mind to become a fag hag, but, as you can imagine, honey, Texas wasn't exactly what you would call a hotbed of flaming faggotry. I managed to sniff out the one or two gay bars in Dallas where you could go dance (McCormack 1976, 14).

At the time, racial diversity did not exist among the homosexual dance community. Puerto Rican and African Americans congregated in a few gay clubs in a small section of east Harlem located between 116th Street and 125th Street and Second and Third Avenues. They would rent lofts and storefronts and have music and dancing. The practice dated back to the Harlem rent parties of the 1920s and 1930s. Within Harlem itself, African American homosexuals and lesbians self-segregated and socialized in their own cabarets and speakeasies in order to maintain secrecy, privacy, and self-preservation (Lawrence 2003, 45–46).

By the early 1970s, in New York City, constant pressure by the Gay Activist Alliance pressured municipal officials to change the archaic laws. In late 1971, New York Mayor John V. Lindsay made a public declaration for reform throughout the city in all areas of social services. One of the agenda items was to eliminate the harassment and brutal attacks upon the homosexual community. On October 12, 1971, a page one headline story of *The New York Times* proclaimed, "City Acts to Let Homosexuals Meet and Work in Cabarets." Lindsay's administration publicly stated that, "The laws are impossible to enforce and have simply been a vehicle for corruption and oppression....Homosexuals have a right to congregate in places of public accommodation." In December 1971, municipal legislation was officially enacted that provided homosexuals with the same "safeguards for citizens against all forms of arbitrary victimization" as was provided to all citizens of New York (Narvaez 1971, 1).

FADING, MIXING, DJ'S, AND DISCOS

The idea of playing continuous prerecorded music for dancing was conceived in the discothèques during the 1960s. The invention of starting one song and overlapping the beginning of a second song as the previous song ended (a practice known as "fading") was most likely started by Terry Noel, who was a DJ at the

Peppermint Lounge (see Chapter 5). Noel employed two turntables, thereby having the second song ready. In the early 1970s, DJ Francis Grasso, who at one time worked as a substitute DJ for Noel, perfected the concept of "mixing" records while working at the Sanctuary in New York (see earlier in this chapter). In all likelihood, Grasso did not invent "mixing" but many attribute him as the DJ who perfected the process (Low, "Hustling Disco," n.d.).

The idea of mixing was to match the drumbeats and beats per minute (BPM) of the records of two different songs and overlapping and intertwining them, creating a seamless segue into the next song, so that the dancer could continue dancing in an uninterrupted flow—without missing a beat. (During the mid-1970s record companies began issuing books known as "Record Bibles" that listed the BPM's of all new releases.) Grasso would literally hold one record with his fingertips as the turntable spun underneath. As the other song played he would determine an appropriate segment to release the record so that both were playing at the same time (known as a "blend"). He would then remove the first record and prepare another record to follow. At the time it was all done by the "feel" of the individual DJ. (In later years, technical features would be introduced such as cross-faders and BPM meters that allowed the DJ to speed up or slow down the song to get an exact match) (Lawrence 2003, 35–36).

In the process, Grasso created a "reciprocal" relationship with the audience: the dancers responded to what he was playing and he, in turn, responded to the reaction of the dancers. According to Bill Brewster and Frank Broughton, who chronicled the history of the disc jockey in their publication *Last Night a DJ Saved My Life*, they proclaimed that Grasso's method was a turning point that "completely changed the relationship between the DJ and his audience." They explained,

> Before him the DJ might have known that certain records had the power to affect the mood and energy of the crowd; only after him did the DJ recognize that this power belonged to him, not the records. It lay in the DJ's skillful manipulation of the dancers, in the way he sequenced or programmed the records (1999, 129).

Grasso also attempted to expand the dancing effect by flipping the switches of the lighting "to the beat of the music."

The idea of synchronizing the beat of the music with lighting effects was first instituted during the late 1960s. At the time, Ron Ferri, a Rhode Island artist, was commissioned by Michael Butler (the producer of *Hair*; see Chapter 5) to design a lighting effect in the Chicago nightclub Le Bison. Ferri designed a 30-foot wall of incandescent light bulbs and wired them through a device he called the "Translator." The device coded the amplified music into electrical pulses that, in turn, flashed the multitude of lights in synchronization with the beat of the music. Strobe lights, borrowed from fashion photographers, were also incorporated. In essence, the Translator stimulated the ear-to-eye body, proving a new sensation for the social dancer (Haden-Guest 1997, 13).

A distinctive feature of the lighting effects was the Disco Ball—made up of hundreds of small square mirrors. The Disco ball was a round ball of varying size from 8 inches to 60 inches in diameter, but the average diameter was about 20 inches. It was usually hung from a motorized hook from the ceiling at the center of the dance floor; the hook spun the ball slowly around. One or more spotlights were directed at the ball, which in turn reflected through the mirrors and created a star-like pattern that continuously moved around the dance floor. During the mid-1970s, the National Products plant in Louisville, Kentucky, employed 27 people who made over 1000 Disco balls per week. By the end of the twentieth century, the company was producing only about 60 balls per week. The name "Disco" was dropped, and they were renamed Mirror Balls.

The ability of the DJs to synchronize the beats of the music with the lighting effects and mixing in a continuous stream of music, from the time a dance club opened until it closed, was a new sensation that the club dancers loved. At the time, *Rolling Stone* writer Tom Smucker described that the Disco "was about ecstasy: a place where the DJ choreographed music and lighting to manipulate the mood on the dance floor until everyone was lost in movement" (1980, 425). *Village Voice* columnist Andrew Kopkind added, "The club DJs prided themselves on psyching out a crowd and then programming them into an ecstatic frenzy, slip-cuing records into a continuous sequence and equalizing them for dancing by boosting the bass" (1979, 29).

A solitary dancer in Disco era top and glitter pants dances under a Disco ball.   Author's Archives.

Record companies took notice, as did the radio stations. Unlike previous years when radio airplay made a record popular, during this era it was the DJ within the Disco clubs who was responsible for making a record a hit. In New York City alone, it was estimated that dancers purchased almost 250,000 of the records that were played in the Discos. As a result, many of the club DJs were as famous as the recording artists. They included Steve D'Acquisto, Jim Burgess, Michael Cappello, Joey Carvello, Francis Grasso, Bobby Guttadaro, Danae Jacaividis, Frankie Knuckles, Larry Levan, John Luongo, David Mancuso, Howard Merritt, Tom Moulton, Richie Rivera, Tom Savarese, Wayne Scott, Nicky Siano, Jimmy Stuard, Roy Thode, and Ray Yeates (Holden, "The Evolution of a Dance Craze," 1979, 29).

And to dance in the Disco was to participate, and in participating one had a sense that he or she belonged. Individuals could go into a Disco, and from the very moment they entered they could be consumed by the music. For many, the dance floor was a safe haven from the daily toils and tribulations of life. Music critic Mikal Gilmore exclaimed, "That was *Saturday Night Fever's* great cheap moral: whatever daily drudgery entraps one it's all erased on the dance floor" (1979, 54). Music critic Lester Bangs added,

> Living the disco life is knowing that as long as you stay inside these glowing, flashing walls, absolutely nothing will change: neither the beat nor your relations with the people around you (1979, 92).

One patron, Cindy McEhrlich, proudly said,

> Disco has brought back the Hangout, a place to go for a few hours that doesn't cost too much….I've stopped answering friends who watch and ask "Doesn't it get boring?" watching is not the point. Watching is boring (1976, 32).

But not all Discos were alike. There was definitely a difference between the Discos that were located within the heart of a city such as Atlanta, Boston, Chicago, Los Angeles, San Francisco, Washington, D.C., Miami, or New York with the Discos that were located in the suburban outskirts. Disco in itself was mainly an urban experience. Journalist Andrew Kopkind of the *Village Voice* article said,

> It is part of a sophisticated, commercial, manipulated culture that is rooted exclusively in an urban environment. Disco music is produced in big cities and its fashions are formed in big cities, at considerable expense, by high-priced professionals….All the sparkle, speed, cynicism, and jaded irony associated with metropolitan life is attached to disco. It is far from wholesome. Provincials may either envy or abhor it. But it belongs to the city (Kopkind 1979, 11).

Most of the urban Discos were open to all and catered to both homosexuals and straights (Lawrence 2003, 37).

One example was Dance Your Ass Off People in San Francisco. It was located in a two-story building and held about 6,500. The crowd was racially mixed and mostly singles, both straight and homosexual. The club's DJ, Pete Struve, noted, "I'm the only person I know in town who plays slow music once in a while. They really like it." He also proudly added, "You should see that whole dance floor full of people doing the Hustle….It's the most fantastic thing you've ever seen in your life" (Robertson 1976, 27).

Many of the other urban Discos catered to an integrated crowd of homosexual and straight dancers. San Francisco also had Oz, City Disco, I-Beam, and Trocadero Transfer. Los Angeles had Studio One, and Scandals. In Manhattan there was the Infinity, Flamingo, Les Mouches, 12 West, and Xenon. The Buffalo area included Club 747 Disco, Frisco's 14, Uncle Sam's, Port Shark, the Hibachi Room, the Coliseum, and Fridays and Saturdays Lounge. Some of the notable Discos in Boston included Yesterdays, 1270, Chaps, and Rhinoceros. In Chicago there was Galaxy, and in Atlanta Phazes. In Washington, D.C., they included, The Apple Tree, the L.A. Café, The Plum, Tramps, and The Sazerac.

However, the colorful descriptions and eclectic crowds were usually confined to the urban areas. Within the suburban Discos it was very rare to see a racially mixed crowd. And for that matter, nor was there any evidence of homosexuals. In 1978, Albert Goldman's contemporary account of the Disco-dancing era in his book *Disco* described the typical suburban Disco dance club.

> Those Saturday-night-fever blisters made famous by John Travolta: the teen-age dance clubs where every boy dresses like Travolta in a white, trim-line suit, and everybody does the same step in the same style till they break for the tables where they all talk the same "towhk" [slang for talk] (20).

Nevertheless, the suburban Disco dance clubs sprung up all around the nation.

Officially by 1978, over 2,500 Discos existed nationwide. At the time, *Disco-thekin'* magazine estimated at least 1,500 discothèques in New York City alone. In addition, they noted that over 37 million people had visited a Disco at least once (Goldman 1978, 11). By 1979, Andrew Kopkind of the *Village Voice* estimated that the number of Disco clubs grew to at least 20,000 and earned over $6 billion per year (13). The reason that the estimates were so high was that just about every club, restaurant, lounge, hotel, or recreation hall opened a Disco. The Emerson Steakhouse franchise in Rockville, Maryland, for example, changed over twelve of its restaurants into Discos. A franchise named The 2001 Club tried to capitalize on the fame of the movie *Saturday Night Fever* and opened 24 similar clubs nationwide. Many of the Holiday Inns, Ramada Inns, Sheratons, and Hyatt Regencys all across the country converted their lounges to Discos (Lawrence 2003, 185, 315).

In September 1979, the city of Buffalo in upstate New York hosted what it billed as "The World's Largest Disco." The one time six-hour event held at the Buffalo Convention Center featured musical artist Gloria Gaynor and The Trammps. The "Disco Event" attracted over 13,000 dancers to a dance floor of over 64,000 square feet. The following November, Richard Nader, who earlier in the decade promoted 1950s revival Rock 'n' Roll stage shows, switched to Disco. He promoted a four-hour "Disco Dance Party" at New York's Madison Square Garden, attracting over 14,000 dancers to "the world's largest discothèque" ("Is Buffalo Gig World's Largest?" 1979). Of all the Disco dance clubs throughout America, however, the most famous was Studio 54.

STUDIO 54, "FREAK OUT," AND THE "SON OF SAM"

On April 26, 1977, Studio 54, located at 254 West 54th Street, opened as a Disco dance club. The name was derived from the street address, and the theme was kept throughout the club. The dance floor was 5400 square feet and had 54 different lighting effects synchronized with the DJ's music. The dance club became known nationwide as a hot spot for Disco dancing and the freewheeling lifestyle associated with homosexuality, bisexuality, and drugs. At Studio 54 it appeared that just about "anything goes," and the more risqué and flamboyant the better. It was a haven for the "beautiful people," the extravagantly dressed, and celebrities. One regular, Danny Tenaglia, said,

> Studio 54 was like going to see a movie…It wasn't about the music. When you went there, it was gimmicky. It was the first club where you had people painting their whole body silver. "Oh there was somebody in there on a horse." People would talk about that instead of the music. So it was all about *who* was there (Brewster and Broughton 1999, 189).

However, the exclusive door policy barred entry to the common person (Driver 2000, 210).

Although in past years, other clubs had restrictive entrance policies, it was Studio 54 that made famous the velvet rope and "policing the door." At the entry to the club was one or more doormen stationed behind stanchions linked by a velvet rope. For those fortunate enough to be selected, the doorman would unhook the velvet rope and allow access. According to dance historian Don McDonagh, "Studio 54 selected a crowd on the basis of fame, notoriety, or far out freakiness" (1979, 113). In 1998, a Hollywood film was made about the flamboyant heyday of Studio 54 simply titled *54*. Other films that portrayed the restricted entry policy included *Summer of Sam* (1999) and *The Last Days of Disco* (1998).

In 1978, a hit song by Dana and Gene told the story of a Disco dancing relationship story. He pleads that all he wants to do is marry her and all she wants to know is "Dario, Can You Get Me Into Studio 54?" As a result of its notoriety, people would do just about anything to get into Studio 54. Some would offer large amounts of money to the door guards, which very rarely worked. And some of the enterprising young doormen exchanged sexual favors (usually in a special room in the basement) with both females and males in exchange for entry into the club, which worked more often than not (Jones and Kantonen 2000, 129).

For those fortunate enough to gain entry, the club was designed in itself for extravagant behavior. *Rolling Stone* columnist Michael Segell described it as follows:

> Entrance is gained through a long, mirrored foyer with an arched, gold ceiling bathed in soft red light. The multi-tiered main room is expansive—half lounge, half dance floor. In the lounge area, boyish custodians brush the glittery black carpet, polish the shrine-like chrome plated bar, dust the sprawling couches, and arrange huge urns filled with blooming calla lilies….A heart-shaped pendulum with an attached strobe swings down over the crowded dance floor, followed by a neon fan, cyclorama, and giant smiling man in the moon with a sparkling spoon perched beneath its nose ("Studio 54: Steve Rubell's Disco Disneyland," 1979, 44–45).

The DJ booth, located well above the dance floor, was staffed by three technicians who constantly checked the lighting and sound equipment. They were in charge of raising and lowering the numerous "neon grids" and lavish backdrops that added to the total dancing experience.

Most of the other well-known Disco dance clubs also held an elaborate entrance policy including the noted velvet rope and bouncer. They included Regine's, El Morocco, Le Club, Doubles, Xenon, and New York, New York. These policies continued throughout the twentieth century, and they were also common in the major cities such as Chicago, San Francisco, and Los Angeles. The basic policy at all these clubs was that if you were not on a guest list or were not a regular you were

Crowd waiting outside Studio 54 in New York City, c. 1978. © Bettmann/Corbis.

turned away. Many celebrities got turned away, including some of the same Disco music stars whose records were playing in those very same clubs. One of those was the group CHIC (pronounced "sheik") whose song "Le Freak" would become a monstrous worldwide hit, and they owed it all to the night they were refused entry to Studio 54.

Nile Rodgers and Bernard Edwards of the group CHIC were typical of many of the Disco musical groups of that time. The group was club and radio famous but they were not recognizable in person. In November 1977, CHIC's first single, "Dance, Dance, Dance (Yowsah, Yowsah, Yowsah)," sold over 1 million copies in the first month and went to No. 1 on both the Pop and R&B charts and also was a hit in the Disco dance clubs. The catchphrase "Yowsah, Yowsah, Yowsah" was mimicked on dance floors throughout America. (The phrase actually echoed back to the chant by the MC in the dance marathons of the 1920s and 1930s; see Chapter 2.) The album also generated another hit single titled "Everybody Dance." Although "Everybody Dance" only went to No. 38 on the *Billboard* Pop charts and No. 12 on the R&B, it quickly went to No. 1 on the newly created Disco/Club charts ("CHIC Fan Club Bio 1979").

On one night in 1978, with all their current success, Rodgers and Edwards "dressed to the nines" and decided to pay a visit to Studio 54. They intended to see Disco singer Grace Jones, who was performing at the club that same night. As it turned out, Rodgers and Edwards were also contracted to produce singer Jones's next record album. But upon arriving at Studio 54, they were stopped at the velvet rope and denied entry. They stood outside for hours hoping someone from Jones entourage would recognize them and get them past the doorman. To top it off, it was cold and snowing. Finally, they were so furious that they just gave up and walked back to Rodgers's apartment that was only a few blocks away.

At Rodgers apartment they tried to calm themselves by jamming with their guitar and bass. But they could not forget their frustration and were still fuming at the rejection. Rodgers said, "We were just having a good time, venting our anger and frustration." He remembered,

> We were just yelling obscenities...*Fuck Studio 54...Fuck 'em...Fuck off!*... And we were laughing. We were entertaining the hell out of ourselves. We had a blast. And finally it hit Bernard. He said, "Hey Nile! What you're playing sounds really good."... we said, "damn! That sounds like a song."... And we wrote a whole obscene song about fucking Studio 54, and those assholes. But it had melody, and texture, and form. And we said, "This is hysterical." We changed "Fuck Off" to "Freak Off." But that sounded lame (Haden-Guest 1997, 81_83).

They eventually arrived at the title "Le Freak" and changed "Freak Off" to "Freak Out." Rodgers explained that "Le Freak" was also a song about a dance style called The Freak "that was the biggest dance in America at that time." The Freak involved trying to get as close to your partner in the most sensual way possible without actually touching. Rodgers described it as follows:

> Most of the time when you're going out to a club to dance, you're dancing with a total stranger. You're using that as a form of communication.... [You might say] Hey, I like what you look like now let's go out and check out our [dance] moves together. The Freak was the closest thing to having sex without winding up...going all the way ("Nile Rodgers talks about 'The Freak' dance," BBC documentary).

As it turned out, Rodgers and Edwards wrote the whole song "within twenty-five to thirty minutes." "Le Freak" quickly sold more than 6 million copies, and it became one of the biggest records of 1979. It was not only the biggest hit for CHIC, it also became the largest selling single in the history of Warner Brothers records, right behind "White Christmas" and "Rudolph the Red-Nosed Reindeer" (Haden-Guest 1997, 81–83).

As a group, CHIC would lose its popularity as Disco itself waned, but Rodgers and Edwards went on to produce such successful songs as "We Are Family" by Sister Sledge (almost a clone-like of CHIC's hit song "Good Times"). Of interesting note, "Good Times" would also become a major part of the sampling in the first Hip Hop hit "Rappers Delight" by the Sugarhill Gang (see Chapter 7) ("CHIC Fan Club Bio 1979").

As with Disco music, almost as quickly as it burst upon the scene Studio 54 closed in the fall of 1978. The club owners Steve Rubell and Ian Schrager were convicted of tax evasion by the IRS and each served a prison sentence. Upon their release, the owners reopened the club, but by that time the scene had passed it by. The club opened sporadically for many years thereafter, eventually closing for good around 1986. The building still stood and was used for private parties and converted back to a Broadway theater. In retrospect, photographer Francesco Scavullo, a Studio 54 regular, said,

> I just went there to dance and forget everything. I never took the camera there. I just let off a lot of steam. I wasn't involved in drugs or drinking, and I wasn't involved with the sex stuff downstairs. I just went there because I loved the music…and because I love to dance (Haden-Guest 1997, 114).

And to dance is what many Disco loving New Yorkers wanted to do. However, during a 13-month stretch from July 1976 to August 1977, a real life fear gripped New Yorkers as the "Son of Sam" serial killer terrorized the city. The victims were totally at random, but the news media tried to draw a pattern, telling the frightened public stories that the .44 caliber killer (so-named because of the weapon used) was targeting young couples in parked cars who had previously attended a Disco. Some newscasters even claimed that the "Son of Sam" lurked inside discothèques looking for victims. The paranoia almost paralyzed the city. Young people were literally afraid to go out dancing. Dance clubs and nightclubs suffered drastically and some just closed.

On August 10, 1977, a "reclusive 24-year-old postal worker" and U.S. Army veteran named David Berkowitz was arrested and charged with the killings. Police found the .44 caliber handgun in his possession and also a loaded .45 caliber machine gun in his car. Police indicated Berkowitz was preparing to enter an unnamed Disco in either Queens or Long Island in preparation for a mass murder (McFadden 1977, 1, 10).

On the same night that Berkowitz was captured, Albert Goldman was in Studio 54. In his classic book *Disco*, Goldman recalled the relief of the dance crowd. He said,

> Right in the middle of [Meco's] *Star Wars*, the sound system died as if someone had pulled the plug. The nearly hysterical voice of Steve Rubell, the club's manic owner, blabbered over the PA: "They got Sam!…Son o' Sam!…They got 'im!" A mighty cheer rose from the disco floor. The sound system soared again to full volume…the [dancers] celebrated the vanquishment of its most implacable enemy (1978, 20).

With the killer captured, New Yorkers celebrated by getting back to dancing.

ROLLER DISCO, BILL BUTLER, AND THE EMPIRE ROLLERDROME

During the late 1970s, the popularity of Disco music and dancing took hold at indoor roller-skating rinks nationwide. Dancing on roller skates to Disco music had many names, including "Rock 'n' Roller Skating," "Roller Rocking," "Jammin" and "Disco on Wheels," but it became most commonly known as "Roller Disco." It was not until 1977 that mainstream America caught on to Roller Disco. Rinks started replacing their old "organ style" of music with the popular Top-40 songs that attracted many youngsters. Many roller rinks installed additional sound equipment and lights to replicate the Disco nightlife in a drug-free and nonalcoholic environment for children, teens, and adults. The popularity was also attributed to the new development in polyurethane wheels on the skates that were versatile enough to be used both indoors and outdoors. Another addition was a "fifth wheel" that was fastened under the forefoot to serve as a toe stop and aid in many of the dance maneuvers (Kollmar and Mason 1979, 25).

Roller Disco is often credited with originating at the Empire Rollerdrome in Brooklyn, New York, by skater Bill Butler. In 1979, Bill Butler published an instructional booklet titled *Jammin' Bill Butler's Complete Guide to Roller Disco.* The book promised, "Step by exciting step, from the first moment you strap a pair of skates on your soon-to-be-happy feet." Some of Butler's basic fundamentals included balancing, going back and forth, keeping the basic beat with the music, learning the all too important "How to Stop," as well as the inevitable what to do when you fall down, and, of course, "Getting up!" Butler recommended,

> Get up as quickly as possible. Never lie around waiting for assistance…When you turn to get up, turn toward the inside of the rink. When skating counter-clockwise (the usual direction), skaters tend to go to the right of an accident. So if you turn to face the outer rail when getting up, the possibility of colliding with another skater with your back or your feet is greater (1979, 36).

The basic moves had names including the Whip, Pivot turns, the Lean, the Snake, Side-stepping, Shoulder-Shaking, and hundreds of others. Butler described the relaxed fun atmosphere that was displayed at the typical Roller Disco. He added,

> Female jammers have always felt free to ask men to skate couples. Men have always jammed with men and women with women, arms linked, holding hands, arms across waists, hands on shoulders playing follow-the-leader, making trains, forming couples, trios, sometimes eight or nine people echoing one another's moves, communicating through movement, moving in sync with the other bodies, with the music propelling, cementing relationships (Butler and Schoen 1979, 21).

In all, more than 4,000 roller rinks and 22 million Americans enjoyed roller-skating. Of that number, the Roller Skating Rink Operators Association reported over 70 percent played Disco music. In 1978, the 10,000 square foot Easy Glider Roller Rink in Westchester County in New York, for example, employed a DJ to play Top-40 songs. On Wednesdays, however, they did retain live organ music playing tunes for Waltz, Fox Trot, Tango, and Jitterbug (Sim 1978, WC8).

In April 1979, *Rolling Stone* journalist Maryanne Vollers visited the Empire Roll-erdrome. She described her initial foray into the Brooklyn roller rink as follows:

> When the door opens, you're clobbered by the full force of the music and the colored lights, sprayed around the room by revolving mirror globes. Before you can even see the skaters, you can pick up the breeze created by dozens of speeding bodies, and with it the odor of sweat and wine and perfume.

Roller Disco skater Vinnie Vinzerilli explained that the simple combination of music, roller-skating, and dancing provided everyone at the Rollerdrome with a sense of sheer joy and exhalation. He added, "You can't worry about racism or family problems because you're afraid of bustin' your ass on the floor" (Vollers 1979, 38–39).

By 1979, according to Joe Shevelson, VP of the Chicago Roller Skate Company, the number of roller rinks topped 5,000 nationwide and there were 25 million skaters. California had about 360 Disco roller rinks, including the Palisades Gardens in San Diego, Sherman Square Rink in Los Angeles, the Stardust in San Bernardino, Skateway in Orange County, and Roller City in West Covina. New York also had Village Skates, Busby's, High Rollers, and Brooklyn's Empire Rollerdrome, all "bopping to a disco beat." New Yorkers roller-skated in Central Park and Californians on Venice Beach and Ventura Blvd. At Venice Beach, they held the Venice Outdoor Disco Roller-skating Championships. Other Roller Discos nationwide included Skateland in Hixson, Tennessee; The Great Skate in Decatur, Illinois; Axle in Niles, Illinois; Disco Wheels in Chicago; Twilight Time in Dallas, Texas; Northland in Detroit, Michigan; and Fast Eddie's Skating and Disco in Atlanta, Georgia (Marzano 1979, 8–9).

In July 1979, The Roxy opened as a roller rink on West 57th Street in Manhattan. Anna Quindlen of *The New York Times* said the "Roxy is to roller skating what Studio 54 was to disco" replete with a "complex light system in hot reds and cool blues, the silver skyline along the back wall and the red velvet ropes outside bespeaking exclusivity." The Roxy maintained the same type of exclusivity as

Roller Disco combined roller-skating and Disco music. In this 1978 photo, skaters Roller Disco at the Roxy Roller Rink in New York City.   © Roger Ressmeyer / Corbis.

Studio 54 had and soon attracted celebrities and the "beautiful people" (Quindlen, "Where to Roller Skate to a Disco Beat," 1981, C13).

During that same year, roller skate sales, which had never topped 1 million pairs sold in any given year, rocketed to over 3 million pairs sold. Newspaper headlines proclaimed, "Skating Revival Rolls On," "Roller Skating + Disco Dancing = Two Hit Rinks," and "Roller Skates: 300,000 Pairs a Month," among many others (McDowell 1979, F13). During that same year, Hollywood capitalized on the fad and produced two movies *Skatetown USA*, starring Patrick Swayze and *Roller Boogie* starring Linda Blair and Roller Disco skater Jim Bray.

Instructional books included, *Roller Disco* by Dale Marzano and *Roller Disco Dancing* by Kerry Kollmar and Melody Mason. Each offered information on the types of skates, the basic steps, and fashion tips. Marzano's book was billed as "The only authorized guide to disco dances for roller skaters." It included, "Basic skating moves," "Hot-doggin'," "Latest rink fashions," and "Ten easy-to-learn dances." Two of the roller-dances were the Conga and the Line Shuffle. Marzano said The Conga was "done exactly the same on skates as on feet" (see Chapter 3). He described the Conga on roller skates as follows:

> The skaters start in a line, one in front of the other, with hands on the waist of the person in front. Skate forward on the left foot. Then skate forward on the right. Now skate forward on the left foot again. Now kick the right leg out to the side. Then the right leg comes down and skates forward, the left skates forward, the right skates forward again. Finally the left foot kicks out to the side. Note that you end in a position to start the series with the right foot again (1979, 56).

"The Conga" on roller skates was prominently featured in the movie *Roller Boogie*. The Line Shuffle was done in a circle facing inward as "the dancers skate in one direction, and then in the opposite direction but all gradually progress down the floor." *Roller Disco* also included tips for freestyle roller dancing and partner dancing with dance names such as the Coffee Bean, the New Yorker, the Goose, and the Tango Split (1979, 57).

Roller Disco Dancing by Kerry Kollmar and Melody Mason provided an interesting beginning to their instructional book. The descriptive introduction was both a sociological reflection of the attitude of the decade of the 1970s as well as an attitudinal reflection of the appeal of Disco, the music, and roller-skating. They wrote:

> It is the end of the 1970's. We have ended a war and gained a new national pastime. The noisy metal and rubber wheels of the jeeps and tanks that destroyed then, have now been replaced by silent, streamlined, polyurethane wonder-wheels of today's Roller Disco skate. Many people have come to fall in love with this new physical and powerful means of expression every day now....It is fun, it is uninhibited, and it is there for you to do. You can do it alone or with a friend or group....Anyone can do it—and every one is! It is Roller Disco Dancing and when you try it, you will fall in love with it! (1979, 5).

Kollmar and Mason also described the fashion of Roller Disco as "the flashy, bright, neon light-and-loose look of the new phenomenon....is a relatively new one" (1979, 5).

In 1981, journalist Anna Quindlen toured the various roller rinks in the New York tri-state area. For the benefit of "those who have never been to a roller disco," she described the colorful atmosphere,

> Where human projectiles from all walks of life, wearing stretch fabrics of every hue, regularly hurl themselves around a fast track to a thumpity-thump beat....Somehow, the stroke-stroke of roller skating seems perfectly suited to the bamp-bamp-bamp of disco...there are computerized light systems, conversation pits, mirrors. There are men in skintight purple pants, women in spangles and chiffon, [and] children in designer jeans ("Where to Roller Skate to A Disco Beat," 1981, C1).

For the most part, however, the best rule of fashion was "safety first." It was advisable not to wear long scarfs, or chains, or even lengthy pants that might restrict the body's smooth movement or, worse yet, get tangled in the skate wheels. Pants or shorts for both genders were also advised. Kollmar and Mason cautioned "Women can wear skirts, but at the risk of displaying more than they might like—in the event of a bad spill" (1979, 27).

DANCE FEVER

Disco took a page from the tradition of *American Bandstand* and the success of *Soul Train* to provide both regional and nationally broadcast dance shows. In 1975, *Disco Step-by-Step* was the first television dance show solely for Disco music and dancing. It was broadcast regionally in western New York, eastern Pennsylvania, and southern Canada. According to Marty Angelo, the show's creator, producer, and host, *Disco Step-By-Step* was "the first television show specifically dedicated only to disco music, dance instruction, and hustle dancing." Angelo said,

> I wanted to make it different than *American Bandstand*...and *Soul Train*. Most of the dance styles displayed on those two shows and in the clubs were just free style type dancing. I really saw disco as the hustle!...I decided to make dance instruction a segment on the television show. I had professional instructors come on and teach people how to dance the hustle right in the privacy of their own home.

Other regional TV Disco dance shows included Boston's *Dancing Disco* and *Disco Fever* in Los Angles, California (Glassman 1979, 47).

The first nationally syndicated Disco dance show was *Disco '77*. It was filmed in a local Disco in Miami, Florida. It followed a similar format that featured musical artists as well as a group of regular Disco dancers. In 1978, the name of the show was changed to *Disco Magic* and was expanded internationally and broadcast to 70 other countries around the globe ("Disco '77," IMDb.com, n.p.).

The most notable of all the Disco dance shows was *Dance Fever* hosted by Deney Terrio (John Travolta's dance coach from the movie *Saturday Night Fever*). The fast-paced weekly half-hour dance show was best remembered for a featured cast of professional dancers known as the Solid Gold Dancers. It ran in first-run syndication from 1979 to 1985. Shortly after the show premiered, Terrio recalled a telephone call from his parents. They said "Deney, somebody's putting bumper stickers on our mailbox." Terrio asked, "What do the stickers say?" His mother replied, "Disco sucks." All he could tell them was "Disregard it" ("Deney Terrio," Disco Step-by-Step Web site).

THE "DISCO SUCKS" CAMPAIGN AND THE DEATH OF DISCO

During the early years of Disco, the criticism was aimed mainly at the new technological amenities such as the sound systems, lighting effects, and even the clothing. One federal agency, the Bureau of Radiological Health, claimed that the laser effects, as part of the light shows, could be damaging to the eyes. In other instances, podiatrists warned that the extreme height of the platform shoes would cause permanent damage to the feet. Others simply resurrected the common complaint against a new genre a music—that it was too *loud*. Many media accounts cited clinical reports about the danger of going deaf. Robert Varc of *The New York Times* sarcastically asked,

> Isn't there a way for people to awaken their senses, to transcend their humdrum lives, without rupturing their eardrums…Can't they get their kicks by standing next to a Con Ed workman jackhammering through a sidewalk?

Occasionally the criticism was simply poking good-natured fun at the fashion. Vare, in obvious reference to the Village People, said that in some of the Discos one could find, "Cops and construction workers in vinyl pants and mylar earrings, unless they are homosexual, in which case they might wear the uniforms of cops and construction workers" (Vare, 1979, A15).

On the other hand, some religious and municipal organizations were not so subtle. In 1977, the Reverend Jesse Jackson, for example, called for a nationwide ban against all Disco music. He claimed that the music promoted "promiscuity and drug use" ("Censorship Incidents 1970s," n.d.). In 1978, the town of Henryetta, Oklahoma (population 6,400) instituted a ban on public dancing. Under pressure from some townspeople, the city council rescinded the ban early the following year. However, the repeal came with a restriction that no "dance hall or disco" within the town limits could be located within 500 yards of a house of worship. The small town did have over 20 churches (*Rolling Stone*, April 19, 1977, 6). In the mid-1970s, in the city of Baxter Springs, Kansas, the town council also placed a ban on "Disco dancing" within the town limits. The case was met with resistance among some town members and was actually taken to the Supreme Court. In 1979, in the case *City of Baxter Springs v. Bryant*, 226 Kan. 383, 598 P.2d 1051, 1057 (1979), the prohibition on Disco dancing was found unconstitutional. The court stated that, "Healthful and harmless recreation cannot be prohibited by a municipal corporation."

During 1979, "Discophobia" was the word most often repeated for those who had an aversion to Disco music and the Disco dance scene. The negative connotation of sexual tales, drugs, and dirty money of the underworld were widely publicized in the media. Although the flamboyance certainly existed in a few select urban clubs, it was not readily apparent in the suburban clubs. In reality, the term that best described mainstream America's revolt against Disco was "Homophobia." Many of the critics of Disco continually applied the words "superficial" and "artificial." At the time, a media consultant researching Discophobia undertook an attitudinal research survey and confirmed that the words "superficial" and "artificial" were "derogatory euphemisms for *gay*" (Lawrence 2003, 377).

And with Discophobia many men lost the inherent desire to dance. Conservatives mounted continuous attacks on the freewheeling nonpartner dancing and reinforced the image that dancing was for "sissies." And with that came the advent of two parallel worlds, one being Disco that embraced the masculinity of dancing with or without a partner. The other created an inherent homophobia that abhorred dancing and was embraced by the supporters of Rock 'n' Roll. At the time, Casablanca record promoter Kenn Friedman said, "There is a big cultural difference between rock and disco, and it's gayness. Some people don't like to talk about it, but it's true" (Kopkind 1979, 13). Cultural historian Bruce Schulman added, "It obviously threatened suburban white boys who found it too feminine, too gay, too black.... Throughout the nation's vanilla suburbs, the white noose surrounding the increasingly black and Latino central cities, white youth rallied behind the slogan, 'Disco Sucks.' Clubs and concert halls sponsored 'disco sucks nights,' occasionally resulting in ugly racial incidents" (2002, 73–74).

In April 1979, journalist Mikal Gilmore admitted that, while writing an article for a *Rolling Stone* issue devoted to Disco, others in the magazine's publishing office began appearing with T-shirts displaying the words "Disco sucks." He observed that it was the "intransigent rocker" who attacked Disco the most. At the time, Gilmore's contemporary account proved quite prophetic and also quite accurate. He added,

> More importantly whenever a phenomenon is given blanket dismissal, you can be sure something deeper is at work. And what's going on here is that rock fans, like the proverbial cake, have been left out in the rain. Disco's principal constituents have been gays, blacks, Hispanics—the presence of the gay culture alone in disco has been enough to ward off a lot of rockers (Gilmore, 54).

In other words, Rock 'n' Roll was uncompromising against blacks, gays, Hispanics, and women. In a 1979 interview with *Rolling Stone*, Nile Rodgers of the group CHIC said:

> When I first started [in the early Seventies], all I played was super heavy-duty rock & roll...To be a guitarist in a heavy glitter band was the whole thing. To be [Jimi] Hendrix or Jimmy Page [of Led Zeppelin] was success to me. Life became more real when I tried to get a record deal. There's a hell of a lot of racism in rock & roll. As a black man playing lead guitar, I could never get a record deal (Farber 1979, 32).

It was not long, however, before Rock 'n' Roll launched an all-out war on Disco.

On July 12, 1979, the Chicago White Sox baseball team sponsored a "Disco Demolition Nite" at Comiskey Park. The promotion included a ticket at the cost of 98 cents if the fan also brought a Disco record for destruction. The Associated Press estimated at least 40,000 fans attended the scheduled doubleheader between the Detroit Tigers and the Chicago White Sox. Between games, Chicago Rock 'n' Roll DJ Steve Dahl of WLUP-FM, dressed in military fatigues, led the crowd in repeated chants of "Disco Sucks, Disco Sucks!" He proceeded to literally blow up thousands of Disco records. The explosion edged on the crowd, and thousands of fans stormed the field in a wild frenzy. In the process, they ripped up the sod and tore down banners—while chanting "Disco Sucks." When order was finally restored (1 hour and 16 minutes after the scheduled start of the second game) the umpires declared "the field unplayable" and postponed the game (the White Sox eventually forfeited) ("Anti-Disco Rally Halts White Sox," 1979, A16).

Unfortunately, the Comiskey Park rally was not an isolated incident. In Columbus, Ohio, radio DJ John Fisher of WLVQ-FM put on a public display as he also dressed in military fatigues as he destroyed numerous Disco records and "torpedoed" the song "In the Navy" by the Village People. In Portland, Oregon, KGON-FM radio personality Bob Anchetta perched himself above a concession stand at a local drive-in movie theater. A crowd estimated at 900, there to see the movie *Animal House*, chanted "Disco Sucks" as Anchetta smashed and burned hundreds of Disco records. In Utica, New York, WOUR-FM's morning show offered a regular prize each day as listeners chose between a method of Disco record destruction by a chainsaw, by a wild-animal stampede, or by a city bus. In Detroit, Michigan, WWWW-FM (known as "W4") set up a morning duo who called themselves the "Disco Ducks Klan." Shortly thereafter, the duo, Jim Johnson and

The "Disco Sucks" campaign often led to violent demonstrations. On July 12, 1979, thousands of fans stormed the field in between games of a scheduled doubleheader at Chicago's Comiskey Park during "Disco Demolition Nite." © Bettmann/Corbis.

George Baier, switched to another rock station WRIF-FM and quickly began a group called DREAD, the Detroit Rockers Engaged in the Abolition of Disco (Rose, "Discophobia: Rock & Roll Fights Back," 1979, 32).

Disco club DJ Tom Moulton surmised that it was easy for the Rock radio DJ's to join in the cause. since prior to Disco it was the radio DJ's who had the power to make a song a hit, but with Disco the role was reverted to the club DJ. Moulton said, "The clubs brought them down a peg or two, so they were the first ones to put a nail in disco's coffin." However, the onslaught was insurmountable, and by the end of 1979, Disco sales plummeted. In essence, Disco was dead (Lawrence 2003, 374).

In 1981, Pop music legend and perennial *American Bandstand* host Dick Clark added,

> Frustrated rock fans just couldn't see Disco for what it actually was—another offshoot of rock and roll. In condemning Disco, these bitter rockers sounded like anti-rock parents of the fifties, with their complaints that the music was unimaginative and monotonous. Nevertheless, people wanted to dance (Uslan and Solomon 1981, 430).

In fact, Americans danced for one simple reason—to have fun. And they would continue to dance as evidenced by the late twentieth century development of Breakdancing, Country line dancing, and the Swing dance revival.

7

Breakdancing, Country Dancing, and the Swing Dance Revival: 1980–2000

We didn't know we were dancing on the edge of our graves.
—Rodger McFarlane, 1999

The Political, Social, and Cultural Climate

By 1980, the memory of the Vietnam War had faded as had the Hippie lifestyle and the call for social change. In 1981, the inauguration of Ronald Reagan as the 40th president of the United States was a return to conservative middle-class values that many felt had come undone during the 1960s and 1970s. The Cold War tensions were also revived (see Chapter 4), and the nuclear arms race with the Soviet Union escalated, spending billions of dollars on a missile and a defense system program known as "Star Wars." The fear of nuclear war with the Soviet Union was resurrected and was reflected in many movies and television shows including *Red Dawn*, *War Games*, and *The Day After* (Giordano 2003, 204–208).

In lieu of social programs, the Reagan administration shifted its approach to support big business with a "Supply-side" economic theory claiming that if business did well the result would "trickle down" to the American worker. (During the time, the American workforce shifted its base from a manufacturing economy to a service economy.) By 1992, the U.S. Census reported that over 60 percent of the American workforce worked in service based jobs. As a result, a shift also occurred in the number of hours worked. Although the U.S. Bureau of Labor statistics indicated the average workweek was at 34.9 hours, what was not factored in was the "unpaid" overtime hours and second jobs that most Americans held or were required to perform. In 1987, a Harris Poll reported that the average number of hours worked per week had actually increased from 40.6 in 1973 to 48.4 hours per week (Kraus 1994, 74).

In 1989, *Time* magazine announced that, "Americans came to worship career status as a measure of individual worth, and many were willing to sacrifice any amount of leisure time to get ahead." A new work ethic was instilled by "Yuppies" who were defined as urban white-collar professionals born in the Baby Boom generation during the years 1945 and 1959 and usually held financial jobs such as in investment banking and the stock market. They flaunted wealth as a symbol of pride through the purchase of material goods and designer clothing. By conservative numbers over 20 million were classified as yuppies and being "busy" was advertised as a sign of status. As a result, the 1980s were sometimes labeled the "Greed Decade" characterized by hostile corporate mergers and acquisitions ("How America Has Run Out of Time," 1989).

Reagan's new Economic Recovery Tax Act allowed significant tax advantages that triggered a "merger mania" as large corporations bought up other corporations. In a few short years over 20 mergers were valued at over $1 billion each, and the gap between the wealthy and poor began to widen. Historian Eric Foner stated, "By the mid-1990's, the richest 1 percent of Americans owned 40 percent of the nation's wealth [including 60 percent of all corporate stock], twice their share twenty years earlier" (1998, 322). In contrast, by 1990, over 33 million Americans were classified in the poverty level and almost one-half million were homeless.

Working hard also translated into "playing hard." Most found that membership in a private health club offering high tech equipment could satisfy the need. By 1987, *Time* magazine announced that Americans spent over $5 billion in over 20,000 health clubs nationwide. They also purchased in-home exercise equipment totaling $738 million. (By comparison, in 1977, sales were only $5 million.) By 1992, membership at health clubs numbered 16.6 million, and all forms of fitness increased.

In 1992, with the election of Bill Clinton, many considered the 12-year period of the Reagan/Bush era over. However, Clinton's proposals for a National Health care plan and stricter Gun Control Laws never mustered enough support among the U.S. Senate or Congress. In addition, acceptance for homosexuals within the military as the "Don't Ask, Don't Tell" policy angered his opponents and never was approved. Although gays wanted equality and did not feel they should have to hide if they were, in the military they were routinely discharged if their sexual preference was revealed. During the fall of 1998 and into the beginning of 1999, Clinton faced impeachment hearings for perjury involving a relationship with a White House intern. On the other hand, during Clinton's tenure, the budget was balanced and the national deficit reduced to levels never thought conceivable.

At the time, Americans were captivated with television as over 98 percent of all Americans owned at least one television set, and many had accompanying videocassette recorders (VCRs) and access to cable. Independent polls reported that almost 72 percent of Americans watched over 2.5 hours of television each day. In addition, Nielson surveys revealed that as Americans partook in other activities such as housework and schoolwork, the television was turned on for an average of over 7 hours a day. More Americans watched sports on television as the sports industry grew into an enormous business. Sporting events such as the World Series, the Super Bowl, and the NCAA basketball finals known as "March Madness" attracted huge audiences and became part of American culture. Americans were also engrossed in many other activities including shopping at malls and gambling at casinos in Las Vegas, Nevada, and Atlantic City, New Jersey.

By the late 1980s, hundreds of thousands of teens and young adults spent countless hours in over 24,000 mall arcades, in over 400,000 street locations, and with millions of home systems playing the new video games. The arcade and video game business made more money than Hollywood movies, casino gambling, and professional spectator sports combined. In 1985, Nintendo Entertainment System (NES) was the number one selling toy—outdistancing perennial favorite Barbie (Kent 2001, 152).

By the mid-1980s, Hacky Sack sold over 1.2 million beanbags and was considered a "national sport" on college campuses. Wacky Wall Climbers sold over 20 million. Other popular toys and fads included Trivial Pursuit, Pictionary, Rubik's Cube, Cabbage Patch Kids, Baseball card collecting, the Teenage Mutant Ninja Turtles, and subculture role-playing games such as *Dungeons and Dragons* (Panati 1991, 434).

In 1981, a devastating disease was discovered among homosexuals at the Saint dance club in New York City. At first it was called GRIDS (Gay Related Immune Deficiency Syndrome) and sometimes the Saint's disease, named after the Manhattan dance club. It was a virus that shut down the body's immune system, had no known cure, and was fatal. The following year the Centers for Disease Control reclassified it as AIDS (Acquired Immune Deficiency Syndrome). At the time, many thought it was strictly a disease spread among homosexuals. Some of the Christian Right and clergy, for example, claimed that it was the "work of God," brandishing the gay lifestyle and the association of the decadent lifestyle of Disco. In addition, many in the federal government, including the White House, refused to acknowledge the AIDS crisis (Giordano 2003, 203).

The reality, however, was that AIDS was not isolated to one community. The epidemic spread throughout all societal factions in America and changed the daily practices of many Americans, who, because of lots of misinformation, were afraid of AIDS transmitted by touching others or their belongings. In essence, as a result of AIDS the inherent lifestyle of the Disco nightlife and dancing was officially "dead." The preceding period of sexual freedom would come crashing down as AIDS captured the headlines and Americans were concerned about "safe sex." By the late 1980s, many of the dance clubs frequented by the homosexual community, including the gay baths in San Francisco and New York were closed. Rodger McFarlane, the executive director of the Gay Men's Health Crisis, summed it up best. He said, "AIDS ravaged the dance community hard...We didn't know we were dancing on the edge of our graves" (Brewster and Broughton 1999, 201).

The Dances

I'll dance as long as I'm still having fun.

—17-year-old Joshua Lozada, 1985

It's more fun to play for dancers than people who sit there and look at you.
—84-year-old musician Bill Stewart, 1998

The music tells me how to dance....Dancing is always fun. There are no mistakes.
—Rafael Infante, *Dance With Me*, 1998

BREAKDANCING, HIP-HOP, AND "GETTING KRUMPED"

During the early 1970s, Breakdancing developed in New York City in direct response to the record manipulation skills of DJs such as Clive "Kool Herc" Campbell and Joseph "Grandmaster Flash" Saddler. It was also intertwined with turntable music mixing and graffiti and collectively part of a culture known as Hip-hop. At the time, Clive "Kool Herc" Campbell began hosting his own block parties in the South Bronx based on the large outdoor sound systems from his native Jamaica. He was considered the first "Break-beat" DJ. That is, he began reciting rhymes over the breaks and instrumental parts of the music. Kool Herc added a cast to rap and rhyme over the breaks known as "MCs," and he also employed dancers during the breaks, which he called "B-boys," short for Break-dancers (Farley, "Hip-Hop Nation," Time.com, 1999).

In order to create longer breaks for dancing, DJ Grandmaster Flash conceived the idea of "scratching" a record album on dual turntables. (Scratching was a method of manipulating the record back and forth and working the mixer's cross fader.) Flash also perfected the idea of listening to one turntable on a set of headphones while playing the other, therefore, overlapping the scratching technique and creating longer breaks. He explained, "I had taken a section that was maybe fifteen seconds and made it five minutes. So that these people that really danced, they could just dance as long as they wanted." As a result, scratching made the turntable an instrument rather than just a device to play records. By the mid-1970s, Grandmaster Flash was a local celebrity in the South Bronx and

---

Breakdancing incorporated head spins, backflips, and acrobatic movements as well as the Locking and Popping style originated by Damita Jo Freeman and Don Campbell (see Chapter 6). B-boys or "Breakers" performed in teams known as "crews." Typically it was performed on a piece of cardboard laid out on the street or sidewalk to facilitate the moves. For music, the B-boys would bring along a large portable cassette player with large speakers sometimes known as a "Boom Box" or "Ghetto Blaster." In July 1984, *Newsweek* described it this way:

Start the spin by standing on your head; then push off with your hands and pump your legs in the air. Sound too tough? Well then try a hand glide instead; crouch down, put all your weight on your left hand, then hoist your body into the air and start spinning by shoving off with your right (McGuigan 1984, 47).

Harlem. He worked at block parties, schoolyards, and two small South Bronx clubs, the Back Door and the Dixie Room. On September 26, 1976, he filled the Audubon Ballroom, the same venue that held the first dance marathon in 1923 and where former Lindy hopper Malcolm X was assassinated in 1965 (see Chapters 2 and 5). Some of the other early clubs that featured Breakdancing were T-Connection, Disco Fever, Club 371, Harlem World, and the Roxy Roller Disco (Haden-Guest 1997, 217).

In 1981, the low-budget movie *Wild Style* accurately captured the essence of the South Bronx street scene of the music, graffiti, and Breakdancing. In 1983, director Freke Vuijst from Denmark filmed a 30-minute documentary titled *Electric Boogie* that featured real-life teens Breakdancing on the streets of New York City. The mainstream Hollywood release of *Flashdance* (1983) brought the dance to wide appeal. *Flashdance* featured a few Breakdancing scenes of the real-life Breakdancing group the Rock Steady Crew from the South Bronx.

The following year, the Rock Steady Crew was also featured in the movie *Beat Street* (1984). The soundtrack album sold over half a million copies, and *Newsweek* described the movie as a "crash course in the hip-hop culture" that combined the elements of graffiti artists, Breakdancing, and a Hip-hop DJ in the South Bronx. *Beat Street* also featured real-life DJs Kool Herc and Afrika Bambaataa. The final scene was filmed at the Roxy Roller Disco in New York (McGuigan 1984, 47). The low-budget movie *Breakin'* (1984), filmed in southern California, was a

In 1984, the low-budget movie *Breakin'* was a surprise hit, and the soundtrack album sold over a million copies. *Breakin'* featured three talented real-life Breakdancers including Michael "Boogaloo Shrimp" Chambers in the center, Lucinda Dickey, directly behind Chambers, and Adolfo "Shabba-Doo" Quinones, second from right.   MGM/UA and Cannon Group / Courtesy of Photofest.

surprise hit, and the soundtrack album sold over a million copies. *Breakin'* featured three talented real-life Breakdancers, Lucinda Dickey, Adolfo "Shabba-Doo" Quinones, and Michael "Boogaloo Shrimp" Chambers. The success triggered a sequel made later that same year titled *Breakin' 2: Electric Boogaloo*.

As a result of these movies and the media attention, Breakdancing soon spread to the suburbs, such as the town of Mamaroneck on Long Island as well as across America, including Houston, Texas; Denver, Colorado; and even small towns such as DeWitt, Michigan (population 3,596) (Callahan 1984, WC27). By 1984, Breakdancing achieved mainstream commercial acceptance. The San Francisco Ballet, for example, opened its season with 46 Breakdancers, and the 1984 summer Olympics in Los Angeles closed with 100 featured Breakdancers. During that same year, the book *Breakdancing: Mr. Fresh and The Supreme Rockers* was No. 1 on *The New York Times* "How To" best-seller list (McGuigan 1984, 47).

Breakdancing: Mr. Fresh and The Supreme Rockers was a complete "how to" manual, including the history, music, slang, fashion, and, most importantly, detailed instructions of Breakdancing's three main components Floor Rock, Uprock, and Electric Boogie. It defined *Floor Rock* as "You support yourself on one hand and kick out with one or both legs; spin your legs and your body about your supporting hand." It also was described as "any dancing you do while you're down on the floor, with one or both hands acting as supports." *Uprock*, which originated in Brooklyn as early as 1970, was a form of "dancing fight." The dancers get as close as possible without actually touching. The movements were fast and resembled King Fu. Uprock was featured in the movie *Breakin'* (10–13). The *Electric Boogie* was defined as "the part of Breakdancing that looks like dancing." It included moves such as the Wave, the Mannequin, the King Tut, the Pop, the Lock It, Floats, and Glides (22–24).

The book *Breakdancing: Mr. Fresh and The Supreme Rockers* was popular among teenagers and was even available in school libraries. Salamanca High School in upstate Salamanca, New York, for example, had the book in its library; however, the school administrators reproduced a "warning" (that was only on the inside of the cover of the original publication) and dutifully placed it on both the front and back cover as well as within many sections within the book itself. The warning stated:

> BREAKDANCING is a demanding form of art which requires careful study. The dance steps in this book are complicated. They are explained and demonstrated by professional dancers. They should not be attempted by anyone without the supervision of a professional instructor. Breakdancing can result in serious bodily injury.

In January 1985, warnings on the hazards of Breakdancing were rampant. Dr. Rodney A. Appell, for example, claimed that two 17-year-old boys "suffered from patchy baldness, caused by a repeated spinning on the top of the head that eroded hair shafts down to the scalp." The American Medical Association Journal claimed torn ligaments, dislocated necks, severe sprains of the ankles and thumbs. Doctors also warned of the potential fatalities, paralysis, and "twisting of the testicles, which could lead to a cut-off of blood supply and [result in] gangrene" (Chenoweth 1985).

But despite the warnings, 17-year-old Joshua Lozada of the Bronx countered, "I'll dance as long as I'm still having fun. It's good to get into...Break dancing is a dance. It's not just rolling on the floors. If you take the time to look at our artistic ability, you realize it's about dancing" (Park, n.d.). In simple terms, the reason most older people did not Breakdance was because most people did not possess either the athletic skills or daring to perform the dance. For the faint of heart or for those over the age of 18, *Newsweek* advised, "Better yet, why don't you just sit this one out?" (McGuigan 1984, 47).

By the late 1980s, Breakdancing was replaced by a new style of Hip-hop dance. It was based more on footwork including the Electric Boogie, Locking and Popping, and Michael Jackson's Moonwalk rather than acrobatics (Driver 2000, 234). By the end of the 1990s a new style of Hip-hop termed "Krumping" emerged from Los Angeles. Krumping contained quick "rapid fire movements" of the upper body and pelvis. Journalist Taisha Paggett of *Dance Magazine* described it as "a freestyle dance form that's full-bodied, adrenaline-driven and confrontational....The dancers are more interactive with each other, sometimes using physical contact and weight sharing....Absent from this dance are moves that traditionally signify hip hop, like uprocking, freezes, and headspins." Krumping hit mainstream after the year 2000 and was filmed in a documentary titled *Krumped* (2004) and the movie *You Got Served* (2004) (2004, 32–34).

SALSA AND "DIRTY DANCING"

In the movie *Saturday Night Fever* (see Chapter 6), the last contestants in the Disco dance contest were Puerto Rican, "Couple No. 15" Hector and Maria. In fact, Hector and Maria danced a version of Salsa to the song "Salsation." "Salsa," in the direct literal Spanish translation, simply means "sauce." Sometimes it translated as "spicy" or in some translations "hot sauce." At about the same time, Venezuelan born DJ Phidias Danilo Escalona began using the term "Salsa" to denote the musical style and dance music. By the 1980s and into the 1990s, Salsa incorporated an amalgamation of styles including Disco, Mambo, Merengue, Rhumba, Cha-cha, and other Latin dances. A scene in the Hollywood movie *My Blue Heaven* (1990) featured a stylized version of the Merengue and also incorporated other Latin styles. The songs were also highly stylized and Pop influenced, creating a "milder" and "more tranquil sound" popularized by artists including Eddie Santiago, Luis Enrique, Ricky Martin, and Enrique Inglesia (Waxer 1994, 4, 91).

Both the music and the dance of Salsa became strongly identified as a symbol of pride and identity among Hispanic Americans and also linked to the growth of the Hispanic communities themselves. After 1965, with relaxed immigration laws throughout the country, more immigrants from the Caribbean Islands entered the United States. A significant number of native-born Cubans, Puerto Ricans, and Dominicans settled in the Spanish speaking sections of New York City and Miami. As a result, the music and dance styles incorporated more influences and also developed regional differences. Basically, there were five styles of Salsa: the first was derived from New York born Puerto Ricans and was sometimes described as "old school"; the second style was derived directly from the island of Puerto Rico; the Venezuelan style was derived from the sounds of the 1960s and 1970s;

Actors Steve Martin, Melissa Hurley, Rick Moranis, and Leslie Cook dance the Merengue in the movie *My Blue Heaven* (1990). Warner Bros. / The Kobal Collection MYB015AV.jpg.

the Colombian style sometimes contained "a little jump"; and the fifth was the Cuban style, more commonly known as the Miami style (Driver 2000, 90).

In New York, for example, clubs featuring Salsa dancing included the Copacabana, Nell's, Babalu, La Maganette, and the Corso Club. In Boston, Salsa dance clubs included El Bembe, Sophia's, and Ryles Jazz Club. In Miami, the Salsa was danced at Palladium Bongo's, Cuban Café, Mango's, Tropical Café, and the

> The basic step in Salsa was the same as the Mambo, but interpreting the step usually came down to either dancing on the "1" beat or the "2" beat (see Chapter 4). Journalist Mireya Navarro observed that "In many Latin clubs in New York, the dancers—white, black, Asian, Hispanic—come from many different cultures, but they are grouped not by ethnicity, but by beat." And it was the dancing on the "1" or "2" that Salsa dancers not only looked for but also argued over. In Miami, for example, Navarro observed two dancers having a difficult time, not because they could not dance but rather because they were dancing on different beats. She noted, "they bumped knees. Then they pulled in different directions. Then the song became interminable. When it was over, they spent time talking but did not dance again." The problem was that one was dancing on the "1" and the other on the "2." Dancing on "2" was sometimes known as the New York Mambo, and it did not contain any pauses. Dancing on "1" was more indicative of the Miami style and was closer to the original Mambo that paused on the fourth and eight beats. Navarro added a further differentiation that the "1" dancers follow the melody and the "2" dancers follow the percussion or the clave ("Battle of the Mambo Is Bruising Some Toes," 2000, 1).

Macarena Tavern. On the west coast, Salsa dancing was featured at Café Cocomo and Pier 23 in San Francisco, and the Mayan Theater in Los Angeles. Regardless of regional styles, Venezuelan musician Miguel Urbina interjected that "the salsa that people like is the salsa that is good for dancing." He added, "orchestras took seriously into consideration…[that the] dancer was the most important thing" (Berríos-Miranda 2002, 44).

But going to a club to dance Salsa was not as simple as it might seem. For example, musician and dancer Willie Colon insisted, "the basic beat is always four-quarter time—four beats to the measure. That's important because you move your feet on three of these beats, the second, third, and fourth, and you hold on the first. If you try to dance on the first beat you'll be fighting the whole flow of the rhythm" (Waxer 2002, 93). And fighting the flow of the rhythm was evident in the Hollywood movies *Dirty Dancing* (1987) and *Dance With Me* (1998).

In *Dance with Me*, the character Ruby (actress Vanessa Williams), a professional ballroom dancer, asks Cuban immigrant Rafael Infante (actor Chayanne), "Do you Mambo?" He replies, "I'm Cuban of course I know how to dance." But they have some difficulty as he continually steps on her toes. The problem is that he is dancing on the "1" beat and she insists that he is doing it wrong and tells him "You're gonna break on the 2 beat." He replies, "The music tells me how to dance…. Dancing is always fun. There are no mistakes."

Dirty Dancing (1987) featured a Catskill resort dance instructor named Johnny Castle (actor Patrick Swayze) teaching a young guest named "Baby" (actress

Dance instructor Johnny Castle (actor Patrick Swayze) and a young guest named "Baby" (actress Jennifer Grey) in a scene from the movie *Dirty Dancing* (1987). In the social dance setting, the term "Dirty Dancing" also came to signify a style of close intimate sensual couple dancing.   Vestron Video / Courtesy of Photofest.

Jennifer Grey) how to dance the Mambo. At first they have difficulty—she is trying to begin the dance on the beat of "1," and he is teaching her to begin the dance on the offbeat count of "2." Although the film did not necessarily settle the cultural debate of dancing Salsa on the "1" or the "2," the movie itself became a cultural phenomenon. At first, many critics simply described *Dirty Dancing* as a "clichéd story" from a fading Catskills resort. However, pop culture critic Melena Ryzik proclaimed, "There are movie fans, and then there are 'Dirty Dancing' fans." The fan mania over the movie was supported by the fact that the soundtrack album sold over 10 million copies and was awarded an Academy Award Oscar. The movie was also translated into a successful Broadway stage production, a nationwide tour, and a short-lived television series. In the social dance setting, the term "Dirty Dancing" also came to signify a style of close intimate sensual couple dancing. Dance studios reported that, as a result of the movie, many new students seeking to learn the Mambo and old favorites such as the Cha-cha also had an interest in the close-contact Lambada (2005, AR:8).

LAMBADA, "THE FORBIDDEN DANCE"

The Lambada evolved from African based rhythms during the early 1930s in northern Brazil. It started as a solo dance but soon developed as a close contact couple dance. It also resembled the late nineteenth century Brazilian Maxixe, a dance that also involved close contact and interlaced legs (see Chapter 1). By the mid-1930s, the Lambada was a sensation in Rio de Janeiro, but was deemed "immoral" and banned by Brazilian dictator Getulio Vargas. The dance survived in the villages and indigenous areas (Hamlin 1990, F1).

In the spring of 1988, while working on a film in Porto Seguro, Brazil, French director Oliver Lorsac witnessed Brazilians dancing the sensual Lambada. Lorsac saw the dance as marketable and teamed with music entrepreneur Jean Karakos. In the process they registered the name, bought the rights to over 400 lambada type songs, and garnered a commercial sponsor. In January 1989, they produced a short video of the song "La Lambada" with a group known as Kaoma and arranged to show the video hourly over 300 times on the French television TF-1 network (a French version of MTV). As a result, the song "La Lambada" quickly went to No. 1 in 15 European countries. By June 1989, both the song and the dance were a craze all over France and in northern Europe. The success encouraged Lorsac and Karakos to launch a media campaign in America (Gonzalez, "Dirty Dancing With a World Beat," 1990, 73).

In December 1989, the video of *La Lambada* was shown in America on *Entertainment Tonight* and also featured on the CBS-TV New Year's Eve show. In January 1990, the media blitz continued as Kaoma, a seven-piece musical group and eight stage dancers, performed a limited four-city tour in New York, San Francisco, Miami, and San Juan, Puerto Rico. In early February the video aired on VH-1 at the same time that the song was released in America on the album titled *World Beat*. The album quickly went to No. 1 on the *Billboard* Latin charts, but only No. 56 on the Pop chart, and No. 27 on the Dance charts (Gonzalez, 73).

The American media quickly picked up on the dance and proclaimed it "The Dance of the 90s." It was featured in newspapers, magazines, television news shows, and entertainment shows including the mainstream *Good Morning America* and *The Today Show*. Two Hollywood films were quickly produced, *The Forbidden Dance* (1989) and *Lambada: Set the Night on Fire* (1990), as well as a short-lived Broadway show *Oba Oba*. The fashion styles included shirts unbuttoned and knotted at the waist for men and short flared skirts and cropped tops for women. For those wishing to purchase the "billowing skirts" for women or "baggy pants" for men, Macy's in New York opened a lambada fashion boutique (Campbell 1990, E1).

The Lambda was danced in a 2/4 rhythm in a closed dance position. A slight variation of the closed position was that the man placed his right hand around his partner's waist and both partners slightly bent their knees as he pulled her very close in a "thigh straddle" in which the man extended his right leg under the woman as she wrapped her thighs around his leg. The basic movement was performed in a slow clockwise rotation to the count of quick-quick-slow. At the same time they remained in a tight embrace and gyrated their hips. It was an accentuated hip movement as the man moved his hips beginning with the left and transferring

The Lambada was a close sensual dance in which the man extended his right leg under the woman as she wrapped her thighs around his leg as seen in this photo from the movie *The Forbidden Dance* (1989).   Columbia Pictures / Courtesy of Photofest.

the weight on his feet left-right-left, right-left-right. It was a dance, however, that definitely required lessons (Hamlin 1990, F1).

Reporter Ben Fong-Torres of *The San Francisco Chronicle* noted that Terry Dye of the Arthur Murray Dance Studio in San Francisco was one of the first in America to teach the Lambada. In December 1989, he described his first lesson with some amazement as follows:

> We assume our position, the Brazilian music begins, and as we take off, while I mentally count off the quick-quick-slow rhythm, I am aware of Dye's legs pressed against my right thigh. This lovely stranger is straddling me! (1989, B3).

The basic steps were demonstrated in an excellent contemporary instructional video titled *How To Lambada*. The 30-minute video, released in conjunction with the Hollywood movie *The Forbidden Dance*, featured the dancers from the movie dressed in the sensual contemporary fashions for the Lambada dance floor. Dance instructor Kathy Blake also produced an instructional Lambada video titled *Let's Learn How to Dance the Lambada*. An illustrated instructional booklet titled *Lambada!* (1990) by Jonathan Pearlroth provided not only the basic step but also added advanced steps, turns, and the Group Lambada. The Group Lambada was performed by three or more people in a "Lambada Chain" similar to the Conga Line (Pearlroth 1990, 51).

The dance was quickly picked up in California and New York, especially among Latins and the young. In New York, it was danced at S.O.B. (Sounds of Brazil) nightclub. In Los Angeles, the Spice nightclub featured Lambada workshops. In San Francisco, it was danced at the Bahia Tropical Club on Market Street on Wednesday evenings. Lambada clubs within the Washington, D.C., area included Brasil Tropical club on Pennsylvania Avenue, Chelsea's on M Street, Christini's on Connecticut Avenue, the Federal Bar in the Vista Hotel, and the Baja in Georgetown. All the clubs featured lambada lessons, music, and live bands (Zibart 1990, N19).

As quickly as the dance spread, so was its sultry reputation as "a vertical expression of a horizontal desire." *Newsweek* called it "an alternative to sex in the age of AIDS." In January 1990, journalist Jesse Hamlin of *The San Francisco Chronicle* shockingly decried, "Thighs straddle thighs, tushies shake, hips circle, groin grinds against groin. Now and then they spin and dip, but rubbing in time is the main event" (F1).

As it turned out, the Lambada craze barely lasted a year. The problem was first and foremost that the Lambada was mainly a media-generated fad that was force-fed to the public. One potential dance student added, "It's an exciting dance, but it's not easy to learn. The steps are rather intricate." Dance instructor Chuck Sloan of the Arthur Murray Dance Studio in Silver Spring, Maryland, claimed that it was "the hardest dance I've ever had to keep up." Another instructor from the Washington, D.C., area said, "The real [Lambada] sometimes isn't even physically possible for most people to do" (Campbell, 1990, E1).

As a result, by December 1990 the Lambada fad fizzled out. That same month, Susan Wloszczyna of *USA Today* claimed that the "lambada was one dance most everyone sat out" (2D). On the other hand, Lena Williams of *The New York Times* recommended, "The lambada is fine if you like being locked into a Latin frenzy on the dance floor. But if you prefer your dancing to be smooth rather than frenetic, think 'electric slide'—the newest dance craze" (1990, 48).

THE ELECTRIC SLIDE, THE MACARENA, AND THE HAMSTER DANCE

The Electric Slide was arguably the most popular line dance of the twentieth century. Unlike the Lambada, where traditionally the women waited to be asked to dance, with the Electric Slide—since no partner was needed—anyone could get up and dance. The line dance was usually performed to the song "Electric Boogie" sung by Jamaican Reggae artist Marcia Griffiths. Musician Bunny Wailer wrote the song in 1978 for Griffiths, who was a backup singer with the legendary Jamaican Reggae group Bob Marley and the Wailers. The song was first released in 1983, and at the time the song was a hit in America, with the dance causing a mild sensation. Griffiths claimed that the song only gave a name to a line dance that was originated by a group of Washington, D.C., seniors around 1970. (The dance, however, may have just been a slight variation on a 16-count Disco era line dance named the Hot Chocolate—see Chapter 6.) In other cities the dance had different names. In Memphis, Tennessee, for example, it was called the Roller Coaster. In Detroit, it was called the Hustle, and in both Dayton, Ohio, and New Orleans, it was called the Bus Stop. All of the name variations were also Disco era line dances (Jones, "Dancers Line Up for a 'Boogie' Charge," 1989, 4D).

In 1989, a remixed record version and an MTV video of the retitled "Electric Boogie/Electric Slide" was released, and the dance became a nationwide sensation. Griffiths could not fully explain why the song that was an almost forgotten hit in 1983 had suddenly become "a cultural phenomenon." In October 1989, for example, Washington, D.C., held "Electric Slide Day" at Freedom Plaza. Over 3,000 people did the Electric Slide continuously for 45 minutes. Griffiths speculated,

> It has something to do with unifying large, diverse crowds of people...the kind of song and dance that every segment of society can relate to...It's a simple, happy song with a light reggae feel, not hard-core, just a nice cross-over touch. Once you hear it, you gotta move....It is really something to behold (Milloy 1989, B3).

And move is what people certainly did. It did not take much enticing for the dance floor to quickly fill once the

---

The Electric Slide was an 18-count four-wall line dance described as follows:

The dance began with a 4-count hop and side shuffle to the right with a hand clap and a 4-count hop and side shuffle to the left with a hand clap. (Some variations substituted a 4-count vine step to the right and a 4-count vine step to the left in place of the Hop and slide). Walk backward right foot (count 9), left foot (count 10), right foot (count 11), touch left toe next to right (count 12), step forward left foot (count 13) touch right toe next to left (count 14), step back right foot (count 15) touch left toe next to right (count 16), step forward left making a quarter-turn to the left (count 17), complete the quarter-turn by touching the right toe next to the left (count 18). The right foot is free to begin the sequence again.

In fact, the Macarena was hardly much of a dance. It was mainly all hand and arm movements with a simple quarter-turn at the end of each 16-count sequence. It was performed as a solo line dance as follows:

Extend the right arm out palm down (count 1); extend the left arm out (count 2); Turn right palm up (count 3); Turn left palm up (count 4); place right hand over left elbow (count 5); place left hand over right elbow (count 6); place right hand behind head (count 7); place left hand behind head (count 8); place right hand in front over left hip (count 9); place left hand in front over right hip (count 10); place right hand in back on right buttocks (count 11); place left hand in back over left buttocks (count 12); sway hips from side-to-side (counts 13, 14, 15); turn and hop to the right (count 16). The sequence was repeated until the music finished. (Sometimes the entire line would hop and turn to the left.)

Electric Slide was announced. In fact, even if a person did not know the dance itself, a quick lesson right on the dance floor was given by many wedding and party DJs. The dance became a staple at weddings, at catered affairs, and on cruise ships, and continued well into the twenty-first century. During the same time, other fad dances that were short-lived included the Smurf, the Bird, Da Butt, Rock the Dinosaur, the Train, the Cha-cha Slide, and the Hamster Dance. One dance even simpler than the Electric Slide and just as popular was the Macarena.

In 1993, the song "Macarena" was recorded by a singing duo from Spain named Los Del Rio composed of Rafael Ruiz and Antonio Romero. Romero, who wrote the song, said that a Flamenco dancer in Caracas, Venezuela, inspired him. Some said that the dance might have been a simplified version of a 1960s Cuban dance style known as El Mozambique ("Itsy-Bitsy Dance Craze," 1996, H25). Both the song and dance quickly became popular in Mexico, Brazil, Argentina, Chile, and Colombia. It was soon popular on cruise ships, and Americans on vacation picked up on the dance and took it home with them. As a result, the song and dance of the same name was continually requested at parties and dance clubs. DJs soon began playing the song every night—sometimes more than once.

Pop culture critic Daisann McLane of *The New York Times* called the Macarena "the no brainer of social dance." She added,

> because it's performed either in a group line or solo, there's no partner anxiety involved; everyone can join in. And although the dance involves a rhythmic hip action, it is secondary to the signature movements that come from the upper body—the Simon Says-like play of the arms and shoulders. Therefore, unlike the daunting dirty dancing of the lambada, the Macarena leaves sexiness as an option (1996, H30).

In December 1995, *The New York Times* announced "Macarena Madness Takes the Floor," as it was performed everywhere, including dance clubs of all kinds, wedding receptions, catered affairs, schools, outdoor restaurants, shopping malls, the Olympics, and even both the Democratic and Republican National Conventions. Many clubs, parties, and organizations held Macarena nights, including major league baseball stadiums. In Key Biscayne, Florida, over 10,000 people showed up at the Fair of Seville to participate in a giant Macarena dance. A January 1996 newspaper report indicated that the "madness" was so widespread that between surgeries at Mount Sinai Hospital in Miami the operating-room staff danced the Macarena. The report prompted journalist Lydia Martin of the *Miami Herald* to ask "Has La Macarena Gone Too Far?" (1996, C1). But the dance had not gone too far—it was still in demand. In August 1996, the song hit No. 1 on the American *Billboard* Pop chart and stayed in the Top 100 for over 35 weeks (Navarro, "Macarena Madness Takes the Floor," 1995, A10).

"MOST REQUESTED, MOST PLAYED, PARTY SONGS" AND "CAN'T MISS" PARTY DANCES

Both the Macarena and the Electric Slide became essential at weddings, block parties, corporate functions, dance clubs of all sorts, and weddings. Pop cultural reporter Daisann McLane of *The New York Times* said, "forget the charts and head for that ultimate bellwether of American cultural style: the wedding reception. There you'll find the Macarena is as much an institution as the conga, the hokey pokey, the alley cat, and the electric slide" (1996, H30).

Some of the "Can't Miss" songs that just got the crowd up on the dance floor included Glenn Miller's "In The Mood," Bill Haley and the Comets' "(We're Gonna) Rock Around the Clock," Chubby Checker's "The Twist," Gloria Gaynor's "I Will Survive," Elvis Presley's "Jailhouse Rock," Billy Idol's "Mony,

---

By the year 2000, any party or wedding celebration that hired a DJ usually included some of the top songs dating from the 1930s through the 1990s. *Mobile Beat*, a trade magazine for mobile DJs, published an annual poll of the Top 200 "Most Requested, Most Played, Party Songs." During the late 1990s the list remained fairly consistent.

1997	1998	1999
1. "Macarena"	1. "Y.M.C.A."	1. "Y.M.C.A."
2. "Y.M.C.A."	2. "Because You Loved Me"	2. "Friends in Low Places"
3. "Because You Loved Me"	3. "Macarena"	3. "Love Shack"
4. "I Swear"	4. "Unchained Melody"	4. "Getting Jiggy With It"
5. "Old Time Rock & Roll"	5. "Wonderful Tonight"	5. "Electric Slide"
6. "Unchained Melody"	6. "Love Shack"	6. "Macarena"
7. "Boot Scootin' Boogie"	7. "Electric Slide"	7. "Old Time Rock & Roll"
8. "Wonderful Tonight"	8. "Celebration"	8. "(You Shook Me) All Night"
9. "Celebration"	9. "Boot Scootin' Boogie"	9. "Boot Scootin' Boogie"
10. "Electric Slide"	10. "C'mon Ride It (The Train)"	10. "Because You Loved Me"

Many of the party songs remained the same, whether it was a wedding, a sweet sixteen, an anniversary party or, for that matter, any celebration in general. At weddings, for example, one could usually expect the grand entry (reminiscent of the Grand March of the nineteenth century); the bride and groom's first dance (see Chapter 4); a father/daughter dance; a mother/son dance; and a "cutting the cake" ceremony, among other traditions.

Mony," and the Isley Brothers' "Shout" usually with the same pantomime antics from the movie *Animal House* (see Chapter 6), and Buster Poindexter's "Hot, Hot, Hot"—usually prompting the guests to do the Conga (see Chapter 3).

Some others of the most requested party dances included the Chicken Dance, Cotton Eye Joe, the Limbo, and ethnic folk dances including the Tarantella, Polka, Hora, or Irish Jig. Some of the "Can't Miss" songs for slow couple's dancing included Elvis Presley's "Can't Help Falling in Love," Glenn Miller's "Moonlight Serenade," Eric Clapton's "Wonderful Tonight," Nat "King" Cole and Natalie Cole's "Unforgettable," The Righteous Brothers' "Unchained Melody," and Patsy Cline's "Crazy." The Top Five most requested songs listed by *Mobile Beat* to end the night were

1. "Last Dance"—Donna Summer
2. "New York, New York"—Frank Sinatra
3. "Goodnight Sweetheart"—The Spaniels
4. "What a Wonderful World"—Louis Armstrong
5. "That's What Friends Are For"—Dionne Warwick

All-in-all, mobile party DJs were usually what made the party fun and were greatly appreciated by the vast majority of party goers. However, despite the wide array of party songs and dances to choose from, the party DJ could not always please all of the people, and they usually found that complaints came from guests who did not dance.

CAJUN MUSIC, A FAIS-DODO, SQUARE DANCING, AND A DOSADO.COM

Cajun music and dancing dates from eighteenth century Louisiana and descended from French people by way of Nova Scotia in Canada. Authentic Cajun music was usually performed with an accordion and a scrub board and was played at a Fais-dodo. A "Fais-dodo" was a place that had Cajun food, music, and dancing. At a Fais-dodo, it was common to have all ages, including children, in attendance, and the food usually included gumbo, jambalaya, and praline. Cajun, however, was not limited to Louisiana; it could be found in many areas of the country, including cities New York and Los Angeles. In 1999, author Eve Babitz went to the War Memorial Hall in South Pasadena, California, to attend a Cajun dance. Babitz exuberantly added, "The great thing about the Cajun dance I recently went to, with the live band and the great floor and space, is that I could dance with practically anyone, which in my opinion, is the way a dance should happen" (90–91).

Three of the basic Cajun dances were the Waltz, Two-Step, and Jitterbug. Each of the dance steps closely resembled the basic steps of the social and ballroom versions of the dances; however, the Cajun style added a bit more bouncing and lively body movements in response to the music. Joyce Luhrs, a contributor to *Amateur Dancers* magazine observed a Cajun dance on a visit to New Orleans. She noted the Cajun Jitterbug incorporated some of the same turns as Jitterbug as well as

Country Two-Step. However, the basic dance style added a motion that looked like a "limp." Luhrs described the variation as follows:

> The woman keeps her right heel up as though she has a tack in it, and her partner keeps the left heel up. The heel stays up during the entire dance. The woman goes forward with a front step and then a back step. The man proceeds with a front step and then a back step with the left foot. The man's left leg is sometimes described as being like a peg leg. Each partner moves his/her arms to the rhythm of the music, and the arms move in a push and pull motion, while continuing to hold hands with a partner (2004, 12).

Another unassuming dance style was Square dancing (see Chapter 4).

During the 1987–1988 Session the Californian State Legislature officially adopted the Square Dance as the official folk dance of the State of California. Section 1. (b) of the bill stated in part:

> The Square Dance has a long and proud history. It is an exciting art form that is truly an original of our country, and has been danced continuously in California since the "Gold Rush Days.". . .California leads the nation with more than 200,000 residents square dancing weekly. It conforms to our ever changing lifestyles and appeals to all ages (Chapter 1645 Senate Bill (S.B.). No. 2460).

DOSADO.com, for example, maintains a listing of hundreds of Square dance clubs and organizations throughout the entire United States, the District of Columbia, and Puerto Rico, as well as International organizations. The wide range of Square dance organizations included specialty organizations for singles, teens, seniors, and even homosexuals. The International Association of Gay Square Dance Clubs (IAGSDC), for example, advertised itself as a "lesbian and gay organization. . . open to all square dancers, regardless of age, race, gender, religion, ethnic background, or sexual orientation." The IAGSDC offered an online directory of clubs, a calendar of events, resources, and a list of annual conventions.

URBAN COWBOY, THE TWO-STEP, AND THE TUSH PUSH

In 1980, John Travolta, fresh off the Disco dance floor in *Saturday Night Fever* (see Chapter 6) once again turned to the hardwood and kicked off another dance craze. Travolta appeared in the movie *Urban Cowboy* (1980) that was filmed in an actual honky-tonk (see Chapter 1) named—*Gilley's* in Houston, Texas. Gilley's provided all of the atmosphere of a traditional honky-tonk with the addition of a mechanical bull. Travolta's mechanical bull-riding in the movie inspired many other establishments to install similar devices. On the other hand, Travolta's dancing inspired many Americans to undertake a new Saturday night activity—the Texas Two-Step. As a result, a whole slew of Americans donned jeans and cowboy hats, headed to similar establishments in their towns, and took a Two-Step twirl around the dance floor.

However, the basic Two-Step that was most commonly taught throughout the United States did not have the partners go into the diagonal motion but rather stayed within the line-of-dance. The partners were also in a traditional closed

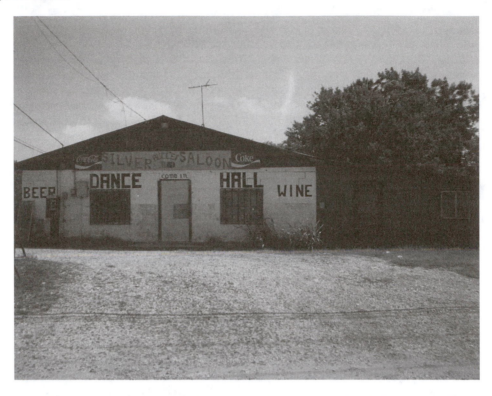

A typical honky-tonk and dance hall outside San Antonio, Texas, c. 1998.   Photo by Thelma Lynn Olsen.

dance position (see Chapter 1). The Texas Two-Step kept the partners together in the dance frame and added a few basic turns without breaking the dance hold. In later years, Two-Step partners added underarm turns, whips, tunnels, and other intricate moves.

During the 1980s, some line dances were also performed including the Cotton Eye Joe and the Tush Push. The Tush Push was probably the most well-known

The Two-Step was danced in a progressive counterclockwise motion along the perimeter of the dance floor known as the "line-of-dance." The Two-Step was similar to the Fox Trot with the feet sliding on the dance floor to the rhythm quick, quick, slow—slow. The handhold and foot pattern had some regional variations. In the version most commonly known as the Texas Two-Step (which Travolta danced in Urban Cowboy) the man placed his right forearm on the lady's left shoulder with his hand behind her shoulder blade (sometimes he placed his palm on her shoulder blade). His left hand grasped the lady's right wrist or palm and held in to the side and below waist level. The lady draped her left arm outside and above the man's right arm. The foot pattern was performed in unison with the man starting going forward and diagonal to the left on his left foot and the lady going backward on her right foot. The pattern was sometimes described as side-together-side—step. The step came after a brief pause at the end of the basic and brought the couple back into the line-of-dance.

of all the Country Line dances. It was danced in 4/4 time to songs that had a Swing or Rock 'n' Roll type beat. Country dancer Jim Ferrazanno wrote the Tush Push combining single step patterns and syncopated Cha-cha steps. The dance was literally written down in describing each beat and step in a similar fashion.

The Tush Push would set the pattern for the line dance craze of the 1990s as did the practice of providing a set of written dance instructions for the line dancer to memorize.

COUNTRY LINE DANCING, "5, 6, 7, 8," AND *COUNTRY DANCE LINES* MAGAZINE

In 1992, the song "Achy Breaky Heart," on the debut album by Billy Ray Cyrus, kicked off a nationwide Country Line dance craze. The album boosted by the popularity of the song sold over 11 million copies. As a result, Country Line dancing caught on all across America—especially in the big cities where country music and dancing

---

THE TUSH PUSH

Description: 40-count, 4-wall Intermediate Line Dance

Suggested Music: *Working On a Full House* by Garth Brooks (slow); *Dumas Walker* by the Kentucky Headhunters (medium); *Honky Tonk World* by Chris LeDoux (fast).

BEAT/STEP DESCRIPTION:

Right and Left Heel Taps With Switch

1 – 2	Tap Right heel forward. Touch Right toe next to left foot.
3 – 4	Tap Right heel forward twice.
& 5	Step Right foot next to left and switch left heel forward.
6 – 8	Touch Left toe next to right foot. Tap Left heel forward twice.

Heel Switches, Tush Push Hip Bumps

& 9	Step Left Foot beside right and switch and touch Right heel forward.
& 10	Step Right Foot beside left and switch and touch Left heel forward.
& 11	Step Left Foot beside right and switch and touch Right heel forward.
12	Clap hands.
13 – 14	Turn Diagonal to Right and bump Right hip forward twice.
15 – 16	Bump Left hip backward twice.
17 – 18	Bump Right hip forward once.
19 – 20	Bump Left hip backward once.

Cha-cha Section Shuffle, Rock Step, Shuffle, Rock Step

21 & 22	Shuffle forward Right, Left, Right (Cha-cha step).
23 – 24	Step forward Left foot rock back Right foot.
25 & 26	Shuffle backward Left, Right, Left.
27 – 28	Step backward Right Foot, Rock forward Left foot.

Shuffle, ½ Pivot Turn, Shuffle, ½ Pivot Turn, ¼ Turn, Stomp, Clap

29 & 30	Shuffle forward Right, Left, Right.
31 – 32	Step forward Left. Pivot ½ turn Right.
33 & 34	Shuffle forward Left, Right, Left
35 – 36	Step forward Right. Pivot ½ turn Left.
37 – 38	Step forward Right ¼ turn Left
39 – 40	Stomp Right foot, clap hands.*

BEGIN AGAIN

(*Note: In some areas of the Carolinas and Tennessee the Stomp and clap were done at the same time making it a 39-count dance).

---

was not considered traditional. (At about the same time, the music and dancing were no longer called Country and Western; they were simply called "Country.") The appeal of Country Line dancing was that a person did not need a partner to dance, and songs specifically for line dancing were played all night long. In addition, anyone of any age could mix on the dance floor, and it was especially appealing to singles.

During a line dance, women were encouraged to hold their hands behind their back. Men either placed their thumbs in their front hip pockets or held their belt buckle. Dance floor etiquette and proper decorum was strongly encouraged. Line dancers were in the middle of the floor, partner dancing went counterclockwise on the outside perimeter, and Swing dancers were on the corners (and on some occasions in the middle).

First time line dancers and the curious would show up in casual attire such as khakis and sneakers. However, by the second or third visit, they usually were "hooked," not only on the line dancing, but also on wearing "Cowboy" gear. Line dancers all over the country started dressing in western wear. Men sported polished belt buckles, denim jeans, and vests. Women also wore jeans, fringed shirts, and frilly dance dresses. And, of course, just about everyone wore cowboy hats and cowboy boots. Some couples took to wearing matching shirts. Some women wore a "boot bracelet" (sort of an exterior ankle bracelet). Many clubs provided small shops within the dance hall, and others bought authentic western attire by mail-order catalog from companies such as Sheplers.

Once properly dressed, Country Line dancers queued up, prompted by a DJ who called out only the specific name of the dance and started the group in unison by counting out "5, 6, 7, 8." Most of the line dances were matched to the song phrasing in set patterns of 16-count, 24-count, 32-count, and 48-count patterns. The counting of 5, 6, 7, 8 set up the line dancers to begin on the proper phrasing of the particular song. (In a Waltz rhythm line dance the count was changed to 4, 5, 6.) The line dances were also defined as either a one-wall, two-wall, or four-wall dance. A two-wall, for example, meant that at the end of the pattern the line dancer would be starting the new sequence facing in a complete 180 degree direction of the dance floor. Typically, it would be started facing "the front," which could be a stage, the bar, or even the DJ booth, and the second wall would be defined as the "back." Conversely, a four-wall dance meant that each sequence began facing each of the four walls of the dance club.

Many people learned the line dances by arriving at the dance club early in the evening. Usually the club hired an instructor and offered two dance lessons free with the cover charge. The dances were practiced to two or three songs and were repeated once or twice during the evening. Throughout the 1990s, the line dances became much more intricate than the earlier Disco era line dances and the Electric Slide. The Country Line dances varied from slow to fast paced, incorporated turns, kicks, hip swivels, and also varied with rhythm styles including Cha-cha, Waltz, East Coast Swing, West Coast Swing, and Two-Step. (In later years, they even incorporated Hip-hop, Disco, 50s Rock 'n' Roll, and Top 40 Dance hits.)

Some of the more common line dances included the Ski Bumpus, the Cowboy Boogie, Waltz Across Texas, Electric Cowboy, Foot Boogie, and Cowboy Rhythm. Many of the line dances either became wedded to or were written for only one specific song. Some of the most requested included "Boot Scootin' Boogie" by Brooks and Dunn, "Trashy Women" by Confederate Railroad, and "Watermelon Crawl" by Tracy Byrd. In the case of "Trashy Women," when the song first came out, line dancers performed a dance titled Horsin' Around. The dance fit the song so well that the dance became almost universally known as "Trashy Women." In the case of "Boot Scootin' Boogie," however, the dance had as many as 14 or 15 regional variations. On the other hand, some popular dances such as Fallsview Rock remained consistent throughout the country. The dance was named after the Fallsview Hotel in Ellenville, New York, where the dance was premiered during a Country Dance weekend. One of the reasons that Fallsview Rock remained the same nationwide was because it was also published in a Country dance magazine.

In July 1984, *Country Dance Lines* magazine started with a mere eight pages. By 1995, the monthly magazine averaged over 110 pages. Many of those pages contained descriptions of dance steps and choreographed dances (mostly line dances). A monthly listing titled "Music for Dancing," provided a track-by-track listing of about 25 to 30 CDs each month. The track listings provided the Beats per Minute (BPM) and a suggested dance. Song titles in bold designated that the song had an especially strong beat for dancing. Each year *Country Dance Lines* published a directory of Country dance instructors. In 1998, it listed over 3,300 instructors in all 50 states and 16 foreign countries, including Australia, England, Canada, France, Germany, and even Saudi Arabia. In the year 2000, at the time that *Country Dance Lines* ceased publication it had over 22,000 subscribers and had cataloged over 5,000 Country Line and partner dances.

Some of the more popular partner dances included the El Paso, Wooden Nickel, Kansas City Four Corners, Blue Rose, Sweetheart Schottische, and the Cowboy Cha Cha (sometimes known as the Traveling Cha Cha). Most of the partner dances began with a couple in a side-by-side position known as the "cape position." It was so named because the man's hands were placed above and behind the woman's shoulders as if was putting a cape on her. The woman held both her arms up, palms outward and held hands with the man right hand-to-right hand and left hand-to-left hand. Other fixed pattern partner dances with various handholds included the Charleston Bump, Shadow, and the Sidekick. People of the same gender could do some of the fixed pattern partner dances side-by-side or without a partner that included the Ten-Step and the 16-Step. Partner dances that traveled along the perimeter included the Two-Step, Waltz, and Triple Step (sometimes known as the Texas Polka). The traditional slow dance among couples was known as a "Buckle Polisher." Many of the dances could be seen on televised dance shows.

CLUB DANCE, THE "WILDHORSE SALOON," AND DENIM & DIAMONDS

In 1991, *Club Dance*, filmed at a "made-for-TV nightclub" in a television studio in Knoxville, Tennessee, first aired on The Nashville Network (TNN). Two to three episodes were taped each week on Friday and Saturday for airing weekday afternoons at 6:30 P.M. and repeated the next day. Within a few months the show was averaging as many as 1 million viewers. Within the studio set, at an upper stage, host Phil Campbell set himself up behind a bar labeled "The White Horse Cafe." A separate area was usually reserved for line dancers and on a lower level usually packed with Two-Stepping couples was co-host Shelley Mangrum. Among the 200 to 300 on the dance floor, ranging in age from teenagers to seniors, was a mix of about 50 or 60 regulars. Similar to *American Bandstand*, viewers started tuning in just to follow the regulars, and the co-hosts played up the personal relationships. *Club Dance* ran for over seven years, ending in February 1999. At the time the network, owned by CBS, changed its program format as well as the name to The National Network (Mansfield 1999).

In 1994, The Nashville Network (TNN) also launched the *Wildhorse Saloon* country dance show hosted by Katie Haas and later Bobby Randall. The dance show was filmed in the actual Wildhorse Saloon that opened that same year in Nashville, Tennessee. The three-story Wildhorse Saloon was centered on a 3,300 square foot dance floor that could hold over 1,000 dancers and boasted over 1 million visitors each year. It offered a combination of live stage shows and DJ music. The Wildhorse was open seven days a week with free dance lessons from 7 P.M. to 9 P.M. during the week and also offered an hourly dance lesson from 2 P.M. to 9 P.M. on Saturdays and Sundays (www.Wildhorsesaloon.com).

There were over 1,000 establishments all across America that offered Country Dancing. In 1994, New Jersey, for example, claimed over 30 Country dance clubs including the Yellow Rose in Manville (which at the time was ranked as the fourth most popular club in America by *Country American* magazine). Others in New Jersey included the Rocking Horse in Belleville; Dance 'n Style in Rockaway; Oakley's in Princeton; the El Paso (later Music Box) in Sayreville; the Colorado Café in Watchung; and the Whiskey Café in Lyndhurst. The Whiskey Café, for example, featured live country music bands on Saturday evenings such as local favorites, The Nashville Attitude and the Tim Gillis Band.

A random sampling of other places to Country dance across the United States included Brandin' Iron in San Bernardino, California; the Mishnock Barn in West Greenwich, Rhode Island; the Cadillac Ranch in Connecticut; Wild West in Houston Texas; Boot Hill in Rapid City, South Dakota; and the Pony Express in Staten Island, New York. In Charleston, South Carolina, Desperadoes had one of the largest dance floors in the country. The dance floor alone was over 3,700 square feet capable of holding over 1,500 dancers. The perimeter bar and seating area was just as large, with an adjacent sports bar, catering hall, and a pool table area.

Country dancers perform a West Coast Swing during the filming of TNN's country dance show at The Wildhorse Saloon in Nashville, Tennessee, c. 1996. © Kevin Fleming / Corbis.

New York, Los Angeles, Kansas City, and Phoenix, for example, contained franchised locations of Denim & Diamonds that advertised itself as "A Shot of Country With a Splash of Rock n' Roll." In March 1993, the New York franchise of Denim & Diamonds opened in midtown Manhattan and offered Country dancing seven nights a week. A distinctive feature at the center of the dance floor mounted from the ceiling, in lieu of a mirrored Disco ball, was a rotating mirrored saddle. The club held over 600 people, but could not accommodate all of them at one time on the dance floor. In an attempt to placate the clientele, Denim & Diamonds had an alternating format of 20 minutes of line dancing and 20 minutes of Two-Step and partner dancing. Later in the evening they added in a 20-minute freestyle

Country dancers doing an East Coast Swing as the band The Nashville Attitude performs at The Whiskey Cafe in Lyndhurst, New Jersey.   Photo by Lynne Riordan.

segment. In August 1996, at the peak of the Country Line Dance craze, journalist Michael O'Regan of the *New York Daily News* observed its effect upon the New York City area. He visited Denim & Diamonds and discovered that many regulars, including an architect, a pattern designer, and a fashion model, counted themselves among some of the regulars who attended two or three times per week. He added:

> New York City will never be mistaken for the wide-open plains of Texas or the Big Sky country of Montana, but even in the Big Apple you can find a place to do the Tush Push, the Boot Scootin' Boogie, or the Watermelon Crawl. Every night thousands of urban cowboys and cowgirls trade in their business suits and briefcases for a pair of old jeans and a 10-gallon hat to stomp the hours away at the few Wild West outposts scattered throughout the area (SP 16).

Throughout the New York Metropolitan area and all across America, people wanted to learn Country Dancing. To meet the demand, it was taught in dance studios, adult education classes, and continuing education classes at high schools, colleges, YMCA's, and senior centers. The local YMCA on Staten Island, for example, offered four classes in Country Line dancing and two in Country couples dancing for approximately 90 people. At the College of Staten Island, the department of

The Country Line Dancing craze took off in the 1990s. In this photo, taken in 1995, a line dance instructor at the College of Staten Island in New York City teaches a line dance class. Note the position of thumbs in the pocket for the man and the hands behind the back for women.   Author's Archives.

Adult Continuing Education offered five classes in Country Line dancing to over 140 students.

At the time, it also seemed that just about any charity event or fund-raiser centered on a Country Dance theme including volunteer firehouses, churches, VFW's, and grade schools. In addition, there was an onslaught of Country Dance weekends and festivals all over the country. The weekends and festivals usually included a hotel room, dance instruction, workshops, and nightly open dancing. In 1997, for example, a sampling of weekend events numbered over 100 in every state across America. Some of the events combined dance competitions sanctioned by the United Country Western Dance Council (UCWDC). The UCWDC listed categories that included professional, amateur, and various age divisions. The dance competitors, and for that matter many of the amateur dancers, became conscious of their footwear. Many of the aficionados who had taken to wearing authentic cowboy boots realized that they were heavy and not all that comfortable. As a result, they sought out shoes made specifically for dancing. Some purchased ballroom shoes such as Diamante, Tic Tac Toe, and Leo's Giordano. However, one company, Evenin' Star Pro Dance Boots manufactured footwear that looked very much like cowboy boots but were specially designed for dancing. A distinctive feature was a "doubled cushioned chrome leather sole," and they were about one-third the weight.

COUNTRY SWING, EAST COAST SWING, AND WEST COAST SWING

Country dancing also included East Coast Swing, West Coast Swing, and by the late 1990s also freestyle Cha-cha. East Coast Swing was the basic Jitterbug (see Chapter 3) with the addition of triple steps in place of the single step. (It also resembled a version sometimes know as Ballroom Swing.) East Coast Swing (sometimes written as simply ECS) was danced in one spot mainly to medium tempo songs with a variety of underarm turns and a minimal amount of break-aways. Slower tempo songs allowed the partners to do a dance called West Coast Swing (sometimes written as simply WCS). The dance was characterized by the Sugar Push, tap steps, coaster steps, and sultry dance movement of the partners.

During the 1987–1988 Session the Californian State Legislature adopted Senate Bill (S.B.) No. 2460, officially making West Coast Swing the official dance of the State of California. (The same bill also designated Square Dance as the official state folk dance.) The Senate Bill cited the origin of West Coast Swing "in California [in] the early 1930's" that was "created at the grassroots level [providing a] healthy and a joyful activity that belongs to all our people."

Although he denied it, Dean Collins (see Chapter 3) is usually credited with developing the forerunner of West Coast Swing. His smooth style Lindy Hop was smoothed out, and some say the crowded dance floors, especially during World War II, forced couples into Swing dancing in a predescribed slot rather than rotating on the dance floor. During the 1950s, Skippy Blair, a former Arthur Murray instructor was one of the leading proponents of teaching the slotted West Coast Swing style in California. As first, since it was done on the west coast, to dif-ferentiate it from eastern Swing it was called "Western Swing." But that actually confused it with the Country and Western style of music. During the late 1950s, Blair began calling it the West Coast Swing. As it slowly grew in appeal, the need arose to differentiate it from the Eastern style of Swing that was mainly Jitterbug and Lindy Hop. Soon the term East Coast Swing was applied to the basic Swing of Jitterbug, either single step or triple step (Lichtmann, "West Coast Swing History," n.d.).

Whereas the other Swing dances could range to above 120 bpm to a very fast 170 and above bpm's, West Coast Swing was usually performed to much slower in the 110 to 126 bpm range. Unlike the Hustle and other Swing dances, which were danced around a "spot," West Coast Swing was danced in a "slot." The slot was determined to be a rectangular area about three feet wide and six feet long. Within the slot, the basic pattern was called the Sugar Push and the basic rhythm was walk-walk, tap-step, triple step. (It was sometimes easier to envision as the man would pull the woman towards him, stop the lady, and then push the lady away.) The Sugar Push was usually a six-count move, but could also be extended any number of counts. The basic Sugar Push was described as follows:

> The man pulled the woman and walked backwards left foot (count 1), right foot (count 2). The man stopped the lady with both arms and tapped the left foot to left side (count 3). Push the woman and walk forward with the left foot (count 4) and triple step in place step right, step left, step right (counts 5 & 6). The woman walked forward right foot (count 1), left foot (count 2). The woman leaned into the man and tapped the right foot behind the left foot (count 3). Walk backward with the right foot (count 4) and tri-ple step in place step left, step right, step left (counts 5 & 6).

The woman traveled up and down within the "slot" and the man would lead her through as he stepped to the side and outside the slot. She would pass back and forth executing stylized footwork and body rolls in six and eight count patterns within the basic rhythm of the music (sometimes called "playing"). Although it was probably the most difficult rhythm to learn, it was also the most versatile. The West Coast Swing styles varied widely as did the places to dance. (Variations to the West Coast Swing included the Dallas Push, Houston Whip, New Orleans Jamaica, and the Shag.) Unlike other dance styles, it was not as widely known, but it did have a loyal following. It could be found in Country dance clubs all across America. It was also danced to Jazz, Blues, Pop, and Disco. A similar dance to the West Coast Swing was the Shag.

BEACH MUSIC, THE CAROLINA SHAG, AND "JUMPING THE JIM CROW ROPE"

Shag dancing existed in a small region of the east coast of the United States, and it involved an entire lifestyle centered on Beach Music. Most Americans, however, were totally unfamiliar with the type of Beach Music that had nothing to do with California beaches or surfing. A good definition of the music was provided within the liner notes from a compilation CD titled *Original Carolina Beach Music*. The definition was presented in dictionary format as follows:

> **Beach music (bēch mü'zik) n., 1.** music that allows one to be young, be foolish and to be happy, again and again. **2.** the art of combining soulful and melodic vocals and harmonies with house rockin', get up on your feet and dance, instrumentation that when listened to in the company of friends with a healthy party attitude, can evoke euphoric bliss. **3.** greatest listening pleasure can be achieved when, **(a)** wishing you were at the beach, **(b)** traveling to the beach, **(c)** actually walking on the beach, **(d)** talking with friends about the beach, **(e)** dancing with the most gorgeous person that you ever met at the beach, **(f)** noticing that you still have sand in your shoes 3 months after your trip to the beach.

In 1982, Steven Levy of *Rolling Stone* magazine described the "classics" of Beach music as "all catchy, upbeat songs dealing explicitly with the niceties of life on Carolina beaches." He described those "niceties of life" on the beach as

> beer cans held in foam-rubber jackets; LaCoste shirts and Topsiders or Weejuns without socks; a love for a dance called the shag; a tendency to get misty upon recalling that one's first kiss...a raw need to observe the ocean on Easter weekend; and a conviction that life at its utmost is a giant fraternity party (50).

In May 1982, *Beach Blast '82*, held at a fairground outside Charlotte, North Carolina, attracted over 5,000 fans (almost exclusively white southerners) drawn to one of the most notable of all Beach Music artists—an African American band named General Johnson and the Chairman of the Board. Some of their hits included "Carolina Girls (Best in the World)," "On the Beach," "Beach Fever," "39-21-46," "Hey Baby," and "You've Got Me Dangling on a String." *It Will Stand*, a magazine devoted to followers of General Johnson (his given name), claimed 2,000 subscribers. Other Beach Music songs included just about anything recorded by groups including the Drifters, Temptations, the Platters, the Coasters, the Catalinas, Rockin' Louie and the Mamma Jammers, The Fabulous Kays, Archie Bell and the Drells, the Embers, the Holiday Band, Steve Jarrell and The Sons of the Beach, and Bill Deal and The Rondell's. However, the simple factor that determined whether a song was or was not Beach Music was simply if you could Shag to it (Levy 1982, 54).

The Carolina Shag was more commonly known simply as the Shag. (In areas outside the Carolinas it was also known as the Florida Beach Bop and New Orleans Jamaica.) The dance, dating back to the 1930s, originated in the beachfront areas of South Carolina and North Carolina. A plausible fact is that, since the dissemination of dance and music was very much regional and also extremely segregated, the Shag developed as an offshoot of the Lindy Hop and Jitterbug (Lichtmann, "Carolina Shag History," n.d.).

Throughout the 1940s and 1950s, the Carolinas maintained strict segregation both on the dance floor and on the radio airwaves. Bill Griffin, owner of Boondocks, a Shag club, explained, "No civilized white person in the South would have let his child listen to a race record." Under the strict segregation mainstream attitude of the Carolinas, the only place that teens could dance to the R&B and Motown records of African American artists was at the beach. In southern society, the beach offered the one place where breaking from decorum was acceptable. At the beaches, away from adult overseers, teens could attend the black nightclubs to hear a selection of Rhythm and Blues artists. They usually watched from the balcony and very rarely, if ever, intermingled with African Americans. In the South this practice was known as "jumping the Jim Crow rope." The musical style that evolved was known as Beach Music, and the dance was the Shag (Levy 1982, 52).

The Shag basic step is actually a slotted East Coast Swing with moves and handholds similar to the West Coast Swing. The six-count basic had the partners push backward and away from each other, man back on the left foot and woman on the right foot (count 1) and pull forward in a rock step, man forward on the right foot and woman on the left foot (count 2). They complete the basic with two series of triple steps in place. Man step left, right, left (counts 3&4), step right, left, right (counts 5&6). Woman steps right, left, right (counts 3&4), step left, right, left (counts 5&6).

The Shag had a bit more relaxed handhold than either the Jitterbug or the West Coast Swing. Rather than the pull-stop-push motion of West Coast Swing, the Shag was a more relaxed push and pull during the rock step and two sets of triple steps. Similar to West Coast Swing, the footwork was stylized and close to the ground, incorporating some dips, twisting turns, and stylized passes. One of the distinct features was "mirror moves" that had the couples passing and tuning in moves that were mirror images of each other. The Shag was so popular and such a dominant dance form that in 1984, by decree of the General Assembly of the state of South Carolina, the official Act No. 329, 1984, declared Shag as the official state dance of South Carolina.

A documentary titled *Shaggin' On The Strand* (1985) and the Hollywood film *Shag, The Movie* (1989) provided a good portrayal of Carolina society and the importance of a Shag dance contest at the beach. By 1990, there were also numerous Shag dance instructional videos available. By 1991, over 200 Beach and Shag clubs were located in a small geographical area, including Virginia Beach, North and South Carolina, to Jekyl Beach in Georgia. (Some reports claimed more Shag clubs in that small area than the combined number of any other type of Swing dance club in the entire United States.) A similar number of individuals were members of the Shag Association of Club DJs.

By the 1990s, record stores throughout the Carolinas had prominent Beach Music sections. In addition, many Carolina radio stations had strictly Beach Music formats. Shag and Beach Music festivals were common, such as the Biannual S.O.S. (Society of Stranders) gathering of Beach Music and Shag fans. In March of each year, the "Spring Safari" at Myrtle Beach, for example, attracted over 15,000 "Shaggers." A fall event, named the "Fall Migration," drew an equal number of Shag dancers (Liner Notes, *Original Carolina Beach Music*, 1999).

THE LINDY HOP, THE NEW YORK SWING DANCE SOCIETY, AND FRANKIE MANNING

Although the Shag was very popular throughout the Carolinas, it was nowhere near as well known as the Lindy Hop. By the mid-1980s, however, the Lindy Hop was basically an extinct dance throughout America. Even those who danced at weddings and family affairs who knew how to "Lindy" were, in fact, not doing the original eight-count Lindy Hop. They were actually doing a six-count version of either Jitterbug, Ballroom Swing, or Rock 'n' Roll that they had learned during the 1940s and 1950s. Throughout the years those versions had all simply become known as the "Lindy." The rediscovery of the authentic eight-count Lindy Hop (see Chapters 2 and 3) can be attributed to one Swing dance society on the east coast and two sisters from California.

In 1982, a Greenwich Village club in New York City named City Limits occasionally booked a Swing band. By word of mouth, a few dancers began showing up, including some of the original Harlem Savoy Ballroom Lindy Hoppers (see Chapter 3). The former Savoy regulars spread the word that the old Small's Paradise had reopened in Harlem, featuring Swing bands on Monday evenings. At Small's were former Savoy Lindy Hoppers, including Norma Miller, Frankie Manning, George Lloyd, Al Minns, and Willa Mae Ricker (Ricker was one of the featured dancers from *LIFE* magazine's 1943 cover story on the Lindy Hop—see Chapter 3). At about the same time on the west coast, two California sisters, Erin and Tami Stevens, opened and began teaching at the Pasadena Ballroom Dance Association. In their research on dancing they had watched old movies featuring the Lindy Hop. Erin Stevens remembered, "We knew we had to go to New York to find the roots of swing." They came across the name Frankie Manning and on a hunch decided to look in a New York City telephone book—surprisingly his name was listed. In order to learn the original Lindy Hop they traveled to New York to meet him and attended the Swing dance nights at Small's and later at the Cat Club (Pener 1999, 50).

By the end of 1984, Small's closed; however, the spirit of Swing dancing was born again. In 1985, a group of 12 of the dancers who had trekked up to Small's to learn the Lindy Hop formed the New York Swing Dance Society. In order to continue Swing dancing, they hosted "Savoy Sundays" at the Cat Club at 76 East

13th Street. At about the same time, the Washington, D.C., Swing Dance Committee formed with the idea of dancing to old big band standards. They sponsored two dances a month in the restored Glen Echo Park Ballroom in Maryland that eventually drew over 600 dancers per event (Harrington, "Back in the Swing," 1998).

By 1990, membership in the New York Swing Dance Society numbered over 800 avid Swing dancers. Each Sunday the dances attracted about 300 people who danced to legendary tunes played by a live orchestra, prompting the society to move to a larger venue at Irving Plaza located a block off Union Square in Manhattan. During the week, they continued dancing in smaller clubs such as Café Society on Mondays and Tuesdays, and the Red Blazer Too, which offered Swing dancing on Tuesdays, Wednesdays, and Fridays.

In December 1990, *The New York Times* noted that, "The 'swing dance,' [was] making a comeback here and around the country." People were also returning to the dance studios. The Sandra Cameron Dance Studio in Manhattan noted that in 1985 they offered three courses in Swing dancing to a total of 88 students. By 1990, they were offering ten classes to over 290 students. Larry Schulz, the executive director, noted that most of the students were in their twenties and thirties. He added, "The thing about swing is that unlike other ballroom dances, you can learn the basic elements fairly easily…It's casual and fun." ("If It's Sunday, It's the Cat Club," 1990, 35).

In 1992, original Savoy Lindy hoppers Frankie Manning and Norma Miller choreographed and also danced in Spike Lee's film *Malcolm X*. The movie had a great

Lindy Hopper Frankie Manning enjoyed a second career as he became the ambassador of the Lindy Hop and toured the nation's dance studios teaching the original Savoy style. In this photo he instructs at a Lindy Hop workshop.   © Ed Kashi / Corbis.

dance scene that depicted, in particular, high-flying aerials and the flamboyant Zoot suit as described by Malcolm X in his autobiography (see Chapter 3). During that same year, Miller and Manning also helped choreograph and appeared in a made-for-television movie titled *Stompin' at the Savoy*, directed by Debbie Allen. At about the same time, the Stevens sisters in California produced a series of three 40-minute instructional videos with Manning titled *Savoy-Style Lindy Hop*. As a result, Manning enjoyed a second career as he became the ambassador of the Lindy Hop and toured the nation's dance studios teaching the Savoy method well into his nineties.

In 1998, on a PBS television interview, Manning not only credited the Lindy Hop with keeping him young and still dancing, but he also felt that it could heal some of the world's problems. He added,

> I think all of the problems of the world could be solved if all of the leaders of the world could learn to Lindy Hop, and if something happens, they say, "Okay, I'll meet you out on the floor—we'll see who can outdance the other one." If they could do that, then there wouldn't be any wars. You know, we could forget all of that other violent stuff and just dance it off (City Arts, "The Uncut Interview with Frankie Manning," n.d.).

The revival of the Lindy Hop also sparked an interest in Swing music.

ROYAL CROWN REVUE, "ZOOT SUIT RIOT," BIG BAD VOODOO DADDY, AND "SWINGERS"

Swing dancing also sparked a renewed interest in the original big bands, including those of Glenn Miller, Benny Goodman, Count Basie, and Duke Ellington. However, Nick Palumbo, of the Flipped Fedoras, one of the first retro-swing bands in the New York City area, called those bands, "Old School type of bands that plays weddings and high society parties." He added, "They have nothing to do with the new scene." The bands that were part of the "new scene" included over 100 Swing bands on the west coast mainly in San Francisco and Los Angeles (Vale and Wallace 1998, 149).

Most publications, however, mistakenly assigned jazz critics to review the retro-swing resurgence in California. Those jazz aficionados brought up the issue of authenticity—many said that contemporary swingers did not play Swing music the way it is supposed to be played. Lead singer Scotty Morris of Big Bad Voodoo Daddy (see later in this chapter) claimed that the critics were unfair. He said, "Comparing us to bands like Goodman and Ellington that had careers of close to fifty years was unfair. Goodman and Ellington were maestros, bands like us were just starting out." In turn, Morris and Big Bad Voodoo Daddy were just as influenced by the big bands as they were by the likes of Rock 'n' Roll and early Rhythm and Blues singer Blue Lu Barker. Other critics, such as Christina Nifong of *CNN Showbiz Today*, commented quite correctly that the retro-swing connected with young audiences because the bands were "not overly concerned with technique and/or doing things by the book. Their ambition and purpose is to reach out and entertain, to make swing relevant in a contemporary context" ("Swing Daddy-o!" 1998).

Many of the bands described as either retro-swing or neo-swing had roots in punk, alternative rock, or even rockabilly bands. Richard Harrington of the *Washington Post* said many of the bands "freely mix traditional swing and jump blues, hot jazz and bebop, honky-tonk and western swing, boogie-woogie, blues and rock" ("Dancing Hip to Hip," 1990, B1). Vocalist and guitarist Carmen Getit of Steve Lucky and the Rhumba Bums described it as "swing encompasses [big] band, jump blues, and the beginnings of rock and roll. The current term *swing* has become a convention for talking about retro dance music in general." V. Vale, author of *Swing! The New Retro Renaissance* (1998), added, "That's why it works…It's a reinvention, a new form of music we just happen to call swing" (Pener 1999, 40). It was within this environment that the band Royal Crown Revue, considered by many to be the first generation of the retro-swing bands, began.

In 1989, Club Deluxe opened in San Francisco as the first retro-swing club with Royal Crown Revue as the featured band. Lead singer Eddie Nichols remembered,

> When I started the band though, I thought, well, maybe we'll just play for grandmas. I didn't know who the hell was going to go to our shows. And all of a sudden there were these young kids getting into it (Pener 1999, 41).

The "young kids" dressed in vintage attire from the 1940s and 1950s, including pinstripe suits, two-tone shoes, bowling shirts, and straight-skirt dresses. (At the time, the clothing was inexpensive and also what the kids could afford.) Royal Crown Revue band member Eddie Achor remembered, "It was surprising. Here was this bunch of people who were into the music and had all the clothes…and yet they didn't have a band in the scene." Royal Crown Revue, as a band, also dressed in vintage attire and was quickly accepted. At the time, however, nobody danced; they just sat and watched. Soon the kids started dancing a combination of Jitterbug, Lindy Hop, and East Coast Swing. In 1993, the Derby in Los Angeles opened an "all-swing" dance nightclub in the same building that once housed the famous Brown Derby of the 1930s and 1940s. The Derby also hosted live Swing bands and booked Royal Crown Revue every Wednesday night for the first two years. The venue was so

The band Royal Crown Revue, shown here in this 1995 photo dressed in vintage attire, was considered the first of the Swing revival bands of the 1990s.   Courtesy of Royal Crown Revue and Kimberly Vollstedt RBC Management.

popular that lines formed around the block as early as 7 P.M. and lasted to well past midnight (Pener 1999, 45–46).

In 1994, the contemporary retro-swing style of Royal Crown Revue crossed into mainstream pop acceptance. Both the song "Hey! Pachuco" and Royal Crown Revue were featured in the Jim Carrey Hollywood movie *The Mask*. In one extended scene, Carrey, wearing a brightly colored Zoot suit, Swing danced with actress Cameron Diaz. The song itself captures the hard driving beat of the big band era, but the lyrics referenced the factual 1943 "Zoot-Suit Riots" in Los Angeles (see Chapter 3). As with "Hey! Pachuco," the song "Zoot Suit Riot" by Cherry Poppin' Daddies also contained lyrical reference of the 1943 incident. "Zoot Suit Riot" was arguably the most recognizable and widely played mainstream retro-swing song during the late 1990s Swing revival. It was a Top 40 radio hit and was also in MTV's prestigious video rotation (Pacenti 1998).

In 1995, as Royal Crown Revue's touring schedule increased, Big Bad Voodoo Daddy replaced it as the regular weekly Swing band at the Derby. In 1996, Big Bad Voodoo Daddy and the song "Go Daddy-O" was featured in the surprise Hollywood movie hit *Swingers*. One scene of the contemporary movie was filmed in the actual Derby in Los Angeles and featured actor/director Jon Favreau Swing dancing with actress Heather Graham. The movie provided exposure to the band and also inspired individuals to learn to Swing dance.

The band Big Bad Voodoo Daddy, shown here in a 1997 promotional poster, was featured in the 1996 surprise Hollywood movie hit *Swingers*.   Courtesy of Chad Jensen and Big Bad Voodoo Daddy.

In January 1998, Big Bad Voodoo Daddy was the featured act for the entire Orange Bowl college football half-time show. Later that same year, the band also made a November appearance at the nationally televised Macy's Thanksgiving Day parade in New York City. In early 1999, they performed during the Super Bowl half-time show. All told an estimated 400 million viewers saw those three television appearances. Their first CD, the self-titled *Big Bad Voodoo Daddy*, sold over 1 million copies and was on the mainstream Billboard Top 100 Album chart (Badasski, "The Inside Scoop," Issue No. 13, 1998, 50).

At one point during the summer of 1998, six retro-swing CD's were listed on *Billboard's* Top 100 Album chart. They included *Big Bad Voodoo Daddy*, *Zoot Suit Riot and Other Swingin' Hits* by Cherry Poppin' Daddies, *Mugzy's Move* by Royal Crown Revue, the self-titled *Squirrel Nut Zippers*, a compilation CD titled *Swing This Baby* and *The Dirty Boogie* by The Brian Setzer Orchestra, which sold over 2 million copies and placed in the Top Ten. Other popular compilations included *Hipsters Zoots & Wingtips*, *The HiBall Lounge Sessions Volume 1*, the soundtrack from the movie *Swingers*, and numerous releases of Louis Jordan, Luis Prima, Benny Goodman, Glenn Millie, Artie Shaw, Duke Ellington, and Count Basie (Badasski "The Inside Scoop," Issue No. 11, 1998, 50).

In addition, hundreds of CD's were released by new retro-swing bands, including *Mortyfied!* by The New Morty Show, who performed Swing versions of Billy Idol's "White Wedding (Rebel Yell) Medley," and Metallica's "Enter Sandman." *Dem Brooklyn Bums* covered KISS's "Detroit Rock City," "Speak Softly Love" (the theme from "The Godfather" movie), as well as an original Swing tribute to Coney Island in "Boardwalk Boogie." Big Kahuna and the Copa Cat Pack added a new sound to *Hawaiian Swing*. Others, such as Amy and Hank Sinatra's *From 'Hank' to 'Frank,'* ran the influences from legendary country singer Hank Williams to pop music legend Frank Sinatra. Big Time Operator's *High Altitude Swing* covered Sinatra's "Fly Me to the Moon," as well as pre–World War II Swing classics including Duke Ellington's "It Don't Mean A Thing," Benny Goodman's "Sing, Sing, Sing," and Cab Calloway's "Minnie the Moocher." The Big Six from England provided 20 songs on each of two CD's with a combination of originals and covers running the gamut from the high energy "We The Boys Will Rock Ya!" to 1950s classics such as "Blue Moon," "Sh Boom," "Rock 'n' Roll Nightmare," "Sincerely," "New Orleans," and "Long Tall Sally."

The Brian Setzer Orchestra closely resembled the bands of World War II; however, Setzer fronted a 16-piece big band with his electric guitar. His music was actually a fusion of the prewar big bands, with 1950s Rock 'n' Roll, Jump Blues, Rockabilly, and Country. The mix of influences is what made the band original. According to Setzer,

> If you just copy what they did in 1947, it's not going to be bad, it's just going to be the same. To make the music viable, you have to make it new, and you have to make it your own. ("Brian Setzer," n.d.).

In 1998, it was Setzer's updated cover version of the Louis Prima classic "Jump Jive an' Wail" that brought his music into mainstream acceptance. As a result of the success of the song, Setzer scored one of the most prestigious spots in music when he closed the 1998 *MTV Video Music Awards* show with his mega-hit "Jump Jive an' Wail."

The music and dancing were in place, but Swing did not become a nationwide dance craze until after it was featured on a television commercial. In 1998, the GAP clothing store premiered its "Khakis Swing" television commercial on network TV during both the highly rated *ER* and *Seinfeld*. As a result of the Gap television commercial, many youngsters under the age of 18 besieged dance studios in search of learning the high-flying antics featured. In addition, television, fashion, and Hollywood jumped on the wave in an attempt to capitalize economically. The dance craze was helped by major media publications such as *Time* magazine, *The New York Times*, *The Washington Post*, and *The Los Angeles Times* that featured favorable articles on Swing. In 1998, two publications, *The Swing Book* by Degen Pener and *Swing! The New Retro Renaissance* edited by V. Vale and Marian Wallace, chronicled the retro-swing music revival and dance culture.

An entire new generation rediscovered Swing dancing and also wore vintage clothing. Many of the dancers copied the fashions from different eras including Zoot suits, fedoras, and two-tone shoes from the 1930s and 1940s, as well as bowling shirts, poodle skirts, bobby socks, and prom dresses from the 1950s. Others wore suits and ties and dresses. Some even wore military uniforms depicting the Andrews Sisters or Army and Navy attire from World War II. Scotty Morris of Big Bad Voodoo Daddy added, "Because the music is connected to dancing, each city has its own interesting scene. I love to watch the dancers from night to night wherever we go; they are incredible. In some cities swing has just gotten going and it's wild, there's so much new uninhibited energy" (Pener 1999, ix). Bill Stewart, 84-year old musician and a member of Lavay Smith's Red Hot Skillet Lickers, enjoyed the fact that kids were dancing once again. He added, "It's more fun to play for dancers than people who sit there and look at you" (Baldacci 1998, NC1).

SWING CLUBS, "SWING KIDS," AND "DO YOU SWING OR DO YOU JUST LOOK THE PART?"

In 1998, Swing spread across America, and numerous cities and clubs sponsored Swing dance events. Places to Swing dance in Seattle, Washington, for example, included the Monday evening "Club Hi-Dee-Ho" event in Seattle's Pioneer Square. Swing nights were also held at The Baltic Room on Fridays, the Shadowbox on Wednesday evenings, and the Century Ballroom on alternate nights. In Boston, the Roxy on Tremont Street sponsored Friday night Swing dancing to live bands, including Bellevue Cadillac, Cherry Poppin' Daddies, the Flying Neutrinos, Steve Lucky and The Rhumba Bums, Ron Sunshine and Full Swing, and the Crescent City Maulers, among many others. In central New Jersey at Club Bené, the Leopard Lounge provided a weekly array of the top retro-swing bands including Royal Crown Revue, Dem Brooklyn Bums, Nick Palumbo and the Flipped Fedoras, the Atomic Fireballs, and Peggy Cone and her Central Park Stompers.

In New York, there was Swing 46 on 46th Street in Manhattan, and a block south was the Supper Club. Lower Manhattan offered Swing dancing at the highest point in America at the Greatest Bar On Earth located atop the World Trade Center. Outdoor summer Swing and dance events were also held in the World

Trade Center Plaza and the plaza at Lincoln Center during *Midsummer Nights Swing*. An event titled "Swing Mania" held on November 14, 1998, at New York's century old Webster Hall filled to a capacity of 1,200 dancers (Stewart 1999, 74).

In Dallas, Texas, were Deep Ellum Live and The Red Jacket Lounge. Charlotte, North Carolina's Swing 1000 advertised "A Complete Evening Of Dining, Dancing and Entertainment." At a dance at Man Ray's in Pompano Beach in South Florida over 300 dancers showed up regularly for a local Swing night. In Minneapolis, weekly Swing events were held at the Fine Line Music Café, Ground Zero, and The 400 Bar. There was Harry O's Groove Gallery in Spokane, Washington, and Leo's Lounge in San Diego. The Val Air Ballroom at Ashworth Road in Des Moines, Iowa, completely covered its 8,000 square foot dance floor with Swing dancers. Toledo, Ohio, claimed one of the earliest retro-swing clubs named the Citi Lounge. In Chicago, the Olive on North Branch was the place to Swing dance as was the Green Mill, a popular dance hall from the 1920s.

In the summer of 1998, the Chicago Summer Dance program in the Northwest corner of Grant Park installed a 2,500 square foot dance floor and offered outdoor dancing from Thursday through Sunday evenings, averaging about 800 dancers on each night. The program offered free instruction and live music. One attendee, 27-year-old Amy Greenman of Rogers Park, Illinois, outside Chicago, admired "Dancing where you're actually touching someone and communicating through your bodies—that's something our generation hasn't experienced before" (Baldacci 1998, NC1).

In San Francisco, Swing nights were popular in many places, including the Regency Ballroom, the Verdi Club, Club Deluxe, Bimbo's 365 Club, the Hi Ball Lounge on Broadway Street, the Allegro Ballroom, and Café du Nord. The Café du Nord on Market Street in San Francisco had "Swingin' Sundays" and special Swing events on Fridays and Saturdays (Zane 1998).

The Catalyst in Santa Cruz, California, was an all ages Swing club that attracted preteens to grandparents. One young Swing dancer, 17-year-old Jessica Reiter, said, "It's all about being cool and courtly like our grandparents were when they were our age. My grandma still has to be one of the most swinging ladies around. She's the one who taught me to dance and helped me get my look together." Max DeNike, also 17, said, "If you're really sharp and you know how to dance and dig the scene, you can sidle up to any girl you want." Reiter, however, countered and said that although Swing dancing involved a partner getting real close, sometimes the guys get "too grabby." Although part of her retro-1940s look involved a hand fan, it also came in handy. She added, "I give guys a swat when they get too frisky" (Relin 1998, 8).

In Santa Cruz, California, four of the six local area high schools had Swing clubs. Some teenagers were too young to get into the Swing clubs so they congregated and danced in local parking lots. Most of the teenagers learned from watching movies and from each other. Many of the high school Swing dancers were inspired by the Hollywood movie *Swing Kids* (1993). One fast-paced energetic dance scene was set against the resounding beat of Benny Goodman's classic "Sing, Sing, Sing" (see Chapter 3).

Although Swing dancing spread nationwide, not all of the clubs danced the same style. Some aficionados only danced the original Savoy-style Lindy Hop, some

The movie *Swing Kids* (1993) inspired many to learn Swing dancing and helped kick off the Swing dance revival of the 1990s. In this scene from the movie, Peter (actor Robert Sean Leonard) and Evey (Tushka Bergen) dance to the Benny Goodman classic "Sing, Sing, Sing."   Photo by Frank Connor, Hollywood Pictures / Courtesy of Photofest.

danced the Dean Collins smooth style, and others danced East Coast Swing or Jitterbug, while others would only dance West Coast Swing or Shag. Some of the dancers would literally moan and groan that some people were not dancing in the "authentic style." On the other hand, most people really did not care. Swing dancer and Santa Cruz resident Katie Spangler, as one example, said she might be out at a dance and someone would ask her to dance preceded with a question like "So, do you six or eight count?" She replied "God, if I only knew myself or, more importantly, if I only cared!...In our club, dancers don't differentiate between six- and eight-count steps...our emphasis is on the mood of the dance and musicality" (Reiter 1998, 48–49).

Mary Keil, on the other hand, had "grown up Lindy Hopping." She remembered that her parents loved dancing so much that sometimes they would just dance in the living room or kitchen. As a child in Maryland, one of her earliest memories was dancing on her father's feet as he would do various dance steps. As a teenager, she continued to dance but mainly partner dancing with other girls because at the time "boys didn't dance." During the 1990s she had moved to California and heard about the emerging Swing revival in San Francisco. Her friend Gennaro Cannelora told her that he had gone to a retro-swing club dressed in vintage attire. A young woman approached him and said, "Do you swing or do you just look the part?" Cannelora realized that dancing was "a great way to meet women"—so he learned to dance. Keil asked to go, and Cannelora took her to a Swing dance club. She remembered that on the first night she just watched all the dancers, and her first reaction was "Oh my god—they were having fun!"

In 1998, Keil drew on her real-life experiences and wrote a script for a movie simply titled *Swing* (2004). During an opening sequence she recreated Cannelora's real-life anecdote and segued into a movie that presented Swing dancing as a metaphor for life. Keil explained, "Swing dancing...requires practice and discipline, but is tons of fun. And so the choice we have is to either jump into the fray or stand on the sidelines."

The movie also set a good contrast of the original Swing music in the flashback scenes of a 1940s club employing the Black Tie Jazz Orchestra and the contemporary retro-swing scene with the band Jellyroll. The DVD release contained a special feature of a 40-minute piece titled *Dance, Dance, Dance*. The special feature contained many additional dance scenes including the audition process where hundreds of local social dancers showed up dressed in their own vintage attire. Many of the outfits were so authentic that they were filmed for the final cut of the movie.

For some, the dancing was incidental to the Swing scene as a whole. Lindy Hop dancer Hilary Alexander, for example, has been completely immersed in the music and the clothing since 1983. Alexander explained, "Personally I love recreating the era, both in the music and the clothes. When I'm dancing I never wear anything but 30s or 40s vintage clothing, including the shoes." When asked to define Lindy Hop, Alexander took a long pause and blurted out,

> Wow! I kind of think of Lindy Hop as a unique completely American invention. It has so much soul and authenticity. Well gosh Lindy Hop has always been just a fun…just a fun wacky fun dance.…It also has a lack of pretense. I see some other people doing other styles of dancing and are taking it way too seriously. But why else do it if isn't fun (Alexander interview, 2004).

Alexander also danced the Lindy Hop at Swing Camp Catalina.

Swing Camp Catalina was an annual three-day "dance camp" sponsored by the Pasadena Ballroom Dance Association held at the century old Casino Ballroom on Catalina Island off the coast of southern California (see Chapters 2 and 3). The Swing camp featured three days and two nights of live bands and workshops including all levels of Lindy Hop, East Coast Swing, Balboa, Charleston, and the Shim Sham. *Swing Camp Catalina* ran continuously through the end of the 1990s and was still an annual event at the beginning of the twenty-first century. Other dance camps included Monsters of Swing in Ventura, California, and Beantown in Boston, Massachusetts, sponsored by Hop to the Beat Studio. Throughout the country other groups held similar weekend events.

In 1998, Hilary Alexander started her own annual *Camp Hollywood* in Los Angeles, California, providing a three-day four-night complete weekend package of dance lessons, competitions, and evening open dancing to live bands. At the first *Camp Hollywood* she was both surprised and a little overwhelmed when over 300 people showed up—she had expected only about 100. The following year she moved it to the Hollywood Palladium (see Chapter 3), where it drew over 1,000 dancers and earned the self-advertised title "the world's largest Lindy Hop dance camp." About two-thirds of the participants flew in from around the country and from as far away as Japan, Australia, Europe, and Canada (Alexander interview, 2004). By the end of the decade many other events included Swing dancing and other styles of dance such as Collegiate Shag and Balboa. The Big Apple Country Dance Festival, for example, in Lyndhurst, New Jersey, featured combined Country Line dancing and Two-Step alongside West Coast Swing and East Coast Swing.

By the year 2000, the Swing dance scene, some said, was fading. But, all over America, Swing dance societies and clubs were prominent in cities such as Boston, Detroit, Des Moines, Houston, Los Angeles, New York, Philadelphia, and

San Francisco. They continued to sponsor Swing dance events attracting anywhere from a small group of 20 or 30 to 400 or more. Many were linked through the Internet, as well, as over 1000 Web sites were devoted to Swing dance. A 17-year-old Santa Cruz, California, high school student and street Swing dancer, Teague Schneiter, simply added, "But, as I see it, the real lovers of the music are the dancers, and we'll always be dancin', whether it's to Cherry Poppin' Daddies... or in a garage with a record player blasting our grandfather's Louis Prima records" (Reiter 1998, 48).

The Places to Dance

Roseland is home—a place to dream and dance until the world burst in at closing time.

—Jennifer Dunning, 1981

Since we will spend a great deal of time dancing in Heaven, it is well to learn to dance here on earth.

—St. Basil, 16th century

NOSTALGIA, TANGO, AND FREESTYLE DANCE CLUBS

During the 1980s, a few nostalgia dance clubs opened in New York and Chicago. Heartbreak in downtown Manhattan and Shout in midtown, for example, played 1950s and 1960s music, including Elvis Presley, Chuck Berry, and Motown. In Chicago, Juke Box Saturday Night was another nostalgia club. They had two locations in Chicago and one in Minneapolis that catered to an afterwork crowd. It was described by *Newsweek* magazine as a "haven for work-weary yuppies who crowd onto the dance floor and do the locomotion, the twist, the stroll, the jerk, [and] the hand jive." In Houston, Texas, a defined entertainment strip on Richmond Avenue contained numerous dance clubs, including Country, Swing, Jazz, Rock 'n' Roll, Hip Hop, and Freestyle.

In 1985, the Tango was revived in a Broadway stage production *Tango Argentino*. (It was reprised on Broadway in 1999.) In 1997–1998, another Broadway production, *Forever Tango*, featured seven couples performing Argentine Tangos from different time periods in the history of Argentina. Each Broadway production contributed to a mild revival of the Tango in the New York City area. At about the same time, some small groups in the Midwest and New England areas performed authentic eighteenth and nineteenth century dances such as the Schottische, Waltz, Mazurka, and Polka.

In New York, the club Area offered Hip-hop music combined with Rock, both new and old. The Limelight, located in a former church, played similar music and attracted over 10,000 dancers per week. In Boston's Kenmore Square, the Metro and Spit shared a 22,000 square foot dance floor. In Los Angeles, Tim Kelly (son of dancer Gene Kelly) started the notion of the Nairobi Room. It was actually a floating after hours dance club that varied from restaurant to restaurant including the Ballroom of the Park Plaza Hotel and the Stardust Ballroom. In San Francisco, at the club I-Beam on Haight Street Metro, the DJ spun a mix of heavy metal music. In Miami Beach, Florida, especially in the South Beach section, dance clubs were the place to be. Club Z, for example, was open seven nights a week. In almost all of these clubs the dancing was freestyle. One 20-year-old dancer at Scooter's, a rock club in Atlanta, said, "I honestly don't think I can dance with a partner...I go too crazy. I gotta have some room" (McGuigan 1984, 47).

"I WANT MY MTV," MICHAEL JACKSON, THE MOONWALK, AND VOGUEING

In 1981, a new concept in music and television was initiated with the Music Television Video network (MTV). MTV presented a format similar to radio only the song was accompanied by a short film that highlighted the musical artist. They became known as music videos. During its first year, the MTV audience, mainly youth aged 13 to 25, was a little over 800,000. In 1984, the viewers increased to 2 million and within a few short months jumped to over 22 million (Pendergast and Pendergast, Vol. 4, 2000, 435–438).

In 1982, Pop singer Michael Jackson was the first to capitalize on the video market with his album *Thriller*. The album, aided by MTV exposure, spent 37 weeks at No. 1 on the *Billboard* Pop charts and eventually sold over 25 million copies nationwide and 40 million worldwide, making it the top-selling album of the twentieth century. Jackson also released three expensive video productions of the singles "Billie Jean," "Thriller," and "Beat It." Each of the videos incorporated highly choreographed dancing.

In 1983, Michael Jackson was asked to reunite with his brothers, The Jackson 5, for a television special honoring Motown Records 25th anniversary titled *Motown 25*. During the course of his performance of "Billie Jean," he introduced a dance step known as the Moonwalk. Moonwalking was a dance step that moved backwards without any indication that the feet were lifted from the floor. The Moonwalk was seen by millions of TV viewers and was quickly copied by Breakdancers and freestyle dancers nationwide (Driver 2000, 239).

As a result, MTV during the 1980s launched a series of dance inspired videos. Some of the artists included George Michael of Wham in "Wake Me Up Before You Go-Go"; Lionel Ritchie in "Dancing on the Ceiling" (1986); Janet Jackson in "Nasty" (1986), "The Pleasure Principle" (1987), and "Control" (1987); and Whitney Houston in "I Wanna Dance With Somebody (Who Loves Me)" (1987). In 1989, Paula Abdul danced her way through "Straight Up," "Forever Your Girl," and "Cold Hearted." Freestyle dancers in the dance clubs copied many of the choreographed dance styles from the videos.

In 1990, Pop star Madonna adopted the club dance style of Vogueing in her song and video "Vogue" (1990). Vogueing was a pantomime dance style that was popular in underground gay dance clubs that replicated poses of fashion models. Madonna had also capitalized on previous videos incorporating choreographed dance numbers in "Like a Virgin," "Lucky Star," and "Open Your Heart." Both her videos and live stage performances featured highly choreographed dance numbers that were copied by many young fans.

SLAM DANCING, ELECTRONIC DANCE "HOUSE MUSIC," CLUB KIDS, AND RAVE CULTURE

During the 1980s and early 1990s, Slam Dancing was often witnessed at live musical performances including Punk or Rock music. In May 1981, Woody Hochswender of *Rolling Stone* described Slam Dancing as, "You bounce up and down, nice and light. You move to the left and you move to the right, then smash the guy next to you with all your might" (1981, 29).

Andy Smith of the Rhode Island *Providence Sunday Journal* added, "From the outside, it looks as though there's a terrible riot erupting in front of the stage—all you can see are waving fists and elbows and bodies tossed overhead." He added, "it is an invigorating opportunity to work out aggression, groove to the beat and even discover a warm bond with fellow fans." The area immediately in front of the stage that was the most crowded and where most of the activity of Slam Dancing took place was known as the "Mosh Pit" (1992, E1, E4).

The art of Slam Dancing expanded to include stage diving and body surfing. Stage diving was when an individual climbed on the stage and literally dove into the crowd. The crowd would be so tightly packed that they would put their hands up in the air to prevent the "stage diver" from falling. And the person was passed backwards by the crowd towards the back where the stage diver was lowered to the floor. That practice was known as "Body Surfing." Sometimes a person would be picked up by the crowd and would Body Surf "up to the stage for a moment of glory before being tossed back into the fray." Sometimes the crowd was so tightly packed that the stage diver did not dive but actually walked on the heads of the crowd; a practice that was appropriately named "Headwalking" (Christman 1992, 1).

By the mid-1990s, slam dancing had basically disappeared. Troy Johnson of the *San Diego City Beat* noted that for the most part the audiences at a Rock show were that of a "stationary spectator event." He added,

> No longer is the rock show a throng of teens trotting out new dance moves. It's no longer a battlefield of bodies slamming against each other. At your normal concert nowadays—from the tiniest rock dive to massive arena shows—the audience is a static entity. Arms aren't thrown in the air—they're folded across the chest or buried in pockets ("How Dancing in Rock Became Uncool," 2003).

The new standard for teenagers and young adults who wanted to dance was electronic dance music.

In the early 1980s, Chicago and Detroit became centers for an emerging new sound of electronic music and dance culture. In Chicago, at a gay club known as the Warehouse, DJ Frankie Knuckles (a New York transplant) began mixing disco and soul tracks with the little-known electronic music from Europe. The sound became known as "House Music," and the dance style was freestyle, incorporating just about any influence. The dance crowd at the Warehouse averaged between 600 to 2,000 people. The scene was described as follows:

> To reach the dance floor at the Warehouse you had to enter through a stair-well from the white, plant-filled lounge above. Heat and steam drifted up to meet you, generated

in the murk of the under-lit room by the glistening black bodies that were down there [dancing] away. And as you descended into the shadowy cavern, you were hit by the power of the sound system; sparked by the energy of the dancers...Frenzied bodies were packed in wall-to-wall throughout the space, their clothes reduced to a minimum of athletic gear, their bare skin dripping with sweat and condensation (Brewster and Broughton 1999, 292–294).

Other Chicago clubs that played similar music included the Music Box and Power Plant.

By the end of the 1980s, the Chicago dance scene and House music was on a downswing. However, it was invigorated by a new development in nearby Detroit, Michigan, that became known as "Techno." It was an electronic form of music that emerged as an amalgamation of Chicago House, DJ turntable, and the combination of the elements of technological and industrial innovations of the time. The dancing was still freestyle (Brewster and Broughton 1999, 304–311).

Another form of dancing to prerecorded electronic dance music was Rave. In the mid-1980s, Raves began in England. At first they were spontaneous underground dance parties sometimes held in an abandoned warehouse or an open-air venue. (News of a party was usually passed by word of mouth.) Soon thereafter, Rave dance parties spread to the United States. In response, some clubs, such as the Tunnel and Limelight in New York, opened specifically for Rave dance parties. The Rave clubs mixed all sorts of theatrical lighting, large blaring sound systems, and DJs playing a continuous stream of music as the parties extended over long periods of time—sometimes 4, 5, 6, or even more continuous hours. Rave dancing did not have any set dance moves and each person usually danced alone. The dancing was more of a reaction to the continuous music as a result of partaking in drugs including LSD, cocaine, and MDMA (more commonly known as "Ecstasy" or simply "X") (Haden-Guest 1997, 321).

Rave dancing, on the other hand, was part of a subculture community that attracted participants, considered to be the "outcasts" of society, from all parts of America. In the large cities such as New York, they found similar individuals and safety among their peers. Most broke from the mainstream and wore outlandish garb. On March 14, 1988, a headline cover story on *New York Magazine* gave them the name "Club Kids"—a term that became widely accepted (Haden-Guest 1997, 318–319).

In 1994, the movie *Rave, Dancing to a Different Beat*, directed by former Break-dancer Adolfo "Shabba-Doo" Quinones, portrayed a sanitized view of the Rave culture. Another movie, *Party Monster* (2003), presented the seedier side of the drugs and Club Kid culture. However, Pop culture critic Stephen Holden of *The New York Times* claimed that *Shampoo Horns* (1998), filmed in the former Limelight club, provided a "fairly realistic" portrayal of the Club Kids in New York City. He added, "*Shampoo Horns* succeeds in capturing the desperation and emptiness of people determined to be legends in their own minds, no matter how many drugs it takes to get them there" ("Club Kids: Starry Eyes and Blurry Minds," 1998, E32).

However, because of reports of widespread drug use, New York City Police eventually closed both the Limelight and the Tunnel. By the year 2000, the

Chicago City Council approved an ordinance that threatened building owners and managers who knowingly allowed Raves on their property with jail terms of up to six months (Sullum 2001, 12). At about the same time, Congress proposed the Reducing Americans Vulnerability to Ecstasy Act—more commonly known as the RAVE Act. (It was officially introduced in October 2002 and passed on April 10, 2003.) The idea behind the bill was to reduce the use of the drug Ecstasy by shutting down the Rave dance parties (Eliscu 2002, 25).

By the beginning of the twenty-first century an underground dance movement sometimes termed "New Age Raves" or "Holistic Raves" promoted all-night dancing to electronic music without the drugs and alcohol. They could be found in Chicago, Los Angeles, San Francisco, and New York. Some of the groups combined the dancing with yoga, meditation, and other spiritual rites. One Saturday night Rave dancer, 27-year-old Kim Schmidt, revealed, "I was a club kid who used to try to get the high with ecstasy...Now, I get it naturally. I like being around people who are celebrating in a healthy way. And I love to dance" (Smalley 2003, 52).

ROSELAND "KEEPS IN STEP WITH THE 1980s"

In 1977, Louis Brecker, the original owner of Roseland Ballroom in New York City, had died. (Brecker had operated the dance hall since its inception in 1919.) Upon his death, he willed the ballroom to his daughter Nancy Brecker-Leeds. In light of the decline in traditional ballroom dancing at the time and in order to keep the ballroom open, she made some changes. One, with some admitted "reluctance," was to open the ballroom to Disco dancing. During that same year, a movie titled *Roseland* (1977) was filmed almost exclusively within the ballroom. The movie was made up of three loosely connected stories titled *The Waltz*, *The Hustle*, and *The Peabody*. The second part of the movie, *The Hustle*, was a contemporary account of the transition of Disco and the Hustle dance into the ballroom.

In early 1981, Brecker-Leeds sold the ballroom to the Roseland Amusement and Development Corporation. Plans were quickly filed to demolish the ballroom and build a housing development in its place. In July 1981, however, journalist Jennifer Dunning of *The New York Times* "discovered" that Roseland was still intact and couples were still dancing. She was surprised to find that many of those dancers were aging "regulars" who still went to Roseland on a regular basis. Most of the regulars were described as "white and middle-aged to elderly." The ballroom dance sessions, however, had been cut back to Friday evenings from 6:30 P.M. to midnight and Saturdays and Sundays from 2:30 P.M. to midnight. She described the scene as follows:

> For them, Roseland is a magical escape from the emptiness of widowhood or dreary marriages....Roseland is home—a place to dream and dance until the world burst in at closing time. But a surprising number of ballroom-dance aficionados stay on when Roseland goes disco and its floor becomes a vast melting pot of all ages and races (1981, C1).

During the ballroom sessions "ties and jackets" were still strictly enforced among men along with appropriate attire for women. However, after midnight on Fridays

The Roseland Ballroom in New York City, c. 2000. The marquis was removed around 1995.   Photo by Author.

and Saturdays the dress code was dropped, as the dance hall transitioned to Disco until 4 A.M. (In later years, the music included Salsa, Latin, and Hip-hop at midnight.)

By February 1996, architectural plans were once again filed to demolish the building for a 42-story apartment house. Most of the patrons were unaware that the ballroom was in danger of being demolished. What they were aware of was that the ballroom dancing had been cut back to prerecorded music on Thursdays and a live band on Sundays. At the time, the dance floor was still described as "magnificent" but the once grand elegant ballroom was "well beyond shabby, with faded carpets and worn paint." By that time, Roseland's main income was derived by rock concerts and special occasion nights including Hip-hop and Latin dance nights. Almost all of the attendees were not even aware of the long dance history of the Roseland Ballroom. Despite it all, Roseland Dance City weathered the storm and was still intact at the turn of the twenty-first century (Gray 1996, R5).

THE NEW AMERICAN BANDSTAND AND "AMERICAN BANDSTAND BOULEVARD"

One long-standing dance tradition that did not "physically" make it to the twenty-first century was *American Bandstand*. In October 1987, after 5,000 shows and 32 years, the show ended as a network television show. From 1987 to 1989, it was syndicated on cable affiliates as *The New American Bandstand*, even acquiring a new host, David Hirsch, in 1989. However, Hirsch lasted only six months, and the show was cancelled. All told, *American Bandstand*, beginning with Bob Horn's October 1952 premier (see Chapter 4) and extending to Hirsch's farewell in September 1989, lasted a combined continuous total of 37 years on local, network, and cable television. The 37-year run on network television exceeded the boast that the perennial host of *American Bandstand* Dick Clark made way back in 1962 when he said, "I think it can run for 30 years." (Jackson 1997, 224, 278–282).

The show was such an important part of the city of Philadelphia's pride that the City Council voted in 1981 to rename the street "American Bandstand Boulevard." In 1986, the show and the WFIL-TV studio received an unprecedented honor as the building was declared an historical landmark and was placed on the National Register of Historic Places. A plaque commissioned by the Pennsylvania Historical and Museum that stood near the studio entrance door at the site read:

> AMERICAN BANDSTAND This television program had a major impact on the music, dance, and lifestyles of American teenagers. "Bandstand" a local show, began in 1952. Dick Clark became host in 1956, and on August 5, 1957, "American Bandstand" debuted on the nationwide ABC network. Until 1964 the show was broadcast from WFIL-TV here. This 1947 building was one of the first designed and constructed exclusively for television productions.

At the beginning of the twenty-first century the original WFIL-TV studio was still intact on Market Street.

On the other hand, Clark continued to keep the show alive through yearly nostalgia reunion shows (see Chapter 6). In addition, during the early twenty-first century, he produced an NBC-TV prime-time series titled *American Dreams*. The show was a drama set in Philadelphia during the early 1960s and the main cast of characters were high school students who rushed home each afternoon to either watch *American Bandstand* on television or actually appear on the show. The show recreated the original WFIL-TV studio set and interspersed some original film clips. In addition, Clark commissioned a series of *American Bandstand Cafes* that opened in numerous malls and airports nationwide. The restaurants were heavily decorated with nostalgic photos of dancing teenagers from the TV show's long history. However, many of the patrons were more interested in grabbing a quick bite to eat and were totally unaware of what television had meant to dancing.

PBS TELEVISION BALLROOM DANCING AND "DANCING CLASSROOMS"

As a result of the television and Hollywood movies, many Americans only viewed the world of ballroom dancing as resplendent with evening gowns and tuxedos with tails, a persistent image that dated to the Hollywood movie dancing of Fred Astaire and Ginger Rogers (see Chapter 3). In 1981, Boston public television station WGBH-TV began broadcasting the Ohio Star Ball dance competition. It was also carried by dozens of other PBS stations nationwide. The show named *Championship*

In 1989, the 37-year run on network television of *American Bandstand* ended. In 1986, the show and the WFIL-TV studio received an unprecedented honor as the building was declared an historical landmark and was placed on the National Register of Historic Places. In the top photo, the original WFIL-TV studio building was still intact on Market Street in Philadelphia at the beginning of the twenty-first century. The historical plaque is evident at the center at curbside, and the stage entrance is to the right of the plaque. Bottom: A close-up of the plaque commissioned by the Pennsylvania Historical and Museum.   Photo by Author.

Ballroom Dancing, hosted by Juliet Prowse and Ron Montez, drew an average audience of 10 million viewers (Carman 1996, E-1).

In North American competitions at the time, competitive ballroom dance was divided into two divisions: International Style and American Style (American Style did not exist in the rest of the world). Each division was split into two categories, which included International Style Standard and Latin; and American Style Smooth and Rhythm (sometimes also known as Latin). The Standard and Smooth dances moved in counterclockwise progression (Line of Dance) around the dance floor. The Latin and Rhythm dances stayed in one place on the dance floor. A comparative list follows:

Category	Dances
International Style Standard	Waltz, Tango, Slow Fox Trot, Quickstep, and Viennese Waltz
American Style Smooth	Waltz, Tango, Fox Trot, Viennese Waltz*
International Style Latin	Cha-cha, Rhumba, Samba, Paso Doblé, and Jive
American Style Rhythm	Cha-cha, Rhumba, Mambo, Bolero, and Swing

*The fifth dance sometimes included the Peabody, or another American style dance.

As a result of PBS-TV exposure, there was a renewed interest in ballroom dancing. By the early 1990s, there were over 580 Fred Astaire Dance Studios and over 280 Arthur Murray Dance Studios as well as numerous private studios and YMCA's that taught ballroom dancing (Malnig 1992, 144).

In 1984, dancers Yvonne Marceau and Pierre Dulaine combined Ballroom dance and the theatrical arts in the American Ballroom Dance Theater (ABRT). By 1994, the ABRT developed an outreach program for participating New York City elementary schools titled the *Dancing Classrooms* project. The program was a ten-week biweekly session held during the school semester and was incorporated as part of the student's school day. During the 20 sessions, the students, mainly 9 and 10 year olds, learned ten dances including the Merengue, Fox Trot, Rhumba, Tango, Waltz, and Swing. In 1999, over 2,500 students in 29 different New York City Public Schools participated. The following year the program was increased to 37 schools and over 3,500 grade school children. A documentary titled *Mad Hot Ballroom* (2005) chronicled the events of one semester of school children in the program ("Dancing Classrooms," n.d.)

Similar dance programs existed across the country. At Edgewood High School in Madison, Wisconsin, for example, more than half of the Edgewood High's 480 students elected to take a social dance class to fulfill a physical education requirement. In Atlanta, Georgia, the Cotillion Group specialized in teaching partner dancing to 11 to 13 year olds. In the year 2000, they had over 800 students enrolled. The Unified School District in San Francisco, California, sponsored six months of ballroom dance lessons to teachers from 14 district schools to pass on to their elementary, middle, and high school students (Marchant 2001).

Various Social and Ballroom dance classes were also offered on college campuses. One university, Brigham Young, had probably the largest enrollment in social dance instruction with over 6,000 students. At the time, Brigham Young University also offered a Bachelor's degree program in ballroom dance (Marchant 2001). Other colleges that had social dance programs included Arizona State, San Diego State, the University of Wisconsin, Cornell, Stonybrook, Yale University, University of Wisconsin, Texas A&M, the University of Texas, University of Houston, Rice, the University of California, The Ohio State University, New York University, Columbia, and Penn State. In 1999, the demand for ballroom dancing at Penn State University was so great that the number of class offerings was increased from 8 to 48 with an increased enrollment from 240 to 1,440 students. The ballroom dance class fulfilled their physical education requirement (Bronner 1999).

CRUISE SHIPS, DANCE HOSTS, "NO HANKY-PANKY AT ALL," AND "GETTING LUCKY"

In 1970, the number of Americans who vacationed by cruise ship totaled less than 500,000. Throughout the 1980s and into the 1990s, the numbers steadily increased. By 1982 the number was over 1.5 million, in 1991 it was over 4 million, and by the year 2000 cruise ships carried over 6 million travelers each year. During that time cruise ships revamped their amenities and offered an array of travel options, lessened the formality of their dining rooms, and increased on-board amenities. New ships were also built of a size and breadth that was never before imaginable. As a result of the increased size, on-board amenities, such as movie theaters, ice-skating, and rock climbing, could be included (Giordano 2003, 267).

The new amenities were in addition to one of the "grand old traditions" aboard cruise ships—dancing. Professional dance instructors Tom and Orelynn Golson, for example, described Norwegian Cruise Line's *Norway* as a "classic ship" with good dance floors and great music for dancing. The Cunard Line *Queen Elizabeth II* was one of the only cruise ships that featured the Queen's Room, described by the Golsons as one of "the only true ballrooms afloat." But in keeping

In 1981, Boston public television station WGBH-TV began broadcasting Ballroom dance competition. It was also carried by dozens of other PBS stations nationwide. The show named *Championship Ballroom Dancing* drew an average audience of 10 million viewers. As a result of PBS-TV exposure, there was a renewed interest in ballroom dancing. PBS / Courtesy of Photofest.

with the new trend in cruise ship amenities, the dancing options also varied. Travel advice columnist Lois Donahue, of *TheWorkingVacation.com*, observed,

> Whatever your joy of dance might be, from swing to waltz, shipboard dancing can be one of the highlights of your cruise vacation. Knowing the steps can enhance the fun, but since the music on board is so versatile there is usually something to dance to for everybody ("Dancing on the Seven Seas," n.d.).

A tour company named Dance Holidays based in Sussex, England, specialized in organizing trips for Americans involving dancing in Europe and Latin America, such as Salsa in Barcelona, Spain, and Tango in Argentina. Another British based group named Dance and Ski combined trips to ski resorts where guests could ski by day and dance at night. The Hustle Dance Cruise on Royal Caribbean combined four evenings of Hustle dancing with a Caribbean cruise. Dance-Visions on the other hand held a five-day dance camp in Las Vegas. Company president Wayne Eng said, "they get to take lessons during the day, and in the nighttimes there's everything else to do" (Catto 2003, 2).

On the other hand, some organizers, such as Marion Hoar of "Dance at Sea," personally inspected each cruise ship and also selected the dance instructors and the DJ to accompany her tour group. Triangle Cruise and Travel agent Betsy Hockaday scheduled not only the professional dance instructors on seven-day Caribbean and Alaska itineraries, she also arranged for a portable 1000 square foot wooden dance floor to be delivered on board the cruise ship. Let's Dance Cruises organized about ten trips per year exclusively on Norwegian Cruise Lines. Each of the dance cruise organizers, such as Loretta Blake of "Gentlemen Hosts," also carefully selected a sufficient number of male dance hosts for woman who were traveling alone.

A dance host (also known as an "ambassador host" or "gentleman host") was almost exclusively male, between the age of 40 and 70, single, and able to perform the basic social dances including the Fox Trot, Cha-cha, Rhumba, Waltz, and Swing. The men did not receive any pay. In exchange for their services, they received a complimentary cabin (usually shared with another dance host), meal privileges, laundry discounts, tips, and a chance to see exotic ports. Some cruise ships provided air transportation but most of the men had to pay their own transportation. In fact, many of the hosts were actually required to pay a small daily fee for each day aboard ship. They were also required to help during the day with dance classes, occasionally escorted groups on shore excursions, and were expected to attend every social function.

A typical evening was a 45-minute predinner set of dancing. After dinner, which could last only 30 minutes or so, was another 45 minutes of dancing. An entertainment show usually lasted about an hour and then dancing from about 9:00 P.M. to midnight. The dance host was expected to dance the entire time, but not with the same partner twice in a row. However, one of the cardinal rules expressed by host coordinator Dorine Nielsen of Fort Lauderdale's Sixth Star was "No hanky-panky at all." Romance with the guests and cabin visits were expressly forbidden —although not always enforceable. The simple policy was that if the dance host broke any of the rules, he would be ejected from the ship, and he would have to finance his own travel home from wherever the ship might be located (Doup 2003).

The idea of a "dance host" became an industry standard and was welcomed aboard the cruise ships. The concept was also parodied in the Hollywood movie *Out to Sea* (1997). Beyond the world of Hollywood, however, dance hosts fulfilled a real need. Phyllis Zeno, who organized the Merry Widows of Tampa, Florida, explained,

> You see women coming onboard in wheelchairs and walkers, but the music starts and they dance…It's like Lazarus throwing down the cane. These women can go all year and never be in the arms of a man. They cuddle up and feel attractive again.

One widow added, "I love to dance, so having someone to dance with is an added plus" (Doup 2003).

Dancing for companionship, however, was not one-sided. Some dance hosts, such as Bill Rohlfing, from Southampton, Pennsylvania, a 73-year-old widower, joined the dance host program to deal with their own loneliness and lack of female companionship. Rohlfing said, "All my life I kind of felt that somebody needed me …You know, I never really thought of it that much, but after my wife passed away I just kind of had that feeling nobody needed me. I was very lonely.…I think I bring happiness into the lives of other people." ("Would You Care to Dance?" ABC-News.Go.com, 2001).

The concept of providing a gentleman dance partner also occurred on land. In August 1995, in an article for the *Miami Sun Sentinel*, journalist Lou Ann Walker wrote of a "secret society" in Florida where gentleman dance partners were paid as dance escorts for elderly women. Most of the women ranged in age from their sixties to their nineties. Almost all were well-off financially and spent their winters in Florida "to dispel the blues of winter." They frequented hotels like the Sun Spa Hotel near Miami, which offered a "cabaret night" of dancing six nights a week. The unique feature was that in a role reversal of a bygone era of Taxi-dancers (see Chapter 2) for a fee of $6, one of the elderly women could "rent a male partner for a two-minute dance." The male dance hosts received $3.60 of the fee, the rest went to the Sun Spa. On a typical night the men dance about 15 to 20 dances. Other ballrooms in the area included Mr. Dance and Margo's. Walker revealed to her own astonishment that,

> Coming from the Midwest, I guess I couldn't really believe that an elderly woman would pay for an escort or that there were such things as ageing gigolos.…But South Florida has a way of working its spell on almost everyone, making the tacky seem normal and the normal seem, well almost idiotic (Walker, "Romance For Sale For $6 A Dance," 1995, 8).

The male dancers, ranging in age from 20 to 85 years old, actively handed out business cards and solicited their services for not only dancing, but also dance instruction and escort services. One of those providing dance services was 70-year-old Lucky Kargo.

In a related story titled "Getting Lucky," journalist Lou Ann Walker claimed that, "Single women of a certain age go to Miami, to retire or just to dance—with ageing gigolos like Lucky Kargo." She described Kargo (see photo in Chapter 4) as a "suave" and "gentlemanly" ballroom dancer with "an 88-key grin." At the time, Kargo, a former dance instructor, Broadway dancer, and cruise ship dance host from New York, was new to the South Florida dance scene. As for the elderly ladies, he knew how to make each one feel that he was "having a splendid time." He said, "They like that sexy man-appeal." One unnamed women said, "That's what money is for. You pay to get your nails done, you pay for a good time [dancing]. What the hell? Tomorrow it could be all over" (Walker, "Getting Lucky," 1995, F3).

FOOTLOOSE: FACT OR FICTION OR NOT? AND "IS DANCING A SIN?"

In 1984, the Hollywood movie *Footloose* portrayed the struggle of a "hip" Chicago teenager named Ren McCormack (actor Kevin Bacon) who moved to a small Midwestern fictional town named Bomont. Ren found that, as a result of the persistent preaching from the local minister, the town of Bomont was convinced that dancing was a sin and therefore prohibited. In the hope of persuading the town council and the minister to rescind the ban and allow dancing at the high school prom, Ren quoted from the Bible. He cited Psalm 149, "praise ye the lord let them praise his name in the dance." Ren rhetorically asks the town council, "What did David do?...David danced before the Lord in all his might...Leaping and dancing." Despite it all, the town council held firm and rejected his appeal. Although the kids promoted their own dance right outside the town limits, the dancing was less a part of the movie than the struggle for the right to dance. The movie was a surprise hit, but many people simply dismissed the idea that the movie was anything but pure fiction. The reality, however, was that, unfortunately, selective bans on dancing were not just in the movie *Footloose*, they actually remained very real throughout the twentieth century and into the twenty-first century.

In November 1986, a real-life "Footloose" scenario occurred in the town of Purdy, Missouri (population 1,000), located in southwestern Missouri near the Oklahoma and Arkansas border. Students at Purdy High School wanted to hold their senior prom in the high school gymnasium but discovered that the local school board prohibited dancing on school grounds. The local school board argued that dancing led to "alcohol abuse, drug use, and illicit sex ("Missouri Students Fight Town's Dancing Ban," 1986, 30).

About half of the schools 137 students and their parents took the case to court, prompting one town member to claim that the dance supporters were "God-hating Communists." The students lost their case and held their prom elsewhere. In 1988 (after the seniors had graduated), a Federal District Judge called the school ban unconstitutional. However, the United States Court of Appeals for the Eighth Circuit overturned the decision. The United States Supreme Court upheld the decision on the school ban on dances (Greenhouse, 1990, A22).

In 1987, the town of Anson, Texas, experienced a similar circumstance; however, the ban on dancing was wholly within the city limits. Many did not even know why the town council so ardently enforced the ban. Ironically, once each year during the Christmas season, one public dance was held at the Old Pioneer Hall within the town. The event, a century old tradition called the Cowboys' Christmas Ball, was always well attended (Ainslie, 1995, xiv, 33–34).

In March 1986, the widely circulated monthly Christian publication the *Firm Foundation* asked, "Is Dancing a Sin?" The author, the Reverend Robert R. Stephenson claimed, "Although the Bible does not come out and say 'Thou shalt not dance,' it does condemn dancing." Stephenson quoted Exodus 32:15–24, Samuel 30:16,17, and Mark 6:18–26 trying to connect some obscure Biblical references to dancing and to twist the logic against the fun of dancing. He purported that "in the scriptures we find no support to justify the claim that dancing is acceptable in the sight of God...but God's wrath fell on those that practiced such." He claimed that Galatians 5:19–21 discussed "the works of the flesh." Therefore he concluded, "Dancing is then a work of the flesh, and therefore condemned by God." Stephenson also resurrected some of the age-old urban legends of the "evils" of social dancing. He added, "No doubt many a girl has been insulted, raped, and abused, after hours of dancing, who would not have been subjected to such had she refrained from the dance." His distorted conclusion was simple: "The true dedicated child of God will not dance because he loves God more than himself. Yes, dancing is a sin, and must be avoided" (Stephenson 1986).

Beyond questioning the conscious of the individual, many towns and Christian colleges maintained century old prohibitions against social dancing. On April 18, 1996, the Associated Press reported that Baylor University in Waco, Texas, held an on-campus student dance. An event of that type would normally not even have been noticed; however, for Baylor students it was the first time in the university's 151-year history that dancing was allowed on campus. The event attracted over 7,000 people, some who came to look, but almost all came to dance.

On the other hand, Cornerstone University in Grand Rapids, Michigan, for example, printed a notice in their Student Handbook that prohibited "social dancing and attendance at dance clubs." Although the ban was lifted in 2004, students were still forbidden to dance in any "indecent, erotic, and violent" manner (Bickel 2004, A1).

Wheaton College, a small Christian college in Wheaton, Illinois, about 25 miles outside Chicago, continued an over 140-year-old prohibition against dancing both on and off the college campus. In the 1990s, the off-campus dance ban was eased as students and faculty members were permitted to dance at family celebrations such as a wedding but only with a relative or spouse. The on-campus dance ban was lifted in early 2003; however, a revised set of rules allowed students to dance but they were required to avoid any behavior while dancing "which may be immodest, sinfully erotic or harmfully violent" (Abwin 2003).

In Arkansas, for example, six of the state's 10 church affiliated private colleges maintained prohibitions and restrictions on dancing on campus. (Some did allow Square or Folk dancing.) John Brown University's vice president for student development, for example, admitted that there were students on campus who wanted the school to allow social dancing. But he strongly rebutted. "Hey, there are enough Christians out there who still believe dancing is problematic" (Branam 2004).

In contrast, author Eve Babitz of *Two by Two: Tango, Two-Step and the L.A. Night*, recalled an unsettling incident at a Cajun dance in South Pasadena, California. She recalled that she was taken aback as she came across "one problematic dance partner." He had asked her to dance but "had *no idea* at all, and who, as we danced, couldn't lead and didn't care." As it turned out, he was only waiting for the dance to end and an opportunity to hand her a pamphlet and ask "Have you given your heart to Jesus?" In fact, she claimed to be quite "horrified" and described it as "a freakish moment." At first she just wanted to forget the incident and remember the happy environment of the Cajun dancing; however, she felt compelled to write the following:

> Imagine one of these Christians determined to convert people, going to a Cajun dance and looking for willing victims! Imagine a man so poor of spirit, he'd invade a place where people were so happy and so free, trying to instill the Christian Coalition freeze! The contrast between the dance's deepest integrity and this poor stranger from an ugly mental state was enormous. It's hard to imagine a division wider than the one between how happy people were and how rottenly he alone danced. In every scene, of course, there are people who don't dance well, but to combine that with burning in hell if you don't by their act, I mean, even Jesus wouldn't expect that of a convert (91–93).

Babitz could not understand the infringement upon the simple fun of dancing.

In 1984, *Newsweek* magazine sarcastically stated, "Fundamentalists do not oppose dancing because they are against fun. On the contrary, fun can be a powerful weapon against sin." As an example, they cited an all-night "rock-a-thon" sponsored by the North Mesquite Assembly of God in Texas. But the "rocking" was neither the music nor the dancing, but rather an event that took place in real-life rocking chairs. Rock-a-thon sponsor Pastor Ronnie Yarbor explained his reasoning for a rocking chair rather than a dance. He reasoned that dancing "is highly provocative and suggestive, which therefore leads to the immoral...A man who says he can take a woman in his arms on a dance floor in a dance hall under the influence of alcohol and not have any physical feelings is just built wrong" (Adler and Burgower 1984, 52).

However, in regards to social dancing, there was one religious quote that was consistently overlooked. In the sixteenth century, St. Basil provided the quote in simple plain words as follows:

> Since we will spend a great deal of time dancing in Heaven, it is well to learn to dance here on earth.

However, the most surprising prohibition on dancing was in New York City.

CABARET LAWS, "BUCKETS OF BLOOD," AND "NO DANCING" IN NEW YORK?

In 1997, New York City Mayor Rudolph Giuliani enacted a widely publicized "Quality of Life" campaign to clean up the city. (Most New Yorkers thought that the Mayor's ban was only against strip clubs, topless dancers, and the cavernous, noisy, and "ecstasy" drug related nightclubs.) His main enforcement tool was to implement the 1920s era Cabaret Laws—which although very rarely enforced were still in effect.

The so-called "Cabaret Laws" were actually listed as Subchapter 20 of the New York City Building Code titled "Public Dance Halls, Cabarets, and Catering Establishments." Sub-Section: 20-359 defined a "Cabaret" as follows:

> Any room, place or space in the city in which any musical entertainment, singing, dancing or other form of amusement is permitted in connection with the restaurant business or the business of directly or indirectly selling to the public food or drink, except eating or drinking places, which provide incidental musical entertainment, without dancing, either by mechanical devices, or by not more than three persons.

Therefore, if a restaurant provided "incidental" music and did not have a specific cabaret license, none of the patrons were allowed to get up and dance.

The Cabaret Laws were originally written in 1926 as part of the New York City Building Code. Historian Paul Chevigny, author of *Gigs: Jazz and the Cabaret Laws in New York City* (1991), claimed that the law was first created to crack down on both Jazz music and the "multiracial Harlem jazz clubs." After the end of prohibition, the Cabaret Laws remained on the books, but were mainly overlooked by city officials. During World War II, nightclubs and restaurants were essential to the war effort, and they continued to flourish after the war. By 1960, there were 12,000 establishments operating with a cabaret license in the five boroughs of New York City. In 1961, the law was revised that cabarets were permitted only in manufacturing and commercial zones. In 1978, prompted by a 1975 fire at the Blue Angel nightclub and a 1976 fire in a Puerto Rican Social Club, the law was amended to include sprinkler systems in clubs seating more than 75 people (Romano 2002).

In 1997, Giuliani claimed that the Cabaret Laws had a twofold reason for safety and against obtrusive noise. Critics charged that Giuliani's real plan was not of enforcement but harassment targeted at "legal" licensed establishments, and the idea was not to make them safer "but to padlock as many as possible." Deputy Mayor Rudy Washington proudly proclaimed, "We've been closing down these little buckets of blood (nightclubs) for about three years and paralyzing them." However, in reality, those "buckets of blood" nightclubs were actually places where New Yorkers engaged in social dancing. From 1997 to 2000, the city temporarily closed 69 bars and clubs for violating the Cabaret Laws in respect to their patrons dancing. Some of those clubs included Coney Island High, Baby Jupiter, Hogs and Heifers, Vain, Rivertown Lounge, No Moore, the Knitting Factory, and Lakeside Lounge (Brown, "Safe to Dance," n.d.).

Actually, the definition of dancing was loosely explained and at times very vague. Attorney Robert Bookman, who represented the New York Nightlife Association, said, "There's no exception in the law." Some city inspectors have described their definition of dancing from "moving rhythmically," to "gyrating up and down," and even "twitching." He added, "I've defended clients who've been ticketed for having six people dancing near their chairs." The vague definition was loosely covered under Rules and Regulations of Sub-Section 20-368, which authorized the commissioner "to adopt such reasonable rules and regulations as he or she may deem necessary for the proper control, operation, and supervision of public dance halls, cabarets and catering establishments" ("Legalize Dancing NYC— Who We Are," n.d.).

The Lakeside Lounge on Avenue B on the East side of Manhattan was one of many establishments that hung a "No Dancing" sign above their bar. The "No Dancing" sign visibly surprised Brian Rubenstein, a tourist from Chicago. He asked, "How can you play music and expect people not to dance? I can't believe, of all the cities, New York would have a law like this." Giuliani defended the enforcement of the Cabaret Laws in an article in the *New York Daily News*. He claimed, "The rule makes sense, and it is helpful in terms of improving the quality of life of all of the neighborhoods of New York City" (Keys 2001).

But aside from Giuliani's enforcement of the Cabaret Laws, during his administration it was very difficult to apply and receive approval for a cabaret license. It was not the cost of a cabaret license, only between $600 and $1,000 for a two-year period, based on capacity, but the real hindrance was the multitude of agency approvals and zoning restrictions that made it prohibitive. In addition, the process was long, costly, and not guaranteed. And to top it all off, all of the agencies operated independently of each other and approvals could not be applied for concurrently (O'Brien 2003).

On the other hand, New York Nightlife Association attorney Robert Bookman claimed the law "focused on the racialized enforcement of the law, which historians say was originally rooted in a fear of race-mixing." At the time, Bookman revealed, "I can't tell you how many clients tell me authorities have taken them aside and said, 'I'll deny I said this, but if you lose the hip hop night or the salsa night, you won't see us here again'" (Neuberg 2001).

What made Giuliani's enforcement of the law all the more mind-boggling was the fact that, according to a survey sponsored by the New York Nightlife Association and conducted by Audience Research and Analysis, over 24.3 million people per year partook in some form of social dancing. In the process, the music and dance lovers contributed over $2.9 billion to the city's economy and were directly responsible for providing over 27,000 jobs. That figure is even more astonishing when it is compared to the fact that the total number of social dancers in New York amounted to more than the combined attendance of all of the City's major league sports teams, all of the Broadway theaters, and visitors to the Metropolitan Museum of Art and the Empire State Building ("Legalize Dancing NYC—Who We Are," n.d.).

In 1997, in response to the Mayor's actions, a small coalition of New Yorkers organized NYC: No Dancing Allowed to repeal the "antiquated laws." (In 2001, the organization changed its name to Legalize Dancing NYC.) The Pro-dance group sadly admitted, "While it sounds like a joke, the NYC Cabaret Law is very real" ("Legalize Dancing NYC—Who We Are," n.d.). The following year, another Pro-dance organization, the Dance Liberation Front, formed in protest against Mayor Rudolph Giuliani's "crackdown on illegal dancing." Some of their actions included "The Million Mambo March," in which over 100 "protesters" literally danced their way from Tompkins Square Park in the East Village to Washington Square Park near New York University. Other events included a Twist-a-thon in Times Square, a Conga line up Avenue A, and the world's largest Hokey-pokey around City Hall. In case the sarcasm was not totally understood by the Mayor, they also held a rally at the Richard

Rodgers Theatre, which at the time was showing a revival of the movie *Footloose* (Katz 2001).

By the year 2000, however, the situation was not any better. Tricia Romano of *The Village Voice* reported, "While there are 4811 liquor licenses in Manhattan, only 276 are licensed cabarets—down from 12,000 in 1961" (Romano 2002).

THE AMERICAN INDIAN POW-WOW, ESKIMOS, THE O-BON FESTIVAL, AND HAWAIIAN HULA

A similar love of dancing existed among Native American Indians, Alaskan Eskimos, Native American Hawaiians, and Japanese Americans. The main difference of these cultures from the American social dance tradition was that the Eskimo, Indian, Hawaiian, and Japanese cultural dance traditions honored and worshiped the spirits and ancient gods. This practice went against the grain of the American Puritan notion of one god, which viewed those dances as devil worship, or evil (Needham 2002, 11).

During the 1970s, the American Indian Movement, which was formed after World War II to end discrimination and stereotyping of Indians, was instrumental in changing the public perception of Native American Indian culture. As a result, in 1976, the United States Congress passed the Indian Self-Determination Act, which gave Indians control of their education and tribal customs. The most important tribal custom was the Pow-wow (Giordano 2003, 177–178).

The Pow-wow, the most important cultural event, was a social gathering among Native American Indians that brought different tribes together to celebrate their culture through group participation in music and dance. Cultural historian Tara Browner described a Pow-wow as "an event where Native North Americans come together to celebrate their cultures through the medium of music and dance.... Pow-wows are inclusive...meaning that all tribal (and non-tribal) people are invited to participate." Some of the traditional Pow-wow dances were gender specific, whereas others included both genders and even nontribal members. The traditional dances were performed individually in a free-form improvised style and had regional variations. Southern Traditional dancing, for example, contained footwork that was more of a slow stylized walk. Northern Traditional women, on the other hand, stood in one place and shifted their heels in different directions. Southern Straight dancing was mainly performed by males who circled during certain points in the music while holding tribal dance sticks and followed one another in a symbolic trail. Grass dancing was practiced by the Lakota nation whose people wore outfits symbolizing the grass of the Plains States. The Fancy Dance style was "codified" from the fancy style of dress and headgear used in the Wild West shows of the 1920s and 1930s (Browner 2002, 47–49). The Thunderbird American Indian Dancers, for example, traveled the United States dressed in authentic headgear and tribal costumes performing the regional Native American dance traditions. Murielle Borst, a dancer from the Kuna Rappahonock tribe, explained, "We show them that not everything is as stereotypical as Hollywood...It is a completely new experience for them to see the different tribes and that we all look different" (Weinman 2004, A21).

At about the same time, Inuit tribes (formerly known as Eskimos) in Alaska were granted Congressional approval of the 1973 Bilingual Education legislation that secured the same basic cultural rights as Native American Indians. Prior to these Congressional acts, the Inuits also were suppressed in public display of their most important cultural tradition, which was dancing. One Unalaklit Inuit chief described its importance this way:

> The Eskimo...had danced long before the white man came, and would not know how to spend the long dark winters if their only form of amusement were taken away.... There was nothing bad about their dances; which made their hearts good toward each other, and tribe friendly with tribe. If the dances were stopped, the ties between them would be broken, and the Eskimo would cease to be strong....No culture survives without its Native arts. Once that is gone, all is gone (Luttmann and Luttmann1977, 20–21).

In Hawaii, the Japanese tradition of the *O-Bon* festival was an important component of the Japanese Buddhist calendar. Japanese sugar plantation workers first brought the tradition to Hawaii as early as the 1860s. It eventually became a regular Hawaiian Island tradition in small rural communities from as little as 100 to over 1000 participants in the city of Honolulu. Cultural historian Judy Van Zile described it this way:

> The *bon* dance is performed out-of-doors, usually in the evenings, and generally follows the *segaki*, a religious ceremony to honor deceased ancestors....the dance formation is typically a circle or several concentric circles, depending on the number of participants. Musicians are usually in the center, in a *yagura* (a tower approximately ten feet square and fifteen to twenty feet high, from which paper lanterns may be strung) assembled for the occasion. Recorded music for modern dances is amplified through speakers (Zile 2002, 77–78).

The most familiar of Hawaiian dances, however, was the Hula (see Chapter 4).

The Hula tradition actually began long before the European/American influence on the Hawaiian Islands. Missionaries, when they arrived in Hawaii in 1820, had originally banned the Hula, calling it "a very great and public evil." However, both during and after World War II, military personnel and tourists considered the dance innocent exotic entertainment. Hula dancer Patrick Makuakane explained, "Hula is about expressing the poetry in the Hawaiian chants...in traditional Hula, there is no dance apart from language. You can't just dance to beats. You must have language." Although in order for the audience to understand the dance, it was spoken in English, Makuakane added, otherwise, "You'd have no idea what we're talking about" (Gold 2004, AR 8).

THE BAYWAY POLISH HOME AND "LIVING ON POLKA TIME"

Another specific American cultural dance tradition was the Polka. Polka music and dancing were a legitimate form of symphonic music as well as folk music in America since before World War II (see Chapter 4). In Elizabeth, New Jersey, for example, in the Bayway area, a close-knit community with a heavy concentration of Polish, Slavic, and Lithuania immigrants, it was not unusual to have crowds of 1000 or more people at a community center listening and dancing to Polka music. After World War II, there were at least four or five community centers within the immediate Bayway area that were strictly Polka dance halls. The Bayway Polish Home, for example, was a community center that would have at least 250 to 300 dancers for Polka every Friday, Saturday, and Sunday evening. By the 1980s, however, the ethnic makeup of the neighborhood changed, and the community centers closed one by one. By 1990, the Bayway Polish Home was the last cultural bastion in the area offering Polka music and dancing. In order to meet the demand and to "pay the bills," however, the directors shifted to a format of Friday night Social Dancing, Saturday night Latin dancing, and Sunday for Polka dancing.

Dave Snyder, both a social dancer and one of the directors of the Bayway Polish Home, attributed the decline in Polka to the fact that not many professional dance teachers "treated it as a legitimate dance." He added, "It seems that Polka dancing always got grouped in the folk tradition." As a result, it did not appeal to the younger generation. Snyder's love of dancing also came in handy in his professional life. Through the dancing and socializing of the close-knit community of the social dance world, it was inevitable that some of the dancers would also become patients. Dr. Snyder, a dentist by profession, added,

> At times, I would show one of my patients a new dance step that I learned in class right there in the waiting room. I can say one thing, it certainly broke down their anxiety from coming to see the dentist! (Snyder interview, 2004).

Polka dancing still remained popular among the Polish community. Most relied on publications such as the weekly *The Post Eagle* published in Clifton, New Jersey, and the *Polish American Journal* published in six regional editions, including Brooklyn, Buffalo, Boston, and New Jersey. *The Post Eagle*, for example, listed regular weekly Polka events in the New England area. They also carried a column titled "Midwest Polkas," which listed Polka events in Pennsylvania, Chicago, Wisconsin, and Indiana. Dozens of Polka bands played the "circuit." One of the most enduring was 14-time Grammy winner Jimmy Sturr and His Orchestra.

One Polka dance that Sturr and His Orchestra played in Bayway, New Jersey, for example, filled the hall to a capacity of well over 350 people—with some who had traveled from as far away as Michigan, Ohio, Pennsylvania, and New York. The dancing certainly matched, if not exceeded, the fun and energy levels of any other form of social dancing including the Lindy Hop. The Polka dancers were exuberant to the point where all of them were completely absorbed in the music and dance. One couple had continually danced to Sturr's Orchestra since he had played at their wedding nearly 30 years before. Polka dancing was such an important part of their life that they had named their modest boat *Living on Polka Time*.

DANCING AT THE YMCA AND THE NEXT DANCE CRAZE

Although the Village People song "Y.M.C.A." (see Chapter 6) was easily recognizable and usually packed the dance floor, there were, in fact, many people who

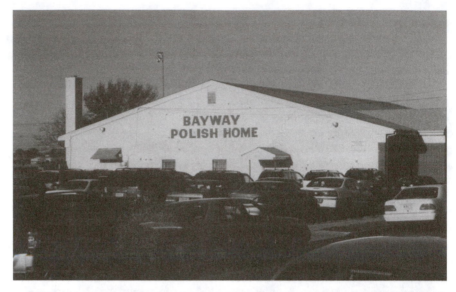

Top: The exterior of the Bayway Polish Home in Elizabeth, New Jersey. Bottom: The Bayway Polish Home during a Sunday afternoon of Polka dancing.   Photo by Thelma Lynn Olsen.

did not get up simply because they did not know how to dance. A persistent problem among the Baby Boom generation was that they did not have the exposure on how to do it right. For most men, the Yuppie work ethic of the 1980s just did not condone dancing, especially freestyle, as an acceptable "manly" behavior. All too often, a young man in a social dance setting was usually on the outside looking in.

Throughout the United States many real life YMCA's offered instructional courses in dancing. The YMCA Broadway Center in Staten Island, New York, for example, offered weekly classes and workshops in all types of social dancing including Country Line dancing, and Swing. Adult program director Stella Bennardello, herself an accomplished Swing, Country, and Social dancer reasoned, "I think the baby boomers are ready for partner dancing. They're not just relating to the [freestyle] dancing of today. After awhile, the classic oldies get stale, and you look for something new." The response from the YMCA students was overwhelmingly positive. One student Robert Neville said, "At all the parties, I never get up, I'm a wallflower. Now I'll be able to get up. I go on a few cruises, and now I'll be able to get up and dance." Thelma Lynn Olsen, a Registered Nurse, said that the dance classes allowed her a release to get out of the house. "It's freedom," Olsen added. "It's just a small amount of discipline to learn the step, and then you're there" (Hynes, "Swing Time," 1997, D1).

As a result, Olsen became "hooked" on dancing and also became proficient enough to teach as a part-time dance instructor. She noticed that, despite the social decorum that "men did not dance," there was actually a suppressed desire to do just the opposite. She reasoned, "I believe that it is not only women who have the secret desire to dance at a social function, such as a wedding or their high school reunion, but men also desperately want to dance with their partners." At one dance workshop of about 30 people, 17 were men. She added:

> I found that all of the men learned the basic swing step quite easily. Yeah, one partner apologized for being "new at it" (being dancing) but he got through the basics…he was smiling…but most important he was there to begin with…I believe he was in the process of sharpening his masculinity not in the process of getting dull.

As a result Olsen surmised,

> Dancing can also be an expression of masculinity. Just look at Vernon Castle, Fred Astaire, Gene Kelly, and John Travolta, as examples through time. They were athletic and masculine. In the past few years, however, men have not had enough role models to dance appropriately as a male. Because in reality, for a man dancing is the best way to meet a partner in life (Olsen interview, 2004).

More so, any couple who danced well together was ardently admired and envied whether at a wedding, dance club, or a sponsored outdoor event. Despite it all, there was a persistent undertone that onlookers who did not dance still viewed those who did dance more as an "oddity." A quote often attributed to an anonymous source, but retold by comedian George Carlin in his publication *Napalm & Silly Putty* (2001) is worth restating. He writes: "Those who dance are considered insane by those who can't hear the music."

The plain and simple fact is that people dance to have fun and forget about the realities of daily life. To those people who live to dance, it is an extremely vital component of their existence within American society. Who is to say what the next dance craze will be. For those who just live (and love) to dance, it does not even matter if there is or is not any "dance craze"—all that is needed is music, a place to dance, and a willing partner.

Bibliography

*Publications within the bibliography preceded by an asterisk provide a good general overview for the student or scholar interested in a reference starting point on the subject of Social Dancing.

Acuña, Rodolfo. *Occupied America: A History of Chicanos.* Reading, MA: Addison-Wesley Publishing Co., 1999.

Adams, Rev. Dr. R.A. *The Social Dance.* Kansas City: R.A. Adams, 1921.

Ainslie, Ricardo. *No Dancin' in Anson: An American Story of Race and Social Change.* Northvale, NJ: J. Aronson, 1995.

Albrecht, Donald, ed. *World War II and the American Dream: How Wartime Building Changed a Nation.* Cambridge, MA: The MIT Press, 1995.

Anderson, John Murray. *Social Dancing of Today.* New York: Frederick A. Stokes Company, 1914.

Angelou, Maya. *Singin' and Swingin' and Getting' Merry like Christmas.* New York: Random House, 1976.

Aron, Cindy S. *Working at Play: A History of Vacations in the United States.* New York: Oxford University Press, 1999.

Asinof, Eliot. *1919: America's Loss of Innocence.* New York: D.I. Fine, 1990.

Babitz, Eve. *Two by Two: Tango, Two-Step and the L.A. Night.* New York: Simon and Schuster, 1999.

Badger, Reid. *Life in Ragtime: A Biography of James Reese Europe.* New York: Oxford University Press, 1994.

Banes, Sally, and John F. Szwed. "From 'Messin'-Around' to 'Funky Western Civilization': The Rise and Fall of Dance Instruction Songs." In *Dancing Many Drums.* Edited by Thomas F. De Frantz. Madison, WI: The University of Wisconsin Press, 2002, 169–203.

*Barzel, Anne. "History of Social Dancing." In *The Dance Encyclopedia.* Edited by Anatole Chuoy and P.W. Manchester. New York: Simon and Schuster, 1967.

Baughman, Judith S., ed. *American Decades: 1920–1929.* Detroit, MI: Gale Research, 1996.

Berríos-Miranda, Marisol. "Is Salsa A Musical Genre?" In *Situating Salsa.* Edited by Lise Waxer. London: Routledge, 2002, 23–46.

Beryl and Associates, eds. *Immorality of Modern Dances.* New York: Everitt and Francis Co., 1904.

Boggs, Vernon, ed. *Salsiology: Afro-Cuban Music and the Evolution of Salsa in New York City.* Westport: Greenwood Press, 1992.

Bibliography

*Borrows, Frank. *Latin American Dancing: The Theory and Technique Explained*. Rev. ed. London, Muller: distributed by Sportshelf, New Rochelle, NY, 1961, 1964.

Braden, Donna R. *Leisure and Entertainment in America*. Dearborn, MI: Henry Ford Museum and Greenfield Village.

Breakdancing: Mr. Fresh and The Supreme Rockers. New York: Avon Books, 1984.

*Brewster, Bill, and Frank Broughton. *Last Night a DJ Saved My Life: The History of the Disc Jockey*. New York: Grove Press, 1999.

Browner, Tara. "Contemporary Native American Pow-wow Dancing." In *I See America Dancing*. Edited by Maureen Needham. Chicago: University of Illinois Press, 2002, 46–50.

Butler, Albert and Josephine. *Encyclopedia of Social Dance*. New York: Albert Butler Ballroom Dance, 1980.

Butler, Bill, and Elin Schoen. *Jammin' Bill Butler's Complete Guide to Roller Disco*. New York: Pocket Books, 1979.

Caffin, Caroline and Charles. *Dancing and Dancers of Today*. New York: Dodd, Mead and Co., 1912.

Castle, Irene Foote. *Castles in the Air: As Told to Bob and Wanda Duncan*. Cambridge, MA: Da Capo Press, 1980.

*Castle, Mr. and Mrs. Vernon. *Modern Dancing*. New York: Harper and Brothers, 1914.

Chalif, Louis H. *The Chalif Text Books of Dancing*. 5 vols. New York: The Chalif Normal School of Dancing, 1914–1925.

Chevigny, Paul. *Gigs: Jazz and the Cabaret Laws in New York City*. New York: Routledge, 1991.

The Chicago Recreation Survey, 1937. Vol. 2. Chicago, 1938.

Chuoy, Anatole, and P.W. Manchester. *The Dance Encyclopedia*. New York: Simon and Schuster, 1967.

Coll, Charles J., and Gabrielle Rosiere. *Dancing Made Easy*. New York: Edward J. Clode, 1922 Edition.

*Collier, James Lincoln. *Benny Goodman and the Swing Era*. New York: Oxford University Press, 1989.

Cree, A.M. *Handbook of Ball-room Dancing, by Paymaster-Commander A.M. Cree, R.N., with an Introduction by George Grossmith; illustrated with diagrams*. New York: John Lane Company, 1920.

*Cressey, Paul G. *The Taxi-Dance Hall: A Sociological Stud in Commercialized Recreation and City Life*. Montclair, NJ: Patterson Smith, 1932, reprint 1969.

Croce, Arlene. *The Fred Astaire & Ginger Rogers Book*. New York: Galahad Books, 1972.

*Dannett, Sylvia G.L., and Frank R. Rachel. *Down Memory Lane: Arthur Murray's Picture Story of Social Dancing*. New York: Greenberg Publishing, 1954.

*Dawson, Jim. *The Twist: The Story of the Song and Dance That Changed the World*. Boston: Faber and Faber, Inc., 1995.

De Forrest, Romayne. *How to Dance & What to Dance*. Chicago: Shrewsbury Publishing Co. S, 1930.

De Frantz, Thomas F., ed. *Dancing Many Drums: Excavations in African American Dance*. Madison, WI: The University of Wisconsin Press, 2002.

*DeMille, Agnes. *America Dances*. New York: Macmillan Publishing Co., 1980.

Dillon, John, and H.W. Lytle. *From Dance Hall to White Slavery: The World's Greatest Tragedy*. Chicago: Charles C. Thompson Co., 1912.

Dodds, John W. "Living in Small-town and Rural America." In *The 1900s*. Edited by Myra H. Immell. San Diego, CA: Greenhaven Press, 2000.

*Driver, Ian. *A Century of Dance: A Hundred Years of Musical Movement, from Waltz to Hip Hop*. London: Octopus Publishing Group Limited, 2000.

Erenberg, Lewis A. *Steppin' Out: New York Nightlife and the Transformation of American Culture*. Westport, CT: Greenwood Press, 1981.

*Erenberg, Lewis A. *Swingin' the Dream: Big Band Jazz and the Rebirth of American Culture*. Chicago: University of Chicago Press, 1998.

Faulkner, Thomas A. *From the Ball-Room to Hell*. Chicago: R.F. Henry, 1894.

Fishwick, Marshall. "The Twist: Brave New Whirl." In *I See America Dancing: Selected Readings 1685–2000*. Edited by Maureen Needham. Chicago: University of Illinois Press, 2002, 123–126.

Fitzgerald, F. Scott. *The Great Gatsby*. 75th Anniversary, Scribner Paperback Edition. New York: Simon and Schuster, 1995.

Fletcher, Beale. *How to Improve Your Social Dancing with the Fletcher Count System*. Canada: The Copp Clark Company, Ltd., 1956.

Flores, Juan. "Cha-Cha with a Backbeat: Songs and Stories of Latin Boogaloo." in *Situating Salsa*. Edited by Lise Waxer. London: Routledge, 2002, 75–99.

Foner, Eric. *The Story of American Freedom*. New York: Norton, 1998.

Frazier, E. Franklin. *Black Bourgeoisie*. New York: The Free Press, 1957.

Freeman, Damita Jo. "Hi, I'm Damita Jo Freeman and I'm Going to Teach You to Dance Funky like on 'Soul Train.'" In *Dancing Madness*. Edited by Abe Peck. New York: Anchor Press/Doubleday, 1976, 98–103.

Gaines, Steven. *Discotheque*. Greenwich, CT: Fawcett Publications, Inc., 1977.

Gambino, Richard. *Blood of My Blood: The Dilemma of the Italian-Americans*. Garden City, NY: Doubleday and Company, 1974.

Gardner, Ella. *Public Dance Halls: Their Regulation and Place in the Recreation of Adolescents Bureau Publication No. 189*. Washington, D.C.: United States Government Printing Office, 1929.

Gargiulo, Vince. *Palisade Amusement Park: A Century of Fond Memories*. New Brunswick, NJ: Rutgers University Press, 1995.

Gilbert, Jeremy, and Ewan Pearson. *Discographies: Dace Music, Culture and the Politics of Sound*. London: Routledge Publishing, 1999.

Gilmour, H.B. *Saturday Night Fever*. New York: Bantam Books, 1977.

*Giordano, Ralph G. *Fun and Games in Twentieth Century America: A Historical Guide to Leisure*. Westport: Greenwood, 2003.

Glassman, Judith. *The Year In Music 1979*. New York: Columbia House and Gladstone Books, 1979.

*Goldman, Albert. *Disco*. New York: Hawthorn Books, Inc., 1978.

*Goodman, Benny, and Irving Kolodin. *The Kingdom of Swing*. New York: Frederick Ungar Publishing Company, 1939 (reprint 1961).

Grover, Kathryn, ed. *Hard at Play: Leisure in America, 1840–1940*. Amherst: The University of Massachusetts Press, 1992.

Gulliford, Andrew. "Fox and Geese in the School Yard." In *Hard at Play: Leisure in America, 1840–1940*. Edited by Kathryn Grover. Amherst: University of Massachusetts Press, 1992.

Haden-Guest, Anthony. *The Last Party: Studio 54, Disco, and The Culture of the Night*. New York: William Morrow and Company, Inc., 1997.

Halberstam, David. *The Fifties*. New York: Metro Books, 2001.

*Hanson, Kitty. *Disco Fever*. New York: The New American Library, Inc., 1978.

Hanson, Kitty. *Touch Dancing*. New York: The New American Library, Inc., 1978.

*Harris, Jane A., Anne M. Pittmann, and Marlys S. Waller. *Social Dance: From Dance a While*. Boston, MA: Allyn and Bacon, 1998.

Harris, Jane A., Anne M. Pittmann, Marlys S. Waller, and Cathy L. Dark. *Dance a While: Handbook for Folk, Square, Contra, and Social Dance*. 8th ed. Boston, MA: Allyn and Bacon, 2000.

*Hazzard-Gordon, Katrina. *Jookin' The Rise of Social Dance Formations in African American Culture*. Philadelphia: Temple University Press, 1990.

Hechinger, Grace and Fred M. *Teen-age Tyranny*. New York: Fawcett Books, 1963.

Hibbert, Toots. "Hi, I'm Toots Hibbert and I'm Going to Teach You to Dance to Reggae." In *Dancing Madness*. Edited by Abe Peck. New York: Anchor Press/Doubleday, 1976, 87–91.

Hilliard, Robert L., and Michael C. Keith. *The Broadcast Century and Beyond: A Biography of American Broadcasting*. 3rd ed. Boston: Focal Press, 2001.

Holleran, Andrew. *Dancer from the Dance*. New York: Harper Collins, 1978.

Horsham, Michael. *20s and 30s Style*. Secaucus, NJ: Chartwell Books, 1989.

Hostetler, Lawrence A. *The Art of Social Dancing: A Text Book for Teachers and Students*. 1st ed. New York: A.S. Barnes and Company, Inc., 1930.

Hostetler, Lawrence A. *The Art of Social Dancing: A Text Book for Teachers and Students*. 3rd ed. New York: A.S. Barnes and Company, Inc., 1934.

Hostetler, Lawrence A. *The Art of Social Dancing: A Text Book for Teachers and Students*. 4th ed. New York: Blue Ribbon Books, Inc., 1936.

The Hullabaloo Discothèque Dance Book. New York: Scholastic Books, 1966.

Humphrey, Don. *What Makes Dancing Wrong?* Great Bend, KS: Don Humphrey, 1963.

Ibrahim, Hilmi. *Leisure and Society: A Comparative Approach*. Dubuque, IA: Wm. C. Brown, 1991.

*Jackson, John A. *American Bandstand: Dick Clark and the Making of a Rock 'n' Roll Empire*. New York: Oxford University Press, 1997.

Jiménez, Carlos M. *The Mexican American Heritage*. Berkeley, CA: TQS Publishing, 1994.

*Jones, Alan, and Jussi Kantonen. *Saturday Night Forever: The Story of Disco*. Chicago: A Capella Books, 2000.

Kaiser, Charles. *The Gay Metropolis, 1940–1996*. London: Weidenfeld and Nicolson, 1999.

Kammen, Michael. *American Culture, American Tastes: Social Change and the 20th Century*. New York: Basic Books, 1999.

Kaplan, Max. *Leisure in America: A Social Inquiry*. New York: John Wiley and Sons, Inc., 1960.

Kent, Steven. *The Ultimate History of Video Games*. Roseville, CA: Prima Publishing, 2001.

Kolata, Gina. *Flu: The Story of the Great Influenza Pandemic of 1918 and the Search for the Virus That Caused It*. New York: Touchstone, 2001.

*Kollmar, Kerry, and Melody Mason. *Roller Disco Dancing*. New York: Sterling Publishing, Inc., 1979.

Kraus, Richard. *Recreation and Leisure in Modern Society*. New York: Appleton-Century-Crofts, 1971.

Kraus, Richard. *Leisure in a Changing America: Multicultural Perspectives*. New York: Macmillan, 1994.

Kraus, Richard, and Sarah Alberti Chapman. *History of the Dance: In Art and Education*. Englewood Cliffs, NJ: Prentice-Hall Inc., 1981.

*Kraus, Richard, Elizabeth Barber, and Ira Shapiro. *Introduction to Leisure Services: Career Perspectives*. Champaign, IL: Sagamore Publishing, 2001.

*K-tel. *Let's Disco: A Complete Instructional System for Disco Dancing*. New York: K-tel International Inc., 1978.

Kyvig, David E. *Daily Life in the United States, 1920–1939: Decades of Promise and Pain*. Westport, CT: Greenwood Press, 2002.

Lambin, Maria Ward. *Report of the Advisory Dance Hall Committee of the Women's City Club and the City Recreation Committee.* New York: The Committee, 1924.

Lanza, Joe. *Bossa Nova: An Original Dance Created by Joe Lanza.* Los Angeles: Labowe and Ventress, 1963.

*Lawrence, Tim. *Love Saves The Day: A History of American Dance Music Culture, 1970–1979.* Durham, NC: Duke University Press, 2003.

Layman, Richard, ed. *American Decades: 1950–1959.* Detroit, MI: Gale Research, 1994.

Layman, Richard, ed *American Decades: 1960–1969.* Detroit, MI: Gale Research, 1995.

Let's Disco: A Complete Instructional System for Disco Dancing. New York: K-tel International Inc., 1978.

Lingeman, Richard R., *Don't You Know There's a War On? The American Home Front, 1941–1945.* New York: Putnam, 1970.

Lundberg, George, et al. *Leisure: A Suburban Study.* New York: Columbia University Press, 1934.

*Lustgarten, Karen. "Hi, I'm Karen Lustgarten and I'm Going to Teach You the L.A. Hustle." In *Dancing Madness.* Edited by Abe Peck. New York: Anchor Press/Doubleday, 1976, 104–109.

*Lustgarten, Karen. *The Complete Guide to Disco Dancing: The Easy Step-by-Step Way to Learn Today's Top Dances.* New York: Warner Books, 1978.

*Lustgarten, Karen. *The Complete Guide to Touch Dancing.* New York: Warner Books, 1979.

Luttmann, Rick, and Gail Luttmann. "Dance In Eskimo Society—An Historical Perspective." In *Focus On Dance: VIII Dance Heritage.* Edited by E. Carmen Imel. Washington, D.C.: AAHPER Publications, 1977.

Lynd, Robert S., and Helen Merrell Lynd. *Middletown: A Study in Contemporary American Culture.* New York: Harcourt, Brace, 1929.

Lynd, Robert S., and Helen Merrell Lynd. *Middletown in Transition: A Study in Cultural Conflicts.* New York: Harcourt, Brace, 1937.

*Maletis, Joelle Rabow. *It's Just a Social, Swing & Latin Thing: A Guide to Social Dancing.* Dubuque, IA: Kendall/Hunt Publishing Company, 2002.

Malnig, Julie. *Dancing Till Dawn: A Century of Exhibition Ballroom Dancing.* Westport, CT: Greenwood Press, 1992.

Marcus, Greil. "Rock Films." In *The Rolling Stone Illustrated History of Rock & Roll.* Edited by Jim Miller. New York: Random House, 1980, 390–400.

Marty, Myron A. *Daily Life in the United States, 1960–1990.* Westport, CT: Greenwood Press, 1997.

Marzano, Dale A. *Roller Disco.* Northbrook, IL: Domus Books, 1979.

*McCarthy, Albert J. *The Dance Band Era: The Dancing Decades from Ragtime to Swing, 1910–1950.*Philadelphia: Chilton Book, 1971, reprint, 1982.

McConnell, Tandy, ed. *American Decades: 1990–1999.* Detroit, MI: Gale Research, 2001.

McCormack, Ed. "No Sober Person Dances." In *Dancing Madness.* Edited by Abe Peck. New York: Anchor Press/Doubleday, 1976, 17–25.

*McDonagh, Don. *Dance Fever.* New York: Random House, Inc., 1979.

McEhrlich, Cindy. "Confessions of the Disco Kid." In *Dancing Madness.* Edited by Abe Peck. New York: Anchor Press/Doubleday, 1976, 31–33.

McQuirter, Marya. "Awkward Moves: Dance Lessons from the 1940s." In *Dancing Many Drums.* Edited by Thomas F. De Frantz. Madison, WI: The University of Wisconsin Press, 2002, 81–103.

Miller, Craig. *Social Dance in the Mormon West.* Salt Lake City: The Utah Arts Council, 2000.

Miller, James. *Flowers in the Dustbin: The Rise of Rock and Roll.* New York: Simon and Schuster, 1999.

*Miller, Norma, and Evette Jensen. *Swingin' at the Savoy: The Memoir of a Jazz Dancer*. Philadelphia: Temple University Press, 1996.

Moore, Patricia Anne. *The Casino: Santa Catalina Island's "Two Million Dollar Palace of Pleasure."* Avalon, CA: Catalina Island Museum Society, Inc., 2002.

Morthland, John. "The Payola Scandal." In *The Rolling Stone Illustrated History of Rock & Roll*. Edited by Jim Miller. New York: Random House, 1980, 101–103.

Moss, George Donelson. *America in the Twentieth Century*. Englewood Cliffs, NJ: Prentice-Hall, 1993.

*Mouvet, Maurice. *Maurice's Art of Dancing*. New York: G. Schirmer, 1915.

Murray, Arthur. *The Modern Dances*. 2 vols. New York: Arthur Murray, 1923.

Murray, Arthur. *Let's Dance*. New York: Standard Brands Incorporated, 1937.

Murray, Arthur. *How to Become a Good Dancer*. New York: Simon and Schuster, 1947.

Murray, Arthur. *How to Become a Good Dancer*. New York: Simon and Schuster, 1954.

Murray, Kathryn, and Betty Hannah Hoffman. *My Husband, Arthur Murray*. New York: Simon and Schuster, 1960.

Myrdal, Gunnar. "Recreation." In *Recreation and Leisure Service for the Disadvantaged*. Edited by John A. Nesbitt, Paul D. Brown, and James F. Murphy. Philadelphia: Lea and Febiger, 1970.

Nasaw, David. *Going Out: The Rise and Fall of Public Amusements*. New York: Basic Books, 1993.

Nash, Gerald D. *The American West Transformed: The Impact of the Second World War*. Bloomington: Indiana University Press, 1985.

*Needham, Maureen, ed. *I See America Dancing: Selected Readings 1685–2000*. Chicago: University of Illinois Press, 2002.

Orlean, Susan. *Saturday Night*. New York: Knopf, 1990.

Orr, William W. *The Christian and Amusements*. Chicago: Moody Press, 1960.

Panati, Charles. *Panati's Parade of Fads, Follies, and Manias*. New York: HarperCollins, 1991.

Pearlroth, Jonathan. *Lambada!* New York: Dell Trade Paperback, 1990.

*Peck, Abe, editor. *Dancing Madness*. New York: Anchor Press/Doubleday, 1976.

Pendergast, Tom, and Sara Pendergast. *St. James Encyclopedia of Popular Culture Volume 1*. Michigan: St. James Press, 2000.

Pendergast, Tom, and Sara Pendergast. *St. James Encyclopedia of Popular Culture Volume 2*. Michigan: St. James Press, 2000.

Pendergast, Tom, and Sara Pendergast. *St. James Encyclopedia of Popular Culture Volume 3*. Michigan: St. James Press, 2000.

Pendergast, Tom, and Sara Pendergast. *St. James Encyclopedia of Popular Culture Volume 4*. Michigan: St. James Press, 2000.

Pendergast, Tom, and Sara Pendergast. *St. James Encyclopedia of Popular Culture Volume 5*. Michigan: St. James Press, 2000.

*Pener, Degen, with foreword by Scotty Morris. *The Swing Book*. New York: Little, Brown and Company, 1999.

Peiss, Kathy. *Cheap Amusements: Working Women and Leisure in Turn-of-the-Century New York*. Philadelphia: Temple University Press, 1986.

Ray, Lillian. *Modern Ballroom Dancing*. Chicago: Franklin Publishing Co., 1936.

*Roberts, John Storm. *The Latin Tinge: The Impact of Latin American Music on the United States*. New York: Oxford University Press, 1999.

Robertson, Frank. "Disco Tech: An All-American DJ Fights the Power." In *Dancing Madness*. Edited by Abe Peck. New York: Anchor Press/Doubleday, 1976, 27–29.

Rollin, Lucy. *Twentieth-century Teen Culture by the Decades*. Westport, CT: Greenwood Press, 1999.

Rose, Kenneth D. *One Nation Underground: The Fallout Shelter in American Culture*. New York: New York University Press, 2001.

Rubin, Lillian Breslow. *Worlds of Pain: Life in the Working-class Family*. New York: Basic Books, 1976.

*Rust, Brian. *The Dance Bands*. New York: Allan Publishing, 1972.

Satori, Rev. Mgr. Don Luigi. *Modern Dances*. Collegeville, IN: St. Joseph's Printing Office, 1910.

Schulman, Bruce J. *The Seventies: The Great Shift in American Culture, Society, and Politics*. Cambridge, MA: Da Capo Press, 2002.

Shomer, Louis. *Swing Steps (Complete Guide to Swing Dancing Self-Taught—Easy! Quick!)*. New York: Padell Book Co., 1943.

*Shore, Michael, with Dick Clark. *The History of American Bandstand: It's Got a Great Beat and You Can Dance to It!* New York: Ballantine Books, 1985.

Silvester, Victor. *Modern Ballroom Dancing*. North Pomfret, VT: Trafalgar Square Publishing, 1993.

Smucker, Tom. "Disco." In *The Rolling Stone Illustrated History of Rock & Roll*. Edited by Jim Miller. New York: Random House/Rolling Stone Press, 1980, 424–434.

Spaeth, Sigmund. *A History of Popular Music in America*. New York: Random House, 1948.

*Stearns, Marshall, and Jean Stearns. *Jazz Dance: The Story of American Vernacular Dance*. New York: Da Capo Press, 1994.

Steiner, Jesse F. *Americans at Play: Recent Trends in Recreation and Leisure Time Activities*. New York: McGraw-Hill, 1933.

Steiner, Jesse F. *Studies in the Social Aspects of the Depression: Research Memorandum on Recreation in the Depression*. New York: Arno Press, 1972.

*Stephenson, Richard M., and Joseph Iaccarino. *The Complete Book of Ballroom Dancing*. New York: Doubleday, 1992.

Stocking, Collis. *A Study of Dance Halls in Pittsburgh*. Pittsburgh: Pittsburgh Girls Conference, 1925.

*Stowe, David W. *Swing Changes: Big-band Jazz in New Deal America*. Cambridge, MA: Harvard University Press, 1994.

Sweet, Jill D. "Keeping the Rituals Alive." In *I See America Dancing*. Edited by Maureen Needham. Chicago: University of Illinois Press, 2002, 40–46.

Thomas, Bob. *Let's Dance with Marge and Gower Champion as told to Bob Thomas*. New York: Grosset and Dunlap, 1954.

Time-Life Books. *Rock & Roll Generation: Teen life in the 50s*. Alexandria, VA: Time Life Books, 1998.

Time-Life Books. *This Fabulous Century: 1900–1910*. Vol. 1. New York: Time-Life Books, 1969.

Time-Life Books. *This Fabulous Century: 1910–1920*. Vol. 2. New York: Time-Life Books, 1969.

Time-Life Books. *This Fabulous Century: 1920–1930*. Vol. 3. New York: Time-Life Books, 1969.

Time-Life Books. *This Fabulous Century: 1930–1940*. Vol. 4. New York: Time-Life Books, 1969.

Time-Life Books. *This Fabulous Century: 1940–1950*. Vol. 5. New York: Time-Life Books, 1969.

Time-Life Books. *This Fabulous Century: 1950–1960*. Vol. 6. New York: Time-Life Books, 1970.

Time-Life Books. *This Fabulous Century: 1960–1970*. Vol. 7. New York: Time-Life Books, 1970.

Tompkins, Vincent, ed. *American Decades: 1900–1909*. Detroit, MI: Gale Research, 1996.

Tompkins, Vincent, ed. *American Decades: 1910–1919.* Detroit, MI: Gale Research, 1996.

Tomko, Linda J. *Dancing Class: Gender, Ethnicity, and Social Divides in American Dance, 1890–1920.* Bloomington: Indiana University Press, 1999.

Trotter, Joe William, Jr. *The African American Experience.* Vol. 2, *From Reconstruction.* New York: Houghton Mifflin, 2001.

U.S. Census Bureau. *Statistical Abstract of the United States: 1987.* Washington D.C., 1986.

U.S. Census Bureau. *Statistical Abstract of the United States: 1995.* Washington D.C., 1994.

U.S. Census Bureau. *Statistical Abstract of the United States: 1996.* Washington D.C., 1995.

U.S. Census Bureau. *Statistical Abstract of the United States: 1999.* Washington D.C., 1998.

U.S. Census Bureau. *Statistical Abstract of the United States: 2000.* Washington D.C., 1999.

Uschan, Michael V., ed. *The 1910s.* San Diego: Lucent Books, 1999.

*Uslan, Michael, and Bruce Solomon. *Dick Clark's the First 25 Years of Rock and Roll.* New York: Dell, 1981.

*Vale, V., and Marian Wallace, eds. *Swing! The New Retro Renaissance.* San Francisco: V/Search Publications, 1998.

Vermorel, Judy and Fred. *Fandemonium! The Book of Fan Cults & Dance Crazes.* London: Omnibus Press, 1989.

*Wagner, Ann. *Adversaries of Dance: From the Puritans to the Present.* Chicago: University of Illinois Press, 1997.

Walker, Caroline. *Modern Dances: Tango, Castle Walk, Hesitation Waltz, One-Step, Dream Waltz.* Chicago: Saul Brothers, 1914.

*Walker, Leo. *The Wonderful Era of the Great Dance Bands.* New York: Da Capo Press, 1990.

Walker, Stanley. *The Night Club Era.* New York: Frederick A. Stokes Co., 1933 (Reprint, Baltimore: Johns Hopkins University Press, 1999).

Walsh, David. "Saturday Night Fever: An Ethnography of Disco Dancing." In *Dance, Gender and Culture.* Edited by Helen Thomas. New York: St. Martin's Press, 1993.

Ward, Ed, Geoffrey Stokes, and Ken Tucker. *Rock of Ages: the Rolling Stone History of Rock and Roll.* New York: Rolling Stone Press, 1986, 524.

Washburne, Christopher. "Salsa Romántica: An Analysis of Style." In *Situating Salsa.* Edited by Lise Waxer. London: Routledge, 2002, 101–110.

*Waxer, Lise, ed. *Situating Salsa: Global Markets and Local Meanings in Latin Popular Music.* London: Routledge, 2002.

White, Betty. *How to Mambo.* New York: David McKay Company, Inc., 1955.

Whitfield, Stephen J. *The Culture of the Cold War.* 2nd ed. Baltimore, MD: Johns Hopkins University Press, 1996.

Williams, Juan. *Eyes on the Prize: America's Civil Rights Years, 1954–1965.* New York: Penguin Books, 1987.

Wrenn, C. Gilbert, and D.L. Harley. *Time on Their Hands: A Report on Leisure, Recreation and Young People.* Washington, D.C.: American Council on Education, 1941.

Veloz, Frank, and Yolanda Casazza. *Tango & Rumba: The Dances of Today and Tomorrow.* New York: Harper and Brothers Publishers, 1938.

X, Malcolm, and Alex Haley. *The Autobiography of Malcolm X.* New York: Ballantine Books Hardcover Edition, 1999.

Youmans, John G. *Social Dance.* Pacific Palisades, CA: Goodyear Publishing Company, Inc., 1969.

Zile, Judy Van. "Japanese Bon Dance Survivals in Hawaii." In *I See America Dancing.* Edited by Maureen Needham. Chicago: University of Illinois Press, 2002, 75–81.

Unpublished Dissertations

Batiuchok, Margaret. "The Lindy: Origin and Development of the Lindy hop 1927–1941." Student paper, New York University, 1988. http://www.swingcraze.com/ussds/Lindy-Hop/LindyThesis/lindy-thesis88-all.html (accessed December 28, 2003).

Chapman, Beverly Armstrong. "New Dance in New York: 1911–1915." Master's thesis, The American University, 1977. Microfilm Copy University Microfilms International, Ann Arbor, Michigan.

Johnson, Celisse Greer. "Popular Dance Styles of the 1920's in Harlem, New York." M.A. thesis, University of California, Los Angeles, 1986.

Youmans, John G. "A History of Recreational Social Dance in the United States." Ph.D. thesis, University of Southern California, 1966.

Periodicals

Abwin, Don. "Wheaton College to Make History by Holding a Dance." *The Associated Press*, November 13, 2003, http://web.lexis-nexis.com/universe/document?_m=241b65a4f6041ab094bdd45aa56f5dc7&_docnum=50&wchp=dGLbVzb-zSkVb&_md5=eb87a237d71eb395b3c1a34c79f02622.

Adler, Jerry, and Barbara Burgower. "Beating the Devil." *Newsweek* magazine, July 2, 1984, 52.

"Admit New Dances to Roofs of Hotels." *The New York Times*, May 31, 1914, Sec. 2, p. 12.

AFI (American Film Institute). "The Apache Dancer." AFI.com (1923 Charles R. Seeling Director), http://www.afi.com/members/catalog/AbbrView.aspx?s=1&Movie=2609 (accessed May 17, 2004).

"Alan Freed." *The History of Rock 'n' Roll: The Golden Decade 1954–1963*. http://www.history-of-rock.com/freed.htm (accessed July 17, 2004).

"Alan Freed Is Out in 'Payola' Study." *The New York Times*, November 22, 1959, 1.

Alden, Robert. "1,000 Twisters and One Floor Swing at Venerable Palladium." *The New York Times*, June 4, 1964, 28.

Alexander, Ron. "Hustling Off to Dance Classes." *The New York Times*, December 4, 1981, B12.

Allen, Mike. "Kathryn Murray Dies at 92; Coaxed Many to 'Try Dancing.'" *The New York Times*, August 8, 1999, 9.

"All New York Now Madly Whirling the Tango." *The New York Times*, January 4, 1914, SM 8.

Aloff, Mindy. "Behind the Scenes: Burn the Floor." PBS.org, http://www.pbs.org/wnet/gperf/burnthefloor/behind.html (accessed May 27, 2004).

"An American Ballroom Companion: Dance Instruction Manuals Ca. 1490–1920." Music Division, Library of Congress, Washington, D.C., http://lcweb2.loc.gov/ammem/dihtml (accessed December 31, 2003).

"American Bandstand's 25th Anniversary." ABC Photo Release, January 28, 1977, Temple University Libraries, Urban Archives, Philadelphia Pennsylvania.

"American Twist or Twisted Americans?" *Senior Scholastic* magazine, January 10, 1962, 13.

"Anti-Disco Rally Halts White Sox." *The New York Times*, July 13, 1979, A16.

Asbury, Edith Evans. "Rock 'n' Roll Teen-Agers Tie Up the Times Square Area." *The New York Times*, February 23, 1957, 1, 12.

Asbury, Edith Evans. "Times SQ. 'Rocks' For Second Day."*The New York Times*, February 24, 1957, 37.

Attwell, E.T. "Recreation in Colored Communities." *The Playground* 19, no. 12 (March 1926): 657.

Badasski, Scoop. "The Inside Scoop."*Swing Time Magazine* Issue no. 11 (1998): 50–51.

Badasski, Scoop. "The Inside Scoop."*Swing Time Magazine* Issue no. 13 (1998): 50.

Baldacci, Leslie. "Swing Sets: 40s Craze Catches on with Modern Club Hoppers." *Chicago Sun-Times*, August 9, 1998, NC1.

Bangs, Lester. "Village People Join the Y." *Rolling Stone* magazine, April 19, 1979, Issue no. 289, 90–92, 95.

Banks, Nancy. "The World's Most Beautiful Ballrooms." *Chicago History*, 2, no. 4, (1973): 206–215.

Barzel, Ann. "The First 75 Years." *Dance Magazine*, June 2002, http://www.findarticles. com/cf_dls/m1083/6_76/87022585/p1/article.jhtml (accessed July 17, 2004).

City of Baxter Springs v. Bryant, 226 Kan. 383, 598 P.2d 1051, 1057 (1979), http://www. constitution.org/becraft/limits1.rtf.

"Beating Chi's Cabaret Law." *Variety*, July 5, 1918, 3.

"Beauty of Old Spain Is Found at the Aragon." *Chicago Evening American*, July 15, 1926, 1.

Bell, Joseph N. "Imagine That—Dr. Kelly, the Old Hoofer." *National Observer*, June 20, 1966 (Source quoted in Stearns and Stearns, *Jazz Dance*, 355).

Berger, Meyer. "Jive Bombers Jamboree." *Colliers*, June 5, 1943, 18–19.

Bickel, Nardy Baeza. "Footloose at Cornerstone; University Drops Six-Decade Prohibition on Social Dancing." *The Grand Rapids Press*, October 6, 2004, A1.

Binford, Jesse F. "Taxi-Dance Halls." *The Journal of Social Hygiene* (1933): 502–509.

Blau, Eleanor. "The Stalking of Random Victims Has Terrified Public Over Years." *The New York Times*, June 29, 1977, 85.

Blum, Howard. "Police To Restrict Parking By Couples." *The New York Times*, August 6, 1977, 1, 42.

"The Bossa Nova." *Newsweek* magazine, November 26, 1962, LX, no. 22, 82.

"Boston Common to Hoot Mon Belt They Rock 'n' Riot Out of This Veldt." *Variety*, May 7, 1958, 1, 58.

Bosworth, Patricia. "At Honka Monka and Roseland, Dancing Their Troubles Away." *The New York Times*, March 7, 1971, 62.

Bowman, LeRoy E., and Maria Ward Lambin. "Evidences of Social Relations as Seen in Types of New York City Dance Halls." *Journal of Social Forces* 3, no. 2 (January 1925): 286–291.

Bracker, Milton. "Experts Propose Study Of Craze." *The New York Times*, February 23, 1957, 12.

Branam, Chris. "John Brown University Content with its Ban on Dancing." *Arkansas Democrat–Gazette*, February 1, 2004, http://web.lexis-lexis.com/universe/document? _m=7aa42c4d3dd1c80825c16e06c305499e&_docnum=12&wchp=dGLbVzb-zSkVb&_md5= d83331c0bdb2731ba9d568de68dbc3a5 (accessed January 7, 2005).

"Breakin', Plot Summary for." IMDb.com, http://www.imdb.com/title/tt0086998/ plotsummary (accessed January 27, 2005).

"Brian Setzer." ArtistInformation.com, http://www.artistinformation.com/brian_ setzer_orchestral (accessed February 10, 2001).

Bronner, Ethan. "Ballroom Dancing Gains New Popularity on Campus." *The New York Times*, January 1, 1999, http://www.nytimes.com/library/national/ 010199educ-dance-ballroom.html (accessed 9 August 2004).

Brown, Ethan. "Let's Dance! A New Move Is Afoot to Change the Cabaret Laws—But Watch Out for Rave." NewYorkMetro.com, http://www.newyorkmetro.com/nymetro/ nightlife/barsclubs/features/6265/ (accessed February 21, 2005).

Brown, Ethan. "Safe to Dance." Cityside NewYorkMetro.com, http://newyorkmetro.com/ nymetro/news/trends/columns/cityside/n_8430 (accessed November 26, 2004).

City of Buffalo. "Dance Halls: Ordinances Governing the Conduct of Public Dances and Dance Halls." Issued by the Common Council 1914 (Library of Congress).

"The Bunny Hug." StreetSwing.com Dance History Archives, http://www.streetswing. com/histmain/z3bunny.htm (accessed March 24, 2004).

"Cabarets Confound the Dance Masters." *The New York Times*, September 12, 1915, 10.

Cab Calloway Web site: http://www.cabcalloway.cc/notes_of_interest.htm.

Callahan, Tom. "Break Dancers Form Crews and Battle To The Beat." *The New York Times*, September 23, 1984, WC27.

Campbell, Gail A. "The Lambada Hype; How A Dance Craze Was Invented." *The Washington Times*, February 13, 1990, E1.

Capeci, Dominick J., Jr. "Walter F. White and the Savoy Ballroom Controversy of 1943." *Afro- Americans in New York Life and History* 5, no. 2 (July 1981): 13–32.

Carman, John. "All the Right Moves PBS Goes Back to the Ballroom." *San Francisco Chronicle*, February 7, 1996, E-1.

Catto, Susan. "Here to There, Cheek to Cheek." *The New York Times*, December 28, 2003: Travel Section 5, 2.

Cedar Point Amusement Park. "A Historical Perspective," http://www.cedarpoint.com/public/news/history/m.cfm (accessed April 9, 2004).

Cedar Point Amusement Park. "A History of Cedar Point," http://www.cedarpoint.com/public/news/history/g.cfm (accessed April 24, 2004).

"Censorship Incidents 1950s." Parental Advisory: Music Censorship in America, http://ericnuzum.com/banned/incidents/50s.html (accessed July 4, 2004).

"Censorship Incidents 1960s." Parental Advisory: Music Censorship in America, http://ericnuzum.com/banned/incidents/60s.html (accessed July 4, 2004).

"Censorship Incidents 1970s," Parental Advisory: Music Censorship in America, http://ericnuzum.com/banned/incidents/70s.html (accessed July 4, 2004).

"Censorship Incidents 1980s." Parental Advisory: Music Censorship in America, http://ericnuzum.com/banned/incidents/80s.html (accessed July 4, 2004).

"Censorship Incidents 1990s," Parental Advisory: Music Censorship in America, http://ericnuzum.com/banned/incidents/50s.html (accessed July 4, 2004).

"Censorship Incidents 2000s." Parental Advisory: Music Censorship in America, http://ericnuzum.com/banned/incidents/00s.html (accessed July 4, 2004).

Chasten, John Charles. "The Prehistory of Samba: Carnival Dancing in Rio de Janeiro, 1840–1917." *Journal of Latin America Studies* 28, no. 1 (February 1996): 29–47.

Chenoweth, N. "Break Dance Warning." *Telegraph*, January 2, 1985.

"CHIC Fan Club Bio 1979." ChicTribute.com, http://www.chictribute.com/glens/texts/text01.html (accessed December 27, 2004).

Christman, Ed. "Inside Mosh: Understanding 'America's No. 1 Dance.'" *Billboard*, May 16, 1992, 1, 22.

"Chubby Checker." WCBSFM.Com, http://wcbsfm.com/halloffame/local_story_1287051039_html/resources_storyPrintableView (accessed 18 May 2004).

Chun, Kimberly. "In The Swing." *The San Francisco Chronicle*, July 10, 1998, http://www.sfgate.com/cgi-bin/article.cgi?file=/chronicle/archive/1998/07/10/PN33635.DTL (accessed October 29, 2004).

City Arts. "The Uncut Interview with Frankie Manning." Transcript City Arts Show No. 11, http://www.wnet.org/cityarts4/week11/my_html/uncut-week11.html (accessed November 11, 1998).

Clark, Roy Milton. "The Dance Party as a Socialization Mechanism for Black Urban Pre-Adolescents and Adolescents." *Sociology and Sociological Research* 58 (1974): 145–154.

"Cleveland's Municipal Dancing Pavilions." *The American City*, January 10, 1914, 34–35.

Clinton, Larry. "Swing Is the Tempo of Our Time." *The New York Times*, February 26, 1939, E9.

Cohn, Nik. "Tribal Rites of the New Saturday Night." *New York* magazine, vol. 9, no. 23, June 7, 1976, 31–43.

Cowley, Susan Cheever. "The Travolta Hustle." *Newsweek*, vol. XCI, no. 22, May 29, 1978, 97.

"Cradle of the Twist." *The Twist* magazine, The Girl Friend–The Boy Friend Corp., New York, 1962, 4–9.

Crease, Robert. "John Lucchese." SavoyBallroom.com, http://www.savoyballroom.com/exp/dancefloor/savoydancers/jlucchese.htm (accessed April 27, 2004).

"Cries of Burning Negroes Heard for Blocks, Identity of Dead Unknown Early this Morning, Many Who Escaped Given Treatment and Many May Die, Fire Caught at Front of Building to Trap Negroes." *The Natchez Democrat*, April 24, 1940, NatchezSites.com, http://www.natchezsites.com/history/rhythmclub.html (accessed June 1, 2004).

"The Dance Craze—If Dying—Is a Remarkable Invalid." *Vanity Fair*, February 1915, 34.

"Dance Craze Stays But Amateurs Rule." *The New York Times*, November 13, 1913, 20.

"Dance Masters Fight Jazz." *The New York Times*, August 7, 1923, 17.

"Dancetime Publications: 500 Years of Dance." http://www.dancetimepublications.com (accessed December 31, 2003).

"Dancing Classrooms." American Ballroom Theater.com, http://www.americanballroomtheater.com/dancingclassrooms.htm (accessed June 17, 2004).

"Dancing Studios Face Coast Study." *The New York Times*, October 1, 1962, 35.

"David Berkowitz." *Court TV's Crime Library*. http://www.courttv.com/schedule (accessed online November 21, 2004).

Davis, Giancarlo. "Royal Crown Revue." *Swing Time Magazine* Issue no. 11 (1998): 27–33.

DeKoven Bowen, Louise. "The Public Dance Halls of Chicago." The Juvenile Protective Association of Chicago, 1917.

Della Cava, Marco R. "USA Is Sampling a Spicy New dance." *USA Today*, January 16, 1990, 1D.

"Deney Terrio." Disco Step-by-Step Web site, http://www.discostepbystep.com/deney_terrio.htm (accessed May 24, 2004).

"Denounces Modern Dances." *The New York Times*, March 2, 1914, 5.

"Dick Clark Had Interest in 17 Music Companies." *Philadelphia Daily News*, March 4, 1960. Temple University Libraries Urban Archives, Philadelphia, Pennsylvania.

Dimitriadis, Greg. "Hip-hop: From Live Performance to Mediated Narrative." *Popular Music*, 15, no. 2 (May 1996): 179–194.

"Disco Fever, Plot Summary for." IMDb.com, http://www.imdb.com/title/tt0118749/plotsummary (accessed November 21, 2004).

"Disco '77, Plot Summary for." IMdB.com, http://www.imdb.com/title/tt0424625 (accessed November 21, 2004).

Donahue, Lois. "Dancing on the Seven Seas." *The WorkingVacation.com*. http://www.theworkingvacation.com/text/dancing_at_sea.html (accessed July 17, 2004).

Dougherty, Philip H. "Now the Latest Craze Is 1-2-3, All Fall Down: Discotheques Greet La Bostela From France." *The New York Times*, February 11, 1965, 43.

Doup, Liz. "High-stepping on the High Seas." *The Houston Chronicle*, November 6, 2003, http://www.chron.com/cs/CDA/ssistory.mpl/travel/cruise/2173587.

Dunlap, David W. "Nightclub to Reopen in Gothic Church." *The New York Times*, May 27, 1998, B8.

Dunning, Jennifer. "Ballroom Week: Let's Face the Music and Dance." *The New York Times*, April 21, 1981, C1.

Dunning, Jennifer. "Roseland: At 62 Keeps in Step with the 80's." *The New York Times*, July 24, 1981, C1.

Eliscu, Jenny. "No *Dancing*: Congress Presses for Anti-rave Legislation." *Rolling Stone Magazine*, October 17, 2002, Issue 907, 25.

Ellison, Ralph, and J. McPherson. "Invisible Man." Atlantic, December 1970, 50.

Errico, Marcus. "Writer Admits Faking 'Saturday Night Fever' Story." *E! Online News*, December 5, 1997. http://www.eonline.com/News/Items/0,1,2190,00.html (accessed May 27, 2004).

Esterow, Milton. "Chubby Checker Twists Upward." *The New York Times*, March 27, 1962, 34.

"Ethics Code Signed By 3 Dance Studios After State Inquiry." *The New York Times*, October 15, 1959, 47.

Farber, James. "Chic Is Less than Meets the Ear." *Rolling Stone Magazine*, April 19, 1979, Issue no. 289, 32.

Farley, Christopher John. "Hip-Hop Nation." *Time.com* February 8, 1999. http://www.time.com/time/magazine/article/0,9171,19134,00.html (accessed June 19, 2002).

Faulkner, Anne Shaw. "Does Jazz Put the Sin in Syncopation?" *Ladies' Home Journal*, vol. 30, August 1921, 16–34.

Felson, Leonard. "Dancers Waltz Back to an Earlier Era." *The New York Times*, December 19, 1993, 12.

Feron, Jeanne Clare. "Roller Skating + Disco Dancing = Two Hit Rinks." *The New York Times*, December 24, 1978, WC9.

Flint, Peter B. "Killer Joe Piro, Who Popularized Discotheque Dancing, Dies at 68." *The New York Times*, February 9, 1989, B15.

Fong-Torres, Ben. "Dirty Dancing in the Next Decade The Lambada—A Sensuous Brazilian Dance Craze." *The San Francisco Chronicle*, December 12, 1989, B3.

"Ford Townsmen Object to His Dances." *The New York Times*, December 16, 1926, 22.

Frank, Stanley. "They'd Rather Dance Than Eat." *Saturday Evening Post*, October 12, 1957, 24–25, 114–120.

Gaines-Carter, Patrice. "A Dance That Has Everyone in Step." *The Washington Post*, July 23, 1989, W10.

Gelb, Arthur. "Habitues of Meyer Davis Land Dance the Twist." *The New York Times*, October 19, 1961, 37, 39.

Gilmore, Mikal. "Disco!" *Rolling Stone Magazine*, April 19, 1979, Issue no. 289, 9, 54.

Gold, Sylviane. "Dancing in Tongues: A New Hula Speaks Every Language from Ancient Hawaiian Chant to Hip-Hop (but Not Waikiki Hotel)." *The New York Times*, August 8, 2004, AR 8.

Gonzalez, Fernando. "Dirty Dancing with a World Beat." *The Boston Globe*, February 15, 1990, 73.

González, Rafael Jesus. "Pachuco: The Birth of a Creole Language." *Arizona Quarterly* (1975): 343–356.

Gray, Christopher. "An Old-Fashioned Dance to the Music of Time." *The New York Times*, October 13, 1996, R5.

Greenbaum, Lucy. "Fighters With a Boogie Beat." *The New York Times Magazine*, December 17, 1942, 10–11.

Greenhouse, Linda. "Supreme Court Lets Stand a Missouri Town's Ban on School Dances." *The New York Times*, April 17, 1990, A22.

"Grizzly Bear." StreetSwing.com Dance History Archives, http://www.streetswing.com/histmain/z3grzber.htm (accessed March 24, 2004).

Hamlin, Jesse. "Flashy, Fleshy SF Debut of Lambada." *The San Francisco Chronicle*, January 8, 1990, F1.

Hammer, Alexander R. "Fad Also Rocks Cash Registers." *The New York Times*, February 23, 1957, 12.

Harrington, Richard. "Back in the Swing." *The Washington Post*, October 26, 1998, http://www.washingtonpost.com/wp-srv/style/music/features/swing1026.htm (accessed July 17, 2004).

Bibliography

Harrington, Richard. "Dancing Hip to Hip; The Erotic Lambada from the Tropics Is a Hot, Hot Topic." *The Washington Post*, March 16, 1990, B1.

"Having Fun Dancing." Nebraska Living History Farm Project, http://www. livinghistoryfarm.org/farminginthe30s/life_18.html (accessed July 17, 2004).

Hazzard-Gordon, Katrina. "African-American Vernacular Dance: Core Culture and Meaning Operatives." *Journal of Black Studies* 15, no. 4 (June 1985): 427–445.

Hiller, Francis H. "The Working of County Dance Hall Ordinances in Wisconsin." *Journal of Social Hygiene* XIII (January 1927): 1–11.

Himmelsbach, Erik, and Jennifer Vineyard. "Swingin' Safari: Americas Moving Their Feet to California's Not So Brand New Beat." *BAM Magazine* 24, no. 17 (August 28, 1998): Issue no. 541, 18–22.

Hinckley, David. "Not the Soda Fountain Type." *The New York Daily News*, May 4, 2004, http://www.nydailynews.com/city_life/big_town/v-pfriendly/story/189750p-164173c. html (accessed June 23, 2004).

Hochsmender, Woody. "Slam Dancing: Checking in with L.A. Punk." *Rolling Stone*, May 14, 1981, 29–31.

Holder, Geoffrey. "The Twist? 'It's Not a Dance." *The New York Times*, December 3, 1961, SM 78.

Holden, Stephen. "The Evolution of a Dance Craze: How Millions Got Happy Feet." *Rolling Stone Magazine* April 19, 1979, Issue no. 289, 28–30.

Holden, Stephen. "Club Kids: Starry Eyes and Blurry Minds." *The New York Times*, March 6, 1998, E32.

"Hot Music At Carnegie." *The New York Times*, January 18, 1938, 22.

"How America Has Run Out of Time." *TIME.com*, April 24, 1989 (accessed June 30, 2004).

Howard, Peter. "The King and Queen of Ballroom Dancing." *Dance Magazine* LXXIII, no. 10 (October 1999): 78–81.

"How HAIR Came to Broadway." *Hair Pages*, http://www.geocities.com/hairpages/ hairhistory.html (accessed November 17, 2004).

"How to Twist." *The Twist* Magazine, The Girl Friend–The Boy Friend Corp. New York, 1962, 22–25.

Hubbell, Sue. "Farewell 'Do-Si-Do,' Hello Scoot and Counter…Percolate!" *Smithsonian*, 26, no. 11 (February 1996): 93–99.

Hughes, Alan. "Though The Fad Is Gone, Twisting Lives On." *The New York Times*, July 28, 1963, 72.

Hynes, Warren. "Yeeee-Ha! It's time to get off the couch and into the barn; country line dancing is sweeping Staten Island." *Staten Island Advance*, June 5, 1995, B1, B6.

Hynes, Warren. "Swing Time." *Staten Island Advance*, June 10, 1997, D1.

"If It's Sunday, It's the Cat Club: Swing Dancing Takes Over Again." *The New York Times*, December 30, 1990, 35.

"Interview with Marty Angelo." DiscoStepbyStep.com, http://www.discostepbystep.com/ martyinterview.htm (accessed July 4, 2004).

"Is Buffalo Gig World's Largest?" *Billboard* magazine, September 8, 1979.

"Is the Twist Immoral?" *TV, Radio Mirror* magazine, June 1962, 72.

"Itsy-Bitsy Dance Craze." *The New York Times*, September 1, 1996, H25.

"Jazz." *Microsoft Encarta Encyclopedia 2000*. © 1993–1999 Microsoft Corporation.

Jewell, Edwin S. "Adults Play in Omaha." *The Playground*, 19, no. 12 (March 1926): 668.

"Jitterbugs." *Life* magazine, 10, no. 8, August 9, 1938, 9.

Johnson, Charles S. "A Survey of the Negro Population of Fort Wayne (Indiana)." Department of Research and Investigations, National Urban League, New York (1928). A machine-readable transcription, http://memory.loc.gov/cgi-bin/query/r?ammem/cool: @field(DOCID+@lit(mu04103) (accessed September 24, 2001).

Johnson, Troy. "How Dancing in Rock Became Uncool." *San Diego City Beat*, January 22, 2003, http://www.sdcitybeat.com/article.php?id=473 (accessed June 30, 2004).

Jones, James T., IV. "Dancers Line Up for a 'Boogie' Charge." *USA Today*, July 25, 1989, 4D.

The Journal of the American Medical Association (December 28, 1918): 2154–2175.

Katz, Lina. "Village Voice." *The Village Voice*, August 22–28, 2001, http://www.legalizedancingnyc.com/articles/katz.html (accessed 21 February 2005).

Kempley, Rita. "A Whole Lotta Lambada." *The Washington Post*, March 17, 1990, D2.

Keys, Lisa. "Gotta Dance? There's Not a Lotta Options in Rudy's N.Y." *Forward* magazine, August 17, 2001, http://www.legalizedancingnyc.com/articles/forward.html (accessed February 21, 2005).

Kihss, Peter. "Calls on .44 Killer Deluge Police, But Few Substantial Clues Result." *The New York Times*, August 3, 1977, A1, A13.

"The 'King of Twist' Tells How It All Started." *The Twist* Magazine, The Girl Friend–The Boy Friend Corp. New York, 1962, 10–14.

Kleiman, Dena. "The 'Hustle' Restores Old Touch to Dancing." *The New York Times*, July 12, 1975, 16.

Kopkind, Andrew. "The Dialectic of Disco: Gay Music Goes Straight." *The Village Voice*, XXIV, no. 7 (February 12, 1979): 1, 11–14.

Kotlowitz, Robert. "Roseland: The Eternal Prom." *Harper's Magazine*, November 1967, 133–136.

Kurutz, Steven. "Funkytown Has a Boardwalk." *The New York Times*, August 15, 2004, CY 4.

Ladd, Bill. "Teen-Agers' Understanding Big Brother—That's Key to Dick Clark's Success." *Louisville Courier-Journal* (Kentucky), April 12, 1959, 1.

"Lambeth Walk." StreetSwing.com Dance History Archives, http://www.streetswing.com/histmain/z3lambth.htm (accessed March 24, 2004).

"Legalize Dancing NYC—Who We Are." LegalizeDancingNYC.com, http://www.legalizedancingnyc.com/whoweare.html (accessed February 21, 2005).

Levy, Steven. "Shag Dancing & Sop Popping." *Rolling Stone*, September 29, 1982, 50–57.

Lichtmann, Kurt. "Carolina Shag History." Cornell University, http://people.cornell.edu/pages/kpl5/f_Shag_rap.html (accessed June 30, 2004).

Lichtmann, Kurt. "West Coast Swing History." Cornell University, http://people.cornell.edu/pages/kpl5/f_Link15_wcs.html (accessed June 30, 2004).

"Life on the Newsfronts of the World." *Life* magazine, vol. 7, no. 8, August 21, 1939, 18–19.

"Lindy by Lanza." *LindybyLanza.com*, http://www.lindybylanza.com (accessed July 17, 2004).

"The Lindy Hop: A True National Folk Dance Has Been Born in U.S.A." A Photographic Essay, *Life* magazine, vol. 15, no. 8, August 23, 1943, 95–103.

Loggins, Peter. "Dean Collins." SavoyBallroom.com, http://www.savoyballroom.com/exp/dancefloor/savoydancers/deancollins.htm (accessed April 27, 2004).

Loomis, Kiku. "The Dean of Style: The Dancer who Taught Hollywood How to Swing." *Dance Spirit* magazine, June 2001, http://www.dancespirit.com/backissues/june01/intheswing.shtml (accessed 12 August 2004).

Low, David. "Hustling Disco: The Transformation of Disco in the Film Saturday Night Fever and Its Origin in the Homosexual and African American Subculture." Disco Step-by-Step Web site, http://www.discostepbystep.com/hustling_disco.htm (accessed July 17, 2004).

Luhrs, Joyce. "Cajun Dance & Music." *Amateur Dancers* Issue no. 152 (November/December 2004): 12–13.

Lustgarten, Karen. "Disco Déjà Vu." December 20, 2002. Disco Step by Step Web site, http://www.discostepbystep.com/karen_lustgarten1.htm (accessed October 19, 2004).

Macías, Anthony. "Bringing Music to the People: Race, Urban Culture, and Municipal Politics in Postwar Los Angeles." *American Quarterly* 56, no. 3 (September 2004): 693–717.

Mann, Judy Luce. "Saturday Night Fever Poses Parental Headache; '*Saturday Night Fever*' A Headache for Parents." *The Washington Post*, July 7, 1978, D1.

"Manning Rules Out a Puritan Sunday." *The New York Times*, February 26, 1926, 16.

Mansfield, Duncan. "Last Dance at Popular Nashville TV Club." *Associated Press*, January 25, 1999, http://www.s-t.com/daily/01-25-99/c01ae078.htm (accessed 18 March 2005).

Marchant, Valerie. "They're Having A Ball." *Time* magazine, March 12, 2001, Time.com, http://time.com/0,10987,,00.html?Qprod=2&qarg=1101010312-10137 (accessed June 18, 2002).

Marks, Peter. "The Argentine Heart: Part Song, All Tango." *The New York Times*, November, 18, 1999, E5.

Martin, John. "The GI Makes with the Hot Foot." *The New York Times Magazine*, January 9, 1944, 14–15.

Martin, Lydia. "Has La Macarena Gone Too Far?" *Miami Herald*, January 15, 1996, C1.

Mason, Gregory. "Satan in the Dance-Hall." *The American Mercury* 2 (June 1924): 175–182.

McDowell, Edwin. "Roller Skates: 300,000 Pairs a Month." *The New York Times*, May 13, 1979, F13.

McFadden, Robert. ".44 Killer Wounds 12th and 13th Victims." *The New York Times*, August 1, 1977.

McFadden, Robert. "'Sam' Suspect, Heavily Guarded, Arraigned and Held for Testing." *The New York Times*, August 12, 1977, 1, 10.

McGee, Celia. "Dance Steps Outside." *The New York Daily News*, August 4, 2004, Section: NOW, 32.

McGuigan, Cathleen, et al. "Breaking Out: America Goes Dancing." *Newsweek* magazine, July 2, 1984, 47.

McLane, Daisann. "In the Footsteps of the Conga and the Alley Cat." *The New York Times*, August 18, 1996, 30.

McMahon, John R. "Unspeakable Jazz Must Go!" *Ladies' Home Journal*, vol. 30, December 1921, 34.

McMahon, John R. "The Jazz Path of Degradation." *Ladies' Home Journal*, vol. 31, January 1922, 26.

Mee, Charles L., Jr. "Discotheque Man." *The New York Times*, January 9, 1966, 92–94, 106.

Meisler, Andy. "The Beat Goes On for 'Soul Train' Conductor." *The New York Times*, August 7, 1995, D7.

Millman, Cynthia. "Frankie Manning." SavoyBallroom.com, http://www.savoyballroom.com/exp/dancefloor/savoydancers/fmanning.htm (accessed April 27, 2004).

Milloy, Courtland. "The Dance That Would Not Die." *The Washington Post*, October 3, 1989, B3.

"Missouri Students Fight Town's Dancing Ban." *The New York Times*, November 2, 1986, 30.

Moynihan, Colin. "In Defense of the Inalienable Right to…Boogie." *The New York Times*, January 10, 1999, 56.

Murray, Albert Murray. "The Blues as Dance Music." *Black Music Research Journal* 10, no. 1 (Spring 1990): 67–72.68.

"Music Show Bows On A.B.C.-TV Aug. 5." *The New York Times*, July 23, 1957, 53.

Narvaez, Alfonso A. "City Acts to Let Homosexuals Meet and Work in Cabarets." *The New York Times*, October 12, 1971, 1.

Navarro, Mireya. "Macarena Madness Takes the Floor." *The New York Times*, December 27, 1995, A10.

Navarro, Mireya. "Battle of the Mambo Is Bruising Some Toes." *The New York Times*, September 3, 2000, A1.

"Ned Wayburn." StreetSwing.com Dance History Archives, http://www.streetswing.com/histmai2/d2waybrn.htm (accessed March 24, 2004).

"The Newest Shuffle." *Time* magazine, April 4, 1960, 44.

Newman, Scott A. "Jazz Age Chicago: Urban Leisure from 1893 to 1934." Page authored July 1, 2000; page retrieved January 25, 2004, http://chicago.urban-history.org/sites/parks/w_city.htm (accessed January 24, 2004).

"New Way to Keep from Getting Tired." Advertisement. *Life* magazine, vol. 7, no. 8, August 21, 1939, 36.

Nicholson, James. "Spotlight Dance: Foxtrot." *Amateur Dancers*, Issue no. 149 (May/June 2004): 6–7.

Nifong, Christina. "Swing Daddy-o!" *CNN Showbiz Today*, Web posting July 17, 1998.

"Nile Rodgers Talks about 'The Freak' Dance" (excerpt from the BBC documentary *The History Of Dance*). ChicTribute.com, http://www.chictribute.com/video/sidor/ledance.html (accessed December 27, 2004).

"Norma Miller: The Survivor Who Wrote the Book." SavoyBallroom.com, http://www.savoyballroom.com/exp/dancefloor/savoydancers/normamiller.htm (accessed April 27, 2004).

Norman, Michael. "Frosty Freeze and Kid Smooth Break for Fame at Roxy Disco." *The New York Times*, October 18, 1983, B4.

Norris, Frank. "Long Lives The King: Paul Whiteman is still the King of Jazz, who lives and works in a great big way after 20 years of piping." *Life* magazine, vol. 5, no. 26, December 26, 1938, 49–53.

Neuberg, Eva. "No Dancing Allowed: Protesting the City's Cabaret Laws Cabaret Laws Outlawing Nightlife." *New York Press*, August 22–28, 2001, http://www.legalizedancing-nyc.com/articles/nypress.html (accessed February 21, 2005).

Nye, Russel B. "Saturday Night at the Paradise Ballroom: or Dance Halls in the Twenties." *Journal of Popular Culture* 7 (1973), 14–20.

O'Brien, Elizabeth. "Most Agree Cabaret Laws Need Changing, But How?" *The Villager* 73, no. 9 (July 2–8, 2003), http://www.thevillager.com/villager_10/mostagreecabaret.html (accessed February 21, 2005).

"Oppose Ragtime Tunes Federation of Music Will Make Every Effort to Suppress Them." *The Brooklyn Eagle*, May 14, 1901, 1, http://www.brooklynpubliclibrary.org/eagle/index.htm (accessed March 24, 2004).

O'Regan, Michael. "They Put the NY into Country: An Architect, a Designer and a Model —Are All Regulars at Manhattan's Top Country 'n' Western Club." *The New York Daily News*, August 25, 1996, SP 16–17.

Pacenti, John. "Swing Comes Back with Big Bands and the Zoot Suit." *St. Louis Post Dispatch —Everyday Magazine*, July 28, 1998, 1.

Page, Ellen Wage. "A Flapper's Appeal to Parents." *Outlook Magazine* 132 (December 6, 1922): 607, http://www.geocities.com/flapper_culture/appeal.html.

Paggett, Taisha. "Getting Krumped: The Changing Face of Hip Hop." *Dance Magazine*, 78, no. 7 (July 2004): 32–36.

"The Palomar Ballroom, Los Angeles." *SatinBallroom.com*. http://www.satinbalroom.com/supplements/palomar.html (accessed May 11, 2004).

Park, Miri. "Breakers: The Next Generation. In the Outer Boroughs, True Hip-Hop Dance Thrives." *The Village Voice*, http://www.villagevoice.com/dance/0217,park2,34137,14.html (accessed January 7, 2005).

Parker, Thomas F. "Recreation for Colored Citizens." *The Playground*, 19, no. 12 (March 1926): 651.

Parson, Thomas E. "News from New York." *American Dancer*, 8 (September 1934): 10.

Pasadena Ballroom Dance Association, http://www.pasadenaballroomdance.com/index.html (accessed January 5, 2005).

Peck, Abe. "The Face of Disco: Macho Men with their Tongues in their Cheeks."*Rolling Stone Magazine*, April 19, 1979, Issue no. 289, 12–14.

Perlmutter, Emanuel. ".44-Caliber Killer Wounds Two In Car Parked on Queens Street." *The New York Times*, June 27, 1977, 1, 39.

Perry, Tenna. "Biography of David Berkowitz, AKA Son of Sam." PageWise, Inc, 2002, http://va.essortment.com/sonsamberkowit_rosa.htm (accessed November 21, 2004).

"A Plantation Cake Walk Makes Much Merriment." *The Brooklyn Eagle*, July 20, 1902, 4, http://www.brooklynpubliclibrary.org/eagle/index.htm (accessed March 24, 2004).

"Police Get a 2d Note Signed by 'Son of Sam' in .44-Caliber Killings." *The New York Times*, June 3, 1977, 65.

Polier, Rex. "Dick Clark and His 'Kids' Go Bigtime." *Philadelphia Inquirer*, August 4, 1957, Urban Archives Temple University.

"Polka History of Dance." CentralHome.com, http://www.centralhome.com/ballroom-country/polka.htm (accessed September 17, 2004).

"Popular Dances from the Cakewalk to the Watusi, Famous Dance Team Traces Fascinating History of American Social Dancing." *Ebony* magazine, vol. XVI, no. 10 (August 1961): 32–38.

"The Psychiatrist Who Analyzed The Twist." *The Twist* Magazine, The Girl Friend–The Boy Friend Corp. New York, 1962, 21.

Pugh, Clifford. "La Macarena; Dance and Song Bridge Cultural Gap." *The Houston Chronicle*, January 23, 1996, 1.

Quindlen, Anna. "Where to Roller Skate to a Disco Beat." *The New York Times*, March 20, 1981, C1.

Quindlen, Anna. "Californians Make a Pilgrimage in Waltz Time." *The New York Times*, August 15, 1981, Sec. 2, 27.

Rabb, John. "How I Stopped Feeling Guilty, Started Jiving, and Got Down to Gyrating and Grooving On the Hardwood; Jiving, Gyrating, Grooving." *The Washington Post*, August 4, 1978, Weekend Section, 1.

Ravo, Nick. "The 70's (Stayin' Alive) Won't Die (Stayin' Alive)." *The New York Times*, November 13, 1991, C1.

Reiter, Jes. "Boombox Saturday Night." *Swing Time* magazine, Issue no. 10, 1998, 48–49.

Relin, David Oliver. "Swing's the Thing." *React* magazine, November 23–29, 1998, 8–9.

"The Rendezvous Ballroom: Queen of Swing." http://www.100megspopup.com/ark/RendezvousBallroom1941.html (accessed May 11, 2004).

"Restaurant/ Discotheque Fires." Emergency-management.net, http://www.emergency-management.net/disco_fire.htm (accessed June 1, 2004).

Rex, Frederick. "Municipal Dance Halls." *National Municipal Review*, July 1915, 414–421.

Rich, Frank. "Discomania, Saturday Night Fever." *Time* magazine, Vol. 110, December 19, 1977, 69–70.

Riley, Clayton. "A 'Train' on the Soul Track." *The New York Times*, February 4, 1973, 121.

"Risk in the Twist Cited by Surgeon." *The New York Times*, December 3, 1961, 154.

"A River of Tears: Happy Land." Court TV's Crime Library, http://www.crimelibrary.com/notorious_murders/mass/happyland/scene_4.html?sect=10 (accessed November 26, 2004).

Roca, Octavio. "Strictly Ballroom It Takes Two to Tango, and Talent to Win, in Competitive Dance." *San Francisco Chronicle*, March 9, 1997, 32.

"Rock-and-Roll Called Communicable Disease." *The New York Times*, March 28, 1956, 33.

Rockwell, John. "Rock vs. Disco: Who really Won the War?" *The New York Times*, September 16, 1990, H36.

Rockwell, John. "Not Merely Nostalgia, It's the Beat, Beat, Beat, and More." *The New York Times*, July 2, 1995, 33, 36.

Romano, Tricia. "A Crash Course in Cabarets: A Historical Overview of New York's Cabaret Laws." *Village Voice*, December 3, 2002, http://www.legalizedancingnyc.com/articles/voice2.html (accessed February 21, 2005).

Rose, Frank. "Discophobia: Rock & Roll Fights Back." *Village Voice*, November 12, 1979, 32.

"Roseland, Plot Summary for." IMDb.com, http://www.imdb.com/title/tt0076639/plotsummary (accessed February 12, 2005).

Rule, Shelia. "The Pop Life: Don Cornelius Steps off the 'Train.'" *The New York Times*, October 20, 1993, C18.

Ryzik, Melena. "The Time of Their Lives, Live: 'Dirty Dancing' moves onstage. But what are Baby and Johnny doing in Australia?" *The New York Times*, January 30, 2005, AR:8, 32.

"700 Dance Masters Ponder New Steps." *The New York Times*, August 19, 1930, 14.

"Seventies Almanac 1973." Super Seventies Rock Sites, http://www.superseventies.com/1973.html (accessed May 30, 2003).

Samuels, Gertrude. "Why They Rock 'n' Roll—And Should They?" *The New York Times*, January 12, 1958, Sec. SM, 16–20.

"Savoy Lindy Hoppers." SavoyBallroom.com, http://www.savoyballroom.com/exp/dancefloor/savoylindyhoppers/savoylindyhoppers.htm (accessed April 27, 2004).

"Says Jazz Will Sing Its Swan Song Soon." *The New York Times*, August 27, 1920, 20.

Segell, Michael. "Studio 54: Steve Rubell's Disco Disneyland." *Rolling Stone Magazine*, April 19, 1979, Issue no. 289, 44–45.

Shanley, John P. "Dick Clark—New Rage of the Teenagers." *Philadelphia Inquirer*, March 16, 1958, Temple University Libraries Urban Archives, Philadelphia, Pennsylvania.

Shanley, J.P. "TV: Teen-Agers Only 'American Bandstand' a Daytime Disk Jockey Show, Bows on Channel 7." *New York Times*, August 6, 1957, 42.

Shanley, J.P. "Television." *America*, February 14, 1959, 587.

Shea, Ann Marie, and Atay Citron. "The Powwow of the Thunderbird American Indian Dancers." *The Drama Review* 26, no. 2 (Summer 1982): 73–88.

Sim, R. Saunderson. "Skating Revival Rolls On." *The New York Times*, February 5, 1978, WC8.

Simon, Bradford S. "Entering the Pit: Slam-Dancing and Modernity." *Journal of Popular Culture* 31, no. 1 (Summer 1997): 149–176.

Smalley, Suzanne. "The New Age of Rave: They chant, they dance, they do downward dog. No drugs or drink allowed. These kids are high on life." *Newsweek* magazine, vol. 142, Issue 1, July 7, 2003, 52–53.

Smith, Andy. "Mosh Pit Madness." *Providence Journal*, November 8, 1992, El, E4.

Sommer, Sally. "Some Like It Hot: Salsa is spicy, sexy, and making waves in dance." *Dance Magazine*, 78, no. 6, June 2004, 46–49.

Sommer, Sally. "Prophets in Pumas: When hip hop broke out." *Dance Magazine*, 78, no. 7, July 2004, 30–32.

"The Spanish Ballroom at Glen Echo Park." National Park Service Web site, http://www.nps.gov/glec/spba/SpBalHis.htm (accessed July 10, 2004).

Spring, Howard. "Swing and the Lindy Hop: Dance, Venue, Media, and Tradition." *American Music* 15, no. 2 (Summer 1997): 183–207.

"Stage Door Canteen." Internet Movie Database IMDb.com, http://imdb.com/title/ tt0036384 (accessed October 14, 2004).

"State Curb Asked On Dance Studios." *The New York Time*, February 22, 1958, 8.

Stephenson, Robert R. "Is Dancing A Sin? Can Biblical authority be found that allows dancing?" *Firm Foundation*, March 11, 1986, http://www.hcis.net/users/dlemmons/ CCD-rrs-Sin.htm (accessed June 23, 2004).

Sternbergh, Adam. "Inside the Disco Inferno: Thiry years ago, a mostly fictional article in this magazine led to the movie *Saturday Night Fever*. But the pictures that ran with that story couldn't have been more real." New York Magazine, July 10, 2006, 98–99.

Strauss, Neil. "You Say 'Soul Train' Is How Old?" *The New York Times*, December 31, 1995, TE3.

Strauss, Neil. "All-Night Parties and a Nod to the 60's (Rave On)." *The New York Times*, May 28, 1996, C11.

Stewart, Doug, and photographs by Gail Mooney. "This Joint is Jumping." *Smithsonian* magazine, vol. 29 no. 12, March 1999, 60–74.

Sullum, Jacob. "Rave Rage." *Reason Magazine*, vol. 33, no. 4, August/September 2001, 12.

"Summary of Principal Bills Acted Upon by the Legislature During 1964 Session." *The New York Times*, March 30, 1964, 24.

Swarden, Carlotta Gulvas. "Whooping and Hollering, It's Country-and-western Dancing." *The New York Times*, April 17, 1994, NJ 8.

Talese, Gay. "Killer Joe Piro: Tireless Dancer." *The New York Times*, December 13, 1964, 88.

"The Tango." Library ThinkQuest.org, http://library.thinkquest.org/J002194F/tango.htm (accessed March 14, 2004).

"Texas Tommy." StreetSwing.com Dance History Archives, http://www.streetswing.com/ histmain/z3tex1.htm (accessed May 24, 2004).

"Thank God It's Friday, Plot Summary for." IMDb.com, http://www.imdb.com/title/ tt0078382/plotsummary (accessed November 21, 2004).

"These Dancers Don't Duck Tradition." *St. Louis Post-Dispatch*, February 7, 1989, 3D.

Thompson, Howard. "Producers Rush Movies On Twist." *The New York Times*, January 6, 1962, 13.

Thompson, Howard. "The Screen: 'Twist Around the Clock.'" *The New York Times*, January 27, 1962, 13.

Thompson, Karen. "Put On Your Dancin' Shoes: The Return of Social Dancing." *Lesbian News*, vol. 24, no. 10, May 1999, 32.

"Thousands Throng Great Aragon Ballroom." *Chicago Evening American*, July 16, 1926, 1.

Tobler, John. "Liner Notes." *Saturday Night Fever*, Soundtrack Album Compilation supervisor Bill Oakes, 1995 CD Polygram International Music No. 42282 5389 2.

Truman, James. "Rollerskating on Wall Street." *Melody Maker* magazine, October 13, 1979. ChicTribute.com, http://www.chictribute.com/arkiv/artiklar/131079mm.html (accessed December 27, 2004).

Turcott, Jack. "Dance Thrill Awaits 18,500 at Garden." *New York Daily News*, August 23, 1935, 1.

"Turkey Trot." StreetSwing.com Dance History Archives, http://www.streetswing.com/ histmain/z3turtrt.htm (accessed March 24, 2004).

"Twist and Get Healthy." *The Twist* Magazine, The Girl Friend–The Boy Friend Corp. New York, 1962, 35.

"United States (History)." *Microsoft Encarta Encyclopedia 2000*. © 1993–1999 Microsoft Corporation.

Vare, Robert. "Discophobia." *The New York Times*, July 10, 1979, A15.

Vollers, Maryanne. "Wheels On Fire: The Rise of Roller Disco." *Rolling Stone Magazine*, April 19, 1979, Issue no. 289, 38–41.

Wade, Judy. "Santa Catalina Island, Southern California's Swing-era Paradise." *The Historic Traveler Magazine*, http://historictraveler.com/primedia/pol_soc/santa_catalina_1.adp (accessed July 26, 2001).

Walker, Lou Ann. "Getting Lucky; Single women of a certain age go to Miami, to retire or just to dance—with ageing gigolos like Lucky Kargo." *The Independent (London)*, May 27, 1995, F3.

Walker, Lou Ann. "Romance For Sale for $6 a Dance, Suave Escorts Help Fulfill the Aging Fantasies of Lonely Women Looking for One More Whirl Around the Floor." *Fort Lauderdale Sun Sentinel*, August 6, 1995, 8.

Walsh, Jeanne Cook. "Dancing Through the Depression." Oldtime Nebraska, http://www.olden-times.com/OldtimeNebraska/n-jwalsh/dancers.html (accessed July 17, 2004).

Waxer, Lise. "Of Mambo Kings and Songs of Love: Dance Music in Havana and New York from the 1930s to the 1950s." *Latin American Music Review* 15, no. 2 (Autumn–Winter, 1994): 139–176.

Wehrwein, Austin C. "Eisenhower Discerns a Decline in Morality." *The New York Times*, May 2, 1962.

Weinman, Heather. "A look at a different culture: Thunderbird American Indian Dancers perform at CSI, teaching school children that tribes still do exist." *Staten Island Advance*, November 20, 2004, A21.

"Welk Show Kept Off TV By a Network Dispute." *The New York Times*, August 6, 1957, 42.

"Western Swing Bands: A History." Big Bands Database, (accessed June 30, 2004).

"WFIL-TV Biography Bob Horn." *News from WFIL-TV*, June 17, 1954, Temple University Libraries Urban Archives, Philadelphia, Pennsylvania.

"Where the 'Son of Sam' Struck, Young Women Walk in Fear." *The New York Times*, June 30, 1977, 38.

Whiting, Sam. "Have A Ball Some Classy Spots to do the Waltz or Fox-trot." *San Francisco Chronicle*, March 3, 1996, 30.

Williams, Lena. "Lifestyle; Three Steps Right, Three Steps Left: Sliding Into the Hot New Dance." *The New York Times*, April 22, 1990, 48.

Wloszczyna, Susan. "The Lambada; Forbidden Dance Stumbled." *USA Today*, December 31, 1990, 2D.

"Would You Care to Dance? Cruise Lines Hire Gentleman 'Hosts' to Entertain Passengers." ABCNews.Go.com, August 24, 2001, http://abcnews.go.com/sections/2020/2020/2020_010824_hosts.html (accessed October 29, 2004).

Zacharias, Patricia. "When Detroit Danced to the Big Bands." *The Detroit News*, http://info.detnews.com/history/story/index.cfm?id=6&category=life (accessed June 3, 2004).

Zane, Maitland. "Passing Up Hip-Hop for the Lindy Hop." *San Francisco Chronicle*, Friday, April 3, 1998, http://www.sfgate.com/cgi-bin/article.cgi?file=/chronicle/archive/1998/04/03/EB64693.DTL (accessed July 17, 2004).

Zibart, Eve. "Get a Leg Up With Lambada." *The Washington Post*, February 16, 1990, N19.

VIDEO/DVD

"America Dances! 1897–1948: A Collector's Edition of Social Dance in Film." Produced by Dancetime Publications Kentfield, California, 75 mins.

Breakin'. Directed by Joel Siberg, MGM, 1984, 86 mins.

"Director's Commentary, John Badham" on *Saturday Night Fever*, 25th Anniversary DVD Edition, 2002, 118 mins.

The Call of the Jitterbug. Jesper Sorensen, Vibeke Winding, and Tana Ross (Green Room Productions), 1988, 35 mins.

Can't Stop The Music. Directed by Nancy Walker (Anchor Bay Entertainment), 1980, 123 mins.

Dance with Me. Directed by Randa Haines, 1998, 126 mins.

Footloose. Directed by Herbert Ross, 107 mins.

How To Lambada. RCA/Columbia Pictures Home Video, 1990, 30 mins.

"Let's Learn to Dance with Laney Cross." Produced by Dan Brown, 4 mins. on Twist documentary, directed by Ron Mann, 1992.

The Mask. Directed by Chuck Russell, New Line Studios, videocassette 1994.

Out to Sea. Directed by Martha Coolidge, 20th Century Fox, videocassette 1997.

Queen of the Stardust Ballroom. Directed by Sam Osteen, VCI Home Video, videocassette 1975.

"Rock 'n' Roll Explodes." The History of Rock 'n' Roll Series. Directed by Andrew Solt Time Life Video and Television and Warner Bros. 1995, videocassette, 60 mins.

Rock and Roll: The Early Days. Archive Film Production, narrated by John Heard, directed by Patrick Montgomery and Pamela Page, TFBI Associates 1984, videocassette, 60 mins.

The Rocky Horror Picture Show. Directed by Jim Sharman, 20th Century Fox 1975, DVD, 100 mins.

Roseland. Director by James Ivory Roseland, Home Vision Entertainment, 1977, DVD, 104 mins.

Saturday Night Fever. 25th Anniversary DVD Edition, directed by John Badham, Paramount Pictures 1977, 118 mins.

"Saturday Night Fever." *VH1 Behind the Music,* director Jill Modabber, VH1 Home Entertainment, 2001, 30 mins.

Shag, The Movie. Director Zelda Barron, MGM, 1989, videocassette, 98 mins.

Swing Kids. Directed by Thomas Carter, Hollywood Pictures, 1992, DVD, 114 mins.

Thank God It's Friday. Directed by Robert Klane, Columbia, 1978.

Twist. Directed by Ron Mann, Sphinx Productions Home Vision Entertainment, 1992, 78 mins.

Zoot Suit Riots. Directed by Joseph Tovares, PBS Home Video, videocassette, 2002.

Record Albums

Arthur Murray presents Discotheque Dance Party. Produced by Herman Diaz, Jr. 1964, RCA Victor Stereo LSP 2998.

Arthur Murray's Music for Dancing—Mambo-Rumba-Samba-Tango-Merengue. Produced by Herman Diaz, Jr. 1964, RCA Victor Stereo LSP 2152.

Learn Disco Dancing. Instructions by Jeff and Jack Shelley. Produced by Michael Goldberg and Eddie Youngblood, 1976, Groove Sound Records No. GS 1001.

Original Carolina Beach Music. Produced by B.H. Edwards, 1999, CD Edwards Music Network Corp., No. 7118.

Saturday Night Fever. Soundtrack Album Compilation supervisor Bill Oakes, 1995, CD Polygram International Music, No. 42282 5389 2.

Twist with Chubby Checker. Produced by Kal Mann, 1962, Cameo-Parkway Records, Inc., No. 7001.

Personal Interviews

Hilary Alexander, December 15, 2004 (telephone).

Dominick Dattilo, May 7, 2001.

Phyllis Giordano, August 9, 2004.

Mary Keil, January 13, 2005 (telephone).

Joe Lanza, November 6, 2004 (e-mail).

Galt MacDermot, November 16, 2004 (telephone).

Vince MacDermot, November 16, 2004 (telephone).
Ann Merlino, August 13, 2004.
Scotty Morris, April 28, 2006.
Thelma Lynn Olsen, May 10, 2004; June 30, 2004.
Georganne Sassano, October 27, 2004.
Carolyn Sgromo, October 27, 2004.
Dave Snyder, October 31, 2004 (telephone).
Bob Soldivera, October 6, 2004 (telephone).
Patricia Wakie (interviewed by John Wakie), May 18, 2004.

A Select List of Hollywood Movies by Type of Dance

Fred Astaire and Ginger Rogers

- *Carefree* (1938)
- *Flying Down to Rio* (1933)
- *Follow the Fleet* (1936)
- *The Gay Divorcee* (1934)
- *Roberta* (1935)
- *Top Hat* (1935)
- *Shall We Dance?* (1937)
- *The Story of Vernon and Irene Castle* (1939)
- *Swing Time* (1936)

Ballroom

- *Dance With Me* (1998)
- *Dirty Dancing* (1987)
- *Mad Hot Ballroom* (2005)
- *Queen of the Stardust Ballroom* (1975)
- *Roseland* (1977)
- *Shall We Dance?* (2004)
- *Strictly Ballroom* (1992)

Breakdancing

- *Beat Street* (1984)
- *Breakin'* (1984)
- *Breakin' 2: Electric Boogaloo* (1984)
- *Flashdance* (1983)

Marge and Gower Champion

- *Give a Girl a Break* (1953)
- *Jupiter's Darling* (1955)
- *Lovely to Look At* (1952)
- *Showboat* (1951)
- *Three for the Show* (1955)

Charleston

- *The Crowd* (1927)
- *The Great Gatsby* (1974)
- *The King of Jazz* (1930)
- *King on Main Street* (1925)
- *Our Dancing Daughters* (1928)
- *A Social Celebrity* (1926)

Dean Collins and Jewell McGowan

- *Always A Bridesmaid* (1943)
- *Buck Privates* (1941)
- *Dance Hall* (1941)
- *Kid Dynamite* (1943)
- *Living It Up* (1945)
- *Playmates* (1941)
- *Ride 'Em Cowboy* (1942)
- *Springtime in the Rockies* (1942)
- *The Talk of the Town* (1942)

Conga

- *Hellzapoppin'* (1941)

Country (Two-Step and Line Dancing)

- *Urban Cowboy* (1980)
- *Pure Country* (1992)
- *Son in Law* (1993)
- *Footloose* (1984)

Disco and the Hustle

- *Carlito's Way* (1993)
- *"54"* (1998)
- *The Last Days of Disco* (1998)
- *A Night at The Roxbury* (1998)
- *Roseland* (1977)
- *Saturday Night Fever* (1977)
- *Summer of Sam* (1999)
- *Thank God It's Friday* (1978)

Fox Trot

- *Around the World* (1943)
- *Is Everybody Happy?* (1929)
- *The Godfather* (1972)
- *Hellzapoppin'* (1941)
- *Here Comes the Band* (1935)
- *Stage Door Canteen* (1943)
- *Swing Fever* (1944)

Freestyle

- *Dirty Dancing* (1984)
- *Footloose* (1984)

- *"54"* (1998)
- *Klute* (1971)
- *Saturday Night Fever* (1977)

Hip-hop and Krumping

- *Krumped* (2004)
- *You Got Served* (2004)

The Lambada

- *The Forbidden Dance* (1989)
- *Lambada: Set the Night on Fire* (1990)

Lindy Hop, Jitterbug, and Swing Revival

- *After Seben* (1929)
- *Around the World* (1943)
- *A Day at the Races* (1937)
- *Buck Privates* (1941)
- *The Godfather* (1972)
- *Groovie Movie* (1944)
- *Hellzapoppin'* (1941)
- *The Jones Family in Hollywood* (1939)
- *Killer Diller* (1948)
- *The Lottery Bride* (1930)
- *Malcolm X* (1992)
- *The Mask* (1994)
- *Ride 'Em Cowboy* (1942)
- *Swing* (2004)
- *Swingers* (1996)
- *Swing Kids* (1993)
- *Swing Fever* (1944)

Mambo

- *Dance With Me* (1998)
- *Dirty Dancing* (1987)
- *Dirty Dancing: Havana Nights* (2004)
- *Mambo Kings* (1992)

Dance Marathons

- *The Lottery Bride* (1930)
- *They Shoot Horses Don't They?* (1969)

Merengue

- *My Blue Heaven* (1990)

Novelty, Fad, or Traditional

- Apache, *The Apache Dancer* (1923)
- Big Apple, *Keep Punching* (1939)
- The Bus Stop, *Saturday Night Fever* (1977)
- Bunny Hop, *Cry Baby* (1990)
- Castle Walk, *The Story of Vernon and Irene Castle* (1939)
- Hand Jive, *Grease* (1978) and *American Graffiti* (1973)
- Hesitation Waltz, *The Story of Vernon and Irene Castle* (1939)
- The Madison, *Hairspray* (1988)
- Mashed Potato, *Hairspray* (1988)
- Maxixe, *The Story of Vernon and Irene Castle* (1939)
- One-Step, *The Story of Vernon and Irene Castle* (1939)
- Time Warp, *The Rocky Horror Picture Show* (1975)
- Toga Party, *National Lampoon's Animal House* (1978)
- Shake a Tail Feather, *Hairspray* (1988)
- Shout, *National Lampoon's Animal House* (1978)
- Sock Hop, *American Graffiti* (1973) and *Grease* (1978)
- The Stroll, *Hairspray* (1988)
- Tarantella, *The Godfather* (1972)
- Wedding, *The Godfather* (1972)
- YMCA, *Can't Stop The Music* (1980)

Rave

- *Party Monster* (2003)
- *Rave, Dancing to a Different Beat* (1994)
- *Shampoo Horns* (1998)

Rock 'n' Roll

- *American Graffiti* (1973)
- *Don't Knock the Rock* (1957)
- *Hairspray* (1988)
- *Rock Around the Clock* (1956)
- *Rock, Rock, Rock* (1956)

Roller Disco

- *Roller Boogie* (1979)
- *Skatetown USA* (1979)

Samba

- *Copacabana* (1947)
- *Down Argentine Way* (1940)
- *The Gang's All Here* (1943)
- *Weekend in Havana* (1941)

Salsa

- *Dance With Me* (1998)
- *Salsa* (1988)
- *Saturday Night Fever* (1978)

Shag

- *Shaggin' On The Strand* (1985)
- *Shag, The Movie* (1989)

Square Dancing

- *The Arkansas Swing* (1949)
- *Hollywood Barn Dance* (1947)

- *Square Dance* (1987)
- *Square Dance Jubilee* (1949)
- *Square Dance Katy* (1950)
- *Son in Law* (1988)

Tango

- *Assassination Tango* (2002)
- *Evita* (1996)
- *The Four Horsemen of the Apocalypse* (1921)
- *Scent of a Woman* (1992)
- *The Sheik* (1921)
- *Strictly Ballroom* (1992)
- *Tango* (1998)
- *The Tango Lesson* (1997)
- *The Tango Queen* (1916)
- *Tango Tangles* (1914)

Twist

- *Doin' the Twist* (1961)
- *Don't Knock the Twist* (1962)
- *Hey, Let's Twist* (1961)
- *It's Trad, Dad* (1961)
- *Twist All Night* (1962)
- *Twist Around the Clock* (1961)

Waltz

- *Roseland* (1977)
- *The Story of Vernon and Irene Castle* (1939)
- *Syncopation* (1929)

Index

ABOUT THE AUTHOR

RALPH G. GIORDANO holds a license as a professional Registered Architect in the state of New York, a Master's Degree in Liberal Studies from the College of Staten Island–City University of New York, and a Bachelor's degree in Architecture from the New York Institute of Technology. His first book, *Fun and Games in Twentieth Century America: A Historical Guide to Leisure*, was published by Greenwood in September 2003. The book is an interdisciplinary study of how Americans spent their leisure time and the political, social, technological, and economic factors that influenced or restricted their activities.

His previous published works include three entries on the Architecture of the Gilded Age, and biographical entries on John Deere and Levi Strauss in *The Historical Encyclopedia of the Gilded Age*. He has also contributed articles to several historical journals on various topics including Rosa Parks, Thomas Jefferson, Cold War Culture, Swing music, Hip-hop, and the integrated use of popular Culture and History. Giordano is also an adjunct Professor of History and American Studies at the College of Staten Island, City University of New York.